# CONTRIBUTORS

JOHN DORNBERG has reported on Germany for more than 30 years and has been based in Munich since 1971. The author of several books, he is also a frequent contributor to *Travel & Leisure, Bon Appetit, National Geographic Traveler,* and the travel sections of *The New York Times* and the *Washington Post.* He is the editorial consultant for this guidebook.

JAMES CLARK, whose travel articles have appeared in *The New York Times,* teaches university English in Heidelberg, where he has lived for ten years.

JOHN ENGLAND, a freelance journalist, has been based in Bonn since 1972. He writes for British and Australian newspapers and magazines.

PETER HAYS, a resident of Germany since 1966, has written for more than 30 German publications and contributed feature articles to many English-language newspapers and magazines.

TED HECK, a freelance travel and sports writer who lived in Germany for five years, contributes regularly to American magazines and newspapers. He returns to Germany every year.

THOMAS LUCEY, a resident of Frankfurt for 25 years, is the German correspondent for *Business International* publications. He has also been a travel editor and columnist and has contributed to two other travel guides.

DAVID MAGEE is a journalist and broadcaster who has lived in West Germany for more than ten years. Now working in Bonn, he was based in Cologne for four years.

PHYLLIS MÉRAS, travel editor of the *Providence* (Rhode Island) *Journal,* contributes travel articles to *Newsday,* the *Chicago Tribune,* and the *San Francisco Examiner.* She travels frequently in East Germany.

ROBERT SAMMONS contributes to *Travel & Leisure, Travel/Holiday,* the *Atlanta Journal/Constitution,* the *Boston Globe,* and many other publications. He reports frequently on Germany and Austria.

DOUGLAS SUTTON, formerly a correspondent for *Newsweek* magazine in Germany, is now an editor with Deutsche Presse Agentur, an English-language wire service in Hamburg.

# THE PENGUIN TRAVEL GUIDES

AUSTRALIA

CANADA

THE CARIBBEAN

ENGLAND & WALES

FRANCE

GERMANY

GREECE

HAWAII

IRELAND

ITALY

MEXICO

NEW YORK CITY

PORTUGAL

SAN FRANCISCO &
NORTHERN CALIFORNIA

SPAIN

# THE PENGUIN GUIDE TO GERMANY 1991

ALAN TUCKER

*General Editor*

PENGUIN BOOKS

# PENGUIN BOOKS

Published by the Penguin Group
Viking Penguin, a division of Penguin Books USA Inc.,
375 Hudson Steet, New York, New York 10014, U.S.A.
Penguin Books Ltd, 27 Wrights Lane,
London W8 5TZ, England
Penguin Books Australia Ltd, Ringwood,
Victoria, Australia
Penguin Books Canada Ltd, 2801 John Street
Markham, Ontario, Canada L3R 1B4
Penguin Books (N.Z.) Ltd, 182–190 Wairau Road,
Auckland 10, New Zealand

Penguin Books Ltd, Registered Offices:
Harmondsworth, Middlesex, England

First published in Penguin Books 1991

1 3 5 7 9 10 8 6 4 2

ISBN 0 14 019.922 5
ISSN 1043-4615

Printed in the United States of America

Set in ITC Garamond Light
Designed by Beth Tondreau Design
Maps by Mark Stein Studios
Illustrations by Bill Russell
Editorial Services by Marian Appellof, Stephen Brewer,
Amy K. Hughes, Anne Lunt,
Lynn Morasco, Mitchell Nauffts, Donald S. Olson
Fact checked by Anne Leo Ellis

# THIS GUIDEBOOK

The Penguin Travel Guides are designed for people who are experienced travellers in search of exceptional information that will help them sharpen and deepen their enjoyment of the trips they take.

Where, for example, are the interesting, isolated, fun, charming, or romantic places to stay that are within your budget? The hotels described by our writers (each of whom is an experienced travel writer who either lives in or regularly tours the city or region of Germany he or she covers) are some of the special places, in all price ranges except for the lowest—not the run-of-the-mill, heavily marketed places on every travel agent's CRT display and in advertised airline and travel-agency packages. We indicate the approximate price level of each accommodation in our description of it (no indication means it is moderate), and at the end of every chapter we supply contact information so that you can get precise, up-to-the-minute rates and make reservations.

*The Penguin Guide to Germany 1991* highlights the more rewarding parts of Germany so that you can quickly and efficiently home in on a good itinerary.

Of course, the guides do far more than just help you choose a hotel and plan your trip. *The Penguin Guide to Germany 1991* is designed for use *in* Germany. Our Penguin Germany writers tell you what you really need to know, as well as what you can't find out so easily on your own. They identify and describe the truly out-of-the-ordinary restaurants, shops and crafts, activities, and sights, and tell you the best way to "do" your destination.

Our writers are highly selective. They bring out the significance of the places they cover, capturing the personality and underlying cultural resonances of a town or region—making clear its special appeal. For exhaustive, detailed coverage of local attractions, we suggest that you also use a reference-type guidebook, such as the Blue Guide or the Michelin Green Guide, along with the Penguin Guide.

As we go to press, the economic and political situation in East Germany is still very much in flux. We have provided the very latest information available on entry to and travel in that area, but it is to be expected that there will be changes after the book comes off press—so we advise you in any case to check carefully with the national tourist offices or with your travel agent and the international carrier you choose.

*The Penguin Guide to Germany 1991* is full of reliable and timely information, revised each year. We would like to know if you think we've left out some very special place.

ALAN TUCKER
*General Editor*
*Penguin Travel Guides*

375 Hudson Street
New York, New York 10014
or
27 Wrights Lane
London W8 5TZ

# CONTENTS

# MAPS

# OVERVIEW

*By John Dornberg*

*John Dornberg has reported on Germany for more than 30 years and has been based in Munich since 1971. The author of several books, he is also a frequent contributor to* Travel & Leisure, Bon Appetit, National Geographic Traveler, *and the travel sections of* The New York Times *and the* Washington Post. *He is the editorial consultant for this guidebook.*

Germany is like a kaleidoscope or a jigsaw puzzle, a land that has baffled many travellers—the Germans included. None less, indeed, than the 18th-century poet and dramatist Friedrich von Schiller, second only to Goethe in stature as a bard and an influence on German literature and thought, once exclaimed rhetorically: "Germany? But where is it? I cannot find such a country. Where the political realm ends, the culture begins." That enigmatic description, written when the territory now called Germany was a patchwork of rival and often warring kingdoms, principalities, duchies, prince-bishoprics, and independent city-states, is as applicable today as it was 200 years ago.

What is Germany and who are the Germans? These are questions that instantly raise new ones: How many Germanys—one, two, a dozen, a score—and which ones?

It is not enough of an answer to speak merely of the former West and East Germanys, divided for 41 years and now united: that is, of the former Federal Republic, with a population of 61 million and an area of 96,000 square miles (a little more than the United Kingdom and a little less than the state of Oregon) whose capital is the small city of Bonn, on the Rhine; or the former Democratic Republic, 16.5 million inhabitants on a territory of 42,000 square miles (about the size of Tennessee and a bit larger than Iceland), which called half the city of

Berlin its capital. It skirts the issue of all the little Germanys within those two political realms—Baden, Bavaria, Hannover, Hesse, Holstein, Schleswig, Brandenburg, Mecklenburg, Saxony, Thüringen, to name just a few—that as recently as 120 years ago were proud independent and sovereign states, some even so-called middle powers, with their own coinage, armies, foreign ministries, and citizenships.

For all its comparatively small size, this land in the middle of Europe is a mosaic of panoramas, as complex and variegated as a patchwork. Although it is a mere 80 minutes by air, or six and a half hours by train, from Munich in the Bavarian Alps to Hamburg near the North Sea—a distance of only 500 miles or so—geographically, architecturally, culturally, even linguistically, it can be like a journey between two different countries.

A trip to Trier on the Mosel river can be almost like a visit to Rome. A day in Nürnberg, Regensburg, or Lübeck will seem like one in the Middle Ages, a weekend in Augsburg a step back into the Renaissance. Or consider Frankfurt-am-Main, the financial center of Germany—indeed, of Europe—a modern metropolis of gleaming steel-and-glass skyscrapers, often derogatorily called "Bankfurt," "Mainhattan," or "Manhattan-am-Main." But within a short radius of this money capital where, they say, it is easier to find a syndicated billion-mark loan than a parking space, there are scores of picture-postcard villages with steep-roofed, half-timbered houses, romantic old market squares, and narrow cobblestone streets—each one a kind of three-dimensional travel poster, a spot where time seems to have stood still.

During an entire life span you could repeatedly travel the length of Germany, about 560 miles from the Danish border in the north to the Austrian and Swiss frontiers in the south, and its breadth, a scant 500 miles as the crow flies from the Rhine and the boundaries with France and the Benelux countries in the west to those of Poland and Czechoslovakia in the east, and still not see everything worth seeing. Nor will you be able to find a common German denominator, for there really is none. Its comparatively small size notwithstanding, Germany is a country of thousands of lifestyles and mores, hundreds of landscapes, scores of regions.

It is a land of craggy, snowcapped mountains and broad, expansive plains; of majestic rivers and sandy ocean shores; of lush, dark forests and vine-covered hills; bustling cities and idyllic hamlets; of graceful Gothic church spires and fairy-tale castles, but also of ugly factory chimneys and the cauldrons of heavy industry. Down south on the Bodensee

(Lake Constance), which Germany shares with Austria and Switzerland, a microclimate creates a subtropical environment where even palm trees grow.

The people are as varied as the topography. The cliché picture of *the German* invariably portrays a man in lederhosen, loden coat, and hat with goat's-hair tuft quaffing beer from a huge mug to wash down a mountain of sausages, sauerkraut, and baseball-sized dumplings, or a buxom blonde, blue-eyed woman garbed in a dirndl. But those are strictly stereotypes of Bavarian highlanders. No Berliner, Frankfurter, Hannoverian, or Rhinelander would be caught dead wearing such duds: It's like suggesting that all Americans wear cowboy hats and boots, bust broncos, and spend their leisure hours square dancing.

The same is true of cuisine. To speak of "German food" is a misnomer. There are no fewer than 1,000 kinds of bread, several hundred distinct *types*—not just brands—of beer, and scores of hams, sausages, and smoked meats, each one a local specialty. Bratwurst comes in a dozen varieties, shapes, and sizes, seasoned with a shelf-full of different spices. No Stuttgarter could survive without a helping of *Spätzle* to accompany the noonday meal. *Labskaus,* a mush of corned-beef hash mixed with red beets, may be the dish of the gods for a native of Hamburg or Bremen, but anathema to the Münchener, who swoons over *Weisswürste,* plump "white sausages" made of minced veal, various herbs, and grated lemon peel.

Nor (except in the written form, called *Schriftdeutsch*) can you really talk about a common language. There is *Hochdeutsch,* High German, and *Plattdeutsch,* Low German, which is very close to Dutch, Danish, and even English. The designations allude to the altitude and geography—Low German being the form spoken in areas close to the Low Countries—not to any refinements of grammar or pronunciation. Beyond those two basic distinctions you will encounter dozens of dialects—not simply accents—that, because they bristle with different words, phrases, and even grammatical constructions, border on being separate languages. To the untrained ear, a busload of Germans conversing in their native Bavarian, Berliner, Hessian, Rhinelandish, Saxon, Swabian, Thuringian, and Westphalian tongues would sound like a Tower of Babel on wheels.

Of course there are the great equalizers. One of them is the spate of Anglicisms that lace the lingo of advertising, business, finance, technology, science, and computerspeak. The other is the uni-language of nightly television. But don't count on that. Several years ago when the Bavarian broadcasting corporation produced a sitcom miniseries for the rest of the national network, station managers up north prudently inserted subtitles in *Schriftdeutsch*.

## The Shaping of Germany

A description of this multifarious and complex land as a single country with clearly defined borders applied, until the autumn of 1990, to fewer than 80 years of its history.

That brief period began in 1871 when Prince Otto von Bismarck, the prime minister of Prussia, created a cohesive nation-state out of a crazy quilt of independent kingdoms, principalities, and dwarf-sized duchies. Called the German Reich, this hodgepodge was ruled by the Prussian kings (known as *kaisers,* or emperors). After World War I and the last kaiser's abdication, accompanied by the overthrow of the still-reigning kings of Bavaria, Saxony, and Württemberg—whose capitals were, respectively, Munich, Dresden, and Stuttgart—Germany became the democratic Weimar Republic, so named because it was in the town of Weimar (now in East Germany), one-time residence of both Goethe and Schiller, that the constitutional convention met; Berlin was the capital. The Weimar Republic gave way to the Third Reich, under the dictatorship of Adolf Hitler and the Nazis. The era of German unity came to an abrupt and destructive close after World War II with the formal establishment in 1949 of West and East Germany as separate sovereign countries. From August, 1961, until November, 1989, those two Germanys were divided by the grim Berlin Wall and a heavily fortified border. Then, miraculously, the Wall crumbled and opened up, and faster than anyone had expected or dared to predict East and West Germany began moving toward unity—a process that first involved currency and economic union in July, 1990, and total political unity expected in the late fall and early winter.

The first sign of human or prehuman life in what is now Germany goes back about 500,000 years: a fossil jaw, found in 1907 near Heidelberg, of an apelike fellow called Heidelberg Man. A cast of the original fragment is on display in that city's Kurpfälzisches Museum. The next indication of habitation is even better known: The remains of Neanderthal Man, who lived 60,000 years ago near Düsseldorf in the Neander valley, were found there in 1856.

Celts, with a high level of civilization and culture, inhabited southern Germany long before the first Germanic tribes migrated from Asia into Central Europe, a process that began around 1000 B.C. and lasted more than 15 centuries. Although those early Germans were mentioned by a Greek navigator who sailed as far north as Norway, it was not until the time of Julius Caesar, who tried but failed to conquer them, that they entered clearly into recorded history.

The bloodiest confrontation between Romans and Germans was during the battle of Teutoberg Forest, near today's city of Detmold, in A.D. 9, when three of Augustus Caesar's finest legions were decimated by the Cherusci, a Germanic tribe led by the chieftain Hermann (Arminius). The battle site is now a kind of national shrine, and Hermann, sometimes confused with the mythological Siegfried, is celebrated as the arch-German hero. Although the Romans continued to clash with the Germanic tribes, even avenging the defeat by Hermann (who was killed by treachery in another battle seven years later), they made no other serious attempts to penetrate more deeply into the Germanic territories. Instead, they colonized the areas south of the Danube and west of the Rhine, establishing strong military forts at Bonn and Xanten and major cities such as Augsburg, Cologne, Kempten, and Trier. Trier ultimately became known as the Rome of the North, a city as populous—with 100,000 people—in the time of Constantius I and Saint Helena, the parents of Constantine the Great, as it is today. To protect their territory, the Romans built the *Limes,* a defensive wall of stone, palisades, and fortresses some 300 miles long, which zigzagged in a generally southeasterly direction from Cologne on the Rhine to Regensburg on the Danube.

These two principal German rivers actually rise not far from each other—the Rhine in the Swiss Alps, the Danube in the Black Forest—but then run off in opposite directions: the Rhine generally northwestward past France and through the Netherlands to the North Sea, the Danube southeastward through Bavaria, Austria, Hungary, the Balkans, and a piece of the Soviet Union to the Black Sea.

A tour of this **Roman Germany** can be a rewarding journey for travellers with a penchant for antiquities. There is much left to see.

**Xanten,** a town on the Rhine between the Dutch border and Düsseldorf, was once a military city with a population of 15,000. Its ruins have been made into an archaeological park with reconstructions of the Roman temples, barracks, private houses, and shops. **Cologne** (Köln) derives its name from *Colonia Claudia Ara Agrippinensis,* that is, Colony of Agrippina II, who was great-granddaughter of Augustus Caesar, sister of Caligula, mother of Nero, and niece as well as wife (third liaison for both) of Emperor Claudius. In A.D. 50 she badgered Claudius into elevating the town of her birth into a "retirement colony" for legionnaires-turned-merchants. It abounds with remnants of its Roman past, the best of which are displayed in the Roman-Germanic museum. This is a city where archaeological treasures just ooze out whenever there are excavations for a new subway line or the foundation for a new building, or when some householder digs in the basement to repair a broken drainage pipe.

**Trier** still has an immense Roman city gate, an amphitheater, several Roman baths, the palaces of Constantine and Helena, and a fourth-century bridge used for modern traffic. In **Baden-Baden**, which Emperor Caracalla made into a health resort more than 1,700 years ago, you can see the Roman baths right underneath the gleaming tiles and chrome equipment of the modern spa. Remnants of the Limes, including a well-preserved fort, can be found north of Frankfurt. **Augsburg** (German for *Augusta Vindelicorum,* Citadel of Augustus in the Land of the Vindelicians) was founded in 15 B.C. as a fortified encampment and then became the provincial capital of Raetia. Nearby **Kempten**, first mentioned in A.D. 18 as Cambodonum, has remains of its Roman forum, walls, and a basilica. **Regensburg**'s Porta Praetoria, Germany's oldest town gate, was built in 179 under Marcus Aurelius and now forms part of a hotel.

The Germanic peoples living within the empire adopted many Roman customs, attitudes, lifestyles, and modes of thought that still distinguish them from their cousins farther east and north. In the late fourth and early fifth centuries, as Rome declined and neared collapse, the Germanic tribes from beyond the Limes expanded south and west. The Vandals, Lombards, and various Goths pushed into Italy and Spain. The Burgundii descended on the region of France that bears their name. Tribes from today's Denmark and the Elbe river valley, the divide between Western and Central Europe—Jutes, Angles, and western Saxons—crossed the sea to England. And there were the eastern Saxons and the Franks, who dominated what is now Germany itself.

By the late seventh and early eighth centuries the face of Europe had been transformed by these various Germanic peoples. Rome itself was politically dead, with all power vested in the eastern emperors at Constantinople. East of the Rhine, between the Limes and the now advancing Slavs, lived the tribes that became the Germans of later times. West of the river a new realm, that of the Franks, had begun taking

shape and expanding its territory under increasingly powerful kings. The most powerful, and important in the subsequent development of civilization, was Charles the Great,
whom the French call **Charlemagne** and the Germans Karl-
der-Grosse. On Christmas Day in 800 Pope Leo III crowned
him emperor in Rome (on a stone that can still be seen in St.
Peter's).

The title *kaiser* (meaning caesar) implied that Charlemagne was the western Christian successor to the Roman
emperors, and with that papal act the Holy Roman Empire
(*das Heilige Römische Reich der Deutschen Nation*) was
born. In name it lasted more than a millennium, until 1806,
when Francis II of Austria, a Hapsburg, renounced the title
under pressure from a new emperor then ruling Europe:
Napoleon Bonaparte. Until the middle of the 16th century,
32 of these elected Holy Roman rulers were crowned in the
cathedral at Aachen (Aix-la-Chapelle) while sitting on a stone
throne that can still be seen there. Starting in 1562 the
ceremony was held in the Frankfurt cathedral, followed by a
gala coronation bash in the Römer (the town hall). For most
of those ten centuries, however, the "empire" was largely a
fiction. In fact, for a while, only the idea of it survived
Charlemagne, for in 843 the West Franks seceded to form
the nucleus of what became France, using Latin instead of
Old High German as the base of their language. The realm
of the East Franks went to one of Charlemagne's grandsons,
Louis (Ludwig) the German. Though another grandson, Lo-
thair, kept the title of Holy Roman Emperor, he got only a
narrow strip of land running from Belgium through Burgundy into Italy—the "Middle Kingdom," over which the
East and West Franks, alias the Germans and French, fought
for centuries. Only when the imperial crown went to King
Otto I in 962 did the empire revive—this time as a purely
German affair.

But as Voltaire pointed out, this German Reich was "neither holy, nor Roman, nor an empire." It was largely an
illusion, with grave long-term consequences for Germany,
for in a sense the Germans are still paying the price. Prussia's Bismarck tried to reconstitute the Reich idea, albeit
excluding the Austrians, whose Hapsburg rulers had been
the Holy Roman emperors from 1273 to 1806.

One trouble with the Holy Roman Empire was that it was an
anemic substitute for the unified monarchy that Germany
lacked. Conversely, it became a major obstacle to the creation
of such a monarchy. The kaisers were not only peripatetic,
travelling from one castle to another with no place they could

call a capital, but, having no real source of revenue, were politically impotent as well. Real power during most of the 1,000 years rested not with the emperors but with the counts, dukes, margraves, electors, prince-bishops, and kings of the various German states. By the middle of the 17th century there were 350 of these states.

While other European countries were unifying under their kings and becoming major powers, the various Germanys, despite the imperial umbrella, became increasingly centrifugal. To complicate matters, there were also the deep religious divisions precipitated by **Martin Luther**, who appeared on history's stage October 31, 1517, when he nailed his Ninety-five Theses attacking the Roman clergy and its abuses to the door of the castle church in Wittenberg (now in East Germany). Thus began the Reformation, which altered the Germanys—and the rest of Europe—dramatically and forever. His Reformation accelerated the atomization of Germany into Protestant and Catholic dwarf states, each of whose local rulers determined the religion his subjects should practice. Moreover, it also triggered a century of violence that culminated in the Thirty Years War (1618 to 1648), during which nearly every German town was sacked at least once and seven million people—one third of the population—were killed.

Though the Germanys flourished culturally and economically during the millennium of the Holy Roman Empire and also in the years of the 19th century following its demise, politically they became increasingly provincial and parochial. Each town, city, county, duchy, principality, and kingdom developed its own laws and lifestyle and cultivated its own customs, even costumes. Some, like Bavaria and Saxony, rose to become middleweight European powers in the 18th century, and one, Prussia (sometimes derisively referred to as "not a state with an army but an army with a state"), even became a heavyweight—so musclebound that by the second half of the 1700s King Frederick the Great was sitting down with Austria's Empress Maria Theresa and Russian tsarina Catherine the Great to divide Poland and make colonial mincemeat of other independent countries of Eastern Europe. By 1870, when Prussia went to war against France, it was so powerful that it could impose hegemonial unity—a kind of "second Reich"—on the other German states. The eight decades of unity from 1871 to 1949, marked by jingoism, chauvinism, military conquest, and racism, failed to create a single picture from the jigsaw pieces. Today—perhaps because most Germans have no clear concept of what Germany is or is supposed to be, especially in light of its division for more than 40 years, until autumn 1990, into West and East—these local differences are being not only preserved but nurtured and encouraged. Cultivating local accents and dialects is a vogue. Provincial museums are sprouting. Hardly a day passes, especially in the balmier months of the year, without dozens of local religious, historical, and folk festivals taking place in small towns and the provinces.

## Germany for Travellers

Given all this diversity, small wonder that Germany is so hard to describe. Which Germany? How many Germanys? They cannot be counted. Yet together they make a traveller's paradise. Nothing is really far away, but visiting Germany does require a *strategy,* for Germany cannot be properly explored fully, or enjoyed to its maximum, in a week or two, or even in a month or two.

Approach the country by selected areas or a region, preferably with a cultural, historical, artistic, or scenic theme, and if that trip whets your appetite, plan to return for a different view some other year. A week or two spent hopping around from Frankfurt to Cologne to Hamburg to Berlin to Munich to Heidelberg, with maybe a short jaunt to the Bavarian Alps, the Black Forest, and the rich northern coastal lands of Schleswig-Holstein—with a day's boat ride on the Rhine perhaps thrown in—will be more frustrating than pleasurable or rewarding. Bear in mind, too, that with a few exceptions, the really large cities offer the least, because virtually all of them were reduced to rubble during World War II and are reconstructions—sometimes good but more often bad—of what they once were. Germany is at its best in the smaller cities and towns, in the villages and countryside.

There are also numerous officially named, and sometimes clearly marked, **touristic routes** that lead through the most historic towns, the most picturesque villages, and the most breathtaking scenery. They are the products of local and regional tourism promoters who began plotting them out in the 1950s and 1960s during the *Wirtschaftswunder* (economic miracle) years, when the Germans yearned for, and started buying, the beetle-shaped cars they were exporting so successfully. These itineraries—which avoid the no-speed-limit multilane Autobahns—go along country roads and numbered federal highways (*Bundesstrassen*), through quaint old villages with cobblestone streets and towns surrounded by turreted Medieval walls—offering proof not only that motoring can still be fun but that there is still a Germany almost as you imagined it to be.

By now there are more than 140 such routes, and quite a number of them intersect. The oldest and most famous, laid out more than 40 years ago, is the *Romantische Strasse* (**Romantic Road**), a 230-mile journey between the Main river city of Würzburg, east of Frankfurt and the Alpine town of Füssen, near Innsbruck, Austria. Others, some of which we have included in our descriptions of various regions, are: the *Deutsche Märchenstrasse* (German Fairy Tale Road), which begins at Hanau, just east of Frankfurt, and winds its way generally northward for more than 300 miles to Bremen; the *Bier und Burgen Strasse* (Beer and Castle Road), which starts just a little south of Nürnberg and then runs westward to the Neckar river and continues along that stream north to Heidelberg; the *Deutsche Weinstrasse* (German Wine Road), a circular itinerary through the wine-growing towns west of the Rhine between the cities of Mainz and Karlsruhe; the *Barokstrasse* (Baroque Road), a convoluted itinerary of dazzling Baroque monasteries and churches in Swabia, south of Stuttgart and north of Lake Constance; and the *Schwarzwald Hochstrasse* (Black Forest High Road) in the country's southwestern corner. Vividly promoted with a plethora of literature, maps, and package deals by local boosters in the communities along their paths, all six rate very high with German vacationers themselves and reveal the country at its best. Moreover, they are easily and quickly accessible to anyone setting out with a rental car from Frankfurt airport, where most visitors arrive.

Our book's more detailed discussion of Germany's attractions begins, ironically, with a city that for most of the postwar period was really two and that was symbolic of the country's Cold War division: **Berlin**. It is the only capital—in both the political sense and by the yardstick of global cosmopolitan values—a unified Germany ever had. It played the political role only during those eight decades of German unity; the global cosmopolitan one only during the 14 years of the Weimar Republic, when Berlin was not only the undisputed heart of literary, musical, theatrical, artistic, fashionable, scientific, and technological Europe but also the Continent's biggest metropolis. Now that the Wall is gone and the city is in effect whole again, it was not yet certain as we went to press whether it would again become the political capital of a united Germany. But is was already girding to resume its role as the country's cosmopolitan center and, with more than 3.2 million inhabitants in the combined sectors, the largest city in Europe between Paris and Moscow.

A half century of dictatorship, wartime devastation, post-war occupation, Cold War division, and isolation from the European mainstream has, of course, left its mark on Berlin. Nonetheless, Berlin remains one of the great cities of the world, and the Berliner, in the face of adversity, remains unique—in spirit, sense of humor, love of art and culture, and zest for life. The city's chic, carefree, tolerant, and enthusiastic atmosphere is infectious. No other German city has as many truly first-rate museums, art collections, symphony orchestras, opera houses, theaters and cabarets, or as vibrant a nightlife.

**Northern Germany** and **the Hanseatic Cities** are a world of their own. Not only is this the heartland of *Plattdeutsch*—Low German—but it is a region that looks out to its Scandinavian neighbors across the Baltic, and across the North Sea to England. Indeed, Hamburgers are said to be more British than the British themselves.

It is a region of proud independence—other Germans call it cold aloofness—spiced by the sinful rambunctiousness that you find in all great harbor towns. **Bremen** and **Hamburg,** the latter West Germany's largest city and Europe's second biggest port after Rotterdam, were always and still are so independent that they are also *Bundesländer,* that is, states of the Federal Republic. **Lübeck**, pristine in its red-brick Romanesque-through-Baroque architecture, is famed not only as the birthplace of Thomas Mann and as the setting of his first novel, *Buddenbrooks,* but for its marzipan. **Lüneburg,** southeast of Hamburg, became rich through the mining of salt—the white gold of the Middle Ages—and today is a perfectly preserved Medieval town. All four cities were members of the Hanseatic League, the protective alliance of mercantile and seafaring city-states that dominated the trade of Europe from the 13th through 17th centuries.

What we call **the Center** is the area bordered by the North German Plain at the top, the densely wooded Harz Mountains and East Germany to the east, the raw hills of the Rhön range—the highlands of Hesse—in the south, and the Westerwald and Sauerland ranges in the west, laced by the lush, romantic valleys of the Werra, Fulda, Weser, Leine, Eder, and Lahn rivers. This is northern Hesse and Lower Saxony, the home base of the Guelphs, who inherited the duchy of Brunswick that became the kingdom of Hannover. One

Hannoverian king, George I, wore the crowns of both this and the English monarchies. **Hannover** has only a few reminders of its prewar splendor, as is the case with **Braunschweig** (Brunswick) and **Kassel**. But the smaller cities and towns—**Hameln**, famed for the Pied Piper legend, **Einbeck**, renowned for its beer, **Celle**, **Goslar**, and **Marburg** and **Göttingen**, the last two both university centers—are perfect gems of half-timbered architecture. North American visitors are still rare in this area, but the Danes, Swedes, Dutch, and English converge on it in droves.

**East Germany**, a term we use now only for its convenient reference value, is Bach-Handel-Luther-Goethe-Schiller country, especially the southern regions of Thüringen, Leipzig, and Dresden. All are commemorated by the houses in which they were born or lived. **Eisenach**, where Luther attended school as a youngster and later translated the Bible, is also the birthplace of Johann Sebastian Bach, whose family home is a magnificent museum. **Erfurt**, where Luther studied and became a friar, is the largest and best-preserved Medieval city in all Germany, rich with treasures of art and architecture. In **Weimar**, capital of a duchy whose rulers lavishly patronized the arts and literature, Bach spent the first two decades of his musical career, and both Goethe and Schiller lived there in the late 18th and early 19th centuries. Their homes, both museums, are among the chief attractions. Handel's birth house in **Halle** is an important musical-instrument museum. The spirit of Luther is indelibly etched in the churches and castle of **Wittenberg**. Bach's name haunts **Leipzig**, where from 1723 to his death in 1750 he was music director of St. Thomas's Church. **Dresden**, the "Florence on the Elbe"—until the February 1945 air raid that turned it into an inferno and wasteland—still has its Zwinger palace, the most exquisite example of Baroque architecture in all Germany, and its famous Semper opera house, where Richard Wagner and Richard Strauss premiered many of their works.

For more than 40 years a journey to East Germany took much advance planning, including a four- to six-week wait for a visa. That situation has improved markedly since mid-1990, but another complication has arisen that will prevail for the next two to three years: The country is virtually booked out. Since travel restrictions were lifted in early 1990, West Germans have been journeying east by the multitudes. Hotels are far too few and it will be a number of years before the deficit can be made up.

Moving back west, we then cover **Cologne** in the heart of the North-Rhine–Westphalia area. Besides the obvious—the cathedral—steep yourself in the city's Roman past and save time to visit some of its dozen Romanesque churches, several of which predate Charlemagne by a couple of centuries. Of the city's many museums, the Roman-Germanic, with its treasures of Roman glass and sculpture, the Ludwig, renowned for its stupendous collection of modern and contemporary art, and the Wallraf-Richartz, loaded with 13th-through 19th-century paintings, are the most important. The Altstadt, the old city quarter, abounds with colorful taverns, all dispensing *Kölsch,* the distinctive, tart local beer.

The **North Rhine area** is that stretch of the river around Cologne from Bonn, the capital of West Germany (immortalized by John Le Carré in his novel *A Small Town in Germany*), to Düsseldorf, the management and financial center of Germany's industrial heartland. The attractions, however, are not the functional government buildings in Bonn or the corporate headquarters and banks in Düsseldorf. Besides being Beethoven's birthplace (naturally, the house is a museum), **Bonn** really *is* a charming provincial town worth more than a detour. **Düsseldorf** lures travellers with its many fine restaurants, the nightlife in its cobblestone Altstadt, its role as a center of contemporary art, and the Königsallee, Germany's most elegant (and expensive) shopping street, a "miraculous kilometer" of conspicuous consumption. Though not a Rhineside city, **Aachen**, with its coronation cathedral, Holy Roman throne, and Charlemagne's bejeweled gold sarcophagus, is vital to understanding what the Rhine is all about. It is less than an hour by car or train west from either Bonn or Cologne, near the Belgian border.

Of the many wine-growing regions, one of the most idyllic (if you shut your eyes to the mobs of weekend and summer visitors) is the Moseltal, the **Mosel river valley**, which twists and winds from Trier near the Luxembourg border east to Koblenz, where it flows into the Rhine. The valley is important not only for connoisseurs of wine, who have long rated those of the Mosel on a par with the vintages of the Rhine, but for **Trier**'s Roman ruins and the picture-postcard Medieval towns along the river. To appreciate this area fully, with perhaps a side trip to the Eifel hills and the backwoodsy Hünsruck region, driving is best, and you ought to spend a week.

**Frankfurt** deserves a better reputation. Derogatorily called "Krankfurt" and "Bankfurt," in the 1970s it was being touted—like New York—as proof that cities as such are doomed. But, also like New York, it has rebounded. Alas, most Germans are either unaware of this or refuse to acknowledge it. Sure, there are the skyscrapers of the many banks, with more to come, but you will also find a reconstructed old quarter, villagelike neighborhoods, lush parks, one of Europe's best zoos, and fine museums supported by 11 percent of the municipal budget—more, proportionally, than any other city in the world spends on culture and the arts.

Frankfurt, moreover, is the ideal takeoff point for the **Central Rhine Region** around it, an area encompassing far more than the **Rheingau**, best known for its wines, the cities of **Wiesbaden** and **Mainz**, and the central **Rhine river route** south of Koblenz. It also includes the **Odenwald** (Oden forest), where spring usually arrives a month before it comes to the rest of Germany; **Heidelberg**, popularized by Mark Twain in *A Tramp Abroad* and by Sigmund Romberg in *The Student Prince;* the loveliest and most dramatic segment of the **Castle Road**, along the **Neckar river;** and the **German Wine Road**, which will introduce you to the wines of the Palatinate, less well known abroad than those of the Mosel and the Rheingau, and take you close to the French border.

**Northern Bavaria** is the part of the former kingdom of Bavaria along and north of the Danube river that bisects Bavaria, today West Germany's largest state geographically and its most important culturally and climatically. **The Danube**, from Ulm to Passau via Regensburg, is almost a journey in itself, so rich in history, art, architecture, and verdant scenery that a few days hardly do it justice. North of it the itinerary focuses on the best of **Franconia** ("land of the Franks"). This area, more than half the size of Switzerland, is a microcosmic version of all of Germany's patchwork attributes. It was ceded to Bavaria by Napoleon as a reward for Maximilian I's loyalty and allegiance to France. No wonder that in Munich people still speak of Franconia as "the colony." Before Napoleon's act of largesse, Franconia was a crazy quilt of independent cities such as **Nürnberg** and **Rothenburg**; powerful church states and prince-bishoprics such as **Würzburg**, the northern tip of the Romantic Road, and **Bamberg**, one of the most beautiful towns in the entire country; and various margraviates and dwarf duchies such as **Bayreuth**, site of the yearly Wagner Festival, and **Coburg**, home of Queen Victoria's beloved Albert. To explore it all would take weeks. Our discussion concentrates on the highlights and a few selected routes.

**Munich** is Germany's "secret capital," the city toward which most tourists—several million annually—gravitate, and where most Germans—60 percent, according to various surveys—would like to live if they could. It has no match in art, music, cuisine, and the joys of life: a fulfillment of Bavarian King Ludwig I's dream to make his capital a city "of which all Germans will be proud." Alas, there is also nothing in Germany to equal its cost, but the visitor will find it a price worth paying. **The Romantic Road** is the tourist route to which we have devoted a separate chapter: a journey that will take you southward from Würzburg through such perfectly preserved, completely walled Medieval cities as Rothenburg, Dinkelsbühl, and Nördlingen, across the Danube to 2,000-year-old Augsburg, and farther to the Bavarian Alps, where you will find "Dream King" Ludwig II's 19th-century fairy-tale castle, Neuschwanstein.

**Upper Bavaria** (southern Bavaria, called Upper because it is higher in altitude) is the region, first of all, of the Bavarian Alps, which stretch in jagged, snow-capped majesty along the Austrian frontier from Berchtesgaden, near Salzburg in the east, to the Allgäu district and the eastern tip of the Bodensee (Lake Constance) in the west: a land of beautiful lakes, highland pastures, neat mountain villages, Baroque churches with onion domes, and the castles built in the 1860s to 1880s by the eccentric Ludwig II, whom the French poet Paul Verlaine gushingly called "the Sun King of the 19th century." But Bavaria also means Medieval towns such as Landshut, Butghansen, and Wasserberg.

**Stuttgart**, once capital of the kingdom of Württemberg, is today the heart of Germany's technological belt, home of two of the country's most expensive and prestigious car brands, Mercedes-Benz and Porsche (BMWs are made in Munich). More important, however, it is the center of **Swabia**, a region that, looking north, includes the Medieval city of **Schwäbisch Hall**, and southward, the lovely old university town of **Tübingen**, the German shore of Lake Constance, and the **Baroque Road**, which will lead you to the spectacular churches and monasteries of Zwiefalten, Ochsenhausen, and Weingarten.

The **Black Forest** and **Baden**, at the southwestern corner of the country, stretching along the right bank of the Upper Rhine, facing France from Baden-Baden to the Swiss border, is Europe's oldest vacation land. Not only did the Romans go for rest and recreation to the spas, but it was in the densely wooded hill country of the Black Forest (Schwarzwald) and in its picturesque cuckoo clock–making villages that modern tourism began in the 19th century, with the advent of the railroads. More important, at least for those who agree that half the fun of travelling is eating when you get there, this small niche of Germany, with its distinct regional cuisine, partly influenced by neighboring France and Switzerland, has the best culinary delights that the country offers, not to mention more starred and top-rated restaurants per capita and per square mile than any other area. To add to the pleasures, the best of them are in centuries-old inns. Our itinerary includes the resort villages of Triberg, Hinterzarten, and Titisee, where you will find as many cross-country skiers in winter as hikers in summer, and, of course, the gold-plated spa and casino city of **Baden-Baden** and Medieval **Freiburg-im-Briesgau**, with its magnificent Gothic minster.

To be sure, there is more to Germany than we can cover in this book: Saarland (West Germany's smallest state, bordering Luxembourg and France) and, sadly, the magnificent old town of **Münster** and the **Münsterland** on the German Plain lie too far afield geographically to relate to our other regions. But there is more than enough variety and pleasure in each of the areas we do present to whet your appetite for a return to other parts of the jigsaw puzzle of Germany year after year.

## USEFUL FACTS

### *When to Go*

Virtually any season is inviting for the visitor to Germany. In the Rhineland and the Altes Land along the Elbe, the showy blossoms of fruit trees brighten the landscape in April and May. Near Mannheim, May and June are asparagus time, when special menus feature that most springlike of vegetables in dozens of ways. Swollen streams rush and seethe in the Harz mountains.

When summer days are hot and thundery, the lakes of Upper Bavaria provide refreshing swimming. Hamburg is hot, but there is cool sailing in the blue waters of the Baltic, off Kiel.

September–October is grape-harvest time in the valleys of the Rhine, Mosel, and Danube rivers. *Altweiber Sommer* (Old Woman's Summer), these fall days are called, when the gold of the grapevines and cornstalks is highlighted by the bright sun and there are wine festivals in the villages along the wine rivers. And late September and early October mean heavy beer drinking in Munich, of course—Oktoberfest.

November can be overcast. December may be, too, but it hardly matters, for the merriment of Christmas markets is everywhere. In Nürnberg, it's toy-market time.

When full-fledged winter comes in the Rhineland there is the gaiety of the carnivals preceding Lent. Munich celebrates with Fasching; the Black Forest with Fasnet. Skiers profit by the snow in the Black Forest and the Bavarian Alps; the more culturally inclined have a wide choice in city centers of operas and concerts and ballets to attend, and castles and museums—sans crowds—to visit.

### Entry Documents

One result of the rapidly paced political changes of the last year is that restrictions on travel between the Germanys have all but disappeared. Only a valid passport is needed for citizens of the United States, Australia, Canada, or New Zealand wishing to visit Germany for stays of three months or less. Identity cards are sufficient for British subjects. For up-to-the-minute reports on entrance requirements contact one of the offices listed under For Further Information at the end of this section.

### Arrival at Major Gateways by Air

From almost anywhere in North America and the United Kingdom, flying to Germany is easy. Lufthansa, Germany's national carrier, offers nonstop service to Frankfurt from Atlanta, Boston, Chicago, Dallas/Fort Worth, Los Angeles, Miami, New York, San Francisco, and Washington. The airline also flies to Frankfurt from Philadelphia and Houston with one stop. Connections can be made through Frankfurt to Hamburg, Cologne/Bonn, Nürnberg, and Stuttgart.

Lufthansa has nonstop service to Düsseldorf from Los Angeles, Miami, New York, and, in the summer months, Chicago. There is also nonstop service from New York to Munich and direct Munich service from Los Angeles, Miami, and, in summer, Chicago. All flights to Frankfurt offer connections to Hamburg, Cologne/Bonn, Nürnberg, and Stuttgart. Lufthansa also now has nonstop service from Newark to Cologne, Hamburg, and Frankfurt, and from Washington, D.C., to Cologne.

A Lufthansa special is the excellent streamlined sightseeing train right along the Rhine, the **Lufthansa Airport Express**, which operates four times a day in each direction and will whisk the air-weary by rail from Frankfurt-am-Main or Düsseldorf airports to Cologne, Bonn, or Düsseldorf rail stations. The trip to Cologne from Frankfurt takes two hours; to Düsseldorf two and a half—only about an hour more than flying. As on an aircraft, food is served to passengers at their seats by uniformed attendants. Booking must be made at the time of air booking, and only ticketed Lufthansa passengers may use the train.

Airlines flying to Germany from the United States, in addition to Lufthansa, are American, Delta, Northwest, Pan American, United, USAir, and the scheduled charter airline LTU. Air France, British Airways, Dan Air, EuroBerlin-France, Pan American, and TWA are the carriers flying to Berlin from West German cities at press time; Lufthansa will undoubtedly be operating into Berlin in the near future.

There is nonstop Lufthansa service to Frankfurt from Montreal, Toronto, and Vancouver, with connections to other points. Air Canada flies nonstop, too, from Toronto to Frankfurt, and provides flights via London to Düsseldorf from Toronto and Montreal. Canadian Airlines International has nonstop Toronto–Munich service and direct service from Vancouver to Frankfurt. Ward Air and LTU scheduled charter service are also offered from various points.

From Melbourne and Sydney, Lufthansa and Qantas fly to Frankfurt via the Far East and Mid-East. Cathay Pacific's Frankfurt flights are from Brisbane and Perth, as well as from Melbourne and Sydney, with a change of aircraft in Hong Kong. Air New Zealand flies to Frankfurt from Auckland via Los Angeles.

The traveller from Britain, like the North American, has an abundance of flights from which to choose: Nonstop Lufthansa service goes from London to Bremen, Cologne, Düsseldorf, Frankfurt, Hamburg, Hannover, Munich, Nürnberg, and Stuttgart. British Airways' nonstop flights are from London to Berlin, Bremen, Cologne/Bonn, Düsseldorf, Frankfurt, Hamburg, Hannover, Munich, and Stuttgart. Pan American links London with Berlin, Frankfurt, Düsseldorf, Hamburg, Munich, and Nürnberg. There is Lufthansa service as well to Frankfurt and Düsseldorf from Birmingham and Manchester, and British Airways service from those cities to many German points. British Airways also flies routes from Newcastle, Edinburgh, and Glasgow to Germany.

KLM offers service from New York, via Amsterdam, to East Berlin; Lufthansa has Frankfurt–Leipzig and Munich–Leipzig flights; and Interflug, the East German airline, flies from Düsseldorf to Leipzig and from Hamburg to Dresden.

## Getting in from the Airports

Efficient bus or train service links major German airports with the cities they serve. At Frankfurt there is a train station directly beneath the airport, and trains make the 11-minute run to the city center every ten minutes for DM 5. There is also regular rail service from the airport station to many other cities in the country. Many InterCity trains stop at the airport station.

Düsseldorf airport also has a rail connection to the center of the city. From the airports in Hamburg, Nürnberg, and Stuttgart, bus service is offered, with an S-Bahn (subway) in prospect for Stuttgart. A bus from the Hamburg airport takes travellers to Lübeck. At all airports, Deutsche Bundesbahn (German Federal Railway) offices will send luggage on to a further destination.

In West Berlin, taxis and the number 9 bus are the links from the airport to the city. A new shuttle-bus service links Berlin's two airports.

West German trains are punctual, up-to-date, and efficient. Even better service is in prospect for 1991, when two new high-speed InterCity expresses are expected to be running between Hannover and Munich, with stops in Göttingen, Kassel, Fulda, Frankfurt, Mannheim, Stuttgart, Ulm, and Augsburg. The new trains will take just six hours between Hamburg and Munich—a trip that now takes eight and a half hours—and just an hour and 25 minutes from Frankfurt to Stuttgart, a journey now of two and a half hours.

Before leaving for Germany, look into the GermanRail-pass, GermanRailpass Junior, GermanRail Flexipass, and GermanRail Junior Flexipass, possession of any of which will do away with waits at ticket counters. Four-, nine-, and 16-day passes are available at rates considerably lower than regular rates, and Flexipasses will allow you to spread the number of days of travel you choose over a 21-day period. Both first- and second-class passes are sold. They may be used on all trains, including the super-express InterCity trains, as well as on selected subways, buses, and ships. With them, reservations are not required (though they are advised). GermanRailpasses must be purchased before you leave home.

Further information is available from travel agents and, in the United States, from GermanRail, 747 Third Avenue, New York, New York 10017; Tel: (212) 308-3100. In Canada, contact DER Tours at 1290 Bay Street, Toronto, Ontario M5R2C3; Tel: (416) 968-3272. In Britain, contact the General Agency of GermanRail, 10 Old Bond Street, London W1X 4EN; Tel: (171) 499-0578.

### Telephoning

The international telephone code for the Federal Republic of Germany (West Germany) is 49; for East Germany it is 37. When calling from within Germany, dial "0" before city codes. In the Federal Republic, both local and long-distance calls can be made from all post offices and coin-operated street booths. Thirty pfennigs is the base charge for a local call from a booth—but from a hotel it is considerably higher.

## Local Time
Germany is nine hours ahead of Pacific Standard Time, six hours ahead of Eastern Standard Time, and one hour ahead of Greenwich Mean Time, and during the changeover to Daylight Saving Time there is a brief period when Germany is another hour behind or ahead. Sydney is ten hours ahead of Germany.

## Electric Current
The electric current is 220 volts AC in both Germanys; North American appliances will require an adapter and adapter plugs.

## Currency
The monetary unit of both Germanys is now the deutsche mark, made up of 100 pfennigs. Coins come in denominations of 5, 2, and 1 mark and in 50-, 10-, 5-, 2-, and 1-pfennig pieces; bills in denominations of DM 1,000, 500, 200, 100, 50, 20, 10, and 5.

## Tipping
In restaurants and cafés in the Federal Republic, a service charge is usually added to the bill, but rounding out the total bill with an extra smaller amount is expected. Tipping is also expected by taxi drivers and porters and in beauty parlors. Be sure to carry small change for tipping attendants in some W.C.s.

## Renting a Car and Driving
Germany has an outstanding toll-free road system with many superhighways where service stations are open 24 hours a day. The traffic signs are international. Unless marked otherwise, there is no speed limit on the Autobahns, but 80 mph (130 km/p/h) is the recommended Autobahn speed; 35 mph (55 km/p/h) is the in-town speed.

When you are buying your airline ticket you can arrange at the same time to rent a car at the airport where you will be landing. Autohansa, Avis, Budget-Sirt, Europa Service, Hertz, Severin and Company, and Inter-rent are among such car-rental companies. Arrangements for car leasing for short and long stays can also be made in North America through

Auto-Europe at Box 1097 in Camden, Maine 04843 (Tel: 800-223-5555). Most major credit cards are accepted for car rental in Germany. Insurance is required, but is usually included in the rental fee. Either a national or an international driver's license is required.

Information desks for motorists are maintained at important border crossing points—at Wassersiebener Bucht near Flensburg (E 3 from Denmark); Ellen near Emmerich on the motorway from Holland; and Kiefersfelden and Schwarzbach on the motorways from Austria. The major German automobile clubs also have border offices and offices in large cities.

Road assistance is provided free of charge (except for the cost of the materials) by the Allgemeiner Deutscher Automobil Club (ADAC), which has emergency patrols on frequently travelled roads and motorways.

### Around Germany

*By Bus.* English-language bus tours in such popular touristic areas as the Grimm brothers' Fairy Tale Road and the Romantic Road through half-timbered towns and villages like Rothenburg, Dinkelsbühl, and Nördlingen are offered by Europa-Bus; bookings can be made by writing to Deutsche Touring, GmbH, Am Römerhof 17, D-6000, Frankfurt-am-Main, West Germany. Among operators providing package tours from North America (with air fare, accommodations, and some meals included) are Cosmos, Gogo Tours, Hapag-Lloyd Tours, Maupintour, Olsen, Travcoa, and TWA Getaway Tours.

*By Boat.* From Cologne to Mainz, vineyards, castles, cathedrals, and half-timbered villages edge the Rhine River, the stretch where the Lorelei sing their seductive songs. Köln-Düsseldorfer (KD) German Rhine Line vessels ply the Rhine and Mosel from April to October, making both day trips and two-night cruises from Cologne to Frankfurt. From April 1991, the line will also cruise the Elbe river between Hamburg and Dresden. Information is available from travel agents or from the KD Line at 370 Hamilton Avenue, White Plains, New York 10601; Tel: (914) 948-3600; in Canada from the KD Line, c/o Holiday House, 110 Richmond Street East, Toronto, Ontario M5C1P1; Tel: (416) 367-5860; in England from G. A. Clubb Rhine Cruise Agency, 80/81 St. Martin's Lane, London WC2; Tel: 836-1876; in Australia from World Travel Headquarters, Kindersley House, 33 Bligh Street, Sydney NSW 2000; Tel: 232-7233.

In summer, Hapag-Lloyd has 13- to 21-day cruises from Bremerhaven. Details can be obtained from Hapag-Lloyd

Tours in North America at 1640 Hempstead Turnpike, East Meadow, New York 11554; in England from Hapag-Lloyd Travel, 15 Maddox Street, London W1; Tel: 409-0894.

Other boat trips are offered by local tour operators in summer on Lake Constance, the Königssee in the Bavarian Alps, Hamburg harbor, and the Danube and Elbe rivers, and to the Frisian Islands of the North Sea; inquire locally.

### Business Hours

Shops and department stores in Germany are generally open in large cities from 9:00 A.M. to 5:30 P.M. Monday through Wednesday, from 9:00 A.M. to 8:30 P.M. on Thursday, and from 9:00 A.M. until 2:00 P.M. on Saturday. On the first Saturday of each month they remain open until 6:00 P.M., except May through September, when they close at 4:00 P.M. A daily lunchtime closing from 1:00 to 3:00 P.M. is common in shops in villages.

Bank hours are normally from 9:00 A.M. to 12:30 P.M. and from 2:30 to 3:45 P.M. weekdays (Thursday until 5:30 P.M.).

Museums are almost always closed on Monday. Hours otherwise tend to be from 10:00 A.M. to 5:00 P.M. year round, with slightly longer hours in summer. Churches—even some of those of historic and architectural importance—are certain to be open only for Sunday services; for other hours of opening it is wise to check with the local Reisebüro (tourist office).

Offices and shops are closed on New Year's Day, Epiphany (January 6), Rose Monday and Shrove Tuesday (Carnival), Good Friday, Easter Sunday and Monday, Labor Day (May 1), Ascension Day (early June), Whit Monday (May or June), Corpus Christi Day (June), National Commemoration Day (June 17), Assumption Day (August 15), All Saints Day (November 1), the Day of Prayer and Remembrance (November 21), and Christmas Eve, Christmas Day, and the day after Christmas.

### For Further Information

German National Tourist Offices are maintained at 747 Third Avenue, New York, New York 10017 (Tel: 212-308-3300); 444 South Flower Street, Suite 2230, Los Angeles, California 90071 (Tel: 213-688-7332); 175 Bloor Street East, North Tower, Toronto, Ontario M4W3R8, Canada (Tel: 416-968-1570); Nightingale House, 65 Curzon Street, London W1Y 7PE, England (Tel: 4953990); Lufthansa House, 12th Floor, 143 Macquarie Street, Sydney 2000, Australia (Tel: 221-1008).

—*Phyllis Méras*

# BIBLIOGRAPHY

ROLAND BAINTON, *Here I Stand: A Life of Martin Luther* (1950). A fascinating and meticulously researched account, regarded by many as the best one-volume Luther biography in any language. Illustrated with many woodcuts and engravings.

DENNIS L. BARK AND DAVID R. GRESS, *A History of West Germany* (1989). This brilliant and provocative two-volume study covers the period from 1945 to 1988, bringing postwar German history alive in vivid detail with an all-star cast of diplomats and politicians including Adenauer, Brandt, Strauss, Erhard, Heuss, Reuter, and many others.

GEOFFREY BARRACLOUGH, *The Origins of Modern Germany* (1946; frequently revised). This short and comprehensive survey by a leading British scholar of Germany begins with the formation of Medieval Germany around A.D. 800 and traces the nation's history to 1939.

FRANZ H. BÄUML, *Medieval Civilization in Germany 800–1273* (1969). Critical assessment by a highly regarded medievalist of the time from the coronation of Charlemagne to the election of Rudolf of Hapsburg to the Imperial throne.

HERBERT BAYER, WALTER GROPIUS, ISE GROPIUS, editors, *Bauhaus 1919–1928* (1938; many times reprinted). This small book is required reading for anyone who is interested in modern art.

JEREMY BERNSTEIN, *Einstein* (1973). The author, a physicist and popular writer, reviews Einstein's scientific achievements and gives an absorbing account of his personality and his life, most of which was lived in Germany before he fled the Nazis.

HEINRICH BÖLL, *The Stories of Heinrich Böll* (1986). Spanning almost four decades, these stories by one of Germany's greatest writers make up a chronicle of 20th-century experience that blends wit with a large and tragic view of life.

JAN CHIAPUSSO, *Bach's World* (1968). This book, which plumbs more deeply than most other studies the religious, philosophical, and social milieu of Bach's time and its effect on his development, offers a rewarding look into the Weimar region's mentality following the Reformation.

NORMAN COHN, *The Pursuit of the Millennium: Revolutionary Millenarian and Mystical Anarchists of the Middle Ages* (1957). Not just about Germany, but an important historical, sociological, and psychological study of the sects that seemed to be especially common in Medieval Germany.

MADELEINE PELNER COSMAN, *Fabulous Feasts: Medieval Cookery and Ceremony* (1976). Though more focused on England than the Continent, this fascinating volume, studded with reproductions of drawings, woodcuts, and illuminations (including many from Germany), will captivate those interested in the food, herbal medicine, literature, and art of the time.

JOHN DILLENBERGER, editor, *Martin Luther: Selections from His Writings* (1961). The viewpoint here is religious rather than historical, political, or autobiographical, but because of Luther's inestimable importance to German cultural history these selections are nonetheless good background for a general understanding of the country.

JOHANN PETER ECKERMANN, *Conversations with Goethe* (1836). Early 19th-century Germany from the viewpoint of the most renowned German figure of the Enlightenment. "The best German book there is," according to Nietzsche. Translated from the German.

BERNT ENGELMANN, *In Hitler's Germany: Everyday Life in the Third Reich* (1985). Gripping and haunting account of the war years in Berlin and elsewhere.

ERIK ERIKSON, *Young Man Luther.* Psychobiography at its best investigates the origins of a rebel.

OTTO FRIEDRICH, *Before the Deluge: A Portrait of Berlin in the 1920's* (1972). A comprehensive, fascinating historical portrait by a noted American journalist of the political, cultural, and social life of Berlin between the wars and the people who created and destroyed it.

H. F. GARTEN, *Modern German Drama* (1959). A lively and readable analysis of dramatists from Hauptmann to Brecht to the Swiss Dürrenmatt, exploring the art form that has served as Germany's main vehicle for spiritual, social, and political thought.

PETER GAY, *Weimar Culture: The Outsider as Insider* (1968). A brief historical introduction by a prominent scholar to the seminal between-the-wars epoch.

A. J. GRANT, translator and editor, *Early Lives of Charlemagne by Einhard and the Monk of St. Gall* (1966). Translation of Einhard's *Vita Karoli Magni imperatoris* and of Notker's

*Gesta Karoli Magni* as published in 1867 in volume 4 of *Bibliotheca rerum germanicarum*.

KARL GEIRINGER, *The Bach Family: Seven Generations of Creative Genius* (1954). Includes a large section on the life and work of Johann Sebastian Bach, tracing his various moves throughout the area around and including Erfurt, Weimar, and Leipzig. Includes map, music, and index of compositions by members of the Bach family.

FELIX GILBERT, *A European Past: Memoirs 1905–1945* (1988). A well-known historian who was born and raised in Berlin reminisces about life in pre-Nazi Germany, with illuminating reflections on German culture, history, and politics—and what might have been.

GÜNTER GRASS, *The Tin Drum* (1959). Probably the most famous novel about life in immediate post–World War II Germany as it struggled to come out from under the devastation of war and defeat. Translated from the German.

MARTIN GREGOR-DELLIN, *Richard Wagner: His Life, His Work, His Century* (1980). An entertaining and masterful analysis of the most controversial figure in the history of opera, recounting his tempestuous life from the early hardships and artistic frustrations to the subsequent triumphs. Translated from the German.

WILHELM GRIMM, *Dear Mili* (1988). With lavish illustrations by Maurice Sendak, this recently discovered fairy tale should delight young Penguins.

KARSTEN HARRIES, *The Bavarian Rococo Church: Between Faith and Aestheticism* (1983). Through careful analysis and lavish illustration, the reader is introduced to a wide variety of Bavarian churches and those features of the Bavarian Rococo that determine its particular style and set it apart from or relate it to the French Rococo and the Italian Baroque.

FRIEDRICH HEER, *The Holy Roman Empire* (1968). In this excellent survey, a noted Austrian historian traces the Holy Roman Empire from the time of Charlemagne through the rise and decline of the Hapsburgs and the attendant political, religious, and social turmoil.

HEINRICH HEINE, *The Poetry and Prose of Heinrich Heine*. Edited by Frederic Ewen. These writings, by one of Germany's all-time literary greats who lived at the end of the Enlightenment in the Napoleonic era, are full of wonderful evocations of the Germany of his day.

CHRISTOPHER HOGWOOD, *Handel* (1984). A famous conductor of Handel's music sketches a comprehensive and entertaining portrait of the developing character and career of Handel, from his early years in Halle and Hamburg to the heyday of opera and oratorio in London.

HAJO HOLBORN, *A History of Modern Germany* (in three volumes: 1959, 1964, 1969). A massive study covering modern German history from the Reformation to the fall of Hitler by an expatriate German scholar who, forbidden to teach by the Nazis, continued his distinguished career at Yale University.

MICHAEL JACKSON, *The New World Guide to Beer* (1977). This comprehensive volume, recognized as the standard in its field, lives up to its name by covering the world, with Germany coming in for a lion's share of the prosits.

MORITZ JAGENDORF, *Tyll Ulenspiegel's Merry Pranks* (1938; many times reprinted). Classic tales of Till Eulenspiegel, the famous prankster who travelled throughout Medieval Germany and is one of its most enduring folkloric figures. Illustrated by Fritz Eichenberg. Translated from the German.

HUGH JOHNSON, *Atlas of German Wines and Traveller's Guide to the Vineyards* (1986). By one of the world's leading authorities on wine. Includes full-color photographs and maps, and a glossary of German wine terms.

KÄTHE KOLLWITZ, *The Diary and Letters of Käthe Kollwitz* (1988). This diary of one of the great German Expressionist artists explains much of the spirit, wisdom, and internal struggle that was eventually transmuted into her art.

BARBARA MILLER LANE, *Architecture and Politics in Germany 1918–1945* (1968). The author shows that Nazi cultural policy was largely the product of conflicting ideas about art held by Nazi leaders.

VICTOR LANGE, *The Classical Age of German Literature* (1982). A survey of the central, or "classical," period of German literature, with special attention to, of course, Goethe and Schiller, as well as Herder, Lessing, Richter, Wieland, and others.

PETER LASKO, *The Kingdom of the Franks: Northwest Europe Before Charlemagne* (1971). An illuminating (and lavishly illustrated) study focusing on the misnamed "Dark Ages," a period with a highly developed civilization and culture, traces of which still survive.

ALEXIS LICHINE, *New Encyclopedia of Wines and Spirits* (1981). This classic compendium for the discerning drinker devotes many pages to the bounty of Germany.

GEORGE LICHTHEIM, *Europe in the Twentieth Century* (1972). A survey of thought and culture in relation to political events, much of it focused on developments in Germany.

DAVID MACAULAY, *Cathedral: The Story of Its Construction* (1973). This award-winning, meticulously illustrated book for children and adults shows the intricate step-by-step process of a cathedral's growth.

GOLO MANN, *The History of Germany Since 1789* (1968). The author, the son of Thomas Mann and one of the foremost German historians of our time, traces the sweep of intellectual developments in Germany since the French Revolution and chronicles political events as well. Translated from the German.

THOMAS MANN, *Buddenbrooks* (1902). A vivid and engrossing account of the transition of a Hanseatic (Lübeck) merchant family from 19th-century stability to early 20th-century uncertainty. The novel, banned by Hitler, endures as one of the classics of German literature. Translated from the German.

GEORGE R. MAREK, *Beethoven: A Biography of a Genius* (1969). A comprehensive and scholarly portrait that is intended, in the words of the author, to "help illumine the artist as a human being."

ANDREW MARTINDALE, *Gothic Art* (1967). One of the best available surveys of this creative period in Western art.

NANCY MITFORD, *Frederick the Great* (1970). Frederick, brilliant military strategist and statesman, scholar, musician, and patron of the arts, is sketched with wit and humor by the author, who draws almost all of her material from contemporary sources. With lavish illustrations.

CHARLES E. PASSAGE, *Friedrich Schiller* (1975). A brief and lively volume providing background and information for each of the nine dramas by the premier dramatist of his time and great shaper of German culture.

DIETHER RAFF, *A History of Germany from the Medieval Empire to the Present* (1985). The concentration here is on the post-Bismarck era and on relationships between Germany and the other nations of Europe (and the United

States), with numerous chapters about the post–World War II era. Translated from the German.

JOHN ROWLANDS, *The Age of Dürer and Holbein: German Drawings 1400–1550* (1988). With particular emphasis on Dürer and Holbein the Younger, this work also surveys the main regions of artistic production, including drawings by Lucas Cranach, Martin Schongauer, and Albrecht Altdorfer.

JEFFREY L. SAMMONS, *Heinrich Heine: A Modern Biography* (1979). The author shows how Heine distilled a pattern of poetic insight and humanistic responsibility in the face of obstacles not unlike those affecting dissident writers throughout the world in our own day.

HORST SCHARFENBERG, *The Cuisines of Germany: Regional Specialties and Traditional Home Cooking* (1989). The book has some cookbook elements, but is also useful for reading about the food itself, as the title indicates. Translated from the German.

ALBERT SCHWEITZER, *J. S. Bach.* (1905; many times reprinted). Schweitzer's great work on Bach treats his subject from the standpoint not of a single art, but of art and science universally, and delves not only into the composer and his work, but into the very essence of music.

WILLIAM L. SHIRER, *The Rise and Fall of the Third Reich: A History of Nazi Germany* (1959, 1960). A three-volume account of the Hitler years in fast-paced, gripping, and exhaustively researched detail by a distinguished American foreign correspondent, news commentator, and historian of the contemporary world.

JACQUELINE SIMPSON, *European Mythology* (1987). One of a series of the world's mythologies and legends, this fascinating, lavishly illustrated book discusses recurring beliefs and stories that for centuries shaped the European peasant's outlook, with considerable attention paid to Germany.

OTTO VON SIMSON, *The Gothic Cathedral: Origins of Gothic Architecture and the Medieval Concept of Order* (1956, 1962; many times reprinted). A highly regarded study that is ranked in its evocative power on a par with Henry Adams's *Mont-Saint-Michel and Chartres.*

LOUIS L. SNYDER, *The Blood and Iron Chancellor: A Documentary-Biography of Otto von Bismarck* (1967). It will be hard to put down this swiftly paced and scholarly account of this enigmatic and larger-than-life personality.

PHILIPP SPITTA, *Johann Sebastian Bach: His Work and Influence on the Music of Germany 1685–1750* (1880). Though more than a hundred years old, this three-volume study is still one of the best and most detailed accounts of Bach's music and life.

WOLFGANG STECHOW, *Northern Renaissance Art 1400–1600: Sources and Documents* (1966). An intriguing assortment of documents, contracts, and letters of the period, the German portion relating particularly to the work of Tilman Riemenschneider, Dürer, Grünewald, and Hans Holbein the Younger.

A. J. P. TAYLOR, *The Course of German History* (1946–1962). A famous historian discusses in a concise survey how the Germans have come to be what they are.

MARIE VASSILTCHIKOV, *Berlin Diaries 1940–1945* (1987). Days in the wartime life of a young aristocrat; extraordinary reading.

C. V. WEDGWOOD, *Thirty Years War* (1962). The classic historical account of the religious wars that tore Germany asunder.

JOHN WILLET, *Art & Politics in the Weimar Period: The New Sobriety 1917–1933* (1978). Germany as a post–World War I center of a new cultural movement. Illustrated.

ARMIN ZWEITE AND ANNEGRET HOBERG, *The Blue Rider in the Lenbachhaus* (1989). Full-color reproductions of masterpieces by Franz Marc, Wassily Kandinsky, Gabriele Münter, Alexei Jawlensky, August Macke, and Paul Klee, with commentaries and brief biographies.

—*Anne Leo Ellis*

# BERLIN

*By John Dornberg*

It's claimed that you can get by with less sleep in Berlin than anywhere else in the world because of *Berliner Luft*— Berlin air. Enterprising souvenir merchants sell it in cans. Today, neither the canned air nor the air that Berliners breathe is as bracingly pure as it used to be, largely due to pollution from the unfiltered smokestacks of surrounding East Germany. However, one thing about the air has not changed: its electrifying quality. And you have to go to Berlin to experience that.

Few cities have made so much news and history. Berlin has usually been associated with something startling, stimulating, and significant, not just in politics but also in business, science, technology, art, theater, music, literature, cinema, fashion, and architecture.

Politically, the city has played many roles. It was the capital of the duchy of Brandenburg, which became the kingdom of Prussia in 1701 when Frederick I crowned himself king. By 1871, Berlin was the capital of the Second German Reich, that of the kaisers; later it was the capital of the short-lived democratic Weimar Republic; and eventually Berlin became the headquarters of Hitler's Third Reich. After the war Berlin was on the front line of the Cold War, the place where two ideologies, two political systems, and, indeed, two different worlds, met and occasionally collided. The city's 3.2 million people were physically divided for 28 years by the grim Berlin Wall that separated West from East.

The Wall opened and began crumbling in November, 1989. This ugly symbol of a dark era is virtually gone, except for the pieces of it being hawked by souvenir vendors. Less than a year after that momentous event, the two halves of

Berlin have virtually joined into one, with no more passport controls and with a single currency. The city is whole again, but in a sense more in the focus of international attention than ever before.

To be sure, at just over 750 years of age, Berlin is still an adolescent compared to other cities in Germany, some of which were urban centers of Medieval Europe when Berlin was still a frontier trading post. Youth notwithstanding, however, Berlin is special. It is delightfully kaleidoscopic, a vibrant city supercharged with high-voltage vitality and, since the Wall began to crumble, imbued with an optimism that seems to underscore its citizens' ability to survive all crises with humor and wit.

Berlin is not a city that can be mastered in three or four hours. To "see" Berlin may take three or four days; to figure out what makes it tick could take a lifetime.

Sheer size has something to do with this. In population— 3.2 million—Berlin is the most populous city between Paris and Moscow. In area, 341 square miles, it is one of the largest in the world. Nearly one third of the city is covered by forests, such as the Grunewald, Spandau, Tegel, and Köpenick, and by farmers' fields. Parts of Berlin are still so bucolic that the city hosts the annual *Grüne Woche,* Germany's biggest agricultural fair. Berlin has three large lakes, the Tegelersee, the Wannsee, and the Müggelsee, and two rivers, the Havel and the Spree. There are 113 miles of rivers and canals and about 1,000 bridges—more than in Venice. Before World War II, Berlin was Germany's second-largest inland port, and both commercial shipping and pleasure boating are still practiced. The Weisse Flotte, or white fleet, of excursion steamers and ferries plies the waterways, and some 75,000 pleasure boats are registered in Berlin.

Life in Berlin is as diverse as its geography. You'll find not just one Berlin, nor even the two once divided by the Wall, but dozens: a jigsaw puzzle of neighborhoods, communities, impressions, moods, and scenes. Within the city limits there are still four 18th-century windmills, one of which was grinding grain as recently as 1980; 55 village churches dating from the 13th century; and 70 weekly outdoor produce markets.

To understand this diversity it helps to know that it was only in 1920 that Berlin became the huge metropolis it is today. That year nearly a dozen independent cities and 59 small towns were incorporated.

If anything here approximates a common denominator, it

is the distinctive Berlin dialect, plus a kind of braggadocio that other Germans call *Berliner Schnauze,* which, loosely translated, means "Berlin lippiness."

*Berlin bleibt Berlin!* "Berlin will always be Berlin!" So goes a popular saying. When it was coined in the 1960s after the Wall was built, it had a political meaning. Now that the Wall is just a bad dream, it has a new meaning: Berlin, with 50 museums, 14 palaces, castles, and châteaus, three opera houses, eight symphony orchestras, five dozen theaters, and 8,000 restaurants, cafés, pubs, and night spots, is a continually fascinating city.

### MAJOR INTEREST

Schloss Charlottenburg and Schloss Bellevue
Zitadelle Spandau
Schloss Köpenick

Dahlem and its museums
Brücke Museum
The Charlottenburg museums
Museumsinsel and the Pergamon Museum

West Berlin's churches, especially the Kaiser-Wilhelm-
     Gedächtnis-Kirche
East Berlin's churches, especially the Dom

Kurfürstendamm, the Zoo, the Tiergarten, and the
     Reichstag
The Brandenburg Gate and Unter den Linden
The Airlift Monument and the memorial to the offi-
     cers who attempted to assassinate Hitler on July
     20, 1944
Memorial to the Victims of Fascism and Militarism
The Grunewald and Tiergarten
Köpenicker Forst

The Wall that divided West from East Berlin from August 13, 1961, to November 9, 1989, did not mark the first separation of this city. Indeed, Berlin started off as two small rival trading settlements on opposite banks of the Spree river in what was then the easternmost region of the Holy Roman Empire, the March of Brandenburg.

This remote area had been settled by barbarian Germanic tribes in the early part of the first century. By A.D. 500 they had moved westward and southward, leaving the land to the

Wends, a Slavic people whose modern descendants, now called Sorbs, still inhabit the Lausitz district in East Germany. Throughout the Dark Ages the Wends and Germans battled frequently. In the eighth century Charlemagne conquered the Wendish lands; by the tenth century, a coalition of Wendish tribes had regained the territory.

In 1147 Emperor Conrad III, Duke Henry the Lion of Saxony, and Count Albert the Bear joined forces against the Wends and defeated them for good. Albert the Bear settled the newly won land and, forging alliances through marriage, became margrave of Brandenburg. His margraviate, or "march," meaning frontier zone, was the cradle of what would become the kingdom of Prussia and the German Reich.

Germans soon began settling and reinforcing the forts the Wends had built, one of which was the Zitadelle Spandau. Around 1230 they founded two towns: Cölln on an island in the Spree river, and Berlin on the river's northeastern bank. Popular legend holds that the name Berlin may derive somehow from Albert the Bear, and it is true that the bear has been the city's symbol for many centuries. However, most city historians scoff at the idea and say that no one knows the origin of the name or what it once meant. Although they profited from commerce on the east-west trade route between Poznan in Poland and Magdeburg, the two towns were bitter rivals. Each had its own Rathaus and was surrounded by its own protective wall. Although only a few yards of water divided them, the towns steadfastly rebuffed attempts at amalgamation. It wasn't until 1307, when robber barons were ravaging the March of Brandenburg, that they agreed on a confederate union. A third city hall, where the combined towns' councillors could meet, was built on the *Lange Brücke* (Long Bridge), now called Rathausbrücke.

Shortly after their union, Berlin-Cölln, which then had a population of some 5,000, joined the Hanseatic League, an alliance of trading and shipping cities along the Baltic and the North Sea. Along with the land route that carried business to the town, the Spree gave Berlin-Cölln access to the Havel river, a tributary of the Elbe that empties into the North Sea, and an overland link was established with the Oder river, which flows into the Baltic Sea.

Berlin's history during most of the 14th and early 15th centuries was tumultuous. In 1323 the last of Albert's descendants died without heirs, and ownership of the Brandenburg margraviate reverted to the Holy Roman Emperor, Ludwig IV. He gave it to his son, but 50 years later Emperor Charles

IV conferred the margraviate on his own son, Wenceslaus, who, in turn, gave Brandenburg to his brother Sigismund, who then transferred ownership to one of his most loyal supporters and lieutenants, Burgrave Frederick von Hohenzollern. On several occasions during this period Brandenburg was also pawned to various moneylenders to finance the wars of its various owners.

Much changed with the advent of Frederick and the Hohenzollerns, who were to rule Berlin, Brandenburg, and all of Germany (not to mention a good chunk of Europe) for the next 400 years. They were a South German clan with vision and a lust for power. They not only routed the robber barons and subjugated the gentry, but they also crushed the independent cities, including Berlin itself. Frederick dissolved the merger of the two towns, disbanded their assembly of councillors, and forbade Berlin and Cölln to enter into alliances. He also confiscated substantial plots of land.

On one of those confiscated plots he laid the cornerstone for a grand palace, thus turning Cölln into his residence, seat of government, and capital of Brandenburg.

The Hohenzollerns, who also acquired Prussia to the east and territories as far west as Kleve on the Rhine, were among the first German rulers to adopt the views of Martin Luther and make Protestantism their state's official religion. To this day less than 15 percent of Berlin's population is Catholic.

Although epidemics and starvation during the Thirty Years War cut Berlin's population from 12,000 to 6,000, its political prospects continued to improve. Duke Friedrich Wilhelm, *der Grosse Kurfürst,* or the Great Elector, who took office in 1640, consolidated and expanded the Hohenzollern lands and encouraged immigration. By 1677 religiously motivated French refugees had already settled in Berlin, and when Louis XIV decided he could no longer tolerate the Calvinist Huguenots in Catholic France, the Great Elector offered them refuge in Protestant Brandenburg.

Of the 15,000 Huguenot immigrants who eventually came to Brandenburg, 6,000 settled in Berlin itself. By the time of the Great Elector's death in 1688, nearly one third of the city's population was French. They were granted the right of self-government and the right to found their own schools and churches. The Französischer Dom, or French cathedral, on the Platz der Akademie in East Berlin, built in 1764 and now restored after more than 40 years as a World War II ruin, is one of their greatest legacies.

The French influence on the city's economic life, administration, armed forces, arts, sciences, language, educational system, and fashions was immense. To this day Berlin's curious dialect contains some French contributions. Berliners still refer disparagingly to weak coffee as *Muckefuck,* which comes from the French expression *moka faux,* meaning a false mocha, or coffee substitute.

Yet when Friedrich Wilhelm died in 1688, Berlin was still a provincial town of fewer than 20,000, a backwater compared to London, Paris, Vienna, Prague, or Moscow.

His son Frederick changed all that. In 1701, after 13 years as duke and elector, he decided that the duchy should become a kingdom. He ordered royal insignia from a jeweler and crowned himself king of Prussia. As a kingdom needs a proper capital, he then set out to create one. He merged Berlin and Cölln into a single city and hired some of the greatest architects to expand and complete the Royal Palace (which was badly damaged during World War II and then demolished by East Germany's Communist regime in 1951). He also built the Zeughaus, or armory (now a museum of German history) on Unter den Linden boulevard, as well as a number of summer palaces, including Schloss Charlottenburg, which has been restored following its devastation during World War II.

Although the city's territory was still limited to what is today the borough of Berlin Mitte (about 4.1 square miles), by the time Frederick I died, in 1713, the capital's population had grown to 60,000. Under his son, Friedrich Wilhelm I, known as the "Soldier King," and his grandson, Frederick the Great, Berlin became grander by the year. Stunning public buildings, including the Brandenburg Gate, were erected along or near Unter den Linden. By 1790, Berlin had a population of 147,000.

The 19th century brought the Industrial Revolution and Prussia's transformation into the German Reich. This was an epoch of explosive growth for Berlin: Between Napoleon's defeat in 1815 and the start of World War I in 1914, the population grew tenfold, from 193,000 to 1.9 million. Yet despite incorporation of some surrounding towns and villages, the city's area was still only one thirteenth of its present size. Some of Germany's largest industrial concerns—Siemens and AEG, electrical engineering companies; Borsig, the locomotive and steam engine manufacturer; Schering, the pharmaceuticals producer—were launched during this period. As many as 50 new factories started up each year. And to work in them, under grueling sweatshop conditions, hundreds of thousands of people streamed into the city.

The barons of industry built their factories to resemble Medieval castles and cathedrals, with crenelated walls and spires. The industrialists also built villas and mansions that rivaled the royal palaces, prompting the kings and kaisers to build even grander edifices in an ornate style that critics dubbed "Reich braggadocio."

There was nothing ornate about the mass housing for the growing labor force: endless rows of five- or six-story buildings of dingy flats, most without plumbing, built around shaftlike inner courtyards as small as 18 by 18 feet. While Berlin was becoming Germany's biggest industrial center, it was also becoming Europe's largest tenement city. This aspect of life in Berlin was eloquently portrayed by the art of Heinrich Zille and Käthe Kollwitz and in the writings of Alfred Döblin, Joachim Ringelnatz, and Kurt Tucholsky.

Although the destruction of World War II, postwar reconstruction, and the urban renewal and renovation projects of the 1970s and 1980s have erased much of this housing, you can get a vivid idea of what it was like in the boroughs of Neukölln, Kreuzberg, and Wedding. These areas are home to the typical *Kneipe,* a tavern that is the focus of a real neighborhood, or *Kiez,* as it's called in Berlin dialect. A good Kiez is an intersection with four corners and four taverns where wheat beer with a shot of corn schnapps flows like water.

There was a brighter side to life in the city. Impressionist painters Max Liebermann, Lovis Corinth, and Max Slevogt were at work; the Expressionist art of Max Pechstein, George Grosz, and Karl Schmidt-Rottluff was winning acclaim; and Jugendstil, or Art Nouveau design, was at its height. With two major opera houses, the Philharmonic orchestra, and the Deutsches Theater, the latter under the direction of Max Reinhardt, Berlin won international stature as a music and drama center. Leading scientists, including Albert Einstein, Max Planck, Fritz Haber, Walther Nernst, Adolf von Bayer, Robert Koch, and Emil Fischer, worked at various times in Berlin. And Berlin became one of the world's greatest museum cities, thanks to its matchless collections of painting, sculpture, and ancient art. Most works survived World War II.

After World War I and the 1918 revolution, which toppled the kaiser and made Germany a republic, Berlin became a center of the Golden Twenties, indeed *the* cosmopolitan crossroads of that decade. Movie stars Marlene Dietrich, Greta Garbo, Peter Lorre, and Pola Negri and directors Fritz

Lang, Ernst Lubitsch, F. W. Murnau, and Josef von Sternberg made the city a cinema capital. Berlin was the home of Dada art and artists Hans Arp, Max Beckmann, Max Ernst, George Grosz, Paul Klee, and Karl Schmidt-Rottluff; of the Bauhaus architects and designers, notably Walter Gropius and Ludwig Mies van der Rohe; of essayists, poets, and writers W. H. Auden, Arthur Koestler, Christopher Isherwood (whose *Berlin Stories* was the basis of the later play *I Am a Camera* and the play and film *Cabaret*), Heinrich Mann, Vladimir Nabokov, Carl von Ossietzky, and Kurt Tucholsky. Berlin was the stage for Bertolt Brecht, Kurt Weill, Erwin Piscator, Carl Zuckmayer and Lotte Lenya. Wilhelm Fürtwängler presided over the Philharmonic. The city had yet another opera house, and the local conductors were Bruno Walter, Otto Klemperer, and Erich Kleiber. It was also in 1920 that Berlin became the sprawling metropolis that it is today. In October of that year eight independent surrounding cities plus dozens of smaller towns were incorporated to create Greater Berlin.

Today, that period seems like a lost paradise. It was lost, of course, because of Adolf Hitler and the Third Reich. Berlin, the mecca of culture and tolerance, became the center of intolerance and anticulture. In their racist megalomania the Nazis even began restructuring the city. The Charlottenburger Chaussee (today called Strasse des 17. Juni), the extension of Unter den Linden west of the Brandenburg Gate, is twice as wide as it was before the Third Reich: Hitler widened it to accommodate his military and political parades.

Worst of all, Berlin became the cauldron for World War II and the Holocaust, a reign of terror and genocide that culminated in the city's own Götterdämmerung.

Of the 4.4 million prewar inhabitants, only 2.8 million remained in 1945, and the city was a wasteland. Streets and squares, especially in the historic center, were strewn with dead bodies, burned-out tanks, and the debris of artillery attacks. Some 75 million cubic meters of rubble—one seventh of all the rubble in Germany—was in Berlin. Of the city's 245,000 prewar buildings, 50,000 were completely destroyed and as many again were near ruins. Transportation was at a standstill; public utilities were nonexistent. And once again Berlin was under foreign occupation—first by the Russians alone, and from August 1945 on by the Americans, British, and French as well.

The situation was worsened by the conflicts between the wartime victors that led to the Cold War. The 1948 Soviet blockade, which the Western Allies met with the 11-month-long airlift called Operation Vittles, was followed by the tragic June 17, 1953, uprising in East Berlin, and finally by the 1961 construction of the Berlin Wall.

To this day, the scars and wounds of World War II, not to mention those of the Cold War, are more visible in Berlin than in any other German city. Large areas of both West and East Berlin are still weed-covered lots on which nothing has been built since 1945, or wastelands created because of the Wall. It may take years before all the scars and gaps disappear.

## Getting Oriented

Berlin's size, and the distances among its most important sites, make the city difficult to master.

Though West and East Berlin were still separate cities as we went to press, all passport controls and formalities of traveling between them had been dropped, and at latest by December 1990 the city was expected to be formally re-united and one again.

But the trauma and scars of division remain, even if the Berlin Wall itself is largely gone, except for the chunks being sold at souvenir stands. And this, of necessity, makes your approach to the city somewhat different. As a result, we have described the city as two—West and East—with separate sections on each. Though the political division is gone, we believe that people will nonetheless continue to refer to the areas as "West Berlin" and "East Berlin" for years to come, by habit and for convenience.

The logical way to explore a city is to start with its old quarter, but that is not the way to do it in Berlin, because of the long postwar division. This historic center, traversed by Unter den Linden boulevard, its east-west axis, is the borough of Berlin Mitte, which is in East Berlin. On and around the avenue, its western end being the Brandenburg Gate, are the most important sites and sights. But the real "weight" of Berlin, that which makes it the throbbing, international city it is, is in West Berlin, and since this is also where you will probably be staying, it is the logical and most sensible part in which to start your tour.

To make sense of West Berlin is also not easy, in part because of its size and the fact that many of its sightseeing highlights are far from its center and main boulevard, the Kurfürstendamm. This avenue runs on a northeast-to-southwest axis for almost 3 km (2 miles) through the heart of West Berlin. Its northeastern terminal, not far from the Bahnhof Zoo, West Berlin's main railway station, is the

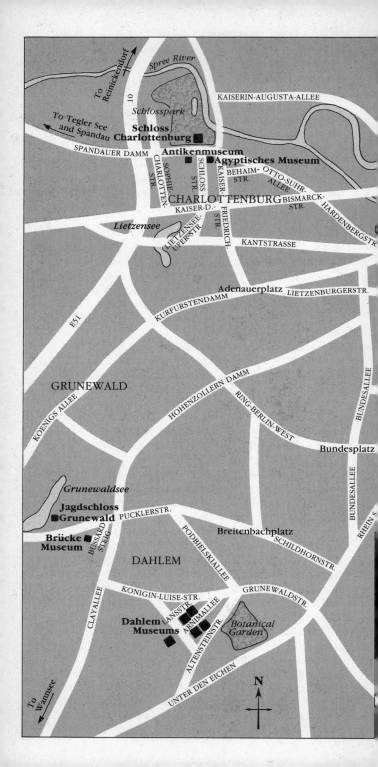

## West Berlin

| 0 | yards | 1,100 |
| 0 | meters | 1,000 |

WILHELM-PIECK-STR.

EAST BERLIN

former Berlin wall

Spree River

TONAERSTR.

STRASSE DES 17 JUNI

*Tiergarten*

UNTER DEN LINDEN

**Brandenburg Gate**

FRIEDRICHSTR.

TIERGARTENSTR.

LEIPZIGERSTR.

former Berlin wall

UDAPESTERSTR.

KURFURSTENSTR.

**Europa-Center**

KOCH-STR.

ORANIEN-WIENER-STR.

STRESEMANNSTR.

*Landwehr Canal*

SCHINERSTR.

**KREUZBERG**

POTSDAMERSTR.

MEHRING-DAMM

**SCHONEBERG**

KOLONNEN STR.      DUDEN STR.

COLUMBIA-DAMM

**Rathaus Schöneberg**

SACHSENDAMM

TEMPELHOFER

AUPT-STR.

**TEMPELHOF**

**Tempelhof Airport**

RING-BERLIN-WEST

To Marienfelde

*Havel River*

N

*Pfaueninsel*

**Schloss Pfaueninsel**

**St.-Peter-und-Paul-Kirche**

PFAUENINSEL CHAUSSEE

*Wannsee*

**Blockhaus Nikolskoe**

NIKOLSKOER

**WANNSEE**

**Schloss Klein-Glienicke**

KONIGSTRASSE

To Dahlem

lienicke Brücke   To Potsdam

**Jagdschloss Glienicke**

| 0 | yards | 1,100 |
| 0 | meters | 1,000 |

Europa-Center, more than 3 km (2 miles) southwest of the Brandenburg Gate. This 22-story office, commercial, and shopping complex, topped by the huge revolving emblem of Mercedes-Benz, is in the center of West Berlin's "downtown" area at the convergence of the Kurfürstendamm, Kantstrasse, Hardenbergstrasse, Budapester Strasse, and Tauentzienstrasse. Since it is central West Berlin's tallest building, replete with 70 stores, 20 restaurants, five cinemas, cabarets, nightclubs, a gambling casino, airline offices, and the Berlin tourist bureau, you can hardly miss it.

A good way to get oriented is to visit the *Multi-Vision Show* on the Center's second floor. There, projectors present images of the city on a 70-foot panoramic screen, with sound in English, French, Spanish, and German. Show times are every one and a half hours, starting at 9:00 A.M. and ending at 1:30 P.M. An observation platform on the 20th floor provides a view of most of the city and a sense of its layout.

Even if excursion-bus rubbernecking is not usually your style, Berlin is where you should make an exception, for no other mode will provide such an excellent overview of the city. There is a variety of tours, all covering basically the same routes. Most have their ticket offices and departure points on or just off Kurfürstendamm, within a few minutes' walk of the Europa-Center. There are two- and three-hour tours of West Berlin and four-hours tours of East Berlin, in both German and English.

The best, fastest, and cheapest way to get around is by public transit, which is excellent in both Berlins. Renting a car may seem inviting because of the city's size, but it is also an invitation to headaches. Traffic is always heavy, parking spaces are rare, and gridlock is common. Moreover, the layout of the city is so complex that you are bound to get lost, no matter how detailed your map. On the other hand, except for a few specific, relatively manageable areas, such as East Berlin's Berlin Mitte and Köpenick or West Berlin's Kurfürstendamm neighborhood, Tiergarten district, the museums in Dahlem and around Charlottenburg Palace, and Spandau's Altstadt, walking tours can become endurance tests.

# WEST BERLIN

## *ON AND AROUND THE KURFÜRSTENDAMM*

The Kurfürstendamm—Ku'damm, or just Ku, for short—is Berlin's grandest commercial avenue: two miles of conspicuous consumption, round-the-clock entertainment, pleasant strolling, and fascinating people-watching. In many ways it symbolizes what West Berlin was during the dark years of the Cold War when it was a *Frontstadt,* or front-line city, and a showcase of capitalism. The boulevard is lined with the city's most expensive shops; dozens of restaurants, cafés, and nightspots; numerous cinemas and theaters; and some of Berlin's best hotels, including its most luxurious, the Bristol-Kempinski, at Kurfürstendamm 27.

The boulevard's name derives from *Kurfürst,* meaning elector, and *Damm,* meaning causeway. The duchy of Brandenburg's elector Joachim II had it laid out in the 1540s as a carriageway between the ducal palace in Berlin-Cölln and his hunting château in the Grunewald. Not until nearly 350 years later, in 1881, at the instigation of Prussia's and the German Reich's prime minister, Otto von Bismarck, was it turned into a 175-foot-wide parkway, divided along its length by a broad strip of grass and trees. Although far from what was then Berlin's governmental, financial, and cultural center, it soon became one of the city's most sought-after strips of real estate, lined by upper-class apartment houses, fancy shops, theaters, hotels, and restaurants. There were so many cafés that American novelist Thomas Wolfe described the Ku as "the biggest coffeehouse in Europe."

One of the most famous cafés is the **Café Möhring** at Kurfürstendamm 213, a favorite hangout of politicians and intellectuals in the early 20th century. Among its habitués were Reich chancellor Theobald von Bethmann-Hollweg, Russian playwright Maxim Gorky, German writers Gottfried Benn and Frank Wedekind, and the painter-poet Else Lasker-Schüler. The Ku'damm was and is to Berlin what the Champs-Elysées was and is to Paris.

Unfortunately, half of its Jugendstil (German Art Nouveau) buildings were destroyed during World War II and replaced by nondescript steel-glass-concrete structures, so

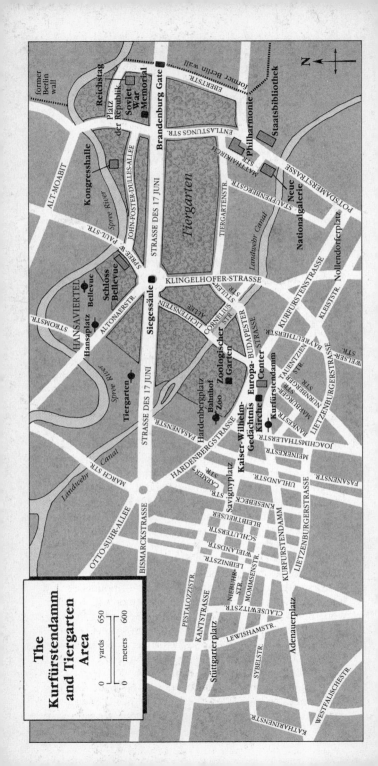

## The Kurfürstendamm and Tiergarten Area

0    yards    650
0    meters    600

N

former Berlin wall
former Berlin wall

Reichstag
Soviet War Memorial
Platz der Republik
Brandenburg Gate
Kongresshalle
Spree River
JOHN-FOSTER-DULLES-ALLEE
ALT-MOABIT
SPREE W. PAUL-STR.
Philharmonie
Staatsbibliothek
ENTLASTUNGS STR.
MATTHÄIKIRCH STR.
STAUFFENBERGSTR.
Neue Nationalgalerie
POTSDAMERSTRASSE
Tiergarten
STRASSE DES 17 JUNI
TIERGARTENSTR.
TIERGARTENSTR.
Landwehr Canal
KLINGELHOFER-STRASSE
Schloss Bellevue
Bellevue
HANSAVIERTEL
Hansaplatz
ALTONAERSTR.
STROMSTR.
Spree River
Siegessäule
LICHTENSTEIN ALLEE
CORNELIUS STR.
STÜLER STR.
STÜLER STR.
BUDAPESTER STRASSE
Tiergarten
STRASSE DES 17 JUNI
Canal
Landwehr
MARCH STR.
OTTO-SUHR-ALLEE
BISMARCKSTRASSE
FASANENSTR.
Hardenbergplatz
Bahnhof Zoo
Zoologischer Garten
Europa-Center
Kurfürstendamm
Kaiser-Wilhelm-Gedächtnis Kirche
KURFÜRSTENSTRASSE
Nollendorfplatz
KLEISTSTR.
BAYREUTHERSTR.
WELSER-STR.
NÜRNBERGER STR.
TAUENTZIEN STR.
MARBURGER STR.
RANKESTR.
JOACHIMSTHALERSTR.
LIETZENBURGERSTRASSE
FASANENSTR.
UHLANDSTR.
MEINEKESTR.
HARDENBERGSTRASSE
KNESEBECKSTR.
CARMER STR.
Savignyplatz
BLEIBTREUSTR.
SCHLÜTERSTR.
WIELANDSTR.
LEIBNIZSTR.
NIEBUHR-STR.
MOMMSENSTR.
PESTALOZZISTR.
KANTSTRASSE
Stuttgarterplatz
LEWISHAMSTR.
SYBELSTR.
CLAUSEWITZSTR.
KURFÜRSTENDAMM
LIETZENBURGERSTRASSE
Adenauerplatz
WESTFALISCHESTR.
KATHARINENSTR.

if you're looking for interesting turn-of-the-century architecture, the supply here is a bit skimpy. The rewards are greater on the streets that intersect the Ku'damm, especially the Meinekestrasse, Fasanenstrasse, Uhlandstrasse, Knesebeckstrasse, Bleibtreustrasse, Schlüterstrasse, and Wielandstrasse.

The best way to see the Ku is to start at the Europa-Center, at its northeastern end, stroll up one side southwest to where it ends at the intersection of Katharinenstrasse and Westfälischestrasse, then cross over and amble back on the other side. You can explore the cross streets according to your mood and fancy. If the mileage seems a bit daunting, don't worry: The myriad eateries and watering places along the route provide ample opportunities to recharge your batteries.

The only "must see" monument on the boulevard, a virtual landmark of West Berlin, is the **Kaiser-Wilhelm-Gedächtnis-Kirche**, or Kaiser Wilhelm Memorial Church, just west of the Europa-Center. Begun in 1891 to mark the 20th anniversary of the second German Reich, and completed in 1895, it was originally a neo-Romanesque structure. Wartime raids leveled all of the church except the western spire and portal, which have been preserved as a memorial to peace. (Berliners, who find humorously cynical names for nearly all their public edifices, call it the "Hollow Tooth.")

For more than a decade after the war there was endless debate about what to do with the ruin. In 1959, Egon Eiermann, one of Germany's leading modern architects, was commissioned to build a new church around it. His complex consists of a hexagonal flat-topped belfry tower, an octagonal central church building, a sacristy, and a chapel. The walls of all are a concrete honeycomb with 20,000 spaces filled by glass mosaics created by the French glass artist Gabriel Loire of Chartres. The bronze crucifix in the main church building is based on a pencil sketch by the early 20th-century German sculptor Ernst Barlach.

## THE TIERGARTEN AREA

*Tiergarten,* literally "animal garden," is the name of one of the largest of West Berlin's 42 public parks and of an entire borough. The 8-square-mile district begins just northeast of the Europa-Center and extends eastward to the border of Berlin Mitte, the city's historical center which is in the former East Berlin. The Brandenburg Gate and Potsdamer Platz are its eastern landmarks.

Although one of the smallest and least populated of West Berlin's boroughs, it is one of the richest in culture and interesting sights. Within its southern half are the Tiergarten itself; the zoo; the Reichstag building; Schloss Bellevue; the Siegessäule (Victory Column); the Soviet War Memorial; Congress Hall, a gift to Berlin from the United States; the Hansaviertel of modern architecture; the Kulturform, including the Philharmonie, the Neue Nationalgalerie, the Kunstgewerbemuseum (Museum of Applied Art), the Bauhaus Archiv, and the Staatsbibliothek (National Library); and the former German army headquarters building.

The Landwehr canal and the Spree river cross the borough. Its main thoroughfare, east to west, is the Strasse des 17. Juni.

To explore the Tiergarten you'll have to do quite a bit of walking, because public transit through it is not the best. The U-9 subway runs along the western periphery of the Tiergarten and stops at the Hansaplatz station, close to the Hansaviertel and Bellevue Palace. The S-3 elevated train runs to the Tiergarten station near the Strasse des 17. Juni and to the Bellevue station, close to Bellevue Palace. A number of bus lines provide access; the most convenient is number 69, which you can board near the Kurfürstendamm station. The shortest walk into the park and district is northeast from the Europa-Center along the Budapester Strasse, past the entrance to the zoo and the Inter-Continental Hotel.

# The Tiergarten

The Tiergarten was originally a hunting preserve of the dukes and electors of Brandenburg. In 1717 it was transformed into a geometric, manicured Baroque-style park, which between 1833 and 1839 was relandscaped in the style of a freely growing, unstructured English garden by Prussia's greatest landscape architect, Peter Joseph Lenné. It soon became Berlin's favorite recreation area, dotted with numerous cafés and restaurants.

The park was also a residential area popular with the rich, famous, and powerful, who built their residences and embassies in its southern sector along the Lichtensteinallee, Corneliusstrasse, and Tiergartenstrasse.

The Tiergarten was one of the most embattled areas of the city during the final month of World War II, and was shelled into a virtual moonscape. What survived the fighting was ravaged in the first postwar winter by desperate citizens who felled the remaining trees for firewood and planted cabbage and potatoes on the open spaces. Most of the foreign embassies were in ruins, and their bricks and stones were carted off to rebuild the rest of the city. Only the Japanese embassy, recently turned into a German-Japanese cultural center, and the Italian embassy, built in the fascist "Duce Style," survived.

Use of the Tiergarten as a source for produce continued throughout the Berlin blockade and airlift. It was not until the spring of 1949, when the division of Germany was already a certainty, that replanting and relandscaping of the park began.

Today the Tiergarten is again full of trees, shrubs, lawns, flower beds, ponds, idyllic little lakes with rowboats, cafés, restaurants, and a staggering 25 km (15.5 miles) of paths and trails.

You might wish to get a bird's-eye view by climbing 285 steps to the observation platform of the Siegessäule, the victory column in the middle of the park on the traffic rotary called Der Grosse Stern, or Big Star. The 224-foot-high Greco-Roman–style column, topped by a gilded bronze Winged Victory, was built between 1869 and 1873 to commemorate Prussia's triumphs in the wars against Denmark, Austria and Bavaria, and France. Originally it was erected in front of the Reichstag, where it stood until 1938. That year, Albert Speer, Hitler's architect and future minister of armaments, had the column moved to the Grosse Stern on Charlottenburger Chaussee (now the Strasse des 17. Juni).

When originally laid out in the late 17th century, the Strasse des 17. Juni (the name commemorates the June 17, 1953, uprising in East Berlin and might be changed back to Charlottenburger Chaussee in light of Germany's reunification) was intended to be a coach road between the royal palace in Berlin Mitte and Schloss Charlottenburg, the new summer palace that Elector Frederick III (later King Frederick I) was building for his second wife, Sophie-Charlotte. In effect an extension of Unter den Linden, it cuts a 4-km (2.5-mile) swath through the Tiergarten in an east–west direction, then changes its name to Otto-Suhr-Allee and continues to Charlottenburg palace. It bisects the park, the northern half of which is the more rewarding.

A short walk northwest from the Siegessäule, along the Altonaer Strasse (or a subway ride from the Kurfürstendamm to the Hansaplatz) will bring you into the Hansaviertel, a residential and shopping district that is a prime example of 1950s architecture and urban planning. In fact, the district's mixture of high-rise apartment houses, boxlike single-family dwellings, churches, and stores was built as an exhibit for the 1957 Interbau, an international construction exposition. Leading modern architects including Egon Eiermann, Walter Gropius, Oscar Niemeyer, Alvar Aalto, and Arne Jacobsen are represented here.

From the Hansaviertel it is a pleasant ten-minute stroll east through the park to **Schloss Bellevue**, a Neoclassical château built in the 1780s for Prince Ferdinand, the younger brother of Frederick the Great. Although severely damaged during World War II, it was completely restored in 1959. Since then it has served as the Berlin residence of West Germany's federal president. You can visit the interior only on Sunday afternoon, and only when the president is not in residence.

Another ten-minute walk east on the John-Foster-Dulles-Allee and along the Spree river embankment will bring you to the **Kongresshalle**, a convention center and auditorium designed by U.S. architect Hugh Stubbins for the 1957 Interbau exposition. Local wagsters have dubbed it the "Pregnant Oyster" because of the shape of its roof. In 1980 the roof came crashing down, killing one person and injuring a dozen others.

Continue east along the John-Foster-Dulles-Allee to the Platz der Republik and the **Reichstag**, Germany's former (and possibly future) parliament building. A colossus measuring more than 450 feet wide, it was built in Neo-Renaissance and "Reich braggadocio" style between 1884 and 1894. Kaiser Wilhelm I personally laid the cornerstone. The Reichstag became the symbol of Hitler's destruction of democracy when the building went up in flames on February 27, 1933. The Reichstag fire remains one of the unsolved mysteries of the Nazi era.

Capitalizing on popular indignation over the blaze, Hitler persuaded aging President Paul von Hindenburg, a World War I hero, to suspend all constitutional liberties and hand him full emergency powers. Thousands of Nazi opponents all over Germany were arrested and put in prisons or hastily created concentration camps. Later that week Hitler and the Nazis handily won their first real majority in national elections. As the embers in the gutted Reichstag building stopped smoldering, democracy disappeared in Germany.

Marinus van der Lubbe, a young Dutchman captured near the fire, was tried with three alleged co-conspirators—Bulgarian agents of the Communist International (Comintern), among them Georgi Dimitrov, who became the first prime minister of Bulgaria after World War II. The Bulgarians were acquitted, but van der Lubbe was sentenced to death and guillotined. Throughout his trial, van der Lubbe insisted that he had acted alone and on his own initiative. The official Nazi version was that the fire had been a Communist plot. However, many suspected that van der Lubbe was a stooge and that the Nazis themselves had set the fire, using an underground passageway into the building to gain access, giving Hitler a pretext for obtaining dictatorial power.

Although the building was partly repaired and restored in the 1930s, Hitler's puppet Reichstag never convened in it again. The "world's highest-paid men's chorus," as the Third Reich's parliament was called, met in the nearby Kroll opera house to rubber-stamp the regime's decisions. The Reichstag was severely damaged during World War II air raids. When the last German defenders of Berlin turned it into a fortress in April 1945, the Soviet army bombarded it with an estimated one million artillery shells. After the Russians captured the city, one of their first acts was to raise the red Soviet flag over the building.

For years the Reichstag stood as a ruin. Reconstruction began in 1954 and was completed, after many delays, in 1972. Since then, along with serving as an exhibition hall, the Reichstag has been the occasional site of caucuses of the Bundestag, West Germany's parliament. What will happen to the building now remains to be seen. In 1987 the West German government issued a proposal to restore the building, including its glass dome, by 1994, the 100th anniversary of its completion. But no final decision has been reached.

There is probably no other spot in Berlin as weighted with politics and history as this easternmost edge of the Tiergarten. During the 28 years that the Wall divided Berlin, the Reichstag, one corner of which was a couple of feet from the Wall itself, represented a kind of outpost against communism. Fifty yards due south of it, on the eastern side of the Wall, now gone, is the Brandenburg Gate, which was East Berlin's bastion against capitalism. These two symbols of Berlin and of Germany, flying the similar but dissimilar black-red-gold flags of the two Germanys, seemed to be facing each other like two huge warships. Now, as people move freely between the two, that feeling is gone.

Just 200 yards west of the Brandenburg Gate, on the Strasse des 17. Juni, is the **Soviet War Memorial**. Constructed in 1946 of marble from the ruins of the Reich chancellery, it bears the bronze figure of a Soviet soldier with fixed bayonet, flanked by the two Red Army tanks that are supposed to be the first to have reached Berlin in 1945. The monument is guarded by two Soviet troopers.

The biggest attraction in the southern half of the Tiergarten is the **Zoologischer Garten**, the West Berlin zoo (there is also a zoo in East Berlin). Entry, however, is not from the Tiergarten itself: The main gate is at Hardenbergplatz, just east of Bahnhof Zoo, and the side gate, called the Elefantentor, is on Budapester Strasse, virtually across the street from the Europa-Center. There is no way to miss the Elefantentor—it resembles a Chinese temple portal with its columns supported by two stone elephants.

Berlin's Zoologischer Garten is not only the largest zoo in the world, with more than 11,000 animals representing 1,575 species, but one of the oldest, begun in 1841, when Prussia's King Friedrich Wilhelm IV consigned his collection of animals to the city. The **Aquarium**, just inside the Elephant Gate, houses another 10,000 animals: fish, amphibians, reptiles, and insects. It's best to get a combined ticket for both. Zoo and aquarium both open at 9:00 A.M. daily; the aquarium closes at 6:00 P.M., the zoo itself at dusk or 7:00 P.M., whichever is earlier.

# The Kulturforum Complex

From the zoo it is a one-mile walk east along the Budapester Strasse, northeast along the Stülerstrasse to the Tiergartenstrasse, then east again to Berlin's **Kulturforum**. Virtually everything in this area was destroyed during the war. Now the Philharmonie, the Staatsbibliothek, the Neue Nationalgalerie, the Kunstgewerbemuseum (Museum of Applied Art), and the Musikinstrumenten Museum are clustered here.

The **Philharmonie**, on the Kemperplatz, home of the Berlin Philharmonic Orchestra, is one of the city's most daring pieces of contemporary architecture. Designed by Bremen architect Hans Scharoun and completed in 1963, it is an asymmetric structure with a tentlike roof. The hall itself, with seating for 2,000, is pentagonal in shape, and the stage is in the center, so that half the audience looks at the backs of the musicians. That arrangement caused a furor at first, but was soon accepted because of the excellent acoustics.

Scharoun also designed the nearby **Staatsbibliothek**, at Potsdamer Strasse 33, which houses the remnants of the Prussian National Library along with newer acquisitions—some three and one half million books at present, with space for another 4.5 million, as well as a huge periodicals department.

The **Neue Nationalgalerie**, at Potsdamer Strasse 50, just

across from the library, is a stunning steel-and-glass pavil-
ionlike structure, the last major work of Ludwig Mies van der
Rohe, completed in 1968, a year before his death. The art
collection consists of paintings, sculptures, and graphics of
the late 19th and 20th centuries.

The architecture of the **Kunstgewerbemuseum** (Museum
of Applied Arts), at Tiergartenstrasse 1, was thoroughly
panned when it opened in 1987: People complained that it
looked like a cross between a fortress and a power plant. Be
that as it may, its collection is superb—with examples of
every kind of European applied art from the Middle Ages
through the 20th century.

At the **Musikinstrumenten Museum**, at Tiergartenstrasse
6, you will find a collection of musical instruments from
around the world, made from the early 16th to the 19th
centuries.

All the museums are open daily, except Monday, from 9:00
A.M. to 5:00 P.M.; admission is free.

A one-block walk west on Tiergartenstrasse will take you
to the Stauffenbergstrasse, named for Claus Graf Schenck
von Stauffenberg, the Wehrmacht colonel who planted a
bomb in the Führer's headquarters on the Eastern Front on
July 20, 1944. The street used to be called Bendlerstrasse and
the grim, gray building at number 14 was the **German war
office**, where Stauffenberg and his three co-conspirators
were executed when the plot failed. A memorial to the four
men stands in the courtyard where they were executed. The
third floor of this old war ministry building, which now
houses various municipal offices, is devoted to a permanent
exhibition of documents and artifacts dealing with the resistance movement. It is open Monday through Friday from
9:00 A.M. to 6:00 P.M., and Saturday and Sunday until 1:00 P.M.

Plötzensee prison in Charlottenburg, where some 7,000
others in the anti-Nazi movement were subsequently executed, is now a juvenile reformatory. The execution shed,
with eight hooks in the ceiling from which the anti-Nazi
conspirators were hanged with piano wire, has also been
turned into a memorial. There is a stone urn symbolically
containing earth from every Nazi concentration camp. It is
open daily from 8:00 A.M. to 6:00 P.M.

## *KREUZBERG*

While the 19th-century entrepreneurs built their cathedral-
like factories and ostentatious mansions, Berlin became Eu-

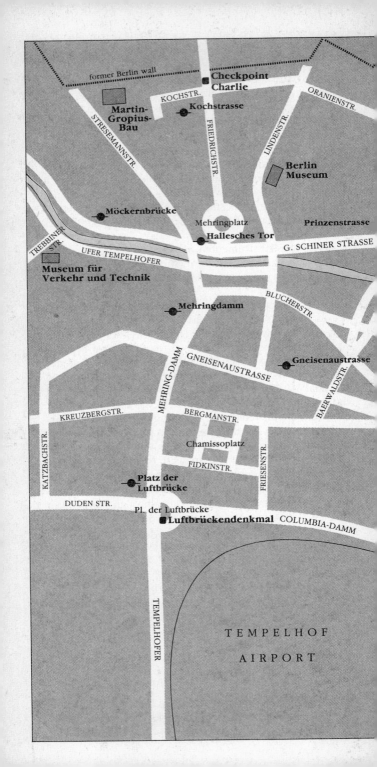

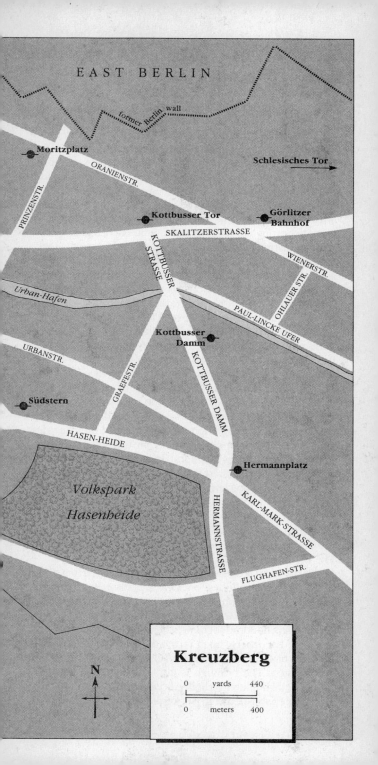

EAST BERLIN

former Berlin wall

Moritzplatz

ORANIENSTR.

Schlesisches Tor →

PRINZENSTR.

Kottbusser Tor

Görlitzer
Bahnhof

SKALITZERSTRASSE

KOTTBUSSER
STRASSE

WIENERSTR.

Urban-Hafen

OHLAUER STR.

PAUL-LINCKE UFER

Kottbusser
Damm

URBANSTR.

GRAEFESTR.

KOTTBUSSER DAMM

Südstern

HASEN-HEIDE

Hermannplatz

Volkspark

Hasenheide

KARL-MARK-STRASSE

HERMANNSTRASSE

FLUGHAFEN-STR.

N

## Kreuzberg

0      yards      440

0      meters     400

rope's largest tenement city. You can still get a vivid idea of what living conditions were like in the boroughs of Wedding, Neukölln, and especially Kreuzberg.

Southeast of Tiergarten, and bordered on the north and northeast by Berlin Mitte, Kreuzberg is just four square miles in area. However, with a population of 130,000, it is the borough that most closely resembles the original scene: rundown, neglected, and crowded. But it is also where Berlin's cultural, subcultural, and countercultural renaissance began in the 1970s. Here is where the Neue Wilden, the "New Wild" artists, had, and in some cases still have, their studios. This is also the borough of punkers and skinheads, of squatters and revolutionaries, of the old and impoverished, of people seeking alternative lifestyles, and of Turkish "guest workers," who account for one third of the district's population.

To be sure, opinions about Kreuzberg vary. Some call it a "zoo," others liken it to New York's East Village, and some consider it "an intellectual prison." The common denominator here is variety. Some streets look as if they had been lifted right out of Istanbul. Art galleries, bookshops, secondhand emporiums, health-food stores, boutiques, hole-in-the-wall theaters, kebab stands, and countless dives line the shabby streets that run through canyons of 19th-century houses. From the Möckernbrücke subway stop in the west to the Schlesischestor station in the east, from the Kochstrasse stop at the northern periphery to the one at the Platz der Luftbrücke and Tempelhof airfield on the southern edge, Kreuzberg is Berlin at its wildest and most confusing.

The easiest and fastest way to get into Kreuzberg is by subway. The U-1 goes west–east through the borough to the Schlesischestor station. The U-6 line runs through Kreuzberg on a north–south axis. The U-8 subway's northern stop in Kreuzberg is Moritzplatz; it then runs southeast through the borough and intersects with the U-1 at Kottbusser Tor. The U-7 line runs generally southeast.

The off-off art scene in Kreuzberg is represented by a string of commercial galleries on Oranienstrasse, and on and around the Chamissoplatz, near the Platz der Luftbrücke. Two of the most interesting cafés in the district are **A Propos**, which offers hundreds of newspapers and magazines to read, and **Café Kreuzberg**, open only from 8:00 P.M. to 4:00 A.M. Both are on the Ohlauer Strasse, near the Görlitzer Bahnhof subway stop. The borough is also going upmarket with a profusion of medium- to high-priced restaurants and bistros. The most established of these, frequented by all the artists, is the **Exil**, at 44a Paul-Lincke-Ufer, near the Kottbusser Tor station.

Kreuzberg is also home to four unusual museums and to what in many respects is the city's most important postwar monument. The **Berlinische Galerie**, located in the Martin-Gropius-Bau, Stresemannstrasse 110, at the northwest tip of the borough, is devoted entirely to late 19th- and early 20th-century Berlin visual arts: painting, sculpture, graphics, design, architecture, and applied art. Only the Brücke group of Expressionists is not included here, as the Expressionists have their own museum: the Brücke, near the Dahlem complex (see below). The building itself is almost as interesting as the exhibits. It was designed in the early 1880s by Walter Gropius's uncle, Martin Gropius, also an architect, and reconstructed after its near-total destruction during World War II. Hours are 10:00 A.M. to 6:00 P.M. daily, except Monday.

Two blocks south of the Kochstrasse station is the **Berlin Museum**, at Lindenstrasse 14. Its displays of art, furnishings, porcelain, handicrafts, and artifacts will tell you just about everything about Berlin and its history that you could possibly want to know. The building is a gem of Neoclassical architecture that was completed in 1735 and served as the city's supreme appellate court for two centuries. From 1816 to 1822 one of the justices was E. T. A. Hoffmann, the painter, composer, conductor, and author of fantasy tales, on whose life and stories the opera *Tales of Hoffmann* is based. Crammed with the bric-a-brac of Berlin's history, the museum is also a great spot for a snack or lunch. On its main floor is the **Alt-Berliner Weissbierstube**, a pub that serves seven varieties of Berliner Weisse, the local wheat beer, and an array of Berlin specialties such as *Soleier* (hard-boiled eggs pickled in salt brine), *Rollmops* (pickled herring), *Hackepeter* (sharply seasoned raw ground meat served on a piece of bread or crisp roll), and *Sülze* (jellied meat). The museum is open daily, except Monday, from 11:00 A.M. to 6:00 P.M.; the pub keeps museum hours except on Saturday and Sunday, when it closes at 4:00 P.M.

Near the Kochstrasse subway station (U-6 line), at Friedrichstrasse 44 on the corner of the Kochstrasse and Friedrichstrasse, the **Haus am Checkpoint Charlie** contains an impressive collection of vehicles and equipment used by East Berlin refugees to flee over, tunnel under, ram through, and get around the Berlin Wall and the East–West German border. Among the exhibits are pint-size automobiles with hidden compartments for refugees, fake U.S. and Soviet army uniforms, and pieces of the hot-air balloon in which two East German couples and their four children flew over the border in 1979. The little museum is a tribute to human wit, courage, and ingenuity. Museum hours are 9:00 A.M. to 10:00 P.M. daily.

Take the U-6 from the Kochstrasse to the Halleschestor and transfer there to the westbound U-1 to the Möckernbrücke stop near the **Museum für Verkehr und Technik** (Museum of Transport and Technology), at Trebbiner Strasse 9. Housed in Kreuzberg's 19th-century market hall and icehouse, its exhibits include one of Otto Lilienthal's original gliders; Baron von Drais's wooden *Laufrad,* the world's first bicycle; and early steam locomotives. It is open 9:00 A.M. to 6:00 P.M. Tuesday through Friday, and 10:00 A.M. to 6:00 P.M. Saturday and Sunday.

Few structures are more symbolic of the division of Berlin than the **Luftbrückendenkmal** (Airlift Monument), on Platz der Luftbrücke at the entrance to Tempelhof airfield. The 65-foot-high stone memorial, with three towering arches symbolizing the three air corridors that linked West Berlin with the Western occupation zones of Germany during the 1948–1949 blockade by the Soviets, is a tribute not only to the airlift itself, which kept the city alive, but also to the 31 American and 41 British servicemen who died in the line of duty during the operation.

The Soviet blockade of West Berlin had its roots in the Western Allies' decision on June 20, 1948, to introduce the deutsche mark of West Germany into the three western sectors of Berlin. The Anglo-American answer to the blockade was "Operation Vittles," the airlift that lasted nearly 11 months until the U.S. and Soviet governments negotiated a settlement of the dispute. During the operation American transport planes alone made 277,728 flights to the city. Tempelhof was the focal point of the operation.

The airfield is virtually in the middle of the city, and it has a history going back to the earliest days of aviation. Indeed, the airfield actually predates airplanes. In 1883 Arnold Böcklin, a Swiss landscape painter who was also an inventor, experimented on the site with two motorless biplanes, but he failed to get them off the ground because of high winds. In 1908 the Wright brothers demonstrated one of their planes here with a 19-minute flight. In 1923 Tempelhof, which takes its name from the 13th-century church built by the Knights Templars, became Berlin's central airport. In 1975 civil air traffic was routed to Tegel because the Tempelhof runways, surrounded by apartment houses, shops, office buildings, a public park, and even a sports stadium, could not be extended to accommodate wide-bodied jetliners. It is now used exclusively by the U.S. Air Force.

# SCHÖNEBERG

This borough, just west of Kreuzberg and Tempelhof and south of Tiergarten, was the "capital" of West Berlin. Once a rich farming area, it became an independent city in 1898 and had a population of well over 200,000 when it was incorporated into Berlin in 1920.

**Rathaus Schöneberg** (also the name of a subway station on the U-4 and U-7 lines, which intersect here), the borough's city hall, is a massive structure that could easily be mistaken for a factory. It was the seat of West Berlin's city-state government from December, 1948 until Berlin became one again.

In the 230-foot clock tower is the Liberty Bell, a replica of the bell at Independence Hall in Philadelphia. It is a gift of the American people to the people of Berlin, and the signatures of 17 million Americans who contributed money for it during the 1948–1949 Crusade for Freedom are preserved in a book in the tower. The ten-ton bell is rung every day at noon and on special occasions.

It was from the tower balcony, facing the square, that President John F. Kennedy delivered his memorable June 26, 1963, speech, in which he said: "All free men, wherever they may live, are citizens of Berlin, and, therefore, as a free man, I take pride in the words '*Ich bin ein Berliner.*' " Berliners have revered him ever since.

# THE DAHLEM MUSEUMS

From Rathaus Schöneberg, or elsewhere in the inner city, it is a 20- to 30-minute subway ride southwest on the U-2 line from the suburb of Tiergarten to the Dahlem-Dorf station, the heart of the great museum area in the leafy residential district of Dahlem.

West Berliners love to confront visitors with a riddle: Who are the city's two most famous residents? The answer: Queen Nefertiti and The Man with the Golden Helmet. The bust of Nefertiti, the world's most beautiful and most photographed woman (even if she does have one eye missing) is the centerpiece of West Berlin's Ägyptisches Museum (Egyptian Museum), near Charlottenburg Palace. Although its authenticity has been challenged, *The Man with the Golden Helmet* is by far the most popular of the Rembrandts in West Berlin's Gemäldegalerie (Picture Gallery), one of the main attractions in the Dahlem complex.

The bust and the painting are two of tens of thousands of art treasures in Berlin's more than 50 museums—collections that are among the richest in the world. But the story behind those collections and museums is one of the strangest in the art world, and inextricable from the history of the Third Reich, World War II, and the Cold War.

The origins of Berlin's hoard go back to the Brandenburg dukes and Prussian kings, who were lavish patrons and collectors of art. In the early 19th century the royal family sponsored the formation of museums open to the public. The first of these galleries, the Altes Museum, on Museumsinsel (Museum Island) in East Berlin, was built between 1824 and 1828, and opened in 1830. It is one of the world's oldest public art museums. Over the next 100 years, the collections were expanded and four more museums were built on the island. Because the collections were state owned, their status remained unchanged during the Weimar Republic and the Nazi Reich.

During World War II the museums were closed and most of their treasures evacuated to safer places: air-raid bunkers in Berlin, warehouses in the suburbs, salt mines in what then became West Germany. Toward the war's end, as the Allied armies advanced through Germany, the Americans and British confiscated the hidden art they found in their occupation zones and sectors of Berlin, and the Russians did the same in the territory under their control.

More than 200 Old Master paintings, for example, were taken to the United States in 1945, exhibited around the country, and kept for many years. The Soviets shipped art to Moscow, where it remained until 1959. By the time the wartime victors were willing to release the treasures, the Cold War was in full swing and both Germany and Berlin were divided. Prussia no longer existed as a legal entity, having been formally abolished in 1947 by the Four Power Allied Military Government. That raised the knotty question of who actually owned the Prussian treasures from Berlin's museums, and to whom they should be repatriated.

For the Russians the answer was easy: They turned over their share to the Communist East German government, which restored most of the buildings on Museumsinsel. In West Germany the matter was finally resolved in 1961 with the creation of the Stiftung Preussisches Kulturgut, or the Prussian Cultural Properties Foundation, jointly owned by the West German Federal Republic, the ten West German states, and the city-state of West Berlin.

That is why Berlin today has two of each kind of museum— one in the west and one in the east. Considering the haste and disorder with which some of the objects were evacuated during the war, it is also understandable why you may find the head of one statue in West Berlin and its torso in East Berlin; or the frame of one painting in the east and the picture itself in the west.

The Dahlem complex, one block south of the Dahlem-Dorf subway station, with entrances at Arnimallee 23 and Lansstrasse 8, includes the Skulpturengalerie (Sculpture Gallery), the Gemäldegalerie, the Kupferstichkabinett (Print Collection), the Museum für Völkerkunde (Ethnographic Museum), the Museum für Indische Kunst (Museum of Indian Art), the Museum für Islamische Kunst (Museum of Islamic Art), and the Museum für Ostasiatische Kunst (Museum of East Asian Art).

The **Skulpturengalerie**, covering two floors in the Lansstrasse building, is full of spectacular pieces dating from the Early Christian–Byzantine period through the 19th century. Among the greatest treasures are wood carvings by Tilman Riemenschneider and other German masters and works by such Italian sculptors as Giovanni Pisano, Donatello, and Bernini.

The **Gemäldegalerie**, located on two floors and in three wings of the Arnimallee building, is a treasure trove of European painting of all schools from the Middle Ages through the Neoclassical period. The German masters section includes paintings by Albrecht Altdorfer, Lucas Cranach the Elder, Hans Holbein the Younger, and Albrecht Dürer. In the Dutch and Flemish division are 25 Rembrandts and 19 Rubenses. In addition there are major works by Hieronymus Bosch, the Brueghels, Van Dyck, Van Eyck, van der Goes, Hals, Memling, Vermeer, and van der Weyden. The Italian section includes a dozen paintings by the Bellinis—father Jacopo and sons Giovanni and Gentile—seven Botticellis, and Giottos, Tintorettos, Titians, and Raphaels. The Spanish school is represented by, among others, El Greco's haunting *Mater Dolorosa* and Velázquez's *Three Musicians*.

The **Kupferstichkabinett** inhabits five rooms on two floors. The collection, only a fraction of which can be shown, includes 23,000 drawings and sketches by 14th- to 18th-century masters, 350,000 etchings, engravings, and woodcuts, and more than 5,000 illustrated books.

The **Museum für Völkerkunde**, whose entrance is on the Lansstrasse, is one of the most important in Europe. Only a small portion of the collection is on display; it is divided into five sections: pre-Columbian American, African, Southeast Asian, East Asian, and Pacific South Seas art.

If, after having visited these four museums, your legs, back, and eyes are still working, proceed to the museums of Indian, Islamic, and East Asian art.

Not far from the Dahlem complex, at Bussardsteig 9, near the edge of the Grunewald forest (see Green Berlin and the Lakes, below), you will find the **Brücke Museum**, named for Die Brücke, a group of early 20th-century German Expressionists. Virtually all of these artists, who collaborated between 1905 and 1913, are represented: Erich Heckel, Ernst Ludwig Kirchner, Otto Mueller, Emil Nolde, Max Pechstein, and, not least, Karl Schmidt-Rottluff, whose own collection of paintings, a gift to the city of Berlin, forms the foundation of this collection. Hours are 11:00 A.M. to 5:00 P.M. daily except Tuesday.

Dahlem also boasts one of Berlin's best French-Italian restaurants—**Ars Vivendi**, at Podbielskiallee 31. It is open for lunch and dinner daily except Tuesday. The ambience is elegantly low key, and owner-chef Salvatore Lanza cooks as memorably as the late Mario Lanza (no relation) sang. The restaurant is just a 15-minute walk from the museum complex or the Brücke Museum.

# SCHLOSS CHARLOTTENBURG AND THE MUSEUMS

It was not until the late 17th century that the electors of Brandenburg began to build grand residences, but once started, they freely indulged in ostentatious pomp and conspicuous Baroque consumption. Most of their lavish digs were damaged during World War II. Nearly all have been restored. The most dazzling palace in West Berlin is **Schloss Charlottenburg** in Charlottenburg borough, a half-hour walk north from Kurfürstendamm and its intersection with Adenauerplatz, or about ten minutes on foot northwest along Otto-Suhr-Allee from the Richard-Wagner-Platz subway station on the U-7 line.

The building was commissioned in 1695 by Elector Frederick III (King Frederick I) as a summer palace for his second wife, Sophie-Charlotte. Many wings were added in the 18th century, along with a manicured park, little pavilions, and various museums. Even a cursory visit takes half a day. The ornate historic apartments, which can be seen only on guided one-hour tours, are open from 9:00 A.M. to 5:00 P.M. daily except Monday. Tours start about every 20 minutes; the last one begins at 4:00.

During the 220 years that the Hohenzollern clan used the palace, the interior decor and furnishings underwent many changes to suit changing tastes. But as frugal Prussians, the Hohenzollerns never threw anything away. Instead, each generation stored its forebears' household goods in Berlin's environs. There, the furniture survived the 1943 air raid that almost completely destroyed Schloss Charlottenburg, and restorers could re-create the palace's interior as it had been during Sophie-Charlotte's time.

The queen was addicted to Oriental decor, which was then quite the rage. Therefore, as you are shepherded through the more than 70 rooms and hallways open to the public, you'll see nearly a dozen decorated in East Asian motifs and one chamber whose walls are entirely covered with Oriental porcelain.

Charlottenburg began rather modestly. The original central building, crowned by an elegant 165-foot copper dome upon which stands a gilded figure of Fortuna, was a summer "cottage" by royal standards, with only a dozen rooms. But Sophie-Charlotte was a lavish hostess who gave brilliant parties and balls, for which she needed more space. Extension of the central building and the addition of the Orangerie began in 1701. Another wing was built between 1740 and 1746 by Frederick the Great's favorite architect, Georg Wenzeslaus von Knobelsdorff, and in 1790 a court summer theater was added. Today, the façade of the entire palace complex, only two stories high, is a mind-boggling 1,666 feet long.

The immense bronze equestrian statue in the center of the courtyard is of Herzog Friedrich Wilhelm of Brandenburg, the Great Elector. Unveiled in 1703, it ranks as one of the finest examples of Baroque bronze sculpture in Europe. Its present location, however, is strictly postwar. Originally it stood on East Berlin's Lange Brücke, and later in front of the royal palace that is no more. In 1943, just before the first devastating air raid on the city, the statue was removed by river barge to safety. Unfortunately, the barge sank in Tegel harbor. The statue was recovered in 1949 and erected in front of Schloss Charlottenburg in 1952.

When the **Schlosspark** was laid out in 1697, it was in the neatly manicured French Baroque style. In the 19th century

Lenné, the landscape architect of the Tiergarten, turned it into a less formal English-style garden. It was restored to its original Baroque form after World War II. The two principal buildings in the park are the **Schinkel Pavilion,** in the style of a Neapolitan villa, and the **Belvedere,** completed in 1788, a late Rococo-style teahouse. The Schinkel Pavilion contains fine examples of late 18th-century furnishings. The Belvedere has a collection of 18th- and 19th-century china from Berlin's state-owned Royal Porcelain Manufactory.

# The Charlottenburg Museums

Four museums that are part of the Prussian state collections are at Schloss Charlottenburg, two in the palace itself and two across the street in the former royal armory and the palace guard's barracks. Before visiting them you might want to fortify yourself with a light lunch in pseudo-royal surroundings at the **Kleine Orangerie,** Spandauer Damm 20, a moderately priced restaurant adjacent to the western Orangerie wing of the palace. Game dishes are among the specialties.

The **Galerie der Romantik,** a division of West Berlin's Nationalgalerie, is in the long Knobelsdorff wing of the palace and contains a collection of fine examples of German Romantic painting. Caspar-David Friedrich (1774–1840) and Carl Blechen (1798–1840) are each represented by 23 pictures. Though best known as an architect, Karl-Friedrich Schinkel (1781–1841) was also a talented illustrator and painter. More than a dozen of his landscapes and pictures of imaginary Gothic cathedrals are on exhibit.

At the opposite end of the long palace façade, in the former court theater, is the **Museum für Vor- und Früh-geschichte** (Pre- and Early History), displaying a collection of artifacts and art from the Paleolithic, Mesolithic, and Neolithic cultures of Asia Minor and of the Bronze and Iron ages in Brandenburg.

The **Ägyptisches Museum,** at Schloss Strasse 70, across the street from the palace, is the home of Queen Nefertiti, whose polychrome limestone bust draws an estimated half-million visitors a year. This 3,350-year-old sculpture alone is worth the visit, because Nerfertiti, wife of Ikhnaton, was surely one of the greatest beauties of all time, and also because the bust is one of the finest pieces of art extant from the Amarna period. But there is much else to see in the museum, including an ebony bust of Queen Tiy, a green stone head of a priest, several mummies, and artifacts of daily life from 2,000 to 5,000 years ago.

The **Antikenmuseum**, at Schloss Strasse 1, directly across the Schloss Strasse parkway from the Ägyptisches Museum, is a dazzling repository of art from the Minoan and Mycenaean periods through early Byzantine times, including Greek vases and amphoras, bronzes, jewelry, worked gold, and ivory carvings.

The Charlottenburg area museums are open daily, except Friday, from 9:00 A.M. to 5:00 P.M.

You can buy replicas of some of the best pieces in West Berlin's state museums at the **Gipsformerei** on Sophie-Charlotten-Strasse 17–18, just past the west end of the palace grounds. This workshop, run by the museums, has more than 7,000 molds of the most famous sculptures and bas-reliefs in Berlin (and elsewhere), from which copies in plaster, synthetic stone or resin, and bronze can be cast. It keeps some of the more popular items in stock. There's a catalogue, and the Gipsformerei will also ship. Small stock items start at around DM 30. A copy of the head of Nefertiti will cost about DM 1,200. Open Monday through Friday, 9:00 A.M. to 4:00 P.M.

# SPANDAU

The formerly independent town of Spandau, half a century older than Berlin itself, now one of its 20 boroughs, and best known perhaps for its Spandau prison, is situated at the westernmost edge of the city and is well worth a day's exploration. Getting there is easy. Take the U-7 subway westbound; the next-to-last two stops on the line, Zitadelle and Altstadt Spandau, are where the attractions are.

The **Zitadelle Spandau** is a thick-walled Medieval castle built on the foundations of one of Albert the Bear's 12th-century fortresses. The present 1,000-by-1,000-foot complex, moated on three sides and bordered on the fourth by the Havel river (more of a lake here) was begun by Elector Joachim II in 1560 and completed in 1594. Since then it has remained virtually unchanged. It is a perfect example of Italian military engineering, and indeed it was an Italian, Francesco Chiaramella di Gandino of Venice, who was its principal architect. Until the age of modern artillery, it was virtually impregnable.

The citadel played a key role in all of the 17th- and 18th-century wars in which Brandenburg and, later, Prussia were involved. Twice it was captured—by the Swedes during the Thirty Years War and by Napoleon in 1806, but each time without battle. The Juliusturm, the castle's central tower, is its oldest part, dating to 1200. The 19th-century kaisers used it as a kind of German Fort Knox, a storage depot for the five billion gold francs they wrested as "reparations" from France after the Franco-Prussian war of 1870–1871. What remained of the hoard after World War I was returned to France in accordance with the 1919 Versailles Treaty.

Most of the buildings in the complex are open to visitors. The most rewarding is the Renaissance-style **Palast**, once the main living quarters of the fortress and now the home of Spandau's **Heimatmuseum** of local history. The collection is actually far less parochial than its name suggests and includes objects dating to the 10th and 11th centuries, when the Slavic Wends inhabited the area. The lower parts of the building incorporate 13th- and 14th-century tombstones with Hebrew inscriptions that were taken from Spandau's Jewish cemetery during a pogrom in 1348.

In the fortress commandant's house is the **Zitadellen-Schänke**, rustic inn and restaurant that serves lunch and dinner as well as Medieval-style banquets. The waiters and waitresses dress as knaves and wenches.

A ten-minute walk southwest from the citadel's main gate, will take you to the heart of Spandau's **Alstadt**. Many of its 18th-century burgher houses have been restored in recent years. There are also remnants of the city's Medieval defensive wall, and most streets are cobblestoned. The **Nikolaikirche**, on Reformationsplatz, is an early-15th-century brick Gothic structure built on the foundations of an even earlier church, and it is typical of the style of Brandenburg. The bronze baptismal basin was cast in 1398; the Renaissance altar dates from 1582.

# SPECIAL TRIPS AND OUTLYING AREAS

Given its size, much of what is worth seeing and doing in Berlin is far from the city center, but still within the city limits. Most of these sites can be reached by public transit. Literature and detailed maps are available for some special tours. Below are descriptions of a few of the best.

# Village Churches

Within Berlin are 55 stone *Dorfkirchen,* or village churches. Seven were built in the early 13th century, before the founding of Berlin itself, by Knights Templars. Three of the most interesting are in the districts of Marienfelde, Lichtenrade, and Buckow, all part of Tempelhof borough. To reach them take the southbound S-2 elevated train from the Anhalter Bahnhof station in Kreuzberg to the Marienfelde station; from there, it's not far by bus to these little chapels.

The **Dorfkirche Marienfelde**, consecrated in 1220, is the oldest village church in Berlin. A Gothic structure built of massive granite blocks, it is located on the tree-shaded, cobblestone village square just off Marienfelder Strasse on a little street named, appropriately, An der Dorfkirche. To get there take the S-2 to the Marienfelde station, then transfer to the number 11 or number 32 bus going south on Marienfelder Allee. The church is about one mile away from the station; the bus stops right at the corner leading to the square.

The 14th-century **Dorfkirche Lichtenrade**, another two miles southeast, is right in front of a farmyard, with a pond inhabited by quacking ducks. Next to the simple fieldstone church is the old village tavern, **Zum Alten Dorfkrug**, where you can lunch, snack, or have a beer. To get there, take the number 52 bus east from the Marienfelde village square to the S-2 elevated line and the Lichtenrade station; there, transfer to the number 82 bus going south to the Lichtenrade village square.

The **Dorfkirche Buckow**, about three miles northeast of Lichtenrade, was built around 1250, and still has five 13th-century stained-glass windows. There are also wall frescoes and gravestones dating from the 14th century. To get there, take the number 52 bus from the Lichtenrade S-Bahn station east to the Buckow village center. The bus stops right in front of the church.

To return to central Berlin, take the number 52 bus east to the Johannisthaler Chaussee subway station on the U-7 line, where you can catch a westbound train to the Adenauerplatz station on the Kurfürstendamm, a ride of about one half hour.

# Industrial Berlin

In the 19th century Berlin was *the* boom town of Europe. Buoyed by the industrial revolution, its population exploded from 172,000 in 1801 to more than 1.9 million by 1900. Though governed by the kings and kaisers, its real power-brokers were the barons of industry. As symbols of their wealth and might, they fashioned their factories, office build-ings, and warehouses after Medieval castles, palaces, and cathedrals. Surprisingly, scores of these edifices—factories, railway stations, power plants, warehouses, streetcar depots, town halls and courthouses, and even breweries—have sur-vived. As recently as a decade ago, they were viewed as architectural monstrosities. But now, in an age of postmod-ern nostalgia, they are being preserved, renovated, and restored.

The city government has mapped a series of 12 walking-or-bicycle tours called *Spazierwege zu Industrie und Technik,* or walking tours to industry and technology. De-scriptive pamphlets and maps in convenient pocket-size plastic holders are available from the information center, Hardenbergstrasse 20, right by the Bahnhof Zoo.

While many of these structures still serve their original purposes, others have been imaginatively converted. In the **Moabit district**, part of Tiergarten borough, for example, dozens of craft and artisan shops are now lodged in the original **Schultheiss brewery** at Stromstrasse 11–17. This biggest of the Berlin breweries (you'll see its name all over town) moved to a new site in 1981. The 110-year-old brew-ing room itself, with its huge, gleaming copper vats, has been converted into a tavern, the **Sudhaus**, which features live jazz and folk music nightly except Monday starting at 8:00 P.M.

# Green Berlin and the Lakes

Vast expanses of Berlin are as pastoral as a landscape paint-ing. West Berlin's Grunewald is 12 square miles in area; the Spandau and Tegel forests are somewhat smaller. East Ber-lin's Köpenicker Forst is the largest, at 22 square miles. The tourist office in the Europa-Center and the information cen-ter on the Hardenbergstrasse provide guidebooks and maps of the marked trails.

The **Grunewald**, in the southwest corner of the city, is bordered on the west by the Havel river and the Grosser Wannsee. The forest begins just beyond the western end of the Kurfürstendamm, which becomes the Königsallee and winds southward through the eastern half of the forest. From the Dahlem museum area, take the U-2 subway southbound, get off at Dahlem-Dorf, walk northwest to the Brücke Museum, and you are at the edge of the forest. The forest is rewarding not only for its greenery and excursion-boat facilities, but also for sheltering several of Berlin's most interesting smaller châteaus and royal mansions.

The **Jagdschloss Grunewald** is a hunting château built for Elector Joachim II in 1542. The château, situated idyllically on the shore of the little **Grunewaldsee**, was restored to its original Renaissance appearance in 1963 and is now a museum. Among its holdings are paintings by German and Flemish masters, including pictures by both Lucas Cranachs (the Elder and the Younger), Barthel Bryn, Jacob Jordaens, Antoine Pesne, and Rubens. There are also 16th- to 18th-century furnishings, hunting trophies, and weapons. The museum is open daily, except Monday, from 10:00 A.M. to 6:00 P.M. April through September, until 5:00 P.M. in March and October, and until 4:00 P.M. November through February. For sustenance, try the delightfully rustic forest inn nearby, **Forsthaus Paulsborn**, right by the lakeside. It is open for lunch and dinner in the summer, lunch only in the winter, and for breakfast, starting at 9:00 A.M., every Sunday.

To see more châteaus and the Wannsee, head to the southern part of the Grunewald. Take either the S-3 elevated train from Bahnhof Zoo or the S-1 from Anhalter Bahnhof in Kreuzberg. Both lines end at the Wannsee. From there you can either walk due west along Königstrasse or north along the lakeshore, or board the number 6 or number 3 bus.

The three main attractions at the western end of the Königstrasse are the Glienicke Brücke, the Jagdschloss Glienicke, and the Schloss Klein-Glienicke. The **Glienicke Brücke**, which crosses the Havel to Potsdam, became famous during the spy trading of the Cold War. This is where Soviet KGB Colonel Rudolf Abel went east (although he actually walked west by the compass) in exchange for U-2 pilot Gary Powers in 1963, and where Soviet human rights activist Anatoly Sharansky walked to freedom in 1983. Until November 1989, the bridge could be used only by Western and Soviet military and diplomatic personnel.

The **Jagdschloss Glienicke**, just south of the bridge, was built as a hunting lodge for Brandenburg's Friedrich Wilhelm, the Great Elector, in 1682. A gem of the Baroque style, it has served since 1963 as a youth hostel and conference center. Only the grounds are open to visitors.

The **Schloss Klein-Glienicke**, just across the street, is situ-

ated in one of Berlin's most beautiful parks, landscaped by
Peter Josef Lenné in 1816. The château, originally a small
country mansion belonging to a wallpaper manufacturer
and then to a chancellor of Prussia, was enlarged and rebuilt
in its present form by Schinkel to serve as a summer residence for Prince Karl, a son of King Friedrich Wilhelm III.
Neoclassical in style, it has a central building with two wings
that enclose an Italian-style courtyard. Prince Karl was an
inveterate globe-trotter who brought back hundreds of souvenirs from his travels to Italy, Greece, and Asia Minor. He
had them all imbedded in the château's exterior walls,
where they can be seen today. One is an old Persian gravestone. The late shah of Iran, on a visit to West Berlin in 1967,
pointed out that it was upside down; apparently Prince Karl
could not read Persian.

A stroll north through the park or on the path along the
Havel river embankment will take you to the **St.-Peter-und-
Pauls-Kirche** and **Blockhaus Nikolskoe**. The onion-domed
church and the log house, which looks as if it is right off the
Siberian taiga, were built by King Frederick William III in
honor of his son-in-law, Tsar Nicholas I, who married Prussia's Princess Charlotte in 1817. The church, consecrated in
1837, was a 20th wedding anniversary gift. The log house,
named for Nicholas, was a present from the king to the
couple in 1819. A fire destroyed it in 1984; it was reconstructed and is now a popular restaurant, serving strictly
German, not Russian, food. This transplanted piece of Russia
provides a panoramic view of the Havel, the Wannsee, and
the Pfaueninsel (Peacock Island), site of one of Berlin's
strangest châteaus, the **Schloss Pfaueninsel**. A ferry will take
you there; the landing is just below the Russian church.

For centuries, the island has been a famous scenic spot.
Toward the end of the 17th century it belonged to an
alchemist named Johann Kunkel von Löwenstern, who was
supposed to make gold there for the Great Elector. Instead
he produced beautiful ruby-colored glasses and goblets,
examples of which are on exhibit in the palace. When the
Great Elector died, in 1688, Kunkel left to ply his trade in
Sweden, and the island went into a long sleep until 1793,
when Frederick William II bought it from Kunkel's heirs,
intending to use it as a hideaway for himself and his mistress, Wilhelmine Encke, the Countess Lichtenau. Together
they designed the château to resemble the ruin of a Roman
country house, with Romanesque elements. They did not
have much use of it—the king died in 1797. But his son,

Frederick William III, and his consort, Queen Louise, loved the place and used it as a summer retreat. During their reign, peacocks were brought here, and Lenné landscaped the parks. The palace is open daily from 10:00 A.M. to 5:00 P.M. April through September, and until 4:00 P.M. in October. It is closed from November through March.

From the island you can catch the number 1 steamer, part of the city's public transit system, back to the landing at the Wannsee S-Bahn station, and from there transfer to the number 2 steamer route, which will take you all the way back north to Spandau for connections to the U-7 subway line. Or transfer to another boat to travel on the Tegeler See to the Tegel forest and Schloss Tegel.

The **Schloss Tegel**, at Adelheidallee 19–20 (a mile north of the boat landing, and near the Tegel station on the U-6 subway line), is also called the **Humboldt Schlösschen**. Built in 1550 for the court secretary of Elector Joachim II, it was later used as a hunting château by the Great Elector. In 1766 it became the property of Georg von Humboldt, father of Alexander, the famous naturalist, and Wilhelm, the equally famous statesman, philosopher, and educator.

Wilhelm von Humboldt commissioned Schinkel to reconstruct the house in the Neoclassical style for his use as a private residence. He, Alexander, and many of their descendants are buried in the family mausoleum on the grounds, not far from an 800-year-old oak under which, according to legend, Margrave Albert the Bear often napped. The mansion and surrounding park are still owned by the Humboldt family.

Wilhelm von Humboldt established Berlin's university and created Germany's public education system. He was also an art collector, with a special interest in Greek and Roman sculpture. Unfortunately, many pieces in his collection were lost during World War II (although some mysteriously reappeared in East Berlin). Until mid-1990, most of the artworks in the mansion were copies, but the East Berlin authorities have began returning them and it is hoped that in a year or two the original collection will again be complete. The house is full of family heirlooms and memorabilia documenting the life and work of both Wilhelm and Alexander. It is open Wednesday and Sunday only, from 2:00 to 6:00 P.M.

From the Humboldt mansion it is a 10- to 15-minute walk (or two minutes on any of the bus lines) back to the Tegel subway station, where you can catch the U-6 to East Berlin.

# EAST BERLIN

Central East Berlin—the 4.1-square-mile borough of **Berlin Mitte**—is Berlin's historic heart, the spot where Cölln and Berlin were first settled. It is still the city's center, with its most important sites: the Brandenburg Gate, Under den Linden, the Deutsche Oper, Humboldt university, the German national library, the armory, Museumsinsel, and Alexanderplatz, now dominated by the 1,200-foot TV tower, Berlin's tallest structure, nicknamed the "Speared Onion." Berlin Mitte also contains the Dom and St. Hedwig's, St. Mary's, and St. Nicholas churches; the Platz der Akademie, formerly known as Gendarmenmarkt, with the Schauspielhaus theater and the French and German cathedrals; and the Rotes Rathaus, so called for its neo-Renaissance red brick façade.

In other words, when the devastated city was divided into four occupation sectors at the 1945 Potsdam conference, the Soviets, and by inference East Berliners, got most of the nuggets. Moreover, though it seemed to take ages, most of it was rebuilt, restored, refurbished, renovated, and enriched with luxury hotels and a profusion of restaurants, cafés, cozy taverns, special shops, department stores, theaters, and cinemas in order to make East Berlin, the capital of the German Democratic Republic, as much a showcase of communism as West Berlin is of capitalism.

The price of rebuilding a few streets, squares, museums, palaces, and monuments was the neglect and decay, or the shoddy prefab restoration, of much of the rest of the city. Moreover, for 28 of the more than 40 years that East Berlin was destined to play its role in the Cold War, it was a showcase within a cage, sealed off from West Berlin by the Wall with its bristling array of guard towers and barbed wire. Many would-be visitors wondered whether a visit was worth it, given the bureaucratic formalities, the surliness of the border guards, and the real or imagined restrictions on freedom of movement.

All that changed dramatically on November 9, 1989, when the Wall opened up and the two Berlins as well as the two Germanys began moving toward reunification. Yet at the same time some things have not changed. The scars of division and of the Wall will long remain, as will those of East Berlin having been the far poorer showcase and the capital of a far poorer country.

# ON AND AROUND
# UNTER DEN LINDEN

Unter den Linden is Berlin's most famous avenue. It runs from east to west for about a mile from Marx-Engels-Platz (known until 1951 as the *Lustgarten,* or Pleasure Garden), to Pariser Platz and the Brandenburg Gate.

The boulevard's pedigree goes back to 1573, when Elector Johann Georg laid it out as a bridle path from his palace to his hunting grounds in the Tiergarten. Three quarters of a century later, in 1647, the Great Elector ordered 1,000 nut trees and 1,000 lindens planted along the road. Although these were cut down in 1680 in order to pave the street and make room for residential and public buildings, the name Unter den Linden stuck, and became official a century later when Frederick the Great widened the street into a parkway and again planted it with linden trees.

In the late 19th and early 20th centuries it was the unchallenged main street of Berlin, divided at midpoint by its intersection with Friedrichstrasse. Along its eastern half were the great palaces, the university, opera, libraries, and other institutional buildings. The western half was lined by foreign embassies, elegant shops, luxury hotels, cafés, and restaurants. Wilhelmstrasse, now called Otto-Grotewohl-Strasse, which intersects Unter den Linden close to the Brandenburg Gate, was the street of government, flanked by the presidential residence, the ministry of justice, and the Reich chancellory. To speak of "Wilhelmstrasse" in those days was like speaking of the White House or 10 Downing Street. By contrast, the intersection of Unter den Linden and Friedrichstrasse was the epicenter of Berlin's political, intellectual, cultural, and commercial life, the location of the Café Kranzler and of the Café Bauer, which was reborn in 1987 as part of the Grand Hotel.

In May 1945, when the bombs stopped falling and the guns were silenced, Unter den Linden was a bleak moonscape of craters and mountains of rubble, with only charred, crumbling façades of gutted buildings still standing. The few linden trees that survived were soon cut down for firewood. Yet today Unter den Linden is again East Berlin's finest boulevard, reconstructed almost as it was. Unfortunately its western half, although again lined with foreign embassies, stores, and government ministries, was rebuilt in faceless steel, glass, and concrete. But from Friedrichstrasse eastward

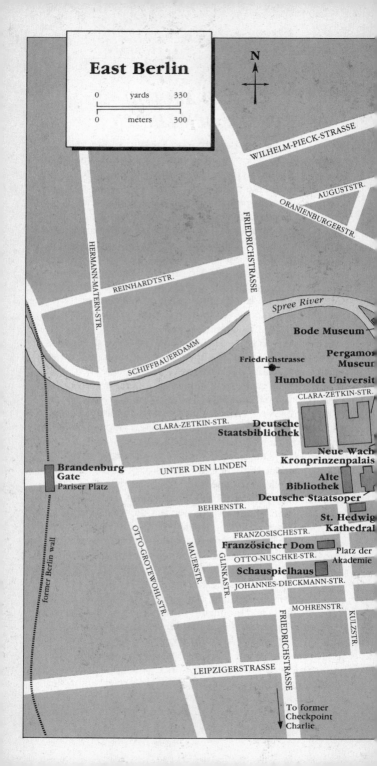

WILHELM-PIECK-STRASSE

SCHONHAUSERALLEE

ROSENTHALERSTRASSE

GR.-HAMBURGER-STR.

RAUSNICKSTR.

MUNZSTRASSE

ROSA-LUXEMBURG-STRASSE

Alexanderplatz

**Nationalgalerie**

BODESTR.

**Fernsehturm**

KARL-LIEBKNECHT-STRASSE

RATHAUSSTR.

**Altes Museum**

**Marienkirche**

**Dom**

SPANDAUERSTRASSE

**Rotes Rathaus**

GRUNERSTRASSE

**Zeughaus**

Marx-Engels-Platz

POSTSTR.

**Nikolaikirche**

WAISENSTR.

**Palast de Republik**

Nikolaikirchenplatz

NIKOLAIVERTEL

STRALAVERSTR.

WERDERSTR.

BREITESTR.

MUHLENDAMM

**Gebäude des Staatsrats**

FRIEDRICHSGRACHT

*Spree River*

NIEDERWALLSTR.

MUSEUMSINSEL

AM MARKISCHEN UFER

**Märkisches Museum**

WALLSTRASSE

*To Treptow and köpenick*

former Berlin wall

virtually every building of note was recreated: Frederick the Great would see hardly any changes. Even the 45-foot-high equestrian statue of "Old Fritz" stands in its proper place in the middle of the avenue. Erected in 1851, it was removed for safekeeping during World War II, then hidden for 35 years behind a clump of bushes on the grounds of Sans Souci palace in Potsdam because East Germany's rulers wanted no reminder of the Hohenzollerns and Prussia. In 1980, in an about-face, they allowed this monument to Frederick the Great to return to Unter den Linden.

The **Brandenburger Tor** (Brandenburg Gate), at the avenue's western end, is the very essence of Berlin. The huge gate—66 feet high, 204 feet wide, and 36 feet deep—modeled after the Propylaeum on the Acropolis, was officially opened in 1791. Frederick William II attended the ceremony. Originally called the Friedenstor (Peace Gate), it assumed a more martial appearance two years later when it was crowned by the bronze **Quadriga**, a four-horse war chariot driven by the Goddess of Victory. The goddess was originally nude, but her appearance triggered so much indignation and so many ribald jokes that the sculptor, Johann Gottfried Schadow, clad her in a sheet of copper. She kept her vigil for 13 years, until 1806, when Napoleon marched triumphantly into Berlin. Like many conquerors before and after, he looted art. He had a policy: "Take a nation's symbols, and you have it in your hands." He dismantled the Quadriga and had it shipped to Paris to be mounted on the Arc de Triomphe. Eight years later, however, the Prussians marched into Paris and recaptured the Quadriga. It was taken to Jagdschloss Grunewald for repair, then replaced on the Brandenburg Gate in June 1814, with one small alteration: The Prussian eagle in the center of Victory's oak wreath was replaced with an Iron Cross.

Few structures have witnessed as many vicissitudes of German history as the Brandenburg Gate. In 1871 it was the stage of the victory celebration after the war with France and the establishment of the kaiser Reich. In 1919 leftist revolutionaries and government troops had a shoot-out around its Doric columns. Battalions of brown-shirted Nazi troops marched through it on the night of January 31, 1933, in a torchlight parade hailing Hitler's appointment as Reich chancellor. In May 1945, like the rest of Berlin, the gate and monument were in ruins. Reconstruction was not completed until 1958. The gate became the symbol of Berlin's division when the Wall was built in 1961, and of the city's reunification when it was opened to pedestrian traffic in 1989. The subsequent celebrations did so much damage to the Quadriga that in the spring of 1990 the monument was removed for renovation and repair and the gate sheathed in scaffolding, all in preparation for celebrations marking the 200th anniversary of the gate in August 1991.

From Brandenburg Gate back to Friedrichstrasse, where the main sights of Unter den Linden begin, is a ten-minute walk. Stay on the north side of the boulevard for a while. The neo-Baroque structure at number 8 is the **Deutsche Staatsbibliothek**, housing a collection of 5.5 million books, manuscripts, musical scores, etchings, and maps. Just past the library, at number 6, is **Humboldt Universität**. Built in 1753 as a palace for Prince Henry, the brother of Frederick the Great, it was given to Wilhelm von Humboldt in 1809 when he founded the university. Twenty-seven Nobel Prize winners have been members of its faculty, and the philosopher Hegel taught here. Statues of both Wilhelm and Alexander von Humboldt flank the elaborate wrought-iron gateway.

Directly across Unter den Linden, at number 11, is the **Alte Bibliothek**, built between 1774 and 1788 by the Prussian architect Georg Friedrich Boumann according to plans made by Joseph Fischer von Erlach for the St. Michael wing of Vienna's Hofburg. Today, the building houses various university institutes.

A few paces beyond is the **Deutsche Staatsoper**, East Berlin's main opera house, commissioned by Frederick the Great, designed by his favorite architect, Georg von Knobelsdorff, and opened December 7, 1742, with a performance of Carl Heinrich Graun's *Caesar and Cleopatra*. One of the world's oldest opera houses and a gem of Neoclassical design, it was thrice destroyed and rebuilt: first by a fire in 1843, then by an air raid in 1943, and finally by bombs and artillery in 1945. The present reconstruction dates from 1955. Erich Kleiber was among its conductors and musical directors. For all its fame, it is just one of two opera houses in East Berlin, and of three in Berlin as a whole. The others are the **Komische Oper** (Comic Opera) and West Berlin's **Deutsche Oper Berlin**.

**St. Hedwige Kathedrale**, the squat, domed structure (modeled on the Pantheon) behind the opera house, is the Roman Catholic cathedral of Berlin and one of the few Catholic churches in this predominantly Protestant city. Construction on it began in 1747. The cast of planners and architects was stellar: Frederick the Great, Knobelsdorff,

Johann Boumann, and the Frenchman Jean Legeay. The Seven Years War halted work, and the church, finally completed in 1772, is named for Hedwig, the beatified wife of Duke Henry of Silesia. It was destroyed by fire during World War II and rebuilt in the early 1960s, with its interior starkly simple and modern and the exterior much as it used to be.

You might enjoy lunch, coffee and pastries, or even dinner at the **Operncafé**, Unter den Linden 5, in the former **Prinzessinenpalais**. This was the Baroque residence of the daughters of King Frederick William III before their marriage. In addition to the Operncafé's daytime functions as a restaurant and coffeehouse, it is one of East Berlin's liveliest night spots, open until 4:00 A.M. On a fair day you can sit on the terrace, which provides a splendid view of Unter den Linden's historic buildings.

Next to the café, at number 3, is the **Kronprinzenpalais**, a mid-17th-century mansion that was enlarged in 1732 for Frederick the Great when he was the 20-year-old crown prince. In later years, the palace served as the official residence of Prussia's and Germany's royal heirs. Heavily damaged during the battle of Berlin, it was reopened in 1969 for use as a government guesthouse for visiting dignitaries. Since the spring of 1990, there have been plans to turn it into an annex of the Nationalgalerie.

On the other side of Unter den Linden, just east of the university, is the **Neue Wache** (New Guardhouse), at number 4. This is one of Karl-Friedrich Schinkel's Neoclassical masterpieces, designed in the style of a Roman temple. After the 1918 revolution that toppled the kaiser and set the stage for the Weimar Republic, the Neue Wache became the Tomb of the Unknown Soldier, a memorial to the fallen of World War I. The East German regime turned it into a Monument against Fascism and Militarism, which presumably it will remain.

The **Zeughaus** (Arsenal), just past the Neue Wache at Unter den Linden 2, is the oldest public building on the avenue. It was completed in 1706 as an armory and gave a fairly clear indication of where Prussia was headed. This four-story structure is the largest and best-preserved example of Baroque architecture in all of Berlin. For nearly a century and a half, from 1730 to 1877, it was used to store captured war matériel. It was then converted into a military museum and a hall of fame celebrating victories by Brandenburg's and Prussia's armies. In 1952 the East German government turned it into the **Museum für Deutsche Geschichte** (Museum of German History).

# THE MUSEUMSINSEL

The **Museumsinsel** (Museum Island) is a complex of museums and galleries at the east end of Unter den Linden. It was on this island that the town of Cölln was founded in the 1230s. Berlin was founded on the east bank.

Of the five original museums at the northern tip of the island—the Altes Museum, the Neues Museum, the Nationalgalerie, the Pergamon Museum, and the Bode Museum—all except the Neues Museum have been rebuilt since the war, are open to the public, and house magnificent collections. Reconstruction of the Neues Museum has been hampered by difficult soil and foundation conditions that strained the East German treasury. Although reunification of the city and amalgamation of the museum collections are expected to accelerate the pace, it is unlikely that the project will be completed in this century. Opening hours for the Altes Museum, the Nationalgalerie, and the Bode Museum are Wednesday through Sunday 9:00 A.M. to 6:00 P.M. The Pergamon Museum is open daily 9:00 A.M. to 6:00 P.M.

The **Altes Museum**, the oldest in the complex, was built between 1824 and 1830 by Schinkel in Greek-temple style. It contains the 20th-century section of the Nationalgalerie, including 40 works on permanent loan from the German collector Peter Ludwig, among them two Picassos. Most of the museum's own contemporary works are by East German artists. It is also the repository of East Berlin's collection of 40,000 drawings and watercolors. Among the museum's treasures are 40 Botticelli drawings illustrating Dante's *Inferno*. (The rest of the original 80 are in West Berlin's Dahlem complex, and the two groups will probably be reunited in 1991.) The museum also houses East Berlin's **Kupferstichkabinett** (Print Collection), an assemblage of more than 130,000 etchings, engravings, woodcuts, and other kinds of graphic art from the 15th century to the present.

The **Nationalgalerie**, built between 1866 and 1876 in the style of a Roman temple with Corinthian pillars, is set on a high base and approached by an imposing flight of stairs. Originally it was intended as a kind of festival hall for state receptions and royal ceremonies, but as the city's collection of 19th- and 20th-century art grew, it took on its current role.

The **Bode Museum**, named for Wilhelm von Bode, director of the Berlin museums from 1872 to 1929, is a triangular two-story structure built in neo-Baroque style. In it are East Berlin's Egyptian museum, the museum of pre- and early history, the Early Christian–Byzantine collection, the numismatic collection, the sculpture collection, and the picture gallery. The Egyptian museum's mummies and its collection of 15,000 papyrus rolls are among the best in the world. The sculpture collection is strong on German, Dutch, and French works from the 12th through 18th centuries. East Berlin's **Gemäldegalerie** (Picture Gallery) features works by German, Flemish, and Dutch artists from the 15th through the 17th centuries, and English and French artists from the 18th. (The best examples of this period are all in West Berlin's Dahlem complex.)

The largest and newest of the museums is the **Pergamon Museum**, completed in 1930. It takes its name from the huge altar from the ancient city-state of Pergamum, in what is today western Turkey. The vast two-story structure also contains the antiquities collection, the Islamic museum, the East Asian collection, the folk crafts museum, and the Western Asian museum. To see it all will take at least half a day. But most visitors make a beeline for the half-dozen main drawing cards on display: the neo-Babylonian collections from the time of Nebuchadnezzar II, including the monumental Ishtar Gate, the Processional Way, and portions of Nebuchadnezzar's throne room; the gate of the Roman Market in Miletus; and the Pergamum Altar. The altar, dedicated to Zeus, ranks as one of the best-preserved examples of Hellenistic bas-relief. It was erected as part of a temple on Pergamum's Castle Hill between 180 and 160 B.C., when Pergamum was a powerful, independent city-state. Portions of it were found in 1871 during excavations at the city's Byzantine wall, and by 1880 almost the entire altar and temple had been dug up. The sections were brought to Berlin in 1902. It took curators until 1930 to reconstruct the altar. Enveloped in sandbags and concrete, it survived the World War II air raids. However, the Russians removed it to "protective custody" in Moscow in 1945 and did not return it until 1957. Two more years passed before the altar was reassembled and the museum reopened. In the spring of 1990 the modern city of Pergamum, now called Bergama, backed by the Turkish government, launched a campaign for the return of the altar. Postage stamps with the slogan "The Pergamum Altar Belongs to Us" were issued. If anything does come of it, it probably will not be for many more years.

# THE MARX-ENGELS-PLATZ AREA

This 1,200-by-600-foot square that extends south from the Altes Museum, called Marx-Engels-Platz since 1951, incorporates much of what used to be the Lustgarten, or Pleasure Garden. Laid out in 1573 as an herb and vegetable garden for the ducal family, it was transformed into an ornamental garden in the 1640s, and then turned into a military parade ground by Frederick William I, the Soldier King, in 1715. Trees were planted here in the 1830s, a portion of the park was ceded to the Altes Museum, and in 1895, on the ground and foundations of an earlier church, work began on the Dom, Berlin's Protestant cathedral.

The **Dom**, 386 feet long, 240 feet wide, and 280 feet high, was completed in 1905. It is an example of ostentatious turn-of-the-century neo-Renaissance, with heavy overtones of Reich braggadocio. In many ways it resembles St. Peter's in Rome; in fact, it was considered the "Mother Church of Prussian Protestantism" and often called the "St. Peter's of the North." Many of the electors of Brandenburg and kings of Prussia are buried in its crypt.

Like everything else in the neighborhood, it was destroyed during the war, but East Germany's Lutheran Evangelical church authorities, with financial help from their brethren in West Germany, restored most of it, and work is expected to be completed in 1991.

The square is flanked on the east by the ultramodern steel, marble, and glass **Palast der Republik**, which occupies the site of the former royal palace. Completed in 1976, the new palace became the home of the Volkskammer (People's Chamber), East Germany's parliament, and did double duty as a community center with cafés, restaurants, exhibition halls, and a central auditorium and theater.

# THE ALEXANDERPLATZ AREA

Once one of Berlin's busiest squares, the Alexanderplatz today is East Berlin's central shopping and commercial district. It bears no resemblance to what it looked like before World War II.

To reach it, go east from the Dom, cross the Spree, and continue along Karl-Liebknecht-Strasse. The left side of the street is lined with shops, the right with a block-wide park whose main features are the Marienkirche, the Fernsehturm, and, on the right side along the Rathausstrasse, the Rotes Rathaus. The church and town hall are virtually all that remain of the prewar district.

The **Marienkirche**, at the foot of the TV tower, is one of Berlin's oldest parish churches. Its austere brick and stone exterior belies its rich decorations and furnishings. Begun in 1270 and first mentioned in town records in 1294, it was in the center of Berlin's Neumarkt (Newmarket Square). A fire devastated the church in 1380, but it was rebuilt. The tower was added in the 16th century.

Among the art treasures inside is the *Totentanz* (Dance of Death) mural—28 depictions of Death painted in 1485 during an epidemic of the plague in Berlin that were uncovered in the course of restoration work 130 years ago. There is also a beautifully crafted 15th-century bronze baptismal font, a Baroque pulpit from 1703, many elaborately carved stone epitaphs, and a fine neo-Baroque organ, on which recitals are frequently given.

The **Fernsehturm** (TV Tower), completed in 1969, presents a mind-boggling accumulation of statistics. If you include the antenna, the "Speared Onion" is 1,204 feet high. The concrete shaft is 825 feet high and 105 feet in diameter, and weighs 26,000 tons. The sphere weighs 4,800 tons. There is room for 200 people on the bulb's observation platform and for another 200 in the revolving **Tele-Café** above it, which makes one complete circle each hour. Two high-speed elevators, with altimeters for the amusement of passengers, take you up into the "onion," and on a clear day you'll have a view extending 25 miles. The observation platform and café are open daily from 8:00 A.M. to midnight in the summer, and from 9:00 A.M. in the winter. (Every second and fourth Tuesday it opens at 1:00 P.M.) On weekends, holidays, and in the tourist season, crowds can be large.

Named for its red-brick color, the Renaissance-revival **Rotes Rathaus** was opened for its first town council session in 1865, replacing several older town halls in central Berlin, including the one that Cölln and Berlin built on the Lange Brücke when they formed their confederation in the 14th century. Since Berlin's enlargement in 1920, the Rotes Rathaus has served as both the borough and city town hall.

# THE NIKOLAIVIERTEL

The St. Nicholas quarter, tucked between the southwest façade of the Rathaus and the Spree river, is the oldest part of
Berlin, the heart of the frontier settlement of the early 13th
century. It certainly looks old, with its narrow cobblestone
streets and gabled Medieval-style houses. But don't let appearances fool you. It's all brand new, as artificial as a movie set. A
scant decade ago the little four-block neighborhood was still
a wasteland, with only the gutted shell of the **Nikolaikirche**,
Berlin's oldest church, still standing. To prepare for the city's
750th anniversary, East German officialdom launched a crash
program to create something "historic," with modern methods. All those "ancient" houses were built with prefab concrete slabs, then covered with cement and stucco, upon
which craftsmen and artisans were free to indulge themselves
with oriel windows, bartizans, Gothic arches, loggias, gargoyles, front stoops, helix ornaments—you name it.

The new "old" buildings added color and atmosphere to a
city very short on both. Moreover, the reconstruction and
restoration of the church of St. Nicholas is a remarkable
achievement. It is now a division of the **Märkisches Museum**
of Berlin history.

Even more remarkable was the re-creation of the **Ephra-
impalais**, at the corner of Poststrasse and Mühlendamm. This
richly ornamented Baroque mansion was built in 1765 for
Veitel Heine Ephraim, a Jewish banker and financial adviser
to the royal court. In 1935, during the Nazi era, the elegant
town house was razed, supposedly to provide space for the
widening of the Mühlendamm. Somewhat mysteriously, hundreds of decorative elements of the façade and interior were
stored in various depots and warehouses, most in what is
today West Berlin. When East German authorities decided to
rebuild the mansion, West Berlin provided some 2,000 sections of the house. They were melded with new pieces of
stone masonry and stuccowork crafted on the basis of old
photographs and illustrations of the house. Today, the Ephra-
impalais is used for art exhibitions.

When it was completed in 1987, the Nikolaiviertel had
become East Berlin's favorite residential and shopping district. Most of the new-old buildings are actually apartment
houses, and specialty stores line the narrow cobblestone
streets. There are numerous cafés, restaurants, and taverns,
such as **Zur Rippe**, at Poststrasse 17, which specializes in
traditional Berlin dishes like pea soup and sauerbraten.

# THE PLATZ DER AKADEMIE AREA

A walk back west on the Werderstrasse, the Nikolaiviertel's northern boundary, will take you back across the Spree, the island, the Spree canal, and along the back side of St. Hedwig cathedral and into the Französiche Strasse. At the corner of Französische Strasse and Külz-Strasse, turn south and go another block to the Platz der Akademie. All told, it should take you ten minutes.

The **Platz der Akademie** used to be called the Gendarmenmarkt because a regiment of 18th-century gendarmes had its barracks and stables there. The name was changed in 1950 on the occasion of the 250th anniversary of the Academy of Sciences, whose main building is on the plaza's eastern side. One of Berlin's finest squares, it was the heart of the French quarter at the end of the 17th century, when Huguenot refugees accounted for one third of the city's population.

Two magnificent churches, the Französischer Dom (French cathedral) and the Deutscher Dom (German cathedral), mark its northern and southern boundaries. The Schauspielhaus, another of Karl-Friedrich Schinkel's masterpieces, fronts the square to the west.

The **Französicher Dom**, a majestic example of late Renaissance-early Baroque style, was designed by two emigré French architects, Louis Cayard and Abraham Quesnay, and built between 1701 and 1705. It is the main church of the Huguenot congregation. In the church tower you can visit the **Hugenottenmuseum**, a small collection of artifacts, applied art, and documents pertaining to the life of the French in Berlin at the turn of the 18th century. It is open Tuesday through Thursday and Saturday from 10:00 A.M. to 5:00 P.M., and Sunday from 11:30 A.M.

The **Deutscher Dom**, a virtual twin of the French cathedral (and not to be confused with the Protestant Dom at Marx-Engels-Platz), was built between 1701 and 1708 according to plans of an Italian architect, Giovanni Simonetti. External reconstruction work was not completed until early autumn 1990, and it will be several more years before the interior has been rebuilt.

The **Schauspielhaus**, a jewel of Greco-Roman–revival style, was one of Schinkel's most notable structures. From the time it opened in 1821 until its destruction during the war, it served first as the Royal Court, then as the Prussian state theater. Since its restoration was completed in 1987, it has been used as East Berlin's main concert hall.

From the Platz der Akademie it is just two blocks west (along either the Otto-Nuschke-Strasse or Johannes-Dieckmann-Strasse) back to the Friedrichstrasse, where you can decide whether you want to leave East Berlin or continue on to explore other boroughs. If you decide to go on, the subway at Stadtmitte station on the Friedrichstrasse or the eastbound S-Bahn at the Friedrichstrasse station will take you to Treptow and Köpenick.

# TREPTOW

This borough, which stretches southeast along the Spree, is named for a fishing village first documented in 1568. In the late 19th century, the area around the old town was turned into the English-style **Treptower Park**. It has been a popular recreation area ever since. Today, one of its main attractions is the **Sowjetisches Ehrenmal** (Soviet War Memorial) and military cemetery. Created in the late 1940s, this is the largest Soviet military monument outside the U.S.S.R. Five thousand Russian soldiers killed in the battle of Berlin are buried here. Although the sculpture is in strictly Socialist Realist style and the architecture is monumentally Stalinist, the memorial is poignantly moving. On the avenue leading to the entrance is a figure of Mother Russia carved from a 50-ton block of granite. Birches line the broad path to a "Grove of Honor," and two walls of red granite symbolize flags lowered in mourning. Atop the cylindrical mausoleum stands a 38-foot-tall bronze figure of a Red Army soldier cradling a small child in one arm and brandishing a sword with which he has just smashed the Nazi swastika.

To get to the park, take the westbound S-Bahn to the Ostkreuz station and transfer to any southbound line to Treptower Park. It is a five-minute walk along Puschkinallee from the station to the memorial.

# KÖPENICK

Stronghold of the Wendish Prince Jaczso, Köpenick predates even Cölln-Berlin. A separate city until its incorporation into Berlin in 1920, it is now the largest of the city's boroughs, and its most pastoral. What the Grunewald and Wannsee are to West Berlin, the **Köpenicker Forst** and **Grosser Müggelsee** lake are to East Berlin: a vast area for hiking, boating, and escaping from the urban landscape. To get there, take the westbound S-Bahn to the Köpenick stop.

**Schloss Köpenick**, south of the train station (walk or take the number 27 bus), occupies the site of Prince Jaczso's 12th-century fortress and is the oldest surviving palace in Berlin. It was completed, in Renaissance style, in 1571 and served as a hunting château for Elector Joachim II. In the early 18th century, Frederick I added two Baroque-style wings. In October 1760, during the Seven Years War, Russian troops plundered the château, and soon after, it went into a long decline. Virtually undamaged during World War II, the palace and its park have enjoyed a renaissance since 1963, when the East Berlin state museums turned the richly decorated structure into the East Berlin **Kunstgewerbemuseum** (Museum of Applied Art). The collection of furniture, porcelain, glass, and goldsmith work here includes more than 900 years of European decorative art from the Middle Ages to the present. The museum is open Wednesday through Sunday from 10:00 A.M. to 6:00 P.M.

Köpenick's neo-Gothic red-brick **Rathaus**, a five-minute walk north of the palace toward the S-Bahn station, would not be worth even a fleeting glance were it not for one Wilhelm Voigt and the playwright Carl Zuckmayer, who immortalized him in the drama *The Captain of Köpenick*.

In the fall of 1906, Voigt, a down-and-out shoemaker with a police record, found, in a pawn shop, a somewhat frayed, oversized uniform of a captain of the imperial guards. He put it on and strolled out of the shop, looking and feeling like a new man. And he was. On the street he spotted a squad of 12 soldiers under command of a lance corporal. Voigt took charge of the troop, marched them to the nearest train station, and rode with them to Köpenick. There Voigt and his soldiers proceeded to the Rathaus, arrested the mayor, and confiscated the municipal treasury. With the cashbox under his arm, the fake captain ordered his soldiers to release the mayor after half an hour and then take the rest of the day off. He strutted back to the station, boarded a train, and disappeared. The story of the Hauptmann von Köpenick, or "Copper Captain," as he was called in the Anglo-American press, made headlines around the world.

However, Voigt wasn't after the money: He wanted blank identity papers. When he didn't find any in the heavy cashbox, he surrendered to the police. He was tried for robbery and impersonating an imperial officer, was sentenced to four years in prison, and served two. For the rest of his life, the cobbler earned a good living by appearing in uniform for a fee.

Zuckmayer turned the episode into a hit play in 1931 and in the 1950s wrote the script for a prizewinning movie starring Heinz Rühmann, then Germany's leading comic actor. The incident gave the German language a new word—*Köpenickade,* a caper that plays on gullibility and blind respect for uniforms and military authority. To Berliners East and West, the phony Captain of Köpenick is still a hero.

# GETTING AROUND

## *When to Go*

The best months to visit Berlin are May through October. The weather in March and April can be fickle, and from November through February it can get grim. Berlin usually has a bracing, temperate climate, with low humidity. Few days are either scorchers or arctic, but you can count on one or the other at least once in a season.

Whatever the season, be sure to reserve hotel accommodations *well* in advance. Berlin's calendar is crammed with trade fairs, festivals, conventions, and congresses. There have been occasions in recent years when hoteliers have put cots and folding beds in lobbies and hallways to accommodate overflow guests. The busiest times are the Green Week agricultural show in late January to early February, the International Film Festival in the second half of February, the International Tourism Bourse (ITB) in early March, the Berlin Festival Weeks in September, and the biannual International Radio-TV-Electronics Exhibition during the last week of August and the first week of September (the next one is this year).

The situation is not much better in East Berlin, where there are fewer hotels. However, even before the Wall fell, it was common practice among business travellers to take a room in East Berlin and commute through Checkpoint Charlie to their appointments in West Berlin. In any case, making hotel reservations in East Berlin yourself, either by telephone or fax from West Germany, West Berlin, or abroad can be daunting. Circuits are totally overloaded, and you may dial futilely for hours. Either book the call through an international operator or use telex. Matters are expected to get a little better in the second half of 1991, after more connections have been installed.

### *Arrival at Major Gateways*

The best way to get to Berlin is by plane or by car. As we went to press, rail connections from cities in West Germany were still few (about 20 trains a day from a dozen cities) and the journey arduously long. Bahnhof Zoo, in the center of West Berlin, five minutes' walk from the Europa-Center, is the main terminal.

Because of the Four Power Agreement, still prevailing as we went to press, West Berlin's Tegel airport is serviced only by American, British, and French airlines (Pan American, Trans World, British Airways, Dan Air, Air France, and Euroberlin). East Berlin's Schönefeld airport is serviced only by Interflug (East German airlines), Aeroflot, other East European carriers, KLM, Austrian Airlines, Finnair, and Alitalia.

An "Airport Transfer" bus connects Tegel with Schönefeld. The 90-minute ride costs DM 15 and departs every 30 minutes. The same bus also takes you from either Tegel or Schönefeld to Bahnhof Zoo and the Budapester Strasse hotel district, costing DM 7 from Tegel, DM 10 from Schönefeld. City bus No. 9 runs between Tegel and downtown West Berlin, stopping at Bahnhof Zoo, Kurfürstendamm, and the hotel area on Budapester Strasse. Departures are every ten minutes, and the ride is 40 minutes. A cab to the city will cost about DM 20 from Tegel, DM 30 from Schönefeld.

There are four Autobahn routes from western Germany, three from the east to Berlin. Driving time from Frankfurt or Munich to Berlin is six to seven hours.

### *Public Transit*

Berliners claim theirs is the best in Germany, if not the world. Their penchant for boasting notwithstanding, the claim has some validity.

The system consists of U-Bahn subways, S-Bahn elevated trains, buses, including many double-deckers in West Berlin, streetcars in East Berlin only, and steamers on many rivers and lakes. Multiple-ride and 24-hour tickets provide use of and free transfers among all systems.

The U-Bahn has ten lines. Service during peak hours is every two and one half minutes; off peak, trains run every five to seven and one half minutes. Late at night it slows to a train every ten minutes.

The network operates on an honor system, backed by spot inspections: You obtain tickets from dispensing machines or ticket windows and cancel them in meters at platform entrances or on buses. The fine for not having a canceled ticket is about DM 60. A single ride costs DM 2.70, five-ride tickets DM 11.50. The best bargains are 24-hour tourist passes, costing DM 9. They give unlimited use of all conveyances, and are for sale at the tourist-office counter at Tegel airport, the BVG-Kiosk Zoo, the Hardenbergplatz, ticket windows in the following subway stations: Zoo, Kurt-Schumacher-Platz, Richard-Wagner-Platz, and Rathaus Spandau, and at most dispensing machines.

### Taxis
Although there are more than 6,000 cabs licensed in Berlin, you can never get one when you need it. They can be hailed on the street or ordered by phone at the following numbers: 69-02, 26-10-26, 21-60-60, and 24-02-02. A one-mile ride costs about DM 6.50.

# ACCOMMODATIONS

The country telephone code for West Germany is 49; the city telephone code for West Berlin is 30. The country code for East Germany is 37; the city telephone code for East Berlin is 2.

## WEST BERLIN

### The Kurfürstendamm Area
If you can afford it, "*die beste Adresse*" in town is the **Bristol-Hotel Kempinski**, in the center of all the action. Totally destroyed during the war, rebuilt in 1952, and thoroughly renovated in 1980, it has all the ambience of a grand hotel, and its guest list sounds like pages from *Who's Who*.

Kurfürstendamm 27, D-1000 West Berlin 15; Tel: 88-43-40; Fax: 8836075; Telex: 183553.

East on the boulevard, and easy to miss because terrace cafés flank the entrance, is the **Hotel am Zoo**, a favorite among visiting journalists, and not just because it's close to where some of them have Berlin editorial offices. It's the size—54 rooms—and the courteous, efficient service. Rooms are moderately priced and have a pleasing modern elegance. The best face the avenue, and some even have little balconies from which to watch the show down below.

Kurfürstendamm 25, D-1000 West Berlin 15; Tel: 88-43-70; Telex: 183835; Fax: 88437714.

The Meinekestrasse is a small side street that intersects the Ku'damm just across the avenue from the Hotel am Zoo.

In what used to be an upper-class apartment house you'll find the **Hotel Meineke**, a small, family-run establishment with some of the advantages of a *pension* and none of the disadvantages. The 60 rooms are high-ceilinged and large, the furniture comfy, the breakfast chamber a delight of neo-Baroque decor with crystal chandeliers.

Meinekestrasse 10, D-1000 West Berlin 15; Tel: 88-28-11 and 883-40-63; Fax: 8825716.

Right next door, in a splendid Belle Epoque building, is the moderately priced **Hotel Residenz**, a reincarnation of old Berlin. Although functionally modern, all of the 85 rooms are agreeably large, and many have elaborate stucco ceilings. Its **Grand Cru** dining room is one of the city's better French restaurants.

Meinekestrasse 9, D-1000 West Berlin 15; Tel: 88-28-91; Fax: 8824726; Telex: 183082.

Moving west on the boulevard, you will find *Pensionen* and small, so-called *Hotelpensionen* on intersecting cross streets. Since many smaller hotels have reception and lobby areas on the second floor, or *belle-étage,* of converted apartment buildings, the distinction between hotel and pension is not always discernible. But there *is* a difference. Hotels have key desks and concierges on duty; in a pension you are handed room and front-door keys for the duration and left to your own devices. The *Hotelpension* is a hybrid of the two, without a concierge but with a few hotel-type amenities. Both are almost endemic to Berlin, and the best are on and right off the Kurfürstendamm.

The **Pension Dittberner**, on the fourth floor of a turn-of-the-century building, will give you the impression that you've entered an art gallery, for it is full of works by contemporary Berlin painters that proprietress Elly Lange collects and exhibits. Among the keys handed to guests is one to the cagelike elevator. Breakfasts, included in the moderate price, are sumptuous. All eight rooms have private showers, but two are without a private toilet.

Wielandstrasse 26, D-1000 West Berlin 15; Tel: 882-39-63 or 881-64-58.

Back on the Ku'damm, between Wieland and Schlüter-strasse, you'll find the **Askanischer Hof**. Established in 1925 by connecting two grand *belle étage* apartments in adjacent houses, it has been a favorite of film and stage folk for decades. Arthur Miller was a guest not too many years ago, as was Heinz Rühmann, the character actor who played the

"Captain of Köpenick." Many movies have been made in its opulent Art Nouveau salon and suites. Proprietress Eva Glinicke personally serves breakfast. All 16 rooms have private baths or showers, but two are without private toilet.

Kurfürstendamm 53, D-1000 West Berlin 15; Tel: 881-80-33; Telex: 181550.

### The Budapester Strasse Area

The southern boundary of the Tiergarten became a hotel street not long after the building of the Wall, specializing in the luxury and first-class category. Among them the **Schweizerhof** is popular, in part because it can boast Berlin's largest indoor hotel pool, replete with ozone-bubble thermal baths, and a balneological department to cure whatever you think ails you. All 430 rooms were recently renovated and redecorated. The atmosphere is a bit sterile, but the Swiss cuisine in the main dining room is great.

Budapester Strasse 21–31, D-1000 West Berlin 30; Tel: 269-60; Fax: 2696900; Telex: 185501.

Just south of Budapester Strasse is another group of first- and luxury-class hotels. The **Ambassador** offers the best in service and amenities at manageable prices. Whatever the 200 rooms may lack in spaciousness is compensated for by the bathrooms. The pool on the top floor is decorated in "tropical Caribbean" style, and there is also a fitness center with solarium.

Bayreuther Strasse 42–43, D-1000 West Berlin 30; Tel: 21-90-20; Telex: 184259.

### Out of the Center

One of the newer additions to the first-class category is the 78-room **Seehof**, just east of the trade-fair grounds and idyllically situated on the banks of the Lietzensee, one of Berlin's smaller lakes. The rooms could be a little larger, but they have all the conveniences and amenities, and when the city is not overcrowded you can choose between modern and traditional furnishings. The service is personal, there's a terrace restaurant and garden bar facing the lake, and for all the pastoral ambience you are within easy walking distance of Charlottenburg palace and only a block from a subway station with a connection to the Ku'damm.

Lietzensee-Ufer 11, D-1000 West Berlin 30; Tel: 32-00-20; Fax: 32002251; Telex: 182943.

# EAST BERLIN

## *The Unter den Linden Area*

For reasons having to do with the Cold War, there was a long-held opinion that East Berlin couldn't possibly have a hotel worth recommending (except maybe to your worst enemy). But long before the Wall crumbled, the state-owned Inter-hotel chain had been doing its utmost, and with considerable success, to dispel that idea.

Indeed, the grandest and most luxurious of all hotels in Berlin, East and West, is the **Grand**, on the block between the Behrenstrasse and Unter den Linden. Opened in 1987, it is built in an eclectic blend of Belle Epoque and postmodern. The Grand is everything its name implies. A splash of marble, thick carpeting, beautifully crafted period furniture, warm wood paneling, exquisite filigree stucco work, crystal chandeliers, and subdued lighting from polished brass lamps with silk shades are some of its best details. Fresh flowers, mostly orchids from the hotel's own greenhouse, decorate the 350 rooms, apartments, and suites. Down pillows and comforters complement soft linens on the beds. Guests have use of the marble swimming pool, saunas, solarium, and squash courts. Classical music plays around the clock on one of the four in-house channels.

Friedrichstrasse 158–164, DDR-1080 East Berlin; Tel: 209-20; Fax: 2294095; Telex: 115198.

Farther north on the Friedrichstrasse is the more functional **Metropol**. The decor is more modern than the Grand's, but amenities and service leave nothing to be desired. Among the attractions are a swimming pool with artificial current, a solarium, a fitness room, massages, and balneological service that will cook you in sulphur, cake you in mud, and twist you into a pretzel to limber stiff muscles.

Friedrichstrasse 150–153, DDR-1080 East Berlin; Tel: 220-40; Fax: 2204209; Telex: 114141.

Right across from the Palast der Republik you will see the huge, modern, Swedish-designed **Palast Hotel**. The ambience in the 600 rooms is uniformly modern, with a warm Scandinavian touch. You have a choice of ten restaurants in the house.

Karl-Liebknecht-Strasse 5 DDR-1080 East Berlin; Tel: 24-10; Fax: 2127273; Telex: 115050.


## *Out of the Center*

Farther afield from Unter den Linden, more typically East Berlinish and certainly more moderate in price, is the **Hotel**

**Newa**, about one and one half miles north of Unter den Linden, but with good bus and streetcar connections. An old-style house behind an old-fashioned façade, it offers especially warm and friendly service. To stay there, however, at least until the regulations have changed, you may need an advance East German visa.

Invalidenstrasse 115, DDR-1040 East Berlin; Tel: 282-54-61.

# DINING

Berlin has more than 7,000 restaurants, cafés, pubs, dives, and eateries of various kinds—6,000 in West Berlin, 1,000 in the East. Berliners, it seems, never eat at home. It also seems they need no sleep. In no other city in Germany do establishments stay open and serve food as late. There are no closing laws, no final drink calls. Most places call it quits at 1:00 or 2:00 A.M.; some stay open much later.

There is a distinct Berlin cuisine; it sticks to the ribs and is not to everyone's liking. A *Bulette* is a cold meatball, or Berlin's version of the hamburger, usually eaten as a snack. *Eisbein,* with sauerkraut, naturally, is pickled pig's feet. *Bockwurst* is a very chubby hotdog, smothered in curry-ketchup sauce or served with potato salad. *Erbsensuppe,* sometimes called *Erbspüree,* is thick pea soup, frequently served with pieces of bockwurst or bacon in it. The *Schlacht-platte* is a platter of blood sausage, liverwurst, boiled beef, and hunks of pork kidney.

On a slightly more sophisticated level you will find *Schlesisches Himmelreich,* consisting of either roast goose or roast pork with potato dumplings and sweet-sour gravy containing dried fruit. *Königsberger Klopse* are veal meatballs, sometimes with pieces of herring ground in, in a caper sauce. *Aal grün mit Gurkensalat* consists of stewed eel in an herb, onion, and sour-cream sauce, accompanied by cucumber salad. A *Berliner* is a person and also a doughnut without a hole, filled with jam and sprinkled with sugar.

Beer is the beverage of Berlin, specifically *Weissbier,* brewed with wheat instead of barley malt and officially called a *Berliner Weisse.* Less officially it is known as a *Molle* or *Kühle Blonde* (cool blonde). With a dash of raspberry syrup it becomes a *Berliner Weisse mit Schuss.* Besides modifying the tartness of the beer, the syrup gives it a Champagnelike effervescence, which may explain why it is always served in a bowl-like chalice.

Finally, the city probably has more foreign than German

restaurants, from simple Turkish *kebab* stands to fine French dining rooms. The profusion of French restaurants should come as no surprise in light of the role the Huguenots played here in the 17th and 18th centuries.

However, Berlin is definitely not Germany's culinary capital. Though the Gault-Millau guide awards 21 Berlin restaurants a single toque, it gives only five of them two chef's hats. Of those, two are at hard-to-reach edges of the city, one is Italian, and another is in East Berlin. The German Michelin is far less charitable, giving only three places in the city a single star.

## WEST BERLIN

### *Gourmet and Foreign Restaurants*

Though it may seem like a journey to the end of the world, **Rockendorf's Restaurant**, at Düsterhauptstrasse 1 in Waidmannslust, Reinickendorf borough, 12 miles north of the city center, is certainly worth the trip. There, Siegfried Rockendorf has converted a lovely villa into what is indubitably Berlin's finest—and also most expensive—restaurant. The moment you have been seated by Rockendorf's wife, Ingeborg, as if you were a family guest, the maestro himself approaches your table to describe the menu. There are no à la carte choices, only multicourse prix-fixe menus that change daily. At lunch you can select either the three- or the six-course presentation, at dinner the six- or nine-course program. The wine list has more than 200 selections. Closed Sunday and Monday, from Christmas through New Year's, and three weeks in summer. Tel: 402-30-99.

**Frühsammer's Restaurant an der Rehwiese**, at Matterhornstrasse 101, near the Grosser Wannsee at the southern tip of Grunewald Forest, is almost as far away. Young Peter Frühsammer, whose wife, Antje, is the hostess and oversees the service staff, approaches German and French dishes in a creative, *nouvelle* style. You are not bound to a prix-fixe menu here, though one or two are offered daily, and 300 wines are listed. Open daily for dinner, and on Sundays for lunch as well. Closed two weeks in January, three in July. Tel: 803-27-20.

Franz and Dorothea Raneburger, both Austrians, moved to Berlin in the early 1980s and opened the **Bamberger Reiter** at Regensburger Strasse 7, a turn-of-the-century corner wine tavern in a residential/commercial neighborhood just two subway stops south of Bahnhof Zoo. Now their restaurant is one of the city's best, frequented by young professionals and intellectuals, scientists and musicians. The late Vladimir Horowitz was served Dover sole when he ate here, but Raneburger's repertoire, which he performs with a staff of five in the kitchen, goes far beyond simple fare. The decor is rustic, with parquet flooring and a growing collection of antiques to make the maximum of 35 diners feel at home. Dinner only; closed Sunday and Monday and January 1–17 and August 1–15. Tel: 24-42-82.

Karl Wannemacher came from a town on the Saar-Luxembourg border in the mid-1970s and eventually opened his own restaurant, the 25-seat **Alt Luxemburg**, at Pestalozzi-strasse 70. The exquisite fare is a blend of French, Luxembourgian, and Saarland cuisine, with occasional touches of Berlin *nouvelle* style to remind you where you are; the decor is wood paneled, with lots of mirrors and antique furnishings that hostess Ingrid Wannemacher has collected. Dinner only; closed Sunday, Monday, the first two weeks in January, and three weeks in July. Tel: 323-87-30.

Udo Kämper is a Berliner, which does not mean, however, that he serves heavy Berlin food at his **Kämper's—Avec**, at Mommsenstrasse 12. Rather, he searches tirelessly in old Huguenot and Prussian cookbooks, including those used by the palace chefs of Frederick the Great, for traditional recipes, which he then prepares in a lighter style. The atmosphere is cozy, with low-hanging lamps, farmhouse bric-a-brac, and flea-market treasures. Kämper's partner, Gabriela Adam, serves her guests at the half-dozen tables as if they were long-lost friends. Dinner only; closed Thursday. Tel: 323-79-25.

Berlin restaurants are proof that good French food can be found at moderate prices. One example is **Restaurant le Paris**, at Kurfürstendamm 211, in the Maison de France, the French cultural center. Open daily for lunch and dinner. Tel: 881-52-42.

The **Paris Bar**, at Kantstrasse 152, is not a bar but a restaurant, and *the* hangout of artists, writers, filmmakers, and theater people. The place is reminiscent of a French working-class bistro. The daily prix-fixe menu averages DM 40 per person. Open from noon to 2:00 A.M. Tel: 3-13-80-52.

Every Berliner has a favorite Italian restaurant among the 800 in the city. One of the best is **La Vernaccia**, at Breitenbachplatz 4, in Dahlem not far from the museums. Proprietor-chef Salvatore Brai is a Sardinian, and he stresses Sardinian regional cuisine. His German wife, Ingrid, supervises the service staff. Open for lunch and dinner, closed Monday and three weeks in July–August. Tel: 8-24-57-88.

## Hotel Restaurants

The best are: **Zum Huguenotten**, in the Inter-Continental Hotel (Budapester Strasse 2), where Birgit Borgschulze, one of Germany's few woman chefs, prepares classic French haute cuisine, Tel: 26-02-12-52; **Park Restaurant**, in the Steigenberger Hotel (Los-Angeles-Platz 1), serving French and sophisticated German cuisine, Tel: 10-88-55; **Kempinski Grill**, in the Hotel Bristol-Kempinski (Kurfürstendamm 27), serving international cuisine, Tel: 88-43-40; **Berlin Grill**, in the Hotel Berlin (Lützowplatz 17), specializing in French and international cuisine in *nouvelle* style, Tel: 25-05-25-62; **Schweizerhof Grill**, in the Hotel Schweizerhof (Budapester Strasse 21–31), serving Swiss cuisine, Tel: 2-69-60; **Conti-Fischstuben**, in the Hotel Ambassador (Bayreuther Strasse 42–43), which is best for freshwater fish and seafood, Tel: 21-90-20; and **Grand Cru**, in the Hotel Residenz (Meine-kestrasse 9), offering French cuisine, Tel: 88-28-91.

## Traditional Berlin Food

There are hundreds upon hundreds of restaurants, inns, and pubs serving what is generally called *Deutsche* or *Berliner* or *gut-bürgerliche* (bourgeois) *Küche*. Prices in most are moderate, as, alas, are culinary skills. On or near the Kurfürstendamm there are quite a few; most stay open until 1:00 or 2:00 A.M.

The **Schultheiss Bräuhaus**, at Kurfürstendamm 220, is the main beer hall of Berlin's leading brewery. **Hardtke**, at Meinekestrasse 27, is typical of old Berlin restaurants, with its bare wood tables and huge portions. The **Mommsen Eck**, at Mommsenstrasse 45, was established in 1905 and is famous for its 100 brands of beer, which you can enjoy out in the beer garden. **Spreegarten**, at Uhlandstrasse 175, embodies the atmosphere of old Berlin with its dark, wood-paneled interior. Although the **Alt Berliner Schneckenhaus**, at Viktoria-Luise-Platz 12a, is a bit pricey, it's hard to beat for atmosphere. The place is crammed with Victorian and Wilhelminian furniture. A little farther afield, the **Wirtshaus Nussbaum**, at Bundesplatz 4, is a bargain if you're looking for Berlin specialties such as Schlesisches Himmelreich or potato pancakes served with onions, bacon, and pumpkin puree.

## Kneipen and In Places

More than 4,000 spots come under the general heading of *Kneipe*. While the term originally meant a corner tavern in a blue-collar neighborhood, today it includes just about any place where people eat, drink, meet friends, or simply hang out.

*Kneipen* close to and around the Kurfürstendamm are the **Cour Carree** (Savignyplatz 5), where billiard and card tables are among the attractions; **Zwiebelfisch** (Savignyplatz 7), which is popular with literati; **Die Kleine Kneipe** (Wielandstrasse 45), popular for its billiard tables as well as its stews and sandwiches; and **Dicke Wirtin** (Carmerstrasse 9), which serves good thick soups.

Among the in places that are likely to stay in for a while are the already mentioned Paris Bar; the **Ax Bax** (Leibnitzstrasse 34), popular among the artist set for its cold buffet; **Dschungel**, or Jungle (Nürnberger Strasse 53), which continues to attract the New Wild painters; **Café Untreu** (it means "unfaithful") at Bleibtreustrasse ("stay faithful") 13; **Chez Alex** (Kurfürstendamm 160), favored for its piano bar, but rather pricey; and **Café Einstein** (Kurfürstenstrasse 58), where the upper-crust leftist intellectual crowd gathers and the novelist Günter Grass may show up to read from work in progress.

### Breakfast

Breakfast, definitely not of the "power" variety, has been a Berlin craze since the late 1980s. At latest count some 300 cafés, bistros, and pubs serve variations of the morning meal at the oddest of hours.

At **Lützower Lampe** (Behaimstrasse 25) the emphasis is on macrobiotic vegetarian breakfasts, with such offerings as grain coffee, rice with tahini cream, and full-kernel rolls. **Café Voltaire** (Stuttgarter Platz 14) serves a choice of French, English, or Dutch breakfast. **Zillemarkt** (Bleibtreustrasse 48) is renowned for gourmet ice-cream concoctions and offers Champagne breakfasts until 2:00 P.M. **Miami** (Kurfürstendamm 100), with billiard and card tables, is open round the clock and starts serving breakfast at 4:00 A.M. **Café Leysieffer** (Kurfürstendamm 218) helps start the day with a breakfast of smoked salmon, Parma ham, fresh baguettes, and Champagne. And most hotels have scrumptious breakfast buffets included in the price of your room.

### Cafés

The word is overused in Berlin, where it can apply to anything from a gay bar or jazz cellar to a place serving *Kaffee und Kuchen*—coffee and calorific German pastries. We have the latter in mind here.

The incarnation of the Berlin café is still the **Café Kranzler**

(Kurfürstendamm 18), which is usually crowded with ma-
tronly ladies wolfing down two (never just one) pieces of
cake topped by mounds of whipped cream. **Café Möhring**
(Kurfürstendamm 213) was not only a favorite hangout of
the bohemian and bourgeois Kurfürstendamm crowd in the
early part of this century, but has two other locations on the
avenue: at Kurfürstendamm 234 and Kurfürstendamm 161–
163. **Café Huthmacher** (Hardenbergstrasse 29d, second
floor) offers daily teatime dancing at 3:30 P.M. in addition to
fine pastries.

## EAST BERLIN

For many years East Berlin was considered a kind of gastronomic no-man's-land. That reputation was unjustified and
undeserved *before* the Wall came down, and the situation is
sure to get even better in the months and years ahead as
private enterprise becomes the rule rather than the exception. Meanwhile, as we went to press these were our
choices.

### *Gourmet Restaurants*

The Grand Hotel's **Le Grand Restaurant Silhouette**, at Friedrichstrasse 158–164, matches the best in the West, in both
decor and creative, impeccably prepared *nouvelle*-style
French and German cuisine. And it surpasses all Western
competitors in friendliness and service. Lunch or dinner
here is memorable, but very expensive. Besides the à la
carte selections, you will be offered a daily six-course prix-
fixe menu. The wine list has 300 labels, among them some
otherwise unobtainable whites from East Germany's own
wine-growing region along the Saale and Elbe rivers. There
is low-key piano music until 10:00 P.M., and after that a
combo with singer always performs, usually until 2:00 A.M.
Tel: (372) 209-24.

For acceptable French cuisine and very good charcoal-
broiled specialties, try the Palast Hotel's **Rôti d'Or**, at Karl-
Liebknecht-Strasse 5. You'll dine by candlelight, with soft
piano music in the background. Tel: (372) 24-10.

If you wish to dine in genuine Rococo surroundings, go
to the **Ermeler Haus**, at Märkisches Ufer 10–12, right on the
Spree canal and about four blocks southeast of Marx-
Engels-Platz. This 16th-century mansion was renovated in
the 18th century and turned into a restaurant in the 1960s.
Tel: 275-51-03.

**Weinrestaurant Ganymed**, at Schiffbauerdamm 5, just off
the Friedrichstrasse and almost next door to Bertolt Brecht's

Berliner Ensemble Theater, has long ranked as one of East
Berlin's top eateries. It still is, and is worth the price. The
atmosphere is genteel, the music—piano and violin—soft.
In the early 1950s it was the favorite spot of Brecht, his wife,
Helene Weigel, and their entourage. It remains a favorite
among East Berlin intellectuals. Tel: 282-95-40.

## German and Berlin Food
East Berlin in many respects has been the better turf for real
local and regional food because it remained closer to "Germany as it used to be"—for better or for worse.

You will find historic surroundings and honest food at the
**Alt Cöllner Schankstuben** (Friedrichsgracht 50), one of the
few surviving old houses along the Spree canal. **Zur Letzten
Instanz** (Waisenstrasse 14–16, south of Alexanderplatz) is
even more colorful. The name means "To the Last Resort" and
comes from the location of this 360-year-old house next to the
former appeals court. The menu reads like a legal proceed-
ing: *Anklage* (indictment), *Kreuzverhör* (cross-examination),
*Plädoyer* (closing argument). Among the specialties are fried
herring with onions, fried potatoes and cole slaw, and jellied
meat with hash browns.

A number of such establishments can be found in the
Nikolaiviertel, although all are reconstructions. **Zum Paddel-
wirt** (Nikolaikirchplatz 6) is worth trying. **Zur Rippe** (Poststrasse 17) serves dishes based on historic Berlin recipes.
The **Bierschänke in der Gerichtsklause** (Poststrasse 28) provides an ambience of vaulted ceilings and Medieval furnishings, and serves traditional Berlin dishes such as Eisbein and
pork roasts, with lots of sauerkraut.

## Kneipen and In Places
Forty-five years of Communist rule and 28 years of the Wall
may have left their mark on East Berlin in many ways, but
*Kneipenleben,* or Kneipen life, remained unchanged.

The **Brandenburger Keller** (Mittelstrasse 29) is indeed a
cellar spot, furnished with stand-up tables and counters, and
popular with journalists. The **Trichter** (Am Schiffbauerdamm) is the favorite Kneipe of the adjacent Berliner Ensemble Theater, as popular with actors and staff as it is with the
after-theater crowd. The **Operncafe** (Unter den Linden 5)
has a bar that is popular with East Berlin's jet set.

Venturing a bit north of Unter den Linden, you'll find the
**Hafenbar** (Chausseestrasse 20, the extension of Friedrichstrasse). Dimly lit, it attracts the younger generation, who
come to dance. Still farther afield, in Prenzlauer Berg

borough, there's the **Alt-Berliner Bierkneipe** (Saarbrücker Strasse 17, near the Senefelderplatz subway station); which attracts the alternative lifestyle crowd. The **1900** (Husemannstrasse 1) is a popular hangout for actors, painters, television people, and folks from the neighborhood.

### Cafés

During the day the **Operncafé** on Unter den Linden is a great spot for coffee and pastries; in nice weather the terrace and garden are open. At **Café Bauer**, in the Grand Hotel at the corner of the Friedrichstrasse and Unter den Linden, the pastries are divine. In the afternoon there is a string orchestra. **Café Spreeblick** (Probststrasse 9, in the Nikolai quarter) has seating for only 50 guests (50 more on the terrace in good weather). There's often a wait, because the cakes and pastries are among the best in town.

# ENTERTAINMENT AND NIGHTLIFE

With three opera houses, eight symphony orchestras, scores of theaters, and some of the country's wildest nightlife, there is no way to run out of after-sightseeing things to do in Berlin. Language may be a bit of a problem for the theater, but in both West and East Berlin you will find musical and revue theaters where the spoken word is not so important.

To find out what's doing and where, check the monthly "Berlin Programm," available at the tourist office in the Europa-Center, at newsstands, in large bookstores, and from hotel concierges; the East Berlin "Wohin in Berlin," obtainable at the Berlin information center at the Television Tower, newsstands, bookshops, and hotels; or the fortnightly program magazines *Zitty* and *Tip,* sold at newsstands in West Berlin.

All theaters, opera houses, concert halls, and cabarets have box offices where you can buy tickets up to an hour before performances. You can also reserve by phone. Hotel desks and any of the central ticket agencies will also obtain tickets for you, but they charge a small fee.

West Berlin ticket agencies close to the Kurfürstendamm are **Theaterkasse Centrum**, Meinekestrasse 25, Tel: 882-76-11; **Theaterkasse Sasse**, Kurfürstendamm 24, Tel: 882-73-60; **Theaterkasse im Europa-Center**, Europa-Center, Tel: 61-70-

51; **Ottfried Laur**, Hardenbergstrasse 7, Tel: 31-37-00-07; **Theaterkasse Kiosk am Zoo**, Kantstrasse 3, Tel: 881-36-03; **Wertheim** department store, Kurfürstendamm 231, Tel: 882-25-00; **KaDeWe** department store, Tauentzienstrasse 21, Tel: 24-80-36.

Tickets for performances in East Berlin can be ordered in West Berlin through **Theaterkasse Zehlendorf**, Teltower Damm 22, Tel: 8-01-16-52. In East Berlin, order through the **Theaterkassen im Palasthotel**, Spandauer Strasse 2, open Tuesday to Friday 10:00 A.M. to noon and 1:00 P.M. to 7:00 P.M., on Saturday 11:00 A.M. to 2:00 P.M.; Tel: (372) 212-52-58 or 212-59-02 for theater tickets, 2-12-71-82 for concert tickets.

## Opera and Musical Theater

The **Deutsche Oper Berlin** (Bismarckstrasse 35) is West Berlin's opera house. The season runs for ten months, with repertory performances nightly. The ticket office is open Monday through Friday 2:00 to 8:00 P.M., Saturday and Sunday 10:00 A.M. to 2:00 P.M., as well as one hour before performances. Tel: 3-41-02-49. Write for reservations to: Kartenbüro der Deutschen Oper Berlin, Richard-Wagner-Platz 10, D-1000 Berlin 10.

**Theater des Westens** (Kantstrasse 12) is West Berlin's operetta and musical theater. The box office is open 10:00 A.M. to 7:00 P.M. daily, and one hour before performances. Tel: 312-10-22 or 312-50-15.

East Berlin's **Deutsche Staatsoper** (Unter den Linden 7) also has a ten-month season. The box office is open Tuesday through Saturday noon to 6:00 P.M. and one hour before performances. Tel: (372) 205-45-56.

Also in East Berlin is the **Komische Oper** (Behrenstrasse 55–57, adjacent to the main entrance of the Grand Hotel). It's in a league all its own, thanks to Walter Felsenstein, who, as general manager and director from 1947 until his retirement in the 1980s, built it into one of the world's greatest houses. Box-office hours are Tuesday through Saturday 2:00 to 6:00 P.M. and one hour before performances. Tel: (372) 229-25-55.

The **Friedrichstadtpalast** (Friedrichstrasse 107) is East Berlin's variety and musical revue theater. Box-office hours are Tuesday through Saturday 1:00 to 3:30 P.M. and 4:00 to 6:00 P.M. and one hour before performances. Tel: (372) 283-64-74 and 283-64-36.

Musicals and operettas are performed on a repertory basis in the **Metropol-Theater** (Friedrichstrasse 100–102).

The box office is open Tuesday through Saturday noon to 1:30 P.M. and 2:00 to 6:00 P.M., Sunday from 4:00 to 6:00 P.M., and one hour before performances. Tel: (372) 207-17-39.

### Cabaret

A *Kabarett* in Germany is a night spot offering food, drink, and entertainment in the form of a politically and socially satirical floor show. To appreciate the humor you should have a fluent command of German and, in Berlin, of the local dialect.

The best cabarets in West Berlin are **Die Stachelschweine**, or The Porcupines (lower level of the Europa-Center), advance ticket sales Monday through Saturday 2:00 to 7:30 P.M., Tel: 2-61-47-95; and **Die Wühlmäuse**, or The Volemice (Nürnberger Strasse 33), box office open daily 11:00 A.M. to 8:30 P.M., Monday only until 7:00 P.M., Tel: 2-13-70-47.

In East Berlin, try **Die Distel**, or The Thistle (Friedrichstrasse 101), box-office hours Tuesday through Friday 3:00 to 7:00 P.M., Saturday and Sunday 5:00 to 7:00 P.M., Tel: (372) 207-12-91.

## NIGHTLIFE

Berlin has always been famous, or infamous, for its nightclubs, discos, dance spots, jazz clubs, and transvestite shows—not to mention prostitution, on the streets and in brothels.

### West Berlin

**La Vie en Rose**, in the Europa-Center, has a show that gets rave reviews. Reservations are essential; Tel: 3-23-60-06. At the **New Eden** (Kurfürstendamm 71), open daily except Sunday 9:00 P.M. to 4:00 A.M., the emphasis is on striptease. The **Scotch Club** (Marburger Strasse 15) features quieter music and more sophisticated striptease.

**Dollywood** (Welserstrasse 24), Tel: 24-89-50, open daily except Monday, has the city's best transvestite show. **Chez Nous** (Marburger Strasse 14) has the second best.

The **Big Eden** (Kurfürstendamm 202) and **Big Apple** (Bundesallee 13) are *the* discos for the younger crowd, with ear-bursting music. The **Metropol** (Nollendorfplatz 5), a former operetta theater, and the **Coconut** (Joachimsthaler Strasse 1–3) are similar. The mid-life-crisis and sensitive-ears crowd prefers **Coupé 77** (Kurfürstendamm 177), which is decorated like an Orient Express railway car, and **Annabelle's** (Fasanenstrasse 64). Both are quite expensive.

Jazz is best at **Flöz** (Nassauischestrasse 37); **Joe's Bierhaus**

(Theodor-Heuss-Platz 12); and **Quasimodo** (Kantstrasse 12). All have varying programs including modern and rock jazz, city blues, new wave, and reggae. For folk music, try **Go-In** (Bleibtreustrasse 17).

### East Berlin

All the big hotel restaurants have music and dancing, and there are also night bars that stay open even later.

The city's most luxurious nightclub is the **Palasthotel Bar** (Karl-Liebknecht-Strasse 5).

You'll find dancing at the **Adria Bar** (Friedrichstrasse 134); at the **Altdeutsches Ballhaus** (Ackerstrasse 114); and at **Ballhaus Berlin** (Chausseestrasse 108).

# SHOPS AND SHOPPING

Although Berlin is a consumer city incarnate, it is actually less pricey than other major German cities. Moreover, in addition to the international names like Cartier, Louis Vuitton, and the inevitable Rosenthal, the city has a profusion of indigenous craftsmen and designers.

The Kurfürstendamm is a mixed scene, with discount stores competing for attention with by-appointment-only jewelry stores, designer clothiers, and chic men's tailors. Serious shoppers usually find the streets that intersect the Kurfürstendamm more rewarding: Fasanen, Uhland, Knesebeck, Bleibtreu, Schlüter, Wieland, and Leibniz. Lietzenburger Strasse to the south and Mommsen, Niebuhr, and Kant streets to the north are also worth exploring. The district on and around **Tauentzienstrasse** is where the biggest department stores are located. There are also interesting shops on the streets that intersect Tauentzien—Rankestrasse, Marburger Strasse, and Nürnberger Strasse.

### Women's Fashions

All the top West German and Berlin designers are well represented on and around the Ku'damm. **Horn** (Kurfürstendamm 213) carries designs by Munich's Manfred Schneider, Cologne's Uta Raasch, and Hamburg's Wolfgang Joop. **Jil Sander** of Hamburg, Germany's most successful designer, has a boutique at Kurfürstendamm 54. Berlin's **Sandra Pabst** has her own salesroom at Kurfürstendamm 67. **La Donna** (Kurfürstendamm 34) features Berlin designer Brigitte Haarke's creations, as does **Oggi** (Bleibtreustrasse 27). **Ritter Moden** (Kurfürstendamm 216) offers Munich's Escada Line; **Zenker** (Kurfürstendamm 45) carries Bogner casuals and sportswear. **Diana Piu** (Kurfürstendamm 72) shows her own collection, and **Univogue** (Mommsenstrasse 2) is the showroom for Berlin designers Marion Ecker and Stephan Woelk.

## Menswear
**Braun & Co.** (Kurfürstendamm 43) and **Sabo & Sabo** (Kurfürstendamm 193) are Berlin's answer to Brooks Brothers, while **Mientus** (Kurfürstendamm 52) leans more toward Italian fashions. **Selbach** (Kurfürstendamm 195) is for those who are (or think) young. Other top-of-the-line menswear shops on the boulevard are **Heinz Brand** (Kurfürstendamm 184), **Kurt Heinemann** (Kurfürstendamm 35), and **Leo Kirsch** (Kurfürstendamm 64–65).

## Children's Apparel
**Elephant's Knot** (Meinekestrasse 8) carries Baby Dior, Floriane, Les Enfants Terribles, and Missoni designs. **Cinderella** (Kurfürstendamm 45) is a little less pricey.

## Leather and Shoes
**Etienne Aigner** is at Kurfürstendamm 197. **Budapester Schuhe** (Kurfürstendamm 199) features handmade Hungarian footwear. **Scarpa Moda** (Kurfürstendamm 52) specializes in the latest shoe fashions.

## Jewelry and Watches
Nürnberger Strasse is lined with jewelry shops. For innovative design and top-of-the-line gold work, visit shops on the Uhlandstrasse and Bleibtreustrasse. **Galerie Lalique** (Bleibtreustrasse 47) has handmade creations from Berlin workshops. **Juwelier Hülse** (Kurfürstendamm 42) represents Blancpain and Audemars-Piguet; **Axel Sedlatzek** (Kurfürstendamm 45) carries Rolex and Patek Philippe watches. Both are also fine jewelers. So are **Juwelier Alt** (Kurfürstendamm 26a); **Wurzbacher** (Kurfürstendamm 36); **Paco** (Fasanenstrasse 73); and **Heinz Wipperfeld** (Budapester Strasse 30).

## Porcelain and Glass
The **Rosenthal Studio-Haus** is at Kurfürstendamm 226, and **Hutschenreuther**, Rosenthal's chief competitor, at Eisenacher Strasse 36. **Helmut Trimberg** (Kurfürstendamm 214) features Meissen as good as that found in the **Galerie** on the second floor of East Berlin's Grand Hotel.

But for the best, shop at the showroom of **KPM**, Königliche Porzellan Manufactur, the state porcelain factory (Kurfürstendamm 26a). Founded as a private enterprise in 1751, KPM was taken over by Frederick the Great and the Hohenzollern dynasty in 1763 and has remained Prussia's answer to Meissen ever since. KPM porcelain is all handmade and hand painted in the original workshops, also open to visitors, at Wegelystrasse 1, near the Tiergarten. Most patterns are from the 18th and 19th centuries—and prices are very *königlich* (royal).

## Designer Furniture

Thanks to a group of 15 avant garde designers who have formed an association called **Berliner Zimmer** (Berlin Room), the city is setting new trends in furnishings and interior design. Their ultramodern chairs, sofas, tables, lamps, and other objects, produced in limited quantities, are as unorthodox as were those of the Bauhaus more than six decades ago. The showroom is at Clausewitzstrasse 1.

## Comestibles

Berlin's, and possibly the world's, greatest food emporium is on the sixth floor of **KaDeWe** department store (Tauentzienstrasse 21). KaDeWe stands for *Kaufhaus des Westens,* or Department Store of the West. This has nothing to do with the city's postwar division, but reflects the fact that when the store was established in 1912 it was in Berlin's western outskirts. Its food section has no match anywhere.

Twenty-five thousand different comestibles are sold in more than 50,000 square feet of sales and display space. Among the delicacies are 1,800 varieties of cheese and 400 kinds of bread, baked fresh daily. Some 60 different salads are prepared hourly. There is a weekly turnover of 40 tons of vegetables and fruit imported from every continent. The meat counter is as long as a football field, and 18 huge tanks contain live fish and seafood that is flown in thrice weekly, to be caught and cleaned before customers' eyes. Paul Bocuse, Fauchon's of Paris, Gaston Lenôtre, and Milan's cheese specialist Peck all have shops here where they prepare and sell their own goodies.

## Art and Antiques

West Berlin is bursting with art galleries—185 at latest count—not to mention antiques stores and scores of bric-a-brac shops. Moreover, it has become a leading art-auction center, thanks to two energetic art promoters, Bernd Schultz and Peter Graf zu Eltz, who have turned the semiannual dispersals at the **Villa Grisebach** (Fasanenstrasse 25) into the most important on the Continent for German modern and classical modern art.

Serious art buyers and collectors should purchase the invaluable *Berlin Arts Guide,* by Irene Bluemenfeld, published by Art Guide Publications Ltd. It is the only guide in English to the Berlin scene. Buy it before you get here; copies are hard to come by in West Berlin.

The best little neighborhood for galleries representing contemporary artists is a one-block stretch on **Fasanenstrasse** between Kurfürstendamm and Lietzenburger Strasse.

**Rudolf Springer** (Fasanenstrasse 13), Berlin's best-known dealer, has been on the scene for some 40 years. He represented Max Ernst, Joan Miró, and Pablo Picasso in the early 1950s, and began showing Georg Baselitz, Jörg Immendorf, Markus Lüpertz, and A. R. Penck in the late 1960s and early 1970s. **Galerie Redmann** (Fasanenstrasse 30) represents many American artists, especially from the Northwest. **Scanart** (Fasanenstrasse 41) shows contemporary Scandinavian art. **Galerie Fahnemann** (Fasanenstrasse 61) is an important dealer of contemporary international painting, as well as prints by Penck, Elvira Bach, and Karl Horst Hödicke, the "father of the Neue Wilden." Reinhard Onnasch (Fasanenstrasse 47) deals in international art of the 1960s and young German artists. **Pels-Leusden Galerie** (in the Villa Grisebach) alternates exhibitions of German classic and modern art and is a good source for works by Lovis Corinth, Käthe Kollwitz, Franz Marc, August Macke, and Erich Heckel. **Volker Westphal** (Fasanenstrasse 68) carries 19th- and 20th-century art, with an emphasis on French and Berlin painting. **Galerie Wewerka** (Fasanenstrasse 41a) emphasizes abstract painting as well as performance art. **Gerda Bassenge** (Fasanenstrasse 73) features work that ranges from the 15th through 20th centuries: etchings and drawings by Dürer and Rembrandt, but also works by Chagall, Beckmann, Kollwitz, Liebermann, and Emil Nolde.

### Antiques and Classical Art

The best and most expensive stores and galleries are on the Fasanenstrasse, Bleibtreustrasse, Schlüterstrasse, and Mommsenstrasse; more line both sides of the Keithstrasse between the Budapester Strasse and Kleiststrasse. Quality of merchandise and prices go down a notch or two on the Motzstrasse, Eisenacher Strasse, and Kalckreuthstrasse; more middle-of-the-market wares are available along the Pariser Strasse and on the Ludwigkirchplatz.

## *Bric-a-Brac, Junk Shops, Flea Markets*

**Pestalozzistrasse**, north of and parallel to the Kantstrasse, is packed solid with bric-a-brac shops for almost its entire distance: a dozen blocks. The **Kudamm-Karree** (Kurfürstendamm 206–208) is a shopping arcade with more than 40 antiques stores, many of which have theme specialties. Every price range is represented.

Huge flea markets are held every Saturday and Sunday on the Strasse des 17. Juni in the Tiergarten and on the Linkstrasse near Potsdamer Platz.

The biggest and most colorful attraction, however, is **Bahnhof Nollendorf**, an out-of-service elevated subway station at Nollendorfplatz, where 16 ancient yellow U-Bahn cars have been converted into junk and antiques shops. Open daily except Tuesday from 11:00 A.M. to 7:00 P.M., it is a collectors' paradise. A 1920s streetcar runs on the abandoned viaduct track at 15-minute intervals to the next station, Potsdamer Strasse, which has been converted into a **Turkish Bazaar** with stands selling copper, cheap jewelry, glassware, and onyx from Istanbul.

In case you get hungry, there are purveyors of Turkish coffee, tea, and delicacies such as kebabs and baklava at the bazaar. Back at the other end of the streetcar line is the **Nolle**, where the fare is strictly Berlinish. Every Sunday morning at brunchtime, there's a Dixieland band.

# THE NORTH
## HAMBURG, LÜBECK, BREMEN

*By Douglas Sutton
and
John England*

*Douglas Sutton, the author of the section on Hamburg, is a U.S. journalist who has lived in Hamburg since 1978. An editor with the Deutsche-Presse-Agentur (DPA) wire agency, he has also written about Hamburg for the* International Herald Tribune, *the* Financial Post, Pan-Am Clipper, *and other publications.*

*John England, a freelance journalist, is the author of the sections on Lübeck, Lüneburg, Bremen, and Bremerhaven. Based in Bonn since 1972, he writes for British and Australian newspapers and magazines and contributes to a Lufthansa airline magazine.*

Travellers sometimes have difficulty in connecting the northern part of Germany with the cliché images of "typically German" landscape and culture. There are no snow-capped Alpine mountains, no lederhosen-clad men in beer gardens quaffing huge steins of beer, no scenic winding river valleys lined with vineyards and dotted with romantic castles, hardly any Medieval towns, with their ancient walls and church-steeple skylines.

Northern Germany is a different countryside with associations of another nature—a historical and cultural amalgamation of Germanic, Slavic, Scandinavian, and Dutch influences. The landscape, both in the Schleswig-Holstein region (squeezed in between the North Sea to the west, the Baltic

Sea to the east, and the river Elbe to the south), as well as in a good deal of the Lower Saxony region just south of the river, is mostly flat and windswept, filled with marshlands and glacial lakes and birches usually associated with Scandinavia. On the North Sea side, you'll find dikes and canal systems for which Dutch know-how was imported three centuries ago. Here and there, south of the Elbe river, you'll run across "round villages," settlements of half-timbered Saxon farmhouses arranged in a circle for defensive purposes, evidence of the influence of Slavic settlements a millennium ago.

With all the bodies of water and waterways in the North, it's only natural that a dominant characteristic of the region is its long tradition of trade and commerce. Hamburg, Bremen, Lüneburg, and Lübeck all belonged to the Hanseatic League, which in Medieval times was the most powerful commercial network linking the eastern Baltic regions, Scandinavia, and northern Germany. Hamburg, Bremen, and Lübeck still retain the term *Hansestadt* (Hanseatic City) in their official titles.

**Hamburg** officially calls itself the "Free and Hanseatic City of Hamburg," and many people consider it the most cosmopolitan and colorful of all German cities. It is immensely wealthy, with one of the highest per capita incomes anywhere in Western Europe, a city-state steeped in international trade traditions with its busy harbor. Hamburg is also alive with artistic and cultural attractions and an entertainment scene that can provide round-the-clock merrymaking.

For those seeking the most traditional Hanseatic city atmosphere, **Lübeck** is unsurpassed. With its Medieval walls and church spires and narrow cobblestone passageways, this small city, once capital of the Hanseatic League, looks and feels like a chapter out of the Middle Ages. It offers nourishment for body and mind alike: Marzipan was created here, and when walking the streets you'll recognize sites from books written by the city's two most famous authors, the brothers Thomas and Heinrich Mann.

The oversized small town of **Lüneburg**, with its German Gothic and Renaissance-style buildings and Medieval market square, is an architectural treasure. Its role in commerce is rooted in both its membership in the Hanseatic League and its former place as an important salt-trading center. About a 40-minute train ride from Hamburg, Lüneburg is an attractive alternative to the big city for an afternoon outing.

Though less than half the size of Hamburg, **Bremen** (with its seaport, Bremerhaven, some 30 miles to the north) is equally steeped in seafaring and world-trade traditions. Situated on the Weser river, Bremen is a major industrial city-state (shipbuilding, electronics, vehicles), but also boasts some architectural gems that survived the bombing of World War II—chiefly Gothic and Renaissance structures like the Rathaus and the cathedral. Attractive side streets attest to the city's merchant and trading heritage.

# HAMBURG

The *Freie und Hansestadt Hamburg*—Free and Hanseatic City of Hamburg—is baffling, not only to the visitor, but, often enough, to its own residents. It has many different faces, which are so often at cross-purposes that visitors may go away with several different impressions of the city, each true, yet taken as a whole failing to render one valid description.

"To write about Hamburg . . . means to write about something withdrawing and denying; it means describing a city that readily lets you grasp it in order to make itself unfathomable," wrote German author Gerhard Mauz.

Hamburg is a bustling place where many different attractions will compete for your attention, be it the arts, the entertainment, the parks and inviting old neighborhoods, or the action along the *Waterkant,* or water's edge, on the Elbe river. You'll come to realize why, with its strongly international flair, the city is often called Germany's "gateway to the world."

Putting Hamburg's statistical parameters down on paper is easy enough, and one of the temptations in trying to describe the city is to quantify it. It has more bridges than Venice and Amsterdam combined, and with upwards of 80 consulates ranks second in the world only to New York City in that category. It is West Germany's media capital and home to the world's biggest mail-order catalog company; it has Europe's second busiest port and, except for West Berlin, is West Germany's biggest city, with 1.6 million residents.

It is not just a city, in fact, but also one of West Germany's ten federal states, with 294 square miles of area. Located on the Elbe river about 100 km (62 miles) from the North Sea, the city looks back on nearly 1,200 years of history, during which it developed from an obscure fishing settlement to one of the most wealthy and powerful cities in the Hanseatic League. Its original name, when it was established as a

Christian outpost in 831 by the missionary Saint Ansgar, was "Hammaburg," a combination of the Old Germanic *Hamma* (marshland) and *Burg* (fortress).

One of the labels that applies accurately enough to Hamburg is *amphibious*. There are miles and miles of Elbe river shorefront and a huge (40-square-mile) bustling port area, plus the 450-acre Alster lake in the middle of the city, the Alster river that feeds it, and an extensive network of canals that connect many of Hamburg's neighborhoods—in all, some 40 miles of navigable waterways within the city's limits.

Is Hamburg a cold, gray, commercial city? Yes. "A city of bancos," sneered Heinrich Heine, who freeloaded off his uncle Salomon Heine, a wealthy Hamburg banker.

A surprising, fun-loving city? Yes. "It was simply, madly wild," said Paul McCartney of the early 1960s when the Beatles were getting their act together in the St. Pauli quarter's red-light Reeperbahn scene of music clubs and brothels.

Hamburg is also a city of high culture—museums, theaters, and opera—as well as of gentility, with its turn-of-the-century districts of tree-lined streets and patrician mansions. "Hamburg is a beautiful city, but perhaps a bit smug," former chancellor Helmut Schmidt, a native son, once commented.

For each label you are tempted to attach to Hamburg the city readily supplies you with evidence to the contrary. "Hamburg enjoys defying description. Because once something gets described, it invites comparison, and Hamburg does not compete for comparisons," observed Mauz.

Doubtless the city will always keep defying description, and will continue to evoke the kind of ambivalence Heinrich Heine felt when he called Hamburg "the sweet cradle of my sorrows."

Your best bet is to take in Hamburg in its *Gesamtheit,* its entirety of contradictory appearances. Consider the existentialist emotion of novelist Wolfgang Borchert when he returned at the end of World War II to Hamburg. Surveying the city reduced to barely more than rubble by the devastating 1943 bombing raids, he wrote: "Hamburg! That is immensely more than a mere pile of rocks. It is Life and Death, work, sleep, wind and love, tears and fog. It is our will to be. Hamburg!"

### MAJOR INTEREST

Elbe river and boat tours of the harbor
Boat tours of Alster lake and canals

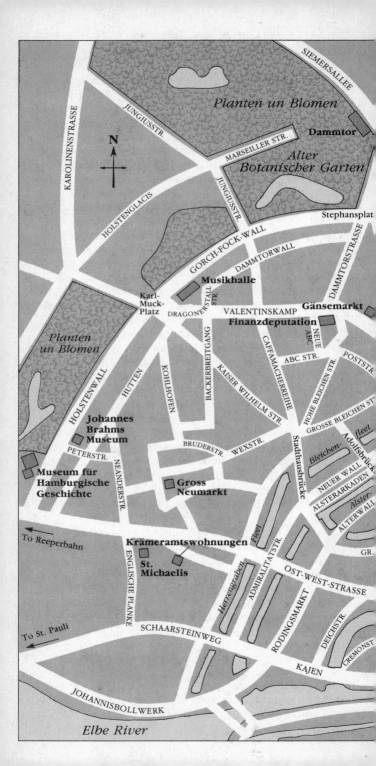

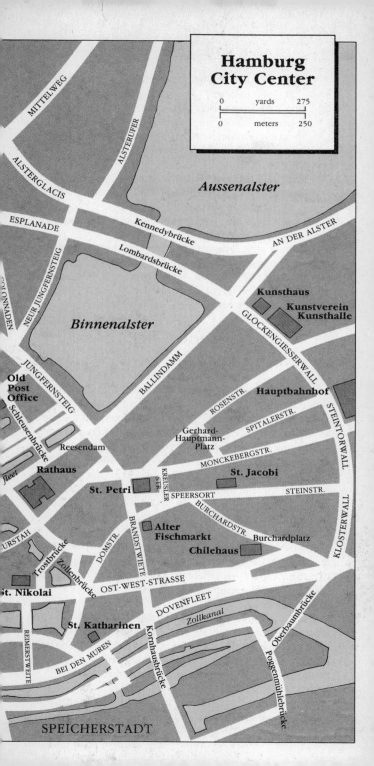

# Hamburg City Center

0 — yards — 275
0 — meters — 250

*Aussenalster*

*Binnenalster*

MITTELWEG

ALSTERUFER

ALSTERGLACIS

ESPLANADE

Kennedybrücke

Lombardsbrücke

AN DER ALSTER

COLONNADEN

NEUR JUNGFERNSTIEG

Kunsthaus

Kunstverein
Kunsthalle

GLOCKENGIESSERWALL

JUNGFERNSTIEG

BALLINDAMM

Hauptbahnhof

STEINTORWALL

ROSENSTR.

Old Post Office

SPITALERSTR.

Gerhard-Hauptmann-Platz

Schleusenbrücke

Reesendam

MONCKEBERGSTR.

St. Jacobi

KLOSTERWALL

Rathaus

St. Petri

KREUSLER STR.

SPEERSORT

STEINSTR.

fleet

BURCHARDSTR.

Alter Fischmarkt

Burchardplatz

URSTAH

BRANDSTWIETE

Chilehaus

Trostbrücke

Zollenbrücke

DOMSTR.

OST-WEST-STRASSE

St. Nikolai

DOVENFLEET

Zollkanal

Oberbaumbrücke

St. Katharinen

REIMERSTWIETE

BEI DEN MUREN

Kornhausbrücke

Poggenmühlebrücke

SPEICHERSTADT

Nightclubs and red-light district of the Reeperbahn,
St. Pauli quarter

Strolls in Aussenalster (the outer lake)
neighborhoods

Shopping arcades, downtown and Binnenalster (the
inner lake) neighborhoods

Rathaus (Town Hall)

Speicherstadt (Free Port warehouse city)

Jugendstil and porcelain collections, Museum für
Kunst and Gewerbe

Museum für Hamburgische Geschichte (Hamburg Historical Museum)

Clipper ship *Rickmer Rickmers*, with museum of maritime history

Churches of St. Jacobi, St. Katharinen, St. Michaelis

Baroque Christianskirche, Altona

Seafaring museums, Altona and Övelgönne

# The Historic City Center

Like most old European cities, Hamburg was once surrounded by defensive walls. Today there is little evidence of
these fortifications, which were torn down in the 18th and
19th centuries, yet many of the names remain as a reminder
of where Hamburg's early roots were planted; for the traveller, they serve to define the historic center of the city.

The ring around the downtown area includes (clockwise,
starting on the western perimeter) the Holstenwall, Gorch-
Fock-Wall, the Esplanade, Lombardsbrücke, Glockengiesserwall, Steintorwall, and Klosterwall. The southern boundary
stretched roughly from today's Oberbaumbrücke on the
southeast perimeter to the Johannisbollwerk on the southwest, and is defined by the riverfront.

Intersecting this semicircle in a northeast to southwest
diagonal are the **Binnenalster** (the inner Alster lake) and the
two main canals, **Alsterfleet** and **Bleichenfleet** (which later
becomes the Herrengrabenfleet), which channel the Alster
into the Elbe.

Using the canals for orientation, two walking tours of the
city center immediately suggest themselves; one on the east
side of the lake and canals, the other on the west. For both,
the convenient starting point is the **Jungfernstieg**, the street
that forms the southern border of the Binnenalster.

At the extreme southeastern corner of the Binnenalster is
the Reesendammbrücke, a good place to pause at the start of

the first, east-side walking tour—if you can do so without getting trampled by the crowds of shoppers pouring in and out of the nearby department stores and shopping arcades. The point marks the spot where, in 1235, a miller named Reese dammed the meandering Alster river, flooding the meadowlands in the river valley to the north and creating the great Alster lake.

As you gaze around the Binnenalster, the most obvious feature you will notice is the harmony of the architecture of department stores and office buildings, chiefly the work of the 19th-century architects Gottfried Semper and Alexis de Châteauneuf. Three buildings that stand out are, on the Neuer Jungfernstieg, the gleaming white Hotel Vier Jahreszeiten, and, a few doors farther up, the Classical-style Übersee club. Facing opposite, on the Ballindamm side of the lake, is the headquarters of the Hapag-Lloyd company.

From here it is just a minute's walk a block to the south to the towering **Rathaus** (Town Hall). Completed in 1897, the German Renaissance–style Rathaus is the sixth in Hamburg's history. Its size alone—647 rooms (more than Buckingham Palace)—is not its only impressive feature, however. Built on marshy ground, its foundations consist of the trunks of 4,000 oaks. The German Renaissance exterior belies the architectural diversity of the interior: Rococo-, Baroque-, and Classical-style rooms and hallways.

The foundations recall Venetian construction. Even more reminiscent of Venice are both the **Rathausplatz** and, across the Klein Alster canal, the arched passageway of the **Alsterarkaden**, with clothing shops, jewelry stores, and boutiques. Both were intended by Châteauneuf to evoke the piazza San Marco when he presented his designs after the Great Fire of 1842.

Entire books have been written on the subject of the Great Fire. One of the ironies was that Hamburg had prided itself on being in the vanguard of progress by having established, in 1676, Europe's first fire-insurance company. The material damage of the inferno—one eighth of the city's population was left homeless—far surpassed the coverage that the Hamburg fire insurance association could offer; the fire wiped the company out. In the aftermath of the four-day fire, it even looked for a while as if the city was financially ruined. But one man, banker Salomon Heine, put his entire fortune on the line to guarantee new credits to help the city rebuild. Heine, whose own mansion was devoured in the flames, asked, "Did the Elbe river burn up? No? Well then, nothing has been lost."

From the Rathausplatz, the next main point of interest, a few blocks uphill on the Mönckebergstrasse to the east, is Hamburg's oldest church, **St. Petri**. The neo-Gothic building here dates only to its reconstruction after the Great Fire, but its foundations go back to sometime around 1050. On the corner of Speersort and Kreuslerstrasse, in the parish basement, is the foundation of the Bishop's Tower, built in 1040, the first stone fortification north of the Elbe river.

In fact, here on this corner, and extending across the Domstrasse and the Speersort to the **Alter Fischmarkt**, was the location of the original Christian mission, set up in the year 831 on the order of Ludwig the Pious, a son of Charlemagne. Today the site is an open-air parking lot.

East up the Speersort, a few blocks away, is the **St. Jacobi church**, which dates from the year 1255 but was almost totally destroyed during World War II. Luckily, what was rescued was one of Hamburg's musical treasures—the Baroque organ built in 1693 by Arp Schnitger, a master craftsman who in his time had built some 150 organs. Johann Sebastian Bach gave a two-hour concert on a Schnitger organ in Hamburg in 1720—at another church, St. Katharinen—and exclaimed, "The beauty and virtuosity of the sounds it makes cannot be praised enough!" The 60-register instrument at St. Jacobi is one of only two surviving Schnitger organs in Germany.

The jump from religion and music to commerce and an architectural treasure is a matter of a few blocks, across Speersort and south on the Mohlenhofstrasse to the Burchardplatz, where the **Chilehaus**, a red brick, wedge-shaped counting house, takes up an entire city block. Completed in 1930 by architect Fritz Höger, the building evokes a merchant ship, symbolic of Hamburg's role in world commerce.

Red brick dominates much of Hamburg's construction. This was the intention of the city's building director of the 1920s, Fritz Schumacher, who wanted to revive North German brick architecture and who himself designed several buildings for the city as well as entire neighborhoods of low-income housing in Hamburg's outer districts.

The triumph of red brick architecture is found across the busy Ost–West-Strasse and down toward the port. There, rising on the other side of the Zollkanal and stretching toward the west for more than a mile, is the **Speicherstadt**, or free-port warehouse city, which was completed in 1888. (The political significance of the free-port status is that it was given to Hamburg by Reichkanzler Bismarck to lure the city into the Prussian customs union.)

The seven- and eight-story warehouses, decorated with

Gothic-style towers and balconies, provide ten square miles of storage space—for Persian carpets, coffee, tea, cocoa, silk, cotton, rubber, and an array of spices from all corners of the globe. It is here, perhaps even more than at the main harbor farther south on the Elbe, that you can sense this city's worldwide trading soul and exult along with prominent 18th-century merchant Caspar Voght: "I am the first merchant to import coffee from Mocca, tobacco from Baltimore, cocoa from Surinam, and rubber from Africa."

It's best to experience this "port within a port" by crossing the Zollkanal at the Poggenmühlebrücke south of the Chilehaus and then walking west among the tall warehouse buildings a few blocks, then recrossing the canal at the Kornhausbrücke, where across the street is the **St. Katharinen church**. Downstairs in the 14th-century Late Gothic church, a slide show depicting a thousand years of Hamburg history is shown several times a day.

What little downtown Hamburg has to offer in the way of authentically old buildings (repaired after the destruction of the war) is found a few blocks west of the church. First there are the half-timbered warehouses of the 18th century at the Reimerstwiete; another block farther west are the **Cremonstrasse** and the **Deichstrasse**, which cover both sides of the curving Nikolaifleet and along which the buildings date back to the 17th and 18th centuries.

Both the Cremonstrasse and the Deichstrasse feature several traditional old-style restaurants—Nikolaikeller, Deichgraf, Alt Hamburger Aalspeicher. More important, these two streets give you a feeling for what Hamburg looked like before the Great Fire of 1842, and before the three weeks of carpet-bombing 101 years later. The Deichstrasse is where the Great Fire broke out—the restaurant Zum Brandanfang ("Where the Fire Began") marks the spot. The buildings also typify the merchants' quarters of the period unique to Hamburg, in which warehouses were built right on the edge of the canal so that goods could be lifted off the boats by pulleys. To get a closer view of the rear of the buildings you can slip through one or two alleyways that lead to a walkway along the canal.

From here, crossing to the north side of the Ost–West-Strasse via a pedestrian overpass, you come directly to Hamburg's starkest reminder of July 1943: the towering, charred Gothic steeple—its original color was yellow—of the **St. Nikolai church**. Completed in 1874, the Gothic-style church is today a blackened skeleton left standing to remind passersby of the horror of war. One block east is the Trostbrücke, on

which two statues, marking the spot where "old" (on the
northeast side) and "new" (on the west) Hamburg were
linked in the 13th century. One statue is of Saint Ansgar, the
canonized archbishop who founded Hamburg in 834, and the
other of Count Adolf III, who set up the New Town in 1188.
Nearby to the east across the way is the Zollbrücke, built in
1633, Hamburg's oldest surviving bridge.

The Trostbrücke also marks the spot where Germany's
first stock exchange was founded, in 1588. The original
exchange burned down in the Great Fire. The present exchange is several blocks farther north, a Classical-style building erected in 1841 and located back-to-back with the
Rathaus, and a few blocks south of the Jungfernstieg, where
we began.

The second walking tour, beginning back at the Rathausplatz
near the Jungfernstieg, covers the west side of the Bleichenfleet and the Alsterfleet. Across the Schleusenbrücke two
blocks northwest on the Poststrasse is the towered Tuscan
Renaissance **old post office** building. It's another contribution by Alexis de Châteauneuf, built in 1847 and now a
shopping arcade of art galleries, bookstores, and clothing
shops.

Turn left at the Grosse Bleichen Strasse and go southwest
on the Wexstrasse through a nondescript area of office
buildings for a few hundred yards to reach the next hospita-
ble attraction, the **Grossneumarkt**. This tree-lined oasis of
restaurants and night spots features two streets worth looking at. A block north of the market square is the **Brüder-
strasse**, consisting entirely of Classical-style buildings from
the last century. The **Peterstrasse**, two blocks farther west, is
a cobblestone street with restored 17th- and 18th-century
red brick town houses reminiscent of buildings in Amsterdam. The **Johannes Brahms Museum** at the western end of
the Peterstrasse is not his birthplace—that is a few streets
away, in the Speckstrasse—but it is a reminder of the neighborhood he grew up in and where he took his first piano
lessons, starting at the age of seven.

Four blocks to the south of the Peterstrasse, Hamburg's
most famous landmark towers high atop a hill on Ost–West-
Strasse: the **St. Michaelis church**. Dating back to the 18th
century, it was twice badly damaged by fire, in 1750 and
again in 1906. The Baroque-style "Michel"—as Hamburg
residents fondly refer to it—easily wins the prize of Hamburg's most beautiful church. Its interior is a symphony of

white and gold, dazzling when the sun shines through the towering stained-glass windows.

One block to the south, Hamburg's Most Tacky Tourist Spot Award goes to the **Krämeramtswohnungen**, the city's last remaining 17th-century apartment buildings, which form a courtyard and were built for the widows of the mercers' guild members. It's worth taking a quick walk among the half-timbered houses—there is also a museum showing the interior of the period—but you'll have to concentrate hard to overlook all the touristy trinkets being peddled.

One museum that should not be missed is a ten-minute walk northwest to the Holstenwall, to the Fritz Schumacher-designed **Museum für Hamburgische Geschichte** (Hamburg Historical Museum). Though not a hands-on history museum, it is a good walk-through one, and includes an exact replica of a 17th-century merchant's home. Most informative are the scale models of Hamburg's development from the earliest times onward, filling in all the architectural gaps in the downtown area created by the Great Fire and the bombings of World War II.

The history museum is especially worth a visit if you have German ancestors and want to do genealogical research. In the museum's office of historic emigration staff members go over microfilms of passenger lists of all the people who shipped out of Hamburg from the 1850s to about 1930. There are literally hundreds of thousands of names on record, but, more important, records of the cities and towns where the emigrants originally came from. The service costs a slight fee, and you should bring records with you that indicate the approximate date that your ancestors left Germany. The office of historic emigration itself is located on the second floor in what was once the captain's quarters of a typical 19th-century steamer. North of the museum building, parallel to the Holstenwall, the museum's parklike grounds contain statues and stone gateways from homes and gardens of the past couple of centuries.

At the grounds' northern end at the Karl-Muck-Platz, where Hamburg's concert hall, the Baroque-style **Musikhalle**, is the chief landmark, turn east and head downhill on the Dragonerstallstrasse, pausing at a little side street, **Bäckerbreitgang**, to see a row of half-timbered houses from the 18th and 19th centuries. Still going east, down the Valentinskamp after the Dragonerstallstrasse, you soon reach the Gänsemarkt. The most imposing structure on the southwest side of the square is another Schumacher building, the **Finanzdepu-**

**tation,** or treasury. A block east and you're back at the Jungfernstieg.

# The Alster

Downtown is about business and commerce and shopping and history, not a place to contemplate Mother Nature. But you need only to go just outside the old city limits to see Hamburg's wealth of tree- and garden-ornamented residential areas. Hamburg is considered one of the greenest of Germany's major cities.

For example, there's the **Alter Botanischer Garten** and the adjoining **Planten und Blomen** park outside the northwest perimeter of the Gorch-Fock-Wall and the Stephansplatz. Besides the greenery, the chief landmark here is the **Heinrich-Hertz television relay tower,** which has an observation platform and a revolving café at its top. The TV tower offers a spectacular view of the downtown area and the vast Elbe harbor.

There is more greenery and almost pastoral serenity along the Alster river and the Aussenalster, the outer lake. You can walk or bicycle all the way from the Aussenalster to the source of the river, some 25 km (15 miles) northeast of downtown Hamburg, along the **Alster Wanderweg** (hiking path).

However, you'll probably settle for hiking around the **Aussenalster,** which is surrounded by parks and footpaths. Along the way are any number of cafés, some doubling as sailboat marinas, where you can rest and get refreshment. "It's the Elbe that makes us wealthy," wrote the 18th-century poet Friedrich von Hagedorn, "and the Alster that teaches us to be sociable." To this day, the Alster—referred to as the "pearl of Hamburg"—remains the focal point of recreational activity: sailing, rowing, and windsurfing, and, around the shores, walking paths and parks as well as cafés.

Ask any jogger—you'll see plenty of them—and you'll learn that the distance around the lake is about 6 km (4 miles). But there are several inviting stops along the way. One of the most favored is **Bobby Reich's boat marina** at the northern tip of the lake, just east of the Krugkoppelbrücke. From there, looking south, you have a panorama of the lake and the downtown skyline. Other favorite rest stops on the circuit around the Aussenalster include the **Mühlenkamper Fährhaus** and the **Uhlenhorster Fährhaus.**

If you do walk the entire circuit, you'll also see a turquoise-colored mosque, on the Schöne Aussicht, used by the many Muslims (chiefly Iranians and Turks) who live in Hamburg. You can also experience the Alster by boat. A fleet provides (April to October) regular transportation between the Jungfernstieg and the neighborhood of Winterhude, some three miles upriver (see more on it below, in Neighborhoods). These shallow-bottomed boats zigzag their way up and down the Alster, linking both shores, and so it gives you plenty of time—about 40 minutes for, say, a trip between the Jungfernstieg and the Krugkoppelbrücke (at the northern end of the Aussenalster proper)—to take in the scenery.

A good way to get a feeling for both the Alster and some of the neighborhoods would be to take an even longer boat ride—about an hour—all the way to the last stop, at the Winterhude Fährhaus, about a mile north of the Krugkoppelbrücke. Across the river you'll notice the 18th-century village church St. Johannis in the Eppendorf district.

To get back downtown you can take the boat again, or the U-1 subway line at Hudtwalckerstrasse just one block east of where you get off the boat, which will take you back, five stations later, to the Jungfernstieg. Or you can walk, in which case you'll be rewarded by going down the **Leinpfadstrasse** along the river's east bank to the Krugkoppelbrücke (where, once again, you can board the boat to get back). The Leinpfad (the name literally means "rope path," describing the path made when people used to tow the riverboats upstream) is one of Hamburg's finest addresses, lined with villas and mansions.

# The Aussenalster Neighborhoods

The debate goes on about whether it is something to be welcomed or condemned, but in any event it seems unstoppable: the gentrification of Hamburg's residential districts around the Alster lake. It's a familiar pattern; what used to be a butcher shop is now a hairstyling salon with a baby grand piano, candles, and mostly Mozart softly emanating from a state-of-the-art sound system.

You can form your own opinion when you look at the Hamburg version of gentrification in the old neighborhoods around the lake. Your tour will reveal that its spread is uneven—some areas have gone to the upwardly mobile and some haven't.

As an example of the latter, there is the western section of the **Rotherbaum district**, in the Hamburg university area on the west side of the lake along the Grindelhofstrasse: You'll find the usual scruffy-looking student pubs and cafés, book-

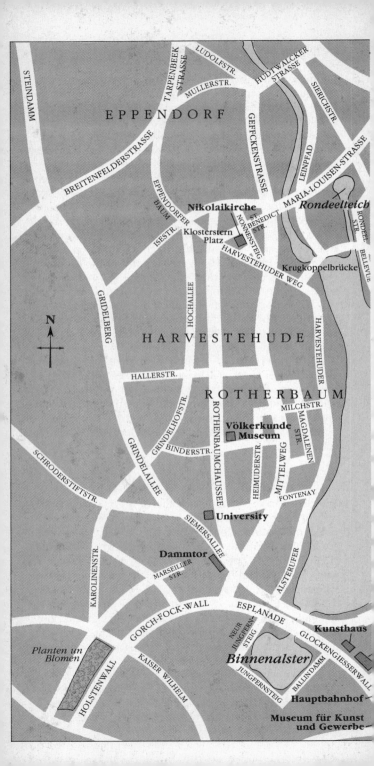

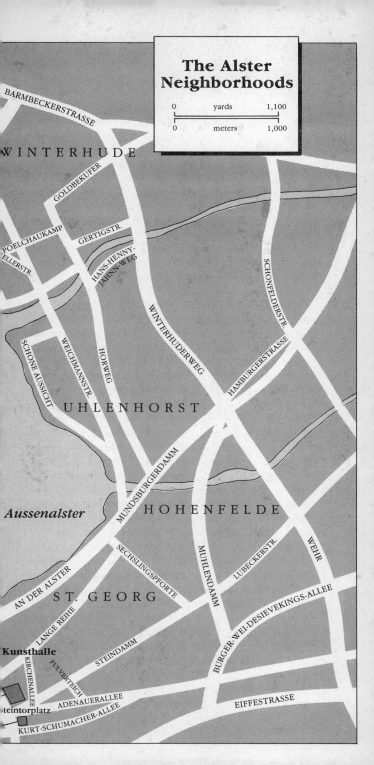

# The Alster Neighborhoods

0      yards      1,100

0      meters      1,000

BARMBECKERSTRASSE

WINTERHUDE

GOLDBEKUFER

POELCHAUKAMP

ELLERSTR.

GERTIGSTR.

HANS-HENNY-JAHNN-WEG

SCHONFELDERSTR.

WINTERHUDERWEG

SCHONE AUSSICHT

WEICHMANNSTR.

HORWEG

HAMBURGERSTRASSE

UHLENHORST

MUNDSBURGERDAMM

Aussenalster

HOHENFELDE

SECHSLINGSPFORTE

MUHLENDAMM

LUBECKERSTR.

WEHR

AN DER ALSTER

ST. GEORG

LANGE REIHE

BURGER-WEI-DESIEVEKINGS-ALLEE

Kunsthalle

STEINDAMM

KIRCHENALLEE

PULVERTEICH

teintorplatz

ADENAUERALLEE

EIFFESTRASSE

KURT-SCHUMACHER-ALLEE

stores and record shops, and one good cinema, the Abaton Kino, where an old film is bound to be showing in the original language. This area also used to be Hamburg's principal Jewish neighborhood. On the western edge of the university campus, on the Grindelhofstrasse, a memorial park features the ground layout of a synagogue destroyed during the November 1938 Kristallnacht. Farther up the street, on the same side, is a former Torah-Talmud school.

The gentrification of Rotherbaum is more in evidence along the Mittelweg, which runs north–south two and three blocks in from the lake, and particularly the so-called **Pöseldorf** section along the perpendicular **Milchstrasse**, a street lined with discos, wine shops, clothing stores, and fashionable restaurants. Pöseldorf is a good nightlife venue.

While you're in the neighborhood you might want to visit Germany's second-largest (after West Berlin's) ethnology museum, the **Museum für Völkerkunde** at the corner of the Binderstrasse and the Rothenbaumchaussee, three blocks west of the Mittelweg. It contains extensive collections of South Seas and African artifacts, plus the largest Siberian-artifacts collection outside the U.S.S.R. From there you can either continue walking north through the next up-market neighborhood, **Harvestehude**, or (more advisable because it's faster) take the subway (U-1 line), boarding at the Hallerstrasse stop in the north of Rotherbaum, on the Rothenbaumchausee, and getting off at the next stop, in Klosterstern in the northern part of Harvestehude.

This puts you right in the middle of one of Hamburg's smartest neighborhoods. Angling off northwest from the Klosterstern into the Eppendorf neighborhood is the **Eppendorfer Baumstrasse**, lined with cafés, restaurants, art galleries, antiques shops, boutiques, and bookstores. Here you won't find the patrician town houses of Rotherbaum, but instead a colorful array of four- and five-story Jugendstil apartment houses—whose rents are skyrocketing. Many people, wanting to avoid the downtown crowds, do their shopping here, although these stores are a shade less chic than those in the downtown arcades.

Just east of the Klosterstern on the St. Benedictstrasse is a modern church, the **Nikolaikirche**, built after the war in remembrance of the downtown church of the same name, now a war memorial. Inside this church is an altar painting by Oskar Kokoschka.

If you continue east on the the St. Benedictstrasse you'll come to a bridge crossing the Alster river just above where it

becomes the lake. Crossing the bridge and continuing on
what is now the Maria-Louisen-Strasse, you'll soon come to a
major north–south street, the Sierichstrasse, and you'll notice a circle of imposing turn-of-the-century mansions on the
right on what is called the **Rondeelteich**, or round pond.
Because the Sierichstrasse is a major traffic lane—beautifully
tree lined, but noisy—continue around to the right on the
Rondeelstrasse, which then turns into the **Bellevue** heading
south. The name needs no explaining; as you follow Bellevue back to the northern tip of Alster lake, a panorama of the
downtown skyline opens up across the lake.

Another interesting neighborhood—and no millionaires'
paradise, like the areas we've just discussed—is a few blocks
east of the Bellevue. Walking east on the Gellertstrasse and
then the Poelchaukamp will take you to the southeastern
edge of the **Winterhude district**, mentioned above in connection with boat trips on the lake. It's less trendy and
upscale than Eppendorf and Harvestehude, and for that
reason, in the eyes of many, more livable. There is plenty of
entertainment here, particularly in the grid of streets east of
the Mühlenkamp and bounded by the Goldbekufer on the
north and the Gertigstrasse on the south. The **Schinkelplatz**,
alive with down-to-earth taverns, restaurants, and small specialty stores, is the heart of the action.

If your legs give out from all the walking, you can simply
hop on the number 108 bus south on the Mühlenkampstrasse
and ten minutes later you'll be back at the Hauptbahnhof
(main railroad station), on a route down through three more
neighborhoods on the east side of the Alster: Uhlenhorst,
Hohenfelde, and St. Georg.

It's worth touring the **St. Georg neighborhood** for several reasons (though it's advisable to do it by day). First, it
is the one area of Hamburg that has seen hardly any
gentrification at all, and so gives you an idea of how some
of the other neighborhoods used to look. Also, many Hamburgers say these blocks between the Steindamm and the
lake northeast of the main train station—their centerpiece
being the **Hansaplatz**—are a less touristy, and therefore
more authentic, version of the red-light St. Pauli district:
hookers walking the street (particularly along the Lange
Reihe), small grocery shops, vegetable stands, pubs, and
kiosks, all in a seedy, rundown setting.

This is also one of Hamburg's polyglot areas, where
Turkish merchants and snack shops compete with Italian,
Greek, Yugoslav, and Lebanese shops. But there's no justice

in romanticizing this area; prostitution goes hand in hand with petty crime and a hard-drug scene, and the down-and-out sleep off their latest binge in doorways.

St. Georg also has its intellectual side, in Hamburg's three chief art museums: the Kunsthalle and the Kunsthaus/Kunstverein, across the Glockengiesserwallstrasse from the Binnenalster northwest of the Hauptbahnhof, and the Museum für Kunst und Gewerbe (Arts and Crafts Museum), south of the station.

The **Kunsthalle**'s collection ranges from the carved 1383 triptych altar of the St. Petri church, by Meister Bertram, to contemporary painters. The collection includes works by Philipp-Otto Runge, Edvard Munch, Edouard Manet, and Caspar-David Friedrich, including his masterpiece, *The Wanderer over the Sea of Mist*. The **Kunsthaus/Kunstverein**, just down the Glockengiesserwallstrasse from the Kunsthalle, is the showcase for current professionals and unknown artists to demonstrate their works in a series of changing exhibitions.

At the **Museum für Kunst und Gewerbe** (Museum of Decorative Arts and Crafts), a block south of the Hauptbahnhof on the Steintorplatz, one of the main attractions is the Jugendstil (German Art Nouveau) collection, with its "Paris Room" from the 1900 World Exhibition. The museum also features stage designs by Oskar Kokoschka, a faïence and porcelain collection, and a collection of antique musical instruments. East Asian and Islamic arts and crafts are also part of the permanent exhibitions. For car buffs, there is yet another museum, a block away on the Kurt-Schumacher-Allee: the **Automuseum**, a branch of the larger car museum in the castle of Tremsbüttel north of Hamburg, which features a wide range of vintage Rolls-Royces, Mercedeses, BMWs, and Opels.

## St. Pauli and Altona

Visiting Altona and St. Pauli, west of the inner city, you are likely to get a feeling of having wandered into a different place altogether—which is exactly what you have done. Altona was only incorporated into Hamburg in 1937. For the 400 or so years before that it often was a fierce competitor with the immensely wealthy and powerful Hanseatic trading city right outside its gates. St. Pauli was a kind of buffer zone between Hamburg and Altona, and with its fishing harbor, its working-class neighborhoods abounding in taverns, and its

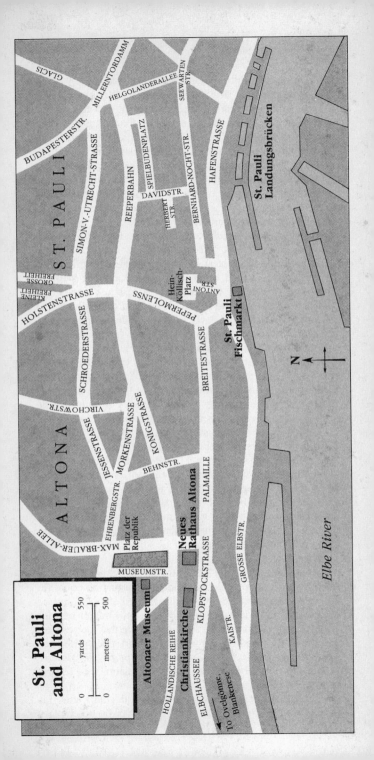

**St. Pauli and Altona**

yards 550
meters 500

Altonaer Museum
Neues Rathaus Altona
Christianskirche
St. Pauli Fischmarkt
St. Pauli Landungsbrücken

**ST. PAULI**

**ALTONA**

GLACIS
BUDAPESTERSTR.
MILLERNTORDAMM
HELGOLANDERALLEE
SEEWARTEN STR.
SIMON-V.-UTRECHT-STRASSE
REEPERBAHN
SPIELBUDENPLATZ
DAVIDSTR.
HERBERT STR.
BERNHARD-NOCHT-STR.
HAFENSTRASSE
GROSSE FREIHEIT
KLEINE FREIHEIT
HOLSTENSTRASSE
Hein-Köllisch-Platz
ANTONI STR.
PEPERMOLENSS
SCHROEDERSTRASSE
VIRCHOWSTR.
JESSENSTRASSE
MORKENSTRASSE
KONIGSTRASSE
EHRENBERGSTR.
BEHNSTR.
BREITESTRASSE
MAX-BRAUER-ALLEE
Platz der Republik
MUSEUMSTR.
HOLLANDISCHE REIHE
ELBCHAUSSEE
KLOPSTOCKSTRASSE
PALMAILLE
GROSSE ELBSTR.
KAISTR.
To Ovelgönne,
Blankenese

**Elbe River**

N

red-light district on the Reeperbahn catering to the world's merchant seamen, it developed a character all its own.

Accentuating **Altona**'s difference was the fact that at one period, in the 17th century, it was under Denmark's rule, and the second-biggest Danish city after Copenhagen. The Danish rulers, never able to subdue Hamburg, set about establishing commercial and civic freedoms and privileges to help Altona compete with Hamburg. Around 1800, at the height of its economic might, Altona had a merchant fleet larger than Hamburg's, and it was around this time that most of Altona's imposing buildings were built.

Today Altona is a largely working- and middle-class residential area where some prominent leftist intellectuals and artists—such as the protest songwriter Wolfgang Biermann—prefer to live instead of in other, more affluent areas of Hamburg. Particularly the little side streets just west of the Altona train station (the Hahnenkamp and the Hohenesch) have the typical Altona flavor of modest shops and taverns.

The best way to tour Altona is to take one of the rapid-transit trains (S-1, S-2, and S-3) from St. Pauli Landungsbrücken a bit southwest of St. Michaelis church and get off three stops later to the west, at the Altona train station. Then head south just across the street to the Platz der Republik, where the Classical-style **Altona Rathaus** dominates the scene. Originally built as a railway station in 1844, it was converted to its present status in 1898. A statue of Kaiser Wilhelm I on horseback stands guard out front.

On the west side of the park is the **Norddeutches Landesmuseum**, which, like its Hamburg counterpart, provides a colorful portrait of the town's seafaring history, including a valuable collection of figureheads. Daily life and customs of the Elbe valley and Schleswig-Holstein are illustrated through costumes, artifacts, old toys, and embroidery, plus an authentic peasant's cottage housing a small restaurant.

Continue south to the Königstrasse, then west a block to reach the Baroque **Christianskirche**, arguably equal in beauty to Hamburg's St. Michaelis. Named after Denmark's King Christian VI, it was completed in 1738. Old gravestones surround the church, but it's the south side that interests us: the grave of Hamburg's most celebrated poet, Friedrich Gottlieb Klopstock, whose most famous work, the *Messias,* was put to music by Georg Philipp Telemann, with its premier in Hamburg in 1759.

After visiting Klopstock's grave several years after his death Heinrich Heine remarked, "I know of no other place where a dead poet could be buried better than [Hamburg]," then added a dig characteristic of his love-hate relationship with the city: "However, as a living poet, living there is much more difficult."

Heine at least knew the area he was disparaging, since he had stayed at his wealthy uncle's country estate about five minutes' walk west of the Christianskirche on the Elbchaussee. Today a modest yellow "garden house" that Salomon Heine had built on the grounds still remains. This spot marks the start of the several miles of palacelike mansions that the merchants of Hamburg and Altona built overlooking the Elbe going all the way out west to Blankenese (for which see below).

Retracing your steps back east on the Elbchaussee, you first come back to the Klopstockstrasse and then pass the Rathaus to reach the **Palmaille**, a tree-lined boulevard flanked on both sides by pure Classic-style houses designed by Danish architect Christian Frederik Hansen. The name derives from the fact that the stretch was first laid out in the mid-17th century as a playgound for ball games—*palla* (ball) and *maglio* (bat). But these houses were built in the late 18th century and, with the exception of a couple of others restored after the World War II bombing, are Hamburg's most architecturally complete buildings in their original state.

Toward the eastern end of the Palmaille comes the Behnstrasse, where you turn left and go one block back to the Königstrasse rapid-transit station. From here you can take the S-1, S-2, or S-3 train back two stops east to downtown Hamburg.

Or you can get off in the **St. Pauli district** at the first station, the **Reeperbahn** stop, and see the "world's most sinful mile," as the boulevard is sometimes called. Many people also call it boring, saying that the live-sex shows and striptease acts lack the joie de vivre and humor of their French counterparts and in no way justify the horrendous prices charged for drinks. One of the landmarks in the district is the red brick Davidswache police station, and just up the Davidstrasse is the infamous little **Herbertstrasse**, an alleyway where ladies of the night display themselves in show windows. A word of caution, however: These ladies do not take kindly to female window-shoppers.

You'll also notice on the Reeperbahn (its name means "rope walk," a reference to the place where rigging for sailing ships was once manufactured) that there's a certain amount of legitimate entertainment. The Operettenhaus expects to be showing *Cats* for several more years, and plans are in the making for reviving the live-music clubs that were once as much a hallmark as the sex trade. This street, after all, is where the Beatles starred before anybody outside of Liverpool had ever heard of them.

To capture some of the flavor of St. Pauli's working-class fishermen's heritage, a walking tour of the crisscrossing network of small side streets (Fischerstrasse, Hein-Köllisch-Platz, the Antonistrasse) just south of the Reeperbahn S-Bahn stop can be recommended. You'll be heading downhill toward the Elbe and the St. Pauli Fischmarkt, from where it is about a half-mile walk east along the river front to the St. Pauli Landungsbrücken.

## Along the Elbe

The most lasting impression visitors take home from Hamburg is very likely a vision of its harbor and the hum of activity on the Elbe river's shores. The main attraction—in fact, the gravitational point of touring activity—is at the **St. Pauli Landungsbrücken**, a 2,300-foot-long floating landing stage where the **boat tours** of the harbor and the downriver excursions to the scenic former fishing villages of Övelgönne and Blankenese embark. It's also the terminal for ferry service to Harwich, England.

The St. Pauli Landungsbrücken building, with its clocktower, is one of Hamburg's best-known landmarks. What you don't see immediately, but is worth seeking out, is the entry to the 1,400-foot-long Alte Elbtunnel beneath the river, built in 1911. You descend steel staircases and then walk to the harbor quays on the other side. Through cavernous quiet, you may hear the engines of huge ocean freighters passing overhead.

Just east of the landing stages is the **Rickmer Rickmers**, a 19th-century clipper ship now serving as a museum for maritime history.

The huge port itself—the second biggest in Europe, employing more than 50,000 people and handling some 16,000 ships a year—goes back more than 800 years. On May 7, 1189, Emperor Friedrich Barbarossa issued an edict granting free-trading privileges to Hamburg. Visitors to the city in the early days of May each year can take part in huge celebrations of the event all along the river front.

Hamburg's harbor is an open tidal port, in which the North Sea tides influence the Elbe river level. Just southeast of Hamburg, the Elbe splits into two arms, the Norderelbe and Süderelbe, to form a kind of circle, which closes again across from the Fischereihafen. The land inside this circle is a giant network of quays, warehouses, and giant floating drydocks, and the skyline is crammed with the skeletonlike steel cranes used to load and unload ships.

The best way to enjoy the harbor is to take a boat tour, from the Landungsbrücken, which takes about one hour. An English-language tour (daily March to November at 11:15 A.M.) departs from pier number 1, near the Rickmer Rickmers. The tour includes the Speicherstadt as well as the main port itself, your tiny boat dwarfed by the huge ocean freighters it passes. Seeing all the activity, you'll gain an appreciation for the role the Hamburg port plays not only in the city's economy, but also in West Germany's foreign trade as a whole.

Some of the best fun all year around, albeit only on Sunday morning, is at the **St. Pauli Fischmarkt**, about a half-mile west of the landing stages. The fishing boats berth at dockside to sell their catch, and a variety of seafood is on sale at booths; every now and then, just to keep people's attention, a hawker will fling a smoked eel into the crowd. The St. Pauli Fischmarkt is also a huge flea market and open-air bazaar, selling clothing, live poultry, Chinese umbrellas, potted plants, herbs and spices—you name it. Along the St. Pauli **Hafenstrasse**, accordion music floats out of the smoke-filled fishermen's taverns.

True appreciation of Hamburg's "amphibious" existence comes with visiting, besides the harbor and the fish market, the string of districts on the Elbe's shores, which stretch northwest from downtown and have over time become incorporated into the city proper: Altona, Ottensen, Othmarschen, Nienstedten, and finally, about 12 km (7.5 miles) to the west, Blankenese.

Bicyclists and hikers can cover the entire distance along a specially marked route starting from the Landungsbrücken. If you're driving you'll head out along the **Elbchaussee**. Atop a ridge overlooking the river, this is Germany's most famous stretch of mansions, belonging to merchants, bankers, and shipping-line owners. The problem is that it is a busy road (on weekends it's mostly bumper to bumper), so you have to look fast to take in the sights.

You can also get out to Blankenese by boat tour—about a 50-minute ride—starting from the Landungsbrücken. The rapid-transit train (S-1), starting from the same place, is faster, of course, but not scenic.

The boat glides past the St. Pauli and Altona districts with their hilltop churches and buildings. Leaving the downtown areas behind, you'll see much more greenery in the outer districts as you stream downriver toward Blankenese. Boat stops along the way include Övelgönne and Teufelsbrück, where passengers can debark to see the sights and then catch the next boat downstream.

At **Övelgönne**, just west of Altona, is the **Lange Jammer**, a row of restored 250-year-old houses and a private maritime museum. At Teufelsbrück is a large park, **Jenischpark**, where the chief attractions are the **Jenish-Haus** and the **Ernst-Barlach-Haus**. The former, a Classical white mansion built in 1932, is now a "museum of upper-class living" showing how 19th-century politician and banker Senator Johann Martin Jenisch lived. Set amid spacious lawns and wooded grounds, the Ernst-Barlach-Haus features more than 100 paintings, 20 wood sculptures, and more than 300 drawings by this North German Expressionist.

The tour boat's final stop is **Blankenese**, another former fishing village hugging the side of the Sullberg hill. It's fun simply to get lost among the labyrinthine tangle of walkways among the thatched-roof cottages, many of them 18th-century structures, each with its own tiny garden plot. At the top of the Sullberg is a restaurant, also called **Sullberg**, offering a grand view of the Elbe river below. Nearby, on the Elbterrasse pathway, is the **Dreehus**, a three-family dwelling built around 1800.

A final point of interest is the **Willkomm-Höft**, or welcoming point, in Schulau, about 8 km (5 miles) west of Blankenese by boat. At a restaurant there passing ships are hailed by a playing of the national anthem of the countries where they originate and a saluting of their colors. There's also a small museum of ships in bottles.

## GETTING AROUND

Hamburg's Fuhlsbüttel airport is a relatively short distance north of the city's downtown area: Barring traffic congestion, a taxi ride downtown takes 20 minutes or less and costs around DM 25. The airport bus service leaves every 20 minutes between 6:22 A.M. and 10:42 P.M. from the three passenger terminals to the Hauptbahnhof; it costs DM 8. A third way in is to take the city bus number 110 (fare DM 3.10), which leaves every ten minutes for the Ohlsdorf station on the U-1 line, and from there you can ride the U-Bahn (subway) downtown. But what you save in money you lose in time.

If you're arriving by train, remember that the Hauptbahnhof is not the final stop. Other stops in the city are the Dammtor, a few minutes away, and the Altona Bahnhof at the end of the line. As a rule, trains arriving from the south, for which Hamburg is the end of the run, will go to Altona. Trains headed for or arriving from Scandinavia stop only at the Hauptbahnhof. It is wise to check with the train conductor about where the train will be stopping in Hamburg. If your hotel is in the Rotherbaum area or others on the west side of the Alster lake, for example, you should get off at the Dammtor station.

The two Autobahn links are the A 1 (Lübeck to Bremen), and the A 7 (Hannover to Flensburg). The A 1 exits for the city are the HH-Horn and HH-Veddel; the A 7 exits are HH-Schnelsen, HH-Stellingen, and HH-Bahrenfeld. The roads leading downtown are clearly marked "Centrum."

Once you've arrived, you'll do your nerves a favor by using the ample mass-transportation facilities instead of driving around the city. If you do drive, remember that three major "ring" roads circle the city. Ring 1, the interior one, follows the old wall fortifications; Ring 2 cuts through the intermediate neighborhoods between downtown and the airport; Ring 3 links with the districts on Hamburg's outer city limits. While technically there is a 50 km per hour (30 mph) speed limit inside the city, you'll have to drive a good deal faster to keep up with traffic. Hamburg drivers, by and large, are aggressive yet disciplined—they tend to drive fast but they won't be dodging in and out without signaling. Still, if you're not up to whizzing along narrow city streets at 50 mph with a car a few feet ahead of you and one just inches behind you, you'll be better off using the mass transportation.

Hamburg has a well-developed network of buses, subways, and rapid-transit trains, which run both above and below ground. The U-Bahn runs on the honor system—if you're caught riding without a ticket (*schwarzfahren,* or "riding black") the fine is DM 60. Tickets for the U-Bahn (U-1, U-2, and U-3) and for the S-Bahn (rapid-transit trains; five main lines, S-1–S-5) are available at the stations from vending machines and in some cases from a clerk. More and more bus stops also have vending machines, but more likely you'll be buying your ticket from the driver. To determine your fare, consult the map with rings portraying the zones you'll be travelling to, and then push the corresponding button.

You'll probably be staying within Zone 1 and Zone 2 to see most of Hamburg's sights. If you think you'll be doing a lot of U-Bahn and bus riding on a given day, get a *Tageskarte,* which is valid for the whole day for all the transportation services.

When packing for Hamburg, think of one element: water. Hamburg's weather all year around is generally a succession of variations on precipitation. In November through February it is foggy and rainy; blustery and rainy from March through May; drizzly and on the humid side from June through August; then sunny with intermittent showers in September and October. So much for the four seasons. Sometimes, however, there is glorious sunshine (pick any month from May through October) and some genuine cold snaps (December through February) when the Aussenalster freezes over. Hamburg's people just shrug about the generally moist climate, borrowing the British maxim to the effect that there is no such thing as poor weather—only the wrong clothing.

Hamburg is one of Germany's foremost bicycling cities, with special paths in many of the downtown and Aussenalster districts. Rentals are available at the tourist information office in the Bieberhaus at the Hauptbahnhof.

From April 1991, Hamburg will be a terminus for Hamburg–Dresden Elbe river cruises on the KD line; the cruises will overnight at various places in East Germany, with land tours available. See Useful Facts (Around Germany) for contact information.

## ACCOMMODATIONS
The telephone area code for Hamburg is 40.

### Downtown
The **Vier Jahreszeiten** (Four Seasons), overlooking the Binnenalster, qualifies as one of the world's hotels of legend. Luxury has its price, of course, but if you can afford it, then go ahead. The hotel ranks second in the world in the *Institutional Investor* hotel survey. It's close to downtown shopping, and its **Restaurant Haerlin**, with a 35,000-bottle wine cellar, is legendary.

Neuer Jungfernstiegg, D-2000 Hamburg 36. Tel: 349-40; Telex: 211629; Fax: 3494602.

Up around the corner is the **Baseler Hof**, several cuts below in price and quality but still an oasis of old-European-style comfort only a few minutes' walk from the downtown attractions. Asking for a room toward the rear of the hotel will mean one without a view, but much quieter than one facing the busy street.

Esplanade 11, D-2000 Hamburg 36. Tel: 35-90-60; Telex: 2163707; Fax: 35906918.

Two hotels more centrally located for shopping and downtown attractions, and also ranking high in terms of luxury and comfort, are the **Ramada Renaissance** (Grosse Bleichen, D-2000 Hamburg 36; Tel: 34-91-80; Telex: 2162983; Fax: 34918431) and the **Hamburg Marriott** (ABC Strasse 52, D-2000 Hamburg 36; Tel: 350-50; Telex: 2165871). Both offer the full range of services to be expected from those well-known chains. A possible drawback to both is that they feel less spacious, having been built into the already crowded downtown area. Traffic is lively, too.

### Around the Alster

Hamburg's one high-rise hotel, the **SAS Plaza Hotel**, is not on the Aussenalster, but if you get a room high up on the east side it will seem like it, with panoramic views of the lake unsurpassed by any other hotel. In some ways it offers the best of two worlds: walking distance both to downtown and to the neighborhoods on the west side of the lake. If you arrive by train you can get off at the Dammtor station, only a few minutes' walk away.

Marseiller Strasse 2, D-2000 Hamburg 36. Tel: 350-20; Telex: 214400; Fax: 35023333.

The new luxury-class **Elysée Palast**, a few blocks north, is at the southern edge of the quieter Rotherbaum neighborhood and is within walking distance of the Hamburg university district.

Rothenbaumchaussee 10, D-2000 Hamburg 13. Tel: 41-41-20; Telex: 212455; Fax: 41412733.

Clean and comfortable accommodations are offered nearby in the **Haus Heimhude**, located on a quiet tree-lined street surrounded by the Rotherbaum neighborhood's turn-of-the-century patrician town houses, one of which this pension-style house once was.

Heimhuder Strasse 16, D-2000 Hamburg 13.; Tel: 44-27-21.

Close to the western shores of the Aussenalster is the **Inter-Continental**. Most of the rooms offer panoramic views of the lake, and a gambling casino is located on the premises. Within a short walking distance from the nightlife neighborhood of Pöseldorf, in Rotherbaum, the Inter-Continental is a place to see Hamburg's trendy fun-seekers.

Fontenay 10, D-2000 Hamburg 36; Tel: 41-41-50; Telex: 211099; Fax: 41415186.

Another peaceful tree-lined side street a few blocks north is the setting for the refined **Garden Hotels Pöseldorf**, two recent efforts to fill a gap in the near-luxury category in Hamburg's hotel landscape. Just around the block from the

Pöseldorf nightlife scene, the two houses (both under the same management) are also just a few minutes' walk from the lake.

Magdelenenstrasse 60, D-2000 Hamburg 13; Tel: 44-99-58; Telex: 212621; Fax: 449958.

A few blocks northwest of the northern tip of the lake, located in the gracious turn-of-the-century neighborhoods of Harvestehude and Eppendorf, are two smaller, quieter accommodations. The **Pension am Nonnenstieg** (Nonnenstieg 11, D-2000 Hamburg 13; Tel: 47-38-69) is midway between the lake and the popular shopping street of Eppendorfer Baum. The **Hotel Smolka** (Isestrasse 98, D-2000 Hamburg 13; Tel: 47-50-57; Telex: 215275; Fax: 473008) is just a block away. Both are only a few minutes from the Klosterstern U-Bahn (U-1 line) station.

On the eastern shore of the Aussenalster three hotels that face the lake offer a variety of nearby attractions. The **Atlantic-Hotel Kempinski,** Hamburg's second most prestigious abode after the Vier Jahreszeiten, offers all the comforts of a traditional grand-style hotel, and its **Atlantic Grill** restaurant. Out front on the lake is a landing for the canal boats that ply the Alster. Just behind this noble hotel is the seedy but colorful St. Georg district.

An der Alster 72–79, D-2000 Hamburg 1. Tel: 288-80; Telex: 2163297; Fax: 247129.

A few hundred yards farther north are the **Hotel Prem** (An der Alster 9, D-2000 Hamburg 1; Tel: 24-54-54) and, nearby, the **Hotel Bellevue** (An der Alster 14, D-2000 Hamburg 1; Tel: 24-80-11; Telex: 2162929). Both are smaller and simpler than the luxury-class hotels, yet (the Prem in particular) offer their guests individualized attention. A lakeside front room in either of these hotels will provide a nice view of the Alster, but they also overlook the busy lakefront street An der Alster. (For their excellent restaurants, see Dining, below.)

Also in the St. Georg district, and right across the street from the Hauptbahnhof, is the **Europäischer Hof**, which provides first-rate services and accommodations often used by out-of-town theatergoers; the city's main stage, the Deutsches Schauspielhaus, is a few doors away.

Kirchenallee 45, D-2000 Hamburg 1. Tel: 24-82-48.

### Elbe River Hotels

For those whose fascination with the busy Hamburg harbor goes so far as wanting to stay close by, the **Hotel Hafen Hamburg,** a converted former seamen's mission on a hillside near the St. Pauli Landungsbrücken, is the place to be.

Seewartenstrasse 9, D-2000 Hamburg 11. Tel: 31-11-30;
Telex: 2161319; Fax: 3192736.

Out in Blankenese, the best address on the Elbe is the
quiet, charming **Strandhotel**. It is very small—only 16
rooms—so a telephone call in advance to confirm a reservation is a must.

Strandweg 13, D-2000 Hamburg 55. Tel: 86-13-44; Fax:
864936.

## DINING

Hamburg's restaurant scene is a mixture of quantity, diversity, and a generous bit of quality. With 4,000 restaurants,
Hamburg is not a town where a visitor is likely to go hungry;
and, reflecting the city's internationalism in the world of
commerce, virtually every nation on the globe is represented in one way or another in Hamburg's eateries.

As might be expected, given Hamburg's seafaring tradition, fish plays a big role in the indigenous cuisine, and most
of the top restaurants offer traditional German dishes as
well. To the outsider, some of Hamburg's self-criticism regarding its restaurants seems too severe. A handful of its
eating establishments have won acclaim beyond Germany's
borders.

One of those is the **Restaurant Haerlin** in the Vier
Jahreszeiten. Like the hotel, the restaurant is a haven of luxury,
where service and food compete for accolades. The menu is a
balance of fish, fowl, and meat dishes in a variety of presentations. Closed Sunday and holidays. Neuer Jungfernstieg 9–14.
Tel: 349-41.

Down on the Elbe waterside, where fishing boats come in
by day and prostitutes ply their trade at night, is what is
widely regarded as Hamburg's best seafood place, the
**Fischereihafen-Restaurant Hamburg**. Guests start with a
crabmeat soup, then usually proceed to filet of red flounder,
one of the house's main specialties, served with a choice of
French and German wines that are just affordable. Grosse
Elbstrasse 143, in Altona. Tel: 38-18-16.

The **Historischer Gasthof Anno 1750** lets you enjoy both
Old World charm (at modern-day expense-account prices)
and a well-rounded, top-quality menu that includes liver
dumpling soup, herring dishes, steak, and filet of pork,
served with salads and ample helpings of fried potatoes. The
beer is brewed on the premises. Closed Sunday. Ost–West-
Strasse 47. Tel: 33-00-70.

A restaurant whose name needs no translating for us, the
**Old Commercial Room**, located across the street to the west

of St. Michael's church, looks and feels like the captain's quarters of an 18th-century sailing vessel. It lays claim to serving the best *Labskaus,* a local dish that consists of corned beef, herring, pickles, and mashed potatoes, topped with a fried egg. Guests usually start with the *Aalsuppe* (eel soup). Englischeplanke 10. Tel: 36-63-19.

A few blocks away, at **Zum Alten Rathaus**, diners who love herring are in 17th heaven: The restaurant offers herring dishes served in 17 different sauces. Sweet-and-sour roast goose is another specialty, as are its rice dishes. Closed Sunday. Börsenbrücke 10. Tel: 36-75-70.

Those searching for Hamburg's top restaurant (and willing to pay handsomely) will head west on the Elbchaussee toward Blankenese to **Landhaus Scherrer**. Among the specialties of chef Heinz Wehmann at this converted 19th-century estate are breaded cod in tarragon sauce served with sauerkraut, stuffed kohlrabi served with lobster, and asparagus in a vermouth sauce. Closed Sunday. Elbchaussee 130. Tel: 880-13-25.

Farther out on the Elbchaussee is another popular restaurant, **Jacob**, which has been in business since 1791. Perched high overlooking the Elbe, Jacob specializes in lobster and other seafood dishes, and is known for having one of Hamburg's best selections of wines. Elbchaussee 401. Tel: 82-93-52.

Outside of downtown Hamburg, but not so far out as the Elbchaussee, are two well-established Eppendorf-district restaurants, best reached by taking the U-1 subway to the Hudtwalkerstrasse stop and then walking that same street over the bridge toward the St. Johannis church. One is **Fish Sellmer**, which has established itself as one of the city's best fish restaurants at very reasonable prices (Ludolfstrasse 50; Tel: 47-30-57). Across the street is the smaller, equally popular **Brahmsstuben**, with its 19th-century bourgeois decor, which specializes in traditional German dishes (Ludolfstrasse 43; Tel: 47-87-17).

Hamburg's most "in" restaurant among the trendy set is the **Mühlenkämper Fährhaus** (on the Alster boat line), which specializes in herring, risotto, and beef tenderloin dishes—at very up-market prices. Hans-Henny-Jahnn-Weg 1; Tel: 220-69-34.

Also on the eastern shore of the Aussenalster are the restaurants of the two small hotels, the Prem and the Bellevue. **La Mer**, in the Prem, specializes in fish (An der Alster 9; Tel: 24-17-26); the cozy **Pilsener Urquell-Stuben**, in the Bellevue, offers top-rate traditional German dishes, washed down by the famous Czechoslovak beer that the restaurant's name bears. An der Alster 14. Tel: 24-80-11.

## NIGHTLIFE

With the possible exception of West Berlin, no German city can match the diversity and sheer range of Hamburg's night-time entertainment. As one popular song notes, "in Hamburg the nights are long," because the partying can go on until the dawn. The variety is overwhelming. From Puccini at the Staatsoper to punk rock at any number of live music clubs, from glittering Postmodern discothèques to 1940s-style gin 'n' jazz dives, from musicals to bawdy live-sex shows, Hamburg's night action bubbles with life and excitement.

As your tour of Hamburg's various districts has already confirmed, the action in this city is not confined to the downtown district area, but is spread around St. Pauli and around the Aussenalster, St. Georg, Rotherbaum, Harveste-hude, Winterhude, and Uhlenhorst. In general, the "serious" artistic entertainment (operas, concerts) is located in the downtown area, while lighter entertainment is to be found elsewhere. The following is a sampling of highlights in what Hamburg citizens call *die Szene,* or "the scene."

### Discothèques

The international set meets at the **Blauer Satellit**, atop the SAS Plaza Hotel, glittering like the lights of the city 26 floors below (open till 4:00 A.M.; Tel: 350-20). On the alternative, low-life side, the **Madhouse** (Valentinskamp 46; Tel: 34-41-93) will blow out your eardrums with its sound system, and the dance floor is crowded with all manner of interplanetary visitors.

### Live Music Clubs

Hamburg's live-music scene is experiencing a revival, with most of the emphasis on rock music and jazz, mostly Dixie-land. Some places offer both, such as the **Fabrik** in Altona (Barnerstrasse 36; Tel: 39-15-65), a former factory converted into a smoky concert hall frequented by Hamburg's leftist/intellectual community. Top U.S. and European artists regularly appear here, the one place in town where the entire spectrum of jazz, not just Dixie, is played.

The most popular Dixieland place is the **Cotton Club**, just off the downtown area's Grossneumarkt (Alter Steinweg 10; Tel: 34-38-78).

Other clubs with a variety of Dixieland and small jazz combos are **Birdland**, bordering on the Eppendorf neighborhood (Gärtnerstrasse 122; Tel: 40-52-77), and **Onkel Pö**, not far away (Henriettenweg 11; Tel: 40-43-96). Across town, on the other side of the Alster lake in the Uhlenhorst district, a good tip is **Dennis' Swing Club**, where Dennis Busby, an expatriate American, has been entertaining people at his piano for more than 20 years. The action usually doesn't get going until around midnight, and, with any luck, you'll catch a wee-hours jam session involving top-name musicians who have already done their gigs at other clubs (Papenhuder Strasse 25; Tel: 229-91-92).

Rock music fans also have a variety of places to choose from. The Fabrik, described above, offers both jazz and rock, so it's best to check first. Among the places that feature solely rock groups, one of the most popular, in the university district of Rotherbaum, is **Logo** (Grindelallee 5; Tel: 410-56-58). Another, near the Hauptbahnhof, is **Markthalle**, a flower market hall converted into a rock music center (Klosterwall 9–12; Tel: 33-94-91).

In St. Pauli, both jazz and rock music await you at clubs on two parallel streets north of the Reeperbahn rapid-transit train station: the Kleine Freiheit and the Grosse Freiheit. The latter street, where the Star Club of early Beatles days was located, is making a comeback after some years in the doldrums (the Star Club burned down). The closest you'll come to the Beatles' turf is **Grosse Freiheit 36** (same address, Tel: 319-36-49), which stands across the street from the former Star Club. Rock music is the main fare here, as well as in the basement called **Kaiserkeller**, where the Beatles sometimes played. At **Blockhütte**, meanwhile, you might catch anything—jazz, rock, or country (Grosse Freiheit 64; Tel: 31-08-01). A block away, jazz awaits fans at **Jimmy's Music Treff** (Kleine Freiheit 42; Tel: 319-11-19).

### Shows

Probably the most popular show in town is the **Hansa Theater** (Steindamm 17; Tel: 24-14-14), which offers an old-fashioned variety mixture of song and dance, juggling acts, sword swallowers, you name it.

Fun, and naughtily entertaining, are Hamburg's two popular transvestite shows. One is **Black Market**, in the Winterhude neighborhood (Mühlenkamp 43; Tel: 279-78-37); the better known is **Pulverfass** (Powder Keg), in the St. Georg district (Pulverteich 12; Tel: 24-97-91).

A club offering a little of everything, including audience participation, is **Schmidt** (Spielbudenplatz; Tel: 31-48-04), near the Reeperbahn.

If your German is good enough and you like political satire, you'll enjoy **Mon Marthe,** in the Eppendorf district, featuring local Hamburg cabaret artists as well as acts from around Germany (Tarpenbekstrasse 65; Tel: 47-54-02).

## Dancing

A review of Hamburg's nightlife is not complete without mentioning one popular institution: **Café Keese,** an old-fashioned dance hall where, under the motto "Ball Paradox," the dancing to live orchestra music is ladies' choice. Coats and ties are required for men, dresses for ladies. Once each hour, the men can choose dance partners (Reeperbahn 19; Tel: 31-08-05).

## SHOPS AND SHOPPING

A visitor could spend an entire day in Hamburg's downtown shopping area and not cover even half of everything there is to see. Hamburg is Germany's leader in creating the labyrinthine *Einkaufspassagen* (shopping arcades) a development attributable in part to mercantile showmanship and in part to Hamburg's often inclement weather. The arcades, some of the more popular of which draw up to 20,000 visitors per day, generally feature the predictable international boutiques and brand names, and have all but supplanted any authentic local Hamburg shops. There are nine arcades in the areas just around the southern part of the Binnenalster.

A block west of the Binnenalster is the **Gänsemarkt-passage,** which links the Colonnaden with the Gänsemarkt. Across that square, on the ABC Strasse, is the **Gerhofpassage,** which leads toward the Poststrasse, where the next arcade, the **Hanse-Viertel,** the largest of all the arcades, is located. Emerging from that on the Grosse Bleichen Strasse, you have a choice of two arcades—the **Alte Post** and the **Kauf-mannshaus.** There's the small **Galleria** on the Neuer Wall, while two other arcades can be entered from Jungfernstieg: the **Hamburger Hof** and the **Alsterarkaden.** Finally, a few blocks east of the lake, is the **Landesbank Galerie,** at the Gerhard-Hauptmann-Platz.

In addition to the arcades, there are the two chief *Fussgängerzonen,* (pedestrian zones): the **Colonnaden,** west of the lake, and the **Spitalerstrasse,** on the east side, which branches off at the Gerhard-Hauptmann-Platz from the Mönckebergstrasse.

A romantic attraction in Hamburg's shopping scene are the weekday outdoor markets, where small grocers and merchants set up booths in the customers' neighborhoods.

Two worth seeing are on the **Turmweg** in the Rotherbaum neighborhood (at the U-1 station Hallerstrasse) on Thursday, and the **Isestrasse** in the Eppendorf district (at the U-3 station Eppendorfer Baum) on Tuesday and Friday. They start closing down around 2:00 P.M. to clear the way for the afternoon rush-hour traffic.

# LÜBECK

Lübeck, once known as the Queen of the Hanseatic League, is a fine old city of red brick and spires and towers on the river Trave near the Baltic coast of Schleswig-Holstein, 65 km (40 miles) northeast of Hamburg via the Autobahn. About one fifth of Lübeck's historic Altstadt was destroyed in an air raid in 1942, but it still has more intact buildings from the 13th to 15th centuries than all other northern German cities combined. Some 1,000 of the old town's buildings are protected historical sites—Lübeck dates from the 12th century—and UNESCO has placed the city on its World Heritage list of international monuments along with bigger cities like Florence, Amsterdam, and Leningrad.

Lübeck is still an important maritime trading center, with a population of about 225,000—swelled by an influx of more than 90,000 refugees from Germany's eastern territories in 1945—and is West Germany's biggest port on the Baltic. The Lübeck area, with excellent sea links for travellers to Scandinavia and connected by canal to the Elbe river (and via that busy waterway past Hamburg to the North Sea), is also a center for heavy industry. The city's medical university, founded in 1973, is now an important research, teaching, and medical-care center. Lübeck is also recognized as the leading city in Schleswig-Holstein—the area between the Elbe and the Danish border—for its wide range of cultural attractions.

The charming historical character of the city—which began as a trading settlement in 1143, was destroyed by fire in 1157, and was refounded by Saxony's Duke Henry the Lion in 1159—is what draws most visitors. Lübeck's waterbound Altstadt, situated on an island, offers fascinating walks through its past, enshrined in its Medieval Rathaus and Markt; its Dom (cathedral), Marienkirche (Church of St. Mary), and other churches; its 15th-century twin-towered Holstentor (Holsten Gate)—Lübeck's emblem, which is also depicted on West Germany's DM 50 bill—and its Burgtor (Castle Gate); its six old *Salzspeicher* (salt warehouses); its charming old red-brick gabled houses on narrow cobblestone streets and alleys; and its two most famous and historic restaurants: the elegant and formal Schabbelhaus, in two Renaissance houses, and the Haus der Schiffergesellschaft (Seamen's Guild House), built in 1535, which belongs to 49 sea captains and offers hearty traditional sailor's dishes.

The home town of Nobel Prize winner Thomas Mann—his *Buddenbrooks* is required reading before a trip to Lübeck— the city is also well known for its Musikhochschule (Academy of Music), which plays a leading role in Schleswig-Holstein's annual summer music festival featuring classical-music concerts in towns throughout the state; for its museums, two of which show how local people lived up to the 19th century; and for its marzipan, its red wine (Rotspon), its many good cafés and restaurants, and its great variety of shopping.

The city also offers enticing day trips to Travemünde, Lübeck's big freight and Scandinavian ferry-boat port and lively beach resort on the Baltic only 20 km (12.5 miles) to the north; and to Lüneburg, the old Hanseatic League salt-producing town dating from 1200, about 100 km (62.5 miles) to the south, whose shipments of the "white gold" to Lübeck helped secure for it the leadership of the Hanseatic League in the mid-14th century. Lüneburg, which also has a historic town hall and market place, as well as interesting old churches and houses, is a good base for exploring the Lüneburg heath, with vast carpets of heather that blossom in August.

## MAJOR INTEREST

Rathaus and Markt
Buddenbrookhaus (birthplace of Thomas Mann)
Schabbelhaus museum and restaurant
Burgtor and Holstentor (old fortified gates)
16th–18th-century salt warehouses (Salzspeicher)
Füchtingshof and other Baroque almshouses
Heiligen-Geist-Hospital (Medieval hospice)
Schiffergesellschaft (historic seamen's restaurant-
    tavern)
Dom and Marienkirche
Altarpiece collection in the St. Annen Museum
Behnhaus (19th–20th-century painting)

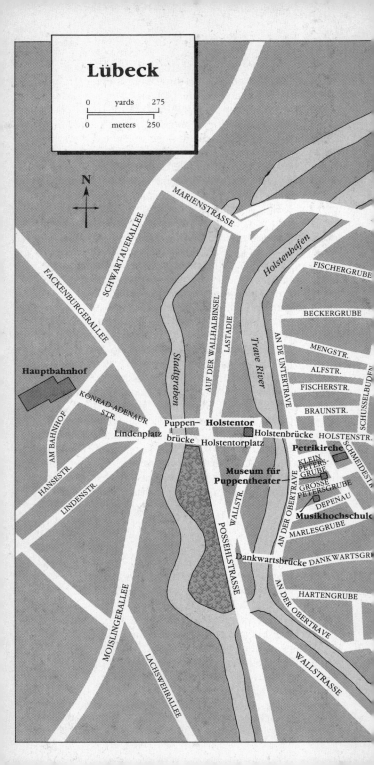

Katherinenkirche
Marzipan at Café Niederregger

Day trips to Travemünde and Lüneburg

Lübeck's compact **Altstadt**, the center of the traveller's attention, stands on an oval-shaped island only a little over a mile
long (north–south) and less than a mile wide (east–west)
that is girted by a ring road that zigzags now and again and
changes its name several times on its route around the inner
town. This island, between the Trave and Wakenitz rivers, is
where the city began as a trading settlement. Eight bridges
across the encircling, moatlike Trave river and Klughafen
waterways connect the old town with greater Lübeck; only
about 12,000 of Lübeck's residents live on the island.

The Rathaus, Markt, and Marienkirche are next to each
other roughly at the center of the old town, surrounded by
shopping streets, with the Breite Strasse, the pedestrian
main shopping street, running north–south past them on
their eastern side. The Königstrasse runs north–south a
block east of the Breite Strasse.

At the northern end of the Königstrasse is the Heiligen-
Geist-Hospital, on the Kobergplatz, and a few blocks north is
the Burgtor gate, at the top of the island. The Holstentor, the
better-known old fortified gate, is at the western side of the
island, toward the main railway station on the mainland. The
cathedral is at the island's southern tip.

One of the city's three tourist information offices is located
on the north side of the Markt (Tel: 451-122-81-06). The other
two offices are at Beckergrube 95, three blocks west of the
Markt (Tel: 451-122-81-09), and at the Hauptbahnhof, or main
railroad station (Tel: 451-723-00), at the western end of the
Konrad-Adenauer-Strasse, on the "mainland" little more than
half a mile west of the Markt across the Puppenbrücke, and to
the west of the landmark Holstentor. (The Puppenbrücke, or
Dolls' Bridge, was given its name by irreverent local folk
because of its seven stone figures of Classical gods and
goddesses.)

The tourist office offers a two-hour guided walking tour of
the Altstadt, well worth taking for initial orientation before
exploring the town on your own. The tour starts outside the
Markt tourist office daily in summer months at 11:00 A.M. and
2:00 P.M., and at 11:00 A.M. on Sunday and public holidays.
The tour is in German, but the guides are usually happy to
explain the main points in English. Individual tours can be
arranged in any of ten languages, and to focus on such

special interests as churches, museums, or Thomas Mann. The tourist office has a good, free booklet in English with maps for do-it-yourself tours, outlining three walks lasting from one to four hours. The longest tour includes visits to seven museums.

Several operators run river boat trips around the town or the port from piers on the north and south sides of the Holstentorbrücke on the east bank of the Obertrave, as well as just north of the bridge on the west bank of the river.

## The Markt and the Rathaus

Whether you are guided or alone, the Markt and the Rathaus, a bit west of the exact center of the island Altstadt, are good starting points for discovering Lübeck on foot. The spacious **Marktplatz** is filled every Monday and Thursday by colorful stalls selling meat, fruit, vegetables, cheese, bread, and handicrafts. In December, the square is given over to a big daily Christmas market of sweets, cakes, and other goodies.

The foundation stone of the multi-winged **Rathaus**, which stands on the north and east sides of the Markt above attractive brick arcades that allow easy access between the north side of the market place and the pedestrian precinct of the Breite Strasse (see below), was laid in 1230. The present-day building is a mixture of Gothic and Renaissance, with high red-brick walls decorated with black glazed-brick courses and round panels emblazoned with coats-of-arms, and topped by slim turrets. Its south-facing wall, built in 1435, is pierced by two large vent holes to allow passage for the keen Baltic wind that often makes walking around Lübeck a bracing experience. The town hall's main entrance on the Breite Strasse has a pointed arch made of green glazed bricks that are believed to date from 1350. Circular bronze fittings on the door wings show the Kaiser surrounded by seven electors. One of the fittings is a 14th-century Gothic original, the other a cast copy. At the front of the building is also a splendid Dutch Renaissance stone staircase built by Tönnies Evers the Elder, completed in 1594.

The Rathaus is one of Germany's oldest and most attractive town halls. Its small entrance hall is heavy modern Gothic Revival, dominated by black glazed-brick arches built in 1887, but the furnishings and decorations of its big audience hall on its ground floor, the former Hanseatic high court, are pure Rococo, dating from 1754 to 1761. Allegorical paintings by Stefano Torelli depict the liberal arts, trade, freedom, mercy, harmony, industry and abundance, vigilance, intelligence, moderation, and discretion. A tall 18th-century iron stove with a decorative brass fretwork screen was the only heat source for the hall—which is now used for receptions, honors awards, and concerts—until 1963. People tried by the court used to leave it by one of two side-by-side doors, depending upon the court's verdict. Those acquitted exited left; those found guilty and sentenced to jail or execution went to their fate by the right-hand door. Both doors have stone steps; the right-hand step is worn down much more than its partner. The 49 members of Lübeck's Bürgerschaft, or Citizenry, as the city council is called, meet in the more modest, wood-paneled Bürgerschaftsaal.

Underneath the Rathaus at the north side of the Markt is the informal and spacious **Ratskeller** restaurant, which serves a wide range of meat, fish, and vegetarian dishes at very reasonable prices. Try the *Labskaus,* a traditional seaman's meal of potato and corned beef mashed together with a fried egg on top, garnished with fresh salt herring and pickles. Another typical local meal is pork and cabbage. The Ratskeller is also known for its *Holstein Ente* (duck) with apple slices. The house brews its own beer, known as "Lübsch," a hearty, yeast-clouded drink with a good head of foam rather like a Pils. Resident brewer Eike Buchholz is happy to let visitors watch him at work.

Try a glass of Lübeck's Rotspon, French red wine from Bordeaux that the city has been importing since the 13th century. French officers of Napoleon's army, which occupied Lübeck in 1806, found that Bordeaux wines stored in the city's cellars tasted much better than the same wines at home. An explanation has never been found, but it is believed that Lübeck's climate and the temperature in its wine cellars has an improving effect on the wines. The word *Rotspon* comes from the north German dialect *Span,* which means a wooden chip, referring to the wooden casks in which red wine was originally stored.

After visiting the Rathaus, you might walk along the bustling **Breite Strasse**, with its many stores selling everything from groceries to electronic goods and musical instruments to fashion clothing, on its way north to the Marienkirche. You might also take a coffee break at the big **Café Niederegger**, on the Breite Strasse opposite the Rathaus. The café was founded in 1806 by Johannes Niederegger, whose firm is now the major producer of the marzipan for which Lübeck is internationally known, employing a staff of 600 to make about 30 tons of the sweet stuff every day and dispatch it around the world.

Local legend has it that Lübeck marzipan was created in 1407 during a famine, when there was no grain available for making bread; the city fathers are said to have told bakers to make bread out of almonds. Racks of marzipan-to-go in all shapes and sizes, from pigs and clowns to floral arrangements and baskets of fruit, fill the entrance hall of the café, where half-a-dozen assistants are constantly busy in summer serving a seemingly never-ending line of visitors. The light and airy café proper at the rear is also always packed in the tourist season, but the waitresses are nimble. Although marzipan cake is (of course) the house specialty, there are plenty of other mouth-watering goodies on offer.

# The Marienkirche Area

The nearby 14th-century **Marienkirche**, just north of the Rathaus, is Lübeck's most outstanding example of brick Gothic and was the model for many other churches in the Baltic area. Built over a span of 100 years by citizens who aimed to outdo the city's cathedral (see below), the Marienkirche ended up being Germany's third-largest church, with a 120-foot-high central nave and the highest brick vaulting in the world. The ambitious townspeople built the church's twin towers to a height of 406 feet, which was 32.5 feet taller than the cathedral's two towers. The church was badly damaged in the 1942 bombings. Its bells crashed down and embedded themselves in the stone floor of its south tower—in which state they have been left, as a reminder and warning of the horrors of war.

A beautiful astronomical clock built in 1566 was also destroyed. It was replaced with a faithful copy that gives a parade of figures every day at noon. The church, where the great Baroque organist Dietrich Buxtehude (1637–1707) played for almost 40 years and counted Handel and Johann Sebastian Bach among his pupils, has the largest mechanical organ in the world (8,512 pipes and 101 stops), built by Lübeck craftsmen in 1968. Like most other big churches in the city, the Marienkirche stages superb organ concerts at various times in the summer and fall. Every day during summer there is at least one organ concert in one of the churches. Ask at a tourist office for the current schedules.

The **Mengstrasse**, a narrow cobblestone street of handsome gabled merchants' houses on the north side of the

Marienkirche (through the arcade of the 15th-century Kanz-
leigebäude, the former Rathaus chancellery), is known not
just for its Schabbelhaus restaurant. At number 4, on the
northern side of the street just west of the Breite Strasse, is
the **Buddenbrookhaus**, which was once the property of
Thomas Mann's family of leading merchants. Mann (1875–
1955), winner of the 1929 Nobel Prize for Literature, was
born in the house and made it world-renowned with his
novel *Buddenbrooks*. Lübeck's most famous son, he was
awarded the honorary freedom of the city in the year of his
death. The 13th-century house was rebuilt in 1758 and was
almost completely destroyed during World War II, but its
façade survived. Now occupied by a bank, the house is one
of the town's major tourist attractions.

The **Schabbelhaus** restaurant, a short walk to the west of
the Buddenbrookhaus at Mengstrasse 48–50, owes its name
to a wealthy master baker and confectioner named Heinrich
Schabbel, who bequeathed 125,000 goldmarks to the city on
condition that it establish a museum for Lübeck antiquities.
The city bought a patrician house at Mengstrasse 36 and
filled it with valuable furniture. Later, they also installed a
wine tavern that became a popular meeting place. The
house was bombed in the 1942 air raid, and postwar reconstruction was not possible. But the Schabbelhaus idea survived, and in the 1950s the city bought the present two
houses, while the local merchants' association raised the
money for their restoration.

The new Schabbelhaus was equipped with antique furniture from old merchants' houses and on loan from Lübeck's
municipal museum. The stylish restaurant, which serves
regional and international dishes, can seat up to 200 in its
various rooms and is a favorite lunch spot for local businessmen and visiting state politicians from Kiel. Supper is served
until 11:00 P.M.; the restaurant is closed Sundays. Reservations are recommended; Tel: (451) 750-51.

**Das Kleine Restaurant**, to the west along the Trave at An
der Untertrave 39, part of the ring road, is in a 300-year-old
red-brick building with Renaissance stepped gables and a
rustic interior decor of dark-brown ceiling beams and light
oak furniture. The restaurant offers refined regional specialties such as terrine of duck with a honey and pepper sauce,
and delicate fish dishes such as salmon and sole. A wide
choice of German and French wines is available. Reservations recommended; Tel: (451) 70-59-59. Closed Saturday
evening and Sunday. Another good restaurant, the **Wullen-
wever**, at Beckergrube 71, three blocks northwest of the

Markt, is in a 400-year-old former brewery. It also offers regional dishes, especially fish, and a choice of 150 wines. Reservations; Tel: (451) 70-43-33.

If you prefer to stay at a quiet, informal, well-located hotel in the center of the old town, the 50-room **Alter Speicher**, the biggest and most modern hotel in the Altstadt, is also on the Beckergrube, in two neighboring buildings. One is a faithful copy of a former gabled warehouse on the site that burned down in 1980. The new building was completed in 1989. Parts of the less attractive, boxlike building next door date from the 12th century. The hotel lives up to its claim of providing first-class accommodation and service at "civil" prices. It has a bar and a cozy pub named **Spökenkieker** (old Northern German dialect for a fortune-teller who is not to be taken seriously), and a rustic **Winzereck** (Vintner's Corner), a good restaurant serving generous portions of regional dishes, with a summer-garden café for light snacks. You can use the two saunas, solarium, and fitness room for an additional charge.

The **Füchtingshof**, the largest and most attractive of Lübeck's several almshouses, built by 17th-century city councillor Johann Füchting for the widows of seamen and merchants, is at Glockengiesserstrasse 23, east of the northern end of the Breite Strasse. It has a richly ornamented Baroque portal leading to a peaceful, secluded courtyard with houses still occupied by widows. The city's oldest almshouses are also on this street: the **Glandorps-Gang** (number 41) and the **Glandorps-Hof** (numbers 49–51), built in 1612 for the widows of merchants and craftsmen. Another old almshouse worth seeing is the **Von Höveln Gang**, dating from 1792, at Wahmstrasse 73–77, one block east of the Markt. The passage, prettily decorated with shrubs and potted plants, is lined with tiny cabinlike rooms.

# The Heiligen-Geist-Hospital Area

The **Heiligen-Geist-Hospital**, founded by some rich and philanthropic local citizens in 1230 and completed 60 years later, is north of the Glockengiesserstrasse on the Königstrasse (which parallels the Breite Strasse to the east). You can recognize it by its four slender turret spires and its spired belfry. The hospice, one of the oldest social institutions in Europe as well as one of the most important monumental building works in the Middle Ages, was converted to a shelter for elderly men and women in the early 19th century, when rows of 130 small wooden cabins with no ceilings were built in its big hall. The cabins, now empty but still intact, were occupied until 1970, when other parts of the building were made into a modern old people's home. The cabins come to life again each Christmas, however, when they are used as stalls for an arts-and-crafts market.

The building's huge vaults were used for centuries to store a wide variety of goods, but are now occupied by an excellent wine restaurant named, in a burst of imagination, **Historischer Weinkeller unter dem Heiligen-Geist-Hospital**. The restaurant has two dining areas: the informal Bürger-keller, serving regional dishes, and the more formal Wein-keller, with silver table service and haute cuisine. The wines come from the best vineyards in Europe, and the house also has some vintages from California. Both restaurants are open for lunch and supper every day except Tuesday (until 1:00 A.M., but cold dishes only after 11:00 P.M.). Reservations are recommended; Tel: (451) 762-34.

At this point in your walk you might be in time to enjoy a good—and "different"—lunch in the **Schiffergesellschaft**, opposite the Heiligen-Geist-Hospital to the west across the Koberg square. The house, with narrowly stepped gables, is one of Lübeck's most beautiful buildings, with a classic, big tavern-restaurant up front and more elegant dining rooms toward the rear. An original building on the site was first chronicled in 1292; the Society of Skippers acquired it in 1535, after which they pulled it down and built the present house.

The front dining area, a big hall that was once the skippers' convention room, is supported by solid painted wooden beams and carved posts, and is filled with long wooden tables at which guests sit on high-backed oak benches under big models of sailing ships suspended from the high, dimly seen dark-brown ceiling. It's fun—and the food is good, too. Regional specialties and seamen's dishes like those at the Ratskeller, including *Labskaus,* are the feature of the long menu (the prices are higher here). A wide range of beers is available, and the restaurant has a good wine cellar. Reservations are recommended for dinner; Tel: (451) 767-76. Closed Monday.

Besides the many gabled houses on the Glockengiesser-strasse, there are fine examples of smaller houses and tiny passages here, too, leading to *Wohnhöfe* (courtyards) at the back of the houses at the north end of the old town on the Kleine Altefähre, the Engelswisch, and the Engelsgrube, off the waterside An der Untertrave above the Beckergrube. Many of these houses are being restored under an Altstadt renewal program, supported financially by the state and federal governments.

# The North Gate

A short walk north from the hospital across the Koberg and along the Grosse Burgstrasse brings you to the brick **Burgtor** (Castle Gate) and the Burgtorbrücke at the junction of two waterways, the Hansahafen and the Klughafen, the latter a long, narrow harbor on the northeast side of the island. The Burgtor was Lübeck's fortified northern city gate, the original built in 1444. It once guarded a small isthmus—now cut by a canal beween the two harbors—that was once the only means of access to the city by land. The roof dates from 1685; part of the remains of the town ramparts, also from the 17th century, can be seen on the Burgtor's eastern side. The remains of the old wall extend down around the eastern side of the old inner city to the southeastern sector, to the site of the old Mühlentor, at the Mühlenbrücke, and now serve as a long parking lot. Also next to the Burgtor to the east is the old customs house, and next to the gate to the west is the red-brick Burgkloster (monastery) whose origins date from 1227. None of the buildings is open to the public.

# The West Gate

The **Holstentor** lies on the Wallhalbinsel (Wall Peninsula) on the Holstentorplatz, two blocks west of the Markt, on the west side of the short Holstenbrücke (bridge) over the Obertrave river. (The Holstenstrasse runs west from the junction at the lower end of the Markt, of Kohlmarkt and Schüsselbuden, two busy shopping streets.) Built in 1469–1478 by *Ratsbaumeister* (city architect) Heinrich Helstede, the Holstentor, with walls up to 11 feet thick, was once a fortified gate with 30 guns guarding the Holstenhafen (the city's western harbor) and the western entrance to Lübeck. It now houses the local **municipal museum** (closed Monday), whose exhibits include a model of Lübeck as it was in 1650, models of Hanseatic *Kogge,* or cogs (single-sail vessels), as well as Medieval torture instruments. The gate was built on a mound of peat that was unable to withstand its heavy load, so the southern tower subsided slightly, and the gate inclined westward. During following centuries the ground sank more and more, and some of the lowest loopholes are now a couple of feet below the surface. The Holstentor is

Germany's best-recognized old city gate, because it is pictured on the back side of DM 50 bills.

The six old **Salzspeicher** (salt warehouses), which stored consignments from Lüneburg for shipment mainly to Scandinavia, where most of it was used to preserve fish hauls, are next to the ancient gate to the south. The oldest of the buildings, nearest to the Holstentor, dates from 1579, while the next three were built about 1600, and the last two about 1745. The buildings are now occupied by a department store, but their original brick exteriors are intact.

A good view of the Holstentor and the rest of Lübeck's romantic skyline is offered by the **Mövenpick Hotel Lysia**, only two minutes' walk due west of the gate on the Auf der Wallhalbinsel between the Trave and, to the west, the Stadtgraben waterways, and just east of the Puppenbrücke and the railroad station. The quiet 197-room hotel, considered the best in town, is favored by visiting business travellers for its good conference and seminar facilities, and is also popular with well-to-do tourists. Its excellent restaurant offers local specialties, especially fish dishes, as well as an international menu, and its **Duell Pub** has a classic English decor and atmosphere.

A quiet family hotel close to the Holstentor is the medium-priced 54-room **Excelsior**, on the Hansestrasse, at its junction with the Lindenplatz, only a few minutes' walk west of the historic gate.

## South of the Markt

The **Musikhochschule**, which runs an open house for visitors, who may listen to lessons, is situated in a graceful 200-year-old Baroque-style former merchant's house at Grosse Petersgrube 21, three blocks southwest of the Markt. The houses on that street numbered 7–29 offer a fine display of various architectural styles ranging from Gothic to Baroque through Rococo to Neoclassical.

Directly opposite the salt warehouses, on the east bank of the Obertrave not far from the Musikhochschule, is the popular medium-priced 46-room **Hotel Jensen**, whose restaurant offers 40 different fish dishes every day. This quiet family hotel has no bar, but provides a 24-hour front-desk service.

The Romanesque **Dom**, a three-aisle basilica with piers, at the southern end of the island, is the oldest church in Lübeck. It was the Episcopal church of Henry the Lion, who

founded it in 1173 on the site of an earlier wooden church.
A Gothic chancel and choir were added in the 13th–14th
centuries. Its huge Triumphkreuz (triumphal Christ on the
Cross) was completed in 1477 by Lübeck woodcarver Bernt
Notke (1440–1509), the leading master of the Late Gothic in
the Baltic region. The cathedral was badly damaged by
bombs in 1942, and restoration work did not begin on it
until 1960, after the reconstruction of the Marienkirche.

(The Marienkirche and the cathedral account for four of
the seven church spires that are Lübeck's "trademark." Another is atop the 750-year-old Gothic **Petrikirche**, one block
south of the Markt near the junction of Holstenstrasse and
Kohlmarkt. From mid-April to mid-October, an elevator
takes visitors 162 feet up to the top of its tower, which gives a
great bird's-eye view of the Altstadt, especially over the
Holstentor area. The 13th-century **Aegidienkirche**, on the
corner of the Aegidienstrasse and the Schildstrasse, three
blocks east of the Markt, has Lübeck's sixth famous spire.
The church has Gothic wall murals and a choir dating from
1587 that was carved by Tönnies Evers the Younger. The
seventh spire crowns the **Jakobkirche**, the seamen's church
four blocks north of the Markt on the Königstrasse, which
runs parallel to and east of the Breite Strasse. The church
dates from 1227 and has an altar built in 1698 as well as two
historic organs—one of them, built in 1504, is one of the
oldest in Europe. The Jakobkirche also contains a lifeboat
from the ill-fated German four-masted training ship *Pamir*,
which sank in the Atlantic in 1957 with all hands, as a
memorial to her 80 dead.)

The cathedral is mirrored in the waters of the **Mühlenteich**, a large pond within the arms of the Trave river as it
circles around the southern tip of the inner town. One block
east of the cathedral, the pond and the river are crossed by
the Mühlenbrücke southeast to the Mühlentorplatz, a traffic
circle, from which you can take the Hüxtertorallee north
toward the B 75 Autobahn to Travemünde or head south
along the Kronsforder Allee toward Lüneburg.

Only about 650 feet south of Mühlentorplatz, on the
Kronsforder Allee, lies the **Kaiserhof**, a peaceful, friendly,
medium-priced hotel formed out of two attractive former
merchants' villas. The 140-bed hotel offers free use of a
sauna, steam bath, and indoor swimming pool; its solarium
costs extra. Its restaurant has only a limited supper menu,
and closes at 9:00 P.M., but its small bar stays open for as long
as guests want it to. The Kaiserhof has two guesthouses one

block to the south; the rooms are comfortable but rather pedestrian, so ask for a room in the *Haupthaus* (main building).

## Music and Museums in Lübeck

Lübeck's cultural life is a lively one. The city's municipal theaters, a complex of three on the Beckergrube—Das Grosse Haus, the Kammerspiele, and the Experimental Studio—offer programs from drama through musicals to grand opera and symphony concerts. Music lovers can also enjoy many concerts given by lecturers and students at the Academy of Music. The Schleswig-Holstein music festival opens with a concert in the cathedral in June and closes with a grand finale in August, in the Marienkirche.

Lübeck's museums are well known for the quantity and quality of their exhibits. The **St. Annen Museum**, in a former Augustinian convent built in 1502–1515 and after the Reformation turned into an almshouse and then a prison, has been Lübeck's museum for art and the history of art, to about 1800, since 1915. Its prize exhibits are an important altarpiece collection, with work by Bernt Notke and by Hans Memling. The museum, at St.-Annen-Strasse 15, four blocks southeast of the Markt, also holds frequent exhibitions of contemporary art.

Also well worth seeing is the Medieval museum-church, the **Katherinenkirche**, at the corner of the Königstrasse and the Glockengiesserstrasse. The towerless church—a former Franciscan monastery built in 1300–1370, secularized in 1806, and now belonging to the city—is one of the most significant brick churches in northern Germany, and is being restored to its original form. The church roof is an original wooden structure, and the floor is covered by centuries-old tombstones. The side aisles have beautiful Baroque chapels. Noteworthy works of art inside the church are a 1578 *The Raising of Lazarus* by Jacopo Tintoretto and a Late Gothic triumphal cross group. Niches of the church's west façade, on the Königstrasse, contain a figure cycle called *The Community of Saints,* sculpted by Ernst Barlach and Gerhard Marcks.

Lübeck's collection of 19th–20th century paintings, including works by Johann-Friedrich Overbeck, Caspar-David Friedrich, Edvard Munch, Max Liebermann, Lovis Corinth, and Max Beckmann, is displayed at the **Behnhaus**, in one of the city's finest "representative" 18th-century burgher houses at Königstrasse 11. The neighboring **Drägerhaus**, at Königstrasse 9, traces the art and cultural history of middle-class urban life in Lübeck from 1750 to 1914, using displays of contemporary art and artistic objects, furniture, and clothing. A special section devoted to Thomas Mann and his elder brother, Heinrich (also a writer—the famous Marlene Dietrich film *The Blue Angel* was based on one of his books), contains documents and letters connected with their lives and works, including the original manuscript of *Buddenbrooks*.

The **Naturhistorisches Museum** (Natural History Museum), next to the cathedral on its south side overlooking the Mühlenteich, has three floors of exhibits of animals, birds, fish, insects, plants, minerals, rocks, and fossils. Its ethnological collection was based on objects brought home by Hanseatic merchants from journeys often far abroad. The Völkerkundesammlung, a collection of objects of many foreign peoples ranging from gold arm bands through carpets and tapestries to saddles and weapons, is in the **Zeughaus**, next to the cathedral on its north side at Grosser Bauhof 12. The Zeughaus is a fine old building that was constructed in 1594 as a grain store, then used variously as an arsenal and wool store; it is now owned by the city.

Lübeck's privately owned **puppet theater museum**, in three old houses at Kleine Petersgrube 4–6, southwest of the Markt, exhibits almost 2,000 puppets from Europe, Africa, and Asia, especially 19th-century models, in what is claimed to be the largest private collection of its kind in the world. Also displayed are puppet stages, props, posters, and barrel organs. The museum, which gives guided tours in English upon request, also stages daily puppet-theater performances.

Just for fun, you might also visit the privately owned "expedition museum ship" MS *Mississippi*, a former river Elbe lightship, moored on the east side of the Holstenhafen just north of the Holstentor, only two blocks west of the puppet museum. The ship displays curiosities from around the world, including more than 500 stuffed tropical animals and fish, collected by its husband-and-wife owners R. and M. Kasten, on what they say were 42 world voyages and jungle and underwater expeditions.

# DAY TRIP FROM LÜBECK
## Travemünde

Travemünde, founded as a fishing village at the mouth of the river Trave on the Lübecker Bucht (bay) in 1187, is a district of Lübeck only 20 km (12.5 miles) to the northeast via the fast B 75. Travemünde is a lively place that offers something for everyone. First, it is a typical and very popular Baltic coast resort (for fun and for health cure) with a beach of fine, golden sand 4.5 km (2.8 miles) long and dotted with 1,700 municipally owned *Strandkörbe,* wicker beach chairs with upholstered bench seats for two and an adjustable hood that protects from sun, rain, and wind—a German invention. The chairs are rented at DM 10 a day.

Travemünde has a busy nightlife, with plenty of bars and discos and a casino. It is a major shipping port and a gateway to Scandinavia, with huge Baltic ferries running every two hours or so to and from Denmark, Sweden, and Finland, as well as Poland in summer months.

Travemünde's long north–south **Strandpromenade**, with the casino lying about halfway along it; the Nordermole, at the mouth of the Trave; and the Vorderreihe, the town's main street on the west bank of the river, south of the Nordermole, are all lined with shops, cafés, restaurants, and bars and offer agreeable strolls or open-air coffee breaks while you watch the big ferries moving to and from the Skandinavienkai (Scandinavia Quay). The 35-floor tower of the up-market **Maritim Strandhotel**, which dominates the southern end of the beach and is now Travemünde's main landmark, offers vast panoramic views of the town, harbor, and bay from its **Dach Restaurant** (Roof Restaurant), a gourmet establishment serving international dishes with a wide choice of fine wines from the great European vineyards. Australian and Californian wines are also available.

The Maritim as a place to stay is better suited for business travellers with generous expense accounts than for tourists. But Travemünde also has a number of comfortable, quiet, middle-class hotels like the 30-room **Atlantic**, on the Kaiserallee, which runs parallel to the Strandpromenade north of the casino. The hotel does not have a view of the sea, but is very near the beach. A small bar serves snacks until 11.00 P.M.

Travemünde's busy yacht harbor, on the east side of the Trave opposite the Nordermole, stages the internationally known Travemünde Woche regatta at the end of July and beginning of August, an annual event that attracts big-time yachters from around the world. The regatta, which celebrated its centennial in 1989 with stirring maritime events including the Cutty Sark Tall Ships Race, is both a folk festival and a sparkling society gathering. The week ends with a grand fireworks display that lights up Lübeck's seven church spires, to the southwest, which can be seen from the top of the Maritim.

The four-masted sailing-ship *Passat,* the sister ship of the lost *Pamir* (see Lübeck), is moored among the yachts in the Passathafen. Now a stationary youth hostel, she may be visited, reached by a small ferry that runs frequently between the two riverbanks from a pier on the Nordermole, near its junction with the Strandpromenade. Small cruise-boat operators offer trips along the river and around the harbors, and the big ferry lines will take you on a day trip on the Baltic on various days of the week. The tourist office at Strandpromenade 1b has all the details; Tel: (4502) 804-30.

Travemünde has a small salient of land, called **Priwall**, hard against East German territory on the east bank of the Trave. The spot has an excellent and popular beach, and a car and pedestrian ferry makes frequent crossings from the Vorderreihe. The B 75 runs from Lübeck to Travemünde through the typically flat but pleasing Schleswig-Holstein countryside. For a look at what until 1989 was East Germany's Iron Curtain, turn east off the B 75 about 4 km (2.5 miles) north of Lübeck onto country road L 104 and drive about 4 km (2.5 miles) to the old border crossing point at Schlutup.

There are hourly trains from Lübeck's Hauptbahnhof to Travemünde's Strandbahnhof, which lies opposite the casino and is only a short walk west of the beach. There is also a good private bus service (LVG) between Lübeck and Travemünde, running from every 15 minutes during rush hours to every 45 minutes in off-peak periods. The bus (no number) leaves Lübeck from the Holstenhafen opposite the MS *Mississippi.*

# LÜNEBURG

The interesting old salt town of Lüneburg, about 100 km (62.5 miles) south of Lübeck along the Alte Salzstrasse, now the B 207–B 209, lies on the river Ilmenau at the northern edge of the Lüneburg heath. (Lüneburg is also only 36 km/22.5 miles southeast of Hamburg on the B 4.) Founded about 1200, and developed by Henry the Lion, the town garnered great importance from its salt pits, and in the second half of the 14th century it was made a member of the Hanseatic League. Salt was transported to Lübeck by horse and cart and by the Stecknitz canal, which became part of the Trave-Elbe canal in 1900.

Its trade in salt—which in the Middle Ages was the only means of preserving food and was almost worth its weight in gold—made Lüneburg one of the richest towns in Germany.

Salt revenues paid for construction of magnificent public buildings like its Rathaus, on the old Marktplatz, dating from 1230; a cathedral and other impressive churches; and splendid **gabled town houses** that today are almost the only example of Northern German Gothic brick architecture still wholly intact. Strong fortifications were built to guard its riches, including, in places, triple ramparts, as well as a moat, watchtowers, and several town gates.

Lüneburg, now with a population of about 60,000, commemorated the salt that it produced for more than 1,000 years—until 1980—by building the **Deutsches Salzmuseum** at the last saline pit to close, at Sülfmeisterstrasse 1, about five blocks southwest of the Marktplatz. Open daily; guided tours last about one hour.

You should begin a tour of Lüneburg, however, by visiting the **Rathaus** (closed Monday), on the northern side of the town, one of the most attractive Medieval town halls in Northern Germany and the largest preserved Rathaus in the country as a whole. It has a handsome Baroque façade built in 1706–1720, with a large clock and belfry tower in which Meissen porcelain bells ring out the hours, and richly furnished and decorated rooms and halls, enhanced by wall and ceiling murals and stained-glass windows that date from the 14th–16th centuries.

Guided 90-minute walking tours in German start daily, April–October, at 11:00 A.M. at the tourist information office (Tel: 4131-30-95-93 and 322-00), located in the arcade underneath the Rathaus and facing the Marktplatz, where a fruit and vegetable market is held on Wednesday and Saturday. Tours in other languages can be arranged. Daily 90-minute bus tours start at the tourist office at 3:00 P.M., but it's best to go around by foot to soak in the town's historic atmosphere.

The **Lüneburger Heide** (heath) is on the town's southern doorstep. Local tour operators offer day trips to the popular excursion area (at its best in August when the heather blooms) by bus, canal, river boats, and a train called the Heide Express. Details of all trips are available at the tourist office.

The Salzmuseum is only one of five museums in Lüneburg, including the Rathaus, that are well worth visiting if you have the time. The others are: the Museum für das Fürstentum Lüneburg (Museum of the Principality of Lüneburg), at Wandrahmstrasse 10, on the river Ilmenau about six blocks southeast of the Marktplatz; the Brauereimuseum (Brewery Museum), at Heiligengeiststrasse 39, four blocks south of the Marktplatz; and the Ostpreussisches Landesmuseum (East Prussian Culture Museum), at Ritterstrasse 10, one street south of the Heiligengeiststrasse.

If you decide to stay in Lüneburg overnight, **Wellenkamp's Hotel**, a comfortable family establishment in an old red-brick gabled house at Am Sande 9, is recommended for both its rooms and its traditional restaurant. Am Sande is the town's second main square, four blocks south of the Marktplatz, and is lined with very good examples of the town's historic houses. A new hotel, opened in 1989 and built in pleasing harmony with its ancient surroundings, is the medium-priced **Bergström**, on Bei der Lüner Mühle along the banks of the river Ilmenau four blocks east of the Marktplatz, and near the 18th-century Alter Kran (Old Crane), the town's trademark. The hotel's Brasserie restaurant and its Greenhouse café directly on the river have big window walls giving views of half-timbered old warehouses across the narrow waterway.

Lüneburg also has historic red-brick tavern-restaurants, such as the 500-year-old **Kronen Brauhaus**, at Heiligengeiststrasse 39–41, which offers good beer and hearty country meals in rooms with Medieval beams or, in summer, in its beer garden, in a courtyard that also contains an interesting brewery museum.

Trains from Lübeck to Lüneburg run every 45 to 60 minutes, but travelling by car gives the opportunity to stop by the historic and picturesque towns of **Ratzeburg**, on an island a few kilometers west of the B 207 about 32 km (20 miles) south of Lübeck, and **Mölln**, on the B 27 about 40 km (24 miles) south of Lübeck, where Till Eulenspiegel died of the plague in 1350.

# BREMEN

The Hanseatic port city of Bremen, on the Weser river 120 km (75 miles) southwest of Hamburg, has all the charm that you would expect from a town that is more than 1,000 years old, with ancient buildings telling the story of its development over the centuries as a hard-working and determinedly independent community. It is also a lively and bustling city of shipping, commerce and industry, art, museums and theater, good shopping, excellent eating and drinking, green

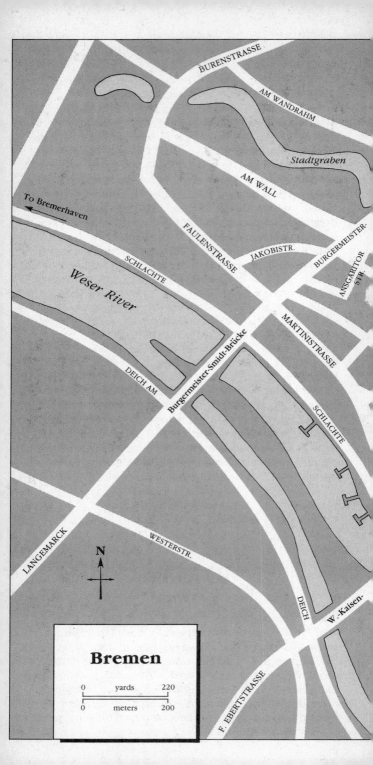

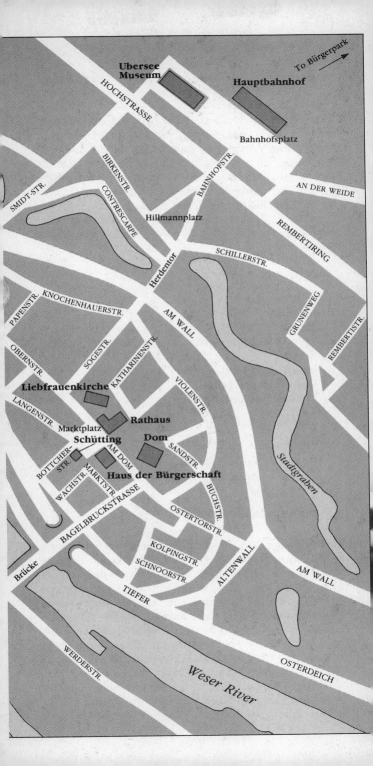

riverbanks and parks—and friendly local people who give
the lie to the cliché that the North Germans are cool and
unapproachable.

The city offers river and harbor boat trips, including an
excursion downriver to the North Sea town of Bremerhaven,
as well as interesting day excursions to the art colony of
Worpswede, for example, on the **Teufelsmoor** (Devil's
Moor) north of Bremen, a lonely land of old peat diggings.
Bremen, the northern terminus of Germany's Märchenstrasse (Fairy Tale Road), is also a good starting point for
exploring the northern part of the route. (Contact the German National Tourist Office for detailed information on this
route.)

### MAJOR INTEREST

St. Peter's Cathedral
Rathaus
Altstadt
15th–18th century "dollhouses" of the Schnoor dis-
    trict
Museums
Weser river and port
Old tavern-restaurants

River excursions

**Bremerhaven**
Deutsches Schiffahrtsmuseum
Open-air museum of 17th-century farmhouses
Zoo am Meer

Excursion to Helgoland

Although more than 100 km (62.5 miles) south of the North
Sea (Bremerhaven is its deep-water port at the mouth of the
Weser), Bremen is very much about ships and their cargoes
from around the world, which still shape the lives and
characters of many of its people. Its port gives work to more
than 40 percent of its population of 545,000. Germany's
oldest maritime city and its second leading port after Hamburg, Bremen is one of the oldest republics still existing in
Europe. Its Altstadt, once walled, is more than 1,000 years
old; its market rights date from 965.

Bremen became a member of the Hanseatic League in
1358 and an Imperial Free City in 1646. The landmark on its
market place, a 30-foot-high stone figure of Roland, a knight

armed with sword and shield, dating from 1404, is its symbol of independence and will for freedom from the rule of princes. Exhibits at the **Focke Museum**, Bremen's state museum for the history of art and civilization at Schwachhauser Heerstrasse 240, trace the city's municipal, ecclesiastical, and maritime history, with many models and pictures of ships as well as displays of bourgeois home decor, porcelain, and costumes.

Together with Bremerhaven, 65 km (40 miles) downstream to the north, which Bremen founded as its deepwater port in 1827 after the Weser had become so silted up that only small boats could navigate the waterway, the city constitutes the smallest West German state. Just over 100 years ago, however, a harbor engineer named Ludwig Franzius solved the silt problem that was strangling Bremen by straightening and narrowing the Weser. The river then flowed faster, washing the silt into the sea and reopening the city to big ships. By that time, unfortunately for Bremen, the port of Bremerhaven had become (and still is) a keen trade competitor with the city that spawned it.

Each of the two ports, among the fastest and most technically advanced in the world, now has its individual specialities: Bremerhaven handles fish, tropical fruits, autos, and containers; Bremen deals mainly with mixed cargoes, especially coffee beans, tobacco, and cotton. Every second cup of coffee drunk in the country comes from Bremen. The internationally known Beck's Beer is also made here; the city is one of the world's biggest tobacco transshipment centers; and it is famous for its spices.

Mercedes-Benz makes cars in Bremen, the aerospace industry carries out major research and development here, and the city is the base of a number of research institutes. With a university strong in high-technology and natural-sciences faculties, Bremen has also become an important center for research projects pursued in close cooperation with industry.

## The Bahnhofsplatz Area

Most of Bremen's compact, oval Altstadt, originally a walled semi-peninsular enclave with the Weser along the south side and the moatlike Stadtgraben along the north, is now a pedestrian zone, and the best introduction to it is the excellent 90-minute guided walking tour offered by the city tourist information office (Tel: 421-30-80-00). The office, well stocked with multilingual maps and booklets, is in a

pavilion on the Bahnhofsplatz, directly opposite the Hauptbahnhof, only a few minutes' walk from the Altstadt to the
northeast. The daily tour, which starts from the office at 2:30
P.M. May through October, is also available in English.

Next to the station to the northwest is Bremen's noted
**Übersee Museum** (Overseas Museum), housing lifelike collections of ethnology and natural and commercial sciences
from around the world, specializing in the South Seas, Australia, South and East Asia, Africa, and the Americas as well as the
Bremen-Weser region. The middle-class hotels **Zur Post** and
**Mercure-Columbus**, on the Bahnhofsplatz, are handy to the
station, the museum, and the tourist office. Behind the station
to the northeast is the big Bürgerpark, where the **Park Hotel**,
one of Bremen's two top establishments, is located. Horse-
drawn carriages tour the park on Sunday at 11:00 A.M. and
Wednesday at 3:00 and 4:00 P.M., leaving from the Mar-
cusbrunnen, near the hotel.

Between the Bahnhofsplatz and the Altstadt to the southwest are the city's other luxury-class hotel, the **Bremen Plaza**,
on the pedestrian Hillmannplatz, and the highly recommended gourmet lunch-only **Grasshoff's Bistro**, at Contres-
carpe 80 (next to the Hillmann-Passage). You will then have
only to cross a moatlike arm of the Weser to get to the Altstadt,
at Am Wall, the northern side of the old semicircular city
fortifications, by the Herdentor bridge at the site of one of
Bremen's eight Medieval gates.

## THE ALTSTADT

The first stop after that, in the Altstadt proper, is the narrow
Sögestrasse (in old local dialect, Sow Street). Butchers used
to keep their pigs on the street in the Middle Ages, and the
practice is commemorated by a swineherd with sows and
piglets cast in bronze in an informal group at the street's
corner with Knochenhauerstrasse, which runs east–west. A
short walk south along the Sögestrasse, past some of the
city's many (summer) street cafés, brings you to the 13th-
century **Liebfrauenkirche** (Church of Our Lady). The former
church of the city council, it has some fine Medieval murals
and stained-glass windows. Behind the church is what the
locals claim is the biggest and prettiest flower market in
Europe. Another short stroll south takes you into the
**Marktplatz** (no longer used as such), with its statue of
Roland standing guard next to the streetcar line (watch your
step), outside the Rathaus.

# The Rathaus

The main Gothic structure of the impressive three-story Rathaus, untouched by World War II, was built in 1405. A Weser Renaissance façade was added in 1612. On the first floor is a huge banquet hall with high arched windows and ornate wooden carvings, and models of old sailing ships suspended over its long tables. City councillors, shippers, businessmen, and ships' captains meet there once a year for a benefit banquet for needy seamen, and the hall is used for many other functions as well.

While Bremen is well known for its beer, it is also Germany's leading wine transshipment center, and down in the Rathaus basement its famous **Ratskeller-Bacchuskeller** restaurant offers a choice of 600 different German wines. Its cellars hold almost one million bottles of German wine alone. Some of the vintages are centuries old, and you had better ask the price. For example, a bottle of a fine German white wine, vintage 1947, can be had for a mere DM 4,400.

The vaulted cellar restaurant can seat up to 600 and serves a wide choice of good, hearty food, including traditional seamen's dishes. Fish, of course, figures prominently on the menu. But you can also enjoy a good North Sea *Scholle* (plaice) at the **Deutsches Haus**, a fish restaurant next to the Rathaus at Am Markt 1.

Before leaving the Rathaus, take a look at the amusing *Bremer Stadtmusikanten* (Bremen Town Musicians) statue at its west entrance, portraying in descending order a cockerel, a cat, a dog, and an ass forming a pyramid. The group, from the Brothers Grimm fairy tale, was created in 1953 by the local sculptor and graphic artist Gerhard Marcks, who felt that Bremen should have something to show its connection with the Fairy Tale Road. The Gerhard Marcks House, Am Wall 208, is dedicated to his works. The **Bremen art gallery**, whose main exhibits are 15th- to 20th-century European paintings and 17th- to 20th-century sculptures, is at Am Wall 207.

# The Dom

Bremen's Dom St. Petri (St. Peter's Cathedral), next to the Rathaus to the east, has a history as a church site going back 1,200 years; construction of its Gothic main building was begun in 1042. A Lutheran church since the Reformation, it was damaged in World War II, and it took 15 years to restore it to its former glory. Special points of interest include a

16th-century Madonna and Child at the chancel, pulpit carvings from the same century, an 11th-century crypt with a 13th-century font (the "Lion's Bowl"), and a Gottfried Silbermann organ dating from 1744.

Excavation work for a new heating system at the cathedral in the early 1970s uncovered a Medieval cemetery containing the graves of 22 bishops. The vestments, miter, and crosier of Bremen's first bishop, which were in incredibly good condition, are now on display in the cathedral **museum**, which also exhibits Medieval murals, stone relics, sculptures, and other treasures found by the excavators. For a chill, visit the cathedral's Bleikammer (Leaden Chamber) containing several mummified corpses believed to have been recovered from dunes along the Weser.

## The Market Place

On the Marktplatz directly opposite the Rathaus to the south is the Schütting, Bremen's chamber of commerce, which bears an inscription above its doors that sums up the mercantile city's can-do philosophy; in regional dialect, it says, "Buten un binnen, wagen un winnen" (Outside the country and in, dare and win). Bremen's *Kaufleute* (merchants) obviously carried that slogan with them around the world. The less attractive modern steel-and-glass building on the east side of the market place is the Haus der Bürgerschaft, the state parliament. The **Übersee Hotel**, favored by business travellers, is in the Wachtstrasse, just off the Marktplatz to the south.

## The Böttcherstrasse

The Böttcherstrasse, another short walk to the southwest of the Marktplatz, is a narrow Medieval street that has been a noted arts-and-crafts center since the 1920s. Its late patron, Ludwig Roselius, made his fortune in coffee. You can see his collection of Medieval art in the 16th-century **Roselius house**, at Böttcherstrasse 6. The Paula Becker-Modersohn house, at Böttcherstrasse 8–10, named after a painter who was one of the founders of the Worpswede art colony (see Day Trips from Bremen, below) in 1889, features many of her works. Workshops and stores of goldsmiths, silversmiths, and other artisans and craftspeople occupy many of the street's interesting nooks and crannies.

A carillon of Meissen porcelain bells, perched high up next to the Roselius house, chimes at noon, 3:00 P.M., and

6:00 P.M. Beer glasses clink at all times of the day at the **Spitzen Gebel**, a tavern behind the Schütting and next to Böttcherstrasse that has a genuine Old Bremen atmosphere.

Going through the pedestrian tunnel at the southern end of the Böttcherstrasse brings you to the Martini *Anleger* (river piers) for 75-minute harbor **boat trips**. Boats depart daily, March through October, at 10:00 A.M., 11:30 A.M., and 3:15 P.M., and at 4:40 P.M. subject to demand.

Evening river-boat parties on the Weser are run every first and third Saturday, April–October, leaving the piers at 7:15 P.M. for a run downstream with an ice-cold schnapps as a welcome-aboard *Aperitiv* before a generous cold buffet. Book well in advance, if possible, through the tourist information office. Bremen's **Kajenmarkt**, a lively flea market featuring a fish auction, arts and crafts, a market crier, and live music, is held next to the piers every Saturday from 8:00 A.M. to 2:00 P.M.

## The Schnoor District and Nightlife

Across the Balgebrückstrasse, a block south of the cathedral, is the charming Schnoor district, at the southeastern end of the Altstadt, on the river. Bremen's oldest, still-intact residential quarter of 15th- to 18th-century "dollhouses" on narrow streets and alleys, the Schnoor is packed with cozy inns, coffee shops and restaurants, arts-and-crafts workshops, antique stores, boutiques, and galleries. The curiosity stores here are big on sailing ships in bottles.

Night owls are well catered to in Bremen by a multitude of pubs, several of them with jazz, and discos. Bremen's oldest "in" disco, the **Lila Eule** (Lilac Owl), is at Bernhardstrasse 10. *Schickeria* (the chic crowd) restaurants include the **Topaz**, Violenstrasse 13, and **Jan Tabak**, Weserstrasse 93.

## Day Trips from Bremen

A day trip to **Vegesack**, a small 18th-century harbor town on the Weser river about 35 km (22 miles) northwest of Bremen, is enjoyable. Many sailing-ship captains built their retirement homes here, and the harbor area is full of faithfully restored old houses and narrow alleys. The town also has many stores and boutiques, and no fewer than 50 hotels, restaurants, cafés, and pubs, several of them on the harbor, so you can watch the busy river traffic go by while you are wining and dining.

A ten-minute walk north from the harbor, through the

green Schönebeck Aue, brings you to the **Schloss Schönebeck**, a 17th-century brick-and-timber former *Wasserschloss* (moated castle) that is now a *Heimatmuseum* (museum of local history). Closed Monday, Thursday, and Friday.

Half-hourly trains from Bremen's Hauptbahnhof take about 25 minutes to Vegesack, and the round-trip fare is only DM6.20.

The attractive art colony village of **Worpswede**, on the Teufelsmoor, 20 km (12.5 miles) north of Bremen, celebrated its centenary in 1989. It has 22 mostly private arts-and-crafts galleries in which to browse, about half of them concentrated in what the locals call the "magic triangle," formed by Bergstrasse-Findorffstrasse-Hembergstrasse in the village center. The **Ludwig Roselius museum of early history**, with exhibits of archaeological finds from throughout Europe, ranging from the late Stone Age to the Vikings, is on the Lindenallee, which runs south from the Bergstrasse. The tourist information office is at Bergstrasse 13.

To get to Worpswede by car from the center of Bremen, drive north via Schwachhauser Heerstrasse–Horn–Lilienthal on *Landstrassen* L 133/L 153. Bus line 140 from the Hauptbahnhof takes 45 minutes to Worpswede; the round-trip fare is DM 8.

The Märchenstrasse (**Fairy Tale Road**), which begins in Hanau, near Frankfurt, where the Brothers Grimm were born, ends in Bremen after a winding journey north of about 600 km (375 miles) through the towns and countryside that inspired their *Märchen*. (We cover this route in our next chapter, The Center.) A day car trip south from Bremen on the B 215, involving a total of about 200 km (125 miles) for the entire round trip, would cover **Verden an der Aller**, with a 1,000-year-old cathedral and a Märchenpark featuring seven fairy tales in life-size pictures; **Nienburg**, with a historic Altstadt and Medieval fortifications surrounded by woods, heath, and moor; and **Minden**, on the Weser river and the Mittellandkanal, with another 1,000-year-old cathedral, the Schachtschleuse (a great lock linking the canal and river), and the Kanalbrücke (aqueduct) over the canal.

# BREMERHAVEN

Bremerhaven, 65 km (40 miles) north of Bremen at the mouth of the Weser river, is well worth a day trip from Bremen, or a longer visit. Its attractions include bracing North Sea breezes, the Deutsches Schiffahrtsmuseum (German Maritime Museum), an open-air museum of 17th-century farmhouses, excellent fish meals at the fishery harbor, and a marine zoo. Bremerhaven is also a departure point for day boat trips to the North Sea island of Helgoland, and handy for a visit to the historic cargo and fishery port and cure resort of **Cuxhaven**.

In historical terms, Bremerhaven is a mere infant—only 163 years old. Founded by Bremen *Bürgermeister* (Mayor) Johann Smidt, the new town quickly became a major maritime gateway to Germany, the home of a big fishing fleet and an important fish market. The port also once held a big ship-building concern, but lack of orders in recent years has caused the yards to concentrate on ship repairing and refitting. The liner *Queen Elizabeth II* was remodeled in Bremerhaven in 1988.

Because of European Community limits on fish catches, Bremerhaven's own fishing fleet has shrunk to only about a dozen vessels, but the city switched successfully to fish processing and handling cargoes from foreign fishing boats, and is now one of Europe's leading transshipment centers for fish. The traditional trade in fish now employs about 55,000 of the city's population of 131,500, and has given the city and its people their salty character. The main port also embraces Europe's largest enclosed container terminal.

## The City Center

The long, slim city center runs north–south along the river front, and most things worth seeing—except for the main Fischereihafen (fishing harbor) and the farmhouse museum—are only a short walk away from the **Theodor-Heuss-Platz**, the town square, with a statue of founder Johann Smidt at its center and the Stadttheater on its riverside flank. The comfortable tourist and business traveller's **Nordsee Hotel Naber** is on the north side of the square. Seagulls provide early morning wake-up calls.

Just around the western corner of the hotel, running north–south, is the Bürgermeister-Smidt-Strasse, the city's main street, which is lined with stores, including the big Columbus center shopping mall on its west side. The local tourist office (Tel: 0471-5-90-22-43) is on the center's first floor, well marked by many signposts that also point the way to stairs down to the open-air section of the **Deutsches Schiffahrtsmuseum** (German Maritime Museum) on the Alter Hafen (Old Harbor).

The first ship in the museum's dock is the U-boat *Wilhelm*

*Bauer,* a World-War-II Type XXI German submarine (ex-U-boat 2450), launched in January 1945 and scuttled by her crew at the war's end in May. Raised in 1957, she has been a floating technical museum since 1984 (independent of the maritime museum), and can be toured daily April through October.

The other ships in the dock include a whale-catcher, a deep-sea tug, an ex-navy PT boat, and an Elbe river lightship. The three-masted bark **Seute Deern** moored here is a good floating restaurant. The museum building itself is about 100 yards to the south. Its halls are crammed with models and pictures and parts of old ships, including the only preserved Hanseatic Kogge, which dates from 1380. This newly launched single-sailed, shallow-draught ship never put to sea; she was torn loose from her Bremen fitting-out dock by a freak flood tide and sank. Found and raised in 2,000 pieces in 1962, she was reassembled and then submerged in a special conservation tank. You may be able to see the ship out of the tank in the year 2000. At present, you have to make do with an indistinct view of her in the greenish gloom of her preservative bath.

A short walk north along the river-front Deichpromenade brings you to the **Zoo am Meer**, containing marine animals, including polar bears, seals, and sea lions. The **Nordsee Museum**, with exhibits of sea animals and plants, is back past the maritime museum and the radar tower to the south between the Weser ferry terminal and the double locks of the Fischereihafen.

The open-air **Farmhouses Museum** is at Parkstrasse 9 in the Speckenbüttel Stadtpark, on the northern edge of the city. Take bus line number 2 from the Theodor-Heuss-Platz to the Parktor stop; the ride takes about 12 minutes

The best fish meals in Bremen are said to be found in Bremerhaven, and the best in Bremerhaven are to be had at the **Natusch** restaurant, Am Fischbahnhof 1, on the Fischereihafen to the south of the city. (It's best to take a cab.) The Natusch has a dark, cozy, old sailing-ship atmosphere, being decorated with ships' timbers, tackle, figureheads, bells, anchors, fish nets, and ship models. It may sound kitschy, but it's not. Owner Lutz Natusch buys freshly landed fish daily at the nearby Fischauktionshalle. Early birds interested in seeing a weekday auction should get to the hall before 7:00 A.M.

# Helgoland

The big passenger ship MS *Helgoland* sails from the Columbus quay, to the north of the city center, daily at 9:35 A.M., May through October, on a nine-and-a-half-hour round trip to the historic North Sea tourist and health resort island of Helgoland, about 90 km (55 miles) northwest of Bremerhaven. A connecting train to the quay leaves Bremerhaven railroad station at 8:50 A.M.

In 1990 the island celebrated the 100th anniversary of its being German. A pagan cult center in the eighth century A.D., it was a pirates' lair in the 14th century and was captured by Denmark in a war with North German Schleswig in 1714. The British annexed the island in 1807 as part of their blockade against Napoleonic France, but exchanged it in 1890 for Imperial Germany's Indian Ocean island of Zanzibar. With an area now of only about one half of a square mile, Helgoland was once four times that size, but its red sandstone cliffs have been eroded by the sea.

In April 1947 the British nearly blew away the then uninhabited island when they tried to destroy World War II U-boat pens with about 6,000 tons of explosive. Helgoland was a German sea fortress in both world wars, and the islanders were moved to the mainland during each conflict. They last returned home in 1952, when the British handed over the island to the new Federal Republic of Germany. The MS *Helgoland,* and the island's stores, sell goods duty free. Passenger ships visiting Helgoland are not allowed to moor alongside the quay; local boatmen, exercising an ancient and fiercely guarded right, transfer visitors to the shore for their four-hour stay.

## GETTING AROUND

For information on Hamburg, see the section on Hamburg, above.

### *Lübeck*

Lübeck's airport is only for small aircraft, but Hamburg's international airport is only 65 km (40 miles) away on the A 1/E 22 Autobahn. There are daily feeder flights between the two cities, but trains between Hamburg and Lübeck run every 30 minutes and the journey takes only a half hour. Lübeck is also on the InterCity and EuroCity railroad network, giving the town frequent links with the rest of Germany and Europe. Its big ferry port at Travemünde makes Lübeck a gateway to Scandinavia.

The town has no subway, but its many bus lines and frequency of service make it easy to reach all districts and suburbs. Bus tickets are bought from the driver, and multi-journey tickets are available at a discount. The taxi service (Tel: 451-811-12 and 451-811-22) is also good.

## *Bremen and Bremerhaven*

Major international airlines do not fly directly to Bremen from overseas airports, but Lufthansa has frequent connecting flights between Bremen and Frankfurt, Germany's biggest aerial gateway. Air Bremen, the local airline, operates daily service between Bremen and London and Brussels, as well as many other European cities (although not Paris). Hamburg's international airport is 120 km (75 miles) away on the A 1 autobahn, and there are hourly InterCity express train services between the two cities.

Bremen airport lies about 5 km (3 miles) south of the city, or a 12-minute ride on streetcar number 5 that costs DM 2.50 to the Domsheide stop, next to the cathedral, or to the Bahnhofsplatz. The taxi fare into the city is DM 6–8. The airport has only one exit, and both the streetcar stop and the taxi stand are located directly outside it.

Bremen has six streetcar and 42 bus lines servicing the city and suburbs, and offers two days of unlimited travel on the entire network for DM 6. On weekends, up to four persons can travel on one ticket. All major international car rental firms have offices in Bremen.

Daily sightseeing bus tours of Bremen (duration about two hours) begin at the central bus depot on the Bahnhofsplatz Monday–Saturday at 3:00 P.M. and Sunday at 10:30 A.M., May through October. Bremen is "bicycle friendly," and you can rent bikes at the Fahrrad station on the east side of the Bahnhofsplatz, which has maps showing bicycle paths in and around the city. Sightseeing flights over Bremen, lasting about 15 minutes, are operated by Roland Air at Bremen airport (Tel: 421-55-40-08), and cost DM 40 per person.

Bremerhaven has seven metropolitan bus lines, and is easy to get around in. The city's radio-taxi service (Tel: 421-400-04) is also good.

## ACCOMMODATIONS REFERENCE
(For Hamburg accommodations, see the Hamburg section earlier in this chapter.)

▶ **Hotel Alter Speicher.** Beckergrube 91–93, D-2400 **Lübeck.** Tel: (451) 755-33.

► **Hotel Atlantic**. Kaiserallee 2a, D-2400 **Travemünde**. Tel: (4502) 741-36.

► **Bergstrom Hotel**. Bei der Lüner Mühle, D-2120 **Lüneburg**. Tel: (4131) 30-80.

► **Bremen Plaza**. Hillmanplatz 20, D-2800 **Bremen**. Tel: (421) 176-70; Telex: 24686; Fax: 1767238.

► **Hotel Excelsior**. Hansestrasse 3, D-2400 **Lübeck**. Tel: (451) 826-26; Telex: 26595.

► **Hotel Jensen**. Obertrave 4-5, D-2400 **Lübeck**. Tel: (451) 716-46; Telex: 26360.

► **Hotel Kaiserhof**. Kronsforder Allee 13, D-2400 **Lübeck**. Tel: (451) 79-19-11; Telex: 26603.

► **Maritim Strandhotel**. Trelleborgallee 2, D-2400 **Travemünde**. Tel: (4502) 750-01; Telex: 261432; Fax: 74439.

► **Mercure-Columbus**. Bahnhofsplatz 5, D-2800 **Bremen**. Tel: (421) 141-61; Telex: 244688.

► **Mövenpick Hotel Lysia**. Auf der Wallhalbinsel 3, D-2400 **Lübeck**. Tel: (451) 150-40; Telex: 26707; Fax: 1504111.

► **Nordsee Hotel Naber**. Theodor-Heuss-Platz 1, D-2850 **Bremerhaven**. Tel: (471) 487-70; Telex: 238881; Fax: 4877999.

► **Park Hotel**. Im Bürgerpark, D-2800 **Bremen**. Tel: (421) 340-80; Telex: 244343; Fax: 3408602.

► **Übersee Hotel**. Am Markt/Wachtstrasse 27-29, D-2800 **Bremen**. Tel: (421) 360-10; Telex: 246501.

► **Hotel Zur Post**. Bahnhofsplatz 11, D-2800 **Bremen**. Tel: (421) 305-90; Telex: 244971; Fax: 305959.

► **Wellenkamp's Hotel**. Am Sande 9, D-2120 **Lüneburg**. Tel: (4131) 430-26.

# THE CENTER

*By Peter Hays*

*Peter Hays, a resident of Germany since 1966, has written for more than 30 German publications and has contributed many feature articles to English-language newspapers and magazines.*

**P**opularly, the river Main, dividing northern from southern Germany, is known as the "Weisswurst Equator." The spicy veal sausage, a traditional delicacy of the south, has proved to be a better way to distinguish north from south than anything geographers can muster.

What we call "The Center" might well be expected to straddle these two halves of Germany, but the whole area actually lies north of the Great Sausage Divide. From a strictly geographical point of view, only our center's southernmost reaches, in particular the volcanic **Vogelsberg** plateau, really qualify as central territory. The **Harz Mountains**, to the east, were bisected for decades by a stretch of the Iron Curtain. Between this range and the **Weser river valley** on the region's western fringe, forested uplands slope down gently from the **Hessisches** (Hessian) **Bergland** to the Northern German plain. Hannover, Celle, and Braunschweig (Brunswick), near the plain's edge, are unmistakably northern cities, where *Hochdeutsch,* at its purest, is spoken.

Often enough, the center-stage role this region has played has had more to do with politics than geography. During Medieval centuries the *Welfen,* internationally known as the Guelphs, ruled large parts of it from their bases in and around Goslar, Braunschweig, Celle, and Hannover. Thanks not least to shrewd marriage policies, the dynasty managed to intertwine its lineage with that of the British Stuarts. In

1714 this led to the Hanoverian Elector Georg Ludwig, a Guelph descendant, succeeding Queen Anne as Britain's King George I. For the next 123 years Hanoverian monarchs held sway simultaneously in Westminster and their home duchy (later kingdom) . At the time, this part of Germany was as close to the hub of Empire affairs as many an English province. Though little Georgian prestige has lingered here, the region has not faded from the royal scene completely. Members of the House of Windsor, notably Queen Elizabeth II and Prince Charles, are regularly sighted on both official and informal visits to the land of their Hanoverian forebears.

Major trade routes have always crisscrossed the center region. In the days of the Hanseatic League, for instance, Goslar lay on the Hanse merchants' road from Lübeck to Padua, Italy. Walled little towns like Herbstein, much farther south, offered a safe night's sleep for long-distance traders on their way from Leipzig to Frankfurt-am-Main. By the same token, today's truckers, en route from, say, Hamburg to Stuttgart, feel they are at the halfway point when they stop for a mug of Autobahn coffee just south of the steep Kasseler Berge.

It's best to take a two-pronged approach to this region. Start by visiting the cities and towns that ring the forested mountains of the Weserbergland and the Vogelsberg, from Celle in the north to Marburg in the south, which will put you in the historical picture. After that, you may feel like diving inside those rings, into the pages of a storybook. Meander upriver from Hameln (Hamelin) along the Weser, into Sleeping Beauty country: the dark, still quite forbidding forests in which some of the best-known German folk and fairy tales are set.

**MAJOR INTEREST**

Hannover
Celle and its Medieval architecture
Braunschweig and its historic backwaters
Goslar and the Harz Mountains

**The Land of Fairy Tales and the Brothers Grimm**
Einbeck
Hameln and the story of the Pied Piper
Bodenwerder and the Baron Münchhausen
Hannoversch Münden
The Reinhardswald and Sleeping Beauty
Kassel

Marburg and the Romantics
Hanau, birthplace of the Brothers Grimm

# *HANNOVER*

Lower Saxony's state capital is a good base from which to
enter the Center proper, especially if you happen to be on the
rebound from a Hanseatic city tour. Hamburg to Hannover is
a comfortable 90-minute Autobahn hop. A good map and
some astute navigating to the freeway called the Messe
Schnellweg will assure you of smooth entry into town, because city planners have pandered to the motorist with a
network of urban superhighways and flyovers. You may be
tempted to cruise right into the heart of the city. But beware:
Parking is tight. Turn right down the Hans-Bockler-Allee and
leave your car in the neighborhood of the **Congress-
Centrum**, where there is far more space.

Hannover's city center suffered a great deal of bomb
damage during World War II. Stately buildings such as the
Oper and the Leineschloss, of which enough survived to
warrant restoring, are generally lone period pieces, separated by several blocks of modern façades. To conjure up
some semblance of cohesion, the authorities had a broad
red stripe, over 4 km (2.5 miles) in length, painted along the
city pavement. Its loops and squiggles lead to some three
dozen interesting buildings and monuments. Consecutive
numbers on the pavement should match those of a compan-
ion booklet (obtainable at the tourist offices in the Neues
Rathaus or the main station), but fail to do so in many cases.
The stripe is badly faded and, here and there, completely
erased. Discovering the remains of Old Hannover under
your own steam can be just as much fun.

Suggesting the **Hauptbahnhof** as your point of departure
may not sound all that exciting. But this is as central a
railway station as you can imagine, with plenty of atmosphere. The trancontinental Milan–Copenhagen and Paris–
Moscow express trains both stop here. The station's exterior
deserves more than just a glance. One of the most palatial
you are likely to see in town, it is a proud, escutcheoned
edifice designed on Classical lines similar to the nearby
**Oper**. Both were the work of Hannover's official architect,
Georg Ludwig Laves, in the first half of the 19th century. A
statue of King Ernst August, who commissioned the work,
rides high in front of the station. At the Vienna Congress in
1814 the Guelph electorate of Hannover had been pro-

moted to kingdom. It survived as such until 1866, when Ernst August's blind son, King Georg V, lost a decisive battle to his cousin, King Wilhelm I of Prussia, whereupon Hannover became a Prussian province.

From the station to the sweeping curve formed by the river Leine and the Friedrichswall highway are some 3 km (1.5 miles) of pedestrian zones to stroll in. Modern urban designers have done their best to create boulevards and squares that invite you to linger. Department stores and fast-food establishments have, unfortunately, replaced patrician architecture, but the **Georgstrasse**, the **Kröpcke** (the liveliest square), and the **Karmarschstrasse** still seem to work the same magic as in prewar times. This area is nearly always teeming with window-shoppers, knots of chatting students, street musicians, and teenage daredevils on skateboards.

A fragment of Medieval Hannover awaits you down by the Leine river. A couple of half-timbered houses on the Kramerstrasse and the Burgstrasse date as far back as the 16th century. A stone arch, the **Marstallstor**, is all that remains of the royal stables built in 1714. The graffiti on it almost eclipse the sculpted coat-of-arms of King George I of Great Britain and Hanover. On the river are a few cafés, their beer gardens basking in the last of the day's sunshine. From here you'll have a good view of the 17th-century **Leineschloss**'s riverside façade. It was here, in 1701, that Electress Sophie was designated successor to the British throne by London's emissary, the earl of Macclesfield. Shortly after Queen Anne's death in 1714, Sophie died too. The British crown thereupon passed to her son Georg Ludwig.

Lackluster rebuilding has recently given way to restoration by stonemasons trained to work in the old-fashioned way. A good example is the **Leibnizhaus** in one of Hannover's most elegant squares, the **Holzmarkt**. The ornately fronted Renaissance house that the mathematician and philosopher Gottfried Wilhelm Leibniz lived in from 1698 on now serves as a scientists' conference center. Equally stylish are the nearby **Ballhof**, built as a badminton hall for Duke Georg Wilhelm in the 17th century, and the **Altes Rathaus**, with its Gothic pinnacle gables, pottery friezes, and its own restaurant, Ratskeller, renowned for its chanterelle dishes. Dining here, you are quite likely to witness Medieval-style banquets re-enacted for the benefit of large tourist groups. Slightly farther down the Schmiedegasse is the candlelit **Brauhaus Ernst August**, where you can have a glass or two of top-fermented *Hannöversch Pils,* Hannover's celebrated beer, available only here. Meals are served until 1:00 A.M. on weekdays and 3:00 A.M. on weekends.

South of the **Friedrichswall** highway the cityscape opens out into spacious greens and parks, ornamental lakes such as the **Maschsee**, and majestic squares such as the **Waterlooplatz**. The column here, another Laves masterpiece, commemorates the June day in 1815 when Napoleon was defeated by the combined efforts of an unprecedented Anglo-Hanoverian alliance. A minor monument in front of the **Hauptstaatsarchiv** depicts Count Carl von Alten, a German general who led an English infantry division at the battle. Hannover-British cooperation has continued: The city hosts an annual "British Week," which features pop stars such as Rod Stewart.

Hannover's many museums attract a large number of *Bildungsbürger,* or culture vultures. Be sure to visit the **Sprengel Museum** on the shores of the Maschsee. It houses a collection of contemporary art with works by Chagall, Picasso, Beckmann, Nolde, and Klee. The museum is named after its patron, the local chocolate manufacturer Dr. Bernhard Sprengel, who donated his private collection and a considerable sum of money to the City of Hannover in 1969. Sprengel started collecting in 1937; a Third Reich exhibition of "Degenerate Art" in Munich that year so dismayed him that he promptly bought two watercolors by one of the abused artists, Emil Nolde.

Hannover's most regal feature is a short tram ride (on the number 1 line) away from the city center, in **Herrenhäusen**, an area that boasts the country's finest example of an early Baroque park. Laid out like a geometrician's idea of floral embroidery, Herrenhäuser Gärten's 120 acres of horticultural symmetry would be best appreciated from a hovering helicopter. The view from a special visitor's "panorama terrace" is almost as impressive, however. Miles of hornbeam hedges and boxtrees shorn like poodles frame potted plants (including a 327-year-old Viennese pomegranate shrub), flower beds, lawns, and gravel paths arranged to reflect gardening styles from Renaissance to Rococo, with some flowery Islamic frills thrown in. The original planting dates from the time of the Thirty Years War, but Herrenhausen owes most of its charm to the period of Hanoverian ascendancy. Electress Sophie, who had a lot of say about its design, called the park "my life," and in fact died while on one of her regular walks through it.

Nowadays, open-air plays are staged at Herrenhausen

within the **Heckentheater**'s immaculately trimmed hedges, and dazzling Baroque-style firework displays are accompanied by high-decibel renditions of Handel's "Music for the Royal Fireworks" and other pieces. No entrance fee is charged, except during the illuminations, which you can see after dusk (on Wednesdays, Fridays, and Saturdays during the summer). The main grounds open at 8:00 A.M., and close at 8:00 P.M. in the summer and 4:30 P.M. in the winter. The **Georgengarten** section is open round the clock.

If you leave town along the Friedrichswall, you can stop at the (relatively) new **Rathaus** for some farewell bombast. Designed by a Berlin architect at the turn of the century, its neo-Gothic dome and turrets were more to the taste of Kaiser Wilhelm II than to that of many Hanoverians. Its dizzying entrance hall contains four scale models of the city, each from a different period. One, of half-timbered Hannover in the year 1689, will give you an inkling of what to expect in Celle.

# CELLE

The fables woven around Britain's royal family by today's tabloids are pretty tame stuff compared to the real-life dramas their Hanoverian ancestors played out. So read on, or, rather, drive northeast on highway B 3 to Celle, less than an hour from Hannover. There, the Herzogschloss, encircled by the river Aller, one of its tributaries, and a stretch of moat, faces some 600 wood-frame houses, most of them listed as historic monuments, which line a compact grid of streets much as they did more than 300 years ago. The original settlement two miles upstream was shifted here lock, stock, and beam by order of Duke Otto the Severe in 1292. The move gave the citizens better protection from marauding barons, and explains the orderly layout, an early example of urban planning.

From here the dukes of Celle ruled their share of Guelph territory, including Hannover. Not until 1705, at the death of Duke Georg Wilhelm, Electress Sophie's brother-in-law, was the seat of government transferred from Celle to Hannover. During Georg Wilhelm's reign, the Hanoverian dynasty acquired a Macbethian flavor. The duke's daughter Sophie Dorothea was coupled with his nephew Georg Ludwig, Britain's future King George I, in a dynasty-buttressing marriage. It was a mismatch from the start. Sophie Dorothea took an aristocrat, Philip von Königsmark, as a lover. When news of the affair leaked out, von Königsmark was murdered in Hannover's **Leineschloss**, supposedly on Georg Ludwig's orders. After divorcing his wife, Britain's monarch-to-be banished her to grim **Schloss Ahlden** on the river Aller. There, Sophie Dorothea languished until her death in 1726. During her 30 years of confinement she was never once allowed to see her two children: Sophie Dorothea, who later gave birth to Prussia's Frederick the Great, and Britain's future George II.

Georg Ludwig, it seems, took some time settling in as George I in London. He never bothered to learn English, conversing instead in French with his new courtiers. After the absolute power he had wielded in Hannover, he also had to accustom himself to his new subjects' watchful parliament.

Prince Charles, who is said to take the Royal Hanoverian motto *ich dien* (I serve) particularly seriously, occasionally turns up in Celle with the Princess of Wales. Union Jacks galore are unfurled to welcome this not-so-distant relative.

The **Herzogschloss** may not match Buckingham Palace for size, but it is certainly as elegant. It is a refined edifice of Weser Renaissance pedigree, with deliberately asymmetrical windows. (For Weserrenaissance, see Hameln, below.) The palace is featured on the country's 30-pfennig stamp. Its beautifully stuccoed theater, the oldest of its kind in Germany, has been active since 1670, and Celle's municipal ensemble performs there almost nightly. The ten-month repertory season of more than a dozen plays includes works by Molière, Calderón, Lessing, Wilde, and contemporary dramatists such as Bodo Strauss.

When Celle's royal residents moved to Hannover in 1705, the city fathers were given the choice of a prison-cum-lunatic asylum or a university as the city's next tenant. They opted for the former, reputedly because they saw students as a greater threat to public morals. The economic slump that ensued is one of the main reasons for Celle's present wealth of Medieval architecture: Funds were not available to replace what later generations tended to scorn as peasant housing.

In those days the **Lüneburger Heide**, now a juniper-dotted heathland, was covered with oak forests that grew slowly and sturdily in the sandy soil. Celle's Medieval builders used whole oak trunks as uprights. Pointed gables added to the haughty demeanor of the long rows of tall town houses still standing today. Tradesfolk evidently thought wattle, daub, and timber anything but fashionable, and at one end of the **Markt** there are still some façades they plastered over in order to distinguish them from those of their *Ackerbürger,* or town-peasant neighbors. Take a short stroll around the **Rathaus** opposite. Pillars and gray brickwork painted on the side are signs of Celle's relative impoverishment at a time when other, wealthier towns were indulging in extravagant Baroque adornments. Note too, in a niche near the entrance, a painted plaster miniature of the town hall's bearded Medieval master-builder Reisz in profile, and, hanging from the front wall, the iron rod with which the merchants of old measured out their cubits of cloth.

In Celle, individual house owners, who receive minimal tax relief for their efforts, have forked out considerable sums restoring their homes. The **Zöllnerstrasse**, the **Poststrasse**, the **Neue Strasse**, and the **Stechbahn** (the former jousting field) are all crammed from end to end with fine half-timbered specimens, and you can spend hours attempting to decipher the dozens of repainted and recarved inscriptions on the beams. Some are in *Hochdeutsch,* others in *Platt,* Northern Germany's anglophonic dialect. A long inscription above the windows of the Lateinschule, on the Roland-strasse, is in Latin, naturally enough, and exhorts young scholars to heed their elders' pearls of wisdom.

It's easy enough to determine the period of the houses because many display their date of construction neatly carved into one of the front beams. At the corner of the Poststrasse and the Rundestrasse stands the town's most profusely decorated burgher residence, **Hoppener Haus** (dated 1532), with its lewdly allegorical wooden reliefs. Next to it is a less ornate house built, according to the first owner's carved caption, "out of necessity, not pleasure," at the end of the Thirty Years War. Next door is an even plainer building, dated 1701. It should come as no great surprise that twice a day—at 6:30 A.M. and 6:30 P.M.—a bugler's brief chorale drifts across town from the top of the **Stadtkirche**'s spire.

Quite a few Hamburgers and Hanoverians travel to Celle to do their Saturday shopping. Along the **Bergstrasse** and the **Grosser Plan**, in particular, a motley band of grocers and old-time purveyors thrive. **Huths Kaffee** has been roasting its own coffee since 1851. In **Café Kiess** you can sample *Schweineöhrchen,* traditional Danish pastries shaped like pigs' ears. A couple of Medieval blocks away, in the Stech-bahn, the **Löwenapotheke** has been in the pharmacy business for well over four centuries. Duck down into the **Ratskeller** beneath the town hall chambers and try some *Niedersächsische Hochzeitssuppe,* a beef broth with aspara-

gus tips and noodles sometimes still served at local weddings. The town's premier hotel, **Der Fürstenhof**, has been
known for its various duck dishes ever since it had access to
the *Endtenfang,* a ducal pond originally patrolled by duck-
catchers who kept Georg Wilhelm supplied with his favorite
fowl. Today, the chefs use only free-range birds.

# *BRAUNSCHWEIG*

As you approach what the Anglo-Saxon world calls Brunswick
along B 214 southeast from Celle, you will see that lush dairy
pastures are being slowly but surely enveloped by the city's
industrial outskirts. The puffing factory chimneys are one of
the less attractive ways that once-aristocratic Braunschweig
now makes its presence felt. This city of 250,000 people, only
42 km (26 miles) east of Hannover, has gone through some
tough times. World War II bombing flattened most of the
noble architecture of this former capital of the Guelph duchy
of Brunswick. Now it is hard to picture the ducal heyday, when
Braunschweig ranked as one of the country's centers of
culture. Gotthold Ephraim Lessing's *Emilia Galotti,* Germany's first non-Classical tragedy, had its premier here in the
**Hoftheater** (since replaced by the **Staatstheater**) in 1772, as
did Goethe's *Faust I* in 1829.

The postwar decades saw a shift in emphasis. Braunschweig is the home of Rollei cameras, and has made the
most of its technical and scientific traditions. The nation's
civil aviation authority is based here. So is the **Physikalisch-
Technische Bundesanstalt**, which possesses the world's
most accurate atomic clock. The country's oldest polytechnic
school, grown out of the Collegium Carolinum founded in
1745, now has more than 14,000 students in some 100
disciplines.

All this has had very little effect on city tourism. Recent
promotional drives, which labeled Braunschweig "The Like-
able City," were aimed at widening the former capital's
appeal. What the image-makers call "islands of tradition"
exist amid the concrete sea of office blocks, department
stores, and parking lots. One such enclave is the **Burgplatz**.
Braunschweig is at its most Medieval here, thanks to the
awe-inspiring **Dom St. Blasius**, which rears up opposite the
**Burg Dankwarderode**. Cathedral and castle are both testimony to a 12th-century building spree unleashed by the
Guelph heavyweight Heinrich der Löwe (Henry the Lion).
He and his cousin Frederick Barbarossa, the rival Hohen-

staufen clan's red-bearded Holy Roman Emperor, were two of the Middle Ages' most flamboyant figures. In youth and early manhood they were friends and even allies, but in 1176 they clashed on matters of principle and power. Henry was consequently stripped of his Bavarian and Saxon holdings by Frederick and exiled for three years in England. On his return he retired to Braunschweig.

During that period, English and German royalty were closely entwined. Henry the Lion's wife, Maud, was the daughter of England's Henry II and Eleanor of Aquitaine. Maud and Henry lie side by side in a delicately sculpted tomb in the Romanesque Dom St. Blasius. The discreet sculptor saw to it that the duke is represented as being several inches taller than his spouse, when in fact the opposite was the case. Maud, who was married off at the age of 12, grew to outstrip her husband by about eight inches. On the tomb Henry is shown clutching a model of the cathedral. Among St. Blasius's main delights is the barley-sugar twist of the pillars, which foreshadows Tudor fluting.

The castle, across the square, now holds a fine collection of Guelph treasures, including the 800-year-old bronze lion that Henry made the Guelphs' heraldic symbol. The one atop the pedestal outside in the square is a more recent replica.

Excellent à la carte meals followed by stylish slumber under 500-year-old oak beams can be had in the city's pricey **Hotel Ritter St. Georg**. For more down-to-earth fare, head for the area called the **Magniviertel** near the bomb-torn and now concrete-supported **St. Magni-Kirche**. In spite of its name, the **Altstadt Bierhaus** regales its guests with Greek snacks and taped pop music. A lot of the surrounding *Gasthäuser* go in for traditional dishes. If possible, sample the variations on the culinary theme of kale and asparagus, two regional specialties, in their respective seasons: the former from October to December (the cabbage tastes best if harvested after a hard frost), the latter usually from mid-May to the end of June.

Any tour of Braunschweig's surroundings should include a visit to the **Bibliotheca Augusta** in **Wolfenbüttel**, a few miles south of Braunschweig on the B 4. The world-famous Baroque library hit the headlines in 1983 when it was decided to give the Gospels of Henry the Lion, commissioned by the monarch as a present for Braunschweig's Cathedral of St. Blasius, a permanent home here. The states of Lower Saxony and Bavaria, the federal government, and an industrial trust forked out a grand total of DM 32.5 million for the beautifully illuminated masterpiece—the highest price ever paid for a single book. The library is named after local Duke August the Younger, one of the greatest scholars and bibliophiles of his day. When he died in 1666, at age 87, the "prince of peace" had amassed some 130,000 imprints. Subsequent librarians, such as the 18th-century dramatist and critic Gotthold Ephraim Lessing, were recruited from the highest literary ranks. One of many famous visitors was Giacomo Casanova, who rated the seven days spent browsing through dozens of volumes "among the happiest in my life." Today there are more than 350,000 books, including some 13,000 Bibles in different languages, on display. Many of the incunabula are unique. One of the most valuable is Ulrich Boner's *Edelstein,* printed in Bamberg by Albrecht Pfister in 1461.

# GOSLAR

Leave Braunschweig south via B 4 (followed by a short spell on B 82) for Goslar. Thanks to its status as a hospital town during World War II, Goslar's core of Medieval buildings, many of them more than 400 years old, is on a par with Celle's. Whichever of the crooked, cobbled lanes you head down, you are more than likely to end up in the central **Marktplatz**. Do not miss the mechanical movie—the glockenspiel—there. In the course of four daily performances (9:00 A.M., noon, 3:00 P.M., 6:00 P.M.) starring life-size figures on the 19-bell carillon facing the **Rathaus**, a knight-errant called Ramm emerges, mounted on a horse that paws the ground and unearths a rich lode of silver. The horse may well be a piece of poetic license, but the fact remains that from the year 969 on, large quantities of lead, silver, gold, copper, zinc, and other non-ferrous metals were mined on the nearby **Rammelsberg**. By the end of the last millennium, a veritable gold and silver rush was on, and, according to one chronicler, Goslar rated as "the fairest and wealthiest city in the whole of Saxony."

From the outset silver was smelted under imperial license. Generations of trouble-shooting Holy Roman Emperors certainly stashed away a lot of it. With the coins talented artisans minted for them, umpteen feuds and political showdowns were funded. Meanwhile, the miners themselves often spent a grueling week at a time down in the shafts.

Those early Holy Roman rulers were as nomadic as Bedouins, with castles all over Western Europe. But Henry III seems to have had a genuine soft spot for Goslar, and it was during his reign that the **Kaiserpfalz** was built. By 1056 the palace had attained its present enormous dimensions: a two-story stone structure 178 feet long and 60 feet wide, the world's largest secular example of pure Romanesque style. Countless sessions of the *Reichstag,* the Imperial Diet, were held here. Henry III is buried in Speyer, but his heart remains enshrined in Goslar's **Ulrichskapelle**. In later centuries the palace either fell into disuse or served intermittently as a courthouse, jail, and granary. Prussia's Kaiser Wilhelm I donated millions for restoration work in 1871 and turned the Kaiserpfalz into a kind of German shrine. It still bristles with the symbolism of a more glorious age: In the imperial hall huge murals, vaguely reminiscent of a Wagnerian opera set, glorify a millennium of Teutonic myths.

Ore was mined until a few years ago. As early as the 13th century, after the decline of imperial influence, the increasingly independent and powerful burghers joined the Hanseatic League, bought the duchy of Brunswick's tithing rights to the mine, and soon enjoyed their own coinage privileges. Periods of slump included part of the 15th century, when the shafts (you can book guided tours down them at the tourist office in the main square) were continually flooded. That problem was eventually solved by Thuringian engineers.

The miners themselves never benefited much from their work. Back in the Middle Ages their houses, now so picturesquely restored on the **Glockengiesserstrasse** and similar lanes, were humble, smoke-filled abodes without chimneys. The affluent classes consisted mainly of merchants, brewers, artisans, and patrician farmers, whose guilds had a lot of political clout. One of the most powerful, the cloth merchants', operated from the **Kaiserworth** (in the Marktplatz), now a hotel-cum-restaurant with some fine old vaulting and atmosphere to match. One corner of the building has a worn ledge at its base; guild bosses once sat persistent debtors there and then made them walk the breadth of the square with their breeches down, to the jeers of the populace. The bronze fountain is more than 700 years old. One of its gargoyles graphically portrays the Old Testament story of Jonah; interestingly, the marine monster shown regurgitating Jonah bears scant resemblance to a whale.

Goslar is still good at grand gestures. Opposite the **Marktkirche** is the highly respected restaurant **Brusttuch**, where diners are ensconced behind mullioned windows and a decorative façade, and given rolled-up menus fastened with a red seal. Slightly more affordable eateries include the **Butterhenne** on the main square, which specializes in barrel-fresh sauerkraut, venison, and salted hamshank, and **Restau-**

rant **Abzucht**, on the Abzuchtstrasse, run by two young chefs from Hamburg who have developed their own version of nouvelle German cuisine. The town's most lauded hotel, **Der Achtermann**, does a brilliant Disneyland impression of the Middle Ages, with sundry halberds, muskets, and suits of armor lining its walls. Bits of roughly hewn masonry, originally part of the town fortifications, are still visible inside the hotel.

## THE HARZ MOUNTAINS

A short, ear-popping climb south up B 241 from Goslar will bring you to the heart of this gently undulating range. The densely forested humps, which rarely rise above 800 meters (2,600 feet), are just about rugged enough to figure as a skiing option in the winter and as a favorite hiking area in the summer. From Clausthal-Zellerfeld take the scenic mountain road, B 242, via Altenau, to **Torfhaus**. The broad swaths of treeless no-man's-land snaking through the forest mark the border with East Germany. Through one of the very popular pay telescopes around here you can pick out **the Brocken**. Crowned by a communications antenna, the legendary granite peak (one of the few above 1,000 meters, or 3,300 feet) towers over East Germany's portion of the Harz.

Superstition had it that every Walpurgis Night, May 1, hordes of witches, described poetically in Goethe's *Faust,* smeared themselves with a secret ointment, and then flew up to the Brocken on winged horses, cats, rams, brooms, hayforks, and even shovels to celebrate their sabbath. Since those wild Harz days, when backwoodsmen still roamed the hills, sleek and efficiently run spas such as **Bad Harzburg** and **Bad Lauterberg** have proliferated. They tend to attract health-conscious visitors who pop pills, follow strict diets, and walk a network of forest trails signposted to the point of urbanity.

To leave this well-beaten and sophisticated track, head for the broad wedge of hill country that slopes down on either side of the **Auf der Acker** ridge. Life in secluded villages such as **Sieber** and **Lerbach** still revolves around lumberjacking and other kinds of forestry work. Although you won't find quite the same love of pageantry here as, say, in Bavaria, local customs are kept alive by folk groups like the one in Lerbach. On festive occasions young men and women don their traditional costumes for a spirited session of whip-cracking, singing, and dancing. Their distinctive yodeling, a means of communicating in the thick forest, is also a sort of high-pitched narrative. The very rural **Herz-Hotel Sauerbrey**, run by the same Lerbach clan for the past five generations, has its own little theater-cum-beerhall that regularly puts on folk plays and fairy tales for children. The present owner remembers how his father would spend weeks on end in the forest burning charcoal to sell. The charcoal burners are no more, but every August **Altenau** hosts a lengthy *Köhlerfest* in remembrance of their vanished craft. It takes weeks to construct and stoke the old-fashioned kiln, so the festivities last just as long.

# GÖTTINGEN

For a modern city of 130,000, Göttingen, 110 km (68 miles) south of Hannover, and southwest of the Harz area, has a remarkably large and lively **Altstadt**. The base of the ramparts is intact enough to challenge early-morning joggers to a long, looping run. Mind you, for several postwar decades the Altstadt's main Medieval feature was the bout of rush-hour jousting by knights in gasoline-powered tin. Eventually, the city council stepped in and "becalmed" its central grid of streets, turning them into a pedestrian zone. So now, while Greater Göttingen throbs away, life in this inner haven of shops and open-air cafés has been decelerated to a pace that would upset no one in the sleepy Harz villages less than an hour's drive to the north.

The lack of exhaust fumes has been good for the ancient building façades, including that of the still handsome, Classical **Aula** in the Wilhelmsplatz, formerly one of the centers of the **Georgia Augusta university**, which recently moved most of its faculties to the outskirts of the city. With its magnificently pillared early 19th-century Great Hall, the Aula is comparatively new. Its architectural elders, such as the row of half-timbered houses down **Paulinerstrasse**, date to the 15th and 16th centuries. There is a reason for the age gap. In 1536, when other German universities were already thriving academic communities, Göttingen had first applied to its imperial overlords for permission to build its own university. Prospects were good, until Göttingen joined the Schmalkaldischer Bund, an alliance of Protestant towns and principalities committed to overthrowing the Holy Roman Empire. After the Protestants' defeat, Göttingen, along with many of its allies, had to eat humble pie. Envoys travelled to the court of Emperor Charles V to beg his forgiveness. Payment of

10,000 gold florins averted the *Reichsacht,* a decree that would have practically outlawed the town. A long period of economic decline ensued, and it wasn't until 1733 that Britain's King George II, alias Hanoverian Elector Georg Augustus, inaugurated and funded the university named for him.

The Georgia Augusta has made up for its late start in academic life, claiming some 30 Nobel Prize winners as its own. More than 250 marble plaques on the house walls honor the prominent academics and alumni who resided or lodged there. The chemist and physicist Otto Hahn, who later regretted splitting the atom with fellow scientist Lise Meitner, lived at Gervinusstrasse 5 from 1953 on. Germany's "Iron Chancellor," Otto von Bismarck, a law student here, spent 1832–1833 at Bürgerstrasse 27a, the last remaining of the ramparts' 30 watchtowers. The poet Henry Wadsworth Longfellow studied belles lettres here for a year in 1829 and is remembered by a plaque at Rote Strasse 25. The boister-ous law student Heinrich Heine, who was sent down from the Georgia Augusta for six months after challenging an acquaintance to a duel, lodged at five different addresses between 1820 and 1825. Originally, four plaques commemo-rated him. Today, only the one at Weender Strasse 50 re-mains. People put the others' disappearance down to the scathing descriptions of academic life with which young Heine, later to become one of the country's most acclaimed poets and writers, spiced his *Harzreise.* The very first sen-tence sums up his feelings: "The town of Göttingen, famous for its sausages and university. . . ."

Almost in the same line, though, Heine praised "the very good beer" in the city's Rathskeller. He often balked at the "iron paragraphs of Roman jurisprudence" he had to memo-rize, although he eventually earned a doctorate in law. Very probably Heine preferred a favorite German student disci-pline: beer-mug philosophy. In a wide range of Göttingen Kneipen (pubs), you can eavesdrop on an interesting mix of bright thoughts and platitudes. Down in the vaulted cellars of the crenellated **Altes Rathaus**, the **Rathskeller** itself has kept good wines and brews on tap since the 14th century. Today it specializes in *Deutsche Küche,* meaning an emphasis on fresh cuts of meat and a variety of the region's spicy sausages. Up above, the old town hall's main hall, used for New Year receptions and official functions, is a beautiful blend of Medieval beams, late 19th-century frescoes, heral-dic friezes, and Gothic windows.

The **Zum Szültenbürger** restaurant in the Prinzenstrasse

has a cozy, unaffected feel to it, and caters to an international clientele in the sense that students bring along any newly arrived overseas friends and treat them to the town's most affordable snack: *Schmalzbrot,* thick slices of bread spread with drippings. The **Junkernschänke**, in the Barfüsserstrasse, a stylish joint with Renaissance carvings, attracts the moneyed class of students and lecturers out to impress. Considered an "underground" establishment by the trendy set, the **Nörgelbuff**, easy to overlook down a passageway off the Groner Strasse, often has live folk music and student mini-theater in its basement. Regulars divide time between quiet card games and discussions. **Zum Altdeutschen**, in the Prinzenstrasse, treats you to generously filled baguette sandwiches and *Pils.*

With any luck you might witness an academic ritual in Göttingen as quaint as any of the surrounding hill country's folk customs. Upon receiving their doctorates, graduates are wheeled out in flower-bedecked carts to kiss the bronze **Gänseliesel** statue opposite the Altes Rathaus. At the turn of the century, dozens of competing sculptors offered designs for a suitable monument. The "Goose Maiden," erected in 1901, won over more orthodox suggestions—thanks to a strong student lobby.

# THE LAND OF FAIRY TALES

The country roads heading northwest from Göttingen up into the **Weserbergland** should be guarded by gossamer checkpoints with elfin border guards on duty. You are entering the land of Sleeping Beauty and the Seven Dwarfs and deep, dark forests like the Solling that have lost none of their mystery. The brooks and rivers hurrying down the hills to meet the river Weser all seem to have age-old tales to tell; even the smallest town prides itself on its stock of fables and legends. Local storytellers have been skillful weavers of fact and fiction for centuries, often providing the raw material on which writers like the brothers Grimm embroidered. Hanau, the Grimms' birthplace, more than two hours' drive south of Göttingen, is the starting point of an officially designated **Fairy Tale Route**, which meanders north to coastal Bremerhaven. We suggest you reverse the route's sequence of towns and head south down it, using it merely as a rough guide (with pertinent and entertaining literature at all the municipal tourist offices along the way). From Göttingen take the B 3 north to Einbeck. This *Bundesstrasse,* followed by the B 64, B

240, and the B 83, will get you to Hameln. You can pick up the Fairy Tale Road there.

# Einbeck

If you skirt the eastern edge of the Solling on the way northwest from Göttingen to Hameln, it is worth making a detour to this half-timbered old town, where some 400 Gothic and Renaissance-style houses still stand, their beams crooked with age and covered with carved reliefs. Their entrances are unusually large, but for practical reasons: In the Middle Ages some families brewed beer at home and stored their hops on the top floor, and it was through the front entrance that the town's master brewer delivered and fetched the jointly owned vats needed for the job. In an early cooperative system, the burghers pooled their *Ainpöck'schen Bier,* as it was called, and exported it as far afield as Stockholm and Amsterdam. During a *Reichstag* in Worms, Martin Luther allegedly did a short commercial for their brew, raising a tankard and calling it "the best one knows." Local people never tire of telling visitors that Munich's Hofbräuhaus started in 1589 with imported Einbeck beer. Sixteenth-century Bavarian brewers were so impressed by it that they stopped mixing spices in with their hops and malt. It was also in Bavaria that *Ainpöck'schen* was slowly but surely abbreviated to *Bock,* the present name, by that region's guttural dialect.

Guided tours of the modern brewery are popular because any beer sampled en route is free of charge. But a more historical approach is to down your *Bock* in **Zum Brodhaus**, the former bakers' guild headquarters and now one of the oldest inns in town. The regulars there prefer *Pils;* they find *Bock* too sweet.

Einbeck was nearly destroyed at the end of World War II. U.S. soldiers were amazed when they saw swastikas on a house at Tiedexer Strasse 8, on a chest in the Rathaus, and, most conspicuously, on an escutcheon outside Zum Brodhaus. Sickened by the sight, their commanding officer was about to have the town shelled when one Heinrich Keim, who later became the mayor, did some eloquent explaining to save Einbeck: During the Middle Ages a patrician family, the von Ravens, cherished the swastika as a symbol of fertility and prosperity.

From Einbeck it is another 50 km (30 miles) to the northwest to Hameln (English, Hamelin), southwest of Hannover.

# Hameln

Even on weekdays (from spring to late autumn) Hameln's two main pedestrian thoroughfares, the **Bäckerstrasse** and the **Osterstrasse**, are full of day trippers admiring the town's lavishly ornamented stone façades. The unusual carvings of masks, pyramids, and gargoyles gave rise to the term *Weserrenaissance*. One alley, the **Bungelosenstrasse**, seems strangely unaffected by the bustle: It was here, on June 26, 1284, that the Pied Piper was last seen with 130 children of the town who followed him, and to this day the locals respect an unwritten rule that forbids music of any kind in this eerie back street.

With the wedding-cake splendor of the 17th-century **Hochzeitshaus** as a backdrop, the mysterious event is enacted every Sunday at noon by a group of costumed residents. The play in the market square sticks closely to the Grimms' version: A young journeyman, resplendent in a gaudily hued doublet, drifts into town, rids it of a plague of rats by luring them into the river Weser with a tune on his silver flute, and then, denied his fee, leads the children away with another enticing tune. Historians speculate that the fairy tale is based on fact, probably an exodus of young colonists to Moravia or Pomerania.

The town, not surprisingly, prefers not to quibble with the Grimm tale: It attributes more than half its tourist revenue to the legend. Indeed, there is not a souvenir shop without a supply of fluffy toy rats. The **Rattenfängerhaus** restaurant serves *Rattenschwänze,* or rat tails, really pork filets flambéd with Calvados. **Zur Krone** offers larger groups *Ratten-Nester,* a similar meat dish (which must be ordered ahead through the tourist office). A ubiquitous chaser in most taverns and restaurants is *Rattenkiller,* an especially potent bitters.

# Bodenwerder

A couple of years ago, this tiny town on the river Weser, 25 km (15 miles) south of Hameln via the B 83, celebrated its 700th anniversary; its oldest houses lean crookedly along the leafy left bank. From the riverboat pier (there is a regular service from Hameln) a narrow street leads to the manor in which Baron Karl Friedrich Hieronymus von Münchhausen was born in 1720. Most of the building is the city hall, but one small chamber serves as a museum brimming with Münchhausen memorabilia, each piece with a baronial tale to tell. Part of an iron stove on display has the British crown embossed on it—not so surprising, as young Hieronymus was born in the heady Anglo-Hanoverian era. In fact, his father held the rank of "Royal Mounted Great-British Lieutenant-Colonel." A page at the duke of Brunswick's court at the age of 12, young Münchhausen soon followed in his father's footsteps and, as an officer in the Brunswick Regiment, saw years of action in Turkey, Russia, and Finland. In 1750, he returned to Bodenwerder with several citations for gallantry, and remained as lord of the manor. From then on, Münchhausen's life became rather humdrum, and the baron evidently relieved the tedium by amusing relatives and friends with far-fetched accounts of his wartime experiences.

The manor grounds used to stretch up as far as today's **Café Berggarten**, which has a fine view of the Weser snaking its way through the Weserberg hill country. Von Münchhausen would invite his friends to the adjoining tower for hour upon hour of storytelling. Down at the museum, you can see the battered old megaphone with which the baron called down to the manor for more ham and wine during such sessions. Münchhausen never wrote down his stories: This was done, apparently without his knowledge, by business-minded scribes with a keen ear for bestselling material. The first collection was published in English, under the title *Baron Münchhausen's Narrative of His Marvellous Travels and Campaigns in Russia*. In England the volume proved to be extremely popular. Translated into German, the baronial bard came out as *Der Lügenbaron* (the lying baron). The harsh title seems to have upset him, even though he deliberately exaggerated his tales to the point of fantasy. Often enough, they were meant as parodies of the usual war veterans' bragging. A classic example: Münchhausen cruises over enemy lines on a cannonball.

The recent film based on the marvelous campaigner's adventures ran for only a couple of days in Bodenwerder. The townsfolk seem to prefer the uproarious Münchhausen sketches as performed by local actors in front of the **Rathaus** (at 3:00 P.M. on intermittent summer Sundays). The biggest event of the year is the *Lichterfest* (every second Sunday in August), when a Münchhausen stuntman on a lightweight cannonball is towed over the town by helicopter. Some 50,000 spectators usually turn up.

## Hannoversch-Münden

From Bodenwerder the B 83 and then the B 80 follow the Weser upstream (south) to Hannoversch-Münden, a leisurely 90-minute drive away. (On the map it may appear simply as "Münden," between Göttingen and Kassel.) In the **Rotunda** here, formerly one of the town's fortified towers, you can sign a chit of paper renouncing any claim to compensation in case of injury, and then climb up a series of ladders to the topmost rafter. Through a hatch you'll have a sparrow's-eye-view of yet another Medieval gem: some 700 mostly half-timbered houses crammed into a triangle formed by the confluence of the rivers Weser, Fulda, and Werra. Nothing much has changed here since Dr. Johannes Andreas Eisenbart, another of the region's colorful characters, walked the streets below.

Eisenbart was an 18th-century itinerant medic who hired jugglers, tumblers, and fire-eaters to herald his rounds through the villages. Due not least to this approach, he was regarded as a kill-or-cure charlatan by his critics. Allegations were made of horrific operations, including the extraction of gallstones with forceps the size of coal tongs. An inscription on the house at Lange Strasse 79, in which he died, seeks to put the record straight: "He was not as reputed." Recent research has revealed that Eisenbart treated penniless patients free of charge, and successfully pioneered the removal of eye cataracts. The doctor is buried outside the **Aegidienkirche**. His headstone describes him as "Royal British, Electoral-Brunswickian, Privileged General Practitioner."

An Eisenbart play reminiscent of the Pied Piper capers is performed every Sunday from Whitsun until late August at 11:15 A.M. in front of the **Rathaus**.

# The Reinhardswald

From Hannoversch-Münden a minor road climbs up via the hamlet of Hilwartshausen toward the Reinhardswald. These darkly inviting hill forests flanking the upper Weser river valley, including the **Bramwald**, are some of Germany's best-kept secrets. This is still a magical world of fir-scented, sun-dappled glades, where any of the toadstools could be the Fairy King's throne.

From Hannoversch-Münden follow the signs northwest to Sababurg. After about 8 uphill km (5 miles), you'll feel the almost primeval forest begin to swallow you up. Some of the oaks and beeches are more than 700 years old. One of the world's oldest game reserves is here, a 530-acre area set aside by a local count in 1589 and containing endangered species such as the auroch and bison.

Six-hundred-year-old **Sababurg** would be perfectly hidden here were it not for many signposts. Part of its castle is in ruins, draped with climbing roses. It is often a summer venue for open-air concerts and the like. The other attraction is a hotel-cum-restaurant (Burghotel Sababurg), where old-world charm comes at a price. This has long been a popular spot for wedding receptions and even has its own registry office. In the nearby castle Jacob (the elder by one year), the story of Sleeping Beauty is supposed to have taken place. From here as far south as Hanau you will be travelling through the landscape in which the Brothers Grimm set most of their fairy tales.

# KASSEL

This city, spread on several steep hills overlooking the Fulda valley 50 km (30 miles) southwest of Göttingen and south of the Reinhardswald, had the misfortune to be saddled with a large tank and locomotive factory during World War II. Bombing reduced most of its once elegant districts to rubble. For a taste of what is left of Old Kassel take a tram from the Hauptbahnhof up to the **Schlosshotel Wilhelmshöhe** which still sports its turreted **Löwenburg,** built in the 18th century on the lines of a Scottish Highlands castle. The Friedrichsplatz, at the bottom of the Treppenstrasse's flights of steps, is still adorned by one of the region's finest Classical buildings, the **Museum Fridericanum.** Every five years it hosts the *Documenta,* a 100-day festival of contemporary art (due next in 1992) that has brought Kassel postwar fame. Shortly before his death, the artist and environmentalist Joseph Beuys, a *Documenta* regular, began a "7,000 Oaks" campaign: He planted oak trees in and around the city, marking each tree with a small block of basalt like the one in front of the museum. One of the square's less conspicuous attractions is a 1,000-meter (3,300 foot) brass rod that the artist Walter de Maria, one of Beuys's contemporaries, drove vertically into the ground.

The Fridericanum once housed the Hofbibliothek, where Jacob and Wilhelm Grimm worked as librarians in their mid-twenties. The brothers had spent the early part of their childhood in Steinau an der Strasse (see below), but after their father's untimely death they were sent to live here with a well-to-do aunt, who was a lady-in-waiting at Kassel's court. After completing their studies in Marburg, the brothers returned to Kassel. At one of the markets on the outskirts they met Dorothea Viehmann, a housewife who seems to have been a gifted storyteller. In her youth she had learned dozens of tales from the soldiers and merchants who passed through her father's inn, **Die Knallhütte** (still in business today), on their way south to Frankfurt-am-Main. The Grimms would invite Dorothea up to their rooms at the corner of the Marktgasse and the Wildemannsgasse, where she supplied them with the raw material for roughly a third of the stories they later published. There was no fee involved. Instead, the brothers would bring out their best china and serve tea. Dorothea, a woman of modest means, regarded the pleasure of stirring her tea with a silver spoon as sufficient recompense, we are told.

The house the Grimms lived in no longer stands. But there are twin statues in the little square named after them at the western end of the Königsstrasse, Kassel's main street. The brothers were inseparable to the end of their days, Jacob, a bachelor, even moving in with Wilhelm and his wife.

# *MARBURG*

Marburg, 80 km (47 miles) southwest of Kassel, has one of the region's most ancient pedigrees. Its municipal records date back to the beginning of the 12th century. The town's core of venerable buildings, on a hill overlooking the river Lahn, emerged from World War II unscathed. Life in the Altstadt still has a tranquil, academic flavor. Nearly a quarter of Marburg's 70,000 inhabitants are students. The university was founded in 1527. It was here that Martin Luther and the Swiss church reformer Ulrich Zwingli met for talks that failed to bridge the doctrinal gap between them. From the **Schloss**, the Altstadt's crowning 15th-century glory, you'll have a splendid view of the Lahn hills. Getting up there from the river Lahn at the foot of Marburg entails a steep climb up cobblestone lanes and more than 400 steps. During their sojourn here as law students, from 1802 to 1805, the Grimm brothers lodged about halfway up, at the corner of the Barfüsserstrasse and the Wendel Gasse. The building, with a shoe shop on the ground floor, is marked by a plaque.

The old part of town, something of a maze, is where the 16,000 university students spend a fair portion of their après-lecture time. Favorite dives are the **Destille** on the Steinweg, famous for its Tequila Sunrises, and **Cavete**, also on the Steinweg, a jazz tavern where the late Chet Baker and Elvin Jones have given live performances. Except on weekends, when an endless stream of provincial shoppers climbs up here from the parking lots, life is a placid round of baguette-crunching and wine-sipping. The last political demonstration, in which stark-naked students protested cuts in grants, took place some ten years ago.

Jacob and Wilhelm Grimm apparently found early 19th-century Marburg idyllic. Walk up through the fragrant gardens, aflutter with butterflies, to the **Forsthof,** now a residence hall, where the brothers had their tutorials with professor Friedrich von Savigny. He introduced them to his brother-in-law Clemens von Brentano, a member of the Heidelberg school of Romantic writers and a collector and publisher of German folk songs. The association furthered their career, much as Dorothea Viehmann did later.

Down in the Unterstadt do not miss the **Elisabethkirche,** named after the city's patron saint, Elisabeth von Thüringen. At the beginning of the 13th century, Elisabeth, the 20-year-old widow of that state's duke, became Marburg's titular ruler. Instead of exploiting the position like many of her predecessors, she gave up all her worldly goods and spent her short life tending to the sick and aged. Elisabeth was canonized in 1235. In the sacristy you can see the glittering gold shrine, studded with jewels, that contained her remains until the Reformation. Grimm connoisseurs identify it as the model for Sleeping Beauty's glass coffin. Latter-day pilgrims to the shrine have included the British royal family, who are Elisabeth's distant relatives.


# *HERBSTEIN*

A pleasant cross-country drive east from Marburg along B 62 and B 254 as far as Lauterbach will bring you back to the heart of Fairy Tale Country. The part of B 275 here climbs south from Lauterbach to the **Vogelsberg,** a bumpy plateau formed by volcanic activity some 30 million years ago. Herbstein, a quiet farming community in the process of restoring its Medieval architecture, is the gravitational center of West Germany. In 1978 a TV network found that a map of the country, cut out along its borders and then mounted on cardboard, can be spun on a perfectly horizontal plane only if it is pivoted almost exactly where Herbstein is. The village now presents its visitors with certificates proudly proclaiming its central location (50° 32′ 18″ latitude and 9° 21′ 41″ longitude). An inscribed stone has even been erected at the exact spot: south of Herbstein on the road to Altenschlirf. If and when West and East Germany are unified, of course, Herbstein's claim to fame will evaporate.

The weaving of legends is an age-old local craft here. Herbstein's name, for example, is said to derive from the ancient Harras, a knight who ruled the area. He had the suitors bidding for his daughter Hermengilde's hand engage in a formidable contest. The first to shoulder a huge basalt rock up to the castle could marry Hermengilde. Hugo, his daughter's favorite, almost made it to the portcullis but then collapsed. With his dying breath he uttered the words *herber Stein*—which translates roughly into the genteel expletive "dratted stone."

Volcanic rocks, which came in handy during the village's restoration work, still dot the surrounding fields. **Hoherods-kopf,** one of the nearby hills, is probably where the ancient volcano's crater once opened. It was here that the eighth-century missionary Boniface, who was born in Devon, England, did some of his early preaching. He had received papal authority to evangelize the German tribes in 718; by 754 he was the Archbishop of Mainz. He and 53 companions were martyred in Frisia three years later.

Ten years before his death Boniface had instructed one of his pupils, Sturmius, to have an abbey built in **Fulda,** 25 km (15 miles) east of Herbstein. Along with its counterparts in Orleans, Tours, and St. Gallen, the abbey school had become one of the Continent's theological centers by 814, the year of Charlemagne's death. Christianity was spread throughout central Germany from here. Boniface lies buried in the crypt of Fulda's cathedral. Built between 1704 and 1712, the existing Dom is the focal point of one of Germany's finest Baroque town centers, which throbs and buzzes into life on market days.

## STEINAU AN DER STRASSE

The B 27 and B 40, running south from Fulda, return you to the "Fairy Tale Route" in Steinau. This town, close to Frankfurt-am-Main to the southwest, was once the first-night stop for merchants on their way from Frankfurt to Leipzig. When the town gates were bolted at dusk, the highway robbers known to lurk in the spooky **Spessart forest** nearby must have felt well and truly locked out, because the walls of the Renaissance castle's keep are more than 30 meters (90 feet) high. The whole of this tiny town has a fortified feel. The Grimm family moved here from Hanau when Jacob and Wilhelm were six and seven years old, respectively. During the five years their father was a magistrate in the **Amtshaus** (now the **Heimatmuseum**), the boys led a carefree and sheltered life. One of their favorite haunts was the spring down by the town wall—follow the sign reading *Stadtborn* to visit it. Jacob and Wilhelm probably felt the same way about their surroundings as their brother Ludwig Emil, who later illustrated many of their books. Looking back on those romantic days as an adult, he recalled "Steinau, nestling between two hills, [as] the wonderland of my childhood."

When their father died in 1796 the Grimms fell on hard times. Widow Grimm had very little money and six children to feed. To help out, her sister Henriette, a lady-in-waiting in Kassel, took charge of Jacob and Wilhelm, who bade a sad farewell to Steinau. The town has kept their memory alive, and the museum in the **Schloss** is amply stocked with their writings, including the erudite philological volumes of their later years. In the market square, opposite the fountain embossed with characters from their best-known folk tales, the **Steinauer Marionettentheater** regularly performs their stories with beautifully carved puppets. One of the cozy taverns, **Zum Weissen Ross**, even serves the brothers' favorite boyhood dishes: pea soup followed by wine-flavored mousse with vanilla sauce.

# GELNHAUSEN

You need considerable time and stamina to explore this old hillside town between Steinau and Frankfurt, with its steep lanes and two main squares, **Untermarkt** and **Obermarkt**, set on different levels. But just walking around Gelnhausen is like turning the pages of a chronicle of a millennium of German history. Down on the banks of the river Kinzig are the remains, including some still elegant arches, of a **palace** (*Pfalz*) built for Emperor Frederick I of Hohenstaufen in the 12th century. It was during the *Reichstag* here in the year 1180 that Barbarossa parceled out the territory of his cousin and rival Henry the Lion—a fateful decision that triggered Germany's *Kleinstaaterei,* its division into hundreds of small states. The Pfalz grounds are open daily except Mondays.

Opposite the palace grounds, in the former fortifications, is the **Hexenturm**, a tower in which alleged witches and heretics were held prisoner by the Inquisition and its torturers during the Middle Ages.

The former synagogue in the Brentanostrasse, built in

1601 and destroyed in 1938, has been reconstructed as a place for lectures and exhibitions. It still contains one of the very few Baroque Torah shrines left in Europe. Its inscription in both Hebrew and German reads: "In the years of hatred our Jewish citizens were deported and their place of worship desecrated. In the hope of reconciliation, this building was dedicated to the spirit of peace and culture on September 25 in the year 1986."

In the **Kuhgasse** you can see the oldest half-timbered house in the state of Hesse (which you entered north of Kassel). It is Gothic in style, dated 1340. The bust in the Untermarkt shows Philipp Reis, born on the Langgasse in 1834. Along with Alexander Graham Bell and Charles Boursel, he is one of the telephone's pioneers.

For some historic accommodations try the **Grimmelshausen-Hotel** in the Schmidtgasse, where Johann Jacob Christoph von Grimmelshausen was born in 1621. As a 13-year-old he witnessed imperial troops sacking the town and had to flee to Hanau with his grandfather. Soon afterward, he was thrown into the atrocities of the Thirty Years War. He survived some nine years in the thick of the fighting: as a groom, imperial musketeer, and regimental clerk. In 1669 Grimmelshausen published *Der Abentheurliche Simplicissimus,* the first German-language novel. His account of a disingenuous young man enlightened and toughened by the horrors of war is allegorical and satirical, but not all that fictional. Simplex, the book's hero, relives much of what Grimmelshausen himself went through. The novel has since been translated into more than a hundred languages, including Chinese.

# HANAU

Fifteen km (10 miles) southwest of Gelnhausen the ragged skyline of Hanau's hasty 1950s architecture rises to meet you. Farther in, a semblance of an Altstadt—just enough for you to picture yesteryear's Hanau—has recently been restored. One of the most ornate buildings is the **Rathaus**, which faces a huge monument in honor of Jacob and Wilhelm Grimm. Hanau has made the most of the fact that the brothers were born here, even though they soon moved on to Steinau with their parents. Later, after their years in Kassel and Marburg, the brothers pursued academic careers in Göttingen, as we have noted, and finally Berlin. There they lived busily ever after, immersed in compiling a comprehensive German dictionary. Wilhelm got as far as the letter D;

Jacob, who died four years later in 1863, continued as far as *Frucht,* the word for fruit. They were buried side by side in Berlin's Schöneberg cemetery. By the time following generations of academics had completed their dictionary, in 1960, *Der Grimm* was 35,000 pages long.

Frankfurt-am-Main lies just to the west of Hanau.

## GETTING AROUND

The region lies within a heart-shaped network of major Autobahns: Hannover–Kassel; Kassel–Paderborn; and Bielefeld–Hannover. These Autobahns are close enough to be useful for A-to-B driving but do not encroach on the scenic interior. Motoring here is a pleasure: Country roads and remote forest roads are relatively free of heavy traffic, thanks to those outer Autobahns.

Hameln, Bodenwerder, Hannoversch-Münden, Kassel, and Marburg are connected to the main Munich–Hannover railroad line with some of the fastest stretches in the Republic's rail network, but there is no line up the Weser river valley. Nature lovers see this as a blessing.

One of the most enjoyable ways to explore the area is by riverboat on the Weser. The **Oberweser Dampfschiffahrt**, the biggest of several shipping companies, runs a scheduled service from the end of April to the beginning of October. Vessels call at most of the villages and towns between Hameln and Bad Karlshafen. Downstream travel (to the north) is considerably faster than upstream travel; for example, the trip from Karlshafen to Bodenwerder takes seven hours, while the return trip can take up to five hours longer. During periods of low rainfall there are some very shallow stretches of river, and schedules cannot always be maintained.

## ACCOMMODATIONS REFERENCE

▶ **Der Achtermann**. Rosentorstrasse 20, D-3380 **Goslar** 1. Tel: (5321) 210-01; Telex: 953847.

▶ **Burghotel Sababurg**. D-3520 **Hofgeismar-Sababurg**. Tel: (5678) 10-52.

▶ **Der Fürstenhof**. Hannoversche Strasse 55/56, D-3100 **Celle**. Tel: (5141) 20-10; Telex: 925293 CEHOG D.

▶ **Grimmelshausen-Hotel**. Schmidtgasse 12, D-6460 **Gelnhausen**. Tel: (6051) 170-31.

▶ **Herz-Hotel Sauerbrey**. D-3360 **Osterode-Lerbach**. Tel: (5522) 20-65.

▶ **Hotel Ritter St. Georg**. Alte Knochenhauerstrasse 11-13, D-3300 **Braunschweig**. Tel: (531) 130-39.

▶ **Schlosshotel Wilhelmshöhe**. Im Schlosspark 2, D-3500 **Kassel**. Tel: (561) 308-80.

# BACH AND LUTHER COUNTRY

## IN EAST GERMANY

*By Phyllis Méras*

*Phyllis Méras, travel editor of the* Providence *(Rhode Island)* Journal, *contributes travel articles to* Newsday, *the* Chicago Tribune, *and the* San Francisco Examiner. *She travels frequently in East Germany.*

Now that the Berlin Wall has toppled, and the Communist government that ruled East Germany for decades with it, the land of Luther and Goethe and Bach should soon be an inviting destination once again. The old regime's stiff regulations and the pitfalls that accompany them—prepayment for accommodations before visas are issued; a wait of three to six weeks to obtain visas; discouraging changes in your itinerary after it has been set—are now things of the past. We still refer to this area as East Germany, however, because that is how people will—by habit or for convenience—be referring to it for some time.

While the postwar rebuilding of West Germany has been all but completed, in East Germany there is scarcely a city or town where streets are not torn up and where scaffolding does not conceal fine Renaissance or Baroque façades.

Small entity that it is—318 miles north to south and 90 miles east to west—East Germany's resources are limited. Brown coal is the fuel of necessity, and smog is inevitable.

Pollution of waterways is considerable as well. Then there is the shortage of paper, which limits the amount and kinds of printing that can be done. Guidebooks in English to historic sites have low priority. In fact, because English in general has had low priority, it is often difficult to find English-language tours or English-speaking help in hotels and restaurants.

But in 1983, the 500th anniversary of Martin Luther's birth in Eisleben, some three million foreign visitors braved the difficulties of entry to see the sites that were important in that great reformer's life. East Germany enjoyed the hard currency that they brought, and it has been wooing visitors from the West ever since.

Five-star hotels that vie with any hotel in the world have been erected in major cities. Avis and Hertz rental cars are available. And, of course, since July, 1990, the West German mark has been East Germany's only legal tender.

Though hotels in lesser categories tend to be lacking in many amenities (toilets leak; windows refuse to open and close; the sink faucet may also be the water supply for the bathtub), prices are relatively low (DM 80 to 100 per person in smaller cities for a satisfactory room with breakfast and a private bath, DM 120 to 140 in Leipzig and Dresden, and more for deluxe hotels).

And East Germany has much to offer. Isolated as it has been behind a wall for decades, it somehow seems still part of a simpler, quieter past. Crossing the border, you step into a place where walks in the woods and strolls in the park are part of the pattern of everyday life. Sex shops and rock music, VCRs and Big Macs have yet to arrive, though given the pace of unification and economic integration, they won't be long in coming.

This is a land rich in culture and historic cities, among them Berlin (see our Berlin chapter) and Leipzig, renowned since the Middle Ages for its trade fairs; Dresden, whose incomparable Baroque architecture, demolished in World War II, is being painstakingly restored; and Potsdam, home of Sans Souci; the dazzling showplace of the Prussian emperor Frederick the Great. In East Germany's little towns and villages, half-timbered Medieval houses crowd cobblestone streets. High Gothic churches tower over marketplaces. Castles loom on forested hillsides. Music is everywhere in the air. Raphael's *Sistine Madonna* and Giorgione's *Sleeping Venus* are in Dresden, along with one of the world's finest collections of porcelain and royal jewelry. Then there is Luther's birthplace at Eisleben; Eisenach, where Johann Sebastian

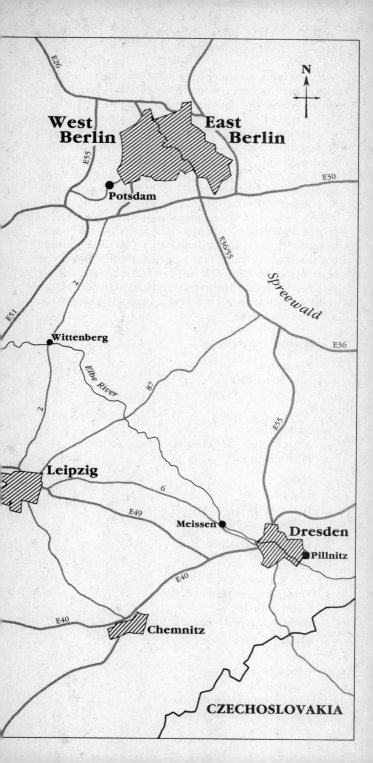

Bach was born; Arnstadt and Mühlhausen, where he played the organ; Wittenberg, where Protestantism began; Weimar, where Johann Wolfgang von Goethe and Friedrich Schiller wrote; and Gotha, once ruled by Queen Victoria's sons. There is Naumberg, with its Medieval cathedral; the Hanseatic towns of Stralsund and Rostock on the Baltic Sea; the sylvan Spreewald with its winding waterway; the wildflowers of the Harz Mountains; half-timbered Quedlinburg and Wernigerode and rebuilt Halberstadt; the Thuringian forest; and the Elbe valley with its brown-gold river.

Only a few of these attractions—the major cities of Leipzig and Dresden, as well as those with close connections to Frederick, Bach, Handel, and Luther—are discussed here, but the venturesome visitor to East Germany should consider exploring further. It will surely require stamina and patience (trains are late; museums close for lunch; historic churches are opened at the whim of church wardens)—but it will be rewarding.

### MAJOR INTEREST

**Potsdam**
Sans Souci palace
Schloss Cecilienhof

**Wittenberg**
Stadtkirche
A stroll along the Collegienstrasse
Renaissance Rathaus

**Halle**
Handel house
Gothic and Romanesque towers
Halloren Museum

**Lutherstadt Eisleben**

**Eisenach**
The Wartburg
Reuter-Wagner Museum
Georgenkirche
Bach and Luther houses

**Erfurt**
Dom
Augustinerkirche
Severikirche
12th-century Krämerbrücke
Thuringian folk art museum

**Gotha**
Schloss Friedenstein

**Mühlhausen**
Kornmarktkirche and museum of the Peasants' War
Marienkirche

**Weimar**
Goethe and Schiller houses, Altstadt
Lucas Cranach the Elder altarpiece, Stadtkirche
Franz Liszt house

**Leipzig**
Altes Rathaus
Naschmarkt
Thomaskirche
Bach archives, Bose house
Neues Gewandhaus
Georgi Dimitroff Museum

**Dresden and Environs**
The Albertinum museum
The Zwinger museum
Semper Opernhaus
Summer palace of Pillnitz
Albrechtsburg and Dom, Meissen
Display rooms of the Meissen factory

We begin at Frederick the Great's palace in Potsdam just
outside Berlin, then move southwest into Luther and Handel
territory, first Wittenberg, then Halle and Eisleben, near
Leipzig.

Bypassing Leipzig for the moment, we continue on to
Eisenach, on the West German border. From Eisenach—of
interest for both Luther and J. S. Bach—we follow the northern edge of the Thuringian forest eastward through towns
famous for their association with J. S. Bach: Gotha, Erfurt,
Mühlhausen, Arnstadt, and Weimar.

From this point the route heads back toward Leipzig, and
after Leipzig we end at Dresden and Meissen on the north–
south route between Berlin and Prague.

# *POTSDAM*

In Potsdam, 30 km (17 miles) southwest of East Berlin (but
just across the Havel river by way of the Glienicke bridge
from West Berlin's Wannsee and Grunewald area), Frederick

the Great of Prussia, longing for a restful place, built a
summer palace near the Havel that is one of Europe's
loveliest 18th-century royal dwellings. The center of this
historic town was severely damaged in 1945, and is only now
being rebuilt for its 1,000th anniversary in 1993. But Frederick's country palace survived the war relatively intact. Indeed, it was to Schloss Cecilienhof that Harry S Truman,
Joseph Stalin, and Winston Churchill (and his successor as
British prime minister, Clement Attlee) came for the Potsdam Conference of 1945 that decided the postwar fate of
Germany.

Small by the standards of its day—**Sans Souci** was built
between 1745 and 1747—Frederick the Great's golden summer palace of ten rooms, plus a vestibule and a marble hall,
is an architectural and decorative gem. It seems to bring the
outdoors indoors in a near-miraculous way.

Frederick was a writer, artist, and musician. He wrote
poetry and prose and played the flute, for which he composed concertos. J. S. Bach wrote his "Musical Offering" for
Frederick in 1747. Though often curt to people, he was
devoted to animals and to nature. Indeed, he asked to be
buried in the garden here beside his beloved greyhounds.
(Instead, he was buried in Württemberg, with his father,
Friedrich Wilhelm I, whom he abhorred.) Frederick drew
the plans for Sans Souci himself, setting his palace at the top
of a terraced vineyard. He wanted a single-story structure so
he could open his doors and step out into the garden. To
make his design a reality he selected an old friend, Georg
von Knobelsdorff, an army officer turned architect.

From the garden entrance, guests entered his long, low,
narrow building with a center dome and mounted a graceful
flight of stairs. There, between the long windows of the
façade, 36 caryatids lean outward.

At the north entrance, where today's guests enter, Frederick's visitors who came by coach would, stepping out, look
through a semicircular colonnade of Corinthian pillars to a
view of artificial Roman ruins in the distance. The palace was
constructed in what has come to be called "Potsdam Rococo."

Bacchus and nymphs dance in relief above the doors in its
cheerful entrance hall. Flora, goddess of flowers, looks
down from the painted ceiling. In the art gallery, paintings of
the school of Jean-Antoine Watteau and sculpture and busts
(including a bust of Frederick made from his death mask)
line the walls. Off Frederick's library—filled in his day with
more than 2,000 books in French, for he admired everything

Gallic—are his study and bedroom. Though the furniture is Rococo, the rooms themselves have since been rebuilt in Classical style. It was in the alcove here, sitting in his wing chair, that Frederick died in 1786, at the age of 74. The French clock that he always took great care to wind himself is said to have stopped at the moment he died.

The ceiling in the bright music room, which especially seems to bring nature indoors, is gaily painted with spiders and birds, baskets of flowers, and dogs chasing rabbits. Murals inspired by Ovid's *Metamorphoses,* done by the French painter Antoine Pesne, seem somehow to expand the walls.

In the reception room, with its painted ceiling of Flora and Zephyr, god of wind, the king thoughtfully hung French paintings that he liked, so that those awaiting an audience could while away their time fruitfully.

Frederick had the central hall of his palace fashioned after the Pantheon in Rome, with Carrara marble columns. The guest rooms are off it—one in Chinese style, based on the paintings on Chinese porcelain; a second done in blue; a third in red. Finally, there is the Voltaire room, with a bust of the French philosopher scrutinizing the parrots flying on its lemon-yellow walls.

A great admirer of Voltaire, Frederick corresponded with him for years and invited him to move to his court so they could talk together of matters the king considered important: philosophy and literature. Voltaire came and stayed for a while, but the pair quarreled and the philosopher left. "He is like a lemon," Frederick remarked afterward. "You can press out the juice and throw the rest away."

A stroll over the extensive grounds of the palace is as important a part of a visit to Sans Souci as seeing its buildings. At the foot of the stairs to the garden, the great fountain plays. Down the Hauptallee from the fountain is the obelisk portal entrance to the park, with two goddesses—Flora of flowers and Pomona of fruit—standing on a wall beside sets of Corinthian columns. In the Neptune grotto, the god of the sea brandishes his trident over a Baroque arch set against a backdrop of trees.

Above the grotto rises the **Bildergalerie** (Picture Gallery), said to be the first building ever constructed solely for the purpose of exhibiting of works of art. Here (poorly displayed) are paintings by Peter Paul Rubens, Lucas Cranach the Elder, Guido Reni, Caravaggio, and Anthony Van Dyck.

On the west side of Sans Souci is the **Orangerie**, built in

Italian Renaissance style. Inside, the decoration is French Regency and Empire, and copies of 47 Raphael paintings hang on the walls.

Also west of Sans Souci is the extensive **Neuer Palais** (New Palace), whose construction at great expense, just after the Seven Years War with France, Austria, Russia, Saxony, and Sweden had exhausted the nation, dismayed Frederick's subjects considerably. The king, who himself called this enormous red-brick palace (with a marble concert hall 100 feet long and a 500-seat theater) ostentatious, seemed to think it important to build it to show off the powers of his state.

There is a gay little Chinese teahouse with a tent-shaped roof, treelike columns, gilded sculptures, and, inside, a Mandarin sitting beneath a parasol. This was a period of great admiration for things Chinese all across Europe, for China seemed to Europeans, from the little they were learning of it, a paradise on earth. This teahouse, designed by John Büring, is one of the finest examples of chinoiserie.

**Schloss Cecilienhof**, now part first-class hotel, part historical museum, is a 1913 copy of an English country house built on the palace grounds for Kaiser Wilhelm II's son, Crown Prince Wilhelm, and his wife, Cecilia. Thirty-six rooms of the palace were renovated and used for the Potsdam Conference. Today, only a few are open to the public (see also Staying in Potsdam, below). The Soviet delegation to the conference met in the former study of the crown princess. The paneled smoking room of the crown prince became the working room of the American delegation. (It was here, reportedly, that Truman learned of the successful completion of the atomic bomb with a telegram declaring cryptically, "A baby is born.") At the writing desk in the crown prince's blue study, Winston Churchill worked for a few days before Clement Attlee's Labor Party came into power and Attlee succeeded him.

Other late additions on the palace grounds, built by Frederick William IV in the 19th century, include **Charlottenhof**, a little palace designed by Karl Friedrich Schinkel in the 1820s in villa style. Its wide lawns, maples, copper beeches, lindens, and extensive flower beds were largely laid out in their present form by master landscape artist Peter Joseph Lenné. Among other late additions are the Römische Bäder (Roman Baths), the Fasanerie (Pheasantry), the Friedenskirche (Peace Church), and a number of gardens.

To the east of the palace grounds, in the town of Potsdam itself, the dome of the **Nikolaikirche**, built by Schinkel in

1849 but bombed in World War II, has been restored along with the **Wilhelm-Staab-Strasse**, a Baroque street. There are the little houses of the Dutch quarter to see; the Russian colony built for singers from Russia at Frederick III's court; the reconstructed 1752 Rathaus topped with Atlas holding the world on his shoulders; and the **Brandenburger Tor** (Brandenburg Gate) of 1770—not, of course, to be confused with the gate of the same name in Berlin that for 40 years separated East from West.

## Staying and Dining in Potsdam

Historic **Hotel Cecilienhof**, built in English country-house style for the family of the crown prince during World War I, is the place to stay in Potsdam. It was here that the Potsdam Agreement was signed in 1945. Much of the palace—42 rooms, many of them elegant and with garden overlooks—is now a hotel. Tours of the city of Potsdam can be arranged; some English is spoken. There is good dining in the Cecilienhof dining rooms.

The **Hotel Potsdam** on the Lange Brücke is an expensive, but less charming, possibility. Some English is spoken. The fare and ambience are Bulgarian at the **Restaurant Bolgar**, at Klement-Gottwald-Strasse 35; Tel: 2-25-05.

# *WITTENBERG*

About 75 km (45 miles) south of Potsdam on route 2, about halfway to Leipzig, is Wittenberg, a major Luther site where, in 1517, the Reformer posted his 95 theses that are the foundation of Protestantism, on the castle-church door. The original door was destroyed in a 16th-century fire; a bronze 19th-century door engraved with the theses has replaced it.

Martin Luther came to Wittenberg in 1508 to study and teach at its university. Before long he was one of its most popular professors, and the reputation of the university had spread far and wide. But Luther was outraged by the practice of selling indulgences—buying pardon, as he saw it, for sin through contributions to the Church. The poster he tacked on the church door took issue with the practice.

The sale of indulgences, however, was profitable to the Church, and the enthusiasm with which Luther's theses were received (unbeknownst to him, they were translated from Latin to German and were widely distributed) was disturbing. He was summoned to Worms to explain himself to Holy

Roman Emperor Charles V. On his return, his supporter-benefactor, Saxon elector Frederick the Wise, fearful that Luther might be in danger, whisked him off to Wartburg castle in Eisenach (see below).

But Wittenberg was Luther's home, and it was there that he returned from the Wartburg. While he was gone, his colleagues in the Reformation had been rewriting the rules. One change allowed priests to marry, and on a bright spring day, at the door of the **Stadtkirche** (parish church) of St. Mary that still towers behind Wittenberg's Marktplatz, the priest and monk Martin Luther married a former nun, Catherine von Bora.

If you visit that Gothic church today, you will see Luther preaching on a panel of the altar triptych that his friend and fellow resident of Wittenberg, Lucas Cranach the Elder, is said to have painted (Luther sometimes was a substitute preacher in the church). He is also there as Junker Jörg—the knight he was disguised as in the Wartburg. His wife, Catherine; his protector, Frederick the Wise; and his friend, adviser, and professor of Greek, Philipp Melanchthon, are also depicted on the altarpiece. Wittenberg today is remembered not only for Martin Luther but also for Melanchthon and the Cranachs, father and son.

An amble along the **Collegienstrasse** from one end to the other is a pleasant way to spend an afternoon. A good starting place is the oak tree at whose site Luther burned the papal bull that threatened him with excommunication. A little way farther is the house where Melanchthon, page by page, checked Luther's translation of the New Testament, sent to him from the Wartburg. Still farther along, across a tree-shaded courtyard, is the **Augusteum**, the Augustinian monastery where first Luther the priest, and, after the dissolution of the monasteries, Luther the married man, lived with his family. Today the monastery is filled with Reformation-period exhibits: richly decorated Bibles, prints, coins, medals, and drawings. In Luther's room is a pulpit from which he preached, and the platform from which he lectured to his students.

In the **Marktplatz** monuments to both Luther and Melanchthon stand in front of the High Renaissance **Rathaus**, with a striking two-story portico. From the town hall balcony sentences for malfeasance were issued, and in the marketplace itself executions were carried out. Modern-day strollers often sit for a while on park benches in the Marktplatz to enjoy a sausage or an ice-cream cone and watch the passersby.

Beyond the Marktplatz, which is edged with gabled Renaissance houses, the Collegienstrasse becomes the Schloss-strasse and leads to the **Friedenskirche**. A side excursion may be made near the church to the house where Lucas Cranach the Elder, mayor and councillor of the town as well as painter and friend to Luther, had his workshop.

In its present form the castle church, which has been many times destroyed and restored, is largely 19th century. Frederick the Wise is buried here beneath an early German Renaissance bronze plaque by the Nürnberg sculptor Peter Vischer the Younger. On one side of the church are Philipp Melanchthon's remains; on the other, under the Late Gothic altar, are those of Martin Luther.

It is probably better not to stay overnight in Wittenberg but to take a day trip here from Berlin or Leipzig. If you must stay over, the best accommodation is at the little **Goldener Adler**. (As always, be sure to book in advance.)

# *HALLE*

Southwest of Wittenberg, and only about 30 km (19 miles) west of Leipzig, is Halle, where George Frederick Handel was born in 1685, and where, at the sprawling yellow Handel Haus at Nikolaistrasse 5, pictures and documents (in German but with an English text available) tell of his defiance of his father's wish that he become a lawyer, and of his musical studies. They recall his education at Halle's university, his post as cathedral organist at 17, and his quitting Halle for Hamburg, then Italy, and finally England, where he spent the greater part of his life. Period musical instruments are in the house and visitors are treated to recorded selections from his work. A Handel festival is an annual June event in town.

Halle's other appeals are its skyscape at dusk and its elaborately decorated turn-of-the-century houses. All around the Markt are towers—the two Gothic and two Romanesque towers, joined by a bridge, of the **Marktkirche**, where Johann Sebastian Bach's oldest son, Wilhelm Friedemann Bach, was the organist for 18 years. The Late Gothic **Roter Turm** (Red Tower) also rises here, with a statue of Roland, symbolizing the town's independence, at its foot. A statue of Handel also stands in the square. Lamentably, a tram crosses the marketplace, and by daylight its tracks and overhead wires destroy the illusion of antiquity the towers otherwise offer.

Handsome town houses rise along the Schmeerstrasse

and on the Rannischestrasse, both in the neighborhood of
the market square, but again the omnipresent trams intrude.

For centuries, Halle was renowned for the *Halis* (salt
springs) from which it takes its name, and in its **Halloren
Museum**, at Mansfelder Strasse 52 (which is open one Sunday
morning each month), is the stunning silver drinking-cup
collection of its old salt workers' guild, the finest silver guild
in East Germany. To find out which Sunday the museum is
open, check with Halle information at Kleinschmeiden 6,
near the Marktplatz.

A leading industrial city and a railroad junction, Halle
suffered considerably during World War II. Much rebuilding
and demolition of badly damaged structures still goes on,
but on narrow lanes, half-timbered buildings bear evidence
of the charm of the Halle of the Middle Ages. Today, however, with brown coal firing many Halle factories, air pollution is a problem.

## Staying and Dining in Halle

**Hotel Stadt Halle**, across from the railway station on the
Ernst-Thälmann-Platz, is an enormous edifice designed in
Eastern European modern. Sometimes its showers work,
sometimes they don't. If its windows refuse to budge, a
helpful housekeeper will hammer them open with a shoe
brush from the closet. There really is no choice of accommodation here.

Russian dishes are the specialty in the **Uta Restaurant**, in
the Stadt Halle. There are a number of simple restaurants in
Halle in historic buildings. These include the Gasthaus **Zur
Goldenen Rose** on Grosse Schmeerstrasse, **Zum Mohren**
near Burg Giebichenstein, and the **Weinkeller Moritzburg**
on Friedemann-Bach-Platz.

## Lutherstadt Eisleben

It was in the pretty little Harz mountain town of Eisleben
(population 27,000), 21 km (13 miles) west of Halle, where
blue and rose and yellow stucco houses with high-pitched
roofs front on the market square, that Martin Luther was
born, in 1483. His father was a copper miner; before Martin
was a year old, the family moved to neighboring Mansfeld,
more of a mining center.

Though Luther spent only the first months of his life in
the square little Franconian *Geburtshaus* (birth house) near
the Markt (now reconstructed), Lutherstadt Eisleben (the

"Lutherstadt" was added to the name in 1946) proudly lays claim to his birth. He was baptized in the **Petri-Pauli-Kirche** (the Church of Sts. Peter and Paul); he died in the town archivist's house at the top of the Marktplatz; and his body lay in state at the **Andreaskirche** (St. Andrew's church), which towers over the Marktplatz.

Both Luther houses—the Franconian-style birth house, where an 1817 Johann Gottfried von Schadow bust of the Reformer sits in the garden, and the Gothic-style death house—have been painstakingly restored, and furnished, albeit sparsely, in 16th-century style.

Of particular interest in the Geburtshaus are period paintings of supporters of the Reformation and the gleaming golden swan that became Luther's symbol, alluding to the martyred Czech Reformer Jan Hus's cry 68 years earlier at the stake: "You are roasting a goose, but after me there will come a swan you will not be able to roast." There is a kitchen with iron pots and wooden buckets on the ground floor, along with old copper-mining tools and copies of Lucas Cranach the Elder's portraits of the Reformer's forbidding-looking parents, Hans and Margaretta Luther.

Luther died of a heart attack on his way back to his home in Wittenberg after settling a dispute between two landgraves of Mansfeld. In the little room where he died are a curtained bed, a chest, and a washstand. Elsewhere in the house are the cloth that covered his coffin and a copy of one of the last letters he wrote to his wife.

An English-language recording describes the displays in the state-owned Geburtshaus. In the church-owned death house, an English-speaking guide offers help and will take you up the cobblestone street to the gray-stone Andreaskirche.

In the marketplace, which is edged with half-timbered and gabled houses, stands a turn-of-the-century statue of the Reformer. The **Goldenes Schiff**, on the Lutherstrasse, offers pleasant meals.

## EISENACH

It has often been said that this town, at the West German border in the Thüringer Wald in southwestern East Germany, has been thrice blessed: Here Martin Luther spent both his teenage years and the months in which he translated the New Testament from Greek into German; here, in 1685, the composer Johann Sebastian Bach was born; and here, in 1842, Richard Wagner saw the castle-fortress that rises above Eisenach and, inspired by it, wrote *Tannhäuser*.

Though World War II wreaked considerable damage, Eisenach, being relatively small (population 55,000), has had enough restoration so that much of it looks today as it must have looked in the 17th century. Its half-timbered houses are nestled in the valley below the forest of oaks and birches and lindens. From the **Wartburg**—once the castle home of the landgraves of Thüringen—you can look down on these pretty pastel houses with their red tile roofs.

From the spring of 1521 until December of that year, Luther remained in the hilltop castle above Eisenach. Charles V, the devoutly Catholic emperor of the Holy Roman Empire, had called the reformer-monk to Worms and ordered him to recant his criticisms. When Luther refused, he was declared a "notorious heretic." Though he was given a safe-conduct to return to his home in Wittenberg, the emperor vowed that action would be taken against him later. En route home Luther was "kidnapped" and spirited off, blindfolded, to the Wartburg. There his protectors had him discard his monk's robe for a knight's garb, grow his hair and a beard, and assume a knight's name and identity: He became "Junker Jörg." For nine months he was kept in the Wartburg in hopes that, while he was away, the furor over his activities would eventually end.

His small, simple room at the Wartburg is restored today largely as it was then, furnished only with a table and a green tile stove, the whale vertebra he used as a footstool, a copy of the copper engraving his friend Lucas Cranach the Elder did of him as Junker Jörg, and Cranach paintings of Luther and Melanchthon hanging on the wall. In this room, Luther translated the New Testament from Greek into German in ten weeks, and in so doing virtually created the modern German language.

He was not happy in the Wartburg, the view of wind-tossed trees and spacious valley and red tile village roofs below notwithstanding. He felt guilty being away from the people he thought he should be serving. When bats wheeled about the nearly deserted castle and owls hooted, he wondered if they were the devil incarnate. (An ink spot on the wall of his room is said to have been made when he threw ink at the devil.) Conquering his guilt and anxiety, however, he worked assiduously, and the visitor to the Wartburg today will find, on the table in his room, a copy of the German New Testament he prepared there.

On German-guided tours of the castle, you also visit the

late Romanesque hall with a cross-vaulted ceiling that has been restored to give it the 12th-century look of the landgraves' time, and you will see the bright mid–19th-century frescoes that recount the history of the landgraves. Devotees of music and culture, their hospitality to the minnesingers of Medieval Germany was renowned, and the *Sängerkrieg* (a contest among minstrels) that is said to have been held in the fortress so captivated Wagner, visiting in the 19th century, that he made it an integral part of *Tannhäuser*.

Bright frescoes and murals recall the Sängerkrieg and the life of 13th-century Saint Elisabeth of Hungary, the landgrave's wife who, as Elisabeth of Thüringen, performed great acts of generosity and mercy. Fifteenth- and 16th-century carvings and sculpture are also on display, and in the Jubilee Hall, notable for its acoustics, concerts are held in warm seasons.

En route into town from the Wartburg you pass the **Reuter-Wagner Museum**, a villa that houses a collection of Wagner memorabilia said to be second only to the Wagner collection in Bayreuth in size, but of minimal interest to any but Wagner aficionados.

The musical memorabilia of Johann Sebastian Bach in Eisenach are quite a different story, however. From 1662 to 1741, Eisenach was a Saxon duchy whose rulers, like the Thüringen landgraves before them, were patrons of the arts. Though they had little money to pay musicians, year after year they invited them to their court. Most soon went on to better-paying positions elsewhere, but not Johann Ambrosius Bach. And that was how it happened that Johann Sebastian Bach was born in Eisenach in 1685 to Johann Ambrosius and his wife, Elizabeth. Johann Sebastian was christened in the simple little **Georgenkirche** (St. George's Church), whose wrought-iron gate today bears both his entwined initials and the cross and heart of Martin Luther. (To earn his keep as a schoolboy in Eisenach, Luther sang in the choir and, later, as a fiery preacher, spoke from its pulpit.)

Heavily damaged in World War II, the interior of the Georgenkirche today is gray and gold. Biblical texts bound in gold gleam from its walls. Though 12th-century in its original incarnation, it bears few reminders of that period today. It is notable for its 17th-century paintings of Luther and his reformer forerunner Jan Hus; of Luther's patron and protector, Frederick the Wise; and of Holy Roman Emperor Charles V; for its Baroque pulpit; and for its 4,835-pipe organ.

Relatively little is known of Bach's early years in Eisenach, except that he sang a joyous soprano in church and was taught to play stringed instruments by his father and the organ by his uncle. When he was nine, his mother died; his father died a year later, and he then moved away to a brother's. Although it is *not* a house in which he ever lived, Bach is remembered in Eisenach in the mustard-yellow, late 17th-century **Bachhaus**, not too far from the church.

The house is furnished much as it would have been in his day and is filled with old engravings, letters, and documents about the Bach family. An English-language tape guide to the exhibitions exists but is generally available only to tour groups. There is also a small brochure in English. On the ground floor is a museum of Baroque instruments: lutes, cornetti, a viola da gamba, flutes, piccolos, a harpsichord, and a clavichord. A visit to the house—even if you are alone—is always accompanied by Bach music (live or recorded) played on one or more of these instruments.

Open to visitors, too, is the **Lutherhaus**, where, for two years, the teenage Martin lived with family friends, the Cottas, and attended Latin school. The little, lopsided, 500-year-old half-timbered house, now the property of the German Evangelical Church, has, over the years, been put to different uses. It has had a stocking factory on the ground floor and has been a restaurant, but now it contains documents, illustrated Bibles of Luther's day, and memorabilia of his school years. The two small rooms that were his, with their windows angled for light, are furnished frugally, as they would have been for him. An English-speaking guide is generally on hand.

Eisenach's other principal visitor sites are the elegant Baroque palace museum of blue Thuringian porcelain, the Romanesque **Nikolaikirche**, the 16th-century Late Gothic red Rathaus, and the many half-timbered dwellings that line the town's winding streets.

## Staying and Dining in Eisenach

Hotel choices, unfortunately, are limited in this lovely town of Bach and Luther.

In the heart of town, the **Parkhotel**, at Wartburgallee 2, sits on a corner, clean and welcoming, but distinctly basic. Many a room is without a bath, and the bathroom down the hall may well have plumbing problems. Little English is spoken, but the welcome is warm; the dining room is adequate.

High up at the Wartburg castle, where Martin Luther stayed, visitors may now stay, too, at **Auf der Wartburg**, a small hotel with a splendid view of the red tile roofs of the city below it. The Auf der Wartburg dining room features wild game and Thüringen specialties in a hunting-lodge ambience. Reservations required; Tel: 51-11.

For good wines and satisfying fare, the **Turmschänke Restaurant** in the old Nikolai Turm is conveniently located just beside the Parkhotel, at Platz der Deutsch-Sowjetischen Freundschaft 23. Reservations required; Tel: 52-91.

There is dancing and drinking and a weekend revue at the **Stadtcafé**, at Karlstrasse 35-35; Tel: 30-54.

# *ERFURT*

One of the oldest cities of all Germany, and the best-preserved, least war-damaged of all, Erfurt was a bishopric in 742. By the ninth century it was a prosperous trading place because it lay on the salt route between the north and south as well as on the road from Spain to Russia. It was even permitted to hold fairs, an honor that later was given to Leipzig.

When 17-year-old Martin Luther arrived here as a student in 1500, Erfurt, due east of Eisenach on the way to Weimar, was called "Little Rome" for its 40 churches and 13 monasteries. There were monks and nuns and priests everywhere, attracted by Erfurt's notable university, which, founded in 1392, was one of Germany's first.

The university is no more, having been closed in 1816, but there are still 22 churches and one monastery, and it is above all to see two of those churches, the Catholic Dom (cathedral of the Blessed Virgin Mary) and the Lutheran Severikirche (church of St. Severus) that visitors come to this Medieval city on the river Gera. To reach them, set side by side high on a hill near the center of town, there are 48 stone steps to climb, but no one seems to mind.

The **Dom** was started in the 12th century and rebuilt in the 14th century in Gothic style. It is constructed on arches of stone that in their day were innovative indeed. Its 15th-century stained-glass window—blue and gold and rose and red—is, art historians say, one of the most precious in all of Germany. There is an enormous 12th-century wall painting of a red-cloaked Saint Christopher; a 16th-century Peter Vischer the Younger bronze, *Coronation of the Virgin;* a 12th-century Romanesque Madonna; and a distinctly modern-looking 12th-century bronze candelabrum of a worshiper. And from one of the cathedral towers, the second-largest bell in Germany, the

Gloriosa (weighing more than 13 tons and surpassed in size only by the bell in Cologne's cathedral), rings out on Christmas and Easter. It was in this cathedral that Martin Luther was ordained, in 1507.

Beside it, the gracefully spired **Severikirche**, built in the 14th century, is known for its late Gothic baptismal font and for the 14th-century reliefs on its altar. Unfortunately, like other Protestant churches in both Germanys, it is not easy to find times when it is open.

Though Luther entered Erfurt university in the faculty of arts, received his master's degree in arts, and began after that to study law, his life plan was irrevocably changed, so the story goes, one July afternoon in 1505 here in Erfurt. Walking in the countryside, he was caught in a thunderstorm. Instead of seeking cover, he hurried on in the lightning and thunder and downpour, for he was only a half mile from shelter in the town. But there in the open country, a lightning bolt seared the ground beside him—close enough to knock him down. He was not injured, but terrified. Realizing how close he had been to death, he promised himself to God. Two weeks later, Luther changed his course of study at the university to theology and entered the **Augustinerkloster** on the Augustinerstrasse. He was launched on the career that was to alter the Christian world. Today's followers of Luther in Erfurt not only visit the cathedral where he was ordained but walk in the monastery's Renaissance courtyard and go to the Gothic **Augustinerkirche** (Church of St. Augustine), where, as a young man seeking salvation, he often flung himself on the cold stone floor.

Erfurt suffered relatively little damage in World War II (500 houses were destroyed but only three of historic value). The monastery, however, was struck by a bomb, and reconstruction has been necessary.

The visitor arriving here by train has only a short walk directly down the Bahnhofstrasse past the 12th-century Gothic **Predigerkirche** (Preacher's Church) to the central square and main shopping area of the town, **Der Anger**. Across it is the Hermann-John-Strasse, which leads in turn to the Fischmarkt in the Altstadt. If you continue west from the Fischmarkt down the Marktstrasse, you reach the Domplatz. In the opposite direction, the street beside the elaborately decorated 19th-century Rathaus goes down to the Gera river. If you cross the Anger and turn left, then right at the Wigbertikirche, you will reach the **Barfüsserkirche** on Barfüsserstrasse, where Luther preached one of his last sermons and which is now used for organ recitals.

# Around in Erfurt

Commercial town that Erfurt was, its enterprising tradesmen built homes and shops on the bridge that crossed its river as part of the Russian route. This 12th-century **Krämerbrücke** (Tradesman's Bridge), not unlike Florence's Ponte Vecchio, still stands, with art and antiques for sale now in what were the goldsmiths' and spice merchants' shops in the Middle Ages. It is the only bridge of its kind north of Italy. From either the span itself or the park below, where the mellow-colored half-timbered houses on top are reflected in the Gera, the bridge is a picturesque sight.

Picturesque, too, are the elaborate Renaissance façades of Erfurt's patrician houses, many of them built from the trade in woad, a locally produced blue vegetable dye that, to the sorrow of the town's businessmen, was displaced when indigo was brought back from the East.

Erfurt's most prosperous periods were in the 14th and early 15th centuries and again in the mid-16th century. These were the years of structures like the golden-yellow 1562 **Haus zum Roten Ochsen** (House of the Red Oxen), on the Fischmarkt, embellished with an ox over the door, a frieze of muses, the heads of gods—and with the Devil on the pediment. (If the Devil saw himself, he would be afraid and stay out of a house, or so it was thought then.) Another Fischmarkt treasure is the step-gabled **Haus zum Breiten Herd** (House of the Broad Hearth; 1582), with its colorful reliefs illustrating the five senses—a woman looking in a mirror, playing music, smelling a rose, eating an apple, and touching a bird. Two other fine Renaissance houses are the **Alter Schwan** (Old Swan) wine restaurant, on the Gotthardstrasse near the Kramer bridge, and the Gothic **Haus zur Hohen Lilie** (House of the Tall Lily; 1538), at the Domplatz. The 1604 **Haus zum Stockfisch**, on the Leninstrasse, is now a museum of the city. Near it, on the Juri Gagarin Ring, is a good museum of Thuringian folk art. Set on the river in Erfurt's Little Venice, the **Bursa Pauperum**, now under reconstruction, was a hostel for needy students in university days.

**Michaelisstrasse**, in the Altstadt, is the site of a number of venerable buildings. The early Gothic **Michaeliskirche** (Church of St. Michael) here, where Luther preached in 1522, dates from the 13th century, the **Haus zum Goldenen Stern** (House of the Golden Star) from the fifteenth, and the few remaining ruins of the university from the fourteenth.

A curiosity of some of Erfurt's old houses is a round hole in the façade. University professors' wives would place a

wisp of straw there on days they brewed beer, signaling
neighbors to come in and have some.

In the quarter off Marktstrasse of the half-timbered,
sprawling **Waidspecher theater**, once a woad warehouse,
many of the dwellings of the past have been reconstructed.

In 1808, during the French occupation, Napoleon stayed
at the **Statthalteri** (Governor's Residence) on the Regierung-
strasse near the Anger district. It was here that he grandly
entertained Alexander I of Russia and the kings of Bavaria,
Saxony, Westphalia, and Württemberg. Among his guests
were Goethe and his fellow poet Christoph Martin Wieland.

Seeking the Russian czar as an ally, Napoleon imported
the Comédie Française from Paris to impress him. He surely
impressed Goethe, who said he considered the emperor of
France "the greatest mind the world has ever seen" and was
rewarded for his admiration by being invited to Paris. There,
Napoleon temptingly told the then-resident of little Weimar,
"You will find a larger circle for your spirit of observation . . .
immense material for your poetic creations."

A totally different aspect of contemporary Erfurt is the
permanent Internationale Gartenbau Ausstellung (International Landscaping and Horticultural Exhibition) at Cyriax-
berg on the southwestern outskirts of town.

## Staying and Dining in Erfurt

Hotels are scarce in this Thuringian city. The venerable
**Erfurter Hof**, near the railway station on the Bahnhofsvorplatz, has a certain charm and a restaurant where you can
sample the sausage for which Thüringen is famous and
*Sauerbraten mit Klossen* (marinated beef with potato dumplings). Accommodations are adequate and the service helpful, but little English is spoken.

In the 17th century, King Gustav Adolf of Sweden made the
step-gabled **Zum Hohen Lilie** (Tall Lily) on the Domplatz his
residence for a year. Today, this is a small restaurant with a
nightclub and a welcoming atmosphere. Reservations required; Tel: 2-25-78.

Also in the Altstadt, at Gothardtstrasse 27, is the **Alter
Schwan**, a cozy restaurant where you can while away an
evening pleasantly with a bottle of wine. Reservations required; Tel: 291-16.

The **Cafe zur Krämerbrücke** offers fine coffee and cake
just at the foot of the Krämerbrücke.

# Gotha

Twenty-five km (about 15 miles) west of Erfurt back toward Eisenach, Gotha, at the entrance of the Thüringer Wald, is today a largely modern city of 58,000. Its limited attractions include, again, old houses and the red Rathaus (Town Hall) at the market square and the early Baroque **Schloss Friedenstein** above the city.

This 18th-century château, with an immense courtyard and a park all around it, contains a **museum of the Middle Ages**, a **theater museum** with stage machinery from Baroque days, and a **museum of folk art and costumes**. Sometimes a 17th-century ivory collection, a globe collection, and richly decorated drinking vessels of Baroque times are on display.

The *Almanach de Gotha,* the registry of royal lineage that the world's royals hold in reverence, was started here in 1765. The court of Gotha in those days was small and quiet. (The disappointed English biographer James Boswell, stopping there in 1764, described the duke and duchess as "plain old people.") Members of the Saxon royal house were literary and scientific in their interests. French was the household language, and it was in French that the first *Almanach,* largely an astronomical calendar, was written. The next year, the *Almanach* was expanded to include the genealogy of the house of Saxony and a list of the emperors of Germany.

By 1765, the considerably expanded *Almanach* was being printed in German and was filled with amusing anecdotes and such assorted information as the names of the best confectioners in Paris and the ambassadors of the leading nations. Though the *Almanach* still exists, it is no longer printed in Gotha and bears little resemblance to what it was when every duke born in the world was listed in it.

The last dukes to reside here were sons of England's Queen Victoria at the turn of the century, invited to rule the dukedom because there were no male heirs in Gotha. Albert, the queen's consort, was, after all, a prince of Saxe-Coburg-Gotha.

Gotha is also known as a town where the painter Lucas Cranach the Elder stayed for a time, when his daughter was married to the burgomaster. His symbol, a crested, winged snake, and the bag that was the symbol of his son-in-law still embellish the house they occupied on the Hauptmarkt.

# Arnstadt

In Arnstadt, 18 km (8 miles) south of Erfurt, Bach enthusi-asts can visit the blue-and-white Baroque **Bonifatiuskirche** (Church of St. Boniface). They must make arrangements in advance at the tourist information office or with the minis-ter. Here, young Johann Sebastian Bach held his first job as an organist, from 1703 to 1707.

Arnstadt is a charming little town with a mauve Rathaus that boasts a gilded clock behind a statue of Bach. One turret of its 16th-century castle still stands, and arcades line its market square. A special delight in the Arnstadt city museum is *Mon Plaisir,* 80 Baroque and Rococo miniature settings put to-gether in the early 18th century by Countess Augusta Doro-thea von Schwarzburg-Arnstadt with the help of Arnstadt craftsmen. The settings depict, among other things, a period cooper's shop, an apothecary shop, a shoe shop, the candlelit Arnstadt market square, a wine cellar, nuns at table, billiard players, a barber, ladies at tea, and a musicale. Four hundred costumed dolls people the settings.

Bach had a light schedule in Arnstadt. Playing only for Sunday services, Monday prayers, and Thursday morning service, he was relatively free to do his own composing—and did. He wrote his first works for the organ here as well as some toccatas and chorale preludes. But he annoyed church officials by overstaying a three-month leave he had requested to go to Lübeck to study with the master organist Dietrich Buxtehude. As the story goes, Bach, who walked the 250 miles between Arnstadt and Lübeck, had hopes of proving to be a good enough student to be offered the opportunity to inherit Buxtehude's position as organist at the Marienkirche. But with the job came Buxtehude's daughter as bride. Bach de-clined her on the grounds that she was too old for him, and was thus not offered the job. When he returned to Arnstadt, church officials complained about the way he played the organ accompanying choirs, and there was continual fussing over money. When Bach was offered the post of organist at the parish church of St. Blaise in Mühlhausen, he accepted.

Today, that soaring Gothic church in **Mühlhausen**, 63 km (39 miles) northwest of Erfurt on the road out of Gotha, is blackened by brown-coal smoke. The visitor tends to be urged, instead, to visit the 14th-century **Kornmarktkirche** (Corn Market Church), now a museum of the 1525–1526 German Peasants' War, for it was here in Mühlhausen that the clergyman Thomas Münzer urged his farmer parishioners to fight the taxation by the Church and the outrageous demands of their feudal landlords.

Inside the museum are exhibits of the clothes of peasants and dukes, craftsmen and patricians of the day, and of the pitchforks and scythes that were the peasants' weapons. There were many battles across German lands in the course of the war. In a single battle against royal forces at Bad Frankenhausen, some 5,000 peasants were slaughtered. There the world's largest painting on canvas (406 feet long by 46 feet high), executed by East German artist Werner Tübke, depicts the battle. A historical panorama, this monumental painting shows more than 3,000 twice-life-size figures of peasants and royal mercenaries. Also included on the canvas are Luther, Erasmus, Melanchthon, Ulrich Zwingli, Lucas Cranach, Albrecht Dürer, and Münzer himself. As a result of his efforts on behalf of the farmers, Münzer was later executed.

Beside St. Blaise's and the Kornmarkt Museum, there is the **Marienkirche**, where Münzer was a clergyman, notable for its 1510 Gothic altar by a pupil of Tilman Riemenschneider, and for the little white-and-gold screened area, built in 1608, in which town council members could sit during church services—when no one else could. There are also the 16th-century Rathaus and several other churches to see—most only from the outside—and half-timbered houses on the town's narrow lanes.

# *WEIMAR*

In a golden-yellow house in this town on the river Ilm 24 km (13 miles) east of Erfurt, Johann Wolfgang von Goethe spent the greater part of his life writing, painting, collecting art and minerals, philosophizing, and theorizing. Here he completed his masterpiece, *Faust*. A street or two away, in another golden Baroque house, his friend Friedrich von Schiller busily worked on his drama, *Wilhelm Tell,* destined to become Rossini's opera of the same name.

A statue of the two writers, side by side, stands today outside the **German national theater building** at the site where many of their works were performed. There, in 1919, the constitution for the so-called Weimar Republic, which sought to bring democracy to Germany after World War I, was drafted. (Weimar itself was never the *capital* of the republic; Berlin was.)

For four centuries, literature, music, and art had lent their glory to this tranquil ducal seat. Then, with the 20th century, the shadows fell as the Weimar Republic faltered and collapsed. Adolf Hitler, risen to power, expounded his Third Reich views from the balcony of Weimar's leading hotel, and the concentration camp of Buchenwald was established in the Weimar woods nearby.

But in the heart of the Altstadt, among Baroque and Renaissance houses, cobblestone courtyards, castle turrets, and onion-domed church towers and in quiet parks, it is easy to forget that more recent past. Seemingly endless construction projects somewhat destroy the illusion, but the very simplicity of East German rebuilding—the bamboo scaffolding and plankways over ditches—can with a little imagination also seem a part of the era when civic-minded Goethe, who had taken on responsibility for street building, was becoming disgruntled and disappointed with what he was able to accomplish in his post.

The modern Weimar of broad avenues and busy trams surrounds the old town, but even it is not intrusive in its modernity. Its streets are tree lined, and 19th-century buildings abound.

The **Altstadt**, in which both the Goethe and Schiller houses stand, is a small, easily walked area on the left bank of the river. From 1782 to 1832 Goethe lived and wrote in his house on the Frauenplan, off the market square. Just up the Frauenstrasse, on the street that today bears his name, lived Schiller. At its other end, on the Theaterplatz, was Duchess Anna Amalia's house, with the German national theater next door. The Stadtkirche on Herder Platz, where the philosopher Johann Gottfried von Herder preached, and the duke's palace at Burgplatz are less than a ten-minute stroll from the Goethe house.

In Weimar's pastoral river park, also within strolling distance, is the rustic dwelling where the young Goethe sowed his wild oats during his first Weimar years, and a Roman Renaissance house that he helped design. At the park's west entrance, on the Marienstrasse, is the house where Franz Liszt summered in the late 19th century. It was across the street that the Bauhaus school of architecture and applied arts developed in the 1920s.

Goethe had arrived in the duchy of Weimar in 1775 at the invitation of teenage Duke Karl August, who wished to fill his court with entertaining, clever people. Thanks to Goethe and his friends, the little duchy, then with a population of about 6,000, gained renown as a center of German Classicism. Goethe's mentor, philosopher-theologian Johann Gottfried von Herder, and poet-novelist Christoph Martin Wieland were fellow members of Weimar's Court of the Muses. Setting the tone for it all was Duchess Anna Amalia, widowed mother of the duke and niece of Frederick the Great of Prussia. Today, Weimar is no longer a town; the population is up to 65,000.

World War II bombing damaged both the Goethe and Schiller houses considerably. Both, however, have been restored, and the former is furnished with Goethe's own belongings. In his first years here, in the little garden house on the river Ilm, Goethe had virtually abandoned writing as he sought favor with the duke, joining him at social events and burdening himself with civic responsibilities. Goethe took charge not only of road building in the duchy but of transportation and mining as well, and he directed the court theater. The inefficiency of the bureaucratic system and the frivolity of court life became too much for him, however, and, in the dead of night, dressed as the artist he had decided to become, he fled Weimar for Italy.

When Goethe returned to Weimar, in 1788, he was overflowing with enthusiasm for things Italian. He replaced the Baroque staircase of the house on the Frauenplan with broad stairs in the Italian Renaissance tradition. Enamored, too, of Classical art, he filled the house with plaster casts of ancient busts and statues, and designed special cabinets to display his Italian majolica plates.

Believing that colors affect one's frame of mind, Goethe painted his dining room a sunny yellow; his study a soothing green; and the reception room, in which he greeted such guests as the philosopher Johann Gottfried Fichte and the geographer Alexander von Humboldt, blue. Minerals were another of his interests, and glass-topped display cases contain part of his collection of 18,000 minerals and gemstones. Copies of Goethe's drawings of his buxom wife, Christiane, and their son, Augustus, are on exhibit here, too.

The house is large but not grand. "A surrounding of comfortable, pretty furniture paralyzes my thoughts and brings me into an easy passive condition," Goethe wrote. "Splendid rooms and elegant furniture unless we are used to them from youth are for people who have no thoughts and desire none."

Goethe was 82 when he died in his sparsely furnished little bedchamber. He and Schiller are buried together in a hilltop mausoleum in the historic Weimar cemetery off Friedrich-Engels-Ring. (Buried there, too, in a curious Russian-Greek chapel, is Duke Karl August's Russian daughter-in-law, Maria Pavlovna.)

The **Schiller house**, which stands where the Frauenplan meets the Schillerstrasse, reflects less of that writer's personality, furnished as it is with period—but not the writer's—pieces. It was on the attic wall here that Schiller one day tacked a map of Switzerland and immersed himself in volumes on Swiss travel and history. Drinking black coffee, pausing for meals and rest (but often falling asleep with his head on his arms), he did not stop working for six weeks until *Wilhelm Tell* was finished. In the rooms below, his wife and children led normal lives.

A short walk along the Schillerstrasse leads to the elegant **Wittumspalais** (Widow's Palace), where Duchess Anna Amalia gathered her salon of artists and poets, doctors and philosophers to discuss contemporary problems of science and thought and art. Silhouettes, popular in her day, and an extensive collection of paintings of costumes decorate the walls of this dwelling, into which the duchess moved after a fire had devastated her castle. Today, the reconstructed onion-domed **Residenzschloss** is a museum rich in the works of Renaissance-Reformation artist Lucas Cranach the Elder and his son, for Cranach too was once a Weimar resident. His house, gaily decorated with the mermaids that were his symbol, stands on the Marktplatz.

On the same square are the Flamboyant Gothic Rathaus and the 17th-century **Hotel Elephant**. Thomas Mann, who wrote of the hotel in *Lotte in Weimar,* and Adolf Hitler have been among its guests; it was from its balcony that Hitler announced delightedly—in 1944—that Germany was winning World War II.

At the foot of the square, Dimitroffstrasse leads to the black-spired Flamboyant Gothic **Stadtkirche**, which holds one of the elder Cranach's finest paintings (completed by his son), an altarpiece depicting the Crucifixion, with likenesses of Luther, Philipp Melanchthon, and the artist himself at the foot of the Cross. Herder, by whose name the church is sometimes known, came to it as court preacher in 1776.

In the **Kirms-Krakow house** nearby, a museum recalls Herder's influence on German literature, his insistence on German writers expressing their own nationality in their works rather than, as was the fashion of the time, aping French masters.

Johann Sebastian Bach lived in Weimar, too, but left in disgrace after he infuriated the duke by asking to leave his post of court conductor and was briefly imprisoned for his ingratitude; no house he inhabited here is dedicated to his memory.

The handsomely furnished, high-ceilinged **Liszt house**, where Hungarian-born Franz Liszt gathered young musicians around him in the late 19th century, sits at the west entrance to Ilm park. In its red-carpeted salon stands one of his pianos and the portable clavichord he used to keep his fingers in training when he was travelling. There, as well, are his Hungarian passport and facsimiles of letters from Felix Mendelssohn, Robert Schumann, and Johannes Brahms.

**Goethe's garden house** residence is in the park on the other side of the river. Often, a shepherd is grazing his sheep on the river bank, and in summer the roses are effulgent. A souvenir of the Goethe Italian period is the **Roman house** on the park grounds here, designed, under the poet's influence, in the style of a Roman Renaissance house.

Across Marienstrasse from the Liszt house is a reminder of another aspect of Weimar's cultural history: The school that now stands there was, from 1919 to 1925, the **Bauhaus school**, where the modern concept of the craftsman-designer originated. Expressionists, among them the Russian Wassily Kandinsky, the Swiss Paul Klee, the American Lyonel Feininger, and the Hungarian architect and furniture designer Marcel Breuer served on its faculty.

About 9 km (5 miles) northwest of Weimar, at the end of a pine-lined road beyond Ernst-Thälmannstrasse, are the remains of the concentration camp of Buchenwald, which stood here from 1937 to 1945. Only the old SS barracks, long, straight roads, and a museum remain of the camp where 65,000 victims of Nazism died. A stone bell tower and a monument depicting the victims have been erected at the camp entrance.

## Staying and Dining in Weimar

Since autumn 1990 there has been a fashionable new hotel in Weimar, the **Hotel Belvedere** on the Ilm, with a swimming pool and sauna and chauffeured limousine service.

For more than 200 years the charming **Hotel Elephant**, on the Marktplatz, has welcomed Bach, Liszt, Wagner, and other notables. The hotel was recently repainted and refurbished, and private baths have been added to many of the rooms. Its sweeping staircase invites climbing (even though there is also an elevator). English is spoken by some of the reception staff, all of whom are courteous and welcoming. The Elephant's restaurants are among the most highly regarded in the city. They are big and lacking in intimacy, but the food is reasonably good in both its **Stadt Weimar** and the **Ele-phantenkeller**. The Elephant's **Nightclub Bajadere** is the place to be on a weekend night, but reservations are essential; Tel: 641-71.

As popular now as it has been for generations of the musical and artistic community of Weimar is the **Alt Weimar** on Steubenstrasse: nothing fancy, but acceptable. Reservations required; Tel: 20-56.

Ballet and opera as well as drama are performed at the historic national theater, whose company Goethe once directed. Ask at your hotel about tickets. (The theater is closed in summer.)

# LEIPZIG

Johann Sebastian Bach spent 27 of the most productive years of his life in Leipzig, northeast of Weimar and 160 km (100 miles) southwest of Berlin. Its concert hall, the **Neues Gewandhaus**, replaces the one that was demolished in World War II and is the most modern (there is not a right angle in it) in Germany—a far cry from its origins in 1780 in a genuine *Gewandhaus,* a cloth merchant's trade hall. Its 200-member orchestra today is ranked as one of the world's finest, and its incumbent director, Kurt Masur, will become director of the New York Philharmonic in 1992. Leipzig's monumental **Opernhaus**, completed in 1960, was the first of its kind to be opened in East Germany after the war. The Thomanerchor (Bach came to Leipzig to be the choir's director) continues to be headquartered at Thomaskirche (St. Thomas church) and to sing on Friday, Saturday, and Sunday. (It is best to check the schedule with the tourist office.) Leipzig was also the birthplace, in 1813, of Richard Wagner and the workplace of Felix Mendelssohn (it was he, as conductor of the Gewandhaus in the 1830s, who first established its reputation). Robert Schumann came to its university, once world famous, to study law at about the same time, but was quickly lured into its musical world instead, and married his piano teacher's daughter, Clara Wieck.

With a population of 549,230, Leipzig is today the second-largest city in East Germany and is accordingly lively. Goethe, who studied here in the 1760s, called it "Paris in miniature." For years to come, Leipzig will be known as the city where the revolt that brought an end to Communist rule in Germany began.

Lying at a crossroads of two trade routes—one running east–west between Poland and the province of Thüringen, the other north–south between North Germany and Bohemia—Leipzig has been a bustling city of fairs since the 12th century. To ensure its success as a fair city, Holy Roman Emperor Maximilian I decreed in the 16th century that no other communities within a wide radius could have annual markets. Twice a year, usually the first week in September and the second week in March, it is still the site of trade fairs that bring thousands of exhibitors and hundreds of thousands of visitors to its more than 24 acres of pavilions and exhibition halls, where heavy machinery, tools, books, clothes, agricultural equipment, chemicals, sporting goods, plants, and furs and skins are shown. (Fair time is *not* the time for tourists to visit, for the hotels overflow with exhibitors and buyers, and some are forced to stay as far as 140 km (90 miles) away, in Dresden.)

Liveliness, too, comes with its thousands of students at its three universities, among them Karl Marx university (on the Karl-Marx-Platz), founded as the university of Leipzig in the 15th century by dissident students from neighboring Prague. It lists among its distinguished students not only Schumann and Goethe but also Wagner and the philosopher Johann Gottfried Fichte. The 34-story jagged tower of today's university (nicknamed the "Broken Tooth") has become a symbol of contemporary Leipzig. To today's visitor, however, the university offers little of interest.

Relatively little of old Leipzig stands. A quarter of the city was destroyed by bombing in 1943, and the emphasis has been much more on constructing the new—square modern apartment complexes and exhibition halls, wide pedestrian streets, and big squares—than on restoring the old. But most of both the old and the new Leipzig that has appeal for visitors is concentrated in a small, easily walked area encircled by ring roads.

The Markt is the center of the old city; the Karl-Marx-Platz dominates the new. Touristic sites outside this center, for which vehicular transportation is needed, are the Giorgi Dimitroff Museum, the monument to the Battle of the Nations, the Russian memorial church, the zoo, the Grassi Museum complex, and the fairgrounds.

# The Old City

At the Markt and the Naschmarkt (Snack Market) and their environs, bits of old Leipzig have been reconstructed. On the east side of the **Marktplatz**, the long, gabled Renaissance **Altes Rathaus** has been rebuilt and is now the museum of the city of Leipzig, containing a history of the fairs. Originally constructed in 1556, the golden-yellow, arcaded Renaissance city hall is notable for its Baroque clock tower. In its elaborate festival hall, which survived the war, hang life-size portraits of the electors of Saxony (the old German duchy of which Leipzig was a part). Also in the Altes Rathaus is a room of Mendelssohn memorabilia and a memorial to J. S. Bach.

Reconstructed on the north side of the square is the step-gabled Renaissance **Alte Waage** (Old Weighing House), where foreign imports to the fairs used to be weighed. Across from the Alte Waage is the 17th-century **Königshaus**, used by the rulers of Saxony on their visits to Leipzig. Later it served as a royal guesthouse, providing hospitality for, among others, Peter the Great of Russia and Napoleon. Today, it houses a shop of expensive fashionable goods.

In the neighboring **Naschmarkt**, behind a statue of Goethe as a student, rises the restored blue-and-white Baroque **Alte Börse** (Old Stock Exchange), with sweeping stairs and stucco garlands above the windows. On sunny days the weary pause under the striped umbrellas of its outdoor café, **Am Naschmarkt**.

But it is to the south of the Markt, in the covered arcade of shops and restaurants that is the **Mädler passage**, that you find Leipzig's most famous restaurant, the **Auerbachs Keller**; the original stood here long before Goethe's student days. The poet immortalized it when he had Faust ride away from it on a wine cask with Mephistopheles. In 1912, the first Auerbachs Keller was torn down and the new one created, with statues at its door of Mephistopheles and Faust and of his fellow student revelers.

Another interesting restored restaurant is the 17th-century **Kaffeebaum** (Coffee Tree), on Kleine Fleischergasse, with its Baroque carving of a Turk under a coffee tree above its front door. Liszt, Goethe, Wagner, and Schumann all came here. It was a particular favorite with Schumann and his musical friends, and they spent long hours in one of the downstairs rooms at work on the *New Journal for Music* that Schumann edited. Today, with its dark wood interior and its pictures of composers, it continues to be a popular gathering place for artists, writers, and musicians who come for an evening of beer drinking.

A short walk in the neighborhood of the Markt leads to the pastel Baroque burgher houses along the **Katharinenstrasse** and the **Brühl**. The most famous and handsomest of these is the tawny yellow **Romanushaus**. Its 18th-century owner, Franz Conrad Romanus, is said to have stolen city funds for the construction of his impressive residence, with its 13 rows of windows, its gables, and pilasters, and an oriel window at the corner, along with a statue of a flirtatious Hermes, a finger to his nose. Romanus's happy days in his house were cut short by a prison term, but he is remembered here in a more favorable light for his introduction of a sedan chair service for theatergoers and for the erection of the city's first streetlights.

The tourist information center, where museum hours and concert schedules can be obtained, is just off the Brühl on the Sachsenplatz, a giant square of modern flats and fountains decorated with Christmas-tree-like balls. **The Brühl** itself, wide and modern, continues to be the center of the fur trade, as it has been for generations. Skins and ready-made clothing of fox, beaver, and mink fill its windows in the fall. In the sweeping pink-and-gray restored building across from it on Richard-Wagner-Platz is the Café Brühl, once popular with the theater world but now, unfortunately, distinctly mediocre.

A block east of the Markt stands the 12th-century Nikolaikirche (St. Nicholas Church), where demonstrators for democracy gathered in 1989. A block west rises the high-pitched roof of the 1,000-year-old Gothic **Thomaskirche**, to which Bach came at the age of 38 to be cantor and director of the boys' choir, and director of music at the university. He stayed in Leipzig for the rest of his life. Here he did his finest work, writing more than 300 cantatas, the *Passion According to St. Matthew,* and the Mass in B-minor. But for all their productivity, these were also frustrating years for him. Bach wanted more and better singers and musicians than the city councillors were prepared to provide. He had not been their first choice for the post he occupied, and they never let him forget it.

The years, however, have surely made Bach Leipzig's most venerated citizen. A more-than-life-size statue of him stands outside the Thomaskirche, and he is buried in its choir. Fresh flowers are placed each day on the tablet beneath which he lies, and he is memorialized in the 19th-century stained-glass windows, along with other luminaries: Martin Luther, who preached in the church in 1539 to herald the Reformation; Luther's friend Philipp Melanchthon; mayors of Leipzig; and electors of Saxony.

Just across the street from the church, the restored house of a Bach family friend, the merchant Heinrich Georg Bose, has a first-floor museum devoted to the composer's Leipzig years, and a lovely small concert hall. Nearly 2,000 Bach books and articles in many languages and tapes and records are now kept in the Bose house's Bach archives.

A good collection of musical instruments of the past, including those of the Bach period, are on display at the **musical instrument museum**, in the **Grassi Museum complex** outside the Ring on the Johannisplatz.

## Outside the Old City

The cultural heart of modern Leipzig is **Karl-Marx-Platz**. The immense, architecturally undistinguished new opera house stands on the north side of the square; the **Neues Gewandhaus** (Bruno Walter and Wilhelm Furtwängler, in addition to Mendelssohn, have been among its distinguished conductors); and Karl Marx university are opposite. On top of the Krochhaus, a 1927 version of a square-towered Florentine building—Leipzig's first high-rise—bell ringers strike the hours.

Even more mammoth than the opera house is the cavernous 1907–1915 Hauptbahnhof (main railway station), a few blocks north of Karl-Marx-Platz, one of the largest train depots in Europe, with 26 tracks inside a shell of steel and glass.

In the southwest part of the city rises the **Neues Rathaus**. Its 13th-century turret, part of the fortress that once occupied the site, is perched anachronistically in the center of the turn-of-the-century structure. Nearby, in the monumental former supreme court building of the German Reich, are the city's fine arts museum and the Georgi Dimitroff Museum. In addition to modern German works, the **art museum** contains paintings by such old German masters as Martin Schongauer and Lucas Cranach the Elder; Flemish masters Jan van Eyck, Rembrandt, and Rubens; and the Italian painters Tiepolo, Guardi, and Raphael. The **Georgi Dimitroff Museum**, on the upper floor, is dedicated to the Bulgarian Communist accused of complicity in the setting of the 1933 fire at the Berlin Reichstag. During his trial in the German supreme court here, he successfully defended himself against Hermann Göring, a prosecution witness. Dimitroff later became Bulgaria's first postwar Communist prime minister. The supremely political museum consists largely of photographs.

About 5 km (3 miles) southeast of the city center, above a man-made lake, is the brown stone mausoleum that com-

memorates the Battle of the Nations against Napoleon at this
site in 1813. Here, Russians, Prussians, Austrians, Bavarians,
and Swedes roundly defeated the French emperor on his
way home from his campaign in Russia. The 150,000 casual-
ties the monument honors include Gustav Adolf, the king of
Sweden, who nearsightedly ran into the enemy army in a
fog. (A golden-domed Russian memorial church near the
fairground commemorates the 22,000 Russians killed here.)
The determined visitor can climb the 500 steps to the
monument's top, pausing to look into the Hall of Honor, and
get a view of Leipzig itself in the distance (on smog-free
days, which are not frequent).

Known as the City of Lions (a pet lion is said to have saved
his knight-master from the Devil here in Medieval times),
Leipzig has a zoo that, appropriately, specializes in the breed-
ing of lions. The zoo is ordinary, not worth a visit unless the
tourist office can verify that cubs are present.

# Staying in Leipzig

Leipzig, as the second-largest city in the country and the site
in March and September of the international trade fair, has
more and better accommodations than most East German
cities. The 474-room Japanese-built **Merkur**, which opened
in 1981, is strikingly modern, with a spacious Italian marble
lobby, four restaurants, and bars and nightclubs (one overlooking a Japanese rock garden, complete with a waterfall).
Its deluxe facilities include a beauty parlor, air-conditioning,
a swimming pool, a sauna, a solarium, exercise rooms, a
bowling alley, limousine service, and sightseeing tours. Massages are available.

The **Astoria**, near the Hauptbahnhof, has been a Leipzig
landmark since before World War II. Partially destroyed in
the war, it has been rebuilt and continues to be popular with
fairgoers and exhibitors. Facilities include two restaurants, a
bar, a café and nightclub, and a sauna.

The **Stadt Leipzig**, opposite the Hauptbahnhof, is sprawling, modern, and reasonably well kept but has no special
charm. It has three restaurants and a bar, a sauna, and
nightclub.

The modern **Hotel am Ring** in the cultural heart of the
city on the Karl-Marx-Platz lacks charm but is convenient. It
offers, in addition to its 400 beds, a restaurant, bar, and
nightclub.

# Dining in Leipzig

Up-to-date Leipzig has been forward-thinking enough to publish a restaurant directory that can be purchased at hotel newsstands and at the Leipzig information office, which is located on the Sachsenplatz near the Brühl. They are, however, in short supply and not always available.

By far the most popular restaurant in the city is **Auerbachs Keller**, at Grimmaischestrasse 2 (Mädler Passage), with its 17th-century paintings of Dr. Johann Faust's visit to and departure from the premises with Mephistopheles, as related in *Faust*. Though the present restaurant is a modern version of the original, Auerbachs Keller has been in existence in Leipzig since the 16th century. The wine cellar atmosphere is enjoyable, the food acceptable. *Mephistofleisch,* strips of spicy beef and pork, is the specialty. Reservations required; Tel: 20-79-90.

**Zum Kaffeebaum**, near the Markt at Fleischergasse 4, is rich in literary and musical connections. Founded in 1718 as a coffeehouse, it is one of the oldest in Europe, but today it is a restaurant as well. Goethe, Schiller, and Bach all dined here, and Robert Schumann was a regular. Pictures of singers and artists decorate its walls. The food, again, is acceptable, not special, but the prices are reasonable and the atmosphere inviting when local artists and musicians come to gossip and dine. Reservations required; Tel: 20-04-52.

**Paulaner,** in the Markt neighborhood at Klostergasse 3, occupies three floors in two buildings. The food is well prepared and pleasantly offered. Reservations required; Tel: 20-99-41.

The **Gasthaus Bartelshof** is in an old courtyard near the Markt, typical of the passageways of oldtime Leipzig. Tel: 20-09-75.

The modern **Restaurant Stadt Dresden**, near the Hauptbahnhof at Wintergartenstrasse 7010, offers national and international dishes. An extensive wall painting here recounts Dresden's history. Reservations required; Tel: 20-92-37 or 28-14-78.

There is an unexpected (for East Germany) degree of elegance to the **Weinrestaurant Falstaff**, near the Opernhaus and the Gewandhaus at Georgiring 9. Prices are accordingly high. Reservations required; Tel: 28-64-03.

Once upon a time, Leipzig lay in swampland and fish were plentiful. That is no longer the case, but there is a fish restaurant here, **Gastmahl das Meeres**, all the same, on the Dr.-Kurt-Fischerstrasse. Reservations required; Tel: 29-11-60.

Right in the Naschmarkt (1–3) is **Burgkeller**, with average food in a good, central location. Tel: 29-56-39.

**Zills Bier Tunnel Plovdiv**, near the Markt at Barfuss-gäschen 9, has been serving the public since the 1880s. Today it specializes in charcoal broiling. Tel: 20-04-46.

The Gewandhaus and Opernhaus are, of course, *the* places to go for an evening out in Leipzig. Ask about tickets at your hotel as soon as you arrive, or, better yet, make a reservation through your travel agent when you book your accommodations.

# *DRESDEN*

On the night of February 13–14, 1945, hundreds of American and English bombers thundered over this historic city on the Elbe, the German Florence. After a fire storm of bombs demolished its elegant 17th-century Baroque churches and palaces, 80 percent of the city was in ruins and 35,000 people were dead.

Dresden had been the repository of some of the world's finest art: Raphael's *Sistine Madonna,* Giorgione's *Sleeping Venus,* Rubens's *Bathsheba at the Well,* Greek and Etruscan sculpture, dazzling 17th-century jeweled utensils and orna-ments, and incomparable porcelain. Though virtually no ar-chitectural monuments still stood after the bombing, at least Dresden's portable art had been removed for safekeeping, and Dresden today is again one of the world's great art-museum cities.

The city is divided more or less in half by the Elbe. On the south side, between the Hauptbahnhof and the river, are the major cultural attractions—the art museums, ruined and restored churches of the Altmarkt and Neumarkt, palaces, and the opera house. The Prägerstrasse, a wide pedestrian mall lined with shops, hotels, and restaurants, and the site, at number 10, of the city tourist office, is the main thoroughfare.

On the north side is the Neustadt, with its own Bahnhof. The Strasse der Befreiung (Street of Liberation) is its main pedestrian mall. There, pretty 19th-century pink-and-gold burgher houses have been reconstructed to house shops, apartments, and restaurants. Also on the north side are a Romantic museum, a folk art museum, and an ethnological collection.

Dresden began to be a great art city in the 16th century when August I, better known as August the Strong because of his physical and sexual prowess, became the ruler of the electorate (later kingdom) of Saxony, wherein Dresden lies, about 130 km (80 miles) east of Leipzig. A lover of beauty in both nature and art, August decreed that every newly married couple had to plant two fruit trees—symbolic, of course, of their union, but decorative, too, for his capital. Then he established a *Kunstkammer* (art chamber), which he filled with paintings, geological specimens, scientific instruments, and natural-history displays. But it was several generations later, during the reigns of Friedrich August I (1693–1733; called "the Strong" because he is said to have been able to break a horseshoe in his bare hands and, in a fit of pique, to have dangled one of his trumpeters out a window in one hand) and his son, Friedrich August II, that Dresden became truly a center of art.

Well travelled in his youth, August the Strong returned to Saxony with an artistic appreciation developed in Italy and France. He soon found that his little *Kunstkammer* would hardly do for the art he was collecting. When there was no longer room for more in his castle, he decorated churches and his country residences with the work he had bought. Even the upper floor of the royal stable became an art gallery.

It was August the Strong, wishing Dresden to be a Florence along the Elbe, with beautiful buildings on both sides of its riverbanks, who had a splendid new palace begun on the river's south side. A fire in 1701 in the 16th-century royal palace where he and his predecessors had lived probably prompted him to realize what had long been a dream—a palace with gardens and Roman baths and promenades with porticoes and graceful fountains—a palace that would equal Versailles. It was to be built with galleries for the display of royal collections, and its gardens and promenades were to be the setting for outdoor entertainments. As architect he chose Matthäus Daniel Pöppelmann. Today's reconstructed **Zwinger**, on the Theaterplatz on the river's south side, was its outer court (see below). Though the Zwinger was not completed in August's lifetime, the world-renowned Meissen porcelain that is now displayed there was a creation of his reign—albeit a forced one.

A Thuringian alchemist, John Friedrich Böttger, was the inventor of the Meissen porcelain technique. Charged in Berlin with the offense of being a magician because of his efforts to turn base metals into gold, Böttger had fled to Saxony. While he had feared imprisonment in Berlin, he actually got it in Dresden; but not for trying to produce gold. Rather, he was instructed that he *had* to produce it. He didn't, but instead, elaborating on attempts already made in Dresden to imitate Chinese porcelain, he invented the first European porcelain, as valued in the West as gold ever was. Previously, this popular delicate tableware had to be imported at great expense from the Orient.

To ensure that no one would learn the secret of Böttger's technique, August the Strong had him shut away—first in a room in the Dresden city walls below today's Albertinum museum, then in a castle at Meissen, 35 km (20 miles) down the Elbe. Böttger died a madman, driven insane, some say, by his solitary work.

It was during the reign of Friedrich August II (1733–1763) that Dresden's greatest amassing of paintings was made. Because his chief minister, Count Heinrich von Brühl, was as much an aficionado of art as August was, the king sent him off on an art-buying spree across Europe. It was then that Raphael's *Sistine Madonna* was acquired, 40 years after August, as crown prince, had first seen it in a cloister. Other masterworks that made their way into the collection at this time included paintings by Rubens, Vermeer, Hals, Titian, Velázquez, and Andrea del Sarto.

# The Albertinum

Today this art is temporarily housed on the Brühlische Terrasse in the reconstructed Albertinum museum, which was built on the Elbe's south side as an arsenal above the walls of Dresden in the 16th century. Later it was used as a royal storehouse, before becoming a gallery and museum in late Baroque times. Its highlights are the **Gemäldegalerie Alter Meister** (Gallery of the Old Masters) and the **Grünes Gewölbe** (Green Vault). In the former, the paintings Friedrich August I and II acquired are displayed. (A joy in a visit to an East German museum is the strict limiting of the number of viewers allowed inside at one time. Though you must therefore get in line early in the day to avoid a long wait, once you are inside viewing can be done with tranquility; neither jostling crowds nor omnipresent guards intrude on contemplation.)

At the top of the stairs in the Gemäldegalerie are Canaletto's views of Baroque Dresden, commissioned by Count von Brühl. The magnificence of the city that World War II destroyed is clearly displayed in them. (In addition to the masterworks on view—not all of them, of course, are shown at the same time—a lesser work, the 18th-century Swiss painter Jean Etienne Liotard's *The Chocolate Girl,* is of interest to those who recognize it from the Baker's Chocolate package.) The early paintings all really belong in the Zwinger palace, which, despite painstaking reconstruction after the war, is now in need of further work and unsuitable for housing such a valuable collection. Its Saxon sandstone walls are disintegrating; speculation is that air pollution is the cause. The restoration and reconstruction are to be completed in 1992, and the Gemäldegalerie will move back in from the Albertinum.

The Albertinum's own collection includes works by such 19th- and 20th-century artists as Manet, Monet, Renoir, van Gogh, Degas, Gauguin, and German Impressionists. There is also a fine collection of ancient, Medieval, and modern sculpture—the Roman sculpture collection is the largest outside Italy—and a numismatic collection.

The most dazzling display of all at the Albertinum is in the Grünes Gewölbe, which contains more than 3,000 jeweled objects in gold, silver, ebony and amber, glass, brass, and bronze. These were originally housed in the royal palace in burglar- and fireproof green-painted rooms (hence the name of these rooms in the Albertinum) whose walls were 80 inches thick. Five of these chambers, whose interior decoration is elaborate Dresden Baroque, were the only rooms in old Dresden to survive the 1945 bombing. When the royal palace is reconstructed, probably by 2015, the city's 800th anniversary, these will be rebuilt and their contents returned to them. Meanwhile, temporarily here in the Albertinum are glittering pendants of diamonds, emeralds, and rubies; Limoges ewers and bowls; a golden crucifix rising from a bed of pearls and emeralds; an elephant-shaped drinking vessel of gilded silver, mother-of-pearl, emeralds, rubies, and sapphires; and 16th- and 17th-century goblets in which rare seashells and ivory are joined with gold and silver and coral. There are gold coffee sets and ivory writing boxes and, most charming of all, the "Delhi Mogul's Birthday Party," an assemblage of miniature court figures of gold, silver, enamel, and precious stones was crafted by Johann Melchior Dinglinger, Saxony's 17th-century Benvenuto Cellini. A ring with a skull on it is said to have been the property of Martin Luther. All this and much, much more was saved from destruction by being hidden in the fortress of Königstein in Saxony in 1942.

In the rebuilding of Dresden—after providing boxlike apartment complexes and pedestrian malls lined with unimaginative fountains and hotels for tourists—first attention was given to the rebuilding of the Zwinger, the masterpiece of Pöppelmann, and the Semper Oper.

# The Zwinger

Though all but the porcelain and the clock and scientific-instrument galleries of the Zwinger museum are closed during the present restoration, you can stroll under the arch that leads into its courtyard and smile at the charming Rococo nymphs and fauns that gaze down from its pavilions. They are from the hand or the workshop of the 17th- to 18th-century craftsman Balthasar Permoser. Inside the porcelain galleries are life-size bird and animal figures by the most famous 18th-century porcelain designers, Johann Joachim Kändler and Johann Friedrich Eberlein, along with delicate smaller pieces—clowns and dancing couples, musicians, flowered vases, platters, and bowls.

There are red porcelain pieces (red was the first porcelain produced), white porcelain created after 1709, and porcelain painted by Johann Gregorious Heroldt. In 1720, after a careful study of Japanese and Chinese porcelain painting, Heroldt perfected German glazing. Soon Meissen china was being decorated in shimmering colors. The scientific-instrument collection, with compasses, telescopes, weights and scales, and terrestrial and celestial globes—some dating from the 13th century—is one of the earliest of its kind in the world.

Unfortunately, during the Zwinger's refurbishment the display rooms are not what they should be. Porcelain viewing is considerably better at the Meissen factory in nearby Meissen (see below). For information on the hours of Dresden's various museums, check with the tourist office.

# Old Dresden

More satisfactorily restored than the Zwinger (at least so far) is the **Semper Opernhaus**, situated beside the Zwinger on the Theaterplatz. Reopened in 1985, the present opera house is the second copy of the first theater erected on this site between 1837 and 1841 by Gottfried Semper. After the original burned down in 1869, it was reconstructed by Semper's son, Manfred. Built in Renaissance style and reconstructed after the 1945 bombing, it faces an equestrian statue of Saxony's scholarly 19th-century King Johannes. There is also a monument in the square to Carl-Maria von Weber, who was in charge of the Dresden opera from 1816 to 1826.

Decorating the Semper façade are statues of playwrights and muses. Inside, it has been stunningly re-created to look as it did in Semper's day, with marbleized stucco and fine wood paneling. The interior fairly glows with light.

Across the Theaterplatz, on the Georgi-Dimitroff-Platz, the colonnaded **Stallhof** (Royal Stables) has been restored as well. Set away from any street, with the parade ground edged with arches decorated with the coats-of-arms of the towns of Saxony, the area is something of an oasis in the noisy city.

Beside it rises the onion-domed tower of the Baroque **Hofkirche**. This Catholic court church was built by the Roman architect Gaetano Chiaveri from 1739 to 1755, and though most of its roof and walls fell during the bombing, the tower stood. Most of the interior art—including a 1722 pulpit by Permoser and the 18th-century master builder Gottfried Silbermann's last and largest organ—was kept safely in a salt mine during the war. Behind the court church, reconstruction of the royal palace is under way.

The visitor can obtain a quick rundown of Saxon history a street away from the Hofkirche on Augustusstrasse. There, an outdoor **mosaic wall** depicts Saxony's rulers from the 12th century to the 20th. Because it was made of Meissen china, which had been prefired, the 19th-century wall withstood the intense heat of the 1945 firestorm. Astride their horses ride the electors and kings.

Across the street along the river are the 42 steps (with their statues of Morning, Noon, Evening, and Night) that lead to the **Brühlische Terrasse**, where Count von Brühl once had his palace (now the site of the academy of fine arts) and where the Albertinum stands. Napoleon called this walkway along the winding brown-gold Elbe "the Balcony of Europe," and although the view is no longer what it once was, it remains a lovely overlook.

Below it, behind the Albertinum in the Neumarkt, rise the ruins of Dresden's most famous church, the Lutheran **Frauenkirche** (Church of Our Lady), whose dome was, from 1740 (when it was completed) until 1945, the landmark of this city on the Elbe. Incredibly, it survived the bombing itself—the only building in the Altstadt that, in its entirety, did. The day after the bombing, however, its mighty sandstone cupola collapsed. A statue of Martin Luther stands before it. Another memorable site on the Neumarkt is the Renaissance **Schöne Pforte**, which once led into the royal palace's chapel. At the neighboring Altmarkt little that is old remains—even in ruins—except the reconstructed Baroque **Kreuzkirche** (church of the

Holy Cross), the original of which was built between 1764
and 1792. The Kreuzkirche has long been notable for its
boys' choir.

Across the Georgi-Dimitroff-Brücke (it was formerly the
Augustusbrücke), on the north side of the Elbe in the
Neustadter Markt (New City Market), sits a golden rider—
August the Strong—on a golden horse. Behind the statue
stretches the **Strasse der Befreiung**. Along this Neustadt river
front, behind an extensive park, the Hotel Bellevue has been
created from a 17th-century burgomaster's house. Beside it,
in the 18th-century, so-called Japanese palace, where Friedrich August II kept his porcelain collection, there is now a
museum of ethnography.

# Staying in Dresden

Dresden's most inviting hotel at the moment is the handsome golden-yellow **Hotel Bellevue**. It was a burgomaster's
house until, in 1733, Pöppelmann, the Zwinger architect,
redid part of it so it could be used for city administration.
Now it is an elegant Interhotel, with a river-front garden,
sunny corridors, period rooms (you can purchase the furniture, if you like), and a music room, where Champagne
accompanies intimate concerts. There are nine restaurants, a
swimming pool, Jacuzzi, sauna, bowling alley, solarium, jog-
ging course, and a gift shop; English is spoken. Leipzig fair
attendees are offered a private bus to the fair, with a hostess
serving breakfast en route. In summer, cruises on the hotel's
boat are available to the castle at neighboring Pillnitz, the
hunting lodge of Moritzburg, and Meissen. The new **Interhotel Dresdenerhof**, right on the Neumarkt, is in the
same five-star category but more functional in decor.

The **Hotel Newa**, near the railroad station, is quite a step
down from the Bellevue and Dresdenerhof, but its restaurant is better than average; its rooms are boxlike but adequate. It has a café, two bars, and a sauna.

Two lesser but acceptable hotels, the **Königstein** and the
**Lilienstein**, stand side by side down the Prägerstrasse. Be
prepared, however, to sleep on a concave bed in a minimally
decorated bedroom. English is limited.

At the **Hotel Astoria**, not the most convenient location in
Dresden (near the zoo), there are simple but clean accommodations, two restaurants, and good fare.

# Dining in Dresden and Meissen

**Kügeln Haus**, at Strasse der Befreiung 14, is what a restaurant might have been like in prewar Dresden. It is in a restored, 19th-century burgher house on the north side of the river. There are engravings and woodcuts of singers and actors of the past on its walls. Service is more painstaking than in most restaurants in East Germany, and the place settings are attractively done, too. Reservations required; Tel: 5-27-91.

Dresden's poshest, most dignifed restaurant, and its most expensive, is the **Gourmet**, in the Dresdenerhof. Reservations essential; Tel: 484-10.

You take a cable car to get to the **Luisenhof**, which overlooks Dresden and the Elbe from the city outskirts. Destroyed in the war, Luisenhof has been rebuilt in a neo-Baroque style. There is dancing some evenings at this romantic spot, at Bergbahnstrasse 8. Reservations required; Tel. 3-68-42.

Try a pastry and coffee in the Bellevue's Baroque **Pöppelmann Cafe**, looking out on a field of flowers inspired by the Moritzburg castle garden. Some afternoons there is music to drink your coffee by.

In the cellar of the Rathaus of August the Strong's day, the **Meissner Weinkeller**, Strasse der Befreiung 14, has an ambience of the past—and good local wine and food. Tel: 5-27-91 (the Kügeln Haus, which will connect you).

Polish cuisine is the specialty at the **Wroclaw room** in the International Restaurant, at Prägerstrasse 15 near the main tourist hotels. Tel: 4-95-51-34.

**Pirnaisches Tor** is a modern restaurant and self-service café not far from the Zwinger; fish is a favorite here.

The Semper Oper, which is closed from early July to mid-August, is, of course, the place to go in the evening. Otherwise, try a Dresden Philharmonic concert at the *Kulturpalast,* on Thälmannstrasse in the Altmarkt. Arrangements for tickets of any sort should be made at your hotel as soon as you arrive. Opera tickets in particular are in short supply, so unless you are willing to gamble on getting one (for much less money) at the door, it is wise to take what you can get when you can get it.

The **Vincenz Richter**, An der Frauenbirche 12, is in a half-timbered house near the Marktplatz in Meissen (see below). If the food in this newly refurbished restaurant is as good as it was in the old place, it is worth trying. In any case, it is worth a visit simply to see the handsome historic structure and have a glass of red or white Meissen wine, considered to be the best in East Germany. Tel: 32-85.

**The Activist**, across the Elbe from Meissen town, at Elbegasse 1, is a little square house on the river with an inviting atmosphere and good food. Tel: 22-86.

After a morning of sightseeing at Albrechtsburg castle and the cathedral (see below), it is pleasant not to have to go back down into town for lunch. The **Burgkeller** (Tel: 30-57) and the **Domkeller** (Tel: 20-34) are recent additions to the historic hilltop Meissen complex.

# Around Dresden

Upriver in the Dresden environs, the Baroque palace of **Pillnitz**, the summer dwelling of the electors and kings, is worth a visit. It is about 11 km (7 miles) southeast of Dresden. Designed by Zwinger architect Pöppelmann, it is a curious architectural mix of Baroque and East Asian styles, with pagoda-like roofs supported by Corinthian columns. Its builder, August I, called it "an Indian pleasure seat." And about 20 km (12 miles) north of Dresden there is the sprawling yellow sandstone **Moritzburg hunting lodge**, set on an island among man-made ponds, first constructed in the 17th century and rebuilt for August by Pöppelmann.

Still farther upstream, the fortresses of **Königstein** and **Lilienstein** loom above the river, and, finally, there are the needlelike peaks of Saxony's "Little Switzerland."

Downriver 35 km (20 miles) northwest toward Wittenberg, the 15th-century fortress castle of **Albrechtsburg** and the 13th-century High Gothic **Dom** tower above the Elbe's left bank at **Meissen**. From 1710 to 1864, Meissen porcelain was manufactured in the castle. A short walk leads down from the castle into the half-timbered town. Today, 19th-century Romantic paintings in the castle recount its history. Also in Meissen, on the Leninstrasse, is today's porcelain factory and museum, where visitors can see how modern Meissen is made and painted. There is also a small shop selling Meissen in the town.

## GETTING AROUND

Travel restrictions between the two Germanys are for the most part a thing of the past. Connections between cities in the two are improving all the time. For the most up-to-date information, contact one the offices listed in the For Further Information section in Useful Facts at the front of this book. There are now regular flights on Lufthansa and Interflug between Dresden and Cologne, Hamburg, Munich, and

Stuttgart, and between Leipzig and Düsseldorf, Frankfurt, Munich, and Stuttgart.

Though it is possible to cross the border with a car or rent one in major cities, only on Autobahns can you be assured of gasoline around the clock. For travel on other roads, it is essential to have a map giving the location of gas stations (whose opening and closing hours may not coincide with your needs).

Rail travel in East Germany is slow, but trains do link most communities. Again, however, station personnel are unlikely to speak English, and train schedules can change and leave you stranded.

A new national computer service allows you to obtain information, and make reservations, on all railroad and airline links; check with German National Railroads, Interflug, or Lufthansa, or with offices of the German National Tourist Board.

In April 1991, KD German Rhine Line will begin Hamburg–Dresden cruises on the Elbe river. Each ship will have 64 double cabins and will dock for the night in various East German river ports, offering shore excursions at some, including Dresden—where it is currently very difficult to get land hotel accommodations—Meissen, and Potsdam (to see Sans Souci palace). For booking information see the Around Germany section in Useful Facts at the front of the book.

Because so little is offered in English in East Germany, it makes sense to forgo the normal desire to travel independently in favor of a packaged tour with English-speaking guides or guides who will see that English-language tapes are available (there aren't many of them) for museum tours.

## Shopping

There really is very little of interest to the tourist to buy in East Germany yet. The possible exceptions are old books, art books, prints, antiques, records, and optical goods. Shops at major hotels sell a few familiar brands of soap, perfume, shampoo, and film, and, in larger hotels, locally made souvenirs and gift items.

## Planning

Even if you ask the concierge in your hotel for theater, opera, and concert tickets or to make a restaurant reservation for you, what you ask for may never be received. Tickets for cultural events are always in demand. Whenever possible, if you are booking with a travel agent, ask him or her to reserve tickets for you.

When planning visits to museums and churches, be flexible. Church openings and closings depend on church officials, who may or may not welcome tourists. Museums, like restaurants, frequently seem to be undergoing reconstruction, or hours change. Many museums close for lunch. In small-city tourist offices, there is often no one who speaks English. Be sure to take a dictionary.

Restaurant hours and days of opening and closing should also be checked at hotels. Hours may not be what you expect.

## ACCOMMODATIONS REFERENCE
The telephone country code for East Germany is 37. Bear in mind that East German hotels in general are overbooked these days—packed with West German and other businesspeople trying to gain a timely commercial foothold in the new East Germany. Even the telephone lines are jammed; it may take you hours or even days to get through—if you get through at all.

▶ **Astoria.** Platz der Republik 2, DDR-7010 **Leipzig.** Tel: (41) 722-20; Telex: 51535.

▶ **Hotel Astoria.** Ernst-Thälmann-Platz, DDR-8020 **Dresden.** Tel: (51) 47-51-71; Telex: 2442.

▶ **Auf der Wartburg.** DDR-5900 **Eisenach.** Tel: (623) 51-11.

▶ **Hotel Bellevue.** Köpckestrasse, DDR-8060 **Dresden.** Tel: (51) 566-20; Telex: 261271.

▶ **Hotel Belvedere.** Belvedere Allee, DDR-5300 **Weimar.** Tel: (621) 24-29.

▶ **Hotel Cecilienhof.** Neuer Garten, DDR-1500 **Potsdam.** Tel: (33) 231-41.

▶ **Hotel Elephant.** Am Markt, DDR-5300 **Weimar.** Tel: (621) 614-71; Telex: 618961.

▶ **Erfurter Hof.** Am Bahnhofsvorplatz, DDR-5010 **Erfurt.** Tel: (61) 511-51; Telex: 61283.

▶ **Goldener Adler.** Markt 7, DDR-4600 **Wittenberg.** Tel: (451) 20-53.

▶ **Interhotel Dresdenerhof.** Am Neumarkt, DDR-8010 **Dresden.** Tel: (51) 484-10; Telex: 26267; Fax: 4954053.

▶ **Königstein.** Prägerstrasse, DDR-8010 **Dresden.** Tel: (51) 48-560; Telex: 26165.

▶ **Lilienstein.** Prägerstrasse, DDR-8010 **Dresden.** Tel: (51) 48-560; Telex: 26165.

▶ **Merkur.** Gerberstrasse, DDR-7010 **Leipzig.** Tel: (41) 79-90; Telex: 512609; Fax: 7991229.

▶ **Hotel Newa.** Leningraderstrasse, DDR-8010 **Dresden.**
Tel: (51) 496-71-12; Telex: 26067.

▶ **Parkhotel.** Wartburgallee 2, DDR-5900 **Eisenach.** Tel:
(623) 623-52-91.

▶ **Hotel Potsdam.** Lange Brücke, DDR-1500 **Potsdam.** Tel:
(33) 46-31; Telex: 15416.

▶ **Hotel am Ring.** Karl-Marx-Platz, DDR-7010 **Leipzig.** Tel:
(41) 795-20; Telex: 51426.

▶ **Hotel Stadt Halle.** Ernst-Thälmann-Platz, DDR-4020
**Halle.** Tel: (46) 380-41; Telex: 4401.

▶ **Stadt Leipzig.** Richard-Wagner-Strasse 1, DDR-7010
**Leipzig.** Tel: (41) 28-88-14.

# COLOGNE
## (KÖLN)

*By David Magee*

*David Magee is a journalist and broadcaster who has lived in West Germany for more than ten years. Now working in Bonn, he was based in Cologne for four years.*

Unlike many of the world's large cities, Cologne—with a population of almost one million—is getting better. Every year there are more things to see and do, more new and innovative buildings, and more greenery. There is a youthful vivacity about Cologne that belies its rather advanced age of more than 2,000 years. Many observers feel that it rivals Berlin among German cities for informality, eccentricity, and relaxed atmosphere.

The largest city on the Rhine, Cologne is a major hub of business and industry—the self-styled "commercial center of the West." The title is one the city might have claimed as long ago as the Middle Ages, for then as now the Rhine was one of Western Europe's main trade routes, and Cologne was a leading member of the powerful Hanseatic League.

The city's history as a trading hub dates to the dawn of Christianity. The Romans built a garrison on the site, in the first century B.C. They made it a proper colony in A.D. 50, calling it Colonia Claudia Ara Agrippinensis, after Agrippina, mother of Nero and wife of the emperor Claudius. The colony quickly developed into the Roman Empire's most important trading and manufacturing center north of the Alps.

The Romans left a lasting imprint on Cologne: The remains of their walls and buildings are scattered throughout the central area, and the layout of the city still reflects its

Roman heritage. As Christianity gained influence in the empire, Cologne continued to grow in importance, and by the fourth century an episcopal see had been established here. When Rome's power faded, Cologne became part of the Holy Roman Empire, and Charlemagne founded an archdiocese here in 785. The archbishop of Cologne was one of the most powerful figures in the Holy Roman Empire.

From the 12th to the 15th century, Cologne was the most populous—and one of the richest—cities in the German-speaking world. One tangible aspect of this success was the great Gothic cathedral, whose construction was begun in 1248. But as fortunes shifted in Europe, Cologne's heyday passed. With the discovery of the New World, the emergence of Europe's nation-states, and the development of new trade routes and new ways of doing business, the city's importance faded. Again, this trend was reflected in the construction of the cathedral, which was halted in 1560.

The decline, hastened by the expulsion of the Jews in the 15th century and restrictions on the Protestants in the 16th, was to last until the late 1800s. In 1794 Cologne was seized by French troops, who used the still-unfinished cathedral as what must have been the world's largest barracks and stables. Under French influence, the city also became famous as the source of the world's best-known toilet water—eau de cologne.

When the Rhine province was annexed by Prussia in 1814, Cologne passed into Prussian hands, and the archdiocese was reorganized in 1824. Ironically, these Protestants saw to the completion of the Gothic cathedral, begun by the Roman Catholic Church 600 years previously. In a celebration of the Industrial Age, which brought with it a revival of Cologne's fortunes, the Prussians placed the main railroad station next door to this architectural showpiece. The station is now one of Germany's busiest, serving about 1,000 trains daily.

Cologne suffered mightily in World War II. Although Allied pilots were under orders not to bomb the cathedral, it was nevertheless hit and still bears the scars of bombs and bullets. Fortunately, the massive rebuilding effort, begun shortly after the war, has repaired most of the devastation. The Altstadt (Old Town), which was all but obliterated, has been skillfully restored. Today it is easy to imagine what this quarter was like in the Middle Ages.

Unfortunately, much of the new construction done in the late 1940s and early 1950s was carried out with economic revival in mind, and not much else. The result is, on the whole, jarring. By contrast, many of the buildings that have gone up since the mid-1970s are both architecturally interesting and attractive.

## MAJOR INTEREST

Cathedral
Wallraf-Richartz-Museum/Museum Ludwig
Römisch-Germanisches Museum
Kölnisches Stadtmuseum
Romanesque churches
Museum für Ostasiatische Kunst
Altstadt

The city has two traditions, both known as *Kölsch*: Cologne's own dialect, much influenced by French and Flemish, and its own top-fermented beer. The slightly bitter beer is easy enough to love—there are more than 4,000 pubs, restaurants, and brewery taverns in Cologne. The dialect, however, is considered by many incomprehensible, and is full of booby traps.

The taverns, where the food is always simple and the blue-aproned waiters are often astonishingly brusque, offer such things as a *Halve Hahn,* which sounds like it might be half a hen, but is actually rye bread with a slice of cheese; *Kölsche Kaviar* turns out to be rye bread with blood sausage and onions.

There are many museums in Cologne, most of them specialized. The city revels in its reputation, acquired in recent years, as West Germany's "secret" art capital, and there are more than 100 private galleries in addition to the public museums. The Romanesque churches are also well worth visiting; many cognoscenti admire them more than the cathedral.

The best panorama of Cologne can be enjoyed right across the Rhine from the cathedral, in the district of Deutz (formerly a separate town). There is a ferry in summer, but the walk across one of the bridges only takes a few minutes; it is especially worthwhile at night, when the cathedral is illuminated. Deutz, where the four-stroke internal combustion engine was invented, also offers the splendid Rheinpark gardens, and Europe's only cable car across the Rhine.

The locals will not agree, of course, but if there is a time to avoid Cologne, it is during the much-vaunted carnival. This

# Cologne

| 0 | yards | 275 |
| 0 | meters | 250 |

N

MARZELLENSTR.

MAXIMINENSTRASSE

To Zoo

GOLDGASSE

Rhine River

**Hauptbahnhof**

**Cathedral**

Domplatte

Heinrich Böll Platz

Hohenzollern Brücke

**Dom Kloster**

allrafplatz

**Römisch-
Germanisches
Museum**

BECHERGASSE

**Wallraf-
Richartz-
Museum and
Museum Ludwig**

olping
Memorial

**Minoritenkirche**

MINORITENSTR.

GROSSE
BUDENGASSE

MUHLENGASSE

**DEUTZ**

**Fischmarkt**

RUCKEN-
STR.

OBENMARSPFORTEN

HAFENGASSE

HOHE STR.

Deutzer Brücke

PIPINSTR.

AM LEYSTAPEL

**St. Maria
im Kapitol**

MUHLENBACH

MATHIAS-FOLLER-STR.

HOLTZMARKT

Rhine River

SEVERINSTR.

Severinsbrücke

TEL-AVIV-STR.

event, whose religious significance has been largely lost in a modern frenzy of partying, can be off-putting if you are not prepared for revels on a large and noisy scale. The climax of the carnival comes in the week before Ash Wednesday.

That the Kölner approach carnival with such exuberance should not be surprising. They like a good time any time— so much so that Germans from other parts of the country often accuse Cologne's natives of being vulgar, lazy, and unreliable. But whether you like the natives or not, their city—a curious blend of Medieval and ultramodern—works very well indeed. And the Kölner have another side: Cologne was one of the few German cities that put up any serious resistance to Hitler. The crusty Konrad Adenauer, who would later be West Germany's first chancellor, was lord mayor of Cologne until the Nazis removed him from office and imprisoned him.

## The Cathedral

Although many people claim that the Cologne cathedral is the purest and most perfect example of High Gothic architecture, not everyone is impressed by those soaring spires: Cologne's most famous writer, the Nobel laureate Heinrich Böll, once referred to them sneeringly as "that Prussian crap."

The cathedral or, simply, the Dom, is not only the most obvious Cologne landmark, it is also Germany's best-known building, among Germans and foreigners alike.

Before entering, it pays to stroll about the square, known as the Domplatte (literally, Cathedral Slab) or the Domterrasse. The towers and main entrance are on the west side, only a few steps south of the Hauptbahnhof, the main railroad station. The Römisch-Germanisches Museum and the Wallraf-Richartz/Ludwig museums complex are just as close, to the south.

There is nearly always something happening on the Domplatte. In addition to the usual contingent of street musicians and sidewalk artists, there could be anything from a political demonstration to a skateboard competition, or even a circus.

On the west side there is a replica of one of the tower finials, which gives some idea of the cathedral's massive size; there are also the remains of a Roman wall here. The Cologne tourism office, with its helpful multilingual staff, is just across the street.

In early Roman times, before Christianity gained a foothold in Roman culture, Christians held services in a building close to the city wall, not on the present cathedral site. Where the Dom now stands was once a Roman temple, later superseded by churches, including the ancient Hildebold cathedral, consecrated in 870. But huge as this building was, it would be surpassed by the achievements of the Gothic master builders.

In 1164 the relics of the Magi (whose crowns are represented in Cologne's coat-of-arms) were transferred to the Hildebold cathedral, vastly increasing the town's significance to Christendom. Plans soon were made to erect an even more magnificent structure to house the relics. The cornerstone for the new cathedral was laid in 1248. The building's design was based on the French royal cathedrals of Amiens and Rheims, but the aim was to outstrip these buildings in elegance, architectural concept, and sheer size.

The choir was the first part of the structure to be finished, and it was consecrated in 1322. Construction of the western façade, the largest church front ever built, began around 1300. For almost 300 years the master builders toiled, but by 1560 they had managed to finish only about half of the cathedral. Still, the main floor area was sufficiently complete for it to be roofed over and used. The huge crane used by the builders, which can be seen jutting out from the top of the unfinished building in many old prints, remained a landmark of Cologne for more than five centuries.

By 1560 the money for construction ran out, and work ceased until well into the 19th century. Thanks to a campaign by concerned citizens, interest in completing the cathedral was revived, and repair work in the choir began in 1823. Nineteen years later, the Protestant king of Prussia and the archbishop of Cologne jointly laid the cornerstone for the final phase of construction.

You can enter the cathedral from the south side, but you can appreciate the full impact of the central nave only by going in at the main, western entrance. The effect has been compared to a forest of great trees shimmering in a mysterious light.

Like many other major Medieval churches, the Dom is a splendid repository of works of art. Not least among these are its **stained-glass windows**, representing every period of the cathedral's life from the 13th century to the present day. Several are of particular significance: two in the ambulatory of the choir illustrating the scriptures, dating from between about 1260 and 1275; the kings' window in the choir's clerestory, with the *Adoration of the Magi* in the central portion (about 1310); and the five Renaissance windows in the northern aisle (1507–1509). The windows opposite were presented by King Ludwig I of Bavaria in 1848, and are among the most outstanding of their kind.

Among the most precious objects in the cathedral are the **Gero cross**, which has been dated to around 975, and which is the Western world's oldest large sculpture; the **shrine of the Three Kings**, an outstanding example of goldsmith work from the Rhine-Maas area, crafted between 1180 and 1225; and the altar painting the **Adoration of the Magi**, a masterpiece of the Cologne school by Stephan Lochner (dated about 1450).

The choir fittings are almost entirely original. The high altar, from 1322, is covered with a single slab of black marble almost 15 feet long. The oaken choir stalls were carved around 1310. The 42 paintings on the choir screens were executed in the early 14th century, and the 14 figures on the choir pillars are regarded as the most elegant examples extant of German High Gothic style.

A 19th-century mosaic depicting Medieval life forms the pavement of the choir and the ambulatory. The **treasury** has been sadly depleted over the centuries, but it still has many riches, including the silver shrine, dating from 1633, of the murdered Archbishop Engelbert.

Visitors to the cathedral are permitted to climb the **south tower**, entered via St. Peter's portal—the only part of the main entrance actually completed during the Middle Ages. The tower provides a stirring view of the city and surrounding area, including (weather permitting) the Siebengebirge (Seven Mountains), south of Bonn. But it is a daunting climb, even for the reasonably athletic: 509 steps up a narrow circular stone stairway take the panting visitor to the 230-foot level, and from there it is another 90 feet up to the observation platform.

On the way up, you pass the cathedral's biggest bells: Pretiosa (installed in 1448, 11.2 metric tons), Speciosa (1449, six metric tons), and St. Peter (1923, 24 metric tons). The bells are rung only on special occasions, as the mighty vibrations could endanger the tower.

Admission to the cathedral is free, but visitors are encouraged to make a contribution to a number of good causes. One of the causes supported by contributions is the Dombauhütte (Builder's Lodge), founded probably before 1248. The lodge's artisans—including more than 60 stonemasons, glass restorers, carpenters, smiths, painters, and other personnel—maintain and restore the cathedral.

The job of maintaining this massive building is never ending. Air pollution makes the task increasingly frustrating and expensive. Matters are complicated by the fact that the cathedral is built of several different kinds of stone that weather at different paces. Air pollution has accelerated the deterioration at an alarming rate; experts now judge that, sooner or later, virtually every part of the exterior—both structural and decorative components—will probably have to be replaced. As one official quipped rather bitterly, the day could well come when the cathedral will be a copy of itself.

If Cologne is merely the object of a *Stippvisite*—a flying visit of three or four hours—then the obvious thing to do after viewing the cathedral is to take in the nearby Römisch-Germanisches Museum and the complex that houses the Wallraf-Richartz and Ludwig museums.

# The Römisch-Germanisches Museum

Situated directly across the Domplatte on the south side of the cathedral, the Römisch-Germanisches Museum was completed in 1974 atop the remains of a Roman villa. The main reason for building the museum was to preserve and display the extraordinary Dionysus mosaic (created around A.D. 220). The mosaic and the imposing reconstructed tomb of the Roman legionnaire Lucius Poblicius (about A.D. 40) are both visible from outside the building.

The beautifully designed building presents the life of Roman Cologne—commerce, the military, culture, the cult of the dead, art and luxury goods, the Roman gods, and the life of early Christians—as if in a book. Upstairs, a reconstructed, still functioning carriage is on display, along with the main part of the collection. The objects on view testify to both the level of technology the Romans achieved and the high quality of the applied arts in their empire. One of the most comprehensive collections of Roman glass anywhere includes numerous glass vessels, together with descriptions of the various production and ornamental techniques used in making them. The key work is the diatreta glass, dating from about A.D. 330–340.

There is also an exceptional collection of ornaments from the period of great migrations that followed the fall of the Roman Empire. The collection was assembled from all over Europe, including southern Russia. Providing a chronicle of the rise of the Franks (A.D. 450–700), the displays make clear the cultural and historical interrelationships of early Medieval ornaments, weapons, glass, and ceramics from the Cologne area.

. The part of the museum dedicated to ancient history enables visitors to trace settlements in the Cologne area from the first century B.C. back to about 100,000 B.C. Objects in this section date from the Iron and Bronze ages, and even from Neolithic, Mesolithic, and Paleolithic times; they were gathered not only from the Cologne area but also from the rest of the Rhineland and certain other sites in Europe. (Open Tuesday, Friday, Saturday, Sunday 10:00 A.M. to 5:00 P.M.; Wednesday and Thursday 10:00 A.M. to 8:00 P.M.)

The Rhine once flowed where the street called the Bechergasse now passes parallel to the east side of the Römisch-Germanisches Museum. Running down along the right side of the museum is the **Hafenstrasse**, paved with its original ancient Roman cobblestones.

# The Wallraf-Richartz and Ludwig Museum Complex

Just a few steps away from the Römisch-Germanisches Museum, in the direction of the Rhine, is the Wallraf-Richartz-Museum/Museum Ludwig complex. While this sprawling modern structure was being built, its design created a considerable local furor, even though the architects, Peter Bussmann and Godfried Haberer, were from Cologne. A former CEO of Ford Europe who had a view of the museum from his high-rise office across the river once likened the building to a "herd of boxcars making love." But the building is gaining acceptance. Certainly, with its red-brick and metal cladding, it offers a startling contrast to both the Römisch-Germanisches Museum and the cathedral.

One man's bequest forms the basis not only of today's Wallraf-Richartz-Museum but also of most other museums in Cologne. Franz Ferdinand Wallraf (1748–1824), a canon and professor, had amassed an extensive collection of art from many periods, and he left it all to the city of his birth.

The money to house the Wallraf collection was provided by a Cologne merchant, Johann-Heinrich Richartz (1795–1861). Opened in 1861, the building was designed in Gothic Revival style and constructed on the site of an old Minorite monastery. During the ensuing years, the collection was enlarged by judicious purchases, gifts, and donations. One of the most substantial additions came in 1930, when the

Carstanjen collection was acquired, considerably enhancing the department of Dutch art.

From its early days, the museum welcomed the works of modern artists; the institution began to purchase contemporary art itself in 1912. In 1937, however, the Nazis confiscated most of the "decadent" modern works. Much of the museum building was destroyed by bombing, but fortunately, most of the contents had been evacuated beforehand. A new building, designed for the same site, opened in 1957.

By the time of this reopening, modern art was a major feature of the Wallraf-Richartz-Museum. To the existing collection were added the bequests of Josef Haubrich—including many important works of the German Expressionists—together with supplementary purchases and donations, and the Modern Department was officially established.

Another new era began in the late 1960s, when the Aachen chocolate manufacturers and art collectors Peter and Irene Ludwig began to make numerous loans of contemporary art to the museum. In 1976, following a donation of 350 works of art by the couple, the Museum Ludwig was founded. The new museum brought together all of the 20th-century art in the complex.

The Ludwigs' donation was conditional upon the construction of a new building, however, which was to be the Bussman-Haberer design, and which opened in the autumn of 1986; its wide range of cultural facilities includes not only the two museums and their various services but also the Cinemathek Köln and the 2,000-seat Philharmonie. (The museums are open Tuesday through Thursday from 10:00 A.M. until 8:00 P.M., and Friday through Sunday from 10:00 A.M. to 6:00 P.M.; closed Monday.)

The **Wallraf-Richartz-Museum** ranks among the world's great picture galleries, and is one of Germany's oldest museum foundations. It has the most extensive collection of paintings from the Medieval Cologne school. This collection, and Gothic works from other areas, provide a comprehensive survey of the development of panel painting from the early 14th century to the mid-16th century. Views of the cathedral through the museum's large windows provide a stunning setting for appreciating these paintings.

There are many Late Gothic Dutch panel paintings by Jan de Beer, Joos van Cleve, and others; works by the so-called "Old German" masters—Cranach, Dürer, Burgkmair—illustrate the new approaches developed in the late 15th and early 16th centuries. Some of the finest works of the masters are found in the collection of Dutch and Flemish painting from the 16th century to the 18th.

From the 17th century there are works by such artists as Rembrandt, Rubens, and Terbruggen. The Italians are also well represented: Canaletto, Tiepolo, and Bordone, including one of the latter's major works, *Bathsheba at Her Toilet*. A vivid impression of Spanish art is provided by works of Murillo, Ribera, Collantes, and Melendez.

The 19th-century collection contains paintings by all of the period's most important artists, particularly those of France and Germany. It ends with the Symbolist painting of Ensor and Munch, the Post-Impressionist developments of van Gogh and Gauguin, and the "Intimist" works of Pierre Bonnard.

There is also a collection representing the graphic arts over eight centuries, with about 8,000 drawings and water-colors, around 200 Medieval miniatures, and more than 45,000 prints from the 15th to the 19th centuries.

In addition to these works, the museum houses a collection, started in 1972, of video tapes by various artists, and there are facilities for both screening and producing videos. There is also a collection of more than 5,000 20th-century photographs. Within the complex as well is the **Agfa-Foto-Historama**, one of the world's most important museums devoted to the history of photography. Altogether the collection contains about 12,000 photographs from the past 150 years; in addition, there are 20,000 historical cameras, viewing and projecting equipment, and a photography library containing books, autographs, and cartoons on the history of photography.

The **Museum Ludwig** exhibits works of the 20th century exclusively. The collections are wide ranging, embracing virtually every important artist and movement of the past 90 years, and the museum already has acquired enormous prestige in Germany and beyond.

Avant-garde works of the early part of this century are shown to good advantage, in a fascinating juxtaposition of past and present. The Museum Ludwig includes splendid examples of the seminal work of the 1920s and of Surrealism, with Schwitters, Ernst, Dali, and Magritte all represented by some of their best efforts. An entire room is given over to Picasso; it features both paintings and sculptures. The influence of German art on the 20th century, beginning with the group Die Brücke (The Bridge) and culminating in Expressionism, is well documented.

Important works by Picasso, Braque, Gris, and Léger give

an overview of the most significant developments in Cubism, while the Italian section extends from Cubism and Futurism to Pittura Metafisica. The Russian avant-garde is represented by works of unusual quality from Malevich, Goncharova, Larionov, Rodchenko, El Lissitsky, and others: The Museum Ludwig has made it possible to measure Russia's contribution to modern art against that of the Bauhaus.

The regeneration of the arts after World War II, with the striking new approaches by artists in both Europe and America, is also superbly documented. Abstraction had become an international language, and French painters who made major contributions, such as Wols, Hartung, and Riopelle, are well represented, along with leading Germans such as Baumeister and Nay. Pop art is represented by Warhol, Wesselman, Lichtenstein, and Johns, among others.

## The Zoo and the Rheinpark

After so much culture a breath of fresh air will doubtless be welcome, along with some refreshment. A short stroll across the red-brick Heinrich Böll Platz—to the right of the railway bridge called the Hohenzollernbrücke—leads to the broad steps that go down to the **Rhine promenade**, past Eduardo Paolozzi's *Rheingarten Skulptur.* To the right is the Rhine side of the Altstadt and a row of reconstructed buildings with distinctive peaked gables.

These buildings, most of which date from the 17th century, stretch down to the next bridge, the Deutzer Brücke. Almost all of them have an agreeable, if undistinguished, pub, restaurant, or café on the ground floor, with outdoor service as well; if the day is warm and bright, the passing show on the Rhine promenade will be entertaining.

Germans are a nation of walkers (despite their devotion to fast driving), and they love going for long hikes. The stroll along the Rhine to the zoo provides a perfect opportunity to emulate them. (Just keep an eye out for fanatic bicyclists, who deal harshly with unwary pedestrians.)

You may want to stop for lunch halfway along at the **Bastei**—a curious round restaurant perched above the promenade, overlooking the Rhine. Walk under the Hohenzollernbrücke, and then straight on. In the distance is the Zoobrücke; as the name suggests, the zoo is nearby.

It is also possible to reach the zoo by the city's small but efficient subway system. From the promenade, double back toward the cathedral—for a change of pace, take the narrow

streets and alleyways of the **Altstadt**. There are some delightful shops in the area, and it is impossible to lose your way.

The central subway station is below the rail station's main
concourse. The way is clearly marked by blue signs with a
large white "U" (*Untergrundbahn*—underground railway).
Passengers buy their tickets from the many-buttoned vending machines, and then cancel them in the little orange
boxes placed at the entrance to the trains. Even many Germans find the subway ticket machines confusing; fortunately,
this station boasts a ticket and information counter, and
usually someone on duty speaks English.

Lines 5, 15, 16, and 18 all go in the direction of the zoo;
follow the black-and-white signs that say *Richtung Zoo*. Large
signs indicate each station, and the stops are announced on a
PA system that—unlike most such systems—can actually be
understood. Get off the subway at the Zoo/Flora station; there
is no difficulty in finding the zoo entrance from the subway,
which by now is above ground. (For more on transportation
in Cologne, see Getting Around.)

Established in 1860, the **Cologne Zoo** receives around 1.5
million visitors a year. The complete tour is about a mile and
a quarter, and there are more than 730 different kinds of
animals, from hummingbirds to elephants, all living in settings designed to be as similar to their native habitats as
possible. The zoo has specialized in lemurs—tiny prosi-
mians from Madagascar—and many members of the ape
family are found in the new Urwaldhaus (Tropical Forest
House). Across from the zoo is the excellent aquarium,
which opened in 1971. Those who like creepy-crawly things
will be delighted to learn that the aquarium includes a
terrarium and insectarium.

The **botanical garden** is adjacent to the zoo. Created in
1862 in the style of an English landscape garden, it has trees,
flowers, and other plants from all over Europe as well as
from tropical and subtropical regions. (The zoo is open
daily from 9:00 A.M. to 6:00 P.M., the aquarium from 9:30 A.M.
to 6:00 P.M. The botanical garden opens daily at 8:00 A.M. and
closes at dusk.)

Another kind of park, and one regarded by many as
Cologne's most beautiful, is situated opposite the zoo on the
other side of the river. Known as the **Rheinpark**, it can be
reached by Europe's only cable car across the Rhine—a six-
minute trip 130 feet above the river that offers a sweeping
view of the city, the Rhine traffic, and the surrounding area.

The Rheinpark was established in 1957 as Cologne's contribution to the Bundesgartenschau (National Garden Show).

The park is famous for its many varied and venerable trees, species from both Europe and North America. A chairlift system departing from the cable-car station carries the foot-weary above the park at a leisurely 5 mph.

In the midst of this beauty is the **Tanzbrunnen** (Dancing Fountain), a 30,000-seat open-air auditorium with a stage protected by an unusual tentlike roof. Free concerts and other events are held here during afternoons and evenings from May to September.

On leaving the Rheinpark, you may wish to take the cable car and subway back into the city center, or to continue on foot along the Rhine in the direction of the Deutzer Brücke. The walk goes past the grounds of the Kölner Messe, one of Europe's biggest trade-fair facilities.

The buildings are dominated by the Messeturm (Trade Fair Tower), from the top of which you have the same perspective as that used by Oskar Kokoschka in 1956 to paint his explosively colorful *View of Cologne,* which can be seen in the Museum Ludwig. There is also the obligatory restau-rant here.

From early spring until late autumn the ferry back to the other side departs with reasonable regularity from opposite the Messe buildings. The boat ride is short, but it can be romantic, especially on one of those sun-dappled, misty Rhineland autumn afternoons. The boat ties up near the Hohenzollernbrücke among the vessels of the White Fleet, the excursion boats of the Köln–Düsseldorfer line.

## West Around the Cathedral

Despite its many parks and its Rhine vistas, Cologne cannot be called a beautiful city. But it is one of those places where turning around a corner can be a step into the previous century—or the next one.

Many such experiences can be enjoyed in the central area west of the cathedral. Start on the **Hohe Strasse**, across the Wallrafplatz just left of the cathedral front. This roadway is one of the main arteries of the biggest of Cologne's ac-claimed pedestrian precincts, which have been praised by urban planners everywhere—and rightly so.

The Hohe Strasse is always bursting with life: locals, sight-seers from all over the world, street musicians and magicians, fruit sellers and beggars—all contrasting with some of Ger-many's most elegant window displays and arcades. The Café Eigel, just off the Hohe Strasse, to the right on the Brücken-strasse, offers welcome respite along the way.

The Hohe Strasse opens to the west into the **Schildergasse**, the east–west axis of the pedestrian precinct. On the left is the flagship store of the huge **Kaufhof department store** chain. Its basement supermarket may not be quite Harrod's, but the displays are eye-catching. Passing up the temptations of this bustling and noisy shopping district and continuing along the Schildergasse, you'll encounter one of Cologne's surprising contrasts: the **Antoniterkirche**, a 14th-century basilica. Inside (the church is always open during the day) there is utter quiet, presided over by the famous *Angel of Death* sculpture by Ernst Barlach.

The Schildergasse ends in a large, open square, the Neumarkt. The square is often the scene of an open-air market, which is liveliest just before Christmas. At the far end of the Neumarkt to the right is the bulk of the Stiftskirche St. Aposteln (Church of the Holy Apostles). Built between 1192 and 1230, it is generally considered the greatest monument of Romanesque church architecture in the Rhineland. Each of Cologne's 12 major Romanesque churches is a jewel in its own way, but St. Aposteln is the one to see if time is limited.

Visit the **Schnütgen-Museum** first, though. Turn left (south) from the Schildergasse and walk along the eastern edge of the Neumarkt and across the Cäcilienstrasse, which runs east and west. The Schnütgen-Museum is housed in the Romanesque **church of St. Cäcilien** (Saint Cecilia).

Ignore the modern annex that forms the entrance hall and offices and proceed into the church, which was built between 1140 and 1160 on the site of a ladies' collegiate church founded in the ninth century; this institution in turn had taken the place of some Roman baths. The walls on the left date from the Hohenstaufen dynasty of the 12th and 13th centuries.

The museum was named for Alexander Schnütgen, a cathedral chapter member and priest who left his collections to the city of Cologne in 1906. Throughout his life, Schnütgen was passionately interested in the art of the Middle Ages; he spoke of this interest as "some dark urge." For 40 years, while he worked at the Cologne cathedral, he acquired examples of ecclesiastical art, slowly building the core of today's collection.

It has been housed in St. Cäcilien since 1956. This museum/monument makes the most of the space and light granted to it by its location. The interior was redesigned in 1977, and the new design underlines more than ever the harmony of the Romanesque basilica.

The aim of the museum is to convey the past. This goal is achieved not simply by displaying the objects; the sculptures, carvings, fabrics, liturgical articles, and other works are arranged, as far as possible, according to their function. The result is an atmosphere in which the art is explained without words.

The collections extend from the early Middle Ages to the Baroque. The most important items are sculptures, stained-glass painting (especially the Ten Commandments window), goldsmith work, ivory carving (for example, the comb of St. Heribert), and liturgical objects. The sacristy contains textiles dating from the sixth to 19th centuries; these are mainly liturgical robes, but the collection also includes secular fabrics and embroidery.

As might be expected, most of the objects are from the Rhineland. Many of the Romanesque works from the region are well known: the Siegburg Madonna, the St. George crucifix, and the Cologne Madonnas of the Gothic period. A number of these works provide information about the world view, history, and life of their times. (Open Tuesday to Sunday, 10:00 A.M.–5:00 P.M.; closed Monday. Guided tours Sunday at 11:00 A.M., and open the first Wednesday in the month from 10:00 A.M. until 8:00 P.M.)

The next destination is St. Aposteln—but on the way there, anyone who is seriously interested in photography should stop briefly at **Foto Gregor**, across the street from St. Cäcilien. The store's display of vintage Leicas—all in first-rate condition—is alone worth the pause.

**St. Aposteln** is one of 12 major Romanesque churches in Cologne. These churches were restored in a lengthy program whose costs were borne by the Roman Catholic archdiocese, the city, the state of North Rhine–Westphalia, and the federal government.

The 12 churches are within walking distance of each other, forming a rough ring within what used to be the city walls. Some incorporate structural elements that date from the fourth to sixth centuries.

Even a cursory tour of all 12 churches would take at least two days. (Some of the guided tours organized by the city tourist office take up to four.) St. Aposteln is an excellent choice for those who can only spend an afternoon looking at the Romanesque glories of Cologne.

Two thousand years ago, the Roman wall marking the boundary of the city stood just in front of what is now St. Aposteln's cloverleaf-shaped choir. Although the building's beginnings were modest, it was consecrated in honor of the

Apostles—a patronage usually reserved only for important churches in Rome or Constantinople. The church began to take on its present form between 1021 and 1036, during the tenure of Archbishop Pilgrim, who founded a canons' collegiate church here. It was taken over by its parishioners eight centuries later, and the present building is still used as a parish church.

The 13th-century walls built by the Hohenstaufen family preserved Pilgrim's original building, encasing it and tracing its shape. Today, the original simple, rectangular eastern choir may still be seen from the stretch of wall bounding the chancel.

St. Aposteln's western steeple, erected in the mid-12th century, is one of the inner city's landmarks, with its striking diamond-shaped spire. A disastrous fire in 1192 destroyed the eastern choir, which was subsequently rebuilt; it was around this time that the status of the church began to change. By the close of the 12th century the Neumarkt had become one of the city's major trading venues; now, for the first time, St. Aposteln was integrated into civic life. Tangible evidence of the church's new position was offered by the great new city wall, on which work had begun in 1180; when the project was completed, St. Aposteln stood within the walls.

The first cloverleaf choir in Germany was built in another of Cologne's Romanesque churches, **St. Maria im Kapitol**, several blocks east of the Neumarkt off the Cäcilienstrasse. But the cloverleaf choir in St. Aposteln, finished in the early 13th century, is regarded as the most mature example of its kind.

Some may consider it profane that St. Aposteln is bounded so closely by the **Mittelstrasse**, one of Cologne's fashion centers. Others may feel this is only appropriate, in view of the church's proximity to the city's commercial and mercantile life for so many centuries.

Not far along is the Bazaar de Cologne, a covered shopping mall with a Mediterranean flair. It stands on the former site of Wilker, Cologne's most elegant china and crystal shop. **Wilker** is now to be found at Mittelstrasse 1: Its displays cover two floors, and there are often special exhibitions along with the wares on sale. **Café Fassbender**, proffering marvelous chocolates, cakes, and pastries, is also on the Mittelstrasse. The Hahnentor, once part of the city's Medieval fortifications, guards the end of the street. Just past the great gate is the Hohenzollernring (named, like the Hohenzollernbrücke, for the family that once ruled Brandenburg, Prussia, and all of Germany).

Once a stretch of functional concrete office buildings, snack bars, and garish strip joints, the Hohenzollernring was recently cleaned up and prettified, and Kölner are now quite proud of it. Follow the Hohenzollernring for a short distance, then head east onto the Ehrenstrasse—an area that is more interesting.

With its blend of shops, boutiques, bistros, amusement arcades, fish restaurants, cafés, and bars, the **Ehrenstrasse** is considered by many to symbolize the authentic Cologne. In the Ehrenstrasse you will find **König's**, one of Germany's finest art-book stores. König's claims to stock, or to be able to find, books that cannot be acquired elsewhere.

Farther east the Ehrenstrasse becomes the Breite Strasse, with more shops and the relatively new *Stadt Anzeiger* fountain outside the press house (the *Stadt Anzeiger* is Cologne's largest daily newspaper). A left turn just before this building leads to the Kolping memorial and the **Museum für Angewandte Kunst** (Museum of Applied Arts), originally established in 1888.

This museum occupies the former quarters of the Wallraf-Richartz-Museum; it was reopened in 1988 after a 50-year hiatus, and it is now one of the four major museums for the applied arts in Germany. Its collection covers European arts and crafts from the Middle Ages to the present day.

The large entrance hall holds examples of the very latest designs. Other rooms trace developments back through the 1960s and 1950s, to the Art Deco of the 1940s and 1930s, and the products of the Bauhaus and Werkbund. From there, the collection goes back through Jugendstil and Art Nouveau at the turn of the century, then through Historicism, Classicism, Biedermeier, Baroque, the Renaissance, and finally the Gothic and Romanesque periods.

The excellent furniture collection is of special interest, with examples dating from the Middle Ages to the present day. There are also important collections of ceramics, glass, jewelry, fashion, textiles, and graphics.

## Other Museums

In this city of museums, there are two more that should not be missed: the Kölnisches Stadtmuseum (Cologne City Museum) and the Museum für Ostasiatische Kunst (Museum for East Asian Art).

The **Kölnisches Stadtmuseum** is easy to find: Turn north into the Auf dem Berlich, the first major street after the Ehrenstrasse becomes the Breite Strasse. The museum is two blocks north, on the Zeughausstrasse, just to the east. Close by is a Roman tower; it dates from about A.D. 50.

The Stadtmuseum is housed in what used to be the city arsenal, built around 1600. Even then the building attracted visitors, because it boasted, among other things, a collection of municipal antiquities. The purpose of this museum is to serve as the "city's memory"—a goal it achieves admirably.

You are first confronted with things associated with the name "Cologne," such as eau de cologne. The journey into the past then takes you to the days of the kaiser, and back further still to the time when Cologne was an imperial city— of the Holy Roman Emperors and, before that, of the Romans.

The first floor is devoted to various themes dealing with the city hall and the council; religion, superstition, and science; wealth and poverty (and Cologne has seen both in good measure over the centuries); food, light, and warmth; trade and transportation; and the transition from crafts to industry. (Open Tuesday to Sunday, 10:00 A.M. to 5:00 P.M.; Thursday, 10:00 A.M. to 8:00 P.M.; closed Monday.)

The **Museum für Ostasiatische Kunst** is Europe's oldest museum devoted to the art of China, Japan, and Korea. Although somewhat out of the way, at the Universitäts-strasse 100, it can be reached easily enough by the number 1 or number 2 tram heading west from the Neumarkt, or by taxi (fares, as elsewhere in Germany, are very reasonable). The building, designed by the Japanese architect Kunio Mayekawa, is in itself worth the trip. The museum was established in 1913, but the present building dates from 1977.

The collections center on Buddhist painting and sculpture. The number and quality of Japanese wood sculptures are unique in Europe. Archaeological finds from China and Japan date back to the dawn of East Asian art. A special section devoted to Korea features a collection of ceramics that is generally regarded as the most important one outside that country.

(Open Tuesday through Sunday, 10:00 A.M. to 5:00 P.M.; first Friday in the month from 10:00 A.M. to 8:00 P.M.; closed Monday; guided tours Sunday at 11:00 A.M.)

# Carnival

Cologne's pre-Lenten carnival is a bit like Niagara Falls: It is something many people feel obliged to experience. The various events associated with carnival actually begin officially on November 11, but begin to reach a peak on

Weiberfastnacht, the last Thursday before Ash Wednesday. On Weiberfastnacht, women get to do pretty much whatever they want, starting with cutting the tie off every man foolish enough to wear one on this day. The activities culminate in the main carnival procession, held on Rosenmontag (Rose Monday—the last Monday before Lent).

In fact, there are four local processions in various sections of the city in addition to the main one, which always goes past the Dom. Furthermore, in the period between Weiberfastnacht and Shrove Tuesday there are more than 50 processions.

Anyone who wants a fighting chance of seeing at least part of the Rosenmontag procession in the vicinity of the cathedral should have a spot picked out hours ahead of time. It is a good idea to put on some sort of costume (it does not have to be anything elaborate—just a funny hat will do). Failing that, old clothes are the order of the day.

In the pre-procession warm-up, perfect strangers will kiss each other, link arms, and sing and prance about while drinking assorted mood-inducing beverages, mainly Kölsch. This activity carries on with increasing hilarity until the procession is long gone. The locals say that if you were at the procession and actually saw it, you were not truly entering into the spirit of things.

A new carnival custom has developed in recent years: Many bars and taverns hang out a straw doll in costume, and at midnight on Shrove Tuesday, as Lent begins, the figure is solemnly cremated on a funeral pyre. This marks the official close of carnival for another year.

## GETTING AROUND

### *When to Go*

As elsewhere in Central Europe, Cologne's weather is totally unpredictable at any time of the year. May, June, September, and October can be quite fine if not cold and rainy. July and August can be hot and muggy.

Although more people are becoming aware of Cologne as a place to go for fun, it is still not overly crowded at any time of the year, except when a major trade fair is on or carnival is in full swing.

### *Arriving*

**By car.** Cologne is accessible from any direction via West Germany's magnificent, but frequently terrifying, Autobahn network. (It is not uncommon to be passed by dueling

Mercedes and BMWs hurtling by at 140 mph.) The city is clearly marked at regular intervals, and the exit to take is the one marked Köln-Zentrum. But be warned: The city radiates from the ancient center, forming a rough circle, and this factor, plus a dense one-way street system, makes Cologne an extremely confusing place for the uninitiated. And the local drivers are not patient with out-of-towners who do not know where they are going. Furthermore, parking is at a premium (and only a few hotels have their own parking facilities). The vacation mood, in other words, is best preserved by choosing another mode of transport.

**By train.** Cologne offers excellent rail connections to and from virtually everywhere in Europe (including Great Britain). It is also a stop on Lufthansa's airport express up the Rhine from Frankfurt airport. The main station could not be more conveniently located, with most points of interest and many hotels within walking distance. On every platform there are Deutsche Bundesbahn (Federal German Railway) personnel in red caps who can provide information. (Every platform also has the German equivalent of a hot dog stand, with *Wurst* and hot and cold drinks.) There is also a clearly marked information booth in the main concourse, along with a variety of shops, restaurants and snack bars, a bank, a post office, lots of pay telephones, an international newsstand offering the European editions of many English-language newspapers, a hotel—and some of Germany's most colorful bums. There are taxi stands on both the east and west sides of the station; porter service is available.

**By air.** Cologne and the capital, Bonn, are served by a common international airport about 16 km (10 miles) from the center of Cologne. (It is, incidentally, widely acknowledged as one of the world's most traveller-friendly airports.) There is bus service to and from both cities every 20 minutes; the city-bound buses make several stops, the last one being, in both cases, the main railroad station. To and from Cologne, take the number 170 bus; service begins at 6:00 A.M.

### Around Town

**Public transportation.** Cologne has a system of streetcars, some of which travel the small subway system, and buses. The service is excellent, with frequent connections from early morning until late evening. The streetcars and buses are clean, comfortable, and free of hooligans (except when a big soccer game is being played).

Tickets are priced according to zone, and they must be purchased from the machines that are to be found at each stop and aboard the streetcars. These can be confusing to use; if in doubt, punch the DM 2.40 button—this fare will take you to just about anywhere within the area that is of greatest interest. The tickets must be stamped in the little orange boxes at the platform entrances and attached to pillars in the cars. Although most of Cologne's sights can be seen on foot, this is one place where public transportation is highly convenient. Your hotel's front desk will be able to provide details on getting to the places you want to see.

**By taxi.** There was a time when every taxi in Germany was a Mercedes, but the Japanese have had their impact here as well. One thing remains unchanged, though: All taxis are a cream color and have a black-and-yellow sign on the roof. They are usually spotless inside and out. Occasionally, a cruising taxi with its light on can be flagged down, but do not be surprised if you are ignored. It is more usual to take a cab from one of the stands located throughout the city, or to telephone (Tel: 28-82). Although some of Cologne's cabbies are capable of providing as hair-raising a ride as any Parisian hack, the fares are more than reasonable: A trip even to the suburbs is not likely to be more than DM 20–25, and travelling around the inner area will never be more than DM 10–15. A tip will be appreciated but it is not necessarily expected. If the fare is, say, DM 13.50, rounding it off to DM 14 will be sufficient.

## ACCOMMODATIONS
(The telephone city code for Cologne is 221).

There are more than 230 hotels and pensions within the Cologne city limits, in all classes and price categories. Reservations are recommended at any time; there may be no rooms available at all if a major trade fair is being held.

In Cologne, as elsewhere in West Germany, it is difficult to find a hotel that is truly a fleabag. On the other hand, reasonably priced accommodation with a touch of atmosphere is equally rare. But right on the Rhine, in the Altstadt, is the hotel **Im Stapelhäuschen**. It cannot be called luxurious (not all the rooms have their own bathroom) but it is, as the Germans would say, *gemütlich,* and offers a certain historical charm.

Fischmarkt 1–3, D-5000 Köln 1. Tel: 21-30-43 or 21-21-93.

The **Domgarten**, situated on a quiet side street near the cathedral, has only 15 rooms (all with shower and toilet). There is a friendly family atmosphere, and guests may find themselves being invited to coffee with the landlady.

Domstrasse 26, D-5000 Köln 1. Tel: 12-04-41.

At the other end of the scale in size and splendor is the **Dom-Hotel**. Just across the square from the cathedral, it has been one of the most exclusive hostelries in the city for more than 125 years. It looks and feels the way a first-class Old World hotel should.

Domkloster 2a, D-5000 Köln 1. Tel: 20-24-0; Telex: 8882919; Fax: 2024260.

The Dom-Hotel's major rival is the **Excelsior Hotel Ernst**. Some say it has the better restaurant; certainly it has Cologne's most elegant piano bar. And it is also near the cathedral.

Domplatz/Trankgasse 1, D-5000 Köln 1. Tel: 27-01; Telex: 8882645; Fax: 135150.

Somewhat out of the way, in the suburb of Köln-Sürth, the **Falderhof**, with its 19 rooms (all with shower/bath and toilet), is one of those places to get away from it all. Sculptor Rudolf Peer and ex-concert singer Gertrud Peer converted the stalls and dairy of a 16th-century farm into a tasteful hotel.

Falderstrasse 29, D-5000 Köln-Sürth 50. Tel: (2236) 642-44 or 655-32.

**Haus Marienburg** is another suburban establishment, in Köln-Marienburg. It occupies a former *Jugendstil* (Art Nouveau) villa surrounded by beautiful gardens. It has ten fully equipped rooms.

Robert-Heuser-Strasse 3, D-5000 Köln-Marienburg 51. Tel: 38-84-97.

Most of the major chains are represented in and around Cologne, including Ramada, Maritim, Inter-Continental, and Hyatt Regency. But the city's most unusual, and possibly most luxurious, hotel is the **Hotel im Wasserturm**. Of its 90 rooms, 42 are maisonettes. It is situated in what was once Europe's largest water tower. The facility underwent an extremely expensive conversion and the hotel was opened in mid-1989. There is a glassed-in roof restaurant, and the rooms are decorated with original (and very valuable) works of art.

Kaygasse 2, D-5000 Köln 1. Tel: 130-20-10.

# DINING

Sadly, despite its long history as an international trading hub, Cologne has an indigenous cuisine that has remained simple in the extreme. There is only one food specialty unique to Cologne, and that is *Kölsch Kaviar*. This is smoked blood sausage with "Musik" (raw onion rings) and a rye bread roll. All the other items on the menu are

Rhineland adaptations of dishes that can be found all over Germany. These include steak tartar, pickled white herring served with green beans and potatoes, Bratwurst and Bockwurst, and the *Schlachtplatte* (virtually untranslatable, but "slaughter platter" would be close), a dish comprising cured pork, bacon, blood sausage, and boiled pork piled on sauerkraut and mashed potatoes.

On the other hand, Cologne can claim to be the only city in the world with its very own type of beer. This is the famous *Kölsch,* always served in slim, cylindrical glasses with a substantial head. By law, it may not be brewed anywhere but in the Cologne area.

During the past 10 or 15 years the Cologne culinary scene has brightened considerably, with an influx of restaurants presenting food from all over the world. The best are probably French and Italian, but there are other possibilities. Here is a sampling:

**Bieresel,** at Breite Strasse 114, is the city's oldest restaurant serving mussels. The atmosphere is strictly pub, but the feeling is comfortable (Tel: 24-85-59). Cologne is full of Turkish restaurants and snack bars because of the many Turkish "guest workers" who came to Germany during the boom years. **Bizim,** at Weidengasse 47 (Tel: 13-15-81, closed Sunday and Monday), offers a sumptuous selection of Turkish appetizers and specialties. **Chez Alex** presents the atmosphere of a Parisian salon at Mühlengasse 1 (Tel: 23-05-60, closed on holidays and during carnival). Its classical French cuisine won it a Michelin star.

Chef Herbert Schönberner of the **Goldener Pflug** did even better than that, becoming the first German cook to be awarded three Michelin stars (Olpener Strasse 121; Tel: 89-55-09 or 89-61-24; closed Sunday). On busy Ebertplatz (number 3) there is a first-class gourmet Italian restaurant, **Ristorante Rino Casati** (Tel: 72-11-08 or 72-74-98, closed Sunday and holidays). Another popular Italian restaurant, whose decor is anything but Italian, is **Luciano,** at Marzellanstrasse 68-70 (Tel: 13-54-53). One of the specialties is a simple but very effective saddle of lamb.

To sample a classic Cologne pub, the only choice, really, is **Päffgen,** in Friesenstrasse 64-66 (Tel: 13-54-61; reservations are advisable). It is located in a somewhat sleazy area, but this does not deter the initiated. The pub has been in this same spot for more than 100 years, but what makes it unique is that it is the last pub in Cologne where the beer is both brewed and drunk under the same roof. People go there for that reason, and for the atmosphere—the food is only so-so.

## SHOPS AND SHOPPING

As far as anybody knows, there is only one consumer product (besides *Kölsch*) that is unique to Cologne: 4711 eau de cologne. But 4711 is to be found all over the world, so the serious shopper must seek satisfaction with other commodities.

On the whole, prices are expectedly high—although bargains, of a sort, are to be found. Clothing, for example, is an excellent buy. It may seem pricey, but take another look. The Germans generally are fastidious, fussy dressers (even the ripped-jeans, frizzly-hair look is usually carefully contrived). They insist on a very high degree of finishing and all sorts of detailing. The result is that off-the-rack clothes here are often of superior quality to tailor-made items elsewhere.

Interesting finds are to be made in the many antiques shops: The selection of English furniture just may be better here than in Britain. And, of course, there are the dozens of private galleries offering every sort of art imaginable—and some examples that are not quite so imaginable. Particularly worth a visit is Germany's oldest art auction house, **Kunsthaus Lempertz**, at Neumarkt 3. Founded in 1802, it features the modern masters as well as older works by both Europeans and non-Europeans. In addition, it deals in fine porcelain and silver. Germany's first female art auctioneer, Carola van Ham, operates the **Kunsthaus am Museum**, at Drususgasse 1–5. The emphasis here is on classic and modern art, and non-European art.

Almost any street in the central area of the city will have an interesting shop, but the best hunting is in the Hohe Strasse/Schildergasse pedestrian precinct and in the vicinity of Ehrenstrasse/Breitestrasse. There are exceptions, one being **Saturn**, at Hansaring 75, a bit farther east of the center. This is possibly Germany's biggest hi-fi and music store. The selection of LPs, CDs, and tapes is almost incredible.

The **Bazaar de Cologne**, on the Mittelstrasse, has mainly high fashion, shoes, accessories, and interior decorators' shops and restaurants; the overall atmosphere is out of the Mediterranean.

Among the central city's specialty shops are **Josef Feinhals Zigarren** (Hohe Strasse 116), the country's oldest cigar shop with more than a thousand sorts. **Tonger** (Am Hof 3) has a superlative selection not only of records but also of instruments, sheet music, and antiques. Fans of joke shops will like **Zauberkönig** (Wizard King) at Grosse Budengasse 3; it also has toys.

One of Germany's best postcard shops is **Walther König**

**Postkarten**, at Breitestrasse 93, with some of the most original cards to be found anywhere. **Käsehaus Wingenfeld**, at Ehrenstrasse 90, has more than 300 different kinds of cheese to tempt the connoisseur, while **Cölner Teehaus**, Benesisstrasse 53, near Mittelstrasse, has a huge assortment of teas and wines. (The Germans drink as much tea as the English, if not more.)

# THE NORTH RHINE AREA

## DÜSSELDORF, AACHEN, BONN

*By John England*

The Rhinelanders have a reputation for being friendly and jovial, with a lust for life that finds expression in their annual Carnival frolics, which brighten up the back end of winter for six boozy days until the arrival of Ash Wednesday. The North Rhine area cities around Cologne—Aachen, Bonn, and especially Düsseldorf—celebrate Carnival with big street parades that are worth seeing at least once.

For travellers who can visit only in the summer, these cities offer many other attractions. Ancient Aachen, Germany's westernmost city—situated not on the Rhine but west of Cologne near the Belgian and Dutch borders—is the town of Charlemagne and his great cathedral, bursting with history but sporting a modern international flair. Düsseldorf, the Rhineside big-business city north of Cologne with more than a touch of flashy materialism, is also a great art center with corners in its Altstadt (Old Town) that tell of its pre-industrial past. Bonn, the small, pleasant university and market town on the Rhine south of Cologne that was turned into the federal capital in 1949, has its own charming character that owes nothing to the *Politiker* (politicians).

**MAJOR INTEREST**

**Düsseldorf**
Altstadt architecture and the Heine Institut

Home-brewed *Altbier*
Art collections and museums
Music and theater
Königsallee shopping, gourmet eating, and stylish
    nightlife
Day trips to nearby *Schlösser* (castles)

**Aachen**
Charlemagne's chapel/cathedral
Rathaus and Markt
Music and art museums
Thermal springs
Casino and spas
Day trips to Holland and Belgium

**Bonn**
Altes Rathaus and Markt
Münster (collegiate church)
Music (Beethoven festival), opera, theater
Museums and Beethovenhaus
Old town houses, student quarter
Government quarter
Suburb of Bad Godesberg
Excursions on the Rhine
Day trips to Siebengebirge mountains and Eifel
    Massif

# *DÜSSELDORF*

Düsseldorf, located on the east bank of the Rhine, the state
capital of North Rhine–Westphalia and the location of a
major international airport, is first and foremost a business
and banking city. It is sometimes called the front office of the
industrial Ruhr river area to the near north (Essen, Dort-
mund, and other cities of little interest to the traveller).
About a dozen of Germany's leading industrial corporations
have their headquarters in Düsseldorf, and many multina-
tionals have chosen it as their German and European base.
The city has 170 banking firms, including 60 foreign houses,
and 200 advertising agencies. No fewer than 3,000 foreign
companies from 50 countries operate out of Düsseldorf.

Düsseldorf handles 15 percent of Germany's foreign
trade, and its stock exchange sees the country's greatest
share volume, more than even Frankfurt, the nation's financial capital. It is also a major center for industrial and
consumer-goods fairs. The city is therefore very much con-

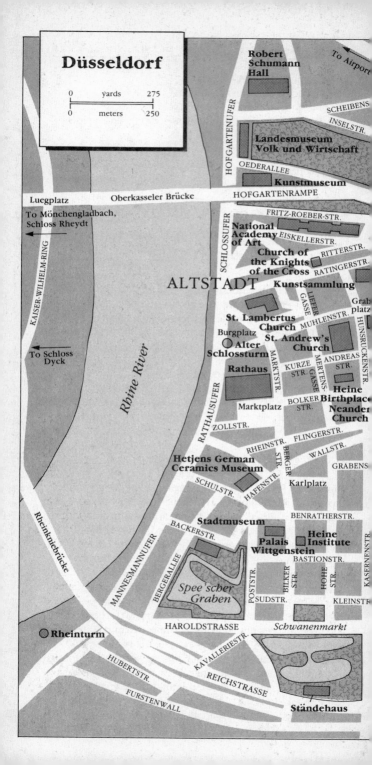

# Düsseldorf

0 yards 275
0 meters 250

Robert Schumann Hall

To Airport

SCHEIBENS

INSELSTR.

HOFGARTENUFER

Landesmuseum Volk und Wirtschaft

OEDERALLEE

Kunstmuseum

Luegplatz

Oberkasseler Brücke

HOFGARTENRAMPE

To Mönchengladbach, Schloss Rheydt

SCHLOSSUFER

FRITZ-ROEBER-STR.

National Academy of Art

EISKELLERSTR.

Church of the Knights of the Cross

RITTERSTR.

RATINGERSTR.

ALTSTADT

Kunstsammlung

KAISER-WILHELM-RING

Grab
platz

LIEFER GASSE

St. Lambertus Church

MÜHLENSTR.

HUNSRÜCKENSTR.

To Schloss Dyck

Burgplatz
Alter Schlossturm

St. Andrew's Church

Rhine River

MARKTSTR.

Rathaus

KURZE STR.

MERTENS-GASSE

ANDREAS STR.

RATHAUSUFER

Marktplatz

BOLKER STR.

Heine Birthplace

Neander Church

ZOLLSTR.

RHEINSTR.

FLINGERSTR.

BERGER STR.

WALLSTR.

GRABENS

Hetjens German Ceramics Museum

SCHULSTR.

HAFENSTR.

Karlplatz

Rheinkniebrücke

BENRATHERSTR.

Stadtmuseum

BACKERSTR.

Heine Institute

Palais Wittgenstein

BASTIONSTR.

KASERNENSTR.

MANNESMANNUFER

BERGERALLEE

Spee'scher Graben

POSTSTR.

BILKER STR.

HOHE STR.

SUDSTR.

KLEINSTR

Rheinturm

HAROLDSTRASSE

Schwanenmarkt

HUBERTSTR.

KAVALLERIESTR.

REICHSTRASSE

FURSTENWALL

Ständehaus

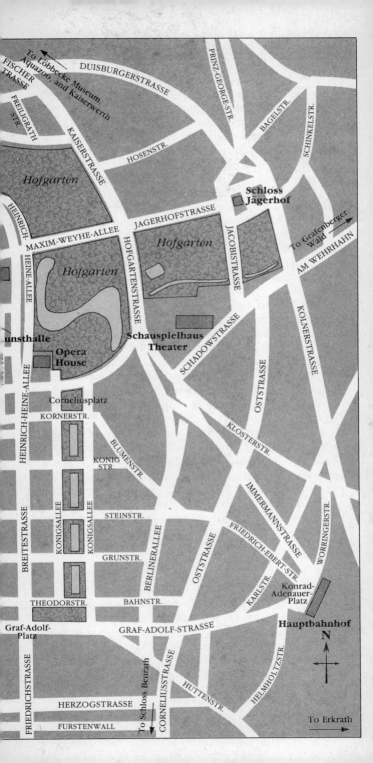

cerned with the making of money. Those who have it flaunt it, spending conspicuously in the elegant and expensive stores on Königsallee and driving the Porsches, Mercedes, and BMWs seen parked outside fashionable cafés.

So what's in Düsseldorf for nonbusiness visitors? If you like shopping you'll love the Königsallee—known as the Kö. But the city has more to offer than that. Its Altstadt down by the river, although now highly commercialized (more than 200 restaurants, bars, and discos are crammed into an area about only a half mile square), still has some interesting and unspoiled historic corners. Düsseldorf is also a leading art center, with great collections to be enjoyed, and is rich in music and theater. Top wining and dining, many good hotels, a stylish nightlife, nearby castles, Rhine boat trips, and horse racing are among the entertainment opportunities the city offers.

Granted town rights in 1288, Düsseldorf (named after the small Düssel river, which runs into the Rhine) is only 700 years old, relatively young compared to Aachen or Bonn. The city blossomed around the year 1400 and became the capital of local principalities in the early 16th century. French revolutionary troops occupied the city for more than a decade; Napoleon even christened it "Little Paris" and for a while considered moving his court there from the French capital.

Düsseldorf expanded again with the coming of industrialization in the 19th century, when it was part of Prussia. The city suffered heavily in World War II; more than 30 percent of it was destroyed. In 1946 it became the capital of North Rhine–Westphalia, a British occupying-power creation constructed of two formerly independent provinces, and went on to take a leading part in Germany's postwar "economic miracle."

## The Altstadt

Visitors to Düsseldorf usually make a beeline for the Altstadt, the old town quarter bounded by the Rhine to the west, the Hofgarten to the north and northeast, and the Königsallee to the east. Most of it is a pedestrian zone, permitting undisturbed strolling along its narrow cobbled streets. Its center is the **Marktplatz** (Market Place), site of the **Rathaus** (Town Hall), the oldest part of which dates from 1573. The daily market these days is on the nearby Karlsplatz, two blocks south along the Marktstrasse and the Bergerstrasse.

The equestrian statue in the Marktplatz is Elector Johann

Wilhelm—commonly known as Jan Wellem—who ruled the city from 1679 to 1716. The small town of Düsseldorf had become the residence of the Palatine electors in 1380, when the county of Berg was elevated to a duchy. But it boomed under the energetic Jan Wellem. A friend of the arts, he brought a shine to Düsseldorf and made ambitious plans to expand it. His residence was one of Europe's centers of culture, and his art collection now forms the core of Munich's Alte Pinakothek (see the Munich chapter). The elector also had an *Antikensaal* (hall of antiques) with a collection of Italian castings of all the best-known sculptures of antiquity, built Düsseldorf's first opera house, supported artists and musicians (and drank with them in the Altstadt), and collected works of artisans and craftsmen.

Under Wellem, many new and imposing buildings sprang up—including Düsseldorf's first Protestant houses of worship and its first synagogue—and its street lighting was made better than that of Paris. The elector also improved trade with other parts of Germany and neighboring European states. But his efforts to turn Düsseldorf into an industrial town were short-lived. Sadly, too, his priceless collections were lost to the city after his death here in 1716. All that was left to Düsseldorf was his statue, completed in 1711 by the Flemish-born Gabriel de Grupello and considered one of the best Baroque sculptures north of the Alps.

The **Burgplatz**, on the Rathausufer (part of the B 1, the main north-south riverside road), a block north of the Rathaus, is an interesting square ringed by restaurants and cafés that put out tables in summer—a good place for a pleasant pause to drink in the Altstadt's relatively quiet daytime atmosphere. There are also some small, smart shops around the Burgplatz. On the west side is the **Alter Schlossturm**, the remains of the city's 13th-century castle, which burned down in 1872. The ruins contain a navigation museum that includes a splendid collection of models of Rhine river ships. At the north edge of the square stands the **church of St. Lambertus**, the oldest in the Altstadt, built in 1349 on the site of an earlier house of worship. It contains the grave of William the Rich, a local 16th-century prince, and has Italian-Flemish Renaissance decorations and a Late Gothic tabernacle.

On the **Mühlenstrasse**, off the Burgplatz to the east, are some handsome 17th- and 18th-century houses and the **church of St. Andrew**, built in 1629, a former court church with a mausoleum of the Palatine electors. The 15th-century Gothic **Kreuzherrenkirche** (church of the Knights of the

Cross), which has two naves, is one block north on the Ratinger Strasse, reached via the Liefergasse or the Neubrückstrasse. Behind the church to the north, on the Eiskellerstrasse, is the **Staatliche Kunstakademie** (National Academy of Art), which under the director Wilhelm van Schadow was the birthplace of the influential Düsseldorf school of art in the mid–19th century. Paul Klee taught there, as did the controversial Joseph Beuys, the *enfant terrible* of post–World War II German art, until he was thrown out. Beuys, known as the "Man with the Hat" because of the fedora without which he was never seen, is considered one of West Germany's greatest artists: His imaginative works in such nontraditional media as felt and lard are now sought after by museums around the world. The academy is open to the public only in February, when works by its students are exhibited.

Just east of St. Andrew's, at Grabbelplatz 5, is the **Kunstsammlung**, offering a fine display of 20th-century art—including almost 90 works by Paul Klee, as well as pieces by Picasso, Ernst, Braque, Léger, Mondrian, Kandinsky, Chagall, Beckmann, Lichtenstein, and Warhol—housed in a building of sweeping lines clad with panels of highly polished black Swedish granite. Many angry taxpayers dubbed the building a "mausoleum" when it opened in 1986.

The **Städtische Kunsthalle** (City Art Gallery), across the street at Grabbelplatz 4, hosts travelling exhibitions of modern art. It is also the home of the tradition-rich *Kunstverein* (art association) for the Rhineland and Westphalia, founded in 1829 by Wilhelm von Schadow.

The Altstadt is also the home of the **Hetjens Deutsches Keramikmuseum** (German Ceramics Museum), in the Palais Nesselrode at Schulstrasse 4, three blocks south of the Marktplatz. The museum, one of the world's greatest ceramics collections, has more than 10,000 exhibits covering 8,000 years of the potter's art from the Orient and Europe.

The **Stadtmuseum** (Municipal History Museum), located in the Palais Graf Spee at Bäckerstrasse 7–9, one block south of the ceramics museum, traces Düsseldorf's history from its beginnings to the present through exhibits of paintings, graphics, sculpture, furniture, weapons, silverware, medallions, excavation finds, and much more. Special features of the museum are local art of the 1920s and contemporary works.

The **Bilker Strasse**, an Altstadt street that runs south off the Karlsplatz, has many of Düsseldorf's other monuments to culture and education. Searchers after the spirit of the poet Heinrich Heine (1797–1856) should visit the **Heinrich Heine Institut** at Bilker Strasse 14. A highly active center of Heine research, the institute not only contains the poet's death mask, archives, library, and various personal possessions but also stages exhibitions and discussions on his life and work. An unusual monument to Heine, a six-foot-high "death mask" lying with its skull in two pieces next to it, is in a small park on the Schwanenmarkt (Swan Market), at the south end of the Bilker Strasse at its junction with the Haroldstrasse. The monument, which includes symbols representing various stages in Heine's life, was created by the Düsseldorf sculptor Bert Gerresheim in 1981 to mark the 125th anniversary of the poet's death. Heine was born in Düsseldorf at Bolkerstrasse 53, east of the Marktplatz, near the 1687 Neander church. The house was reconstructed in 1950.

The former **home of Robert Schumann,** who was the conductor of the city orchestra (now the Düsseldorf Philharmonic) from 1850 to 1854, is at Bilker Strasse 15, opposite the Heine Institut. Headquarters of the Robert Schumann Research Institute, the house is not open to the public, but the Heine Institut contains a Schumann collection, including letters, music, paintings, and opera glasses, as well as a dress worn by Clara Schumann. The Düsseldorf post was Schumann's last; he died in 1856 and is buried with his wife in Bonn's Alter Friedhof (Old Cemetery).

The Bilker Strasse also embraces the **Palais Wittgenstein,** at number 7–9, a spacious, cream-colored, former burgher's house with an inner courtyard that was turned into an entertainment complex in the early 1980s, housing a chamber concert hall and a puppet theater. There is also a small **café** set in a re-created 19th-century butcher's shop moved from another part of Düsseldorf. Old meat hooks, a wood-paneled ceiling, and colorful enameled flower decorations provide a rustic atmosphere. The café is open only during concerts and puppet shows.

Next to the Palais Wittgenstein is **Das Alte Haus** (The Old House), another former burgher's home; open to the public, it contains a private collection of paintings and engravings depicting Düsseldorf's history.

South of the Bilker Strasse and the Heine monument, the impressive colonnaded building on an ornamental lake is the **Ständehaus,** the former seat of the Prussian provincial government and the postwar state parliament. The state assembly is now housed in a new building on the Rhine.

# Eating and Drinking in the Altstadt

Düsseldorf's beer is called *Alt;* it is a pure, dark brew made with an extra dash of caramel malt and roasted malt to impart a darker hue. It contains more hops than Cologne's Kölsch, and is foamier. There is no lack of *Altbier* in the Altstadt (sometimes called "Germany's longest bar"), which has old pubs and tavern-restaurants galore. **Zum Schiffchen**, at Hafenstrasse 5, built in 1628, destroyed in 1944, and restored in 1963, offers good traditional eating and drinking. One of Düsseldorf's best-known pubs, **Zum Uerige**, at Bergerstrasse 1, brews its own Altbier, and has a real Altstadt atmosphere, but in summer you often have to stand in line to get in. Another "home-brew" pub, **Das Füchschen**, at Ratingerstrasse 28, is also worth a visit.

Most of the pubs serve hearty meals; **Zum Schlüssel**, Bolkerstrasse 45, also offers fresh herring snacks. For a classier fish meal, perhaps of oysters or lobster, try the French-style **Carl Maassen** restaurant on the Bergerstrasse, which also serves Champagne (Veuve Clicquot) by the glass. It has its own fresh-fish shop next door. If you fancy other French food—or Italian, Chinese, Thai, Japanese, Egyptian, or Viennese—the Altstadt has it.

The quarter also has some small and simple, but comfortable, hotels, such as the **Rheinblick**, on the Mühlenstrasse, and **Am Rathaus**, on the Rheinstrasse. The Am Rathaus hotel is next door to Düsseldorf's most popular—and noisiest— jazz club, at Rheinstrasse 5, which is open seven nights a week. The Rheinblick can be noisy, too, especially on Friday and Saturday nights.

A short distance south of the Altstadt, near the **Kniebrücke** (Knee Bridge), which is named for a bend in the river at that point, is the **Rheinturm**, a telecommunications tower. At a height of 761 feet, it is Düsseldorf's tallest structure. It has a self-service restaurant, **Panorama**, at 546 feet, and a formal restaurant, **Top 180**, at 560 feet. The latter is named for its 180 window seats, which give all diners a chance to enjoy a magnificent view of the city and river as the restaurant makes one rotation an hour around the tower's axis. Bus route 834 stops at the Rheinturm, and there is plenty of parking space for cars.

# The Hofgarten Area

Düsseldorf has played a leading role in art and music not only within Germany but also elsewhere in Europe. The influence of the Düsseldorf school of art reached out far beyond the city. Robert Schumann, who spent only four years in Düsseldorf, left an indelible mark on its music scene. The city today is more than ever a great center of art, music, theater, and opera. And many of Düsseldorf's cultural venues are located in the **Hofgarten**, the big, elegant swath of greenery that curves around the northern and northeastern borders of the Altstadt.

The **Ehrenhof**, Düsseldorf's riverside museum and music center, sits at the Rhine end of the Hofgarten, immediately north of the Oberkasseler Brücke. The **Kunstmuseum**, located at the north end of the Ehrenhof, houses magnificent collections of paintings, sculptures, and arts and crafts from Medieval days to the present, devoting much of its space to 19th-century art, especially works of the Düsseldorf school. The museum's comprehensive glass collection spans more than 2,000 years from the development of luxury glass in pre-Roman days to the products of our times. An especially attractive feature of the collection is the exhibit of *Jugendstil* (Art Nouveau) pieces by Gallé, Tiffany, Köpping, and Lötz. The graphics collection consists of about 80,000 drawings, watercolors, and lithographs, including 14,000 Baroque sketches.

The east wing of the Kunstmuseum contains the **Kunstpalast** (Art Palace), which stages private travelling exhibitions, as well as the **Robert Schumann Saal**, a 500-seat hall where various concerts, ranging from chamber music to jazz, are given. The **Tonhalle**, at the south end of the Ehrenhof, was built in 1926 to accommodate a health and sports exhibition. Later, it was a planetarium. Rebuilt and reopened in 1978, it is now what Düsseldorf proudly claims is Germany's most beautiful concert hall after the Berlin Philharmonic. Its auditorium seats about 2,000 people, but is steep enough for all to feel close to the stage. The Tonhalle has been host to the world's leading orchestras and conductors, and presents as many as 20 concerts a month between September and June. Old and new works of art are displayed in the foyer and concert hall, and the Tonhalle also houses part of the Kunstmuseum's glass collection.

The Ehrenhof is also the home of the **Landesmuseum Volk und Wirtschaft**, on the west side of the complex, with continually updated working models, dioramas, photographs, videos, lectures, and special exhibitions on German agriculture, industry, and commerce.

If you feel like some refreshment, take a short walk north to the big riverside **Rheinterrasse Restaurant**, to the west of the Kunstmuseum, and watch the busy river traffic go by. The restaurant also operates a *Biergarten* in good summer weather. The **Hotel Germania**, on the Freiligrathstrasse, a quiet side street only two blocks east of the Ehrenhof, across the north end of the Hofgarten, is pleasant and friendly, and conveniently located for exploring the museum quarter.

The city's other musical flagship, the **Deutsche Oper am Rhein**, run jointly since 1986 by Düsseldorf and nearby Duisburg, is at the south end of the Hofgarten at Heinrich-Heine-Allee 16A. Its repertory includes many works by Mozart, but it is also known for its modern musical productions and has a good ballet company as well. The **Schauspielhaus** theater stands across from the opera house at the Gustaf-Gründgens-Platz.

The **Goethe Museum**, in the Schloss Jägerhof (Jacobistrasse 2, at the northeast corner of the Hofgarten's eastern arm), pays homage to the great man of letters, who often visited Düsseldorf. Completed in 1772, the **Schloss Jägerhof** was the residence of the electors' huntmaster and parks superintendent. Since 1987 it has been the repository of the Anton and Katharina Kippenberg Foundation's superb collection of memorabilia from Goethe's time. Anton Kippenberg, who owned the Insel publishing house in Leipzig, spent 50 years putting the collection together. It includes 17,000 books, 3,000 pieces of music, and more than 35,000 writings, paintings, graphics, busts, medallions, and coins. About 1,000 exhibits, displayed in chronological order in 11 rooms, trace Goethe's work and life. They include vitrines containing first editions of his writings, drafts and letters, and likenesses of the poet and his friends. The museum also owns a collection of precious Meissen porcelain and 18th-century silverware.

## Königsallee

Königsallee runs south of the Corneliusplatz at the south end of the Hofgarten, more or less parallel to the Rhine. The Kö, as it is called, is one of the most stylish, and expensive, shopping boulevards in Europe. Along its half-mile length are more than 300 luxury stores. The Kö also has about three dozen fashionable cafés and restaurants, as well as Düsseldorf's grandest hotels, where the prices reflect their top quality and convenient central location.

The 135-room, neo-Baroque **Breidenbacher Hof**, on the corner of the Heinrich-Heine-Allee and the Theodor-Körner-Strasse, near the north end of the Kö, is considered by many experienced travellers the best hotel in West Germany. It has three restaurants, a beauty salon, a sauna, and a solarium. The **Steigenberger Parkhotel**, on the Corneliusplatz, another neo-Baroque building, put up in 1902, has 160 rooms. Overlooking the Hofgarten, and with the Kö at its door, it is another of the city's best addresses. Its gourmet **Rotisserie Restaurant** has summer dining on the terrace with a view of the park, and there is a bistro in the hotel lobby for quick meals. The **Etoile bar**'s piano player provides late-night entertainment.

A posh **Holiday Inn** is on the Graf-Adolf-Platz, at the south end of the Kö, with 177 luxury rooms. Its **Düsseldorfer Restaurant** offers a wide choice of German and international dishes, and its **Bistro Bar** (a nighttime *Treffpunkt*—meeting place—for the chic crowd) has draft *Altbier* as well as a wide range of "fantasy-inspired" cocktails. The hotel also has a heated indoor swimming pool, a sauna, and a solarium.

Chic cafés on the Kö include the **Nachrichtentreff** (the N. T.), a "news" meeting place with ticker machines relaying news-agency reports, at Königsallee 27, on the west (river) side at the corner of the Trinkausstrasse; and the **Café Koenig**, in the Kesting Galerie, at Königsallee 36, directly opposite the N. T., which serves excellent lunches and suppers until midnight to a mixed clientele of businessmen, show-biz people, fashion models, and artists and bohemian types.

The top restaurants include the **Victorian**, an expensive French-cuisine establishment on the first floor of Königstrasse 3A, on its corner with the Kö. Reservations are recommended; Tel: (211) 32-02-22. On the ground floor is the **Victorian Bar**, another popular *Treff* for night owls, and behind the bar the **Victorian Lounge**, a popular bistro. The **Casserole Restaurant**, Königsallee 92, at the south end near the Graf-Adolf-Platz and the Holiday Inn, offers formal dining in its rotisserie as well as snacks in its bistro.

The Kö crowd's other haunts include **Bei Tino's** piano bar, at Königsallee 21, almost next door to the N. T., where the custom is to drink Champagne while sitting around a grand piano played by visiting performers. Open until 3:00 A.M., Tino's also serves good food. **Checker's Club**, an all-night disco with food, at Königsallee 28, opposite the N. T., is not for what Germans call the *Spiesser* (bourgeois-minded). It's a high-decibel *Treff* for the far out, but in small doses it can be fun. **Sam's West**, a nightclub at Königsallee 27, where no fewer than three doormen assess your admissibility, is considered Düsseldorf's number-one night spot. Its prices match its reputation.

# The Outskirts of Düsseldorf

The **Löbbecke Museum and Aquazoo**, a scientific living nature museum, with fish, reptiles, birds, and insects, is located in the riverside **Nordpark** off the Kaiserswerther Strasse, north of the Ehrenhof. Take the U-Bahn (subway) lines U-78 or U-79 from the main railroad station or from the Heinrich-Heine-Allee U-Bahn station (at the south end of the boulevard at its intersection with the Grabenstrasse and the Königstrasse) to the Nordpark stop.

The Kaiserswerther Strasse runs on past the Nordpark exhibition grounds and the Rheinstadion, a sports complex that's home to the Federal League soccer club Fortuna Düsseldorf, and farther north to the village of **Kaiserswerth**, only a few minutes away. Kaiserswerth is a pleasant, quiet village worth a visit for its neat cafés, antiques shops, old houses, and the ruins of the **imperial palace**, enlarged in the 12th century by Emperor Barbarossa, as well as its peaceful square at the church of St. Suidbert.

The **Grafenberger Wald**, about a ten-minute drive east of the city center, has a park in which deer and wild boar roam free. A horse-racing track (*Pferderennbahn*) and the Rochus tennis club are nearby. On the Rennbahnstrasse, next to the racetrack, stands the **Rolandsburg Hotel**, a modern country house opened in 1988, with 59 luxury rooms, an excellent restaurant, and a good lounge bar. In summer the hotel opens its park terrace for drinks and meals.

Germans use the word *Schloss* (castle) somewhat loosely for what most foreigners would call a château. There are three Schlösser in the Düsseldorf area worth a day trip out of the city.

**Schloss Benrath**, on the southern outskirts of Düsseldorf, about 15 km (9 miles) from the city center, was built in 1755 by Elector Karl Theodor as a private summer residence and hunting lodge. Set in a beautiful, thickly wooded park that runs down to the Rhine, the castle is mirrored in a large *Spiegelweiher* (reflecting pool) on its south side. Its 80 rooms, open every day but Monday, are decorated in Rococo style. The S-Bahn (commuter train) line S-6 from Düsseldorf's main railroad station travels to the Benrath station in about ten minutes; from there the Schloss is only a five-minute walk.

A group of four buildings set in a historic park at Jüchen, 20 km (12 miles) southwest of Düsseldorf, **Schloss Dyck** was built in 1650 on the ruins of an 11th-century moated castle, parts of whose walls can still be seen. Long the residence of

the van Dyck family of landowners, politicians, and church-
men, the Schloss now contains an interesting weapons museum, claimed to be Europe's most comprehensive private
collection of hunting guns dating from 1520 to 1933. Its
elegant rooms are noted for their ceiling frescoes, antique
furniture, and splendid hangings of hand-painted Chinese
silk and gold-tooled leather. The main building, with an
inner courtyard, has towers at each corner topped by Baroque domes. The informal park, with a big pond reflecting
the Schloss, contains 190 different types of trees, some of
them 200 years old, as well as large flower beds filled with
narcissus, rhododendrons, and azaleas. Paths through the
park, which is open year round, offer pleasant walks. The
museum, and a cafeteria, are open daily from April through
October, except Monday. By car from Düsseldorf, take the A
46 Autobahn southwest to the Grevenbroich exit, then take
B 59 north and follow the signs.

**Schloss Rheydt**, near Möchengladbach, 24 km (15 miles)
west of Düsseldorf, is a moated Renaissance château in three
parts, consisting of an outer bailey, gatehouse, and manor
house. It was built between 1560 and 1590 under Otto von
Bylandt, a member of a noble Lower Rhine family that can be
traced back to the 13th century. Its manor house has a 13-
room museum displaying arts and crafts, mainly of the
Renaissance and Baroque periods, including Gobelin tapestries, paintings, wood carvings, Greek and Roman pottery,
furniture, glass, ceramics, handwritten books, ecclesiastical
and domestic objects, maps and globes, works of gold and
silver, coins, graphics, textiles, and old weapons. The outer
bailey houses a museum that documents the history of
Mönchengladbach from prehistoric and Roman times, and
includes a weaving section with six hand looms, in recognition of the city as an important textile-making center since
the 19th century. Schloss Rheydt is only about ten minutes'
drive northwest on the B 57 in the direction of Korschen-
broich from Schloss Dyck, so you can visit both castles in
one day.

The 60,000-year-old skeleton of a Neanderthal man was
found in 1856 in a cave near **Erkrath**, in the Neander river
valley, only 15 km (9 miles) southeast of Düsseldorf, and
some of his bones can be seen in the **Neandertal Museum** at
the site (his skull is in the Rheinisches Landesmuseum in
Bonn). A green *Wildgehege* (game reserve) surrounds the
museum, set in the middle of a wood. The reserve is home
to animals that roamed the area when the Neanderthal man
was alive—aurochs, tarpane, and bison.

By car from Düsseldorf, take the A 46 Autobahn in the direction of Wuppertal and get off at the Hochdahl-Haan exit. Take the Haanerstrasse through Hochdahl and follow the signs to the museum. The S-Bahn line S-8 from Düsseldorf's main railroad station takes only about ten minutes to the Millrath stop at Erkrath. From there, take the well-signposted footpath through the Wildgehege for a pleasant 15-minute walk to the museum.

# AACHEN

Germany's main western gateway, lying directly on its frontiers with Belgium and Holland about 65 km (40 miles) west of Cologne, Aachen (Aix-la-Chapelle, or Aken, as its neighbors call it), is a traditional meeting place for the people of three nations. Aacheners are a cosmopolitan, friendly lot who are used to foreign visitors, and their city enjoys a pan-European identity.

Aachen has the feel of pleasant, small-town convenience about it and at the same time offers much to visitors of widely differing interests. There is lots of history in this former imperial capital, including Charlemagne's magnificent ninth-century chapel/cathedral and a 14th-century town hall. Charlemagne's palace court here—the palace itself is no longer extant—was the wellspring of Western Europe's first great cultural renaissance at the end of the "Dark Ages." Charlemagne, himself devoted to learning and the establishment of civil order, brought the scholar Alcuin from York to Aachen in 782 to educate him and his circle in grammar and other subjects. The short-term result—chronicled in Einhard's *Life of Charlemagne*—was a dramatic increase in learning throughout northern Europe. The long-term results are incalculable; Aachen is one of the very great sites of Western civilization.

Aachen was badly damaged by air raids and ground fighting in World War II: Three-fifths of its dwellings were partially or fully destroyed. But by 1966 it had largely completed its reconstruction. Coal mining was once an important industry for the city; now textiles have taken its place and Aachen produces 20 percent of Germany's woolen products. The city is also noted for its marzipan, chocolate, and gingerbread. And for the visitor there is much more: culture, museums, fountains, international riding events, a famous spa and health resort, good hotels, dining and shopping, conventions, and a noted casino.

Aachen's Innenstadt (Inner City) is surrounded by a ring road that traces the circle of its first *Stadtmauer* (City Wall), which was built from 1171 to 1175. An outer ring road follows the course of the city's second wall, built from 1257 to 1357. Both ring roads change names in the course of their sweep around the city.

## The Innenstadt

Two-thousand-year-old Aachen was settled by the Celts and Romans. Much of the city's history took place in the Innenstadt area, and many of its historic monuments can be found there.

Charlemagne, king of the Franks, chose it as his capital in 794, six years before he was crowned Holy Roman Emperor of the West. His **cathedral**, a domed octagonal chapel or basilica modeled on churches in Rome's Eastern Empire and inaugurated in 805, was his greatest legacy to the city.

The cathedral lies near the top of a steep cobbled hill at the center of the Innenstadt, with the Münsterplatz (the cathedral square) on its south side. It was the coronation church for no fewer than 32 German kings over more than seven centuries. Its high-tiered marble throne was used until 1531; the Gothic choir hall was built between 1355 and 1414. Some of Charlemagne's bones are preserved in an exquisite golden shrine created after his canonization in 1165. The top of his skull is worked into a gold-and-silver bust-shaped reliquary held in the **Domschatzkammer** (Cathedral Treasury), one of many precious articles that make the treasury one of Germany's greatest repositories of religious relics and art. Daily tours of the cathedral start from the Domschatzkammer on the Klostergasse, on the west side of the cathedral. From March through August, organ concerts are given at various churches around the city; some of these are performed on the cathedral's 1840 Zoboli organ.

A short walk uphill (north) from the cathedral is the spacious old **Markt** (Market Square), on which sits the Gothic **Rathaus** (Town Hall), built in the early 14th century out of Charlemagne's then-dilapidated imperial palace. The **Reichssaal** (Imperial Hall) on the second floor is where newly crowned German kings held their coronation banquets. Nowadays, every May, Europe's political leaders gather there for the presentation of the prestigious Charlemagne Prize for contributions to European unity. Winston Churchill and Henry Kissinger are on the roll of honor.

The Rathaus's roofs and towers have been destroyed three

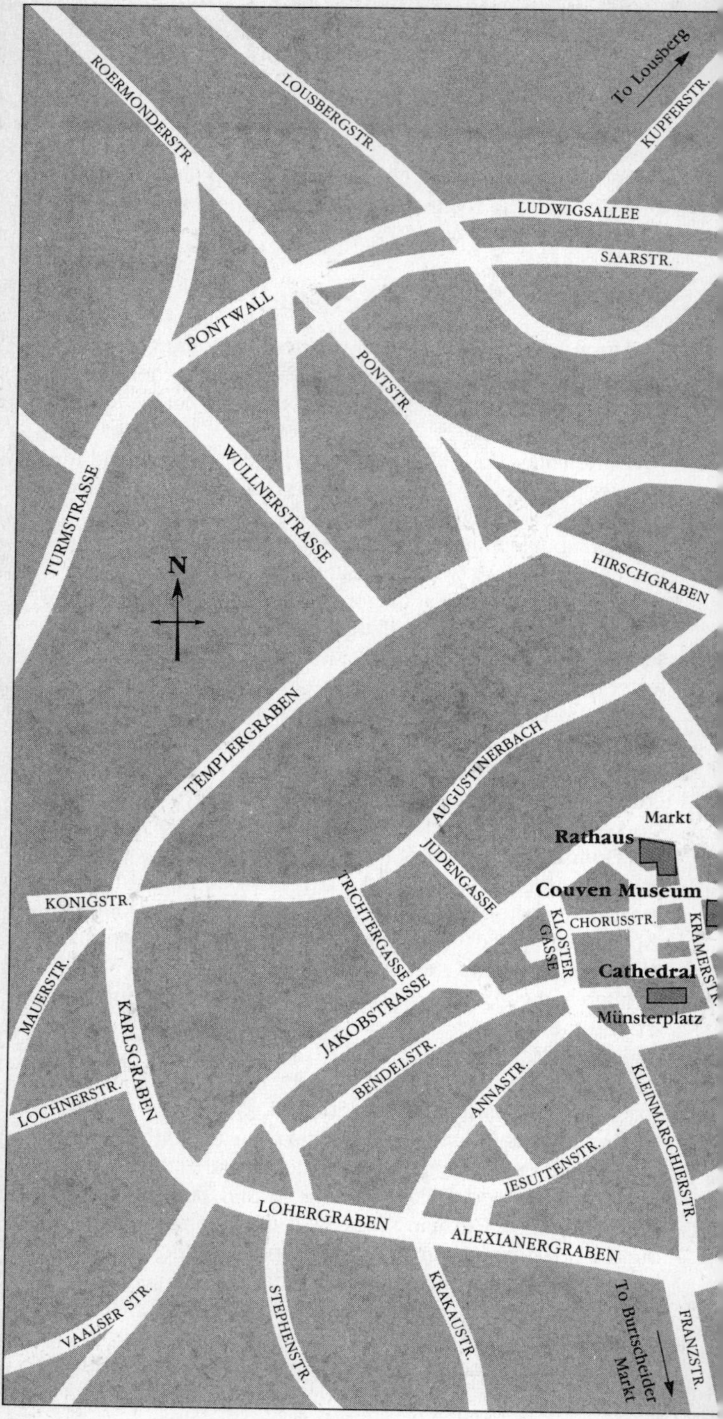
ROERMONDERSTR.
LOUSBERGSTR.
To Lousberg
KUPFERSTR.
LUDWIGSALLEE
SAARSTR.
PONTWALL
PONTSTR.
TURMSTRASSE
WULLNERSTRASSE
N
HIRSCHGRABEN
TEMPLERGRABEN
AUGUSTINERBACH
Markt
Rathaus
JUDENGASSE
Couven Museum
KONIGSTR.
TRICHTERGASSE
KLOSTER GASSE
CHORUSSTR.
KRAMERSTR.
Cathedral
MAUERSTR.
KARLSGRABEN
JAKOBSTRASSE
Münsterplatz
BENDELSTR.
LOCHNERSTR.
ANNASTR.
KLEINMARSCHIERSTR.
JESUITENSTR.
LOHERGRABEN
ALEXIANERGRABEN
VAALSER STR.
STEPHENSTR.
KRAKAUSTR.
To Burtscheider Markt
FRANZSTR.

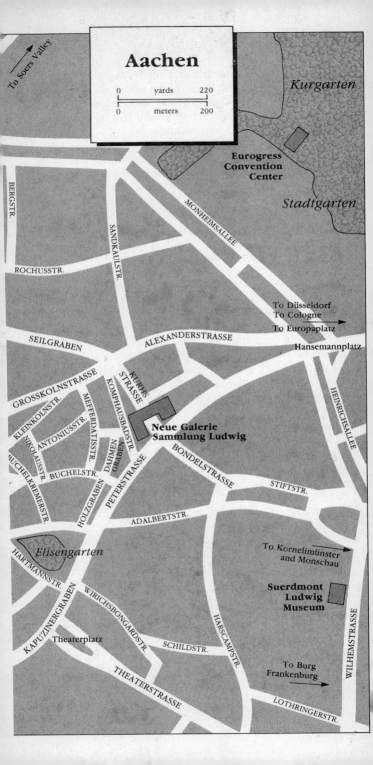

times: in Aachen's great fire of 1656; in another blaze in 1883; and by bombs and shells during World War II. But the Rathaus was patiently restored after each disaster, with a Baroque character added in the 17th and 18th centuries that was, in turn, re-created faithfully thereafter.

There are no regular daily tours of the Rathaus; sightseeing must be arranged with the tourist information office at the restored Gothic Haus Löwenstein opposite the Rathaus at Markt 39; Tel: (0241) 180-29-60. (The office also has a bureau at Bahnhofplatz 4, in the railroad station.)

The tourist office offers a one-hour *Stadtbummel,* a guided walking tour of the inner city that gives a quick general overview of the area. It covers the Markt, the Rathaus, the cathedral, and the Münsterplatz, then drops south downhill along the Hartmannstrasse to the **Elisengarten**, a park with a rotunda sheltering a public drinking fountain that splashes forth Aachen's healthy thermal spring water. From the Elisengarten the tour turns north and goes window-shopping along the pedestrian Holzgraben, the Dahmengraben, and the Grosskölnstrasse, en route back to the Markt. The three streets have some of the chic boutiques for which Aachen is noted. Take a look, and a pleasing sniff, at **Pfeifen-Schneiderwind**, an old-style pipe and tobacco shop at Krämerstrasse 13–15 dating from 1846; it stocks up to 15,000 pipes.

After the tour, for a cup of real coffee and a taste of Aachen's famous Printen gingerbread cookies or rice cakes in a charming "Granny's parlor" atmosphere, go southeast from the Markt down the Büchelstrasse to the corner of the narrow Körbergasse and pop into the **Altes Aachener Kaffeehaus van den Daele**, founded by a Belgian 160 years ago in a house built in 1655. The house has its own bakery. The modernistic, brick-fronted **Aquis Grana Cityhotel** is nearby at the Buchkremerstrasse. The hotel has spa facilities and is conveniently located near the cathedral and the Rathaus.

Aachen has a variety of interesting museums; several of note are in the Innenstadt. The **Couven Museum**, on the Hühnermarkt, southeast of the Rathaus, has a fine collection of furniture and furnishings from the Regency to Biedermeier periods (1740–1840). The **Internationales Zeitungs** (newspaper) **Museum**, Pontstrasse 13 (the street runs out of the northwest corner of the Innenstadt), has more than 120,000 newspapers in 30-some languages.

The **Neue Galerie Sammlung Ludwig**, at the old Kurhaus on the Komphausbadstrasse, on the northeast edge of the Innenstadt, houses a modern-art collection of Peter Ludwig,

Aachen's leading chocolate manufacturer, who holds a doctor-ate in art history and is Germany's biggest art collector.

On fine summer evenings the **Markt** is crowded with hundreds of locals and visitors enjoying a glass of beer or wine and a meal at tables that the old tavern-restaurants set up outside at the first ray of sunshine. All offer good, basic German pub food, including seasonal specialties such as *Matjes* (young Dutch herring) and white asparagus begin-ning in June.

Underneath the Rathaus at its southeastern corner are the old **Ratskeller** restaurant and **Postwagen Inn** (1657), with low, vaulted ceilings and rustic wooden tables and benches. On the other side of the square is the "Gold Strip," a row of old, dark-wood bars and restaurants with such names as Golden Swan, Golden Unicorn, and Golden Chain. A better culinary nugget is the **Goldener Apfelbaum** (Golden Apple Tree), to the south of the Markt, just a short way downhill from the town hall on the Krämerstrasse. It offers a large number of traditional dishes from *Oma's Küche* (Granny's kitchen).

An informal evening's fun can be had touring the many *Studentenkneipen* (Students' Pubs) on and around the **Pont-strasse**, northwest of the Markt. Aachen has more than 45,000 students at its technical university and technical col-lege, and so the pubs are a lively scene.

# Aachen Outside the Innenstadt

To start off your exploration of Aachen outside the Innenstadt, head for the 660-foot-high **Lousberg** mini-mountain for a bird's-eye view of the entire city. Located northeast of the Innenstadt, outside the outer ring road, the Lousberg is a quick cab ride or about a 20-minute walk from the Markt. From the Ludwigsallee stretch of the outer ring, turn up the Kupferstrasse and then follow the winding road to the top. Even if you go on foot, it's worth the effort, and from the **Belvedere** revolving tower restaurant on the peak you can see for miles. (The restaurant is better for *Kaffee und Kuchen*—a coffee break—than for meals.)

We'll continue clockwise around Aachen, using the inner and outer ring roads as reference points.

Just off the Monheimsallee, the northeast stretch of the outer ring road, in the green **Kurgarten**, is the **Eurogress convention center**. The center has two halls for concerts and plays, and is directly connected to the elegant **Steigen-berger Parkhotel Quellenhof**, which has its own spa facilities and an indoor swimming pool.

For many, a visit to Aachen would not be complete without a trip to the neo-Classical **Internationales Spielcasino**, in the former Kurhaus (spa house), next to the Eurogress. Take a turn at roulette, blackjack, or baccarat, or simply enjoy the atmosphere over a glass of *Sekt* (German sparkling wine). The **Gala**, the casino's award-winning restaurant, specializing in German cuisine, is the city's finest, and one of the top culinary establishments in Germany.

Aachen is a convention and tourist town and has many good hotels with and without thermal waters, in all categories, several convenient to the Eurogress and casino. They include the middle-range and functional **Novotel Aachen**, due east of the Kurgarten on the Europaplatz, the terminus of the A 4/A 544 Aachen–Cologne Autobahn at Aachen's eastern city limit; and the pricier **Best Western Hotel Regence**, southwest of the Kurgarten, which has a good Japanese restaurant and a bar called the Hippo Pub. The Best Western is close to Aachen's main shopping area, centered on the **Adalbertstrasse**, a pedestrian zone that runs east of the Innenstadt, off the Peterstrasse stretch of the inner ring.

Aachen's symphony orchestra, founded in 1852, enjoys an international standing and has been led by many famous conductors. Renowned artists and leading orchestras visit the city often, giving concerts at the **Stadttheater**, on the Theaterplatz (just outside the southeastern corner of the inner ring), where plays, operetta, and opera are also performed.

Just south of the theater is a small, friendly, family-run hotel, the 33-room **Benelux** on the Franzstrasse, which runs south from the inner ring road. A short walk south of the cathedral, the Benelux is also convenient to the Innenstadt. The hotel's plain, compact bar-restaurant serves supper until midnight. Another small, but chic, accommodation handy for walking the Innenstadt, and just north of the theater, is the 20-room **Hotel Krott**, on the Wirichsbongardstrasse, a narrow street that runs east off the inner ring. The hotel has a cozy, inviting restaurant.

Following the Theaterstrasse southeast out of the Theaterplatz will take you to Wilhelmstrasse, where at number 18, art collectors Peter and Irene Ludwig sponsor the **Suermondt Ludwig Museum**. The museum exhibits 13th- to 18th-century sculptures and German and Dutch masters of the 15th to 17th centuries, as well as some modern art.

Southeast of the Ludwig, beyond the outer ring road, is Aachen's own "hometown" museum, the **Burg Frankenburg** (Bismarckstrasse 68), which traces the city's history from the Romans through the Middle Ages.

Aachen's more than 30 curative springs, containing 19 minerals, bring many people to the city. The municipal spa house and numerous private thermal baths and rheumatism clinics are located in and around the **Burtscheider Markt**, south of the outer ring road and the Hauptbahnhof (main railroad station). The springs here were already popular with the Romans in A.D. 100 when they built a spa for their Rhineland legions, calling it *Aquae Grani*. Napoleon renovated the baths.

## Excursions from Aachen

Thanks to Aachen's frontier location, the tourist office (across from the Rathaus) offers (by appointment) a four-hour "three countries" bus trip that takes in Valkenberg and Maastricht in Holland and Tongeren, Belgium's oldest town.

The office also runs a four-hour trip into the rolling Eifel hills to **Kornelimünster**, a picturesque Medieval village only 10 km (6 miles) south of the city on route 258, and then 35 km (21 miles) onward to **Monschau**, a pretty, 18th-century cloth- and mustard-making town of cobbled streets and gabled houses.

Aachen's excellent public transportation system—with a total of 145 bus lines running from the Bushof (depot) on the Peterstrasse—also takes in Kornelimünster and Monschau (line 35), but it's best to go by car and take your time. Try to avoid weekends, when visitors pack Monschau.

The world's best riders and horses gather in the Aachen area each June for the international equestrian tournament (CHIO) at the riding stadium in the Soers valley, about 5 km (3 miles) north of the Innenstadt.

## *BONN*

The quiet university and market town that became Europe's newest and smallest capital city in 1949 was immediately dubbed the "Bundesdorf" (Federal Village). To be sure, Bonn, situated on the left (west) bank of the Rhine 28 km (17 miles) south of Cologne, is tiny for a European capital. The city itself has a core population of only about 145,000, but Greater Bonn, embracing Bad Godesberg (also on the left bank, 5 km/3 miles south), Beuel (opposite the city on the right bank), and other formerly independent municipalities, has a total of about 296,000. But it's a nice small town and definitely worth a visit.

As the city hall puts it, *"Bonn ist mehr";* more than merely a "city of politics with those gray eminences in black limousines." And that is true, despite the fact that the 30,000 federal employees are the largest group in the 125,000-strong local work force. The federal-government quarter is located on the Rhine, but to the south and well away from the cobbled town center. Old Bonn takes pride in its long precapital history as well as in its attractions as a relaxing and rewarding town to discover.

Settlement at Bonn goes back more than 2,000 years, to the Celts. It celebrated its second millennium in 1989, based on records showing that the Romans set up a military camp here in the years 13 to 9 B.C. The town was fortified in 1244, occupied by the French in 1794, and taken over by Prussia in 1815, and its center was badly damaged in World War II. Largely reconstructed along its old lines, Bonn has retained its human-scale character and continues to charm.

As Beethoven's birthplace, Bonn offers much in the way of music, including the triennial International Beethoven Festival (the next one is in 1992) at the Beethovenhalle on the Rhine. There are also opera and theater at the riverside opera house, a lively summer program of open-air cultural events, and museums, ancient churches, elegant villas, good restaurants, old taverns, a student milieu—and the Rhine.

Bonn is a compact town, much of it a pedestrian zone, with shops everywhere. It takes no more than ten minutes to cross the inner town in any direction from the city ring (shaped more like a triangle). Like Aachen's ring roads, the Bonn city ring changes its name several times, and its southern and southeastern sections are narrow town-traffic streets.

Europe's greenest capital, with 1,200 gardens and parks, Bonn, in contrast to some other cities along the Rhine, also has 18 miles of promenades on both banks of the river along one of its most attractive stretches. Pleasure boats from Bonn cruise past castles perched on top of wooded hills that are part of huge nature reserves near the city.

## The Markt Area

Bonn's cobbled Markt, on the east (river) side of town, in the inner city, dates from the Middle Ages. The fruit-and-vegetable market, with its raucous stall holders, began in the 11th century. The foundation of the obelisk-fountain at the Markt's center was laid in 1777. In summer the Markt's cafés, restaurants, and pubs set tables outside in good weather, providing a vantage point from which to see the local action.

The pink-and-white Rococo **Altes Rathaus** (Old Town Hall) of 1738 stands on the site of a Gothic building destroyed by the French in 1689. The "new" building was badly damaged in an air raid in October 1944, but was restored.

The Altes Rathaus long ago became too small to house Bonn's administration. In 1977 the city fathers, despite protest from their burghers, built an ugly, towering, concrete new one, called the Stadthaus, on the Berlinerplatz, the northwestern section of the city ring. The building is totally out of scale with the rest of the town's mostly old and pleasing architecture and dominates its western skyline, especially when seen from the Markt.

The Altes Rathaus still has its moments of glory, however, when foreign heads of state visit Bonn. It's routine for them to sign the city's Golden Book, kept in the Altes Rathaus, and then wave to the crowds from its high, richly ornamented, double-flighted perron. General Charles de Gaulle did so in 1962, followed by John F. Kennedy a year later. Queen Elizabeth II has visited the Altes Rathaus twice, in 1965 and 1978. Among a long list of other royals and world authorities who have dropped by, one of the most recent was Soviet leader Mikhail Gorbachev, who played to a packed Markt in June 1989.

Now the Markt is also the setting for the *Bonner Sommer,* Bonn's summer entertainment event, featuring a musical program that ranges from classical through international folk to jazz. The plain, but excellently located, **Sternhotel** on the Markt overlooks it all. Near the hotel, tucked into a corner next to the Rathaus, is **Em Höttche**, a small historic tavern and restaurant serving good German pub food.

A stroll north off the Markt down the Bonngasse across the narrow Friedrichstrasse will lead you to the well-preserved **Beethovenhaus**, the birthplace of Ludwig van Beethoven. A private museum dedicated to the composer, it contains many of his possessions, among them stringed instruments and his last grand piano. **Im Stiefel**, a nearby tavern-restaurant on the Bonngasse, is another good, "scrubbed tables" type of old German pub. Back up the Bonngasse toward the Markt is the Jesuit **Namen Jesu Kirche**, dating from 1717, with a notable Baroque façade. Also just off the Markt, to the northeast, on the Brüdergasse, is the **church of St. Remigius**, a Gothic basilica consecrated in 1317. Beethoven played its 18th-century Baroque organ, which was destroyed in an air raid in 1944 (its keyboard is now on display in his house).

# Bonn

| 0 | yards | 330 |
| 0 | meters | 300 |

*Rhine River*

To Airport

Kennedybrücke

RHEINAUSTR.

**Opera House**

BRASSERTUFER

MARKT STR.

**Alter Zoll**

*Stadtgarten*

ERST FAHRGASSE

**Academic Art Museum**

HNRYSTR.

ARNDTSTR.

AN DER ELISABETHKIRCHE

KAISERSTR.

SCHEDESTR.

BUSCHSTR.

**Alexander Koenig Zoological Museum**

SIMROCKSTR.

## Bad Godesberg

| 0 | yards | 330 |
| 0 | meters | 300 |

AUGUSTA-STR.

PLITTERSDORFERSTR.

BONNERSTRASSE

To Bonn

AENNCHENSTR.

**Godesberg**

BURGERSTR.

To Königswinter

RHEINALLEE

DURENSTR.

MOLTKESTRASSE

RUNGSDORFERSTR.

KOBLENZERSTR.

VON-GROOTE-PLATZ

To Rüngsdorf

WINTER-STR.

MICHAEL PLATZ

FRONHOF

*Theaterplatz*

AM KURPARK

LOBESTR.

BURGSTR.

BRUNNENALLEE

KURFURSTENALLEE

*Stadtpark*

**Redoute**

**Stadthalle**

ELISABETHSTR.

*Redoutenpark*

FRIEDRICH-EBERT-STR.

THEODOR-HEUSS-STR.

ZANDERSTR.

*Rhine River*

KAISER-FRIEDRICH-STR.

To Freizeitpark Rheinaue

WILHELM-SPIRITUS-UFER

**Villa Hammerschmidt**

To Bad Godesberg

**Palais Schaumburg**

# The Münsterplatz Area

A short stroll southwest of the Markt along the narrow Marktbrücke into the Remigiusstrasse brings you to the Remigiusplatz, with its flower market and the traditional **Bonner Kaffeehaus**. Farther up the Remigiustrasse you enter the **Münsterplatz**, the big cobbled square dominated by Bonn's premier church, the 900-year-old **Münster** (cathedral). Built over a third- to fourth-century memorial chapel to Roman martyrs, it was expanded over the centuries and saw the coronations of two German kings, in 1314 and 1356. The church has a restored 11th-century cloister and towers. Also on the Münsterplatz is a statue of Beethoven, Bonn's favorite son, in front of the 18th-century–style Postamt (Post Office).

Bonn's tourist information office (Tel: 0228-77-34-99) is a short walk south of the Münsterplatz by way of the Poststrasse at the Cassius Bastei, Münsterstrasse 20. The office is well stocked with multilingual guides to easy strolls around the town.

Farther south on the Poststrasse, the small Kaiser-era Hauptbahnhof (railroad station) faces the newish **Continental Hotel**, which offers good, medium-priced comfort. Behind the station to the southwest, on the Colmantstrasse, lies the **Rheinisches Landesmuseum**, with exhibits on the Rhineland's history, art, and culture from prehistoric times to the present. Its prize is the skull of Neanderthal man, dating from 50,000 B.C., which was found in the Neander valley, near Düsseldorf.

# The University

Bonn's 40,000 undergraduates make up the largest student body in this part of Germany. The Rheinische Friedrich-Wilhelm-Universität—just south of the Markt with its west side, or Am Hof, making up part of the southeast section of the city ring—was founded in 1818 by the third Prussian king of that name, to replace another academy that was closed by the occupying French in 1798. Quartered mainly in the long, spacious Baroque former elector's palace, it made its name early with its excellent philosophy faculty and is now also noted for law, medicine, mathematics, physics, and chemistry. Its alumni include Heinrich Heine, Karl Marx, and Prince Albert, Queen Victoria's consort. (The couple had their first "date" in Bonn during the prince's student days.)

The university's big public park, the **Hofgarten**, embraces its academic **art museum**, which houses a fine collection of antique sculptures and Greek and Roman artifacts. East of the Hofgarten, across the Adenauerallee (part of route B 9), is the riverside **Pullman-Hotel Königshof**, an upscale tourist and business traveller's hotel whose noted **La Belle Epoque** restaurant offers international cuisine. The hotel has a terrace overlooking the Rhine, a pleasant spot for a coffee break in summer. Another hotel with a good restaurant convenient to the university area is the new, 258-bed **Residence**, on the Kaiserplatz, southeast of the Hofgarten.

## East and West of the Inner City

West of Bonn's inner city area, one block southwest of the overbearing Stadthaus, on the west side of Am Alten Friedhof, is the peaceful **Alter Friedhof** (Old Cemetery), where Robert and Clara Schumann are buried side by side in graves that are always decorated with flowers. Schumann spent the last two years of his life as a mental patient in a private sanatorium in Bonn (now the **Schumann Haus**, at Sebastianstrasse 182, in the southwestern suburb of Endenich, which is also the home of the **Bonn Music Library**). He died in 1856; his wife, Clara, lived for another 40 years and spent many of them in Bonn, composing her own works as well as playing on the world's stages.

Other important people buried in the cemetery include Maria Magdalena van Beethoven, the composer's mother; Friedrich Schiller's wife, Charlotte von Schiller; Adele Schopenhauer, sister of the philosopher; Elsa Reger, wife of the composer Max Reger; and the 19th-century writer-politician Ernst Moritz Arndt.

To the northeast of the inner city is the **Kennedybrücke**, which you can reach via the Bertha-von-Suttner-Platz and the Berliner Freiheit, which links Bonn with **Beuel** on the right (east) bank of the Rhine.

The city **opera house** stands on the Rhine three blocks east of the Markt and just south of the Kennedybrücke. Five blocks north of the bridge is the riverside **Beethovenhalle**, home of the Beethoven festival and many other events and exhibitions. It is here that the federal assembly elects the president.

A hotel convenient to the area is the 504-bed **Scandic Crown**, on the Berliner Freiheit, at the Bonn end of the Kennedybrücke. The hotel offers a five-course "Royal Swedish" smorgasbord in its restaurant and has an indoor swimming pool.

## The Südstadt

Bonn's attractive Südstadt (South Town), southwest of the Hofgarten and west of the river, is worth visiting to see the façades of the many fine old town houses built between 1860 and 1914. The tourist office has a guide to 11 of the best of them, beginning on the Poppelsdorfer Allee, a beautiful, wide avenue of chestnut trees that borders the Südstadt, and heading southwest before turning east into the Königstrasse. The route zigzags through numerous narrow streets and ends back where it began.

At the end of the Poppelsdorfer Allee, in the Südstadt's southwestern corner, is the **Poppelsdorfer Schloss**, the 18th-century former elector's palace, given to the university by the Prussian king who founded the school. The palace was begun by Elector Joseph Clemens in 1715 and completed by his successor, Clemens August, in 1753. The university has converted its park into a fine **botanical garden**, with ten greenhouses and many rare plants.

A daily two-and-a-half-hour city bus tour starting at the tourist office, escorted by an English-speaking guide, includes the Poppelsdorfer Schloss and part of the Südstadt after covering the government quarter and Bad Godesberg. It's well worth taking for an overall view.

Many houses in the Südstadt are honeycombed with student apartments, and the quarter has plenty of students' pubs. Some of these stay open later than those in the rest of the city, which usually close at 1:00 A.M.

If you wish to stay in the Südstadt area, try the **Hotel Bristol**, at the city end of the Poppelsdorfer Allee at the corner of the Prinz-Albert-Strasse. The city's finest hotel, the Bristol regularly puts up delegations of visiting VIPs.

## The Government Quarter

The federal government carries on its business in a clutch of old and new buildings on the Rhine in the government quarter, south of the city along the Adenauerallee and the river. The **Alexander Koenig zoological museum**, on the west side of the Adenauerallee, was where West Germany's founders held their first parliamentary council when they met to create a new country in 1949. They conducted their affairs of state before an audience of the museum's stuffed elephants, giraffes, and gorillas.

The quarter's old (19th-century) government buildings are the most interesting. Provincial Bonn at that time was a retirement town for the idle rich, many of whom had made their money in the industrial Ruhr, which accounts for the city's many splendid villas and town houses. The **Villa Hammerschmidt**, the federal president's office and residence, is on the west side of the Adenauerallee almost opposite the museum. The **Palais Schaumburg**, the old chancellery next door, is interesting because its earlier past was marked by scandal. In the late 19th century it was the home of Prince Adolf zu Schaumburg-Lippe and Princess Victoria of Prussia, a sister of Kaiser Wilhelm II, who lived there together in sin and debauchery, racking up debts by the millions. The **Wasserwerk**, on the Hermann-Ehlers-Strasse, at the river end of the Heussallee, a former pumphouse on the Rhine, is now being used as a temporary *Bundestag* (Parliament) chamber while the regular building, on the nearby Görresstrasse, to the north, is being remodeled.

Near the government quarter, to the south, is the **Freizeitpark Rheinaue**, a highly popular park on both sides of the Rhine created in 1979 for the federal garden show. Crossed by the Konrad-Adenauer-Brücke (also known as Südbrücke, or South Bridge), the park has a boating lake, a Japanese garden donated by the Japanese Embassy, and two restaurants serving good, basic German dishes. Pop, rock, jazz, and classical concerts are given there in the summer, and a big flea market is held there every third Saturday in summer months.

The Konrad-Adenauer-Brücke also leads to the **Schlosshotel Kommende Ramersdorf**, a turreted and towered former castle of the German Order of Knights that dates from 1220. Located in the southern Beuel suburb of **Ramersdorf**, not far from the Freizeitpark, the Kommende has 18 tastefully furnished rooms, a restaurant that serves Italian and international food, a museum with furnishings covering five centuries, and 20 showrooms filled with antique furniture and icons for sale. By car take the B 9 south along the Adenauerallee—which becomes the Friedrich-Ebert-Allee—and take a left turn at the sign for Bonn-Beuel-Süd at the traffic light opposite the Polizeipräsidium (Police Headquarters), to pick up the A 562. Across the river take the Niederholtorf exit, turn left at its end, and drive uphill to the well-marked entrance on the left on the Oberkasseler Strasse.

# Bad Godesberg

Bad Godesberg, Bonn's pleasant, leafy suburb, rates a special mention. An independent spa and retirement town until 1969, when Bonn annexed it, Bad Godesberg has retained its own character. It is the home of most of the capital's 136 foreign embassies and their 1,600 diplomats; many of the embassies are housed in graceful villas. To get to Bad Godesberg by car, drive south from Bonn on route B 9. At the intersection of the Bonner Strasse and the Moltkestrasse, bear right into the Burgstrasse and then immediately bear left into the **Koblenzer Strasse**, Bad Godesberg's narrow, shop-lined, one-way main street. Parking in town is tight; a more practical—and often quicker—route is the U-Bahn (subway) line U-16 or U-63 from Bonn's main railroad station or from the University/Markt U-Bahn station on the north side of the Hofgarten. The trains take only 15–20 minutes from the main station to the Rheinallee terminus in Bad Godesberg.

Bad Godesberg is a neat little town, with a pedestrian center (except for the Koblenzer Strasse) running four blocks north–south and four blocks east–west. The **Theaterplatz** is lined with shops selling everything from meat and groceries to electrical goods and designer clothing. It has a rotunda in the middle where pop- and folk-music concerts are given in summer. The square is named for Bad Godesberg's highly popular **Kammerspiele** theater, located on its southwest corner, which stages a wide range of classical and modern dramas and comedies.

On the east side of the theater is the medium-priced, somewhat plain but centrally situated and comfortable **Insel Hotel**, with its traditional German **Café Insel** (which serves supper, but only until 8:00 P.M.) on its ground floor. The Theaterplatz has a western arm that juts out and runs into another shopping area called **Am Fronhof**, dominated by a Hertie department store, which marks the western boundary of the inner town.

Immediately to the north of the Theaterplatz, between it and the Burgstrasse, is the so-called **Altstadt**, whose name is seen by many as a cruel joke. Bad Godesberg's real Altstadt, with its little old houses and alleys, was demolished a decade ago to make way for a two-level shopping area that does nothing for the town. A bit farther to the north, across the Burgstrasse, the town is overlooked by the 13th-century **Godesburg castle**, half destroyed by Napoleon's troops. The castle contains the comfortable, medium-priced **Godesburg**

Hotel, with 25 beds, and has panoramic views over the town and the Rhine. Its restaurant offers the same views, but the food does not match the location.

Bad Godesberg's inner town is bounded to the south by the tree-filled **Stadtpark** (Municipal Park). The **Stadthalle**, on the park, is a concert and convention hall that also has a pavilion with a spring from which you can sample the local spa water. Tucked into the middle of the park is the **Kleines Theater**, which stages productions similar to those of the Kammerspiele.

At the northwest end of the Stadtpark, across the Kurfürstenallee, is the handsome **Redoute**, a late-18th-century ballroom and gaming hall that is now used for concerts and government banquets for visiting VIPs. The Redoute also has an excellent restaurant for formal wining and dining. Next to it, to the north, the gabled **Redüttchen pub** offers a cozy old inn atmosphere with plain, but good, food. The **Redoutenpark**, running south of the building, matches the Stadtpark as one of Bad Godesberg's finest green spaces.

Opposite the Stadtpark to the north, on the Am Kurpark, is the simple, comfortable **Hotel Eden**, whose front rooms offer a relaxing view of greenery.

The "in" restaurant in Bad Godesberg—although not so much for its food as for its clientele—is the **Maternus**, Löbestrasse 3, east of the Stadtpark off the Koblenzer Strasse. It's long been a favorite haunt of politicians, and Ria Maternus, its elderly but sprightly owner, was awarded a Federal Order of Merit for her motherly services to them.

Better food in an Old World atmosphere can be found at the **Rheinhotel Dreesen**, Rheinstrasse 45–49, on the river in the suburb of Rüngsdorf, southeast of town. The hotel, built in 1893, has an elegant, formal **restaurant** with river views and holds popular, old-fashioned tea dances in the summer on its vine-shaded southern terrace.

The Dreesen was Hitler's base for his meetings with British prime minister Neville Chamberlain in 1938 to discuss the fate of the Sudetenland. U.S. presidents Hoover and Kennedy also stayed there. Public transport stops some way short of the hotel, so it's best reached by car or taxi.

A reasonably priced, romantic riverside hotel is the 18th-century, half-timbered **Schaumburger Hof Hotel**, a 62-bed establishment at the Rhine end of the Plittersdorfer Strasse, northeast of the B 9 and Bad Godesberg's inner town. Legend has it that in 1839 the young German Prince Albert von Coburg-Gotha and Queen Victoria of England held hands under the stone tables shaded by the row of linden trees that still lines the hotel's riverside terrace above the von Sandt Ufer (Rhine promenade). The couple married the following year and revisited the Schaumburger Hof in 1845.

After the founding of Bonn University in 1818, the Schaumburger Hof became a favorite stop for students and professors, such as Heinrich Heine, out for walks along the river from the city. Known then and now for its good restaurant and well-stocked wine cellar, the hotel's other prominent guests have included Kaiser Friedrich III; Theodor Heuss, West Germany's first president; and Chancellor Konrad Adenauer. The hotel is not particularly well located for exploring Bad Godesberg's center, but the walk to town up the Plittersdorfer Strasse takes only about 15 minutes. With the Rhine promenade at its doorstep, the hotel is a good base for strolls along the bustling river.

## Day Trips from Bonn

Bonn is well located for day trips up and down the Rhine and into the surrounding landscape. Koblenz is 52 km (32 miles) south, by way of the A 565 to the A 61, and Cologne is 27 km (17 miles) north, via the A 555. The Siebengebirge nature reserve, the resort town of Königswinter, and the Eifel Massif are all within easy reach.

A day cruise up the Rhine to Koblenz and back passes tidy riverside towns and tree-clad mountains and hills topped by castle ruins. The mighty, fast-flowing waterway is always busy with powerful barges and cruise boats flying different European flags, pushing upstream or sliding down on the strong current between Switzerland and Holland. The Rheinpfeil hydrofoil, for example, stops at Koblenz en route to Mainz, and you can spend a few enjoyable hours ashore exploring this old city at the confluence of the Rhine and Mosel rivers (see the Mosel valley chapter, following) before boarding another boat for the return journey. The line also runs *Mondfahrt* (moonlight) trips on the Rhine from Bonn on summer evenings, with dinner and dancing, and many other trips as well. Check the schedules at the KD kiosk on the Brassert Ufer, or at the Bonn tourist office.

The heavily forested **Siebengebirge** (Seven Mountains) rears up from the east bank of the Rhine opposite Bad Godesberg. The town of **Königswinter**, 10 km (6 miles) south of Bonn via the Konrad-Adenauer-Brücke and the A 59 Autobahn, is a handy point of entry to the mountain area. Königswinter can also be reached by car ferry from Bad

Godesberg, by U-Bahn (lines 64 and 66), and by boats that
depart frequently from Bonn.

In summer Königswinter is packed solid with German
day-trippers and young families, who go there to enjoy
convivial eating and drinking on the river against the backdrop of the Siebengebirge. The town is also especially
popular with Dutch visitors, which inspired local wits to dub
Königswinter the "Holländische Hauptstadt" (the Dutch capital). The **Rheinallee**, a riverside promenade lined with hotels and restaurants that put tables out front in summer, is a
good spot from which to watch the Rhine cruise boats come
and go.

If you'd like to get a little local history while in Königswinter, the **Siebengebirgemuseum**, with exhibits of documents,
pictures, and artifacts tracing the region's social, religious,
and municipal past, is in a fine old villa at Kellerstrasse 16, on
the north side of the Marktplatz. The tourist office is also on
the Marktplatz, at Drachenfelsstrasse 7; Tel: (2244) 88-93-25.

A pleasant excursion into the Siebengebirge is the trip to
the top of the **Drachenfels**, one of the seven mountains and
the legendary home of a dragon's cave. At its peak are a
ruined castle, a restaurant just below, and a 19th-century
castle farther down. The German mythical hero Siegfried,
immortalized by Wagner, is said to have slain the dragon that
haunted the Drachenfels, then bathed in its blood to become invincible.

The Drachenfels Zahnradbahn (rack railway) makes the
trip to the top every half hour from May to September. The
station is on the Drachenfelsstrasse, which runs east off the
Rheinallee and the south side of the Marktplatz, a short walk
from the river.

The Zahnradbahn cars stop on request halfway up (or
down) the mountain for those who want to visit **Schloss
Drachenburg**, built for the Bonn banker Baron Stephan von
Sarter between 1882 and 1884. The many-towered Gothic-
style castle, which looks like a relic from the *Nibelungen* saga,
is set in a park with exotic plants and a herd of deer. It was
bought in 1989 by a state trust that plans to turn much of it into
an active museum for nature protection. The castle's interior
features high, vaulted ceilings and grand staircases guarded
by suits of armor. Two imposing halls, the **Nibelungenhalle**
and the **Valhalla Saal**, are used for classical and jazz concerts
and travelling art exhibitions.

At the mountaintop are the ruins of the once-imposing
**Schloss Drachenfels**. Completed in 1149, the castle was
undermined and damaged by centuries of quarrying for

stone to build Cologne's cathedral. In 1836 the Prussian government bought the castle ruins, closed the quarry, and strengthened the castle structure. Further preservation work was carried out after 1970, when the ruins were buttressed with cement.

The commercially run **Burg Restaurant**, just below the castle, has a great view of the Rhine valley, the Westerwald forests, and the Eifel hills—but it's best to stick to *Kaffee und Kuchen*, and enjoy the panorama.

A short walk down a well-marked path from the Zahnradbahn stop at the top is the privately owned—and somewhat kitschy—**Nibelungenhalle**, containing pictures, sculptures, and music related to the Wagner saga, complete with a Disney-like dragon's cave, a model of the monster that Siegfried slew, and a snake and crocodile farm.

The châteaulike building perched high on a plateau of the Siebengebirge behind Königswinter, and dominating the view of the east bank from Bad Godesberg, is the **Petersberg**, a former luxury hotel that Chamberlain stayed in during his meetings with Hitler in 1938. From 1945 to 1952 the hotel was the headquarters of the Allied high commissioners who ran postwar Germany, and later a federal government guesthouse for visiting VIPs, such as Queen Elizabeth II, Charles de Gaulle, the Shah of Iran, and Emperor Hirohito. After years of neglect, the government is rebuilding the Petersberg as its guesthouse and will make rooms available to the public as well. The work is expected to continue through 1990.

The **Eifel Massif**, with its densely forested hills, volcanic crests, and peaceful pastures, lies west and south of Bonn and stretches to Belgium and Luxembourg. **Bad Münster-eifel** is a peaceful Eifel town, a one-hour drive (50 km/31 miles) southwest of Bonn, that makes an interesting day trip. Take B 56 due west from the Endenich traffic circle and, just before reaching Euskirchen, turn south on B 51 for Bad Münstereifel.

Well-preserved fortifications from the 13th century, with a *Stadtmauer* (City Wall) that boasts four gates and 18 defense towers, run for about a mile around the town. The narrow river Erft, crossed by ten small bridges, runs through it. **Das Rote Haus**, the red-painted town hall, housing the tourist office, dates from 1350. The town's ruined **Burg** (castle) dates from 1270, and the **basilica of St. Chrysanthus** has an 11th-century Romanesque façade. There are well-marked paths in the woods surrounding Bad Münstereifel and along the town wall for leisurely, scenic walks.

# GETTING AROUND

## *Düsseldorf*

Düsseldorf's international airport, only 6 km (3 miles) from the city center, is a major gateway into the North Rhine area. The S-Bahn local train service from the airport's underground station to the Hauptbahnhof (main railroad station) is the fastest and cheapest way to town. The fare is DM 2.60; a cab costs about DM 12.

The city has a good bus and U-Bahn (subway) system, and is one of the towns of the Rhine-Ruhr joint transport operation, which means you need buy only one ticket for a journey involving any combination of buses, streetcars, and trains in their area.

Düsseldorf is well served by InterCity and EuroCity express trains linking it with the rest of Germany and neighboring European countries. Its central station is linked to the Frankfurt airport station by hourly InterCity trains; the Lufthansa Airport Express train, which stops at Cologne and Bonn, also travels from the station to Frankfurt airport.

Düsseldorf is also at the center of a network of four north–south, east–west Autobahns. Cologne is only 47 km (29 miles) south, 35 minutes by train. All major international car-rental firms have offices in the city. For radio cabs, Tel: (211) 333-33.

The tourist office (Verkehrsverein) on the Konrad-Adenauer-Platz, opposite the railroad station, runs a daily two-and-a-half-hour guided bus tour of the city, departing at 2:30 P.M. from bus stop 14 on the Friedrich-Ebert-Strasse, also across from the station; Tel: (211) 35-05-05.

Düsseldorf is a main port for the KD Rhine cruises; see Around Germany in the Useful Facts section at the front of the book.

## *Aachen*

As a major European road and rail junction, Aachen is easily reached from all points of the compass. Its railroad station is served by almost 200 trains a day, including many InterCity and EuroCity expresses making direct links to other major German cities and numerous foreign capitals, from Paris to Moscow, to Copenhagen and Vienna.

Aachen has fast freeway links to Amsterdam, Brussels, and Paris. The A 4 Autobahn goes to Cologne and Bonn, and the A 44 to Düsseldorf. The city lacks an international airport, but is not far from aerial gateways at Maastricht, in Holland

(35 km/21 miles west); Cologne/Bonn (85 km/53 miles east); and Düsseldorf (90 km/56 miles northeast).

## Bonn

Cologne/Bonn International Airport is only about 20 minutes north of the city by way of the A 59 Autobahn. Shuttle buses run every 30 minutes between the airport and the central bus depot; the fare is DM 5. A cab costs DM 50 to 55. Bonn also sits on one of the busiest rail routes in Western Europe, providing frequent express links to the rest of Germany and other countries. Hourly InterCity trains and Lufthansa's Airport Express train link Bonn with the Frankfurt airport.

Bonn's public transportation system is good, and the city radio-taxi service is efficient; Tel: (0228) 55-55-55. All major international car-rental firms have offices in Bonn.

## ACCOMMODATIONS REFERENCE

► **Am Rathaus**. Rheinstrasse 3, 4000 **Düsseldorf**. Tel: (211) 32-65-56.

► **Aquis Grana Cityhotel**. Büchel 32/Buchkremerstrasse, 5100 **Aachen**. Tel: (241) 44-30.

► **Benelux Hotel**. Franzstrasse 21-23, 5100 **Aachen**. Tel: (241) 223-43.

► **Best Western Hotel Regence**. Peterskirchof/Peterstrasse, 5100 **Aachen**. Tel: (241) 390-55.

► **Breidenbacher Hof**. Heinrich-Heine-Allee 36, 4000 **Düsseldorf**. Tel: (211) 130-30; Telex: 8582630; Fax: 1303830.

► **Continental Hotel**. Am Hauptbahnhof 1, 5300 **Bonn** 1. Tel: (228) 63-53-60.

► **Godesburg Hotel**. Auf dem Godesberg 5, 5300 **Bonn** 2. Tel: (228) 31-60-71.

► **Holiday Inn**. Graf-Adolf-Platz 10, 4000 **Düsseldorf**. Tel: (211) 387-30; Telex: 8586359.

► **Hotel Bristol**. Prinz-Albert-Strasse 1, 5300 **Bonn**. Tel: (228) 269-80; Telex: 8869661; Fax: 2698222.

► **Hotel Eden**. Am Kurpark 5A, 5300 **Bonn** 2. Tel: (228) 35-60-34; Telex: 885440.

► **Hotel Germania**. Freiligrathstrasse 21, 4000 **Düsseldorf**. Tel: (211) 49-40-78.

► **Hotel Krott**. Wirichsbongardstrasse 16, 5100 **Aachen**. Tel: (241) 483-73.

► **Insel Hotel**. Theaterplatz 5-7, 5300 **Bonn** 2. Tel: (228) 36-40-82; Telex: 885592.

► **Novotel Aachen**. Europaplatz, Joseph-von-Görres-Strasse, 5100 **Aachen**. Tel: (241) 168-71.

► **Pullman-Hotel Königshof.** Adenauerallee 9, 5300 **Bonn** 1. Tel: (228) 260-10.

► **Residence Hotel.** Kaiserplatz, 5300 **Bonn** 1. Tel: (228) 269-70.

► **Rheinblick.** Mühlenstrasse 15, 4000 **Düsseldorf.** Tel: (211) 32-53-16.

► **Rheinhotel Dreesen.** Rheinstrasse 45-49, 5300 **Bonn** 2. Tel: (228) 820-20.

► **Rolandsburg Hotel.** Rennbahnstrasse 2, 4000 **Düsseldorf.** Tel: (211) 61-00-90.

► **Scandic Crown Hotel.** Berliner Freiheit, 5300 **Bonn** 1. Tel: (228) 726-90.

► **Schaumburger Hof Hotel.** Am Schaumburger Hof 10, 5300 **Bonn** 2. Tel: (228) 36-40-95.

► **Schlosshotel Kommende Ramersdorf.** Oberkasseler Strasse 10, 5300 **Bonn** 3. Tel: (228) 44-07-34.

► **Steigenberger Parkhotel.** Corneliusplatz 1, 4000 **Düsseldorf.** Tel: (211) 86-51; Telex: 8582331; Fax: 131679.

► **Steigenberger Parkhotel Quellenhof.** Mohnheimsallee 52, 5100 **Aachen.** Tel: (241) 15-20-81.

► **Sternhotel.** Markt 8, 5300 **Bonn** 1. Tel: (228) 65-44-55.

# THE MOSEL VALLEY

*By John England*

Winding and looping from the southwest to the northeast, through the steep hills of the volcanic Eifel and Hunsrück regions, the Mosel valley follows the course of the Mosel river for more than 100 miles. A journey in this region takes you from the ancient city of Trier, in the southwest near the city of Luxembourg, to Koblenz in the northeast, where the Mosel river joins the mighty Rhine. The valley encompasses thousands of acres of vineyards in the heartland of Germany—10 percent of the national total. Its beautiful scenery, fine wines, Roman ruins, Medieval castles, and riverside towns with cobbled streets and half-timbered houses merit a leisurely visit.

Thanks to its favorable climate and ideal soil, the Mosel valley is wine country, and vineyards are found practically along the entire length of the valley. The Romans began producing wine here more than 2,000 years ago when they imported vines from France. The white Mosel wines are now known around the world, but the valley also produces some fine—if lesser-known—reds. Riesling grapes once dominated, producing white wines with a piquant, fruity taste; in recent years, Riesling production has dropped as the drier Müller-Thurgau vintages have gained ascendancy. There are many fine wines in the area, but the most famous is the "Doktor" of Bernkastel-Kues, 38 miles down the river from Trier to Koblenz.

The area is also rich in history; even a cursory study of the Mosel valley's past will take you from Roman times through the Middle Ages, the Renaissance, and the rampages of Napoleon's soldiers. Castles are perched protectively on the heights above riverside towns; around the perimeters of cities and towns stand walls built by the Romans to keep out their enemies. Within those walls are the remains of Roman baths and theaters; hard by are Medieval houses on narrow streets. Everywhere, there are wine cellars and vintners, all part of the trade that has been this valley's constant through 2,000 years of turbulence.

### MAJOR INTEREST

River cruises
Vineyards and wine tasting
Roman ruins, Medieval castles, and wine villages

**Trier**
Ancient Roman gate of Porta Nigra
Early Gothic cathedral and treasury
Aula Palatina, former Roman imperial throne room
Rheinisches Landesmuseum
Kaiserthermen, fourth-century imperial palace and
    baths
Day excursions to Mosel valley wine villages

**Bernkastel-Kues**
Medieval market square surrounded by half-timbered
    houses
Ruin of Burg Landshut
Church tower of St. Michael
River cruises

**Cochem**
Altstadt's cobbled streets and half-timbered houses
Reichsburg castle
Chair lift to Pinnerkreuz peak

**Koblenz**
Deutsches Eck, confluence of Mosel and Rhine rivers
Altstadt
Florinskirche
Chair lift to Ehrenbreitstein fortress
Mosel and Rhine river boat cruises

# TRIER

The people of Trier, Germany's oldest city, say that if you dig down a few feet anywhere in their town there is a good chance you'll unearth a bit of Roman history. Certainly, the

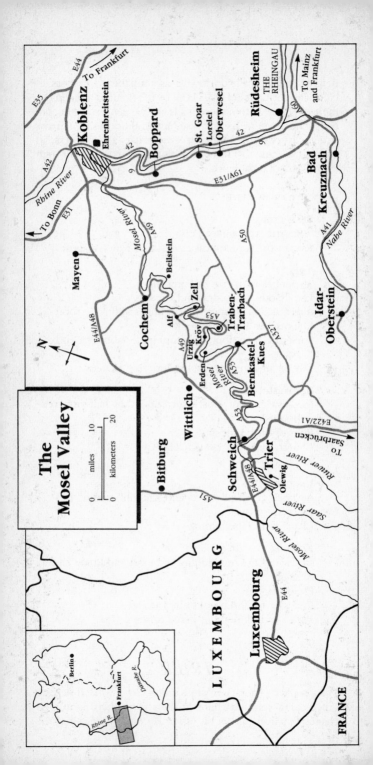

place has an ancient heritage—its bimillennial was celebrated in 1984. Trier may be even older than this: Legend
says the city was founded in 2000 B.C. by Trebeta, son-in-law
of Queen Semiramis of Assyria.

The city's history continues to reveal itself in unexpected
ways. In 1987, construction workers excavating the old
**Viehmarkt** (Cattle Market) for an underground garage un-
earthed the walls of a monastery built in 1617; beneath them
were the remains of Roman baths dating from the first to the
fourth century A.D.

The bulldozers were halted as archaeologists stepped in
to clear the rest of the site, while civic planners went back to
the drawingboard with their plans for the much-needed
garage. At last report, it was to be built underneath the
Roman ruins, which were to be encased in glass.

The **Lenz Weinstuben**, on the east side of the Viehmarkt
square and opposite the latest Roman excavations, is one of
Trier's many good wine restaurants and well worth a visit. Its
several rooms, panelled in dark wood, are frequented at
lunchtime by executives, and in the evenings by a mix of
local people and tourists. The menu is limited but good, and
you can choose from several hundred wines.

On the south side of the Viehmarkt and next to the big
Europahalle convention center is the **Europa Parkhotel**, on
the Kaiserstrasse; a modern, 162-bed hotel, it has a pleasant
breakfast room, restaurant, and a covered terrace for open-
air dining in summer.

On the west side of the Viehmarkt at Am Augustinerhof
and opposite the Rathaus is the Stadttheater, where opera,
operetta, musicals, and plays are staged from the end of
September through the beginning of July.

Although the people of Trier are proud of the Roman link
in their history, the city is not fossilized in its Roman past. It
is a lively, bustling regional capital and an important communications center of 100,000 inhabitants, with a population of
13,000 university students thrown in to keep it young. It is
located only six miles from the Luxembourg border and 30
miles from France.

But history practically oozes out of its pores, not all of it
Roman history—for Trier was not only the home of Roman
Emperor Constantine, but also of Karl Marx. Located at the
intersection of two main trade routes (north–south and
east–west), Trier has always been an important strategic
base. As a consequence, the city's history includes many
bloody episodes. Trier suffered occupation and destruction
by the Franks in the second and fifth centuries, the Nor-

mans in the ninth century, slaughter during the Thirty Years War (1618–1648), and capture by French revolutionary troops in 1794 and by Prussian forces in 1814. In this century, about 60 percent of Trier was badly damaged or destroyed in 1944–1945.

The best way to get a feel for Trier's past is to take the city tourist information office's excellent two-hour, one-mile guided walking tour ("2,000 steps through 2,000 years of history"), which is offered in German and in English. It starts at the tourist office (Tel: 651-480-71) in the same building as the Simeonstift (Municipal Museum) next to the Porta Nigra, the huge north gate built by the Romans to the once-walled city. You continue through the streets of Trier past Roman, Medieval, Baroque, and Rococo landmarks that attest to the area's rich heritage.

Whether you take the guided tour or not, a good place to start your exploration of Trier is the **Simeonstift**, housed in the monastery of Saint Simeon. The collections of art and cultural artifacts reflect Trier's later history into the 20th century. Exhibits include Gothic sculpture, paintings and graphics, furniture, handicrafts, and folklore. The monastery also houses the **Brunnenhof**, a restaurant featuring local wines. The restaurant's courtyard is the setting for the Sommertreff, an open-air program of concerts, plays, and dancing, held every weekend from June to August.

A few steps away is the **Porta Nigra**, built when Trier was known as Colonia Augusta Treverorum—named after its founder, Augustus Caesar. The city served as the supply base for Roman troops manning the Rhenish Limes, the boundary marking the limits of the empire. On the other side of the Limes were the fierce and feared Germanic tribes.

The double-gated building is an architectural masterpiece, believed to have been constructed between A.D. 175 and 200. It is built of rough-hewn sandstones laid one on top of another in a staggered pattern, totaling 52 layers. The Romans used no mortar to bind the stones, employing iron clamps instead. The building has an inner courtyard intended to lay a deadly trap for any attackers who breached the outer gate, because once they were inside the defenders could hurl missiles at them from the galleries above. But the great gate failed to save the citizens of Trier from capture by the Franks in the fifth century when Roman troops withdrew from the boundaries of their empire, and the remaining civilians could not hold the city's fortifications.

The Porta Nigra was abandoned for about 600 years until the 11th century, when it became a church, and a tower with a tall spire was added to the gate's western side. But in 1800, Napoleon, whose troops had occupied the city, ordered the church to be secularized and four years later decreed that the Porta Nigra should be preserved as a Roman monument and cleared of all its later architectural additions. Restored to its original form, the gate is now a pedestrian entrance to the city. You can go inside the building for a look at the defense galleries.

A few yards south of the Porta Nigra, at Brückenstrasse 10, is the **Karl Marx Haus**. (Marx was born in Trier in 1818.) Now a museum run by the Social Democratic Party, its exhibits document Marx's life and the development of socialism in the 19th century.

Two good hotels near the ancient gate are the 32-room B & B **Altstadt Hotel** and the 106-room, modern **Dorint Hotel Porta Nigra**, both of which are on the Porta Nigra Platz. The Altstadt, opened in 1987, is a former patrician house (and a listed historical monument), with an attractive gabled and turreted façade and a slate roof with dormer windows. All rooms are well equipped, including a mini-bar, and the hotel is handy to the inner-city pedestrian zone. The Dorint, by contrast, is built like a box. But, located opposite the Porta Nigra on its north side, it offers great views of the old gate from its front-facing rooms and from its gourmet **Restaurant Porta**, one of its four dining areas. The others are: the **Café Latinum**, serving business lunches with a hot and cold buffet; the **Atrium**, an Italian bistro; and the Espresso Romano, where you can have light snacks. If you just want a beer in cozy surroundings, you can pop into the Salong, a pub on the ground floor.

# The Hauptmarkt

From the Porta Nigra, head south along the Simeonstrasse, the old Roman main street (now a pedestrian shopping area), past the 13th-century **Drei Königenhaus** (Three Kings' House), one of Trier's oldest residences, to the Hauptmarkt (Main Market). The stone cross at the center of the large square was erected in 958 when Trier was granted the right to have a market. (On weekdays, the market still flourishes here.) The delightful old gabled and half-timbered buildings around the Hauptmarkt—many with shops or restaurants on the ground floor—are representative of the city's post-Roman history, from the Middle Ages through the Baroque and Rococo eras. They include the **Ratskeller zur Steipe**, a 15th-century municipal wine and festival house; and the Early

Baroque **Rotes Haus**, next door, which bears the inscription "Trier lived for 1,300 years before Rome." The Rotes Haus has a café on the ground floor.

At the Hauptmarkt's center is a 1595 fountain topped by a statue of Saint Peter that tests the mayor's head for heights on Saint's Day (June 29), when he is obliged to place a bunch of flowers in the saint's arms (a fire department ladder-truck now provides the necessary elevation). On the Sternstrasse—a narrow little street off the east side of the Hauptmarkt, toward the Dom—is the **Palais Walderdorff**, a Rococo palace built in 1765 by an electoral prince of that name. Now housing municipal offices, the palace occupies the site of a Medieval mint whose coins are still turning up in Trier's earth.

If you would like to buy some genuine ancient coins, drop into **Antiken Haubrich**, a small and friendly antiques store at Palaststrasse 15. (The narrow street, southeast of the Hauptmarkt, is given over to foot traffic.) Antiken Haubrich also offers a large collection of Roman pottery and earthen-ware oil lamps, as well as Victorian dolls, miniatures, and thimbles. It is one of the few really interesting stores in Trier (despite the city's pride in its merchants). There is also an abundance of shops on the many pedestrian streets in the neighborhood.

After shopping for Roman artifacts at Antiken Haubrich, you could walk back the few yards to the Hauptmarkt and dine in a cozy Roman atmosphere at the informal **Römer-keller** (Roman wine cellar), in the basement of the Zum Domstein Restaurant on the east side of the Hauptmarkt. It's not exactly the food Augustus Caesar might have enjoyed, but you'll find good, basic German food, a wide selection of wines, and an interesting array of Roman pottery in glass cases.

Two blocks south of the Hauptmarkt is the delightful **Spielzeug Museum** (Toy Museum), at Nagelstrasse 4–5, which has a collection of more than 5,000 toys—from dolls and stuffed animals to a miniature railroad and steam engines.

# The Cathedral

The huge Trier Dom, which looms a short distance from the market, is the oldest cathedral on German soil. It is an unusual conglomeration of architectural styles of different periods, from the central fourth-century Roman structure to the 1901 vestry. Trier was the residence of Constantine the Great, who in the early fourth century made Christianity the official religion of the Roman empire; he built the Dom on the site where his mother, Helena, had had her palace.

In the **Domschatzkammer** (Treasury), built about 1470, are a great many relics, a number of them attributed to Saint Helena, who made several pilgrimages to the Holy Land. (She was canonized after her death.) Among the relics and treasures are her amethyst drinking vessel; a golden case bearing the Holy Nail from the crucifix; a foot of Saint Andrew, whose portable altar is also here; and a large ivory tablet from the fifth century, depicting the transfer of a relic to Constantinople. The Dom's most important relic, which is shown to the public only once every two or three decades, is the Holy Coat, which is said to have been worn by Christ on his way to the Crucifixion. Nowadays the Dom is host to an international organ festival held on Wednesdays during May and June.

The nearby **Bischöfliches Museum**, Windstrasse 6–7, exhibits early Christian finds from excavations at the Dom and cemeteries on the edge of the city, and religious art such as ceiling paintings from the time of Constantine.

Next to the Dom, across a peaceful Gothic cloister, is the 13th-century **Liebfrauenkirche**, (Church of Our Lady) built in the form of a Greek cross. Completed in 1260, it is the second oldest early Gothic church in Germany, after St. Elisabeth's in Marburg.

If you are ready for a meal after touring the Dom and the Liebfrauenkirche, head for the most elegant restaurant in Trier, the **Palais Kesselstatt**, just a few steps from the Liebfrauenkirche at Liebfrauenstrasse 10. The Baroque (1740–45) palace has terrific atmosphere, international cuisine, and fine wines. Reservations are recommended (Tel: 651-402-04).

# Elsewhere in Trier

A short walk south along the Liebfrauenstrasse and east across to the Konstantinplatz leds to the **Aula Palatina**, the lofty and once richly decorated former Roman imperial throne room, believed to have been constructed by Constantine in about 310; now it is the simply furnished Protestant church of Our Savior. Built to awe common folk turning up with petitions to the emperor, the massive hall is more than 220 feet long, and its ceiling is about 100 feet high.

The ever-efficient Romans heated the vast space with cellar furnaces, some of which can still be seen. Today the basilica hosts a series of organ concerts on Wednesdays in July and August.

A few steps from the Aula Palatina, but a big leap forward in time, is the attractive pink-and-white **Kurfürstlicher Palais** (Elector's Palace), with its formal gardens just around the corner. The palace's east and north wings, known as the Red Tower and St. Peter's Portal, were built in Renaissance style in the 17th century, the Baroque south wing in the 18th. Today the palace is the seat of the district government. Walk southeast through the gardens and down the tree-shaded Ostallee to the city's largest museum, **Rheinisches Landesmuseum**, at number 44. Extensive collections of prehistoric, Roman, early Christian, Frankish, and Medieval art and artifacts such as burial monuments, floor mosaics, glassware, terra-cotta and bronze figurines, gold discs, metal harnesses, and about 40,000 coins minted in Trier are the high points of this museum.

Opposite the Landesmuseum, to the east across the palace gardens, is the **Schatzkammer der Stadtbibliothek** (Treasury of the City Library), at Weberbachstrasse 25. It contains manuscripts, documents, and prints from as early as 895, including a 42-line Gutenberg Bible and letters from Goethe and Karl Marx.

A short way south of the Landesmuseum are the massive **Kaiserthermen**, ruins of a fourth-century imperial palace and baths. The baths, which may be explored, are included in the tourist office's walking tour of Trier. The masonry of the hot-water baths and the extensive narrow basements are impressive to see.

A few minutes' stroll southeast along the Olewigerstrasse are the ruins of the **Roman amphitheater**, an arena built about A.D. 100, from which up to 20,000 bloodthirsty spectators could watch gladiators battling with wild animals.

If by now you have not had enough of the Roman era, return to and pass the Kaiserthermen and walk east down the Südallee toward the Mosel river to the **Barbarathermen**, Roman baths dating from the second century. Then go the short distance to the river bank, and turn north (right) on the St.-Barbara-Ufer to the **Römerbrücke** (Roman Bridge), which has pillars from the second century and arches from 1717–1718. Farther along the river, on the Johanniterufer and the Krahnenufer, are two old river-freight cranes dating from 1413 and 1774.

A short walk north from the cranes along the Kranenufer brings you to the Kaiser Wilhelm Brücke and the city harbor on the Zurlaubener Ufer—a busy scene, full of pleasure boats and tourists. The **Pfeffermühle Restaurant** here (Zurlaubener Ufer 76) comes close to the Palais Kesselstatt for elegance and fine food. Reservations are recommended (Tel: 651-261-33).

The large and rather formal **Scandic Crown Hotel**, part of a Swedish chain, is on the Zurmaienerstrasse, which heads northeast from the city end of Kaiser Wilhelm Brücke. The hotel has a pool, sauna, and solarium, as well as two restaurants—one of which, **La Brochette**, is a gourmet's dream. The Lobby Bar is a favored rendezvous at cocktail time.

# Wine Tasting and
# Side Trips from Trier

After so much history, a glass of wine would be refreshing—and there is no lack of refreshment in Trier, Germany's oldest wine-producing city, where more than 3 million vines grow. The many winery cellars near the city (open for tastings daily year round, 10:00 A.M. to 8:00 P.M., except for the Christmas holidays) are great places to relax on a hot day and sample the local vintages in a cool, subterranean atmosphere. (You can try four wines for DM 4, or eight for DM 7.) Tastings must be booked, and schedules rotate weekly, so ask at the tourist information office for the program, or do some wine tasting downtown at any of the *Weinstuben* and restaurants mentioned above. Also highly recommended are **Das Weinlädchen**, Hotel Haag, on the Stockplatz, one block northwest of the Hauptmarkt; and the **Wine Cabinet**, at Weberbach 75, a block west of the Kurfürstlicher Palais garden. You can also taste wine at the wine information center on the Konstantinplatz (six glasses for DM 6). The **Hotel Haag** is a comfortable bed-and-breakfast, and the owner also sells bottles of good local wine for as little as DM 4.20.

For really keen wine buffs, Trier also has a year-round, two-mile-long wine tour with 35 points of interest covering the cultivation and life cycle of the vine, grape varieties, and soil formations. Tours end with a visit to a winery cellar and a wine tasting. The tourist office has a brochure in English giving all the details.

Equestrians can take advantage of the indoor riding facilities at the **Trimmelter Hof**, in the Olewig wine village, a short walk east of the amphitheater on Olewigerstrasse.

The Trier tourist office provides information regarding the bus trips that run several times a week during the summer months to the city of Luxembourg, only 47 km (30 miles) to the west, as well as into the Trier countryside (one third of the area is forests and parks), and to the Eifel hills across the Mosel and the Hunsrück hills on the Trier side of the river. There are also day excursions to wine villages along the Mosel and the nearby Saar and Ruwer rivers (two other noted wine-growing areas).

The Trier area has a lot to offer visitors besides wine and history. Take the cable car from the Zurlaubener Ufer, on the north side of the Kaiser Wilhelm Brücke, up to the Weisshaus terrace for a great view of the city and easy access to the Wildfreigehege (Animal Park). There are more than 90 miles of marked hiking trails on both sides of the Mosel, and the river itself offers sailing, water skiing, boat trips from the Zurlaubener Ufer, and fishing (ask the tourist office about a license).

## ALONG THE VALLEY

To get to Bernkastel-Kues, the next major stop on the Mosel, take the A 602 expressway from Trier to the A 48 Autobahn and then head north toward Koblenz, crossing to the left bank of the Mosel, and shortly afterward taking the exit to Schweich, an old bridge town on route 53. That road, called the Römerweinstrasse (Roman Wine Road) and later the Moselweinstrasse, runs alongside the river, following and crossing and recrossing its serpentine course all the way to Koblenz. (Its number changes to route 49 at Alf, a wine village about halfway down the valley.) The road runs into Bernkastel's Gestade on the riverfront, where it is best to park before exploring the town on foot. As throughout most of the valley, charming wine villages along the 60 km (37.5-mile) stretch between Trier and Bernkastel-Kues present plenty of temptations to stop. Village cellars offer free samples of their wine and the growers sell their products at a discount.

The Mosel river is at its picture-book best as it meanders through the Rhineland-Palatinate between Trier and Koblenz before flowing into the Rhine. It is worth taking at least a couple of days to explore the valley between the two cities, making overnight stops at Bernkastel-Kues and Cochem, two of the Mosel's most delightful Medieval wine towns, before ending at Koblenz and the Rhine.

# Bernkastel-Kues

Bernkastel and Kues are 700-year-old "twin" towns lying on opposite sides of the river. Apart from its fine dry Riesling wines (more on those later), the area's main attractions are Bernkastel's intact Medieval townscape and its romantic quarters, Andel and Wehlen.

**Bernkastel**, granted municipal rights in 1291, was put on the map in 1017 with the building of a castle above the town. That castle was replaced by another in 1280, which burned down in 1693 and has been a ruin ever since. **Burg Landshut**, as it is known, dominates the town and offers a magnificent panorama of Bernkastel-Kues and the Mosel Valley, worth the steep but well signposted two-mile hike that starts on the Karlstrasse, off the Bernkastel Markt. For the less energetic, a bus (Burg Landshut Express) runs from the Bernkastel Gestade every hour on the hour from April through October.

The Romans grew wine grapes in the Bernkastel-Kues area, and viticulture has shaped and influenced the region and its people ever since. One famous wine of the area is the Bernkasteler Doktor Riesling, which is said to have been named in the late 13th century by an archbishop who, having fallen mortally ill, drank it and was cured. Other renowned vintages are the Kueser Kardinalsberg and Wehlener Sonnenuhr. With so much wine around, the twin towns naturally have plenty of taverns, cellars, and stores to choose from, and hold a lively (and crowded) wine festival with fireworks during the first weekend in September.

The small, cobbled old **Markt**, two blocks east of the Gestade in Bernkastel, seems like a holdover from the Middle Ages and the Renaissance. The square is surrounded by 400-year-old half-timbered houses and has a fountain dating from 1606 and a Rathaus built in 1608. Radiating from the market place are streets no wider than alleys. Just around the corner on the Karlstrasse, leaning almost drunkenly over the narrow street, is a quaint, slim house with a sharply peaked roof. Known as the **Spitzhäuschen**, it dates from 1583. It is a private house, but there is a public wine bar in the cellar.

Another historical landmark in Bernkastel is the huge 600-year-old tower of the parish **church of St. Michael**, which houses many art treasures. Across the river in **Kues** is the 500-year-old **hospital of St. Nikolaus**, whose vineyards still produce enough grapes to provide a healthy income. The hospice was founded for the needy by Nikolaus Cusanus, Kues' greatest citizen. Born in 1401, the son of a river boatman, Cusanus became a scholar, scientist, philosopher, and cardinal. The hospital's library contains more than 300 manuscripts dating from the ninth to the 15th centuries.

The noted **Mosel Weinmuseum** at Cusanusstrasse 2 in Kues is worth a visit. Local wine growers also welcome visitors to their vineyards at various times. Check with the tourist information office at Gestade 5, on the riverfront (Tel: 6531-40-23).

To make the most of Bernkastel's Medieval atmosphere, book a room at the **Hotel Binz** on the market place. The hotel's modern structure and restaurants are well run but lack romance; the location, however, is superb. The old **Ratskeller** and the **Cusanus Weinstuben** are right on the market for some simple, cozy wining and dining. The **Gildenhaus Weinstube** is just around the corner at Moselstrasse 6, and the **Weinstube Schmitz**, at Karlstrasse 13, and the **Zum Landsknecht** wine tavern and restaurant, at Römerstrasse 36, are also nearby. All are local favorites as well as tourist hangouts.

**The Gestade**—the river road that runs into Bernkastel past the bridge to Kues—is lined with several of Bernkastel's many family-run restaurants and hotels. Park at the north end of the Gestade and walk south a short distance to the **Altes Brauhaus**, a restaurant in a building that was once a brewery, with a terrace overlooking the busy riverboat dock. The huge lid of an old copper beer vat mounted on the main restaurant wall testifies to its past. The food is typical of Bernkastel's restaurants, which is mostly *rustikal* (rustic)—consisting of plain but tasty meat or fish dishes, served up in generous portions. Mosel eel is the specialty of the region.

The Altes Brauhaus family also owns the informal and comfortable **Hotel Behrens** on the Schanzstrasse, a terrace near the town park, a few blocks south of the Markt overlooking the Mosel. Other noteworthy restaurants and wine taverns on the Gestade include the **Alte Kanzlei** and the **Bacchuskeller**. Informal hotels on the Gestade giving good views of the river include the 30-room **Burg Landshut**, named for the castle. A family-run business for more than a century, it has a Tanzkeller (dance cellar) and a Hofgarten Terrasse for open-air dining in summer. The home-style cooking is good, and there are many wines to choose from.

The Gestade north of the bridge is also the depot for regular bus lines running up and down the Mosel and into

the surrounding countryside, as well as being the dock for
river cruise boats.

# Cochem

Cochem, probably the prettiest town on the Mosel, is dominated by the Medieval-style Reichsburg castle that overlooks it
from the top of a steep hill. It is certainly the most popular
excursion and vacation resort on the river, attracting many
German and foreign visitors. It is a good idea to visit midweek
if possible. But the compact, hilly town is well equipped to
handle mass tourism and manages to absorb even the milling
summer weekend crowds. From Bernkastel-Kues drive north
on route 53/49 through the wine villages of Ürzig, Erden, and
Kröv and the towns of Traben-Trarbach and Zell, until
Cochem's turreted and towered castle comes into sight on its
high perch. The road then runs along Cochem's **Moselpromenade**, which is faced with a long, frontline battery of
hotels and restaurants. Parking space is tight, and finding one
demands patience, but old Cochem is worth it.

The town's history in Celtic and Roman times and the
early Middle Ages is not well documented. But discoveries
of swords from the Bronze Age, Roman foundations, and
graves from the time of Charlemagne long ago confirmed
that Cochem occupies the site of one of the Mosel's earliest
settlements.

**Reichsburg,** the castle that dominates Cochem physically
and historically, has seen some turbulent times. It was seized
by the German emperor in 1151, pawned to the archbishop
of Trier by another German ruler in 1294 (it stayed in hock
for another 500 years), and totally destroyed by French
soldiers in 1689. The castle remained a ruin for 200 years,
until it was bought by a wealthy Berlin merchant and reconstructed according to old plans. The Reichsburg is therefore
not genuinely Medieval, though its lower part was built
around 1000. Its furnishings are largely those of a 19th-
century chateau with a mix of styles that can be a little
jarring.

Most first-time visitors to Cochem make a beeline for the
castle, so take the steep walk up the Schlossstrasse (southwest of the Markt, off the Herrenstrasse) to the Reichsburg
for one of the regular 40-minute tours. English-language
tours must be booked in advance at the Verkehrsamt (Tourist Office) on Endertplatz near the river (Tel: 2671-39-71).
The castle has a souvenir shop that sells replicas of Medieval

weapons, as well as a restaurant with a small terrace that has sweeping views of Cochem and the valley. The **Pinnerkreuz** peak, on the northeastern outskirts of the town, is reached by chairlift from the Endertstrasse, a continuation of the bridge road. The peak is also an excellent lookout point.

After visiting the castle, a trip to the Altstadt (Old Town)— with its cobbled streets and half-timbered and gabled houses—is called for. Start at the Markt, which has a fountain at its center, and the Rathaus, which dates from 1739. Nearby, at Brückenstrasse 3, is the picturesque **Hotel Alte Thor- schenke**. Built in 1332 into part of the old city wall at the Enderttor (one of the three still-intact gates), it was origi- nally a guardhouse and town prison. The Alte Thorschenke offers the most elegant atmosphere, and probably the best food, in town. A suit of armor stands guard in the lobby, and the restaurant of several low-ceilinged rooms is tastefully decorated with antique furniture.

Other antiquities worth seeing are a former Capuchin monastery dating from 1623 on the Klosterberg (a block north of the Markt, up the steps of an alleyway called Hinter Kempeln); the defense tower at the Balduin gate, at the end of the Obergasse, northwest of the Markt; and defense galleries or walkways at the Burgfrieden gate, on the Moselpromenade at the western, or upriver, end of town. Across the Mosel is **Cond**, Cochem's oldest district; dating from 694, it sits at the foot of lush vineyards.

Cochem has a lot to offer beyond its fascinating history— most visitors revel in its beautiful scenery and its many informal wine taverns and restaurants. Several winery cellars, such as the **Weinstube Schlossbergkeller** at Schlossstrasse 15, offer wine tasting by candlelight with hearty snacks and crusty, oven-fresh, whole-wheat bread. The Schlossberg wines, as well as the Herrenberg and Pinnerkreuzberg labels, are among the best produced by Cochem's vineyards.

Another attraction in Cochem is the busy river front; here the cruise boats of three operators (Kolb, Undine, and Köln- Düsseldorfer; all have ticket kiosks on the Moselprome- nade) come and go on the scenic Mosel. It is also pleasant on summer evenings to indulge in a popular local spectator sport—sitting on the terrace of a hotel or restaurant on the Moselpromenade, enjoying a meal and a bottle of wine, and watching other people go by.

Hotels on the Moselpromenade are informal and comfort- able, if lacking the elegant character of the Alte Thor- schenke. The **Germania**, however, has a history dating back to 1749; this 15-room family-run hostelry has a good restaurant and a dining terrace overlooking the river. The **Burg Hotel**, with about 50 rooms, has several dining rooms, some decorated with suits of armor, fine porcelain, and antique paintings; here, if you are in the mood for romantic accommodations, you may ask for a room with an old-fashioned four-poster bed. The hotel also has a pool, sauna, and solarium. The **Hotel Weinhof**, with 35 beds, offers jolly "Mosel Evenings," with dancing and dining by candlelight. On these occasions, strangers link arms and sing and sway together to the strains of local music.

## Around Cochem

The tourist bus operators Knieper (at Endertstrasse 30) and Dä Schmandelecker (Bahnhofsvorplatz 3, at the railroad station, six blocks northeast of the Markt) run half-day and full-day trips to places outside Cochem, such as **Burg Eltz** (a Medieval castle); **Idar-Oberstein** and its precious-stones museum; the **Vulkan Eifel**, hills showing traces of their volcanic origin; Koblenz and the Ehrenbreitstein fortress; and the famous Nürburgring auto-racing circuit.

A boat trip to the wine village of **Beilstein**, a few miles upriver on the opposite bank and known locally as the Sleeping Beauty, is highly recommended. Its Medieval marketplace, half-timbered houses, and dreamy, peaceful atmosphere are watched over by no fewer than four castles. The local Beilsteiner Schlossberg wine is quite good.

## *KOBLENZ*

Koblenz is an ancient but lively city of about 110,000 people; it is situated at the confluence of the Mosel and Rhine rivers. Two thousand years ago the Romans called it Confluentes. This highly popular tourist town has something for all tastes. Wine lovers can enjoy the great vintages that grow along the banks of the two rivers. History buffs can explore the Altstadt, the castles and palaces dating from the Middle Ages through the 18th century, and the Ehrenbreitstein fortress across the Rhine.

There are 20 miles of scenic paths for rambling along the banks of the Rhine, and drinking and dancing at the Weindorf, a replica of a wine village with its own vineyard that is a favorite summer evening haunt for locals and visitors alike (see below). An important hub of road, rail, and river traffic, Koblenz is also an ideal base for trips up and down the Mosel and the Rhine and into the countryside around both rivers.

The best way to explore historic Koblenz is on foot. The tourist office opposite the Hauptbahnhof (Tel: 261-331-34) and its Rhineside kiosk on the Konrad-Adenauer-Ufer (Tel: 261-12-92-07) offer multilingual guidebooks and maps of the city. Begin your tour at the **Deutsches Eck** (German Corner), at the confluence of the Mosel and the Rhine, where the Teutonic Order of Knights founded a settlement in 1216. A massive equestrian statue of Kaiser Wilhelm I was built there in 1897, but the Allies blew him out of his saddle in 1945. The monument's base remains, providing a platform for all-round views of the city, the two rivers, and Ehrenbreitstein fortress.

Close at hand is the **Deutschherrenhaus** (with its Blumen-hof, or flower garden), a former administrative building built by the Teutonic Knights. The Romanesque **church of St. Castor** was consecrated in 836 and completed in the 11th and 12th centuries; its more modern fountain is meant to symbol-ize the rise and fall of Napoleon. The garden is open to the public. Walking back up the Mosel a short distance along the Peter-Altmeier-Ufer past the dock for international river cruise boats, you come to the **Deutsche Kaiser**, an early 16th-century residential tower with battlements (and a wine tavern underneath them). A left turn on the Kornpfortstrasse brings you to the bay-windowed Dreikönigenhaus (Three Kings' House) of 1701 (now the Stadtbibliothek, or city library), then the Franconian royal palace, an early-18th-century Baroque building, with rear towers belonging to the fourth-century Roman **town wall**. The **Hotel Kornpforte** on the Kornpfort-strasse, an 18-room bed-and-breakfast, is handy to them and to the Florinsmarkt, a compact cobbled square and former market a few steps away along Auf der Danne, in the Altstadt. The hotel has a wine parlor for pleasant evening sampling; light snacks are also served.

## The Altstadt

The **Florinsmarkt** is dominated by the Romanesque **Florins-kirche** (Church of St. Florin), dating from the 11th and 12th centuries, with a 14th-century Gothic chancel. Nearby is the **Mittelrhein Museum** in the Altes Kaufhaus, Koblenz's oldest residential house, built in 1419, and next to it the Schöffen-haus (old Courthouse), dating from 1530.

Taverns on the Florinsmarkt offer good wine and simple but tasty food. Try the gabled **Weinhaus Hubertus**, built in

1695, or the **Weinhaus zur Alten Burg**, which also has a beer parlor. Then take a short walk toward the end of the Burgstrasse, off the Florinsmarkt, to its junction with the Balduinbrücke, begun in 1337, to see the **Alte Burg**, a 13th-century castle built by an elector of Trier to dissuade the people of Koblenz from thoughts of secession. The castle now houses the Stadtarchiv (City Archives); only the impressive spiral staircase, decorated with ancient coats of arms, is open to the public.

Along Gemüsegasse from the Florinsmarkt is the **Liebfrauenkirche** (Church of Our Lady), begun in the late 12th century and completed in the mid-13th. You are now in the Altstadt center, near the **Alte Münze** (Old Mint) and **Münzplatz**, a small, charming market place. The mint master's house, built in 1763, is still standing.

Also on Münzplatz is the Medieval **Haus Metternich**, birthplace of the Austrian chancellor Prince Metternich in 1773; the first and second floors are used for travelling exhibitions of modern art. The comfortable, family-run **Cityhotel Metropol**, also on the square, serves up good German food in a pub-style restaurant. A short way down the Marktstrasse (which together with its continuation, the Löhrstrasse, forms the city's main pedestrian shopping zone), is the **Plan**—a large square and popular meeting place on the edge of the Altstadt. Its **Ratskeller** and the neighboring **Ratsstuben**, wine restaurants, are worth a visit. Where the Marktstrasse becomes the Löhrstrasse are four turreted houses built in 1689–91.

There is much more of historical interest in Koblenz, especially the Neoclassical elector's palace (1777–1786), on the Rhineside Augusta Anlagen. The upmarket **Scandic Crown Hotel** is located opposite the elector's palace, on the south side of the Pfaffendorfer Brücke, the city's northern bridge. The hotel provides luxurious accommodations and two restaurants, the **Rhapsody** and **Le Gourmet**; in the **Sky Bar** on the tenth floor you can enjoy panoramic views of Koblenz and the mighty Rhine.

Other attractions include the Neoclassical Stadttheater, built in 1787 on the Deinhardplatz, offering a rich program of plays, ballet, and operetta; **Schloss Stolzenfels**, a 13th-century castle rebuilt by the king of Prussia in 1836–1842 on a hill in the Stolzenfels district at the south end of the city; and the commanding **Ehrenbreitstein fortress** across the Rhine, the site of a tenth-century citadel destroyed by the French in 1799 and rebuilt by the Prussians in 1817–1828.

To get to the fortress, cross the Rhine by ferry from the

Konrad-Adenauer-Ufer, or, by car, take the Pfaffendorfer Brücke on route B 49, and then go left on route B 42 and follow the signs for the few minutes' drive to the base of the fortress. You can drive up to the top, walk, or take the chair lift. Whichever way you go, the tour and the views from the battlements are worth the trip. The fortress, as well as Schloss Stolzenfels, are great vantage points for the "Rhine in Flames" fireworks spectacular along the river every year on the second Saturday in August.

## Other Eating and Drinking in Koblenz

Koblenz has many agreeable wine taverns and restaurants outside the Altstadt. There is a row of restaurants on the **Rheinzollstrasse**, a terrace above the Konrad-Adenauer-Ufer with good views of the Rhine and Ehrenbreitstein fortress. Try the **Wacht am Rhein**, the **Stresemann**, or the **Rheinzollstube**. For a hearty fun night out, go to the **Weindorf** on the Rheinallee next to the Pfaffendorfer Brücke. Built in 1925, it is an exact replica of a wine village with a square enclosed by a vineyard and four half-timbered taverns. There is seating for 700 inside and 1,300 in the square.

There are music, dancing, and entertainment here every night from Easter through October. Of course, it's a crowd scene.

## Excursions from Koblenz

Tour bus services offer day trips from Koblenz to such favorite spots as the Rhine wine town of Rüdesheim (75 km/ 47 miles south of Koblenz); into the Eifel and Hunsrück hills along the Mosel; and into the **Westerwald** forests on the east bank of the Rhine. Check with the tourist office opposite the main railroad station for details. On the west bank of the Rhine just south of Koblenz is Boppard and the beginning of the Lorelei Valley/Rheingau wine area; see the Rhine Around Frankfurt chapter.

### GETTING AROUND
Koblenz is the major gateway from the rest of Germany into the Mosel valley. Cologne/Bonn and Frankfurt are the nearest airports.

The A 61 Autobahn links Koblenz with Bonn (only 52 km/ 32.5 miles away) and Cologne (90 km/56 miles to the north). The fastest way to Frankfurt (126 km/78 miles away) is to take route B 9 north to the Koblenzer Kreuz Autobahn junction, take the A 48 across the river, and join the A 3 to Frankfurt. A slower but prettier route along the Rhine takes you across the river by the Koblenz city bridge, south on Route B 42 to Rüdesheim and Wiesbaden, and then into Frankfurt on the A 66.

Koblenz is well served by rail to and from the rest of Germany and neighboring European countries, with hundreds of passenger trains, including InterCity and EuroCity expresses, daily.

The freeway parallel to the Mosel valley is the A 48 Autobahn, which runs between Koblenz and Trier. The Mosel Express trains, which run from Koblenz to Luxembourg via Trier, stop at several towns along the way, including Cochem, but they no longer stop at Bernkastel (there is no rail traffic to Bernkastel). There is also bus service between Koblenz and Trier, which makes local stops along the way.

Trier is an important junction for road and rail traffic to and from nearby Luxembourg and the rest of Germany. The local A 602 expressway links Trier with Koblenz (124 km/ 77.5 miles away) via the A 48 Autobahn (which also runs a short distance into Luxembourg). Saarbrücken is 94 km (59 miles) to the south, via the A 1 autobahn.

Trier has a small airport for sport and small passenger aircraft. The nearest full-service airports are Luxembourg, Saarbrücken, Cologne/Bonn, and Frankfurt.

Trier itself has reliable public transportation, with 11 bus lines serving the city and surrounding areas. Visitors can buy a 24-hour ticket for rides on the entire urban network. Koblenz's location on the Rhine and Mosel rivers makes it a major base for the "great white fleet" of the Köln–Düsseldorfer (KD) line (Tel: 261-310-30), and such smaller operators as Holzenbein (Tel: 261-377-44). Boats leave from the Konrad-Adenauer-Ufer starting at 9:00 A.M. daily on various trips along both rivers. Boat trips range from a few hours to several days, going as far as Trier on the Mosel and Cologne on the Rhine and even to Frankfurt on the Main.

The Kolb passenger line, based at Breidern/Mosel (Tel: 2673-15-15), has daily boat trips from mid-May to mid-October from the Zurlaubenufer dock in Trier. There are one-hour tours of the local shoreline as well as longer excursions to places like Bernkastel. Three times a week, the big modern passenger ships of the Köln–Düsseldorfer line make excursions from Trier to Koblenz and Cologne on the Rhine. The KD agency in Trier is at Georg-Schmitt-Platz 2; Tel: (651) 766-61.

Most other towns along the Mosel offer tours by boat as well. Check with local tourist bureaus for information.

## ACCOMMODATIONS REFERENCE

▶ **Alte Thorschenke.** Brückenstrasse 3, D-5590 **Cochem.** Tel: (2671) 70-59.

▶ **Altstadt-Hotel.** Am Porta Nigra Platz, D-5500 **Trier.** Tel: (651) 480-41.

▶ **Behrens.** Schanzstrasse 9, D-5550 **Bernkastel-Kues.** Tel: (6531) 60-88.

▶ **Binz.** Markt 1, D-5550 **Bernkastel-Kues.** Tel: (6531) 22-25.

▶ **Burg Hotel.** Moselpromenade 23, D-5590 **Cochem.** Tel: (2671) 71-17.

▶ **Burg Landshut.** Am Gestade 11, D-5550 **Bernkastel-Kues.** Tel: (6531) 30-19; Telex: 4721565.

▶ **Cityhotel Metropol.** Münzplatz, D-5400 **Koblenz.** Tel: (261) 350-60.

▶ **Dorint-Hotel Porta Nigra.** Porta Nigra Platz 1, D-5500 **Trier.** Tel: (651) 270-10; Telex: 472895; Fax: 2701170.

▶ **Europa Parkhotel Mövenpick.** Kaiserstrasse 29, D-5500 **Trier.** Tel: (651) 719-50; Telex: 472858.

▶ **Germania.** Moselpromenade 1, D-5590 **Cochem.** Tel: (2671) 261; Telex: 869422.

▶ **Karl Müller.** Moselpromenade 9, D-5590 **Cochem.** Tel: (2671) 13-34.

▶ **Kornpforte.** Kornpfortstrasse 11, D-5400 **Koblenz.** Tel: (261) 311-74.

▶ **Zur Post.** Am Gestade 17, D-5550 **Bernkastel-Kues.** Tel: (6531) 20-22; Telex: 4721569.

▶ **Römischer Kaiser.** Markt 29, D-5550 **Bernkastel-Kues.** Tel: (6531) 30-38.

▶ **Scandic Crown Hotel.** Julius Wegeler Strasse 2, D-5400 **Koblenz.** Tel: (261) 13-60; Telex: 862338; Fax: 136199.

▶ **Scandic Crown Hotel.** Zurmeiener Strasse 164, D-5500 **Trier.** Tel: (651) 14-30; Telex: 472808; Fax: 1432000.

▶ **Weinhaus Haag.** Stockplatz 1, D-5500 **Trier.** Tel: (651) 723-66.

▶ **Hotel-Pension Weinhof.** Moselpromenade 27, D-5590 **Cochem.** Tel: (2671) 74-62.

# FRANKFURT-AM-MAIN

## By Thomas C. Lucey

*Thomas Lucey, a resident of Frankfurt for 25 years, is the German correspondent for* Business International *publications. He has also been a travel editor and columnist, and has contributed to two other travel guides.*

Johann Wolfgang von Goethe believed Frankfurt, his home town, to be the nation's secret capital. Actually, Frankfurt has traditionally been associated with business and finance more than politics. It is true that after World War II this badly bombed city wanted to become the capital of the new Federal Republic and even rebuilt the bombed Paulskirche as a new house of parliament in anticipation. But the national nod went to Bonn, a small town on the Rhine; Frankfurt's would-be parliamentary building now houses meeting and exhibition halls.

Instead, Frankfurt has become Germany's financial capital. The Bundesbank (Federal Central Bank) and leading commercial banks, as well as the country's principal stock exchange, are headquartered here, and if a central bank of Europe is created in coming years, it too may well be located in Frankfurt. The city has already officially bid for it—as it has bid to replace New York City as the venue of the men's tennis Masters tournament. A 55-story office building, Europe's tallest, opened here in 1990 next to the Frankfurter Messe (Frankfurt Trade Fair), an institution that dates to the Middle Ages. Frankfurt is now a major stop on the international exhibition circuit.

The Middle Ages are still evident in this city, especially in

the Altstadt's (old city's) coronation cathedral of the Holy
Roman Empire. Also, as part of a municipally financed campaign to show that Frankfurt knows there is life beyond
business, the Museumsufer—a long outdoor showcase for
the fine and decorative arts, and for movies—has been
created. This city is also designed for walking, with wide,
often tree-lined *Fussgängerzonen* (pedestrian zones) in the
downtown area. Frankfurt is the home, of course, of the
genuine Frankfurter sausage, as well as a tangy apple cider
called *Ebbelwei*. Since Ebbelwei (or *Apfelwein*) doesn't
travel well, or at least not very far, people must travel here to
drink it.

And they do. Frankfurt is the third most visited city in West
Germany, after Munich and West Berlin. The Messe deserves
a good part of the credit, drawing thousands of visitors to its
chemical, book, textile, car, antiques, and modern-art fairs.
Therein lies a warning: If you are not coming to Frankfurt
for a fair, you should avoid the biggest crowd-drawers,
particularly on weekends. There is a lot to see in Frankfurt,
and you don't want your view blocked.

### MAJOR INTEREST

The Dom and Römerberg
Museumsufer (The Museum Embankment)
Sachsenhausen and its Apfelwein taverns
The Alte Oper
Goethehaus
The Zoo
Day trips to Bad Homburg, and the Roman camp at
    Saalburg

## The Dom and Römerberg

Voltaire was partly right when he remarked that the Holy
Roman Empire was "Neither holy, nor Roman, nor an empire." It certainly did have longevity, however: Created by
Charlemagne and dissolved by Napoleon, it lasted from the
ninth century to the 19th. Frankfurt was a Free Imperial City
within the empire; for centuries, it was also the city in which
the emperor was elected (from 1356 on) and crowned
(from 1562 to 1792).

The coronations took place in the **Dom** (Cathedral),
which celebrated its 750th anniversary in 1988. The Dom
does not have a massive presence; its spiky Gothic tower
dominates the skyline of Frankfurt's **Altstadt** (Old City) only

because high-rise buildings are banned in the area. In truth, this red sandstone church is not even a cathedral and never was one. The Roman Catholic cathedral for this diocese is in the town of Limburg, and Frankfurt's Dom is actually a collegiate church named after Saint Bartholomew. Because ten Holy Roman emperors acquired their crowns here, the church of Saint Bartholomew has gone down in history as the Kaiserdom (Emperor's Cathedral), or simply the Dom, as it is called by everyone in Frankfurt.

Its lack of colossal proportions—and of streams of organized sightseeing groups—make the Dom approachable. It contains a few outstanding artworks. The *Kreuzigungsgruppe* (Crucifixion Group) was made in 1509 for the cathedral cemetery. The recently restored frieze, *Bartholomäus Fries,* designed in 1427, goes around the finely carved choir stalls that date to 1352. The *Maria-Schlaff-Altar,* completed in 1434, depicts the death of the Virgin. The *Wahlkapelle,* behind the choir, is the chapel where the Holy Roman emperors were elected.

The Dom was badly damaged in World War II, but it was one of the few structures to survive the March 1944 bombing that destroyed the surrounding complex of wooden houses and alleylike streets that had been Germany's largest surviving Medieval Altstadt. (A model of the Altstadt can be seen in the nearby Historisches Museum; see below.)

The cathedral's treasures had been doubly protected behind brick walls, and in 1987 a small museum was opened in the Dom's Kreuzgang (Cloister). Many citizens were surprised to learn that the Dom even had a cloister. But it turned out that the area, next to the main entrance, dated only to the last century and was being used as a storage room. On display are Catholic liturgical vestments, pictures, and statues, including one of Saint Bartholomew, as well as models of two earlier versions of the Dom.

After his coronation at the Dom, a new emperor and his entourage would parade to the **Römer,** now the city hall, a route you should follow, too. While this area had settlers as early as the Stone Age, the small cluster of ruins near the Dom dates only from the Middle Ages. The Romans settled this piece of high ground, which is still called the **Römerberg** (Roman Hill), and also constructed a bridge across the river Main. But to the Romans, Frankfurt was very much an outpost. The northernmost frontier of the Roman Empire, the Saalburg camp, is only a few miles to the north (see Day Trips, below). After the Germanic tribes defeated the Romans, the settlement fell into ruins and was forgotten until 20th-century

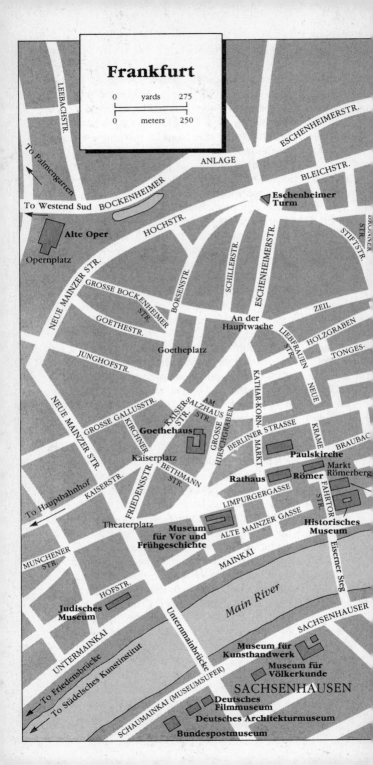

# Frankfurt

| 0 | yards | 275 |
| 0 | meters | 250 |

LEEBACHSTR.

To Palmengarten

ANLAGE

ESCHENHEIMERSTR.

BLEICHSTR.

To Westend Sud  BOCKENHEIMER

Eschenheimer
Turm

HOCHSTR.

Alte Oper

Opernplatz

NEUE MAINZER STR.

GROSSE BOCKENHEIMER
STR.

GOETHESTR.

BORSENSTR.

SCHILLERSTR.

ESCHENHEIMERSTR.

DRONER
STR.

STIFTSTR.

ZEIL

An der
Hauptwache

LIEBFRAUEN
STR.

HOLZGRABEN

TONGES-

JUNGHOFSTR.

Goetheplatz

NEUE
KATHAR-KORN-
MARKT

NEUE MAINZER STR.

GROSSE GALLUSSTR.

KIRCHNER

KAISER-
STR.
SALZHAUS
STR.

AM
GROSSE
HIRSCHGRABEN

BERLINER STRASSE

KRAME

BRAUBAC

To Hauptbahnhof

Goethehaus

Kaiserplatz

FRIEDENSSTR.

BETHMANN
STR.

Paulskirche

Rathaus

Römer

Markt
Römerberg

FAHRTOR
STR.

KAISERSTR.

LIMPURGERGASSE

Theaterplatz

Museum
für Vor und
Frühgeschichte

ALTE MAINZER GASSE

Historisches
Museum

Eiserner Steg

MUNCHENER
STR.

MAINKAI

HOFSTR.

Judisches
Museum

Main River

SACHSENHAUSER

Untermainbrücke

Museum für
Kunsthandwerk

Museum für
Völkerkunde

UNTERMAINKAI

To Friedensbrücke

To Städelsches Kunstinstitut

SCHAUMAINKAI (MUSEUMSUFER)

SACHSENHAUSEN

Deutsches
Filmmuseum

Deutsches Architekturmuseum

Bundespostmuseum

construction workers stumbled across its remains. The Römerberg is also the site of **Villa Franconofurd**, one of the residences of Charlemagne. A document dating to 794 contains the first written reference to anything resembling the word "Frankfurt." The origin of the city's name may have been Charlemagne's way of commemorating the Frankish conquest of this crucial north-south river crossing in a war some 300 years earlier. The vanquished in that battle were the Alemanni, the same Germanic tribe that had originally driven out the Romans.

The area between the Dom and the Römer has been built up in recent years. Near the Dom is the **Schirn Kunsthalle**, where major art exhibitions are held. In 1988, the only West European showing of Kandinsky paintings from the Soviet Union was held here. If there is an exhibition at the Schirn while you are in Frankfurt, it is probably worth seeing. You might rest your feet at the airy Kunsthalle café outside the entrance.

The fresh-looking half-timbered houses facing the city hall are quite new. Purists were shocked when the city built them, but they provide a picture of the long-gone Altstadt, and they brighten a once drab area. Even when fairs, complete with merry-go-rounds, are not being held here, this square (Römerberg) and the surrounding cafés, ice-cream parlors, and restaurants fill up on sunny Sundays. Crowds have been drawn here for many years. Medieval city officials and their families watched plays and tournaments from a specially built gallery on the **Nikolaikirche**, the small chapel in front of the city hall. This chapel has a rare, 35-bell carillon that plays softly at 9:05 A.M., 12:05 P.M., and 6:05 P.M.

The large corner building with the layer-cake appearance, another architectural provocation of some years ago, houses the **Historisches Museum**. The history here is Frankfurt's for the most part, and the exhibits provide fascinating glimpses of yesterday's quotidian life, with whole rooms of furniture, pictures, and posters. On the museum's ground floor is a historic-looking café-restaurant.

**Haus Wertheim**, the half-timbered corner house across the square from the museum's entrance, is one of Frankfurt's few original structures to have survived World War II. An important part of Frankfurt's—and Germany's—history is the **Paulskirche**, which is just across the street from the city hall, toward the Berliner Strasse. This is where Germany's first, short-lived democratic parliament met in the heady days of the 1848 revolution. The present structure, rebuilt from the ruins of the original destroyed in the 1944 bombing, is used for ceremonies and exhibitions.

The Limpurgergasse, a small street between the Historisches Museum and Haus Wertheim, leads to the river Main. Excursion ships dock here, including some that cruise the Rhine. Schedules and tickets are available near the dock. The wide iron footbridge nearby, the **Eiserner Steg**, is the subject of a 1922 painting by Max Beckmann. The bridge crosses to the south bank, with its new Museumsufer (Museum Embankment), and the Sachsenhausen district.

Savor the view of the Museumsufer from the Eiserner Steg, then cross to the south bank and admire the top of the Dom, the three centuries of architectural styles that make up the Historisches Museum, including a 15th-century corner tower that was part of the city's defenses, and the white excursion boats docked next to the Eiserner Steg in spring and summer. These are two of the best views in town.

## The Museumsufer

There are seven museums on the half-mile-long museum embankment, where architects have expanded 18th- and 19th-century patrician houses and in some cases combined them with structures of a contemporary style to create some of Germany's best museums.

All museums on the embankment are open Tuesday through Sunday from 10:00 A.M. to 5:00 P.M., Wednesday to 8:00 P.M. The same hours apply to the Historisches Museum, with special collections open mornings only, and the Jüdisches Museum and Liebighaus. The Schirn is open from 10:00 A.M. to 9:00 P.M., weekends and holidays till 7:00 P.M.; closed Mondays. The Goethehaus operates from 9:00 A.M. to 6:00 P.M. Monday through Saturday, Sunday from 10:00 A.M. to 1:00 P.M.; 9:00 A.M. to 4:00 P.M. October to March.

To the right as you step off the footbridge is the **Museum für Kunsthandwerk** (Museum of Applied Arts), at Schaumainkai 15–17. Inside is one of those collections that got out of hand. Begun at another site in 1877 with only 50 articles, the collection was generously endowed by local benefactors until it became internationally known in the field of decorative arts. Unfortunately, until this structure was expanded in 1985, the collection did not have sufficient display space; even now, only two thirds of the 300,000 objects in the collection can be shown (the rest is in storage). Those on display include rare examples of German furniture and woodwork, porcelain, rugs, glass, tapestries, and bronze and gold works, as well as decorative art from other European countries and the Near and Far East. There is also a special collection of books and calligraphy. The European furniture collection is the best of its kind in Germany.

The building itself attracts visitors. The original villa, which the museum occupied in 1967, was far too small to house the collection. Richard Meier, a New York architect who will renovate the Getty Museum in Malibu, California, designed the airy addition. The Café im Museumpark provides outside tables in summer.

Next in line is the **Museum für Völkerkunde** (Museum of Ethnography), which is at Schaumainkai 29, in the direction of the Untermainbrücke. The original museum was destroyed by bombs in World War II; this new building is not nearly large enough. Only 300 of the collection's 50,000 articles are on display, consisting mostly of artifacts from South Pacific, African, and South American cultures that are dying out. The museum seeks to use its display space to give visitors an appreciation of those cultures. Exhibitions are regularly held on various aspects of the contemporary Third World as well.

There are plans to increase display space by moving the education section to what is now the police station at Schaumainkai 37. Efforts to expand the building itself have encountered a problem: Some of the surrounding trees are locally rare specimens. If a way is found to save the trees and expand the museum, the Völkerkunde will be Frankfurt's third largest.

On the intersection at the Untermainbrücke, at Schaumainkai 41, is a five-story house that contains the **Deutsches Filmmuseum**, which opened in 1984, the first of the new museums on the embankment to open and the most popular. Special exhibitions on King Kong, special effects, and cartoon characters, along with a permanent display of historic movie equipment, draw a quarter of a million visitors annually. A movie theater shows classic and foreign films; in summer, a large outdoor screen is erected next to the river. Visitors can also use an extensive research library.

The Deutsches Filmmuseum was a pet project of Hilmar Hoffmann, who headed Frankfurt's Cultural and Leisure Department for 20 years, until he retired in 1990. Hoffmann was the driving force behind Frankfurt's cultural makeover and has worked hard to create the museum embankment. He is also an author and lecturer on motion pictures, especially those of the Nazi era.

The **Deutsches Architekturmuseum** is next door, at Schaumainkai 43. It, too, offers special exhibits, which have covered subjects as varied as the Postmodern movement and the New York architectural boom of the past two decades. Only 20th-century architecture is on display. The collection includes more than 10,000 plans and drawings by German and foreign architects and 700 models of architectural projects.

Your next stop is a few steps away at the **Bundespost-museum** (Federal Post Office Museum), at Schaumainkai 53. This collection of historic post-office signs, uniforms, telephone and telegraph equipment, mail coaches, and special stamp exhibitions reopened after renovation in September 1990.

The nearby **Städelsches Kunstinstitut und Städtische Galerie** (Städel Art Institute and City Gallery), at Schaumainkai 63, occupies the only building on the museum embankment that was actually intended from the start to be a museum. The Städel, as it is called, has its own art school and park, and occupies a full block. The museum, the city's first, set a pattern that Frankfurt's museums have followed until recently. They are started by private foundations and supported by private wealth. The Städel is named for Johann Friedrich Städel, a banker and art collector who lived on the Rossmarkt, near the Goethe family. He bequeathed his collection of 500 paintings to a museum upon his death, in 1816, at the age of 88. The museum is still organized to fulfill Städel's goal of showing European paintings since the 14th century, and it is one of the best of its kind in Germany. Although the period it covers is vast, the collection is not overwhelming because only outstanding works from each period and school are on display. You'll see works by Botticelli, Rembrandt, and Rubens, along with the German masters Albrecht Altdorfer, Lucas Cranach, Adam Elsheimer, Matthias Grünewald, Hans Holbein the Younger (notably his altar from the local Dominican church), Max Beckmann (who lived nearby and taught at the Städel's art school), Ernst Nolte, and Ernst Ludwig Kirchner, whose graphics make up part of the **Kupferstichkabinett** collection of prints, drawings, and engravings. The museum suffered a blow in 1937 when the Nazis confiscated "decadent" works by Picasso, Oskar Kokoschka, Beckmann (who had left Frankfurt in 1933), and others. The building itself was badly damaged by wartime bombing and wasn't restored until the 1960s.

While the Städel has some sculpture, that form of art is really the domain of the **Städtische Galerie Liebighaus**, at Schaumainkai 71, in the direction of the **Friedensbrücke**

(Peace Bridge). (Note that the Liebighaus is not on the Liebig-strasse, which is in another part of town.) When this mu-seum opened in 1907, the rest of Frankfurt's museums showed mostly paintings and decorative arts. As a temporary measure, the new museum was installed in the house of Baron von Liebig, and by now the museum has permanently acquired the house's name, the house itself, and its parks, planted with locally rare trees. The collection spans 5,000 years and includes sculpture from the Egyptian, Greek, and Roman eras; the Far East; and Medieval and Renaissance Germany, France, and Italy. The exhibits have been carefully selected so that they fit in the old building without crowd-ing. To do justice to the collection, the Liebighaus has been expanded, and works that have never been on display have been brought out of the basement storerooms. The gem of the collection, the *Frankfurter Athena,* a first-century Roman copy in marble of a lost Greek bronze, will be shown henceforth in a new light—in a glass-roofed tower that should do justice to the armless goddess.

From here, you can stay on this side of the Main river and begin to explore Sachsenhausen.

## Sachsenhausen

When people in Frankfurt refer to "dribb der Bach," they mean the area "across the stream," Sachsenhausen. This district south of the river Main has long enjoyed the reputa-tion of being the place to go for fun. The mood in its many taverns is informal. Everyone sits together at long plain wooden tables, and as the night goes on, the singing starts and new-found friends link arms and sway in rhythm, more or less. Here, the drink is not beer or wine but the dry apple cider called *Apfelwein,* or *Ebbelwei,* as it is pronounced in the local dialect. Ebbelwei is the drink of Frankfurt. It is poured from a gray-and-blue stoneware jug called a *Bembel,* into glasses decorated with an embossed diamond-shaped pattern. The first sip of this *Stöffche* (little stuff) may pucker your whole body and convince you that the waiter or wait-ress brought you some kind of vinegar. If so, try a *Gespritzte,* a mixture of Apfelwein and plain mineral water (*Sauerge-spritzt*), or lemonade-flavored mineral water (*Süssgespritzt*). Many local people drink the tangy cider this way. Apfelwein is an alcoholic drink of about 10 to 12 proof.

While Apfelwein is available year round, it also comes in different versions, depending on the season. *Süsser* (sweet) is a dark, cloudy product of the freshly pressed apple harvest and is sold in the autumn. When Süsser starts to ferment, it is called *Rauscher,* a darker, slightly more acidic drink. Thanks to an ancient magic formula, the third glass of Rauscher has special properties that will clear the digestive tract. Süsser and Rauscher are meant to be taken straight, not mixed with mineral water. Apfelwein is drunk with meals, but Süsser and Rauscher are probably too strongly flavored to go well with most dishes. Apfelwein mixed with hot water, cinnamon, and cloves makes a nice toddy.

Sachsenhausen's Apfelwein taverns, which display a pine wreath outside when a new barrel has arrived, tend to serve traditional food such as *Rippchen mit Kraut* (pickled pork chops with sauerkraut), *Haspel* (pigs' knuckles), and *Handkäs mit Musik* (strong tasting—and smelling—cheese with vinegar, oil, and chopped onions). A dish that you will not find outside Frankfurt is *grüne Sosse,* a green sauce made from seven herbs and other seasonings, chopped hard-boiled eggs, and sour cream, usually served with boiled eggs, boiled beef, or poached fish. In Sachsenhausen you are likely to find real Frankfurters made from pork, flavored with spices, and then smoked. The sausage originated in the traditional butchers' area between the Dom and the Römer, in the Middle Ages; the oldest know recipe dates from 1487. The local product has been labeled "genuine Frankfurt sausage" since about 1900 in order to distinguish it from its New World upstart, the American hot dog, which is now for sale in Frankfurt under that name. Unlike the hot dog, Frankfurters are always served in pairs.

For nibbling, there are usually hard rolls, salted bread sticks, and *Brezeln* (pretzels) on the tables. They will go on your tab.

The taverns in Sachsenhausen are especially popular during the summer, when tables are set up outdoors. But getting a seat can be difficult any time of the year, especially on weekends. One trick is to get in just before the "shifts" change from the lunch crowd to the afternoon drinkers to the supper shift, patrons who may linger on with the drinking-only evening crowd. Hot meals are usually not available after 10:00 P.M., and closing time is midnight or 1:00 A.M. While there are no class or age barriers in Apfelwein taverns, patrons who appear to be slumming probably are; it has become fashionable for the local *Schickeria* (chic set) to drop by.

Unfortunately, the traditional Apfelwein *Lokal* has been losing ground in Sachsenhausen to fast-food places, discos and bistros, and trendy restaurants. Nonetheless, establishments that serve the "national beverage" on plain wooden tables are holding their own, and the narrow, tavern-lined streets between the Paradiesgasse and the Grosse Rittergasse have been turned into a pedestrian zone. On sunny days this area seems to be one vast outdoor café. Here you'll have a good chance of meeting folks from back home. (For a list of some of the best Apfelwein *Lokale,* see below.)

If you wish to take in a very wide view of the district, visit the **Henninger Turm**, atop the Henninger brewery's storage silo. An observation platform here provides a vista of the city and surrounding countryside. The same view is available from the tower's revolving restaurant. The Henninger Turm also houses the **Frankfurter Brauerei** (brewery) **Museum** (open Tuesday through Sunday, 10:00 A.M. to 7:00 P.M.).

## Alte Oper

Frankfurt's network of pedestrian zones makes a stroll through the downtown area very pleasant. You can combine shopping with stops at several interesting and historic buildings. One is the Alte Oper, which opened in 1880 and was a copy of the lavish Paris opera. Kaiser Wilhelm I was so impressed with the opera house that when he arrived for the first performance he exclaimed, "Only the city of Frankfurt could afford such splendor!" The building was bombed in World War II and then restored, at great cost, during the urban renewal of the late 1970s. The opera house now serves as a grand setting for concerts, musicals, conventions, and other festive events. You can see the elaborate entrance and lobby whenever the main doors are unlocked. The broad **Opernplatz**, the large fountain, and the Paris-style streetlights make this a pleasant place indeed.

## Goethehaus

Germany's greatest writer lived in Frankfurt until 1765, when he was in his mid-twenties. The Goethehaus actually consists of two houses that were joined by Goethe's father, and they have been in foundation hands since 1863. They were restored to their 18th-century appearance in 1900 and again after being bombed in World War II. The Goethehaus und Museum is near but not on the Goetheplatz or the Goethestrasse. It is located at Grosser Hirschgraben 23 and can be visited conveniently while you are sightseeing or shopping downtown.

# Palmengarten

Not far from the university and next to the American Consulate-General is an oasis called the **Palmengarten**, a botanical garden with tropical, subtropical, and domestic plants. Some grow in an airplane-hangar-sized greenhouse, others in the well-kept park, with a restaurant and café, where old-fashioned outdoor concerts are held in summer. The Palmengarten tends to be crowded on Sundays and holidays. You can enter at Siesmayerstrasse 61, next to the American Consulate-General, or from the Palmengartenstrasse, a small street off the Bockenheimer Landstrasse. The number 36 bus, which stops outside the Siesmayerstrasse entrance, goes to Sachsenhausen. There is also a subway station a few blocks away.

# The Zoo

The late Professor Bernhard Grzimek made Frankfurt's **Zoologischer Garten** internationally known through his books, his encyclopedia of animals, and, most of all, through his films and television series. The zoo has some 3,500 animals in all. Be sure to visit the **Exotarium** (open until 10:00 P.M.), where you'll find especially exotic creatures, and the **Grzimekhaus**, named after the former director, where you can observe nocturnal animals during the day as if it were night. Both are in the middle of the zoo, behind the large lake near the entrance; both also require an additional admission charge. There is also a small extra fee to take pictures in the zoo. The zoo is easy to reach by U-Bahn (subway), with its own station right outside the entrance. It is best to avoid the zoo on Sundays and holidays because it is one of the most popular places in Frankfurt.

# Other Museums

The Rothschild family originally came from Frankfurt, and Anne Frank, the writer of *Diary of a Young Girl,* was born here, too. Anne Frank died in the Bergen-Belsen concentration camp in 1945, near the end of the war; a Frankfurt school has been named after her.

On November 9, 1988, the fiftieth anniversary of the Third Reich's *Kristallnacht,* when Jewish-owned shops were destroyed and their owners terrorized in a nationwide pogrom, Germany's first **Jüdisches Museum** (Jewish Museum) was opened in the Rothschild Palais, the former

home of the Rothschilds. The building, which dates to
1821, is at Untermainkai 14–15.

The museum explores the history of Frankfurt's Jewish
community. On the second floor is a large, plain wooden
model of Frankfurt's Medieval ghetto, which consisted of
small houses tightly packed along the Judengasse (Jews'
Lane), which extended from the Konstablerwache, the large
square along the Zeil shopping area, to the Börneplatz, a
long block to the south. Mayer-Amschel Rothschild, the
founder of the Rothschild dynasty, was born here in 1744.

The ghetto was torn down in the second half of the 19th
century and wasn't seen again until construction workers
uncovered the remains of houses on the Börneplatz a few
years ago. A movement to declare the site a monument
began; eventually it was decided that the houses would be
saved and that a small museum will open in the spring of
1991.

To reach the museum from the Theaterplatz U-Bahn station, follow the Neue Mainzer Strasse to the river and turn
right on the Untermainkai. The Jüdisches Museum is open
Tuesday through Sunday, 10:00 A.M. to 5:00 P.M.; Wednesday
until 8:00 P.M.

The **Museum für Moderne Kunst** (Museum of Modern
Art), on the Berliner Strasse, opened this year. Showing only
art made after 1945, the museum displays Pop Art works
from the Ströher collection, sold to the city by the heirs of
the Wella hair-care products and cosmetics fortune. Of equal
interest is Joseph Beuys's *Blitzschlag mit Lichtschein auf
Hirsch* (*Lightning Bolt with Glow of Light on Stag*), an
environment consisting of 39 pieces of bronze and alumi-
num. The museum also is a venue for major exhibitions.

If you are interested in natural history, you should not
miss Frankfurt's largest museum, the **Naturmuseum Senckenberg**. Housed in an imitation Baroque palace built at the
beginning of this century, the Senckenberg contains the
usual fossils and dinosaurs plus extensive collections in the
fields of zoology, geology, paleontology, and botany. The
founder, Johann Christian Senckenberg, a physician, originally created a foundation to support a hospital. Goethe, a
genius for all occasions, urged that it support the study of
nature instead. Today, the Senckenberg research society has
more than 3,000 members worldwide and is actively engaged in numerous projects. Located at Senckenberganlage
25, two blocks north of the Messe in the university area, the
Senckenberg keeps its own hours: Monday (when the museum embankment is closed), Tuesday, Thursday, and Friday,

9:00 A.M. to 5:00 P.M.; Wednesday, 9:00 A.M. to 8:00 P.M.; and weekends, 9:00 A.M. to 6:00 P.M. Free guided tours are offered on Wednesday at 6:00 P.M. and Sunday at 10:30 A.M.

Struwwelpeter, the dirty little boy who wouldn't cut his hair or fingernails, was "born" in Frankfurt, the creation of Heinrich Hoffmann, a humanitarian, psychiatrist, and children's book author. Two museums are dedicated to their memory. The **Struwwelpeter Museum**, opened in 1982, displays sketches and manuscripts by the author, various editions and parodies of the original book, and other items on loan from Hoffmann's heirs. The museum is located near the Alte Oper, at Hochstrasse 45–47, where the author lived from 1851 to 1859; it is open Tuesday through Sunday, 11:00 A.M. to 5:00 P.M., Wednesday until 8:00 p.m. The **Heinrich Hoffmann Museum** at Schubertstrasse 20, a block from the Senckenberg, collects works about the author and puts on special exhibitions. The small museum is open daily except Monday, from 10:00 A.M. to 5:00 P.M.

The remains of a Roman garrison and the contents of the graves of an early Iron Age warrior and Frankish settlers from the fourth to eighth centuries—all found in Frankfurt—can be seen in the **Museum für Vor- und Frühgeschichte** (Museum of Pre- and Early History). Exhibits also span the period from the Stone Age to the Dark Ages and include primitive tools, ceramics, jewelry, cult figures from the Mediterranean and Near East, and Persian bronze works. The museum is housed in a new building, a virtually windowless, candy-striped "wall" wrapped around the Late Gothic Karmeliterkloster (Carmelite Monastery), whose frescoes have been painstakingly restored. (Putting the two together displayed a "crude lack of taste," complained the prestigious local newspaper, the *Frankfurter Allgemeine*.) The monastery-museum is near the Goethehaus, at the beginning of the broad and busy Berliner Strasse behind the Hotel Frankfurter Hof; it is open Tuesday through Sunday, 10:00 A.M. to 5:00 P.M., Wednesday until 8:00 P.M.

## Day Trips from Frankfurt

Frankfurt's central location, which has helped make it a prosperous city since the Middle Ages, also makes it a good base for day trips. (Many of the places within easy traveling distance from Frankfurt are covered in the next chapter, The Rhine Around Frankfurt.) **Heidelberg** is only an hour away by InterCity (IC) and EuroCity (EC) fast trains, and can be reached via the Autobahn in about the same time.

**Wiesbaden** and **Mainz**, both on the Rhine and near charming wine districts, can be reached easily by Schnellbahn (S-Bahn) and regular Bundesbahn trains. The S-Bahn starts at the Konstabler Wache Untergrundbahn (U-Bahn) station and runs underground to the Hauptbahnhof (main railway station). Bundesbahn trains depart from the Hauptbahnhof. The trips take about a half hour; the quickest S-Bahn does not go via the airport. The Baroque, wine-growing city of **Würzburg** in northern Bavaria is only an hour and 20 minutes away by IC or EC; see the Romantic Road chapter. Wiesbaden, Mainz, and Würzburg can also be reached by Autobahn.

**Bad Homburg** is a famous spa with a traditional casino, where gamblers in dark suits and even black tie (there is a dress code) sedately play roulette and blackjack (but not slot machines). The **Spielkasino**, which opened in 1841, was the world's first and served as the model for the casino in Monte Carlo. The town preserves a turn-of-the-century atmosphere, especially in and around the Kurpark, or spa park; elsewhere, the modern office buildings and fast-food shops can be ignored. The homburg hat was created here and is commemorated by a hat section in the Heimatmuseum. Originally a hunting hat, the homburg was popularized for street wear by Edward VII of Great Britain, who was a frequent visitor to Bad Homburg and the casino. Just 22 km (14 miles) from Frankfurt, Bad Homburg can be reached easily by car, S-Bahn; and the casino's courtesy bus.

Nearby (linked by local transportation) is the **Saalburg**. This reconstruction of a Roman fort on the Limes, the northern wall of the Roman Empire, conveys the feeling of a place where 600 legionnaires were stationed almost 2,000 years ago, although to purists it may look too tidy.

A tip for day-trippers: About half the people who work in Frankfurt commute by train (especially via the Hauptbahnhof) and car. Avoid rush hours (7:00 A.M. to about 8:30 A.M., 4:30 P.M. to about 6:30 P.M., and Friday afternoons). Drivers should avoid the Messe area during large fairs.

## GETTING AROUND

Frankfurter Flughafen, once the home port of Germany's zeppelin fleet, has become one of Europe's busiest airports. With scores of international direct flights every day (about 50 to and from New York alone), this airport will likely be your gateway to Germany.

Ground transportation to and from the Flughafen, including quick and easy access to downtown Frankfurt, runs smoothly. **Taxis** seem to be always available, even late at night. The fare to downtown Frankfurt is about DM 35. At the train station, a floor below the arrival area, an S-Bahn departs every 20 minutes for the Hauptbahnhof, a 12-minute journey. S-Bahn tickets for Frankfurt can be bought at blue machines just before going down to the platform. Never get on a German subway or bus without a ticket. Inspectors make periodic checks, and the fine for "schwarzfahren" (travelling black) is DM 60, payable on the spot.

**Airport trains** run to and from the Hauptbahnhof via the Bundesbahn (federal railway) tracks on the main floor; those serving the Konstabler Wache U-Bahn station are downstairs. Airport trains, marked with the figure of an airplane, are announced in English as well as German. The fare is DM 4.60 during rush hour; at other times it is DM 3.30. The fare is slightly higher in outlying parts of the city and the surrounding area.

Some long-distance Bundesbahn trains also stop at the Flughafen. Information and tickets are available in the arrival area.

Since you don't need a car for local sightseeing and driving downtown is best left to others, the clean and efficient S-Bahn/U-Bahn system is the best way to travel. Many visitors complain that they find it confusing. It isn't if you don't try to grasp all the fine points but just concentrate on what you need to know. A ticket is good for one ride in one direction to any stop in the same color-coded area. The trip may include transfers to other S-Bahn and U-Bahn trains and city buses, and may not last longer than one hour. (Some bus stops have ticket machines; otherwise the bus driver sells tickets.)

Trains are identified by S or U and a route number (the letter is important because there are S and U routes with the same number). The direction is indicated by the name of the last stop. On trains, number and last stop appear on the front of the first car and on electric platform signs. On buses, they are on the front, and all the stops are listed on a schedule displayed at each stop. The same route numbers and destinations mark stairways at entrances and transfer points, with a large white U on a blue background or an S against green posted at station entrances.

The S-Bahn, mostly above ground, links the center of the city with the suburbs, as far as Wiesbaden and Mainz, Hanau, and Friedberg (where Elvis Presley was stationed as a GI in the 1950s). The U-Bahn, which serves Frankfurt proper, covers the points of most interest to visitors, with stations at the Alte Oper, Hauptwache, Römer, the zoo, and Schweizer Platz (for Sachsenhausen and the museum embankment). Buses complement the U-Bahn routes.

The few streetcar lines are part of the city system, and use the same tickets.

If you want to go only a few stops, it is best to purchase a cheaper Kurzstrecke (short-route) ticket. A Kurzstrecke ticket costs DM 1.20 (DM 2 during rush hours, Monday through Friday, 6:30 to 8:30 A.M. and 4:00 to 6:30 P.M.). A 24-Stunden Frankfurt ticket is good for 24 hours; the price is DM 8.

No matter what kind of ticket you buy, the ticket machine shows the price when you press the color-coded destination button. Train service phases out at about midnight or 1:00 A.M. and resumes at 5:00 A.M.

You should take advantage of the network of pedestrian streets, or Fussgängerzonen, for shopping and sightseeing. Start at the Alte Oper, stroll along the Grosse Bockenheimer Strasse (better known as Fressgass', or Gluttony Lane, because it is lined with food stores and restaurants), and continue to the Hauptwache square. A block to the left, at the end of the Schillerstrasse, stands the **Eschenheimer Turm** (the Eschenheimer Tor station on the U-Bahn), a restored Medieval tower and gateway that most photographers can't resist. The Hauptwache is at the beginning of the broad **Zeil**, which claims to do more business than any other shopping street in Germany. To the right, via the Liebfrauenstrasse and the Neue Krämer, are the Römer and the Dom. A footbridge leads to the Museumsufer. This route crosses only five streets open to cars.

The Hauptbahnhof, its subterranean passage, and the tough honky-tonk area around it are not safe for evening strolls.

The city operates tourist information offices in the Flughafen, Arrival Hall B; opposite track 23 in the Hauptbahnhof; and at the northern corner of the Römer. In addition to stocking city maps, calendars, and brochures, these offices sell tickets for the city-run bus tours (there are three a day). At the train station office helpful staffers will also find hotel rooms for visitors. Tel: (69) 212-38-49/51. Hours: Flughafen, 7:00 A.M. to 10:00 P.M.; Hauptbahnhof, varies seasonally, but at least until 8:00 P.M. every day and until 10:00 P.M., except Sunday, from April 1 to October 31; Romer, until 7:00 P.M. weekdays and 6:00 P.M. weekends and holidays.

Almost all weekends and holidays, the **Ebbelwei Express**, a brightly painted old streetcar, runs every half hour from 1:35 P.M. to 5:35 P.M. from the zoo through Sachsenhausen and the Altstadt. There is piped-in music, and Apfelwein and pretzels are served. You can board anywhere en route; the price is DM 3.

Major car rental agencies are at the Flughafen, with offices at the leading hotels; in smaller hotels the desk can make arrangements. The agency will bring the car to you. Frankfurt has wide streets feeding into the various north-south and east-west Autobahns that twist around and through the city. It is considerably easier to drive in and out of Frankfurt than inside it. Autobahns run along three sides of the Flughafen. The nearby clover-leaf intersection, Frankfurter Kreuz, will point you toward Hannover, Cologne, Mannheim, or Nürnberg.

## ACCOMMODATIONS

First, a warning: Major trade fairs overburden hotels and pensions in and around the city, including the large river excursion boat/hotels docked along the Main. Prudent business people attending the fairs make reservations a year in advance. Room prices are also higher during fairs, so if possible, time your visit to avoid a large Messe. The telephone area code for Frankfurt is 69.

### Downtown

The **Arabella Grand Hotel**, which opened in 1988, targets top business travellers, with a VIP floor, conference rooms, and a fitness center, plus restaurants and bars. It is in the shopping area, just half a block from the Konstabler Wache station, where you can catch the train to the plane.

Konrad-Adenauer-Strasse 7. Tel: 298-10; Fax: 2981810.

**City** is a small hotel on a quiet residential side street about a 20-minute walk from the Hauptwache. Only breakfast is served.

Sommerring Strasse 23. Tel: 59-31-97.

**Frankfurter Hof**, the flagship of Germany's Steigenberger group, is a 19th-century grand hotel that offers guests an atmosphere of almost-hushed elegance in a central location.

Kaiserplatz 17. Tel: 215-02; Telex: 411806; Fax: 215860.

**Hessischer Hof**, opposite the Messe, is similar to the Frankfurter but smaller. Both it and the Marriott (below) are popular with trade-fair guests.

Friedrich-Ebert-Anlage 40. Tel: 754-00; Telex: 411776; Fax 7540924.

The **Intercontinental** stands on the Main, two blocks from the Hauptbahnhof. Its upper floors offer panoramic views of the city, as does the top-floor Silhouette bar.

Wilhelm-Leuschner-Strasse 43. Tel: 260-50; Fax: 252467.

The **Mozart** is a small, modern hotel tucked away in the gentrified Westend. It is quiet; only breakfast is served.

Parkstrasse 17. Tel: 55-08-31.

**Mövenpick-Parkhotel-Frankfurt**, owned by a Swiss company, calls itself "a small grand hotel." It is also a convenient pied-à-terre across from the Hauptbahnhof.

Wiesenhüttenplatz 28. Tel: 269-70; Telex: 412808; Fax: 26978849.

When Marriott bought the Plaza from Canadian Pacific in 1989, it promised a complete renovation by mid-1990. Renamed **Frankfurt Marriott Hotel**, it is located in the upper stories of a highrise across from the Messe main entrance. The entrance is through a ground-floor lobby.

Hamburger Allee 2. Tel: 795-50; Telex: 412593; Fax: 79552432.

The **Savoy** is a modern hotel, across from the Hauptbahnhof.

Wiesenhüttenstrasse 42. Tel: 27-39-60; Fax: 27396795.

**Schwille**, a small hotel next to the popular café of the same name, is in the Fressgass' section of the Fussgängerzone, near the Alte Oper.

Grosse Bockenheimer Strasse 50. Tel: 28-30-54; Fax: 92010999.

**Turm**, new, efficient, and expanding, is a medium-sized hotel on a wide, busy street near the Eschenheimer Turm.

Eschenheimer Landstrasse 20. Tel: 15-40-50; Fax: 553578.

**Pension Uebe**, in a corner house half a block from the Turm Hotel, is an institution to which many faithful guests return year after year. Only breakfast is served.

Grüneburgweg 3. Tel: 59-12-09.

### Out of Town

**Gravenbruch Kempinski-Frankfurt** provides a posh country-resort atmosphere within a short drive of the city and the airport. However, the avid sightseer may find it remote. Top executives, who can hold large and small meetings here with breaks for tennis, love it.

Gravenbruch Ring, 6078 Neu-Isenburg. Tel: (6102) 50-50; Telex: 417673; Fax: 505445.

**Schlosshotel Kronberg**, built in the 19th century for Kaiser Friedrich III's young widow, Victoria (daughter of Britain's Queen Victoria), is furnished with antiques and has an Old World atmosphere. This is a place to relax in old-fashioned elegance.

Hainstrasse 25, 6242 Kronberg. Tel: (6173) 7-01-01; Fax: 701267.

Easily reached by pedestrian bridges from the airport passenger terminal, the **Sheraton** provides meeting facilities, including an adjoining convention hall, for business travellers, as well as R & R for transient passengers. This is the second-largest hotel in Europe.

Hugo-Eckener-Ring 15. Tel: (69) 697-70; Telex: 4189294; Fax: 69772209.

Nearby is the **Steigenberger Hotel Frankfurt Airport,** which recently added an Executive Tower with a tenth-floor VIP lounge, where breakfast as well as evening cocktails are served. Although it overlooks an Autobahn, this hotel is surrounded by woods and is actually quite peaceful. It provides frequent courtesy bus service to and from the passenger terminal.

Unterschweinstiege 16, Frankfurt 75. Tel: (69) 697-50; Telex: 413112; Fax: 69752505.

Each of these hotels has a fine restaurant.

# DINING

## *Luxury Gourmet*
**Weinhaus Brückenkeller,** a 300-year-old wine cellar with vaulted ceilings and wandering musicians, had long been popular with visitors to Frankfurt. In 1988 Michelin awarded it a star, and Frankfurters rediscovered it. The menu is small and changes daily; the wine list is extensive and pricey. Schützenstrasse 6. Tel: 28-42-38 and 28-50-92. Evenings only, from 7:00. Closed Sunday.

**Restaurant Français,** which occupies a comfortably small room in the Hotel Frankfurter Hof, feels old-fashionedly French; that is, formal and elegant. The menu, however, is not limited to French dishes. Tel: 202-51. Closed Sunday and holidays, and for four weeks during July and August.

**Humperdinck** (which also has a Michelin star) is in the careful hands of two serious cooks. The mostly French dishes are works of art, but some people feel the staff is too serious, and so it is best if you know a little about gourmet food and wine. Engelbert Humperdinck, the composer of *Hänsel und Gretel,* and Struwwelpeter author Heinrich Hoffmann lived in this building long ago. Grüneburgweg 95. Tel: 72-21-22. Open weekdays for lunch and dinner, and on Saturday for dinner only (from 7:00). Closed Sunday.

Finally, bear in mind the **Gourmet Restaurant** in the Hotel Gravenbruch Kempinski and the restaurant in the **Schloss-**

**hotel Kronberg** (see Accommodations, Out of Town). Reservations are required for all these restaurants.

## Moderate

**Bistrot 77** would be in the preceding category if it did not offer a four-course meal for DM 50 as well as a splurge on a nine-course feast for DM 135 (pricey French wine). This is not a bistro but a gourmet restaurant located deep in Sachsenhausen's Apfelwein district. Bistrot 77 is the achievement of the brothers Mosbach, Guy and Dominique, sons of an Alsatian wine grower whose products can be sampled here. Ziegelhüttenweg 1–3. Tel: 61-40-40. Open for lunch and dinner weekdays, dinner only on Saturday (from 7:00); closed Sunday. Reservations required.

A Frankfurt restaurant critic noted recently that traditional German dishes have become "almost exotic" here. And indeed, you'll have no trouble finding Italian, Yugoslav, Chinese, and Indian restaurants. But what of the German restaurants? In addition to those in Sachsenhausen (see below), you might try:

**Dippegucker** for its rustic decor, good beer, affordable wine, and hearty meals. It is at two locations: Eschenheimer Anlage 40, facing the Eschenheimer Turm; and Münchner Strasse, facing the Hauptbahnhof. The former opens for lunch and then from 5:00 P.M.; the latter is open all day until midnight.

**Gutsschänke Neuhof** is in a class by itself: a 500-year-old half-timbered farmhouse in a setting complete with pond, ducks, and swans. There is outdoor dining in good weather. The large menu includes homemade *Wurst* and *Schinken* (ham), both also sold to go. It is in Dreieich-Götzenhain, between Götzenhain and Neu-Isenburg. Tel: (06102) 32-14. Open every day from 10:00 A.M. to midnight, and warm meals are served from noon to 2:30, and 6:00 to 9:30 P.M. Coffee and cake are served from 3:00 P.M. on. The place tends to be mobbed on Sunday.

**Apfelwein Klaus** is at Meisengasse 10. Everything here is genuine—the long tables, the blackboard menu, and, of course, the Ebbelwei. Open for lunch and dinner.

## Sachsenhausen

Picking an Apfelwein place here is a matter of personal preference and available seats. Some of the most traditional and popular establishments include:

**Zum Eichkatzerl**, at Dreieichstrasse 29; open from 3:00 P.M. to midnight, closed Wednesday.

**Zum Fichtekränzi**, at Wallstrasse 5; open 5:00 P.M. to midnight, closed Sunday and holidays.

**Zum Gemalten Haus**, at Schweizer Strasse 67; open 10:00 A.M. to midnight, closed Monday and Tuesday, and mid-June to the end of July.

**Germania**, at Textorstrasse 20; open from 10:30 A.M. to 12:30 A.M.

**Kanonesteppel**, next door at Textorstrasse 16; open week-days from 4:00 and weekends from 11:00 A.M.

**Adolf Wagner**, at Schweizer Strasse 71; open 11:00 A.M. to midnight.

All of the above are *Gartenlokale;* that is, they move their tables out under the trees in nice weather.

### Cafés

Germany's rich cakes and strong coffee are served not as desserts but as late-afternoon fare at 4:00 P.M. The Frankfurt specialties are **Frankfurter Kranz**, a ring-shaped cream cake with vanilla flavoring, and **Bethmännchen**, almond and marzipan cookies named after the Bethmann banking family. A good place to sample them and other Konditorei goodies is **Altes Café Schneider**, Kaiserstrasse 12 (near the Frankfurter Hof), closed Sunday in summer; and **Café Schwille**, on the Fressgass', Grosse Bockenheimer Strasse 50. The **Café Boulevard le Opera**, in the Mövenpick restaurant complex on Opernplatz, facing the Alte Oper, has even richer, Swiss-style cakes.

## SHOPS AND SHOPPING

### Hauptbahnhof-Kaiserstrasse

**Etienne Aigner**, Kaiserstrasse 9, stocks fashions and leather goods by the Munich-based designers. **Behagel**, Kaiserstrasse 3, is a long-established shop for porcelain, including Meissen, and crystal. **Friedrich**, Kaiserstrasse 17, sells antique and modern jewelry and silver, including their own award-winning designs. **Gerson**, Düsseldorfer Strasse 1–7 (near the Hauptbahnhof), is a large and leading fur retailer. **Gold-Pfeil**, Kaiserstrasse 22, carries its own leather goods, made in nearby Offenbach. **J. A. Henckels Zwillingswerke**, Kaiserstrasse 20 and Rossmarkt 11, sells scissors and knives made of Solingen steel. **John Montag**, Kaiserstrasse 41, deals in porcelain, and has a permanent Meissen exhibition. **Rosenthal Studio**, Friedenstrasse 10 (near Hotel Frankfurter Hof), stocks everything Rosenthal, including avant-garde china patterns.

## Goethestrasse

**Annabel of Königstein**, number 9, carries a wide selection of Armani and Ungaro fashions. **Bogner Sportmoden**, number 21, sells fashions and sportswear by the skiing family. **Christofle-Pavillon**, number 29, stocks French silverware and gold and silver jewelry. **Escada**, number 13, is an outlet for another famous Munich fashion name. **MCM—Modern Creation Munich**, number 26–28, is a large store with a wide selection of mostly men's, and some women's, clothing. **Spangenberg**, number 29, sells furs, many custom made. **Vonderbank**, number 11, one of Frankfurt's oldest art galleries, deals in paintings, prints, and graphics.

## The Hauptwache

**Frankfurter Kunstkabinett**, Börsenplatz 13–15, is a traditional leading art gallery. **Lorey**, with entrances at Schillerstrasse 16 and Grosse Eschenheimer Strasse 11, is a small, upscale department store that stocks porcelain, glass, handicrafts, and other luxury goods. **Prange**, at Hauptwache 1, carries Bally and other well-known shoe brands. **Wempe**, at Hauptwache 7, sells watches and clocks by the Hamburg concern, plus top international brands.

## Near the Dom/Römer

**Wilhelm Dobritz**, Braubachstrasse 10–12, deals in 17th- to 19th-century paintings, antique furniture, silver, porcelain, and pewter. **Joseph Fach**, Fahrgasse 8, sells antiques. **Pia Forner, Kunst um 1900**, Fahrgasse 1, carries turn-of-the-century artworks. **Maison Phoenicienne**, Fahrgasse 87, specializes in ancient Roman archaeological finds. **Galerie Prestel**, Braubachstrasse 30 (opens at 11:00 A.M.), is a prestigious art gallery. **Thomas Poller**, Kirchnerstrasse 1–3, sells antiques. **Stor**, Fahrgasse 9, sells antique dolls and toys.

## Flea Market

The Saturday-morning flea market, with 700 vendors and 150 stands for children, is located on the south bank of the Main river, along the museum embankment. The **Flohmarkt** is not noted for gems; it deals in used household goods and bric-a-brac. It is open from 9:00 A.M. until 2:00 P.M.

# THE RHINE REGION AROUND FRANKFURT

*By James A. Clark*

*James Clark, who has contributed to* The New York Times, *teaches at a university in Heidelberg.*

The Rhine region south and immediately west of Frankfurt delights in Germany's warmest and driest climate. Thomas Mann, speaking as confidence man Felix Krull, says: "The Rhine valley brought me forth—that region favored of heaven, mild and without ruggedness either in its climate or in the nature of its soil, abounding in cities and villages peopled by a blithe and laughter-loving folk—truly of all the regions of the earth it must be one of the sweetest." In this case, Felix Krull is trustworthy. The Rhine valley from Koblenz south to Alsace, with its almond, cherry, fig, and other fruit trees and its sheltered sunny slopes covered as far as the eye can see with vineyards, has often been described as a sort of northern annex to Italy—as in fact it was under the Romans. Though wine grapes were indigenous here, it was the Romans who taught the Rhinelanders how to make the best of their grapes, skills later encouraged by Charlemagne, who spread viticulture as assiduously as he did Christianity. This part of the Rhineland not only turns out fine wines, but has been fundamentally formed by the culture of wine: its economy, traditions, festivals, and innate magic. That very Mediterranean deity, Dionysus, holds sway over the northern gods as far down the Rhine as Boppard, near Koblenz and the mouth of the Mosel.

To the beneficent climate and the congenial customs of this middle Rhine landscape add its varied, pervasive beauty, and you have a guaranteed formula for attracting vacationers. The charms of the area are diverse. If the stately progression of the Rhine from Wiesbaden west to Rüdesheim is too slow for you, head south of Frankfurt to the Odenwald, where every bend in the road—and roads here consist mostly of bends—brings a surprise: a hidden valley, an unsuspected village, a gallows in ambush on a windswept hilltop, a Renaissance palace in a little market town. The steep wooded banks of the Neckar, itself a wine-producing area, with its Medieval castles brooding unassailably over the silent river, are only an hour away from the Weinstrasse's hearty, convivial welcome: There is a festival practically every day somewhere here on the west bank of the Rhine south of Mainz, between Grünstadt and Schweigen on the French border.

Fortunately for the millions of visitors attracted by all this atmosphere, cultural wealth, and fine wine, the well-known German efficiency and industry are also steadfast in the area. Its hotels and restaurants are impeccably managed; trains, buses, and trams run everywhere and on time; the roads are superb (and so are the maps, luckily, because German road signs tend to be useful principally to natives). Despite some lapses, on the whole this region's historical riches and romantic associations have been preserved and made accessible rather than immoderately exploited. The region is superb for walking, which brings blessings denied those who rely on wheels. The Rheingau and the Weinstrasse (Wine Route) have instructive, well-marked trails of all lengths through their famous vineyards; in the Odenwald and around Heidelberg you are never more than a few moment's walk away from a solitude enriched by traces of the past and drenched in the natural beauty of the land.

This chapter, setting out westward from Frankfurt, begins with visits to ancient Mainz and the spa city of Wiesbaden before following the Rhine downstream (west and north) from Frankfurt through the Rheingau and the valley of the Lorelei. We then move south of Frankfurt, upstream, to Darmstadt, and from there plunge south into the Odenwald, traversing it to see a selection of its historic towns.

Farther south, we pick up the river Neckar at Bad

Wimpfen and follow the river north and west to Heidelberg, with excursions to the cathedral cities of Speyer and Worms on the Rhine. Finally, west of the Rhine, we trace the Deutsche Weinstrasse (German Wine Route) south through the Pfalz (Palatinate), from Grünstadt down to Schweigen on the French border.

MAJOR INTEREST

**Mainz**
Cathedral
Gutenberg Museum
Altstadt

**Wiesbaden**
Thermal springs
Altstadt
Bath district (casino, parks)
Shopping, theater, cultural events

**The Rheingau**
Landscape (vineyards, Rhine)
Strausswirtschaften (vineyard taverns)
Historic towns
Eberbach Monastery
Johannisberg (Spätlese wine)
Brömserburg wine museum

**Valley of the Lorelei**
Bingen (Burg Klopp)
Rhine castles (Mäuseturm, Rheinstein, Reichenstein)
Lorch (picturesque village)
Bacharach (old-city houses)
Oberwesel (Schönburg castle, city walls)
The Lorelei and St. Goar (Rheinfels castle)
Boppard (Roman walls, Altstadt, Rheinallee)

**The Odenwald**
Nibelungenstrasse (legends, landscape)
Half-timbered Medieval villages
Handicrafts (pottery, beekeeping)
Darmstadt (Art Nouveau)
Lorsch (Königshalle)
Michelstadt (Rathaus, Fürstenau castle)
Amorbach (abbey)
Miltenberg (*Fachwerk* houses)

**Castles on the Neckar**
Landscape

Bad Wimpfen
Burg Guttenberg (falconry, museum)
Burg Hornberg (Götz von Berlichingen)
Schloss Zwingenberg
Hirschhorn
Dilsberg (walled village)

**Heidelberg**
Romantic associations
Altstadt
University
Castle
River Neckar (Old Bridge, Philosophers' Walk)

**Speyer and Worms**
Cathedrals
History
Pfälzer wines and food

**The German Wine Route**
Haardt foothills landscape
Wine tasting
Deidesheim's Marktplatz
Rhodt's Weinhöfe
Dörrenbach's Rathaus

# *MAINZ*

The capital city of the state of Rheinland-Pfalz, Mainz is on the left bank of the Rhine, opposite Wiesbaden, across from the mouth of the Main, a convenient 20-minute drive west of Frankfurt's international airport on the A 60. Most of Mainz's points of interest lie in a compact area within or immediately adjacent to the Altstadt (Old City), between the Rhine and the low hills to the west. Although Allied bombing obliterated 80 percent of the city in 1945, the Mainzers have succeeded in preserving many remnants of a history that began with the Romans in 38 B.C., saw the construction of one of Germany's great cathedrals and the invention of the printing press, and culminated with Mainz's emergence as an important modern commercial and cultural center.

Like other Rhineland cities, Mainz has lubricated the passage of the centuries generously with wine; in fact, it has a larger expanse of vineyards (1,111 acres) than any other large German city, enough wine taverns to consume most of its own output, and a citizenry known for its willingness to try. Mainz's reputation for riotous merrymaking is renewed each winter when one of Germany's major TV networks brings the costumes and buffoonery of the city's traditional winter carnival festivities (the Mainzer *Fastnacht*) to viewers across the country.

# The Cathedral

Behind the zany makeup and clownish humor it adopts in February, Mainz has historically had another visage: a stony-featured ecclesiastical power that for a thousand years stared unblinking into the faces of electors and emperors, princes and popes. The strong-willed prince-archbishops of Mainz rarely gave way.

Ceremoniously robed, mitred, and bearing their Episcopal croziers, a procession six centuries long of these imperious and acquisitive prelates glares down at you from the columns and walls within the Mainzer Dom (in the center of the Altstadt), one of the three great imperial cathedrals of the land (with those of Speyer and Worms). The Archbishop of Mainz, as one of the seven electors of the Holy Roman German emperor, held enormous temporal power. He accumulated domains, fortresses, and rights of taxation from the monarchs his vote helped to the throne, thus increasing the worldly riches and might of the archbishopric.

The original seat of the archdiocese was an eighth-century church built over a pre-Christian temple site where the Protestant church of St. John now stands, west of the Dom across the Leichhof square. This edifice, however, was too modest to support such magnificence. So, in about 978, shortly after becoming archbishop of Mainz, Willigis, the emperor's chancellor, began building the present cathedral. Now the chief landmark and focus of the Altstadt, the Dom is an enormous structure whose exterior is best seen from some distance: Though its six towers are impressive, it lacks the soaring spires that make some other cathedrals, such as Cologne's, awe inspiring even viewed from directly below. A thousand years of building, destroying, and rebuilding have given the Dom a somewhat heterogeneous character, but recent restorations have shaded its mixture of Romanesque, Gothic, and Baroque elements a uniform ochre that emphasizes their essential harmony.

The great **bronze doors** through which you enter the Dom (north entrance, facing the Marktplatz), the gift of Willigis himself, are the second oldest in Germany (Aachen's are older). Within, on the left, flanking the steps to the east apse, you will find the earliest grave markers, beginning (to the right) with that of Siegfried III, who died in 1249. A walk down the nave and aisles takes you through 600 years of German funerary art, from the Romanesque period into the 19th century.

Across the Marktplatz from the Dom, a few steps to the north and facing the square, is a row of 18th-century houses. The **Café Korfman** (Markt 11–13) occupies one of these houses, whose ornate and flowery façades are confections as delightful as the café's house specialty, homemade *Apfelstrudel* with ice cream. A table in front of the café makes a good vantage point from which to watch the spectacle of a German market (every Tuesday, Friday, and Saturday) unfold against the backdrop of the venerable Dom.

# The Gutenberg Museum

On the east side of the Marktplatz, the Marktbrunnen, with its colorful saints and cherubs, was erected in 1526 to celebrate Emperor Charles V's victory over the French at Pavia. Beyond this fountain, across the Liebfrauenplatz east of the Dom, you will find a fascinating museum: the World Museum of Printing, better known as the Gutenberg Museum, established in 1900. With the invention of a hand printing press using movable cast type, Johannes Gutenberg, a native Mainzer, opened the floodgates to the sea of information that inundates us today. About Gutenberg himself we know almost nothing, other than that he was rarely out of debt. The numerous portraits adorning the museum are fanciful, as no artist portrayed the legendary inventor in his own lifetime. The museum houses a complete reconstruction of his workshop; judging by the amount of muscle required to work the printing press, Gutenberg must have had shoulders like a football player or else had very burly assistants (he employed as many as 20 craftsmen). The museum's proudest possession is the B 42, one of the few remaining copies of the original Bible Gutenberg printed between 1452 and 1455. Housed in a barred vault among other precious volumes, it is displayed under controlled light and temperature conditions to prevent fading and deterioration of the paper.

Set aside an hour and a half or so to wander through the whole of this well-lit, attractive compendium of printing history. Tours in English can be arranged for groups. The shop in the entrance hall offers a rich choice of mementos and gifts, including facsimile manuscripts, printing devices, and books.

## In the Altstadt and Environs

To the right as you leave the Gutenberg Museum, the Mailandsgasse takes you east toward the Rhine (streets leading down to the river have red signs; streets parallel to the Rhine have blue signs). Just behind the museum you come to the restaurant **Heilig Geist** (Rentengasse 2), a convenient and atmospheric setting for a hearty Mainzer meal under the vaults of a 13th-century hospital. Two blocks north along the Rheinstrasse, past the city's ultramodern convention center, the Rheingoldhalle, you can't miss the adjoining **Hilton International Mainz**. Equipped with minibars, color television, and lavish furniture, this expensive hotel is more than comfortable, it is almost overpowering. For a Rhine view, you should specify quarters in the older of its two sections; a glassed-in walkway above the street leads west, away from the river, to the 1982 addition, containing sauna, fitness center, solarium, and other facilities. The hotel's **Rheingrill** restaurant is a fashionable rendezvous for Mainz's young professionals.

Starting from the Dom, explore the wine bars, shops, and cafés of the Altstadt neighborhoods just south and west of the Dom, clustered on the Augustinerstrasse, the Kirschgarten, and nearby streets. Half-timbered façades and steep slate roofs with ornate gables, elaborate moldings, and colorful trim give the area its architectural flavor, but it is the Mainzer's fondness for a good time that gives the Altstadt its character. You'll find *Weinstuben* everywhere; featuring wide selections of Rheingau and other local wines, they usually do not open until late afternoon. At Rotekopfgasse 3 (immediately behind the Gutenberg Museum), for example, is the Weinstube **Rote Kopf**, whose warm wood paneling, Art Deco lamps, and friendly service attract locals as well as visitors. The **Kartäuser Hof** (Kartäuserstrasse 14, off the Augustinerstrasse a few streets south of the Dom) claims the honor of being Mainz's oldest inn (the first records of it date from 1171); it has a cozy vaulted cellar with many authentic Old German details. Across the street the **Klosterschänke** boasts a terrace shaded by two enormous chestnut trees whose roots are said to reach all the way down to the Rhine. **Mac Boss** (Augustinerstrasse 57) features a rib dish called *Altstadt Knochen* (Old Town bones). Guests here, if they are feeling expansive (as Mainzers often are), may drink their beer out of something called a "guzzle machine."

The nightly festivities reach their crescendo at Carnival time—from New Year's Day to Ash Wednesday—when Mainzers greet one another with an exuberant "*Helau!*" and mock ceremonies lampooning German pomp and bureaucratic ritual, and parades, masked balls, and street parties are the order of the day. Mainz welcomes summer around June 24 with the three-day festival of Saint John, Gutenberg's name day. Highlights are the hilarious reenactments (on Gutenbergplatz, west of the Dom) of Medieval initiations undergone by printers' apprentices and the jousting matches between boats on the Rhine. In late August and early September, the Mainzer *Weinmarkt* marks harvest time with the appropriate consumption of wine on a grand scale and a fireworks display over the river.

Above the merrymaking in the Altstadt is **St. Stephen's church** (from Gutenbergplatz, follow the Ludwigstrasse west to the Schillerplatz, then take Gaustrasse southwest one street to the Olgasse, which leads directly up to the church). Behind its plain exterior St. Stephen's shelters a set of remarkable stained-glass windows on Old Testament themes by Marc Chagall, executed between 1976 and 1979. One hundred thousand visitors annually lose themselves in the meditation-inducing blue of Chagall's windows, but many overlook the magnificent Late Gothic **cloister** adjoining the south wall of the church, considered the finest of its kind in the Rheinland-Pfalz.

Not far from the church (two blocks east down the Stefansbergstrasse and then left into the Ballplatz) is the moderately expensive **Drei Lilien**, the best-known French restaurant in a city not distinguished by *haute cuisine*. Chef Hans-Joachim Stuhlmiller's creative use of fresh local ingredients draws a mix of business and academic folk as well as out-of-towners.

Southwest of the Altstadt, a few streets beyond St. Stephen's, the heights on which the Romans once built their fortifications are crowned with strips of parkland where a stroll offers a panorama of the city and the Rhine. In the southern section of this park, directly above the Weisenauerstrasse on the Rhineside (about a mile south of the Dom, with a convenient streetcar line a block away) is the **Favorite Parkhotel**. It offers modern accommodations in exceptionally pleasant surroundings, with views of the river or the park in which the hotel lies. In good weather, the large sun terrace is particularly attractive, and the hotel has all the facilities one expects in its higher-price range.

The more moderately priced **Central Hotel Eden** is one of several in its category in the immediate vicinity of the main railway station. Rooms are spacious and quiet, service is good, and the hotel's air-conditioned restaurant enjoys a solid reputation among business travellers.

# *WIESBADEN*

A city of elegance and charm, Wiesbaden, west of Frankfurt right across the Rhine from Mainz, invites you to indulge your senses: to bathe in a splendid Art Nouveau setting; to taste Rheingau food and wines at their best; to enjoy music or theater in Baroque palaces; to savor a little risk at the casino or a little self-indulgence in the fashionable shops. Though it's easy to spend money here, some of Wiesbaden's most characteristic pleasures are free, such as strolling in the many parks or exploring the city's fanciful and extravagant architecture.

People have been using the hot springs here since 3000 B.C. Those indefatigable bathers, the Romans, built their baths where today the **Kochbrunnen** fountain steams to the surface in the Kranzplatz. The Romans called the baths *Aquae Mattiacorum,* "the waters of the Mattiaci" (the local Germanic tribe); in these waters many a pensioned legionnaire bathed, attempting to soothe the soreness acquired in long night watches here at this outpost of the empire's forward boundary. Some four hundred years after the Romans decamped (A.D. 400), Charlemagne's biographer Einhard was the first to record, as Wisibada, the city's present name, meaning "baths in the meadows."

The baths remained Wiesbaden's focus and source of prosperity as it attained the title of imperial city (1215). The last of the great Hohenstaufen emperors, Frederick II, attended Mass here in 1236: He had just issued the imperial decree at the Diet of Mainz by which he hoped to establish lasting peace; instead, this proclamation marked the beginning of the end of the Holy Roman Empire. Barely six years later, the archbishop of Mainz conquered and destroyed the city. When Wiesbaden emerged again it was as the ruling seat of the counts of Nassau, the family whose history was to be Wiesbaden's for the next 600 years.

Wiesbaden's 26 thermal springs produce 528,000 gallons

of hot water daily. Rainwater seeping into mountain fissures heats up in the volcanic depths and bubbles out under pressure at 150 degrees Fahrenheit. The Kochbrunnen alone supplies 132,000 gallons daily to curative baths in nearby hotels and in the Aukamm district, site of the largest clinics. Wiesbadeners often pause for a sip of these bitter waters that flow from the spigots under the cupola near the fountain. The second largest spring, the Adlerquelle, rises in the **Kaiser-Friedrich-Bad**, a public bath and sanatorium a block south of the Kochbrunnen. When suitably cooled, the Adlerquelle's steaming waters not only supply the baths in this turn-of-the-century palace of the cure but also heat its interior—which is worth a visit. Vibrant Art Nouveau frescoes, decorative windows, and a massive carved oaken staircase hint at luxuries to come. A sauna, steam bath, or swim in the opulent majolica-tiled bath is a memorable experience.

The **Römertor**, just south of the Kaiser-Friedrich-Bad, is a 19th-century notion of what a Roman gate should have looked like. It bridges a gap in the **Heidenmauer**, a genuine Roman fortified wall from the time of Valentinian.

## The Altstadt

In the narrow lanes of the Altstadt below the Römertor you can browse among antiques stores and secondhand shops in the quarter called **Schiffchen** ("shuttle," as in loom), washing down the dust with a glass of cold Riesling in one of the taverns you'll find here. The crooked streets, whose names evoke the district's Medieval past (Gold lane, Ditch street, Weaver lane) converge on the **Marktplatz**, the focal point of the Altstadt. On Wednesdays and Saturdays the Marktplatz becomes a cheerful jumble of vendors' stands where you can haggle over homemade sausages, fresh fruit, vegetables, and flowers.

Since 1946, Wiesbaden has been capital of the state of Hesse, and the Hessian Landtag, or Parliament, meets in the Neoclassical palace bordering the Markplatz to the northwest. The Schloss was built for Duke Wilhelm of Nassau in 1842, though he didn't live to occupy it; it sits where the castle of his ancestors probably stood in the 17th century, surrounded by fortifications of which no trace remains. Just a stone's throw across from the Schloss stands the one visible relic of that time, the **Altes Rathaus** (Old Town Hall), but restorations have left only the bare outlines of its former Renaissance glory.

The Gothic Revival **Marktkirche** (Market Church) dominates the square, and its five sandstone steeples (the tallest is 290 feet) distinguish Wiesbaden's skyline. Carl Boos succeeded in 1862 in imparting an improbable lightness to this red-brick basilica, whose lofty lines draw the eye upward. Don't miss the weekend organ concerts played on the church's two organs.

## The Bath District

When the house of Nassau gained ascendancy in 1750, the city prospered, but despite half a century of recovery and growth, the Altstadt's grim history of war, plague, fire, and famine remained. In 1820 Christian Zais, the duke of Nassau's construction chief, set out to remake Wiesbaden. He cordoned off the Altstadt's bad memories in a pentangle of five broad boulevards. Then, to the east, he made a fresh start, envisioning a resort for the wealthy and titled elite who might wish "to enjoy and experience a heightened Life and a better Existence, and not to be introduced to common Scenes." When he completed his first *Kurhaus,* in 1810—far from any actual thermal springs—Wiesbaden's glory days began. When Goethe first took the cure in 1814, the city had about 4,000 inhabitants; less than a century later there were more than 100,000, of whom more than 200 were millionaires, more than in any other German city.

The present-day **Kurviertel** (bath district), including the Kurpark, spreads out like a fan. Seen from the top of the Wilhelmstrasse, a vast expanse of lawn bordered with alleys of plane trees and flanked by two Neoclassical colonnades stretches away to the ponderous standstone front of the present **Kurhaus**, which has engulfed Zais's original structure. The gaming room incorporates a reconstruction of the old *Kursaal;* even if you don't try your luck at roulette or blackjack, you can enjoy a concert or a meal here. You may also eat elegantly and well at the **Belle Epoque**, attached to the **casino** (no need to patronize the gaming tables to reach the dining tables), or in the more casual, less expensive **Bistro**, accessible without entering the casino. Wilhelm exemplified Hohenzollern aesthetics in his praise of the Kurhaus as "the most beautiful in the world"; but echoes of the old Hohenzollern puritanism could be heard in his objections to some of the Art Nouveau frescoes. In fact, there was no gambling in the present Kurhaus when Kaiser Wilhelm II inaugurated it in 1907, for the Prussians had long since forbidden games of chance.

Another of the kaiser's enthusiasms was the Hessian State

Theater, south of the Kurhaus: a private entrance for his coach allowed him to be driven through the cellars directly to his box. An opera, ballet, or play should be part of any visit to Wiesbaden. Especially during the May Festival (book well in advance), artists of international repute appear in the Stadtstheater's splendidly Baroque **Grosses Haus**.

North of the Kurhaus, across the Sonnenbergerstrasse, you can take a winding path up to the **Schöne Aussicht** (Beautiful View) district, from which the city's finest villas look out over the Kurpark. In the past century and a half, Wiesbaden's growing wealth has manifested itself here in a profusion of showpieces, each house outdoing the next in grandeur. Somehow the mélange of striking details from the Baroque, Neoclassical, Gothic Revival, Renaissance, and turn-of-the-century Jugendstil styles manages to form a harmonious whole. Zais, whose inspiration this Villa Quarter was, would have been pleased.

## Staying, Dining, and Shopping in Wiesbaden

Wiesbaden's senior hostelry, the **Schwarzer Bock** (Kranzplatz 12), has been looking out on the Kochbrunnen for 500 years, a tradition reflected in its opulent furnishings. The place has a rich history, abounding with such tales as that of Dostoevski, who managed to stay away from the roulette wheel long enough (26 days) to write *The Gambler*—and to pay his hotel bill. The rooms are spacious and luxurious: Try for one on the courtyard with a tanning terrace. The Bock's restaurant, **Elizabeth**, very successfully mixes traditional German fare with nouvelle cuisine; the setting is a superb room paneled and ceilinged in oak and walnut with 16th-century carvings.

Back to back with the Bock, at Kaiser-Friedrich-Platz 3–4, is the recently modernized **Nassauer Hof**, a luxury hotel with rooftop thermal pool and sun terrace; many of its rooms have fine views down the Kurpark. It also has the distinction of housing two prime eating places: the **Orangerie**, a sunny pavilion looking out on the square and featuring homey dishes served with urbane grace; and **Die Ente vom Lehel**, whose guiding spirit, Hans-Peter Wodarz, has been called Germany's answer to Paul Bocuse. At Die Ente (The Duck), if you get a table, you can marvel at the spectacular presentations for which Wodarz is famous—at corresponding prices. Try his breast of quail in goose-liver gravy, or a filet steak garnished with horseradish-ginger sauce. Tel: (6121) 13-36-66.

A hotel on the far side of the Kranzplatz, **Am Kochbrunnen** has an attractive location, friendly service, and comfortable (if assertively wallpapered) rooms around a sunny court. Under the same management, **Am Landeshaus** (Moritzstrasse 51), two blocks from the main railway station, is newer than its counterpart but has the same cheerful atmosphere and moderate prices. Another popular, moderately priced hotel is the **Klee am Park**, with a bar, café, and restaurant in a quiet setting on the Kurpark. It has 60 comfortable rooms with their own balconies.

As its name implies, the **Restaurant de France** (Taunusstrasse 49) is a temple of nouvelle cuisine, and its quiet but elegant decor and unobtrusive service encourage concentration on such dishes as pickled saddle of venison with candied red cabbage or giant shrimp in leek and onion butter served with cherry tomatoes. The wine cellar boasts more than 300 labels.

Roam the **Taunusstrasse**, bordering the Kranzplatz to the northwest, for fine antiques, then head down the Wilhelmstrasse, which starts at the southern end of the Taunusstrasse, for a series of ultrachic shops stretching south for a flag-draped mile. (The shops are on the west side only; on the east is the Warmer Damm park with its exotic trees and cooling fountains.) Known as **The Rue** to Wiesbadeners, and commemorating Duke Wilhelm of Nassau, the Wilhelmstrasse is where you'll find purveyors of furnishings, fashions, jewelry, and art, as well as glassed-in shopping arcades screened by hanging plants. Take time to think carefully about an expensive purchase at **Café Blum** (Wilhelmstrasse 44), which has a century's experience in making Wiesbaden's favorite confection, *Nusstörtchen,* a tart with walnut-cream filling.

## Outside the City

For more than a century the princes and dukes of Nassau resided not in Wiesbaden but on the Rhine just to the south, in the majestic Baroque palace in **Bieberich**. Napoleon came here in 1804 to persuade Prince Friedrich August to join his Rhine Alliance, a pact that in 1806 formally killed off the long-moribund Holy Roman Empire. Napoleon rewarded Friedrich with a dukedom, and it was as the duke of Nassau's guest that Goethe, in 1815, heard the news of Napoleon's defeat at Waterloo. A tour of the Schloss ends in the *Festsaal,* with its beautiful inlaid parquetry, marble columns, and frescoed cupola depicting the Olympian deities, where Goethe and the duke were dining when the news came.

Approached from Wiesbaden along the Biebricherallee, which is lined with chestnuts and silver beeches, the Schloss lies at the southern end of a mile-long park in which the International Horse Show is one of the spring's splendid social events.

The best view of Wiesbaden is from the observation platform built atop the iron lampposts that once illuminated Wilhelmstrasse. The platform is atop the **Neroberg**; you can get there most scenically on the Victorian cable car. Counterweighted with 1,850 gallons of water, it trundles from the top of the Taunusstrasse to the peak (altitude 800 feet). The car takes you over the vineyards that furnish Wiesbaden's prized (and pricey) Neroberger, a light, fragrant Riesling.

Five minutes from the observation platform (directional signs mark the path) is the small, delicately domed **Russian Orthodox chapel** (called the Greek Church) that has become a symbol of Wiesbaden. It is the burial place of the last duke of Nassau's first duchess, Elizabeth Michalovna, niece of the czar and a Russian princess. Beneath impressive frescoes by Hopfgartner and Jacobi, the sculptured likeness of the 18-year-old, who died in childbirth, lies atop her tomb.

From the Neroberg you can see another high point rising on the west of Wiesbaden: **Schloss Frauenstein**, about a 30-minute drive westward. From the south end of the Wilhelmstrasse, take the Rheinstrasse west to the Ringkirche and continue west on the Dotzheimerstrasse, following the signs for Frauenstein. Entering Frauenstein village, take the first left (sign for Nürnberger Hof). A short walk north of the parking area at the road's end brings you to a curious rough stone obelisk commemorating Goethe's 1814–1815 visit. Should you come in May, the surrounding hillsides will be a white blanket of cherry blossoms, and at any season the views of the Rhine and the vineyards falling away toward it are rewarding. A one-lane farm road descends through the Herrnberg vineyards from the Nürnberger Hof to the village of Frauenstein below.

Here the knights of "Frowensteyn" built their Burg (fortified citadel) in the 13th century. A railed walk leads up its ruined ramparts to an overall view of the town. In its protective shadow stand a number of handsome half-timbered houses. The one directly across from the early 16th-century church may be as old as the Burg itself, but Frauenstein's oldest citizen is the gnarled linden tree in the churchyard, estimated to be 700 to 1,000 years old.

The place to eat in Frauenstein is the **Weinhaus Sims**, where game, meat, and vegetables are fresh from the area, and the wine is exclusively the local vintage. Try the Grorother Spätburgunder red wine if you can persuade Herr Sims to part with some from his special stock. It is lighter and less sweet than its French counterpart, Burgundy; Frauenstein shares with Assmannshausen (see below) the distinction of being the sole growers of this wine in the Rheingau.

## THE RHEINGAU

In the same latitude as Winnipeg and northern Mongolia, the world-renowned Rheingau wine district ought to be too far north for wine growing. Yet nowhere in Germany is the climate milder than along this 45-km (27-mile) jog to the west (at Mainz and Wiesbaden) in the Rhine's generally northward course. The wind-sheltered southern slopes of the Taunus range, on the river's right—in this case, northern—bank, get plenty of sunshine and comparatively little rain. The Romans recognized these conditions, together with the fertile soil, as ideal for vineyards; the Roman influence on Rheingau wine is commemorated still in the distinctive glass, the *Römer*, from which it is traditionally drunk.

For centuries monks and peasants cleared and terraced the ground and planted the vineyards. Today one Rheingauer out of three lives, directly or indirectly, from the wine trade. The Rheingau wine grapes, not as sweet as most, produce a delicately fruity wine, full in aroma and capable of aging superbly. Eighty percent of this wine comes from the Riesling grape, and Rheingau Rieslings are considered to be among the best white wines made anywhere.

The area has more than wine, though. It contains so much of historic and scenic interest that you should plan at least two days here or more if possible. Like its Rieslings, the Rheingau should be sipped, not gulped. Its essence is in its deliberate tempo: the quiet flow of the river, the slowly ripening grapes, the vintner's patient watch over his maturing wine, the centuries of weathering that have given the monasteries and castles their fabled *Romantik.*

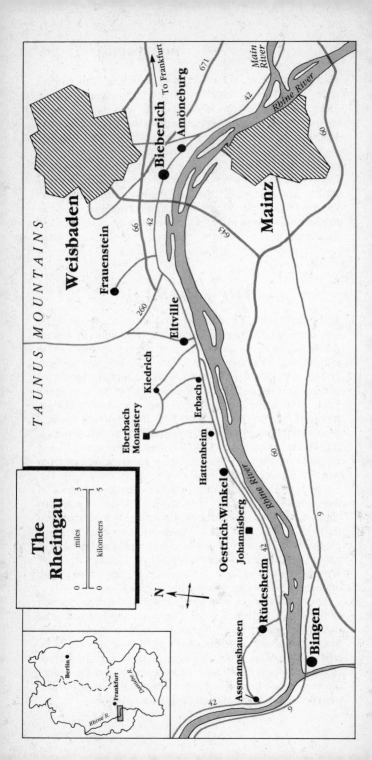

# The Rheingau

miles 3
0
kilometers 5
0

N

TAUNUS MOUNTAINS

Weisbaden

Frauenstein

Eberbach Monastery

Kiedrich

Erbach

Eltville

Hattenheim

Oestrich-Winkel

Johannisberg

Rüdesheim

Assmannshausen

Bingen

Bieberich

Amöneburg

To Frankfurt

Mainz

Main River

Rhine River

Rhine River

Rhine River

671

42

60

643

66

42

260

60

9

42

9

Berlin

Frankfurt

Rhine R.

Danube R.

# Eltville

Of Eltville, the Rheingau's unofficial capital, right outside Wiesbaden to the west, on the Rhine's right bank, Goethe wrote: "Everyone has a peaceful, by no means hurried, appearance." Thomas Mann chose Eltville as an appropriate birthplace for Felix Krull, his charming swindler, and says of it: "Everywhere nature smiled." All this relaxed good humor may stem, in part, from the tranquillity of the town's historic center, directly on the river. Here, undisturbed by the highways and rail tracks that crowd the Rhine's banks farther downstream, you can stroll under the plane trees along what was once a tow path as the barges chug by. The sun terrace of the **Café zur Rheinhalle** is a good place from which to watch the gulls circle the turreted tower of Eltville's landmark, its 14th-century **castle**.

For a century and a half following the tower's completion in 1348, successive archbishops of Mainz cast an acquisitive eye from its windows on the free imperial city of Mainz across the Rhine. Finally, in 1462, Archbishop Adolph II of Nassau conquered the prize, but the ensuing street fighting drove many of the Mainzer patricians from the city. One of those displaced was Johannes Gutenberg. Generous in victory, the mighty archbishop took the aging and impoverished inventor into Eltville castle and later made him a noble of his court, with an annual pension of one ton of grain and 2,000 liters of wine. Gutenberg in turn brought Eltville the distinction of being one of the earliest centers of printing; here he and his relatives set up a small press beside the castle. In the Gutenberg room in the castle you can see pages from a dictionary printed on this press.

The **Bechtermünzer Hof**, site of the press, is one of several imposing noble-family residences near the castle. Here, as in the neighboring complex of the Baron Langwerth von Zimmern (just behind the castle, in the Kirchgasse), you can visit the wine cellars for a tasting. If you prefer, like the Eltvillers, to savor their Sonnenberger Riesling on the banks of the Rhine, go to the **Gelbes Haus**, on the Burgplatz, where you also get a substantial meal in the garden terrace with a river view. For help in arranging wine tastings go to the *Verkehrsamt* (Tourist Office), Schmittstrasse 2.

In the Rosengasse, among a section of pretty half-timbered houses, the 14th- to 15th-century **Pfarrkirche** harbors a wonderfully expressive Gothic fresco of the Last Judgment and a pensive Madonna, the *Madonna of the Half Moon,* the work of a 16th-century master.

The **Sonnenberg**, a small, comfortable hotel, occupies a quiet corner at the foot of the Sonnenberg vineyards at Friedrichstrasse 65.

# Kiedrich

Three kilometers (2 miles) northwest of Eltville, Kiedrich nests in the shadow of the ruined **fortress of Scharfenstein**, once a stronghold of the archbishops of Mainz. Kiedrichers are hill folk, less open and friendly than their Rhineside neighbors, with a name for shrewd bargaining and tight-fistedness. They keep their showpiece Gothic church, **St. Valentine's**, locked tight when there is no service. If you come on Sunday, however, you'll hear, inside this little treasure box of carved wood furnishings and tracery windows, two matchless sounds: the authentic 15th-century notes of Germany's oldest playable organ, and Gregorian plainsong rendered by the Kiedrich men's choir in the Gothic-Germanic idiom now heard only here. For both of these Medieval treats, and for much else that he restored and preserved in the village, Kiedrich has to thank an Englishman, Baron John Sutton; he adopted the village in the mid-19th century, and the street that leads to its famed Gothic square and St. Valentine's is named for him. In German, the first syllable of Valentine sounds like "fall"; for centuries the church was the goal of pilgrims wishing to cure the "falling sickness," epilepsy. The artistic riches of the church, which Sutton rescued after years of neglect (the chapel of St. Michael was about to be demolished and its stones used to pave the road to Eltville), stem from the gifts of the grateful healed.

To try Kiedrich's celebrated wines, seek out a *Strausswirtschaft*—a wine tavern run by proprietors of small vineyards on their own premises. There are several Strausswirtschaften in the area, but they are open only seasonally. This institution dates back to Charlemagne, who ordered the *Strauss* (bouquet) of fir boughs to be hung out as a sign of hospitality. To protect the trade, no vintner could hang out his Strauss for more than four months a year, and each was restricted to serving his home-grown wine only. In these family-run, informal establishments there is nearly always someone among the regular local customers who speaks enough English to advise you about wine, a subject that melts the reserve even of the shyest Kiedricher. The proper accompaniment to the wines you will be offered are home-made delicacies such as *Handkäse mit Musik* (strong farmer's cheese with raw onion), *Spundekäs* (a soft cheese mixture), or *Hausmacher Wurst* (home-cured sausage). Strausswirtschaften are found everywhere in the Rheingau, but do not open before 5:00 P.M. Charlemagne's taste for wine was equaled by his distaste for drunkenness, and he forbade any drinking before the sounding of the wine bell at day's end or the end of Mass on Sunday.

Larger wine estates may qualify as *Gutsausschänken* (wine restaurants), operating all year and offering a wider range of food, often in a centuries-old private residence the likes of which you couldn't otherwise see. In Kiedrich, the historic **Klostermühle** (Eltvillerstrasse 2) seems an appropriate venue to sample Kiedrich's Klosterberg Riesling wines. *Klostermühle* means "monastery mill," and the homemade appetizers set out on a millwheel table include a potent Handkäse called *Klosterduft,* "a whiff of the cloister."

# Eberbach Monastery

Across the valley a few kilometers west of Kiedrich, the monastery of Eberbach was built up between the 12th and 14th centuries by Cistercian reformers, who were not only religious purists but also industrious wine makers. Following their ascetic rule *"Ora et Labora"* (pray and work), they worked so hard that the monastery, at its peak, possessed Europe's largest vineyards and its own fleet to take the wine down to Cologne for sale. Eberbach's wealth and power ultimately led to slackness, corruption, and internal dissent, and the declining monastery was practically wiped out in the Thirty Years War. Following secularization in 1803, Eberbach passed to the dukes of Nassau; they seized choice bits to ornament their palace grounds in Bieberich and converted the dormitorium into an asylum. Since 1945 the Hessian State Wine Authority has administered Eberbach and its vineyards (still Germany's most extensive), staging artistic events and wine seminars in the restored splendor of the Medieval buildings, which also provided authentic backgrounds for the film of Umberto Eco's book *The Name of the Rose.*

The mighty Romanesque basilica, a monument of cold serenity, becomes a magnificent setting for the festivities when Rheingau vintners celebrate their Thanksgiving—on the first Sunday in December. In the apse of the church, the tombs of two Nassau archbishops are adorned by a remarkable *Resurrection,* a masterpiece of the late 14th century. The vaulted ceiling of the adjacent chapter hall is of the same era. Beneath the dormitorium, whose echoing length is matched by few Gothic halls, is the cabinet cellar; here you can taste the product of eight centuries of refinement: Eberbach's pride, the Steinberger Cabinet Riesling. (For information on a week-long, English-language wine seminar, including room and festive dinners in the monastery, write the German Wine Academy, Reisebüro Bartholomae, Wilhelmstrasse 8, D-6200 Wiesbaden.)

# Oestrich-Winkel

Between Eltville and Oestrich-Winkel farther west along the river, the Rhine highway passes through Erbach and Hattenheim, two pretty and prosperous wine centers. **Erbach** has the famous Marcobrunner vineyard, of whose robust, full-bodied wine Prussian novelist Theodore Fontane wrote: "It's wonderful how many buffets the heart can endure if you can fend them off with a bottle of Marcobrunner." **Pan zu Erbach** is a small but elegant outpost of haute cuisine concealed in Erbach's outskirts (Eberbacherstrasse 44): For starters, have a glass of Riesling Sekt (a sparkling wine) from the restaurant's own vineyard.

As you approach Oestrich, you'll see on the Rhine side of the road a curious squat tower with a conical roof, topped by a crane that projects over the river. For centuries, starting in the early 1500s, the **Oestricher Kran** has hoisted casks of Rheingau wine into moored barges. The crane machinery was operated by an ingenious wooden treadmill. The present structure was built in 1745. Another Oestrich landmark, the **Schwan** (5–7 Rheinallee), is the best place to stay here, and its riverside terrace is the best place to watch the Rhine flow past the Kran or arrange to take a cruise in one of the excursion boats that dock here. You can taste the hotel's own vintages by candlelight in its wine cellar; taste moderately, however, before mounting the winding 17th-century wooden stairway (only one flight) to your room. Just behind the Schwan's homey Renaissance horizontals rise the severe Gothic verticals of **St. Martin's church**. This handsome but heavily restored church contains several interesting works, including a Late Gothic Holy Sepulcher in which three virgins in low relief seem to look askance at three drunken knaves in Medieval armor.

Oestrich's twin is **Winkel**, and the two towns, with Mittelheim in the middle (naturally), form a single community "so long-drawn-out as to make those driving through impatient," Goethe commented. The 65-year-old poet had first been lured to the Rheingau by young Bettina von

Brentano's seductive letters describing it. In the **Brentano house** (89 Hauptstrasse), Goethe's study is preserved as it was when he visited in 1814–1815. Other visitors—Beethoven, the brothers Grimm, Bettina's brother Clemens—made Winkel a focus of Rhine Romantik and the associated nationalism that followed Napoleon's defeat and the expulsion of the French from the area. Winkel has a culinary focus, too; the **Graues Haus** (Graugasse 10), the oldest stone-built house in Germany, has since 1981 been the home of one of the Rheingau's best restaurants. The plain ninth-century exterior conceals an equally uncluttered modern interior; from the wine cellar you can select from 400 labels the best accompaniment to such delicacies as calf's head stew with oysters.

## Johannisberg

In about 1100, the Benedictine brothers established the Rheingau's first monastery at Johannisberg, between Winkel and, to the west, Rüdesheim. Unfortunately, these monks met with less success than their Cistercian colleagues at Eberbach. Despite its excellent wines, the monastery, battered by wars and deep in debt, was dissolved in the 16th century. The abbots of Fulda (see the Center chapter) built a Baroque castle over the monastery's cellars in the 18th century, but that was bombed out in 1942, and today's Schloss is a postwar reconstruction. But one of history's happier accidents also happened here. In the fall of 1775, a mounted messenger was sent to bring the abbot of Fulda's permission for the start of the grape harvest; but the messenger was delayed, and by the time the grapes were picked they were overripe and covered with fungus. Then came the historic discovery: Instead of ruining the wine, this *Spätlese* (late harvest) actually improved it by intensifying the sugar content. Highly prized today, Spätlese wines are also high priced, because late picking reduces the wine's volume.

Goethe's best-loved stroll from the Brentano house was into the vineyards below Johannisberg, and the Brentano housekeeper was shocked at the amount of Schloss Johannisberg 1811 he could put away. Heinrich Heine later exclaimed: "*Mon Dieu!* If only I had the faith to move mountains [*Berge*]! The Johannisberg would be the *Berg* I'd summon, wherever I was!"

The **castle** has been in the possession of the house of Hapsburg ever since the Austrian emperor presented it in 1816 to the wily chancellor Metternich, who retired here to scheme out a new Europe after the Congress of Vienna and who asserted of his feeling for the Rheingau, "The Rhine flows in my veins." Visit the 900-year-old cellars for a taste of the wine that inspired poets and statesmen, and visit the Schloss for its unmatched views.

# Rüdesheim

Like a lot of travellers, the tranquil Rhine loses its composure at Rüdesheim, where it plunges into the turbulent Bingen gorge. Though a canal was blasted out here in 1935, Rhine captains still take a pilot through the gorge, whose once-wild waters prompted many a Medieval merchant to leave his ship at Rüdesheim and go overland to Lorch (or vice versa). As a Rhine harbor, the city embarked on the prosperity that it still enjoys. Now it is tour buses that harbor here; Rüdesheim embodies Rhine Romantik for three million visitors a year, and its hotels and taverns thrive.

Rüdesheim has always been someone's gold mine. In the 13th century the archbishops of Mainz squeezed river tolls out of Rhine ships from a former Frankish castle. Today known as the **Brömserburg**, the castle houses a fascinating museum of wine making. The display of more than 1,500 drinking vessels reminds visitors that wine has also, since Roman times, brought riches to Rüdesheim. Later, the archbishops moved a mile or so downstream for an even tighter grip on the Rhine's gorge from **Ehrenfels castle**. Their toll booth was the **Mäuseturm** (Mouse Tower), a fortification on a rocky islet below Ehrenfels. Legend has it that the cruel and miserly Archbishop Hatto, whose granaries bulged while the peasants were starving, was devoured in the tower by mice from one of his own grain stores. The tale reflects the commoners' view of the extortionate prelates from Mainz—but in fact the word *Mäuseturm* derives from *Maut* (toll). Now the restored tower is a navigational aid and, like the ruins of Ehrenfels, a romantic milestone along the Rhine.

Little remains of three other castles, besides the Brömserburg, that once guarded Rüdesheim, but town houses built by lords still ornament the city's center with their Gothic slate roofs, bay windows, and half-timbering. The best known is the **Brömserhof**, a picture-book example of Late Gothic residential architecture; it now houses a display of automated musical instruments.

If a stroll down the Rheinstrasse reminds you of a seaside boardwalk minus the beach, a turn up the **Drosselgasse** places you firmly back in Romantic Germany; you can't mistake the aromas of sizzling bratwurst and wine and the thumping rhythm of drinking songs coming from the many taverns packed into its 158-yard length. Right in the middle of it all, the **Lindenwirt**, with its vaulted cellars, wine-cask bedrooms, and a talking suit of armor named Kunibert, offers concentrated doses of extroverted Romantik. The **Hotel Felsenkeller** (Oberstrasse 39), a few steps from the action, has comfortable rooms and a pleasant wine tavern in its Medieval cellars. Still quieter, the **Central Hotel** (Kirschstrasse 6), directly opposite St. Jakob's church, is a pleasant family-style hotel with quite a good restaurant.

# Niederwald and Assmannshausen

Atop the grandiose Niederwald monument over Rüdesheim a 32-ton bronze lady called Germania reminds us that Rhine Romantik is tied historically to the German longing for a national identity. The tide of nationalism rose through the 19th century to flood proportions following Germany's victory over France in 1871, and on that tide Bismarck launched the Second Empire. "The Rhine is Germany's river, not its boundary," proclaimed romantic poet E. M. Arndt in 1813; 60 years later, Germania raised the imperial crown above the river, representing an attempt to recapture the glories of the past. The effort was doomed; the near-assassination of Kaiser Wilhelm I at the monument's inauguration was an accurate portent of the Second Empire's eventual fate.

A 20-minute walk through the woods west of the Niederwald monument, the hotel **Jagdschloss Niederwald** brings the German search for an identity down to our own times. In 1948 Konrad Adenauer presided here over the meeting of leaders that produced the *Grundgesetz,* the Federal Republic's equivalent of a constitution. The state of Hesse modernized the hotel, formerly a hunting lodge, in the 1960s, without sacrificing its pleasantly old-fashioned charm. Rooms are large and the setting lovely.

A short, scenic cable-car ride away farther downstream on the Rhine, **Assmannshausen** is a smaller and quieter version of Rüdesheim. You can relish its main attractions simultaneously: a glass of fine Spätburgunder, sipped on the Rhineside terrace of the hotel **Krone Assmannshausen** at the foot of the Hollenberg vineyard from which the wine comes. Although it has been here since 1541, the Krone most vividly evokes the Romantics of the early 19th century. The Freiligrath room commemorates the fiery poet who completed his revolutionary credo, his *Glaubensbekenntnis,* here in 1844; following which he lost his government

pension and had to flee to England. Manuscripts and autographs of other Romantic figures are also on view here, but
the most romantic figure of all, the Rhine, is your compan-
ion in the Krone's spacious dining room, where you dine
in style on the freshest fish and game. For a room in one of
the corner bays with views of the river and the vineyards
above, book well in advance.

## *VALLEY OF THE LORELEI*

Beyond Rüdesheim, the Rhine races through the Binger Loch
(gorge) and resumes its mostly northward course toward the
sea. From Bingen (on the Rhine's left bank opposite Rüdesheim) you follow the river for 60 km (37 miles) north to
Koblenz (for which see the Mosel Valley chapter), through
the valley of the Lorelei, where the swift current has gouged a
sinuous bed between steep terraced and forested cliffs of
slate towering hundreds of feet above you. With its dramatic
scenery, its legends, its wine, its pretty towns graced by
Medieval churches and lofty fortresses, the valley of the Lorelei is still seductively veiled in the mists and clouds of German
Romanticism.

From her perch on the sheerest of these precipices (on
the right bank near St. Goarshausen), the Lorelei, a legendary siren, is supposed to have lured voyagers to their destruction on reefs still visible today. Clemens von Brentano was
the first to associate the rock formation with a dangerously
seductive woman, Lore Lay; in 1827, Heinrich Heine, in his
poem "Die Lorelei," created the story of the siren perched
on high.

For most of its history, the Rhine gorge between Bingen
and Koblenz hindered and frightened more travellers than it
enchanted. The place is also the setting for a body of grimly
fascinating Rhine legends, such as those of the Nibelungen,
the warrior dwarfs who guarded a fabulous treasure—the
Rheingold—in the cliffs of the gorge. Merchants and pilgrims on the Rhine avoided this stretch of the river or, if
necessary, made a white-knuckled, prayerful passage
through its narrows and rapids. Those who escaped the
dwarfs and the reefs still had to cast an apprehensive glance
at the looming Gothic castles, from which parties of armed
toll collectors were all too likely to descend.

With Germany's reconquest of the Rhineland from France
in 1814, a wave of Romantic enthusiasm brought the first
travellers who had come to see the valley of the Lorelei,

rather than merely to survive it. Many of them were English, inspired by the adventures of Byron's gloomy wanderer Childe Harold, whose creator toured the Rhine in 1816— even before the first steamboat braved the river as far up (south) as Koblenz. By the mid-1820s boatloads of diligent English tourists were already careening past the Lorelei, prepared to exchange their sterling for improvised lodgings, leftover wine, and souvenir etchings of dubious quality. Hardship and danger were all part of the romantic thrill of a Rhine cruise in the 19th century.

Though the hardships are fewer nowadays, the valley of the Lorelei still offers most of the scenic charms of the past century. Foremost among them is the dramatic beauty of the Rhine gorge itself, through which the river prowls past rocky cliffs and deep, vineyard-clad side valleys that appear by turns starkly shadowed or blindingly sunny. You can join a boat cruise at any of the riverside towns, and many of these outings feature wine-tasting and sightseeing stops along the way. Historic structures such as churches, city walls, and towers ornament the communities, as do some grim and grand castles. Some of the latter offer accommodations at costs surprisingly low in view of their amenities (saunas, swimming pools, and effectively restored Medieval surroundings—not to mention memorable views). It is possible to see a good sampling of both sides of the Rhine in one very busy day, but two to three days allow you more leisure to attune your hearing to the Lorelei's siren song.

# Bingen

Directly across the Rhine from Rüdesheim (see the Rhein-gau, above), Bingen grew up around a Roman fort guarding the heights between the Rhine and the mouth of the **river Nahe**, which itself drains a well-regarded wine-growing region and flows into the larger river here. Drusus Germanicus, the younger brother of Emperor Tiberius, made his name—literally—by keeping the German tribes down; he may have built the original wooden bridge across the Nahe, around 10 B.C. A thousand years later Archbishop Willigis of Mainz constructed the present **Drususbrücke**, probably the oldest surviving stone bridge in Germany, on the original Roman foundations (crossing the Nahe about 1 km/1½ mile south of the Rhine).

Crowning Bingen's central hill on the site of the Roman fort, **Burg Klopp** houses the city's administrative offices in a handsome stone palace, a 19th-century reconstruction in the gabled Late Gothic style. Parkland and vineyards surround the Burg, which you can reach from the Rhine side by a steep stairway leading up the hill from Bürgermeister-Frans-Neff-Platz, or by car from the east over a bridged moat by way of the Mariahilfstrasse (there is a parking area just outside the moat). From the Burg's pleasantly shady grounds, an airy view across the Rhine of Rüdesheim, Ehrenfels castle, and the Niederwald monument rewards your efforts.

From Burg Klopp, follow the Rochusallee (from the east end of Mariahilfstrasse) 2 km (1.5 miles) east up to the **church of St. Rochus**, perched on vineyard-clothed heights looking out over the Rhine. Pilgrims flocked to the original 17th-century chapel to appeal for St. Rochus's help against the Black Death. Destroyed by German artillery during the French occupation in 1795, the church was hastily reconstructed in 1813, when St. Rochus's intervention was again urgently needed: Napoleon's armies, now in headlong retreat from defeat at Leipzig, had brought typhus to Bingen. Goethe describes the St. Rochus festival of August 1814, following the consecration of the rebuilt church, and its processions, feasting, and much wine. The surrounding Rochusberg park has inviting footpaths.

Back in town, parallel to the Rhine, between it and Burg Klopp, a lively pedestrian zone leads you from the foot of the Burg down Basilikastrasse west to the Nahe to Bingen's stately Gothic **basilica of St. Martin**. (Don't panic when all roads seem to lead back to the water: Remember, two rivers come together here.) An 11th-century crypt, in which some remains of a Roman temple have been found, is the oldest surviving part of the church, which went up in flames along with most of Bingen in the great fire of 1403 and has been rebuilt and restored frequently since then. One work of art survived the fire: an enthroned Madonna and Child from about 1320 (northeast corner of the church, near the crypt), but the finest pieces are the lovely early-15th-century figures of Saint Catherine and Saint Barbara gracing their respective altars to the left and right of the nave.

A few blocks north and east of St. Martin's, you can stroll through Bingen's gracious park along the Rhine, past the docks of the various cruise boats plying the river; you can also cross over to Rüdesheim in a passenger ferry from here. Facing the river (and, unfortunately, the busy railway tracks) is a whole row of hotels on the Rheinkai, across the tracks from the park; the chief virtue of their accommodations and restaurants is the view. Most put out tables on the street in good weather, and conviviality reaches its height here during the first two weekends of September, during the Bingen wine festival.

## Castles on the Rhine

Leaving Bingen by rail or car (highway B 9) toward the west, you cross the Nahe and pass Bingerbrück, an important rail junction. Just off the left bank, the **Mäuseturm** appears on its islet in the Rhine. This was once the toll station of the archbishop of Mainz (see the section on Rüdesheim, above). A chain anchored at the foot of the tower spanned the river to Ehrenfels castle on the right bank, blocking passage until long-suffering Rhine skippers crossed the palms of the archbishop's toll collectors with sufficient silver. A ruin in the 18th century, the Mäuseturm was restored in its present Late Gothic picturebook style by the Prussian king Frederick William IV in 1855, for the more benevolent purpose of aiding navigation.

Directly above the road, 3 km (2 miles) beyond the Mäuseturm, **Burg Rheinstein** clings to its cliff as naturally as if it had been growing there for millennia. In fact, Rheinstein castle in its present form dates back only to the 19th century. In 1825 Prince Frederick Ludwig, a cousin of Frederick William IV, employed Karl Friedrich Schinkel, virtuoso of the Gothic Revival, to rebuild what was then the ruin of Schloss Vogtsburg, as it had been known for 600 years. Dubbing it Rheinstein, the prince turned his 13th-century rubble heap into a romantic fantasy with Gothic battlements and turrets, where the Prussian aristocracy, dressing up in "authentic" costumes, could play at Middle Ages. Leave your transportation at the parking lot and walk up the zigzag path to the castle for the short tour, offered daily in season. It features delicate frescoes by Ludwig Pose and some lovely cast-iron staircases among other period details, with fine views of the Rhine and Assmannshausen from its terraces.

Linked to Burg Rheinstein by legend as well as history, **Burg Reichenstein** is about 1.5 km (1 mile) north on the B 9 (in the village of Trechtingshausen, turn left at a sharp angle off the B 9 at the sign for Burg Reichenstein). Legend has it that the handsome Kuno von Reichenstein loved the lady of Rheinstein (or Vogtsburg, as it was then), but her family had pledged her to marry a rich old knight. Luckily, as the wedding procession set out from Rheinstein, a horsefly stung the bride's mount, and the runaway steed took her straight to the arms of her lover in Burg Reichenstein. History tells the less-romantic tale of Philip von Hohenfels

and his son Dietrich, the robber knights of Burg Reichenstein. They so assiduously "robbed the ladies, imprisoned
the clergy, mistreated their vassals and plundered merchants," according to one complaint, that in 1253 the League
of Rhenish Cities razed the fortress. The indefatigable von
Hohenfels family rebuilt it, and it had to be pulled down
once and for all by King Rudolf of Hapsburg (see the section
on Speyer, below) in 1282. Rudolf put an end to the robber
knights by the simple expedient of beheading them; the
executions took place at the pretty Early Gothic **church of St.
Clemens**, one of the oldest churches on the Rhine, near the
B 9 on the south edge of Trechtingshausen. For centuries
largely a ruin, in 1899 Reichenstein came into the busy
hands of Baron Nikolaus Kirsch-Puricelli, whose family
manufactured cast-iron stoves. He restored the Burg in grandiose Romantic style. You can visit its salons, bedrooms,
library (complete with concealed staircase), business office,
chapel, and battlements, all in one entertaining (if somewhat
chronologically confusing) tour. The Burghotel, just north of
the castle gate, is small and in need of repair; but the
grounds and view are still delightfully unspoiled.

Four kilometers (2.5 miles) north of Trechtingshausen on
the B 9 lies Niederheimbach, west terminal of a car-ferry
service to Lorch on the right bank.

# Lorch

Besides making a pleasant excursion across the winding
Rhine, a side trip to Lorch allows a stroll (plentiful parking in
the riverside park in front of the city gates) through a quiet,
picturesque Rhine village that played an important role in
history. Medieval merchants who dreaded the swift whirl of
current at Bingen could unload the goods they had brought
by ship this far up the Rhine and pack them through the
Taunus hills south to Rüdesheim or Geisenheim in the placid
Rheingau. Lorch grew up on the mouth of the river Wisper,
thriving on the wood and wine trade as well as on the skills of
its weavers. The finest extant example of this prosperity is the
**Hilchen house**, whose noble façade rises above the Rhine in
Renaissance step gables crowned with mussel-shell ornamentation. The city honors its builder, Johann Hilchen, a 16th-
century imperial field marshal, with an annual wine festival
celebrated in Renaissance dress. (The date varies from year to
year.) Just north of the Hilchen house, a steep cobbled lane
leads to the **church of St. Martin**, where Hilchen's gravestone,
bearing his coat of arms, can be seen. A magnificent 15th-

century carved altarpiece, one of the finest in the Middle Rhine, depicts Saint Martin, patron of wine makers, and the Virgin. At her feet kneel the master carvers who created this work.

# Bacharach

Returning to the left bank of the river, 4 km (2.5 miles) beyond Niederheimbach, you enter Bacharach. Here, cut off from the Rhine by the railway and the B 9, half-timbered houses with steep Gothic slate roofs picturesquely line a narrow valley and the narrow bank. For Victor Hugo, who visited here in 1838, Bacharach was a "fairytale village, drenched in saga and legend." Hugo describes the Ara Bacchi (Altar of Bacchus), a rocky outcrop in the Rhine just downstream from Bacharach, where according to legend burnt offerings to the Roman wine god ensured a good vintage. The legendary rock didn't long survive the romantic French novelist's visit; unromantic German engineers considered it a navigational hazard and blasted it out of the water around 1850. Nor is it any longer thought that Bacharach's name derives from that of the vinous deity; it has been traced to the Celtic *Baccaracum* (settlement).

Nevertheless, for centuries Bacharach and wine were practically synonymous. Until the Thirty Years War, all wine shipped down the Rhine was indiscriminately called "*Bacharacher.*" The wine that had come through the perilous Binger Loch—on craft small enough to navigate the narrows—was stored, traded, taxed, and reshipped from Bacharach.

A stroll along the 14th-century **city walls** from one Medieval tower gate to the next affords views of the Rhine on one side and the village on the other. From the market square, almost everything worth seeing can be encompassed in a glance: the handsome Gothic Peterskirche, the old Posthof with its half-timbered gables and courtyard, and the well-known **Altes Haus**.

Built in 1568, the Altes Haus is one of the few structures that survived the manifold occupations and destructions that beset Bacharach in the 17th century. Behind its charmingly crooked, steep-roofed façade, crowded with flower boxes and tracery windows, you can partake of ponderous Rhineland fare in one of several beamed and paneled rooms heavy with atmosphere. (Take home a souvenir brochure bearing a sketch of the Altes Haus by Victor Hugo himself.) Around the corner, at Rosenstrasse 16, is the **Jost Beerstein Factory Outlet**; even if you don't find the array of German crafts to your own taste, it's an economical place to buy the sort of gifts people expect you to bring back from the Rhine. Though there are no hotels of distinction in Bacharach, adequate rooms simply furnished can be found at the **Altkölnischer Hof** (two doors south of the Altes Haus) and at **Zur Post**, Oberstrasse 35, near the market square. Both have beautiful *Fachwerk* exteriors and atmospheric dining rooms. (For more on *Fachwerk* see the Odenwald section, below.)

Directly south of the Peterskirche on the Oberstrasse, a flight of one hundred steps leads up to the famed **Wernerskapelle** (Chapel of St. Werner). Built at the end of the 13th century to commemorate a youth who purportedly was the victim of ritual murder by Jews (a tale refuted by modern scholars), the chapel was not completed for 140 years; then it was destroyed in the 17th century. By the beginning of the 19th century its ivy-covered roofless ruin was one of Bacharach's romantic sights, and its legend was echoed by Heinrich Heine in "The Rabbi of Bacharach." (Don't climb all those steps unless you want exercise—the chapel is boarded up for repairs.)

The finest view of Bacharach is from its Medieval fortress, **Burg Stahleck**. Most of its present inhabitants don't mind the steep 15-minute climb from Blucherstrasse above the market square—since 1926, when it was restored, the Burg has been a youth hostel. Begun in the 11th century, the Burg served as a Hohenstaufen stronghold until the interregnum of the 13th century; it then became the site of the hotly disputed 1314 election, which finally named Ludwig IV of Bavaria as Holy Roman Emperor. The Burg's massive walls also looked down on the festivities when Emperor Charles IV consolidated his iron grip on the Rhine by marrying Anna, daughter of the prince elector of the Pfalz, in 1349.

## The Pfalzgrafenstein and Kaub

About 4 km (2.5 miles) downstream from Bacharach, rounding a river bend on the B 9, you catch your first glimpse of one of the most remarkable of the Rhine's castles, the Pfalzgrafenstein. Rising out of an islet in center of the stream, the Baroque-turreted Pfalz looks like a red-and-white fortified steamer plowing up the Rhine. Take the Engelsburg auto ferry over to Kaub on the right bank; from Kaub you can visit the castle via a second ferry (time for transit and tour is about one hour). The Pfalz was first built in 1327 by Emperor Ludwig IV in order, as his political opponent Pope John XXII complained, "to squeeze out even

more harshly... his cursed taxes and tolls." Increasingly
heavily fortified, the Pfalz carried on despite the pope's
excommunication of Ludwig. Its toll collectors, sounding
trumpets to halt passing ships, boarded and searched them
mercilessly for contraband. Always vulnerable to high water,
the Pfalz is entered through a gateway in the third story,
defended by a portcullis and surmounted by the quarters of
the commandant.

**Kaub**, known since the 14th century for its slate quarries
from which came much of the Rhineland's roofing material,
also benefited from the toll station; sailors and passengers
had to come ashore for food and accommodations while
fees were being settled. The best known of the inns that
catered to this trade was the 18th-century **Stadt Mannheim**,
from which Field Marshal Blücher directed on New Year's
Eve 1813 the monumental Rhine crossing of 83,000 Prussian
and Russian troops on their way to Paris in pursuit of
Napoleon's armies. Today the Stadt Mannheim has been
converted to a **military museum** (Metzergasse 6) exhibiting
documents, weapons, and portraits associated with Blücher
and the Napoleonic Wars. **Burg Gutenfels**, high above the
town, dates from 1200. Until recently this oft-restored, scenic
fortress served as a popular city-run hotel, but now it is
privately owned, and its massive gates open only for a select
clientele. Its bulwarks have reverted to their Medieval function of keeping the common folk out.

# Oberwesel

About 3 km (1.5 miles) below the Engelsburg ferry (again on
the left bank), visitors get a hearty welcome at the delightfully romantic **Burghotel Auf Schönburg**. High above the
village of Oberwesel is perched the handsome 12th-century
**Schönburg castle**, which was for more than 500 years the
property of the Schönburg family and is now the hotel. The
castle was burned and pillaged by Louis XIV's rampaging
troops in 1689, and the Schönburg clan died out a few
decades later. This tragedy is not surprising, in view of the
stubborn virginity attributed to the seven lovely and legendary Schönburg sisters, who were driven out of their home
and across the Rhine by a sudden onslaught of frustrated
suitors one misty morning. Father Rhine is said to have
commemorated the proud ladies and their stony virtue in
the form of seven man-killing reefs that plagued rivermen
passing Oberwesel until the mid-19th century, when dyna-

mite finally forced the maidenly barriers. In 1885 an American industrialist (with the unlikely but appropriate name of T. I. Oakley Rhinelander) purchased and began restoring the dilapidated Schönburg castle, a labor of love that ended only with his death more than 60 years later. The **Restaurant auf Schönburg**, occupying the proud towers and Medieval chambers of the restored castle, combines the charm and atmosphere of a romantic past with modern service and comfort. Reserve accommodations as far in advance as you can, particularly for weekends. In view of what it offers, the hotel is still very reasonably priced.

Oberwesel is distinguished by its unusually well-preserved **city walls** and fortified towers, despite some ill-advised 19th-century planning for railways and highways. Back in the 1850s, when the railroad was still a novelty, enterprising Oberweselers vied to have the tracks laid as close as possible to their inns, so that guests could enjoy watching the trains pass. Today the most prominent fortified tower, the 14th-century **Ochsenturm**, trembles as the trains brush past its inland side, while the B 9 traffic whizzes by on the Rhine side. Serene above the turbulence of modern life, however, stands Oberwesel's great treasure, the Gothic **Liebfrauenkirche**, often referred to by locals as the "red church" because of its red plaster exterior. The high altar, constructed in 1331, is one of the oldest and most beautiful of its kind. With a double row of expressively carved saints and apostles, it depicts events in Christ's redemption of man, centered on the crowning of the Virgin. Many of the figures that were lost in a sensational 1975 robbery have been recovered, but restoration is still going on and access to the high altar is barred. Fine side altars in the north and south choirs are devoted, respectively, to Saint Nicholas, patron of sailors, and Christ and the Apostles with Mary and Martha. Both were donated around 1500 by Canon Peter Lutern, whose memorial stone carved by the famous master Hans Backoffen graces the west side of the south aisle. Carved memorials of the Schönburg clan, vivid 16th-century frescoes, and many other details make a visit to this church fascinating. Organ concerts here, a memorable experience, can be arranged for groups at the tourist bureau (Rathausstrasse 5).

Apply at Bäckerei Heinrich, at Rathausstrasse 14, near the tourist bureau, for a tour of the Oberwesel **Bakery Museum**, whose century-old oven still produces incomparable German bread and where you can see three centuries worth of bread-baking implements. Local folk drop in at Klaus Weiler's gabled, half-timbered **Weinhaus Weiler** at Marktplatz 4 for a typical Rhineland meal in a pleasant atmosphere; the tidy rooms upstairs are moderately priced.

## The Lorelei and St. Goar

Below Oberwesel, the Rhine foams through a narrowing channel between steeper and steeper cliffs until it reaches the fabled Lorelei. Here the river passes a rock face on the right bank towering 433 feet above it. For ages rivermen feared this passage and wove stories around the echo that followed them through it: In the cliff's caves lived a tribe of dwarfs, warrior guardians of the golden treasure of the Nibelungen. Today the roar of auto and train traffic on both banks has drowned out the echo, but the somber cliff looming over the Rhine has lost none of its fascination. In 1801, in his first novel, *Godwi,* Clemens von Brentano invented the legend of a golden-haired temptress calling to passing ships from the heights: 22 years later Heinrich Heine immortalized Brentano's siren in the poem "Die Lorelei," which begins *"Ich weiss nicht, was soll es bedeuten, dass ich so traurig bin"* (I know not what this sorrow of mine may mean). You too will be sorry—if you join the masses who drive to the top of the Lorelei, unaccountably compelled to visit the only spot in the area from which its chief attraction is not visible.

Seven kilometers (4 miles) downstream from Oberwesel, the lively, colorful town of **St. Goar** has since the sixth century been the home of the Rhine pilots who guide river traffic through the Lorelei narrows. But the relation between town and Rhine shipping has not always been friendly. St. Goar's redoubtable fortress, **Burg Rheinfels**, was built on the heights above the town in 1245 by Count Diether III of Katzeln-bogen, one of the toll-collecting lords who preyed on passing ships. Only a decade after the construction of Rheinfels, 26 cities of the Rhine Alliance, fed up with the count's extortion-ate rates, unsuccessfully besieged his castle for more than a year—the first of many sieges the mighty fortress withstood. Finally, at the end of the 18th century, the French brought down its walls for good. Today the **Schloss-Hotel auf Burg Rheinfels** (at the top of the Schlossbergstrasse) once more stands for a warm welcome to travellers, who can stay in its charming period-furnished rooms with views of the Rhine. The present-day toll, though still higher than average, is justified by the amenities offered, which include indoor swimming pool, sauna, and fitness center. The hotel occupies the restored part of the ruined castle, and you can follow a tour of the Medieval battlements with a quick swim or dinner on the outdoor panoramic terrace.

Below, in the town, the Protestant **Stiftskirche**, on the Marktplatz just east of the railway station, dominates St. Goar with its Gothic tower. Built on the foundations of an earlier Romanesque church by the counts of Katzenelnbogen in about 1469, the Stiftskirche is dedicated to St. Goar, whose image appears repeatedly among the church's Late Gothic **frescoes**, among the finest on the Rhine. The saint himself came to the Rhine from Aquitaine in the sixth century, and tales of miracles wrought at his grave made the town's fortune as a place of pilgrimage until the Reformation lowered the stock of saints.

St. Goar is further blessed with several agreeable middle-priced hotels, a very good place to eat, and a staggering collection of cuckoo clocks, all on the same street. Next to the Stiftskirche at the south end of the Heerstrasse, **Schneider am Markt** is convenient, quiet, and friendly, and it has a nice Rhine view. A few steps (north) down the street, Sebastian Burch not only offers clean, comfortable rooms at the family hotel **Zur Lorelei**, but has also built a local reputation for the best food in town. Try Burch's Lorelei steak, which comes to your table sizzling on a hot slate slab. Among St. Goar's numerous souvenir shops, the best known and most original is Doris Mühl's **Cuckoo Clock Center**, toward the north end of Heerstrasse. Besides having the "world's largest free hanging cuckoo clock" (restored in 1983—and "technical improvements are always being made"), the shop has an awesome array of gifts in the same genre.

On the east bank, across the Rhine from St. Goar and linked to it by a convenient ferry, **St. Goarshausen** is a small community watched over by Wilhelm II of Katzenelnbogen's 14th-century Gothic castle, usually referred to as **Burg Katz**. Count Wilhelm's "Katz" was his response to the construction by his rival, the archbishop of Trier, of **Burg Maus**, a similar fortress at Wellmilch, 2 km (1.2 miles) down the Rhine. Though Burg Katz was destroyed by Napoleon in 1806, the restored fortress of the robber knights served in modern times to house retired officers of the German federal revenue service, a sequence that draws ironical smiles from local taxpayers. Burg Maus has also undergone extensive restoration and today houses an aviary, with daily exhibitions of falconry.

# Boppard

Tucked into an elbow of the Rhine 12 km (7.5 miles) north of St. Goar and just south of Koblenz at the mouth of the Mosel, Boppard is a compendium of Rhineland attractions: Roman walls and Medieval fortress, Gothic churches, Renaissance half-timbered houses, Rhine wines, and Rhineside hotels. Entering the town from the south on the B 9, follow the parking signs to the Marktplatz in the center of town. Unlike most Lorelei valley towns, Boppard has not allowed the highway and the railroad to sever it from the Rhine. The city's tenacious hold on the river dates back to the middle of the fourth century A.D., when the Roman emperor Julian ("the Apostate") anchored the Roman Limes (fortified boundary) here with a fort called "Bodobrica." Parts of the massive **Roman foundations** can still be seen (south of the Marktplatz at the top of the Kirchgasse, for example), and elaborate baths have been found under the Marktplatz itself.

A century later the Roman baths became baptismal basins, when early Christians turned the bathhouse into a church. The fifth-century church was succeeded by the Romanesque **St. Severus**, which today dominates the Marktplatz; on the floor of St. Severus you can still trace the outlines of the earlier building. As you enter St. Severus from the Kirchgasse, notice inside on the righthand wall a stone with two stylized birds; this is a memorial to one Besontio, a deacon of the earlier church, dating back to A.D. 500. St. Severus, completed around 1234, boasts two Early Gothic masterpieces: the great crucifix over the high altar, considered one of the finest examples of its period, and a joyous enthroned Madonna inside the arch on the right aisle nearest the altar.

Boppard enjoyed the power and privileges of a free imperial city until 1312, when Emperor Henry VII presented both Boppard and Oberwesel to his brother Baldwin, archbishop of Trier, to whom the townspeople were required to swear oaths of fealty. The resentful citizens of the proud Rhine city balked, and eventually Baldwin had to besiege and storm Boppard. Baldwin then built, just east of the Roman walls (one block north down the Burgstrasse from the Marktplatz), the 1327 fortress known as the **Alte Burg** (Old Fortress), of which only the original tower remains. In it (and in the newer, 18th-century parts of the Burg) Boppard's **civic museum** invites you to visit a cabinetmaker's workshop, a forestry museum, and displays from Roman and prehistoric times. But the proudest exhibit is a gallery of lovely bentwood furniture created by Boppard's best-known native son, Michael Thonet, the founder of the firm that furnished the cafés of Vienna, Paris, and the world with the familiar bentwood chair. It is doubtful whether Baldwin's own seat in this fortress on the Rhine was ever so comfortable.

As the wine and shipping trade grew and Boppard flourished, its noble families dwelt in increasing luxury. Two blocks (east) up the Rhine from the Alte Burg you come to the imposing Late Gothic **Ritter-Schwalbach house**, one of the finest examples; a stroll back down the Rheinallee takes you past many other fine façades. At the corner of the Karmeliterstrasse you reach the 14th-century **Karmeliterkirche** where the Ritter (Knight) Siegfried von Schwalbach himself stares combatively out from under his helm on a memorial stone. The church's rich collection of Late Gothic art is one of Boppard's gems.

Boppard's 3-km- (1.5-mile-) long **Rheinallee** is a festive and colorful promenade along the great river past hotels, cafés, and boat landings, all competing for your attention. Queen of the lot is the luxurious **Bellevue Rheinhotel**, near the Alte Burg. Relatively expensive, the Bellevue is a fine old Jugendstil dame with her turn-of-the-century airs and graces still intact, despite the thoroughly modern facilities (sauna, steambath, pool, and tennis). Rooms 412 to 416 have terraces on the Rhine; the rooms in general are spacious and handsomely furnished. Have a festive dinner in the hotel's **Pfeffermühle** dining room, where you can have, for example, a Belle Rose mystery aperitif followed by a Swabian snail plate and *medaillons* of wild boar stuffed with mushrooms in red-wine sauce. Just down the Rheinallee, a moderately priced hotel with a friendly atmosphere is the **Baudobriga** (Boppard's Celtic name), most of whose rooms have balconies overlooking the Rhine. The hotel's proprietors, the Ries family, have their own wine estate, and you can sample their estate-bottled wines from the slopes of the famous **Bopparder Hamm**. This slate-covered slope, situated downstream and around the bend of the Rhine north of Boppard, rises at such a steep angle that wine growers practically have to rope up to tend their vines. You can view it and Boppard from the sky if you take the 20-minute chair-lift ride (don't forget your Dramamine) up to the lookout point **Vierseenblick** (from the foot of the Mühltalstrasse at the west end of Boppard).

Take the ferry across the Rhine from Boppard to the B 42 on the right bank and drive downstream for an almost equally dramatic view of these vertical vineyards from the road between Filsen, where there are some fine *Fachwerk* houses, and Osterspai. In about 8 km (5 miles) you reach **Braubach,** the northern terminus of our Lorelei valley route, triumphantly crowned by the **Marksburg castle.** Never successfully besieged, this regal 13th-century fortress is the only castle on the Rhine that has withstood the centuries intact. The counts of Katzenelnbogen were responsible for its construction around 1283 on an older foundation, insuring their grasp on Braubach's profitable lead and silver mines. Though never taken by storm, the Marksburg suffered from neglect over the centuries as it lost strategic significance. Following its acquisition by the German Castle Society in 1900 it was painstakingly restored by Bodo Ebhardt to serve as the society's headquarters. Today a tour of the castle with its authentic and reconstructed furnishings and collections of Medieval weapons makes a fitting climax to a trip through the valley of the Lorelei.

# THE ODENWALD

Coming south from Wiesbaden on the eastern side of the Rhine, the A 5 at Darmstadt (29 km/18 miles due south of Frankfurt) begins to parallel a line of castle-crowned steep hills overlooking the Rhine valley. These heights are the western edge of the Odenwald (Oden forest) upland, whose ancient woodlands and narrow, winding river valleys are rich in Medieval legend. Medieval, too, seem its towns, with their half-timbered buildings clustered around market squares, carved stone fountains, and arched bridges. The Odenwälders themselves keep old-fashioned trades alive— farming, ivory carving, beekeeping, and innkeeping—but they live very consciously in the 20th century. Many commute to work in the industrial centers beyond the Neckar, which bounds the Odenwald to the south near Heidelberg. Others take advantage of the Odenwald's own industry, the tourist and health-resort trade. Fresh mountain air, spring water, and a judicious use of Frankfurt ad agencies keep their ubiquitous little pensions and hotels full of German vacationers as well as foreign guests, so advance bookings are advisable in this area.

Measuring some 50 miles long (between the Main and the Neckar) by about 40 miles wide, the Odenwald is compact enough to "do" in a day or so, but its storybook scenery, hearty food, and mild, sunny climate often cast their delaying spell; three or four days are none too many.

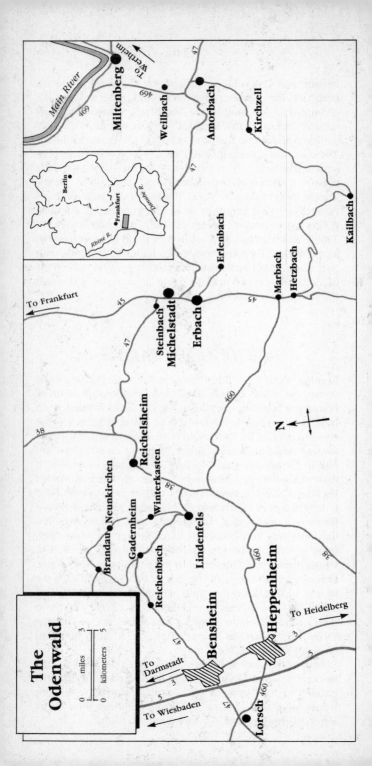

# The Odenwald

miles
0    3
kilometers
0    5

# Darmstadt

The bombs of 1944 left little intact of the former capital of the grand duchy of Hesse-Darmstadt, and the postwar economic success has overwhelmed what remained in cement waves of modern construction. The most significant survivor is the Jugendstil artists' colony on the **Mathildenhöhe**, the eastern heights of the city. At the turn of the century, the last grand duke of Hesse, who was himself only 21, brought together a group of young German-speaking artists whose goal was not just to produce art, but to live it. On the Mathildenhöhe they built homes, studios, and exhibition areas based on their own design philosophy, and in 1901 they staged their first and most original exhibition, A Document of German Art. A walk through the area today will recall some of the freshness and daring of that artistic vision. The stark boldness of the **wedding tower**, in particular, will surprise those for whom Art Nouveau has come to mean flowery trivia; it was built on the occasion of the grand duke's marriage in 1907.

From the Mathildenhöhe, less than a kilometer west down the Dieburgerstrasse you come to the historic center of the city and Darmstadt's **Schloss**, immediately north of the Marktplatz, which is a busy pedestrian shopping zone. The Schloss, a charming résumé of seven centuries of German architecture, is worth visiting for its furnishings and collections. Its finest possession is the *Madonna of Burgomeister Meyer,* a masterpiece of Renaisssance character portrayal painted in 1526 by Hans Holbein the Younger. Also among its respectable collection of Old Masters is Pieter Brueghel's last work, *Magpie in the Gallows* (1568). The Schloss looks north across the Friedensplatz to the Neoclassical façade of the **Hessian state museum**, built in 1902 to house the collections of the grand duke. The museum's attempt to display objects in an authentic environment reflects the influence of Art Nouveau ideas: Roman finds are displayed in an atrium, Gothic religious art in a Gothic chapel. One flight down from the Roman exhibit you progress through a beautiful display of Art Nouveau utensils, jewelry, and furniture to a wonderland of stained-glass windows glowing in a dimly lit hall.

Beyond the museum, the former Schloss park, the **Herrngarten**, reaches north in a refreshing expanse of lawns, paths, and trees. On its northeast corner, in the Prinz-Georg-Garten, the Rococo **Prinz-Georg-Palais**, often called the **Porzellanschlösschen**, harbors the grand-ducal porcelain collection, including pieces of Sèvres, Meissen, Wedgwood, and Kelsterbach.

The **Weinmichel** is ideally located across the street to the west of the museum at Schleiermacherstrasse 10–12. It has recently undergone discreet renovation and offers accommodations moderate in price. The restaurant, popular with locals, has an excellent wine list. Near the Hauptbahnhof, west of the center, is the **Maritim Hotel**, at Rheinstrasse 105; its prices match its elegance.

# Lorsch

Today an unremarkable village of small shops and farms, Lorsch, about 25 km (15 miles) due south of Darmstadt, was once a spiritual and political power center of Charlemagne's empire. The slight elevation that kept it dry during the Rhine's periodic floods made Lorsch a north–south crossroads and a gateway to the Odenwald. Here the Romans erected a temple to Mithras, and here in 767 an abbey was founded that, under imperial patronage, was to achieve immense influence and wealth. A beautifully preserved remnant of that glory is the **Königshalle**, the triumphal gateway through which Charlemagne paraded into the abbey of Lorsch in 774 to dedicate its new church. The emperor made the Lorsch abbots independent princes, answerable only to Rome and to himself; many were imperial relatives. During the next two centuries the abbey acquired enormous holdings through patronage; in turn, it bolstered the emperor against rebels and spread Christianity through the pagan darkness of the Odenwald, founding many churches and monasteries. Today the Königshalle is the only intact edifice of the Carolingian Renaissance remaining in Germany. Emblematic of Lorsch's importance as a cultural crossroads, its steep-pitched Germanic royal hall (with festive Gothic frescoes) rests on the classical arches and pillars of a Roman triumphal gate.

Opposite the Königshalle, across the flower-decked market square, is Lorsch's handsome Baroque **Rathaus**; beneath its turreted and gabled roof is a small museum, whose exhibits include relics of Lorsch as a tobacco-growing center. Cool off with Frau Dreyss's homemade ice cream in a dozen flavors at the **Café am Kloster** on the square. For the serious appetite, try for at least a share of a table at the small and popular restaurant **Zum Schwanen**, down the Nibelungenstrasse. Antique curios occupy the space here not filled with diners intent on Heinz Metz's French-accented New

German cuisine. Book, or come very early; Nibelungen-strasse 52; Tel: (6251) 522-53.

# Fachwerk

No region met the necessary conditions for the building of *Fachwerk* (half-timbered) houses better than the Odenwald, with its mild winters, plentiful wood, and skilled native craftsmen. The frames of heavy squared timbers were assembled on the ground according to coded marks, then hauled upright with block and tackle or windlasses manned by chanting villagers. Wooden pegs or large iron nails held the frames in place, while spaces between the beams were filled with the most convenient and economical materials at hand: wattle and daub, stone, brick, timbers, or plaster. Fachwerk's endlessly varying patterns give the Odenwald villages much of their charm, and you could hardly find a more delightful introduction to the Odenwald than the village of **Heppen-heim**, 5 km (3 miles) east of Lorsch and once its possession. Leave your vehicle in the parking area and walk up to the market square. Its central fountain is a good vantage point from which to take in the surrounding 16th-century façades, each prettier than the next.

# The Nibelungenstrasse

East from Lorsch you can explore the Odenwald along the Siegfriedstrasse, by way of Heppenheim, or the Nibelungen-strasse, which begins at Bensheim, a few kilometers north. From Bensheim, follow the B 47 northeast through the Lauter valley to the foot of the Neunkirchener heights, then south-east to Lindenfels and generally eastward to Michelstadt and Amorbach, where the Nibelungenstrasse follows B 469 north to Miltenberg on the Main. Conjecture makes one of the abbots of Lorsch the author of the *Nibelungenlied,* that grim and vengeful epic of the winning of the warrior maid Brunhilde through Siegfried's magical prowess, and his death by Hagen's dagger beside a forest spring. The Odenwald, hunting ground of the Nibelungen, is dotted with enough "Siegfried's Springs" to backdrop half-a-dozen Wagnerian arias. About 8 km (5 miles) along the Nibelungenstrasse beyond Bensheim, turn left (north) at Reichenbach on the Lauter to see the first of these springs. In this case, though, the fatal spring, which is about 1 km (.6 miles) from Reichenbach, is only incidental to the main event, the **Felsenmeer** (Sea of Boulders). Produced perhaps by a legendary battle of Titans, or perhaps as the result of granitic erosion, these photogenic rock cascades (some bearing the marks of Roman quarriers) tumble down from a ridge that commands a fine view of the forested valley. (A trip to the Felsenmeer makes a nice week-day hike; it fills up on weekends.)

# Neunkirchen and Lindenfels

At the Brandau junction, 11 km (7 miles) east of Bensheim, just before Gadernheim, turn left off the B 47 and follow the winding secondary road to 3 km (1.8 miles) north to Brandau, and then 4 km (2.4 miles) east to Neunkirchen. The German passion for unsullied mountain air and long walks has made Neunkirchen, the highest village in the Hessian Odenwald, a popular health resort. Founded by the abbey of Lorsch in the 13th century, the village church occupies the site of an earlier chapel dedicated to the twin saints of healing, Cosmos and Damien.

Neunkirchen's true patron spirit is no saint, but a tormented ghost. The lords of **Schloss Rodenstein**, whose ruin lies a mile east of Neunkirchen, held the village and its environs from the Middle Ages until the last one died of plague in 1671. The tale is told of the 14th-century knight Hans von Rodenstein, who won a beautiful lady in a tourney in Heidelberg, then basely deserted her. Dying in battle, the unchivalrous knight was doomed to be hunted ever after by the hounds of hell, who chased him across the lonely peaks of the Odenwald. Through the ages, Odenwälders have heard—but not seen—repeated passages of the knight's spirit, a droning, wordless wail suddenly traversing a cloudless sky, presaging fire and war if it comes to the ruined castle, but a good omen if it flies north.

From Neunkirchen it is a scenic 8 km (4.5 miles) due south back to the B 47 (Nibelungenstrasse) at Lindenfels (by way of Winterkasten). Like Neunkirchen, **Lindenfels** lives on air. Perched on a high ridge from which five river valleys fall away into the blue distance, it offers pine-scented breezes to refugees from urban smog. Fill your lungs well before mounting to the **castle** ruins: The ascent is short, but the view from the remaining ramparts is breathtaking. Erected in 1123 by the first Hohenstaufen emperor, Conrad, the castle survived countless assaults and sieges, mostly while it was in the possession of the electors of the Palatinate, only to be ignominiously sold and pulled down for building materials at the end of the 18th century. On your left as you descend from the castle along the Burgstrasse, the city museum, housed in the Medieval **tax house**, has four floors of ingenious displays recreating the daily life of an Odenwald village since Medieval times.

"The Pearl of the Odenwald," as Lindenfels likes to be called, is a good base for exploring the surrounding hill country. Get a *Wanderkarte* (hiking map) because the forest is laced with trails of every imaginable length and degree of difficulty. You won't soon forget the tranquil beauty of the landscape through which they take you.

Lindenfels has many pensions and hotels. Especially central is the well-reputed **Hessisches Haus**. Facing the castle and the lion's head fountain, it offers rooms with spectacular views across the valleys. (Rates are cheaper from the third night on.) Directly across the Burgstrasse from the hotel, the **Altes Rauch'sches Haus** has homemade confections and good, solid Odenwald food. Both of these establishments are in the heart of the festivities on the first August weekend when Lindenfels celebrates its Castle and Costume Week with folk dancing, singing, and parades.

## Michelstadt and Erbach

Every German community believes that its Rathaus is the fairest in the land. Surely the most photographed is the one in Michelstadt, on the eastern side of the Odenwald, 25 km (15 miles) east of Lindenfels on the Nibelungenstrasse (and also on route B 45, which runs south from Frankfurt). Framed between the flower-decked fountain and the Gothic steeple of the church behind it, the Michelstadt **Rathaus** adorns countless brochures and guides. Across from the church (Braunstrasse 5), the restaurant **Drei Hasen**'s three gilded rabbits beckon you to such hearty dishes as *Schweinshaxen* and Holsteiner *Schnitzel*. Around the corner (Grosse-Gasse 17), the **Grüner Baum** restaurant also claims a 300-year history, which the meticulously kept building reflects (perhaps too abundantly), inside and out. Rooms—small, tidy, and laden with tradition—are available in both hostelries.

After Charlemagne died in 814, his son Louis presented Michelstadt to the emperor's courtier and friend Einhard, who retired here to begin his *Vita Caroli*. The pious biographer, who was also an abbot, built a church in Steinbach (the town through which the Nibelungenstrasse enters Michelstadt) and stocked it with the requisite relics, which he had sent his secretary to filch from the graves of Christian martyrs in Rome. Not much remains of the **Einhardsbasilika**—what you see is largely restored—but just down the path, on the

wooded bank of the river Mümling, is the lovely Renaissance
**castle of Fürstenau**. Originally a moated 13th-century stronghold of the archbishops of Mainz, the castle was rebuilt later
by the counts of Erbach, who added its graceful and distinctive arched gateway.

The elegant Baroque façade of **Erbach castle**, since 1736
the residence of the counts of Erbach, forms the west side of
the market square in **Erbach**. Behind it, the stern cylinder of
the castle keep, a remnant of the original 13th-century fortress, looms above an array of Renaissance and 18th-century
buildings. The castle's several museums are as worthwhile
for their vaulted Gothic interiors, stained-glass windows,
and parquet floors as for Count Franz I's collections of
armor and weapons, Roman artifacts, stuffed animals, and
objets de vertu. On the square, a colorful farmers' market is
held on Saturdays against the festive backdrop of the castle,
the Mümling and its bridges, and the half-timbered buildings of the **Städel**, Erbach's Medieval minivillage.

American visitors will of course be mindful of U.S. prohibi-
tions against importation of ivory—the carving of which is a
specialty here—and may choose to bypass the ivory shops
that seem to pop up on nearly every street corner and seek
out Erbach's pottery instead. At the **Müller-Dönig** workshop,
just south of the market square at Bahnhofstrasse 21, you can
watch master potter Hermann Dönig and son Bernd at their
potter's wheel, continuing a 350-year family tradition of
Odenwald ceramics, turning out dishes, bowls, pitchers, and
a thousand other forms; their patterns are naive folk motifs
in red and beige, blue and green. Beekeeping, another
ancient tradition, is practiced by Hermann Gabel in nearby
Erlenbach. He welcomes English-speaking visitors, and you
can call to arrange a visit to his *Imkerei* (apiary); Tel: (6062)
25-37 or 48-46. Interesting by-products are candles, candy,
and cosmetics, all made of honey.

## Amorbach

Amorbach, 25 km (15 miles) east of Erbach on the Nibelungenstrasse, has a particularly beautiful example of late
Baroque architecture, its **abbey church**. Starting in the eighth
century, the abbey was the nucleus around which Amorbach
grew. As it celebrated its first millennium in 1734, it was in the
hands of the archbishops of Mainz, under whom Mainz was
bursting into its Baroque flowering. Shortly before the
French Revolution put an end to the power and glory of the
Church's earthly dominion, church architecture had reached

its peak of opulence. Amorbach's church was one of many Romanesque and Gothic churches transformed by Baroque builders such as Maximilian von Welsch, court architect to the archbishop. He retained the church's twin Romanesque towers as he conceived the restrained and harmonious sandstone façade above which they now rise. Within, outstanding stucco work by Bavarian masters Uebelherr and Feichtmayer magically blends with Matthäus Günther's paintings in fascinating trompe l'oeil effects. Come on a Wednesday or Friday to enjoy an afternoon concert on the famous organ, which has 3,000 pipes and is one of Europe's largest Baroque instruments. The abbey tour includes another late Baroque gem, the **library**, housing 30,000 volumes collected by the prince of Leiningen, now proprietor of the abbey.

Amorbach boasts two hotels with a storied past. The **Post** (Schmiedgasse 2) traces its lineage to 1546 and was once a post station; its rooms, in a modern addition behind the restaurant, are quiet and comfortable. Directly across the street, the somewhat less expensive **Badischer Hof** groups its rooms around the former farmyard, which now serves as a garden café. The hotel's Biedermeier hominess brought physicist Max Planck back year after year. Both hotels have good restaurants.

# Miltenberg

In a deep bend of the river Main, 10 km (6 miles) north of Amorbach on the B 469, the wealthy merchants of Miltenberg lined both sides of their long Hauptstrasse with imposing Medieval and Renaissance houses, Fachwerk abutting Fachwerk all the way from the foot of the Burg to the grandiloquent city gate on the Main bridge. Midway down this parade of patrician pomp is the **Zum Riesen**, which claims to be the oldest hostelry in Germany—its first guest having been Emperor Frederick Barbarossa in 1158. Other guests in its annals are Martin Luther, Albrecht Dürer, and an endless list of kings, generals, and notables down to Richard Strauss and the late Franz-Josef Strauss. Accommodations in its undeniably atmospheric precincts range from regal to merely comfortable, and a tiny elevator supplements the spiral staircase. Here you can dine on such favorite Medieval delicacies as bear chops, stuffed partridge, veal with smoked oysters, and shredded ox marinated for two weeks and flavored with 22 herbs, washed down with quince wine.

Miltenberg began as a Roman fort on the Main where the Limes (fortified imperial boundary) emerged from the

Odenwald to run north along the river. The archbishops of Mainz, their eyes fixed firmly on potential income from river traffic, built the Burg about 1200, and the merchant community prospered in its protective shadow, as evidenced by the Gothic grandeur of the **Altes Rathaus**, now called the Merchants' Hall, on the Hauptstrasse. Here goods were stored and traded, and duties were levied.

Miltenberg's prettiest corner is its **Marktplatz**, from which a low gateway leads through the Schnatterloch tower (where witches are said to have been burned) up to the Burg. The **Weinhaus am Alten Markt** has attractive, moderately priced rooms, many with views over the square (request a room with a bay window). A few steps farther down the street—and farther up the price scale—the **Altes Bannhaus** has uncluttered, quiet rooms. In the Medieval cellars of the Bannhaus, once a prison, such specialties as venison liver grilled with sesame, partridge terrine with homemade quince jelly, and dove stuffed with chanterelles and garnished with Port sauce are served with unobtrusive attentiveness.

The Nibelungenstrasse continues northeast (upstream) along the Main toward Wertheim, in the direction of Würzburg; or you can return to Amorbach to pick up the **Siegfriedstrasse**. It runs southwest from Amorbach through Kirchzell to Kallbach, then swings northwest to join the B 45 at Hetzbach. From there it runs north to Marbach and follows the B 460 back to Heppenheim—for another route through the endlessly scenic Odenwald. Contact the German National Tourist Office for detailed information on the Siegfriedstrasse and the Burgenstrasse (see below).

## CASTLES ON THE NECKAR

From below (downstream of) Heilbronn, a medium-sized town north of Stuttgart, the river Neckar winds north and west across the southern flank of the Odenwald and past Heidelberg toward its rendezvous with the Rhine at Mannheim. You can follow the river up the **Burgenstrasse** (Castle Road), which begins to the southwest in Nürnberg and of which this section, along B 27 and B 37, is the northwestern end. A gentle landscape of vineyards, fields, and orchards alternates with the somber beauty of wooded hills, which predominate as the river nears Heidelberg. For centuries a trade artery in wine, wool, wood, salt, and iron, the Neckar provided natural sites for fortified castles, protecting their approaches while offer-

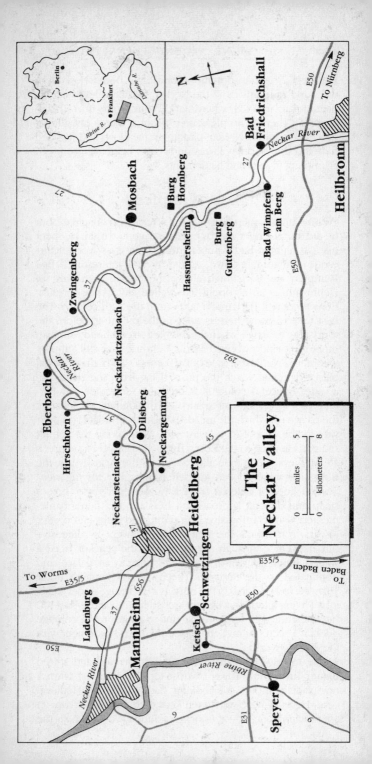

# The Neckar Valley

| miles | 0 | | 5 |
| kilometers | 0 | | 8 |

Bad Friedrichshall

Heilbronn

To Nürnberg

E50

Neckar River

27

Bad Wimpfen am Berg

Burg Guttenberg

Hassmersheim

Burg Hornberg

Mosbach

E50

292

27

Zwingenberg

37

Neckar River

Neckarkatzenbach

Eberbach

Hirschhorn

Neckarsteinach

Dilsberg

37

Neckargemund

45

Heidelberg

656

37

Mannheim

Neckar River

E35/5

Schwetzingen

To Baden Baden

E50

To Worms

E35/5

Ladenburg

E50

Ketsch

Rhine River

9

E31

Speyer

6

Berlin

Frankfurt

Rhine R.

Danube R.

N

ing their lords transportation—and often booty. Now highways and railroads flank the Neckar, but its valley is still as
beautiful as in 1878, when Mark Twain wrote in *A Tramp
Abroad,* "There is no pleasanter place . . . than a raft gliding
down the winding Neckar, past green meadows and wooded
hills and slumbering villages, and craggy heights graced with
crumbling towers and battlements."

# Bad Wimpfen

Twain's famous raft trip down the Neckar was imaginary, but
he did tour the river area by boat, carriage, and train. He spent
his first night at Bad Wimpfen, describing it as "very picturesque and tumble-down, and dirty and interesting." **Bad
Wimpfen am Berg**, high above the Neckar northwest of
Heilbronn, is an acropolis-like walled city whose fortifications Frederick Barbarossa laid out in the 12th century. The
best time to come here is early in the morning, before the
tourist buses arrive, when the cobbled streets lined with half-
timbered, window-boxed Medieval houses are still slippery
with dew. From the arcade of Barbarossa's **Pfalz**, the imperial
palace, you can watch the mists rising from the river. The
arcade's graceful columns framed the same view for Barbarossa's successors as they strolled through the great hall of
the palace (of which the arcade is the only remnant) on their
way to the chapel at its west end. Walk along the rebuilt
ramparts leading to the **Roter Turm** (Red Tower) to appreciate Medieval siege mentality. Scenic as they usually are, the
Burg sites were chosen for defensibility, not for the view.
Several lines of defense barred the besieger's way: first, a
steep and difficult approach, such as a moat; then a battle-
mented wall with massive iron-reinforced gates and corner
towers from which the wall could be swept by defensive
missiles. Once through the outer wall the attacker faced a
walled inner courtyard, containing the actual palace and
dominated by the *Bergfried* (keep). Bad Wimpfen's Roter
Turm served the lords of the Burg as a last refuge under siege;
it had living quarters, a hearth, arched niches, and even a WC
(at the end of a long, zigzagging passage, to discourage
odors). A secret tunnel connected the keep's basement with
the outside world.

The town's landmark is the Gothic turreted and spired
**Blauer Turm** (Blue Tower), whose top, 196 steps up, offers a
fine vantage point overlooking Bad Wimpfen's Medieval
core. Here—where watchmen kept their vigil for fire or an
approaching enemy—at noon on a Sunday you can hear the

fanfares and alarums of the tower trumpeters. The hotel adjacent to the tower, the **Blauer Turm**, offers panoramic views from its rooms and a breezy terrace where you can have *Maultaschen* (meat pies) high above the Neckar. Nearby is the **Steinhaus**, once the queen's dwelling and one of the largest surviving secular Romanesque buildings. Now a museum, it houses displays of Medieval armor, weapons, furnishings, tools, and art, as well as artifacts from the salt industry, long a major source of income for Bad Wimpfen.

The town's prosperity reached its acme in the 15th century when, as a Free City, it joined the influential Swabian League, but the terrible 17th century saw it twice occupied, pillaged, and burned to the ground. Few of the Fachwerk houses along the Klostergasse and Hauptstrasse predate the Thirty Years War, and those, handsome as they are, represent but a shadow of the town's former riches.

As an official *Kurort* (health resort), Bad Wimpfen has plenty of accommodations. The **Sonne** combines a cheerful, homey atmosphere and central location (where it has been for four centuries) with moderate prices. If tramping the battlements has given you a hearty appetite, try the **Gasthaus Barbarossa** on the shady Market Square for roast pork with fine herbs and *Spätzle* or their specialty, *Stauferlendchen*.

Down on the edge of the river below, **Bad Wimpfen im Tal** was known as Cornelia in the days when Roman sentries sent up smoke signals from their wooden watchtowers. This was one of the strongest anchor points of the Limes, the 300-mile-long fortified road that was the empire's northeast frontier from the Danube to the Rhine. On the foundations of the Roman fort stands the church of Saints Peter and Paul, now part of a Benedictine abbey. Its notable **cloisters** illustrate the decline of the Gothic from 13th-century opulence to 15th-century austerity.

# Burg Guttenberg

On a high ridge between the Neckar and Mühlbach valleys 7 km (4 miles) north of Bad Wimpfen, Burg Guttenberg may forever form your image of the complete Medieval castle. Its preservation has been in the capable hands of the Gemmingen family since 1449, when Hans von Gemmingen paid 6,000 guldens for it. Its uncompromisingly square Hohenstaufen tower keep betrays its 12th-century origins, when vassals of the emperor held Guttenberg. During the Reformation it became a refuge for hunted Lutherans, but the Gemmingen family, though staunch Protestants, were clever enough to play one side off against the other during the Thirty Years War and so preserve Guttenberg from the reduction to rubble suffered by many such castles.

By turns amusing, fascinating, and horrifying, the six-tiered **castle museum** takes you through the castle's past. Tin soldiers fight out the battle of Wimpfen (1622) on a dusty plaster plain; an ivory ladies' flea-catcher reminds you of the casual view of hygiene that prevailed; and instruments of torture bear witness to the right of high justice exercised by the lords of Guttenberg for 400 years. Most memorable of all is the twice-daily (March to November) display of falconry staged on the castle's Neckar valley terrace. Claus Fentzleff keeps and trains more than 100 birds of prey at Guttenberg, helping replenish threatened species by periodically releasing young eagles, falcons, hawks, and owls bred in his aviary. The beauty and the savagery of the Middle Ages are both manifest in a falcon's deadly swoop on the bait. After the show, have a hot *Würstchen* and a cold beer in the **Burgschenke**, adjoining the Burg.

## The Hornberg and the Minneburg

At Hassmersheim, 5 km (2 miles) north of Burg Guttenberg, you cross the Neckar on an auto ferry; a mile to the north on the east side is the **Burg Hornberg**. At the surprisingly luxurious hotel of the same name right in the castle precincts, balconied rooms open on views of the forest or (more expensive) the Neckar; the view is an attraction they share with a restaurant and a terrace grill.

The dominant figure at Burg Hornberg had an iron fist; since he bought the castle in 1516 with the ransom wrung from a hapless captive, the one-handed robber knight Götz von Berlichingen has been identified with Hornberg. Mark Twain reports: "In an assault upon a stronghold in Bavaria, his right hand was shot away, but he was so interested in the fight that he did not observe it for a while." Goethe made Götz a romantic hero in the eponymous play, idealizing him considerably, but it is historically accurate that he led a band of rebels against the oppressions of the feudal lords—his own class—during the Peasants' Revolt in 1525. The castle, from which Götz conducted raids on Neckar shippers to finance his campaigns, is as satisfyingly picturesque a ruin as the old rascal himself must have been before expiring at the unusually ripe age of 82.

A lovely oasis of Medieval houses clusters around the

Marktplatz in the predominantly modern city of **Mosbach** on the B 27, down the river and a mile inland from Hornberg. Outstanding in the richness and variety of its Fachwerk is the **Palm'sches Haus** (1610), across from the 16th-century Rathaus.

Downstream beyond Mosbach, now along the B 37 forking northwest off B 27, the Neckar valley narrows and deepens, edged by steep, forested slopes. As you go north along the east bank, the ruined towers of the **Minneburg** loom above the trees on a bluff across the river. Cross the bridge here, at Neckargerach, and continue about 5 km (3 miles) inland to Neckarkatzenbach, where a right turn at the fountain before the village takes you another mile to a parking place on the Schlossberg. From here, a pleasant 45-minute stroll along a broad level path leads to the castle of Minneburg, whose mossy remains date largely from the 16th century. The Minneburg can only be reached on foot, so the quiet beauty of its surroundings remains undisturbed except by the occasional picnicker (bread, cheese, and a bottle of wine are indicated).

## Schloss Zwingenberg

Six hundred fifty feet above the Neckar, beyond the village of Zwingenberg farther down route B 37 and the river, Schloss Zwingenberg is not only not a ruin, it is handsomely preserved and serves as the residence of the margravine of Baden. Tours are allowed from 2:00 to 5:00 P.M. on Tuesdays, Fridays, and Sundays, and you should not miss this chance to see a particularly fine castle (tours are in German, but the guide speaks some English). If you leave your car in the parking lot of the last restaurant downstream, you can walk (15 minutes) up a heavily wooded, idyllic gorge, the **Wolfschlucht**. The path circles behind the Schloss to its entrance. The tour gives you fascinating glimpses of the stronghold from which the 14th-century nobles of Zwingenberg preyed on the river traffic; so merciless were they that in 1364 the Palatinate and Württemberg sent a combined force to seize and raze the castle. Beyond the Schloss, the Wolfschlucht path goes on up past Gothic crags and waterfalls through the romantic scenery in which Carl Maria von Weber set his opera *Der Freischütz* in 1820. A milestone of German Romanticism, it is performed annually in the open courtyard of Schloss Zwingenberg.

## Eberbach to Neckarsteinach

Staying at the **Hotel Krone-Post** in Eberbach, 9 km (5 miles) down the Neckar from Zwingenberg, may be as close as you can get to the sort of raft cruise Twain fantasized. Your room has a window over the river, and you dine on a grape-arbor–shaded Neckar terrace. On Eberbach's historic market square, a few paces inland, facing the 15th-century Rathaus, is another hotel, the **Karpfen**; you can't miss its façade, which is covered with frescoes depicting the city's prominent figures and events. The hotel is friendly and personal, and the food consistently good. At the **Altes Badhaus** restaurant on the Lindenplatz, a few blocks west of the Marktplatz, Sigrid and Heinrich Götzenberger prepare fish and game specialties with imagination and a sure instinct for public relations that has won their gourmet table recognition from all over southwest Germany; Tel: (6271) 56-16. For an informal meal from the same kitchen go downstairs to the **Badstube**; try the *Kaninchen* (rabbit) ragout with marjoram sauce and *Bubespitzele*.

The Neckar nearly ties itself in a knot at **Hirschhorn**, 9 km (5 miles) below Eberbach. Dominated by its 12th-century **castle** (much of it later rebuilt), Hirschhorn's Medieval houses cluster around the 15th-century **Carmelite abbey church**. Here you can see some interesting, though over-restored, 16th-century frescoes. Up on the Burg, a café terrace looks out across the river's hairpin bend and back into the lush Odenwald. Mark Twain, who described Hirschhorn's "packed and dirty tenements," would delight in today's tidy and conscientiously restored village, whose 17th-century half-timbered façades invite you to explore its lanes; especially noteworthy is the line of river-front houses built next to or on the old city wall. At number 25 on the Hauptstrasse, which parallels the Neckar, the **Weinstube zum Hirsch**, in a building that dates in part to 1621, features such delicacies as home-smoked salmon created from an old Norwegian recipe.

Halfway from Hirschhorn to Heidelberg, the walled fortress village of **Dilsberg** looks north across the Neckar toward Neckarsteinach with its four castles. Imagine, Twain suggested, "a comely, shapely hill, rising abruptly out of the dead level of the surrounding green plains . . . and with just exactly room on the top of its head for its steepled and turreted and roof-clustered cap of architecture," and you have Dilsberg as it still looks today. The prince-elector took refuge here when the French overran Heidelberg castle, and Dilsberg's walls held General Tilly at bay in 1622 and 1629, during the Thirty Years War. Not until 1827 was the central fortress dismantled. From the 52-foot-high defensive wall you can look deep into the Neckar valley across grazing lands and forest toward Heidelberg. Below the fortress wall, the restaurant **Zum Deutschen Kaiser** offers homemade sausages and pastries, and a terrace with a view.

Grilled saddle of lamb in herb sauce with fresh mushrooms is one of many lamb, fish, and poultry specialties at the little restaurant **Zum Letzten Heller** down in Neckargemünd, at the foot of Dilsberg's hill (Brückengasse 10). You can escape the town's heavy traffic at the hotel-restaurant **Zum Ritter**. Not cheap, the hotel has many rooms directly on the Neckar; its glassed-in dining terrace has the same view. Across the bridge and back upstream about a mile, you come to a roadside parking area shortly before you reach **Neckarsteinach**. From here a path winds up the hillside past three of the area's four castles; persevere until you reach the **Schwalbennest**, the highest and prettiest, about 30 minutes from the road. From the restored watchtowers of this early 13th-century ruin a vista of villages, river, fields, forest, and hills stretches away into the distance.

# HEIDELBERG

Like most European cities, Heidelberg has a modern and a historic face. Unlike most, however, its Altstadt is not its center but its eastern extremity: a long wedge of slate-roofed sandstone buildings jostling for space along the narrow south bank of the Neckar. The Altstadt began upstream under the protective ramparts of the elector's hillside castle; through the centuries it edged westward down the river, squeezed between the last heights of the Odenwald. Reaching the Rhine plain, Heidelberg at last expanded into the Weststadt, whose research towers, high-tech industries, and chain hotels form most visitors' first, rather disappointing, impression of "romantic" old Heidelberg.

From Bismarckplatz, Heidelberg's present-day center, a walk east along the **Hauptstrasse** takes you progressively back in time into the Altstadt. The Hauptstrasse is now a broad and busy pedestrian mall, but narrow Medieval lanes on both sides frame glimpses of looming green hills; on the south, the Königstuhl (Throne), on the north, the Heiligenberg (Holy Mount), omnipresent representatives of State and Church.

The **Kurpfälziches Museum**, at Hauptstrasse 97, about halfway to the castle, is prettily housed in an early 18th-century *palais* with a courtyard café. The museum's master-piece is Tilman Riemenschneider's 1509 altarpiece of Christ and the Apostles, their realistically carved faces gaunt with pathos. Anthropology buffs will seek out the cast of the 300,000-year-old lower jaw of Homo Heidelbergensis, dis-covered in the vicinity 80 years ago. Not far from the mu-seum, the restaurant **Zum Güldenen Schaf**, at Hauptstrasse 115, has an herb garden for open-air luncheons and an atmospheric interior; the proprietor has created a droll museum of the city's history in a back room.

# Heidelberg University

The key event in Heidelberg's history was the founding, in 1386, of the first university in Germany; it was the brainchild of Elector Ruprecht I of the Palatinate. Ruprecht's university got off to a roaring start when the German emperor backed the Italian candidate for the papacy during the Great Schism rather than the French; part of the fallout from this political event was the exodus of German intellectuals from the Sorbonne. The professors of Heidelberg's four faculties, modeled on the Sorbonne, were partly paid by Ruprecht but depended mostly on benefices granted by Pope Urban VI, who also issued the bull authorizing the university.

When the university's rapid growth caused a space prob-lem, Ruprecht II had a simple solution: He drove the city's Jews from their homes and synagogues and converted them to faculty housing for the university's clerical professors. But the university grew up outside the walls of the original city, whose limits the **Universitätsplatz** marks. Here, where the building known as the Old University now stands, stood Martin Luther in 1518 to dispute with a faculty still loyal to their benefactor in Rome. Only 45 years later its members, reflecting the Calvinist convictions of Elector Friedrich III (the Pious), composed the Heidelberg Catechism, the defini-tive statement of reformed Christian faith.

If the Baroque façade of the Alte Universität does not match your conception of a Medieval university, it is because the Wars of the Orléans Succession at the end of the 17th century more or less erased Heidelberg, and the then-existing univer-sity, from the map. Built in 1728, the Old University has its own considerable tradition; among more recent lecturers have been Karl Jaspers, Martin Heidegger, Arnold Toynbee, and Somerset Maugham. A few steps past it and up the Augustinerstrasse, visit the best-known relic of Mark Twain's and Sigmund Romberg's Heidelberg: the **Studentenkarzer** (student prison). Generations of unrepentant scapegraces confined to its cramped second-floor rooms for minor offences have scribbled with candle smoke and chalk on the walls, immortalizing their plaints and witticisms.

The Universitätsplatz is usually alive with students perched on the central fountain, draped on the Old University's steps, and flowing in tidal rhythms through the portals of the New University and the library. The New University, built in the 1930s with funds collected by a former American ambassador, is on the south side of the square. The library, the **Bibliotheca Palatina**, is worth seeing, not only for its wonderfully exuberant entrance on the Seminarstrasse but also for its exhibit of Medieval manuscripts. The most significant is the Codex Manesse, a beautifully illuminated 14th-century collocation of earlier courtly love lyrics (facsimile display). The oldest church in Heidelberg, the 12th-century **Peterskirche**, stands opposite the library; within are the gravestones of three centuries' worth of university professors and Palatine courtiers.

# Heilig-Geist-Kirche

In 1400, Elector Ruprecht III celebrated his ascension to the imperial throne (as Ruprecht I) by building a new church on the Marktplatz, a few blocks east of the Universitätsplatz. Though his reign lasted only one inglorious decade, Ruprecht's Heilig-Geist-Kirche (Holy Ghost Church) has raised its Gothic flanks over the attached merchants' stalls for almost 600 years. The tombs of more than 50 prince-electors ornamented the church until 1693, when French troops smashed them and scattered the bones of the dead; oddly, the only surviving gravestones are those of Ruprecht himself and his wife, Elizabeth, who still smile naively up at you from their place in the north aisle.

If you attend—and you should—one of the frequent concerts in the Heilig-Geist-Kirche, be sure to sit in the gallery, opposite the performers. These galleries were specially built in 1440 to house the library the prince-electors had begun with manuscripts commandeered from the abbey of Lorsch. By the end of the 16th century the Bibliotheca Palatina was one of Europe's most important. Though Heidelbergers still grind their teeth over the story, its seizure in 1622 and presentation to the Vatican by General Tilly no doubt saved its 5,000 books and 3,500 manuscripts from destruction.

Across from the church, the **Hotel zum Ritter St. George** is another treasure that survived the holocaust of 1693. Built by a cloth merchant in 1592, its richly ornamented gables and bays reflect the growing self-confidence of the rising middle class. Its small rooms are rather sparsely appointed and its services are limited, but the hotel's prices are not out of proportion to its central location.

# The Castle

For six centuries the Heidelberg Schloss, seat of the princes and electors of the Palatinate, watched over the city; but in 1774, a fire completed the destruction begun by the French 80 years earlier. Ironically, now that the invading hordes are composed of tourists, the castle has done Heidelberg more good as a ruin than it ever did intact as a fortress. Among the first waves of seekers of the Romantik to come down the Rhine was a French nobleman, Charles de Graimberg. Falling in love with the castle—which was being carted away stone by stone for building material—he battled for 50 years to save and restore what his countrymen had almost obliterated. The result, Europe's quintessential romantic ruin, is worth the 15-minute climb (from the Marktplatz, cross the Kornmarkt and take the Burgweg; a cable car also ascends from this point). The green terraces surrounding the castle were once Renaissance gardens whose ornamental hedges, trees, and fountains were considered a wonder of the early 17th century. Join one of the English-language tours that form hourly in the castle courtyard for an entertaining and comprehensive history of the ruin. Its finest points are evident at first glance, though: the Renaissance beauty of the northern and eastern walls, the latter now only a façade, but with a wealth of ornament. Don't miss the pharmaceutical museum in the Apothecary Tower.

Originally a formidable stronghold securing the Neckar ford and ferry, the castle was gradually converted by the prince-electors into a palace, an increasingly vulnerable stage setting for their own family dramas, one of which proved disastrous. In 1671 the young Princess Elizabeth-Charlotte was commanded by her father, the elector, to marry the epicene duke of Orléans, brother of Louis XIV. Over the ensuing 50 years "Liselotte," who had been born in the Heidelberg castle, wrote 4,000 homesick letters about her existence as a "royal slave" in Paris. When her brother died without an heir, the Sun King used her supposed claim to the Palatinate as a pretext for invading it. Heidelberg fell without resistance in 1688, and French troops later razed the city and demolished the castle.

# Along the Neckar

The Neckar crossing that the castle had been built to guard was first bridged in 1310, but in the next four centuries fire, ice, and flood destroyed four successive wooden bridges between the Altstadt on the south bank and Neuenheim on the north. The last elector to live in the castle, Karl-Theodor, left a more enduring stone bridge as a memorial to his tranquil 57-year reign (legend has it that he also left 200 children, by as many different mothers). The twin towers at the south end of the **Karl-Theodor Brücke** (or, simply, the Old Bridge) were the Medieval city's main gate. Today, crowned with Baroque helms and graced with a classical arch, the gate and bridge have become Heidelberg's symbol. Friedrich Hölderlin, in his "Ode to Heidelberg" (1799), likened the bridge to the graceful arc of a bird in flight, and Goethe called it one of the world's wonders. Germany's greatest poet visited Heidelberg eight times and, like so many others, lost his heart here (to Marianne von Willemer, another poet's wife). In 1795 Goethe *almost* stayed at the **Goldener Hecht**, facing the Old Bridge across the square, according to a plaque the hotel now proudly displays. The Hecht's popular restaurant is crowded every evening with young locals who enjoy its plain fare under fanciful wall frescoes highlighting its history.

From the Old Bridge up to the Heilig-Geist-Kirche, the **Steingasse**, Heidelberg's oldest paved street, has some of the city's best antiques and curio shops. Nearby, at Haspelgasse 18, the quiet **Weinstube zum Backofen** serves traditional Heidelberg dishes; try the *Leberknöpfle* with *Specksalat* and a Schwarzer Riesling wine. Another good place to eat is the **Schnookeloch** (Haspelgasse 8), filled with mementoes of student life; more staid, but even richer in student atmosphere, is the **Café Knösel** (Haspelgasse 20), a favorite in the Altstadt since 1863. Frau Knösel invented the *Heidelberger Studentenkuss,* a bittersweet chocolate confection filled with nougat and praline.

Cross the Old Bridge and climb the Schlangenweg, zigzagging steeply through vineyards and orchards (20 minutes) up to the **Philosophenweg**. No visitor to Heidelberg should pass up this view of the bridge, Altstadt, and castle. For six centuries university students and teachers have, like Aristotle, done their best thinking on their feet—to what effect may be judged by the seven Nobel prizes they have won.

From the middle of the Philosophenweg, high above the Neckar and paralleling it for about half a mile, follow the signs for paths leading even higher up the Heiligenberg to its peak (another hour of easy walking). At the top (1,562 feet) the ruined **Michaelskloster**, founded in 870 by the abbey of Lorsch, stands in a grove that has been a place of worship since Celtic times. The ruins here have recently been tidied up and fenced in, but the scene still evokes the pure religious ardor of the Carolingian founders.

If you prefer an easier walk, follow the Philosophenweg east (and gradually downhill) to its juncture with the Hirschgasse, which will take you down to the Neckar. Mark Twain came to the Hirschgasse to observe the bloody ritual duels fought by student fraternities "in a two-story public house": the **Hirschgasse**, at Hirschgasse 3, where an inn has stood since 1490. The hotel enjoys an unequaled location directly across the Neckar from the castle. Renovated after a recent fire, the Hirschgasse features Laura Ashley–style suites, a restaurant aspiring to the gourmet level, and an eager, friendly young staff. Under the same management, and slightly less expensive, the **Prinz-Hotel Heidelberg**, at Neuenheimer Landstrasse 5, overlooks the river from the other (western) end of the Philosophenweg, with such extras as an oversized thermal whirlpool, steam sauna, waterfall shower, and a kitchen serving Italian cuisine.

**Neuenheim**, the north bank suburb where the Romans fortified and bridged the Neckar, now has many handsome turn-of-the-century houses; riverside joggers pant through its park, and elderly ladies feed crumbs to the swans along the riverbank. The Theodor-Heuss bridge leads back to Bismarckplatz, hub of Heidelberg's excellent streetcar and bus network. Two blocks south is the city's premier hotel, the **Europäischer Hof–Hotel Europa**. Generously proportioned in 19th-century grand-hotel style, the Europa has built its new wing around a garden court that many rooms overlook. You can choose between these and more spacious quarters in the old section—all are comfortable.

Diagonally across the park to the west, **Holiday Inn** has taken over another old-timer, the Schrieder Hotel, renovating it within municipally imposed limits and adding no-smoking rooms and a basement pool and sauna. You can, of course, dine sumptuously at both hotels, but epicures should read further: A few blocks south, at the **Alt Heidelberg**, the food, particularly the seafood specialties, of the **Restaurant Graimberg** attracts as many locals as lodgers. Upstairs, the accommodations are roomy, and prices are moderate. Two other convenient hotels in the same category are the **Monpti** and the **Acor**, both in tastefully converted town houses.

The gourmet restaurant **Simplicissimus**, at Ingrimstrasse 16, strikes a French note in the middle of the Altstadt. The decor is classic Parisian café style, the food light, delicate, and fresh. The Old City abounds in Greek, Turkish, and especially Italian restaurants to which Heidelbergers flock: **Piccolo Mondo**, at Klingenteich Strasse 6, grills its fresh fish and meat specialties with finesse and serves them with humor.

If you should notice that the Heidelberg streetcars are flying the city's colors on little flags during your visit, head for the Philosophenweg or the Theodor-Heuss bridge, two good vantage points for an evening fireworks display over the castle. The Schloss is artfully lit to simulate its siege and destruction, and the climactic blaze of pyrotechnics over the Neckar is a heart stopper.

# Outside Heidelberg

Less than 10 km (6 miles) down the Neckar, **Ladenburg** gives the impression of having been touched up with fresh paint just before your visit. The village's original Celtic name, Lokwodunon (Swamp Fortress), indicates how muddy things could get here before the Rhine and the Neckar were tamed. Now you can explore with dry feet the city walls and gates and the network of curving lanes lined with immaculate half-timbered houses, many bearing their 15th- and 16th-century dates in Gothic flourishes. Proud of their 2,500-year history, Ladenburgers have marked the courses of Roman roads on the Kirchenstrasse near the pretty 14th-century **church of St. Gallus,** built over the Roman forum. The **Lobdengau museum** occupies the 17th-century Bischofshof, once the resort of the bishops of Worms. The most notable, Johann von Dalberg, privy councillor to Elector Philipp I, brought humanist scholars and teachers to Heidelberg during the university's late-15th-century flowering.

It is almost impossible to avoid eating asparagus all over the Rhine area between April and June, when every café and restaurant displays a banner proudly proclaiming *Spargelzeit* ("asparagus time"). Though you don't have to go to **Schwetzingen**, 10 km (6 miles) west of Heidelberg, to eat that delicacy so beloved to the German, Schwetzingen's plump white asparagus is thought by connoisseurs to be the best. Have a helping of it covered with hollandaise (or in some 50 other forms) at the restaurant **Löwen**, at Schloss Strasse 4–6, across from the castle; if you have a place to cook, buy it fresh by the kilo at the Spargelmarkt.

Schwetzingen's **Schlossgarten** is not only one of the prime examples of formal landscape gardening in 18th-century Europe, it is also a delightful place to spend a day. The park combines Baroque opulence with romantic lavishness, reflecting the sequence of architects employed by Elector Karl Theodor, whose summer residence this was, and for whose delectation they created fountains, lakes, a mosque, a ruined aqueduct, and a "Roman" fortress.

# *SPEYER*

About 25 km (15 miles) southwest of Heidelberg on the far side of the Rhine, Speyer is most easily reached by car by way of Schwetzingen and Ketsch (the train trip from Heidelberg to Speyer, because it requires several transfers, takes an hour to an hour and a half). Originally a Roman fortification, Speyer became a bishopric in the seventh century, but it first assumed importance as a town in the 11th century with the construction of its **Dom** (cathedral), the most enormous building project of the day. As you approach the Rhine bridge from the east, the Dom rules the town's skyline and is its main attraction for visitors.

Emperor Conrad II began construction of the Dom in 1030, ushering in a new, monumental phase in European religious architecture. One of the most important Romanesque structures in Germany, it was also the land's largest church until it was eventually surpassed by the Cologne cathedral. Whether you approach it from the Rhine through the shady park on whose west edge it stands or along the Maximilianstrasse through the town, the cathedral's red sandstone bulk with its massive Romanesque domes and towers confronts you majestically. From its steps on St. John's Day in 1146 Bernard of Clairvaux summoned Conrad III with the voice of God ("O Man . . . I have raised you to the heights of royalty. And you, what have you done for me?") to set off on the disastrous Second Crusade. Here in the Dom the second Diet of Speyer in 1529 annulled religious freedoms previously granted, provoking the protests of six princes and 14 cities, the followers of Martin Luther—who were from that time known as "protestants."

Entering the Dom from the west, you cross the lofty nave, whose bare sandstone walls and massive columns emphasize its airy, clean proportions. To the right, at the end of the south aisle, a flight of stairs leads down into the **crypt**. Begun in 1025, the crypt, the largest north of the Alps, is considered one of the world's most beautiful. Four emperors, three empresses, and four German kings rest here in stone sarcophagi (with modern covers). "Nothing is more magnificent, nothing nobler, nothing in Germany and Europe holier than these Imperial tombs," Victor Hugo wrote.

When the French razed Speyer in 1689, Louis XIV's soldiers played football with the heads of royalty from the pillaged crypt—but they found only the top level of graves. Not until 1900 did excavations reveal the graves of the Salian emperors, Conrad II and his descendants Henry III, IV, and V, identified by their wooden orbs and copper crowns. At the base of the vault where they now lie, the image of Rudolph of Hapsburg, the first of a great dynasty, is sculpted upon his gravestone holding the orb and scepter. His furrowed brow and tense mouth give the impression of a conscientious, somewhat harried man doing his best in a difficult position.

A few steps south of the Dom is the massive towered and turreted 19th-century **Historisches Museum der Pfalz**, scheduled to reopen after renovation in June 1990. One of the best and largest museums of viticulture is here; on display is a Roman flask, found in a sarcophagus near Speyer, containing wine from the third century A.D. The museum's best-known exhibit is the so-called **Golden Hat**, a Bronze Age cult object (circa 12th century B.C.) of pure gold.

Behind the Dom and the museum, a wooded park full of benches and paths reaches down to the Rhine. You can stroll along the river or take a two-hour cruise around it in the little steamer that docks here. The north boundary of the park is the Speyerbach, which you can follow back up toward the Dom from the Rhine to reach the **Sonnenbrücke**, a picturesque Medieval bridge in a quarter of half-timbered houses and cobbled streets in the shadow of the Dom.

Speyer's main street, Maximilianstrasse, once the triumphal way by which monarchs and princes of the church proceeded ceremoniously to the Dom, is now a pedestrian mall leading west to the Altpörtel, Speyer's best-known landmark after the cathedral. About halfway between the two, just off the Maximilianstrasse at the head of the Korngasse, you'll find, in a carefully renovated Fachwerk structure, the restaurant **Zur Alten Münze**. Here moderately priced Pfälzer cooking is tastefully dished up in the wood-beamed interior or, in good weather, at tables on the square in view of the cathedral.

The **Altpörtel**, one of the few structures that survived the conflagration of 1689, is Speyer's only remaining Medieval gate. The **Altpörtel Café**, with its pretty Baroque façade, makes an excellent vantage point from which to admire the ponderous portal—actually a tower—of which the base is 13th century, the top story with its Gothic arched arcade 16th century, and the steep slate roof 18th century. Just a few steps south down the Karmeliterstrasse at number 11–13, the **Backmulde** is a cozy (but not cheap) restaurant featuring Alsatian specialties and a fine selection of French and Pfälzer wines. The Backmulde is small enough that owner-chef Gunter Schmidt can personally advise his guests, so be sure to reserve a table; Tel: (6232) 715-77.

# *WORMS*

Worms lies on the Rhine's west bank about 30 km (18 miles) northwest of Heidelberg (follow the A 5 to Bensheim, then go 20 km/12 miles west of Bensheim on route B 47, the Nibelungenstrasse). Daily excursions by boat leave for Worms from Heidelberg's Neckarside docks on the left (west) bank of the Rhine for a pleasant half-day trip down the Neckar and the Rhine.

Larger than Speyer, Worms too is dominated by its mighty Romanesque **Dom**, practically the sole memorial to Worms's century-long status as one of the the leading imperial cities of the Holy Roman Empire. Whether you arrive by car or boat, you will have no difficulty finding the Dom in its park on the highest hilltop of the Altstadt. Here, safely above high water, the Romans built the forum of their Civitas Vangonium, one of Rome's earliest bases on the Rhine, at a trade-routes crossroads settlement the Celts had called Borbetomagus. Later the Frankish kings held court where the forum had been; on this historic hill, Charlemagne celebrated two of his five weddings and received the homage of the defeated Tassilo, duke of Bavaria.

The Dom, graced by Romanesque round towers and arches, and enlivened by many grotesque and fanciful exterior carvings intended to drive off evil spirits, was largely constructed between 1130 and 1200. The main entrance (on the south side) is through a soaring Gothic arch flanked by lively early-14th-century sculptures of biblical scenes. Cross the nave and go left down the north aisle past a series of intricate and expressive Late Gothic sandstone reliefs commissioned by the great humanist bishop of Worms, Johann von Dalberg. Standing in the characteristically pentagonal west chancel under three Gothic rose windows, you look down the years to the ornate Baroque high altar in the east chancel.

Though the Dom's crypt (entrance at the head of the south aisle) shelters no imperial graves, it does hold the ancestors of the Salian emperors, particularly the tomb of Conrad the Red, father of Emperor Conrad II and founder of the Salian line. Worms remained a steadfast rock for the Holy Roman Emperors in a stormy sea of rivalry through the centuries, and it was the scene of many historic imperial meetings. The Concordat of Worms in 1122 ended the struggle between church and state over investiture (the power to invest bishops and abbots); the agreement provided that this privilege resided solely with the papacy, but granted the state a certain amount of veto power in the decision. Not long after completion of the Dom, Frederick Barbarossa made Worms a free imperial city, recording this action on a bronze tablet over the cathedral's north portal.

This north entrance was once the ceremonial portal of the emperors and bishops, whose courts were situated in the **Schlossplatz** north of the Dom. Here, where the Romans had met in their forum, where the Nibelungen and the Franks had held court, Martin Luther faced Emperor Charles V on a spring day in 1521 and refused to retract his criticisms of the Catholic Church. The Diet of Worms had taken up the question of Luther; the Edict of Worms declared him an outlaw. With his words, "Here I stand. I can do no other. God help me. Amen," Luther provoked his own excommunication and laid the foundation of the Reformation. A few steps up the Stephansgasse to the north is a park where a 19th-century memorial to that historic day centers on the robed and adamant figure of Luther towering over other great reformers such as Wycliff, Hus, and Savonarola.

In Charles V, Worms had a champion of Catholicism; in Luther, the founder of Protestantism; and in Rabbi Salomon Ben Isaak—called Raschi—Worms had, from 1055 to 1056, the definitive Medieval Talmudic scholar. Follow the Martinsgasse north from the Luther memorial to the handsome 13th-century church of St. Martin. One block north, at St. Martin's Gate in the former city walls, begins the **Judengasse**, the only surviving Jewish ghetto in Germany and the best-preserved Medieval street in Worms. Turn right into the Hintere Judengasse to find, at the center of what used to be one of Germany's oldest and most important Jewish communities, the Men's Synagogue. First built in 1174, the synagogue was destroyed and rebuilt several times during outbreaks of racial persecution (most recently in 1938). As the Talmudic scholar's memorial, the **Raschi Judaic museum** was set up here in 1982 in a modern building on Renaissance foundations, with a valuable collection of documents, pictures, and religious objects, many from Worms's silversmith workshops. Nearby, in the synagogue garden, a stairway leads down into the ritual **Mikwe** (women's bath), which also dates to the 12th century. A block southwest of the Dom, on the busy Andreasring, Germany's oldest **Jewish cemetery** is an overgrown jumble of 2,000 gravestones, many ancient and illegible, the oldest dating back to the 11th century.

Follow the Andreasring east one block to the Andreaspforte (gate), through which, to the right, you find the 12th-century **cloister of St. Andrew**, which since 1928 has housed the city's archaeological and historical museum. Don't miss its fascinating display of Roman artifacts, especially the glass. The Romanesque abbey church now houses a display of Medieval and later sacred objects.

Though nothing tangible remains of Worms's fifth and sixth-century Burgundian royal courts, the resounding names of mythological Nibelungen heroes, derived from Burgundian times, still adorn the city's streets, parks, and squares. Siegfried came to Worms to woo Kriemhilde, sister of Burgundian king Gunther; before he could attain his own heart's desire, Siegfried had to win the Valkyrie Brunhilde for Gunther. Blood oaths, treachery, magic, and revenge characterize the story, best known to us in Wagner's operatic cycle of operas, *Der Ring des Nibelungen.* The story ends in Hagen's murder of Siegfried and his casting of the Nibelungen gold into the Rhine. No visit to Worms is complete without a pilgrimage to the Hagen statue in the Rhineside park, just north of the bridge, where the bard is immortalized in the act of disposing of the troublesome treasure.

## *THE GERMAN WINE ROUTE*

West of Heidelberg and Mannheim, the broad Rhine valley stretches 35 km (22 miles) to the foot of the Haardt massif overlooking the left (west) bank. On that bank, below the heights, lies the **Deutsche Weinstrasse**, the German Wine Route. The northern section reaches from Grünstadt (20 km/12 miles southwest of Worms) south on the B 271 through Kallstadt, Bad Dürkheim, Wachenheim, and Deidesheim to Neustadt, the Weinstrasse's unofficial capital. From

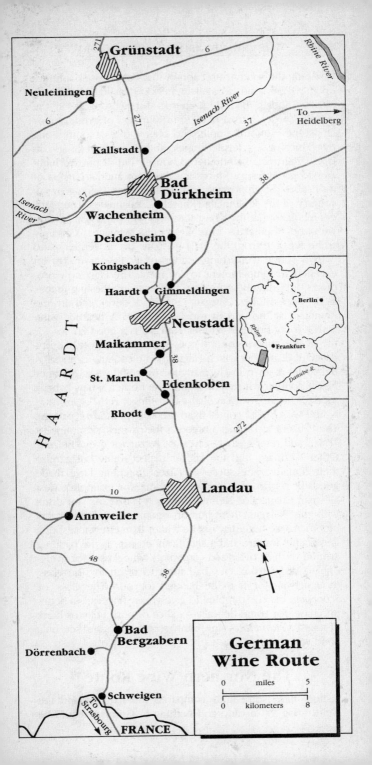

Neustadt, the southern section of the Weinstrasse continues on the B 38 south to Maikammer, St. Martin, Edenkoben, Rhodt, Landau, Bad Bergzabern, and Schweigen on the French border, a total of 80 km (50 miles) of gentle, sunny landscape. Almond, apple, and cherry trees bloom along the Weinstrasse's fertile slopes, and the charm of its villages, with their half-timbered houses and distinctive high-arched gateways, produces an abundant annual harvest of tourists. Most important, this is the finest wine-growing country of the Rheinpfalz (Rhineland-Palatinate). The Pfälzers maintain that their best Rieslings will stand comparison with the Rheingau's most aristocratic vintages. Certainly white Riesling from the Pfalz—usually dry to semidry, and with a subtle, refreshing, rather fruity flavor—makes an excellent accompaniment to any meal. The Pfalz now produces only slightly more than half as many Riesling grapes as it does Müller-Thurgau, a hybrid developed in the Rheingau at the end of the last century. A heartier wine with a fruity bouquet, Müller-Thurgau is a good choice for the novice wine taster and goes well with the sort of spicy, flavorful dishes for which Pfälzer home cooking is noted. A light wine known in Germany for over 300 years, Sylvaner is still popular with snacks, while the Kerner, a new hybrid, modifes Riesling with a touch of Trollinger red.

The word *Pfalz* comes from the Latin *palatium* (palace). The Pfälzers, as distinct a breed as their wines, pronounce it "Palz," and refer to themselves as "Pelzer" or even "Belzer." Other Germans find the Pfälzer dialect funny but admire their initiative and success: Pfälzer emigrants have made good the world over (in Pennsylvania, for example); West German Chancellor Helmut Kohl is a Pfälzer. As you drink with the Pfälzers, their humor, openness, and hospitality bloom. A joke here may not be wittier than elsewhere, but it is certainly louder, and a significant custom is the handing around of their oversized (one-pint) wineglasses for everyone to drink from. (It's bad form to reach for the glass, though; wait for it to be handed to you.) The glass, or *Schoppen,* may be dimpled to give greasy fingertips a better purchase, for some delicacy—a slice of pork belly or hunk of fragrant *Handkäse*—invariably accompanies and sets off a good wine here.

# The Northern Wine Route

Visitors have sometimes compared the land around the Weinstrasse to Tuscany, and nothing in Germany could be more Tuscan than the little fortified town of **Neuleiningen**, near Grünstadt, with its cliffside houses overshadowed by the ruined 13th-century castle of the Leiningen counts. (From Grünstadt, take the Weinstrasse, B 271, 1.5 km/1 mile to Kirchheim, and follow the signs from Kirchheim 3 km/2 miles west to Neuleiningen.) Here, in 1525, the Countess Eva is supposed to have quelled a peasant uprising by stuffing the rebels with good food until they forgot their grievances. The restaurant **Burgschänke** at the base of the castle still sends its patrons away in the same happy condition; its specialty is thick beefsteaks. Down the lane, **Liz's Stuben** (Am Goldberg 2) is tiny, intimate, and friendly, offering whatever Frau Gissel feels like cooking that day—the menu is light and Italianate. Neuleiningen has a jewel of a small hotel, the **Alte Pfarrey**, housed in three buildings of a 15th-century farm court, its guest rooms furnished with Italian antiques and Baroque reproductions. The Mozart room at the hotel is the right setting for a glass of local Höllenpfad wine.

About 10 km (6 miles) south, **Bad Dürkheim** rises like an amphitheater up the lower slopes of the Isenach valley. On the first and second weekends of September the town stages a Rabelaisian spectacle, the Dürkheimer Wurstmarkt, which Dürkheimers claim is the world's largest wine festival. Shaded by gigantic tents from the late-summer sun, half a million celebrants consume a quarter of a million liters of wine. A gargantuan wine cask, the Dürkheimer *Fass,* contains not the wine but the drinkers—450 people can crowd into its two levels. Lurching in unison from side to side in time with traditional drinking songs, the merry Pfälzers pass around their giant wine tumblers in a scene worthy of Brueghel, from whose brush could have come the procession of vintners wheeling in wine kegs on Medieval-style wheelbarrows. This custom recalls the original 15th-century Wurstmarkt: Pilgrims came in such numbers to the chapel of St. Michael on the hill above Dürkheim that the local merchants trundled their wares, including sausage and wine, up the Michelsberg in barrows.

Known also for its Michelsberger Riesling, Bad Dürkheim has become equally famous for its water, and today many pilgrims come to be cured by immersion or inhalation rather than by prayer.

**Haus Boller** is a small, highly respectable hotel with moderate prices and a convenient location near the spa. The restaurant **Tenner**, Römerplatz 12, serves up *Saumagen* and *Leberknödel* with a good assortment of local wines—which you can also sample in the homey atmosphere of one of the Strausswirtschaften found in the Gaustrasse (after 5:00 P.M.).

Overlooking Bad Dürkheim from the west, the 11th-century **abbey of Limburg**, once the repository of the symbols of imperial power (crown, orb, scepter, and sword), was destroyed in 1404. Today its roofless abbey church, with two rows of plane trees replacing its monolithic sandstone columns, is part of an impressive ruin in which the city often stages concerts.

According to tradition, one of the abbots of Limburg lost a drinking contest to the *Bürgermeister* of **Wachenheim**, south of Bad Dürkheim (now on route 271), and had to forfeit the tax paid to the abbey by the Wachenheimers. It is easy to see that Wachenheim has always prospered from its wine by its numerous handsome *Höfe* (estates) belonging to prosperous wine proprietors. One of the most interesting to visit is that of Dr. Bürcklin-Wolf in the **Kolb'schen Hof**, at Weinstrasse 65. Its vaulted cellars, where the abbot is said to have lost his wager, can hold 1.4 million liters of wine. Tours of the cellars, in which modern wine-making technology has not excluded the use of traditional wooden casks, are conducted with characteristic Pfälzer gusto and spontaneity; you can take home such fine vintages as a 1986 Wachenheimer Gerümpel Riesling Kabinett to conjure up memories. Right around the corner, the wine restaurant **Alte Münz** (Langgasse 2) would remind you that Wachenheim was the 15th-century *Münze* (mint) for the dukes of Zweibrücken—if you weren't preoccupied with your *Münzplatte,* a platter of solid Pfälzer *Wurst* specialties, and your choice of 14 different open wines.

Like Wachenheim, **Deidesheim**, to the south of Wachenheim, conceals an underground labyrinth of wine cellars. Deidesheim's great wine estate is **Bassermann-Jordan**, whose Forster Kirchenstück vineyard received the formal military salute, with flourished saber and drumroll, of the withdrawing Spanish army of occupation following the Thirty Years War. Known for its traditional wine-making methods, Bassermann-Jordan stores its wines only in oaken casks. Make an appointment for a tour and a tasting session at the **Ketschauer Hof**, just behind the Gothic church of St. Ulrich on the Marktplatz.

An excellent complement to your visit to Bassermann-Jordan—or any of the other fine wineries—is a tour of the **cultural wine museum** next to the church. Among many other displays are wine labels and bottles, wine glasses from Roman times to Jugendstil, a cooper's shop, and the grandly furnished city council chambers—and the museum is still expanding. It is housed in Deidesheim's pretty Baroque Rathaus, from whose steps on the first Tuesday after Pentecost, between 5:45 and 6:00 P.M., a billy goat is auctioned off with great ceremony, the final bid coinciding with the 6:00 bell. The goat, which is paid to Deidesheim as a "grazing fee" by the hill town of Lambrecht, is presented by Lambrecht's most recently married couple; the offering must be "well-horned and potent," leaving the ceremony's significance in little doubt. You can watch the billy-goat auction from your window if you get a front room facing the square at the **Deidesheimer Hof**. The large comfortable rooms, though not cheap, are a good value, and the hotel's **Schwarzer Hahn** dining room is now under the direction of Manfred Schwarz, a name that generates excitement among German gourmets. Tel: (6326) 18-12.

On the other side of the Marktplatz, at Weinstrasse 31, the restaurant **Zur Kanne** has a 700-year tradition, elegantly rustic interior, and refined Pfälzer cooking: for instance, a hearty saddle of venison, a delicate *carpaccio* with green beans, and foie gras on sliced apples with truffle sauce. The white wines come from Bürcklin-Wolf, and some good reds from France. Credit cards are accepted—luckily, considering the prices.

Farther down, north of Neustadt, the Weinstrasse closely skirts the green slopes of the Haardt. Between Gimmeldingen and Königshof (on the left 2 km/1.2 miles from the Weinstrasse's Gimmeldingen exit), the **Hotel Burckshof** stands in its own wooded park. Its tranquil garden terrace looks far across the plain, as do many of the rooms in this turreted 19th-century villa, which is comfortable and moderate in price.

In a similar situation, but better known and pricier, the **Hotel Haardter Schlösschen**, at Mandelring 35 in Haardt, also offers fine views from its vantage point above Neustadt in a lush park surrounded by the walls of a 700-year-old ruined fortress. (Entering Neustadt from the north on the B 38, turn right on the Haardterstrasse at the first major junction, following signs for Haardt, Neustadt's northern suburb, to the Mandelring, and continue to the hotel at number 35.) The comfortable rooms are furnished in part with the products of the innkeeper's own carpentry skills, and meals on the panoramic terrace overlooking the vineyards include Pfälzer specialties prepared from local organically grown ingredients.

**Neustadt an der Weinstrasse** is a bustling, cheerful market

town with an exemplarily restored Altstadt harmonizing recent construction with older buildings. The Gothic church
contains the tomb of Elector Ruprecht I, founder of Heidelberg University, and boasts the world's largest cast-iron bell,
capable of loosening roof tiles with its thunder. In the
Marktplatz in front of the church, the queen of the wine
harvest is chosen every October, the climax of a week of
festivities. Ever ready for a party, the Neustädters are a
friendly, gossipy lot, with the trick of making a guest feel at
home. The prettiest *Weinstube* in the Altstadt is the sunny
**Liebstöck'l**, at Mittelgasse 22, in a gabled 18th-century building facing the huge linden tree that shades its garden. Try
Annette Heinzmann's *Ochsenfetzen* in a garlic-bacon sauce
with a salad and homemade Spätzle; she will advise you about
wine. Equally delighted to discuss his food and wine, Jürgen
Reis runs the **Altstadtkeller** at Kunigundenstrasse 2, one
street south of the Marktplatz. He brings you the day's menu,
chalked on a large slate, usually featuring thick steaks or a veal
filet—hearty food suited to the Keller's vaulted stone interior
and backed by 18 open Pfälzer wines.

Right across the Kunigundenstrasse, the tiny **Hotel Légére**
is still an inside tip. Olympic cycling champion Gregor Braun
(he won a medal in Montreal in 1976) and his wife, Ilse, have
designed and furnished the half-timbered interior, which is
flooded with light from the central stairwell; the four rooms
are simple but charming, and the price is moderate.

## The Southern Wine Route

The southern Weinstrasse begins north of **Edenkoben** (on
route B 38 below Neustadt), noted for its columned Neoclassical palace, the former summer residence of King Ludwig I
of Bavaria. Surrounded by chestnut groves and vineyards,
the **Villa Ludwigshöhe** now houses the paintings of German
Impressionist Max Slevogt. Below, on the west edge of
Edenkoben, the former Cistercian **abbey of Heilsbruck** is
now a private estate and winery, boasting the largest wine
cellar in Germany to use oak casks only. Manager Rudolf
Nagel will conduct groups of 20 or more through the refec-
tory and cellars and supervise wine tastings in the picturesque courtyard; Tel: (6323) 28-83 for information. Among
the estate's fine wines are Edenkobener Klostergarten Riesling, Silvaner, and Ruländer vintages.

Just south of Edenkoben, on the lower slopes of the
Rietburg, is the village of **Rhodt**, one of the Weinstrasse's
treasures. A stroll down its Theresienstrasse under a line of

venerable chestnut trees takes you past one imposing example after another of the distinctive Pfälzer Höfe from the
17th and 18th centuries; most have high-arched stone carriage gates, elaborately carved and set off with fig trees,
flowers, and vines.

Rhodt's real treasure is its Traminer vineyards, which
produce a wine so prized during the Renaissance that in
1603 the margrave of Baden-Durlach traded the duke of
Württemberg *two* of his villages for Rhodt. As part of Baden-
Durlach, Rhodt escaped the general destruction that Louis
XIV visited upon the Pfalz in 1693, so the wine not only built
Rhodt's proud Weinhöfe, it also rescued them. Some of these
Traminer vines, in the Rosengarten vineyard at the village's
edge, are thought to have been producing fruit since the
17th century, a fact that would make them the oldest bearing
grapevines in Germany and possibly anywhere in the world.

For a look behind the village's massive gates, which are
kept protectively closed on its liquid gold, visit a Weinstube
established in a Hof. A good choice would be the **Weinstube
Waldkirch,** at Weinstrasse 53. At tables set out in the cobbled
courtyard, Frau Dorothea Waldkirch offers you a tray of
wine-taster's glasses from which to select your wine and a
palette of some two dozen local specialties from which to
select your dinner. (Insiders go for the simple, homemade
*Bratwurst* with fried potatoes and *Kraut*).

In a landscape as dramatic as its history, one of the
grimmest fortified castles in Germany, **Burg Trifels,** rises
from the limestone precipices above **Annweiler,** 15 km (10
miles) beyond Edenkoben west of route B 38 on route
B 10. Here the Salian emperors kept the symbols of imperial majesty—crown, orb, and scepter—for 150 years, and it
was to Burg Trifels that Emperor Henry VI, son of Frederick Barbarossa, returned in 1196 from his savage conquest
of Sicily with 150 pack mules laden with treasure. Henry
pursued his vision of a Hohenstaufen world empire with
ruthless single-mindedness. When he captured Richard the
Lion-Hearted of England, Henry not only held him for
ransom for a year at Trifels, but also forced the English
king to acknowledge him as his feudal overlord. Malaria
struck Henry down in Sicily before he could realize his
dream of conquest. His castle, destroyed by lightning in the
17th century, was restored and enlarged by his spiritual
successors from 1937 to 1942. The view from Burg Trifels'
parapets west across the rugged Wasgau compensates you
for the 20-minute hike up. In Annweiler, a flower-bordered
stream, complete with functioning Medieval waterwheel,

reflects the quaintly irregular old houses of the **Altstadt**. Try the *Flammkuchen,* a kind of Pfälzer pizza, fresh out of the cast-iron oven at the **Weinstube S'Reiwerle** (Flitschberg 7) on Wednesday or Friday evenings, or the good wine selection any time.

In **Bad Bergzabern,** south down either route B 48 from Annweiler or route B 38 down from Edenkoben and Landau, you are just 5 km (3 miles) from the wine gateway that marks the southern end of the Weinstrasse. The **Petronella,** directly behind Bad Bergzabern's Kurpark, is in the middle of this spa-resort's prettiest scenery; every large, airy room has its own balcony on the park. The Altstadt is rich in historic buildings, most built by the counts and dukes of Zweibrücken. The oldest and finest is the **Gasthaus zum Engel**; with its ornate gables and bays, it is the Pfalz's most notable Renaissance construction. The proximity of the French border is evident at the restaurant **Wilder Mann**, at Weinstrasse 19, whose Alsatian food goes well with its Pfälzer open wines.

At the head of a valley just southwest of Bad Bergzabern, shaded by chestnut and fir trees and accented by roses, **Dörrenbach** is already planning its millennial celebration in 1993. Plan to get here early in the day to make the best of this gemlike village's genuinely Medieval atmosphere. Everything is concentrated in the space around the Renaissance Rathaus, across from the Late Gothic defensive towers of the fortified churchyard. Standing between them is like being caught in a time warp. Don't linger too late; by the time the tourist buses are pulling in down at the square, you can already be tucking into your lunch at the **Altdeutsche Weinstube**, at Hauptstrasse 14. A suitable Medieval dish here would be the *Kunsthammelfleisch* (mutton roast), marinated for three days in red wine and spices and served with a garlic-cream sauce. And by now you'll know which Pfälzer wine to order.

## GETTING AROUND
Frankfurt International Airport is the main gateway to the region. Rail service from the airport itself to Frankfurt and from there to Wiesbaden, Darmstadt, and Heidelberg is frequent and fast (see the Getting Around section in the Frankfurt-am-Main chapter).

From Wiesbaden you can visit the Rheingau by train, supplemented by bus: For example, a bus takes you from Eltville to Kiedrich and Eberbach abbey. From Mainz, trains down the valley of the Lorelei stop at Bingerbrück (across the river Nahe from Bingen) before racing on to Koblenz; plenty of local trains also stop at all the villages along the left bank of the Rhine.

From Darmstadt you can reach the central Odenwald by train, traveling down to Eberbach on the Neckar by way of Michelstadt and Erbach. Buses link the towns and villages of the Odenwald with a reliable, though not necessarily very frequent, service. The Neckar valley is accessible by rail from Heidelberg all the way up to Stuttgart, a scenic trip of a few hours. East–west rail connections in the whole area, however, are rather complicated, when they exist at all; it is difficult, for example, to get from Heidelberg to the Weinstrasse. Once you reach Grünstadt, however, the rest of the Weinstrasse can be explored by the rail-bus combination.

Though river cruises allow little latitude for independent exploration, they are scenic and relaxing. Short-distance cruises with local lines operate out of most Rhine and Neckar ports, often featuring shoreside wine-tasting and sightseeing arrangements. The cruise ships of the well-known KD German Rhine Line White Fleet, based in Cologne, are floating hotels complete with swimming pools, bars, glassed-in observation decks, and English-speaking crews. You can see the Rhine between Frankfurt and Cologne on a three-day cruise with stops at Mainz, Rüdesheim, Bacharach, Boppard, and Braubach (Marksburg castle). Other cruises go up the Rhine to Worms, Heidelberg, Speyer, and beyond. It is possible to join KD Line cruises in progress for short stretches as well, provided there is space available, and you can (for an extra charge) also convert your railway ticket to a boat ticket (or vice versa) at any KD dock. The KD line also offers daily Rhine service between late March and November 1 to all points of interest between Cologne and Frankfurt, including Boppard, St. Goar, Oberwesel, Kaub, Bacharach, Lorch, Bingen, Rüdesheim, Eltville, Wiesbaden-Biebrich, and Mainz. Normal crusing time from Boppard to Mainz is eight hours, but you can do it by KD hydrofoil in less than two. Local tourist information offices can furnish current schedules and help with bookings; see also "Getting Around Germany" in the Useful Facts section at the front of the book.

By far the most flexible and convenient way to get around the area is by car. The major rental agencies have offices in all the larger towns. But your aim should be to get rid of your car as soon as you reach your destination because everything described in this chapter is best seen on foot. (The local *Hauptbahnhof*—train station—is often the best place to park.) Heidelberg, for example, which is an exasperating city for drivers, has an excellent bus-streetcar system with special daily and weekend rates for sightseers. All of the major towns and cities in this region have pedestrian zones embracing their most interesting districts, and so have most of the smaller ones. By all means get a hiker's map from the tourist office and explore the outlying areas. The trails are well maintained and much used.


## ACCOMMODATIONS REFERENCE

▶ **Acor.** Friedrich-Ebert-Anlage 55, D-6900 **Heidelberg.** Tel: (6221) 220-44.

▶ **Alte Pfarrey.** Untergasse 54, D-6719 **Neuleiningen.** Tel: (6359) 54-15.

▶ **Altes Bannhaus.** Hauptstrasse 211, D-8760 **Miltenberg.** Tel: (9371) 30-61.

▶ **Alt Heidelberg.** Rohrbacherstrasse 29, D-6900 **Heidelberg.** Tel: (6221) 91-50; Telex: 461897.

▶ **Altkölnischer Hof.** D-6533 **Bacharach am Rhein.** Tel: (6743) 13-39.

▶ **Badischer Hof.** D-8762 **Amorbach/Odenwald.** Tel: (9373) 12-08.

▶ **Baudobriga.** Rheinallee 43, D-5407 **Boppard am Rhein.** Tel: (6742) 23-30.

▶ **Bellevue Rheinhotel.** Rheinallee 41–42, P.O. Box 126, D-5407 **Boppard am Rhein.** Tel: (6742) 10-20; Telex: 426310; Fax: 6742-102602.

▶ **Blauer Turm.** D-7107 **Bad Wimpfen.** Tel: (7063) 78-84 or 225.

▶ **Hotel Burckshof.** D-6730 **Neustadt an der Weinstrasse.** Tel: (6321) 660-16.

▶ **Burg Hornberg.** D-6951 **Neckarzimmern.** Tel: (6261) 40-64; Telex: 466169.

▶ **Burghotel Auf Schönburg.** D-6532 **Oberwesel am Rhein.** Tel: (6744) 70-27.

▶ **Central Hotel Eden.** Bahnhofsplatz 8, D-6500 **Mainz.** Tel: (6131) 674-00-12.

▶ **Central Hotel.** Kirschstrasse 6, D-6220 **Rüdesheim.** Tel: (6722) 23-91; Telex: 42110.

▶ **Deidesheimer Hof.** Am Marktplatz, D-6705 **Deidesheim.** Tel: (6326) 18-11; Telex: 454657.

▶ **Europäischer Hof–Hotel Europa.** Friedrich-Ebert-Anlage 1, D-6900 **Heidelberg.** Tel: (6221) 51-50; Telex: 461840.

▶ **Favorite Parkhotel.** Karl-Weiser-Strasse 1, D-6500 **Mainz.** Tel: (6131) 820-91; Telex: 4187266.

► **Hotel Felsenkeller.** Oberstrasse 39, D-6220 **Rüdesheim am Rhein.** Tel: (6722) 20-94. Telex: 42156. Fax: 47202.

► **Grüner Baum.** Grossegasse 17, D-6120 **Michelstadt/ Odenwald.** Tel: (6061) 24-09.

► **Haus Boller.** Kurgartenstrasse 19, D-6702 **Bad Dürkheim.** Tel: (6322) 14-28.

► **Haardter Schlösschen.** Mandelring 35, D-6730 **Neustadt/ Haardt.** Tel: (6321) 326-25.

► **Hessiches Haus.** Burgstrasse 32, D-6145 **Lindenfels.** Tel: (6255) 24-05.

► **Hilton International Mainz.** Rheinstrasse 68, D-6500 **Mainz.** Tel: (6131) 24-50; Telex: 4187570.

► **Hirschgasse.** Hirschgasse 3, D-6900 **Heidelberg.** Tel: (6221) 499-21 or 403-20; Telex: 461474.

► **Holiday Inn.** Kufürsten-Anlage 1, D-6900 **Heidelberg.** Tel: (6221) 91-70; Telex: 461170.

► **Jagdschloss Niederwald.** D-6220 **Rüdesheim.** Tel: (6722) 10-04; Telex: 42152.

► **Karpfen.** Am Alten Markt 1, D-6930 **Eberbach am Neckar.** Tel: (6271) 23-16.

► **Klee am Park.** Parkstrasse 4, D-62 **Wiesbaden.** Tel: (6121) 30-50-61.

► **Am Kochbrunnen.** Taunusstrasse 15, D-62 **Wiesbaden.** Tel: (6121) 52-20-01/2.

► **Krone Assmannshausen.** Rheinuferstrasse 10, D-6220 **Rüdesheim.** Tel: (6723) 20-36.

► **Krone-Post.** D-6930 **Eberbach am Neckar.** Tel: (6271) 20-13/14.

► **Am Landeshaus.** Moritzstrasse 51, D-62 **Wiesbaden.** Tel: (6121) 37-30-41/3.

► **Légére.** Kunigundenstrasse 13, D-6730 **Neustadt an der Weinstrasse.** Tel: (6321) 8-29-52.

► **Lindenwirt.** Drosselgasse, D-6220 **Rüdesheim.** Tel: (6722) 10-31/2; Telex: 42167.

► **Zur Lorelei.** Heerstrasse 87, D-5401 **St. Goar.** Tel: (6741) 16-14.

► **Maritim-Hotel.** Rheinstrasse 105, D-61 **Darmstadt.** Tel: (6151) 87-70; Telex: 419625.

► **Monpti.** Friederich-Ebert-Anlage 57, D-6900 **Heidelberg.** Tel: (6221) 234-83.

► **Nassauer Hof.** Kaiser-Friedrich-Platz 3–4, D-62 **Wiesbaden.** Tel: (6121) 13-30; Telex: 4186847.

► **Petronella.** Kurtalstrasse 47, D-6748 **Bad Bergzabern.** Tel: (6343) 10-75.

► **Post.** Schmiedgasse 2, D-8762 **Amorbach/Odenwald.** Tel: (9373) 410 or 13-10.

► **Zur Post.** Oberstrasse 35, D-6533 **Bacharach am Rhein.** Tel: (6743) 12-77.

► **Prinzhotel Heidelberg.** Neuenheimer Landstrasse 5, D-6900 **Heidelberg.** Tel: (6221) 403-20; Telex: 461125.

► **Zum Riesen.** Haupstrasse 97, D-8760 **Miltenberg.** Tel: (9371) 25-82.

► **Ritter.** Neckarstrasse 40, D-6903 **Neckargemünd.** Tel: (6223) 70-35/37; Telex: 461837.

► **Zum Ritter St. Georg.** Hauptstrasse 178, D-6900 **Heidelberg.** Tel: (6221) 242-72 or 220-03; Telex: 461506.

► **Schloss-Hotel auf Burg Rheinfels.** D-5401 **St. Goar.** Tel: (6741) 20-71.

► **Schneider am Markt.** Markt 1, D-5401 **St. Goar.** Tel: (6741) 16-89.

► **Schwan.** 5–7 Rheinallee, D-6227 **Oestrich/Rheingau.** Tel: (6723) 30-01; Telex: 42146.

► **Schwarzer Bock.** Kranzplatz 12, D-62 **Wiesbaden.** Tel: (6121) 15-50; Telex: 4186640.

► **Sonne.** Hauptstrasse 87, D-7107 **Bad Wimpfen.** Tel: (7063) 245.

► **Sonnenberg.** Friedrichstrasse 65, D-6228 **Eltville/Rheingau.** Tel: (6123) 30-81/83.

► **Weinhaus Weiler.** Marktplatz 4, D-6532 **Oberwesel am Rhein.** Tel: (6744) 70-03.

► **Weinhaus am Alten Markt.** Marktplatz 185, D-8760 **Miltenberg.** Tel: (9371) 55-00.

► **Weinmichel.** Schleiermacherstrasse 10–12, D-61 **Darmstadt.** Tel: (6151) 268-22.

# NORTHERN BAVARIA
## THE DANUBE AND FRANCONIA

*By John Dornberg*

**B**avaria is Germany's largest state; at more than 27,000 square miles, it is a substantial chunk of territory and not only by European standards. You could fit Belgium, Holland, and Luxembourg into it with room to spare, or Massachusetts, New Hampshire, and Vermont. Moreover, none of the other German *Länder,* as the states are called, has so completely preserved its 19th-century territorial integrity as this proud one-time kingdom, which still, in contrast to the other *Länder,* calls itself a *Freistaat,* a "Free State."

Bavaria is bordered on the south by Austria, on the east by Czechoslovakia, and along its western boundaries by the states of Hesse, whose principal city is Frankfurt-am-Main, and Baden-Württemberg, whose capital is Stuttgart. It is traversed from west to east by the Danube river, which enters Bavaria from Baden-Württemberg as it passes between the twin cities of Ulm and Neu-Ulm, and leaves at Passau, to the east, where it enters Austria, from there to continue past Vienna, Budapest, and Belgrade, before eventually reaching the Black Sea. The Danube divides Bavaria—which is named after the Germanic Baiuoarii tribe, who inhabited the area during the so-called Dark Ages and were subsequently conquered by the Franks—into northern and southern halves, in what is more than just a geographical division: There are significant topographical and climatological differences between the two halves, as well as cultural and linguistic ones.

In this chapter we will first follow the Danube from west (Ulm) to east (Passau), with occasional side trips into the Bayerischer Wald (Bavarian Woods) to the north, as well as special places in Niederbayern (Lower Bavaria) to the south. Then we will discuss the half of Bavaria *north* of the river, a region that is centered on Nürnberg and known historically and geographically, as well as politically, as Franconia (Land of the Franks—the Franks being the same general Germanic group that later produced the Merovingians and Carolingians).

(The *southern* half of the state—alpine Oberbayern, or Upper Bavaria, upper meaning higher in altitude—is covered in a separate chapter following the chapter on Munich. The chapter immediately after this one covers a band that stretches down the *western* side of Bavaria, from Würzburg in the north to Füssen in the Alps, on the Austrian border: the so-called Romantic Road. The Romantische Strasse, as it is called in German, intersects the route we cover in this chapter as it crosses the Danube at Donauwörth.)

Northern Bavaria is agreeable country, largely bottomland and gently rolling hills covered with dense forests around the Danube basin, becoming somewhat more mountainous as you travel farther north into Franconia. In the towns of the region, the Middle Ages lie spread out before you, and every hill seems to be crowned by a castle or a fortress—though the sounds you'll hear will most likely be those of a tractor in a nearby field. Still, as you travel the region's smooth roads, with good hotels and picture-book inns awaiting you at every turn, you will feel as if you have been transported into the past.

Some of the most breathtakingly beautiful Gothic, Renaissance, and Baroque architecture in Europe dots this peaceful, modest landscape. In the course of your tour you will encounter the magical work of Cosmas Damian and Egid Quirin Asam, brothers who in their day were the most celebrated masters of Bavarian Baroque architecture and stucco work; the deeply moving wood carving and sculpture of Tilman Riemenschneider and Veit Stoss; and the painting of Lucas Cranach and Albrecht Dürer. You will see splendid palaces built by prince-bishops, the powerful ecclesiastical and temporal rulers of once-sovereign states. And you will stay in rustic country inns that have been in business for centuries. The air is clean here, and if you keep off the Autobahn and avoid following signs that point the way to a town's *Industrieviertel* (industrial district), you will never realize that Bavaria, in addition to being Germany's second most populous state, has also become the country's high-tech "sunbelt."

MAJOR INTEREST

**Along the Danube**
Ulm and the world's tallest church spire
Ingolstadt's fortified Medieval old city
Well-preserved Regensburg and its Roman ruins
Straubing's Baroque architecture
Passau and the convergence of the Danube, Inn, and
   Ilz rivers
Naturpark Bayerischer Wald; Metten; Grafenau

**Franconia**
Nürnberg, city of the Meistersinger
Bayreuth and the Wagner festival theater
Kulmbach (beer)
Coburg, ancestral home of Prince Albert
Baroque churches of Banz and Vierzehnheiligen
Bamberg, jewel of Romanesque, Gothic, Renaissance,
   and Baroque architecture

# The Food of Northern Bavaria

Northern Bavarian food is hearty and should be approached with gusto. It is influenced by the cooking of neighboring Austria, Czechoslovak Bohemia, and Swabian Württemberg, and encompasses a variety of local traditions. In villages and small towns the noon meal is the main one, and always starts with a soup that usually has something substantial floating in it—a farina or liver dumpling, or sometimes a soft, thin pancake cut into noodlelike strips and eaten with a happy slurp. If the soup is thick, like lentil soup, it will contain slices of wurst. From there the meal usually moves on to a meat dish with gravy, accompanied by potatoes or a baseball-sized dumpling, cabbage, or sauerkraut. Dessert is rarely served, though when it is it is usually compote or custard.

*Brotzeit* (literally "bread time") is the evening meal in more tradition-bound homes and small towns. The bread is dark, usually rye, with a crisp crust, and there are countless variations on the basic theme. Sausages of all kinds, and cured and smoked meats (especially hams of infinite variety) are the standard accompaniment.

Michelin stars and Gault-Millau toques are rare in this part of Germany. Nürnberg is a bit more rewarding for the discriminating gourmet, as is northern Franconia, where you will find top-rated restaurants in and around Bayreuth, Coburg, and Bamberg. Nonetheless, you will be able to eat well though the portions may seem formidable.

In Franconia, there are some distinctive regional specialties you should try when you find them on menus. Though pork seems omnipresent, veal is also a popular entrée, and one particularly delicious dish is *Kalbshaxe Blau,* which translates as "blue leg of veal," though it isn't blue at all. The meat is first browned in butter, then simmered in vinegar with a variety of vegetables. Nürnberger *Bratwürste* are different from other bratwurst you may have tried, especially in terms of their size: They're about the same size as a little finger in both thickness and length. Six of them are considered a snack, a dozen a light meal. Although those from Regensburg look like their twins, they are in fact just cousins (the ingredients and spices are somewhat different). Both kinds are usually accompanied by sauerkraut, however. Up in Coburg try *Taschnudeln,* which, in effect, are potato noodles, buttered and baked. *Pfifferlinge* (chanterelles) abound in Franconia as well as in the Bayerische Wald. Sautéed, they make a wonderful side dish, and don't pass them up when offered in a soup such as *Pfifferlingsuppe.*

Of course, sweets and pastries abound in this part of Germany. A *Fränkischer Käsekuchen* is a cheesecake with apples baked across it; *Zwetchgenblootz* is plum cake buried under almonds and crumbs. *Honigkuchen* is made with half a pound of clover honey and a cup of walnuts, and traditionally is sliced extremely thin—mercifully, because of its richness. *Coburger Makronen* are different from other macaroons in that they are made of equal amounts of almonds and hazelnuts. Last but by no means least are *Nürnberger Lebkuchen,* the Christmas specialty that is exported around the world and to which the loosely translated term "gingerbread cookies" does not do justice (in part because they do not contain any ginger).

Beer is as prevalent as water in Northern Bavaria, and it seems that every town has its own brewery, whose suds the locals invariably praise as the best in the world. Indeed, of Bavaria's remaining 1,500 independent breweries (there used to be more than 6,000, but mergers and takeovers have swallowed up many), two-thirds are in the northern part of the state and some of the most famous brands and varieties are brewed in Franconian Kulmbach and Bamberg.

Elsewhere in Franconia *the* beverage is wine, and the *Frankenweine* (Franconian wines) grown along the Main river and its numerous tributaries, especially in the area around Würzburg, are among the most prized in Germany. Generally fuller-bodied and drier than those from other German regions, *Frankenweine* are also known to be earthier and less aromatic. What distinguishes all of them is the flat, dark-green *Bocksbeutel* (literally "goat's scrotum") bottle in which they are sold.

# ALONG THE DANUBE

The Danube, which meanders its way for 1,725 miles through eight countries to its estuary at the Black Sea, making it Central Europe's longest river, is also its most celebrated—in story, song, poetry, and legend. No other river in Europe is as scenically varied, and none has been witness to as turbulent a history—from the first-known settlement of Celts along its banks around 800 B.C. right through the extraordinary political changes of the past few years.

Yet, when you mention the Danube, most people think of Vienna, Budapest, Belgrade, and the Balkans. That its origins are actually in Germany's Black Forest, and that 400 of its more than 1,700 miles pass through West German territory, is both a little-known and oft-forgotten fact. However, it is along this section, as the river passes by and through picturesque villages and towns, old moated castles, frowning fortresses, and majestic Medieval cities such as Ulm, Ingolstadt, Regensburg, Straubing, and Passau, that the Danube valley is often at its loveliest.

## *ULM*

Ulm, the first stop on our itinerary, is 90 km (56 miles) southeast of Stuttgart by way of the Stuttgart-Munich (A 8) Autobahn. Legally, this city of 100,000 is part of the state of Baden-Württemberg, thanks to the way Napoleon carved up the region in 1810, a rather arbitrary process that caused the Bavarians to create a new city—Neu-Ulm, current population

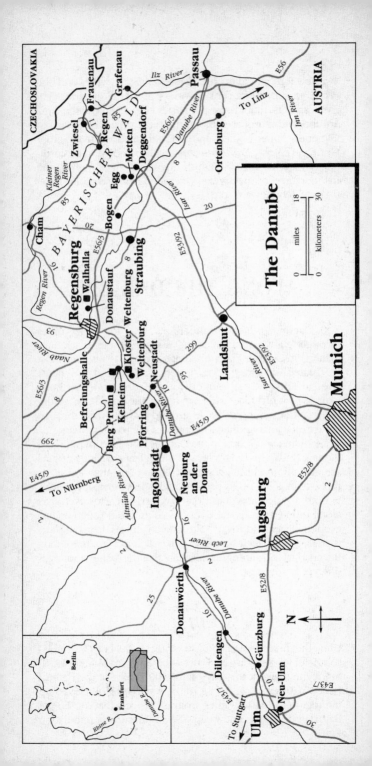

about 50,000—on the right bank of the river. All the important sites and attractions are in "old" Ulm.

And old it certainly is, having started as an Alemannic
settlement in the seventh century. It obtained a municipal
charter in 1164, and 110 years later became a *Freie Reichsstadt,* that is, a free city of the imperial realm, with its own
coinage rights and judicial jurisdiction, and answerable
only to the Holy Roman emperor. The weaving of fustian (a
blend of linen and cotton), trade, and shipping accounted
for much of its prosperity in the Middle Ages. In fact, it is
in Ulm where the Danube first becomes navigable for
small craft—flat-bottomed boats called *Ulmer Schachteln*
(Ulm boxes). Long before a string of locks interrupted the
river's flow from here to Vienna, Ulm's quays bustled with
these fragile vessels as they prepared to navigate what were
then very treacherous waters. Powered by strong men
wielding massive oars, they carried their cargo (and sometimes passengers) as far downstream as Belgrade.

Ulm's two most famous native sons are Albert Einstein,
son of a local merchant (who moved the whole family to
Munich when Albert was a little boy), and one Albrecht
Ludwig Berblinger, known as the "Flying Tailor of Ulm," a
poor but inventive tailor who was the first human being after
Icarus to attempt flight, and actually had mastered it quite
successfuly until an embarrassing mishap in 1811. In honor
of a visit to Ulm by King Frederick I of Württemberg,
Berblinger decided to demonstrate his flying machine pub-
licly. With some 10,000 onlookers on hand, he leaped from
the town wall with his weird-looking wings and proceeded
to plummet like a stone into the Danube.

The wall from which the tailor attempted his flight is
Ulm's oldest, dating well back into the 12th century. An outer
ring of defenses was built in the 14th century, enclosing an
area so large that the town did not outgrow it until 500 years
later. Both sets of walls were so formidable that Ulm was
able to withstand all the furious conflicts of the Middle Ages,
including the Thirty Years War, unconquered. In fact, it took
the Allied air forces to destroy the city—more than 65
percent of which was leveled by air raids in 1944 and 1945.
Miraculously its two most famous landmarks, the brightly
frescoed Rathaus (City Hall), with its fanciful clock, and the
Münster (Minster), with its 528-foot-spire, the highest church
tower in the world, were both spared.

# The Münster

The Münster, which is visible from miles away, dominates the Münsterplatz, the center of the city. One of the largest cathedrals in the world, its vaulted ceiling soars 137 feet above the central nave. But the Münster is also one of the finest examples of Gothic craftsmanship in Europe, as well as one of the richest in terms of its interior decoration.

The foundation stone was laid in 1377, and according to local lore the mayor and townspeople covered it with gold coins and jewels, all of which have long since been encased in mortar. Ulmers continued to build and add to the church over the next five centuries, and though most of the work was done by the early 16th century, the two eastern towers and the tall western steeple, Ulm's landmark, weren't completed until 1890.

Not surprisingly, given its grand scale, the construction of the cathedral attracted some of the greatest architects, sculptors, and painters of Medieval Germany—each of whom seemed bent on outdoing the others. Among the main interior features are the magnificent 15th-century choir windows, striking for their size and coloring; the beautifully carved choir stalls, which were created by Jörg Syrlin the Elder between 1469 and 1471; the 1471 fresco of the Last Judgment, considered one of the most important examples of Gothic wall painting; and Syrlin's 85-foot-high limestone-and-sandstone tabernacle.

Atop the roof of the central nave is a carved stone figure of a sparrow with a blade of grass in its beak—the *Ulmer Spatz*—the town's legendary mascot. According to legend, a group of laborers had unsuccessfully tried to bring a long log through one of the city's gates. Finally, they noticed a nest-building sparrow carrying a blade of grass that had to be negotiated through a small hole before it could be added to the nest. The observant laborers watched as the clever bird turned the blade lengthwise and brought it easily through the hole, and then, their lesson learned, they put their shoulders to the task and got the log into town.

"Ulm Sparrows"—in porcelain, ceramic, plastic, tin, chocolate, and marzipan—are sold all over town. And if you wish to completely immerse yourself in the legend, you'll find the **Hotel Ulmer Spatz**, Münsterplatz 27, right in the shadow of the church, a moderately priced place to eat and stay. The hotel also has a wine tavern and garden restaurant.

# Around in Ulm

Ulm's Rathaus, just south of the Münster on the Rathausplatz, dates back to 1360 and has presented the same façade to the town since 1420. The statues that grace the upper story depicting various electors and emperors of the Holy Roman Empire, have been there since 1427. The astronomical clock, with its Zodiac signs, positions of the moon and planets, and countless other bits of incidental information, was added to the façade in 1520, but the one you see nowadays—in perfect working order—is a 1580 replacement. The Renaissance-style *Neuer Bau* (New Wing) was incorporated into the original structure in the late 16th century, and looked so palatial when completed in 1593 that Ulm's burgomaster and town councilors moved right in, figuring they could make better use of it than the grain merchants for whom it had been built.

The **Ulmer Museum**, just east of the Rathaus, with its entrance at Neue Strasse 92, has a fine collection of Gothic and applied art, as well as a substantial collection of modern regional painting and sculpture.

A short stroll south from the museum, along the Marktplatz, will bring you to the **Metzger Turm** (Butcher's Tower), which is part of Ulm's Medieval wall. This "leaning tower of Ulm" has been listing more than six feet in a northwesterly direction for well over six centuries. The nearby *Adlerbastei* (Eagle's Bastion) is the section of the wall from which Berblinger made his leap into the Danube in 1811.

If you walk west along the fortifications you'll come to the idyllic **Fischer-und-Gerberviertel** (the Fishermen's and Tanners' Quarter), which is laced by canals and outlets of the Blau river, a small tributary of the Danube. Dubbed "Little Venice," the quarter is one of the city's loveliest. It is also a perfect spot to stop for lunch, and you won't find a more delightful or historic choice than the **Restaurant zur Forelle**, Fischergasse 25, an elegantly rustic 16th-century inn specializing in fish dishes—notably trout—that have won it recognition throughout Europe.

About 2 km (a little over a mile) upstream along the Danube is the **Deutsches Brotmuseum** (German Bread Museum), Fürsteneckerstrasse 17. Germany has more odd and specialized museums than any other country in Europe, and this one is devoted entirely to the cultural history of bread. Among the exhibits are a 5,000-year-old Mesopotamian bas-relief illustrating the bread-baking process, Medieval bakers' utensils, and documents and paintings dealing with the role of bread in religion.

Most of Ulm's hotels are located north of the Münster and within walking distance of the railway station. The biggest and most modern is the **Intercity Hotel**, Bahnhofsplatz 1, directly across from the station. If you prefer a more personalized atmosphere, consider the **Neutor-Hospiz**, Neuer Graben 23, about a ten-minute walk from the Münsterplatz.

The city's most highly rated restaurant, the **Florian Stuben**, is located about 2 km (a little over a mile) north of the Münsterplatz at Keplerstrasse 26. It's a perfect evening place, and offers silver, crystal, and fine porcelain service in a rustic wood-paneled environment. But be sure to reserve ahead; Tel: 61-02-20.

# Between Ulm and Ingolstadt

To continue your exploration of the Danube valley, cross the river to Neu-Ulm and follow the signs and B 10 out of town in the direction of **Günzburg**, a drive of about 16 km (10 miles). If you're not in a hurry, stop off in the center of town for a look at the **Frauenkirche** (Church of Our Lady), a fine example of Baroque architecture by the Swabian-Bavarian stucco master Dominikus Zimmermann completed in 1741.

Close to the church is a major road junction. Instead of continuing on B 10, you will want to bear left (north) onto B 16 for the 51-km (32-mile) drive to Donauwörth.

The road, which follows the left (north) bank of the Danube, passes through the town of **Dillingen**, which is exuberantly rich in Baroque churches and monasteries, and also boasts a magnificent palace. The **palace**, on Schlossstrasse, served as the residence of the bishops of Augsburg after the burghers in that city rebelled against their temporal rule in the 15th century. The Augsburg bishops soon turned Dillingen into a major ecclesiastical center, complete with a **university**, whose 17th- and 18th-century buildings you will find on the Kardinal-von-Waldburg-Strasse. The **Maria Himmelfahrtkirche** (Church of the Assumption), completed in 1617 and renovated in Rococo style in 1768, is part of the complex. The church's rich decoration is equaled only by that of **St. Peter**'s, a former parish church elevated to the rank of a papal basilica in 1979, on the Klosterstrasse, adjacent to Dillingen's Franciscan monastery. In both you will find sculptures and stucco work by Johann Michael Zimmermann and Johann Georg Fischer, two of 18th-century Bavaria's finest and most prolific architect-artists.

**Donauwörth**, the next destination, is where the **Romantic Road** crosses the Danube, and you will find a description of it in the following chapter. B 16 then continues east from Donauwörth along the Danube's right bank for 32 km (20 miles) to Neuburg.

**Neuburg an der Donau**, population 25,000, has its roots in Roman times and, thanks to its strategic location, became a major stronghold and customs station of Bavaria's Wittelsbach dynasty as early as the eighth century. In fact, the foundations for its **castle** were laid in 788, though most of the huge complex that now rises above the river was built between 1530 and 1545 by Count Ottheinrich of the Wittelsbach family's Palatinate line, one of the most prolific builders of the German Renaissance period.

Besides the castle, be sure to see the **Frauenkirche** (Church of Our Lady) on the Karlsplatz, completed in 1618 and regarded as a perfect blend of late-Gothic design with Renaissance interior ornamentation. Italian stucco artists did much of the work. Worth seeing, too, are the 17th-century **Rathaus** and the **Church of the Holy Cross**, an 18th-century structure with a high altar by Zimmermann.

Neuburg is ideal for strolling and soaking up Medieval atmosphere. And just 2 km (a little over a mile) northwest of the city, in Neuburg-Bittenbrunn at Monheimer Strasse 119, you will find the **Kirchbaur-Hof** (Tel.: 25-32), a rustic country inn with moderately priced rooms and a prodigious kitchen that specializes in fish dishes, notably trout, pike, carp, and perch. Even if you don't spend the night or stop for lunch, consider the Kirchbaur for an afternoon coffee and slice of cake; its apple strudel is some of the best to be found along the Danube.

B 16 crosses the Danube again at Neuburg and continues along the left bank in an easterly direction for another 23 km (14 miles) to Ingolstadt.

# INGOLSTADT

Though better known today as both the center of Bavaria's oil-refining industry and the home of Audi cars, Ingolstadt (current population 90,000) has roots that go back 2,500 years. And while it began to burgeon as a powerful Danubian citadel as early as the sixth century A.D., its golden age didn't begin until 1255, when Bavaria's Duke Ludwig the Severe built a fortress here, now known as the Altes Schloss. Two centuries later another Bavarian ruler, Ludwig the Rich, founded the duchy's first university in Ingolstadt, which put the city on the map as a center of learning, science, and culture. Thanks to a massive defensive system comprised of three walls completed in 1430, it was also one of the best-fortified towns in southern Germany—so well protected, in fact, that it withstood several onslaughts by the armies of Sweden's King Gustav Adolf during the Thirty Years War.

The crafts played a key role in the life of the town during the Middle Ages, and because of its advantageous position on the Danube Ingolstadt retained its industrial importance well into the 17th century. It really began to boom after World War II, however, and now is not only a major car-manufacturing center and the terminus for three transcontinental oil pipelines but also has four oil refineries. Fortunately, all of this heavy industry lies well to the east of the historic old city, which, snuggled safely within its ancient walls, looks much as it did in the Middle Ages.

The old city is a semi-circular maze of narrow streets, many of them cobblestone, lined by gabled houses, and measures a little more than half a mile in diameter. You can, if you wish, still walk around the **wall**, which was reinforced at strategic spots by formidable towers, all of which have survived. Of the main gates, however, only one remains— the **Kreuztor**, at the western end of the Kreuzstrasse.

Just a few steps from the latter is the **Liebfrauenmünster** (Basilica of Our Lady), one of the finest examples of brick Gothic architecture in Bavaria. Though commissioned in 1425 by Duke Ludwig the Bearded, it wasn't completed until more than a century later. Its high altar, dating back to 1572, is made up of 91 painted panels depicting bearded, learned men of the time. Be sure also to see the richly carved 16th-century pulpit and choir stalls.

Continuing along the Kreuzstrasse, which changes its name to the Ludwigstrasse and becomes a pedestrian mall, you will eventually come to the center of the city and its other architectural treasures.

The **Stadtpfarrkirche** (City Parish Church) **St. Moritz**, Moritzstrasse 4, a late-Romanesque structure that was consecrated in 1234, was expanded in the 14th century with Gothic additions. The Baroque stucco work inside the church was done by Johann Baptist Zimmermann in the 18th century. The **Minorite Church**, on the Harderstrasse, is a 13th-century basilica, noteworthy for its finely carved stone epitaphs. Munich's Asam brothers, Cosmas Damian and Egid Quirin, left their magnificent imprint on the small **church of Maria Viktoria**, Neubaustrasse 1, which was begun in 1732 as the prayer hall of the Marian student congregation. The enormous ceiling fresco, one of the Asam brothers' master-pieces, is unusual for its brilliant colors, and was probably a collaboration between them. The high altar is the work of Johann Michael Fischer.

Ludwig the Severe's original castle in Ingolstadt, the **Altes Schloss**, on the Hallstrasse, is also known as the *Herzogskasten* (Duke's Box), and served the Wittelsbach rulers for almost two centuries. After that the Duke's Box was turned into a grain warehouse, which is fitting enough, for that is what it looks like. (Today it's the municipal library.) The **Neues Schloss** (New Castle), Paradeplatz 4, which looks a bit more like a ducal palace, was commissioned by Ludwig the Bearded and built between 1418 and 1432, then expanded in the 16th century. Today it houses the **Bavarian army museum**, a collection of weapons and military paraphernalia that will tell you everything you ever wanted to know about soldiering.

For lunch or dinner you might consider stopping at the **Restaurant im Stadttheater**, Schlosslände 1, almost adjacent to the Neues Schloss and Army Museum, and with a terrace looking out over the Danube. The menu is rather international, but the sole garnished with crab, asparagus, olives, and mushrooms stands out.

The **Restaurant Tafelmeier**, Theresienstrasse 31, at the corner of the Kreuzstrasse and close to the Liebfrauen basilica, is both more rustic in its decor and more traditionally regional in the food it serves.

The best spot to spend the night in the old city is the **Hotel Rappensberger**, Harderstrasse 3, near the Minorite Church. The rooms are clean and comfortable, and you sense instantly that it is family run.

# Between Ingolstadt and Regensburg

B 16, which brought you into Ingolstadt, will also take you out of town again. If you want to continue driving along the Danube, however, take a left turn at the fork in the road about 12 km (7 miles) outside of Ingolstadt and follow the unnumbered county road, which hugs the left bank of the river, as far as the town of Pförring; signs will point the way. Just beyond Pförring the road intersects with a wider one that will take you into Neustadt; again, signs will point the way. In Neustadt, make a left turn onto the river road, and follow the signs to Bad Gögging, Weltenburg, and Kehlheim. Using these directions, it will be about a 35-km (21-mile) drive along the river from Ingolstadt to the next stop on our itinerary, Weltenburg.

**Kloster Weltenburg**, located on the Danube's right bank at a sharp bend in the river, is Bavaria's oldest monastic community. It is also almost impossible to find. From Kehlheim (see below) it is best reached by boat. Coming from Ingolstadt, your best bet is to leave your car at the parking lot upriver, even if the attendant on duty does little to encourage you. Your persistence will be well rewarded, however, for the abbey church of St. George and St. Martin is one of the most vibrant masterpieces of the Baroque, not to mention one of the finest works ever created by the Asam brothers.

Despite its remoteness, Weltenburg was thoroughly plundered by iconoclasts in 1546, and the abbot was subsequently forced to sell what remained of the monastery's library to pay for minimal repairs. For more than a century and a half the place gradually declined. Then, in 1716, the Asam brothers were called in to do some badly needed restoration. Cosmas Damian was then 29, his brother Egid Quirin 23. Both had only recently returned from their studies in Rome. What they brought back to Bavaria—and to Weltenburg—was an artistic vigor and brilliance unmatched in a period that was characterized by its artistic exuberance. The elder Asam, who was responsible for most of the architectural work, also painted the ceiling fresco (in which he portrayed his younger brother as an angel). The finest feature of the church, however, is its high altar, on which the brothers collaborated, and which portrays the struggle of Saint George against the dragon.

**Kehlheim**, 8 km (5 miles) downstream from Weltenburg, is where the Altmühl river meets the Danube, and is also the start of the Rhine-Main-Danube canal, which is scheduled to open in 1992. The waterway, when completed, will enable freight barges to operate between the North and Black seas.

A Celtic settlement for almost 500 years before the Romans came along and turned it into a military base, Kehlheim owes its present appearance to Duke Ludwig the Severe, who commissioned its construction as a totally planned city in 1206. Unlike other Medieval towns, with their narrow, twisting streets, Kehlheim was laid out as an orderly grid and is surrounded by a protective wall that bends at right angles. While you're here, be sure to see the 15th-century parish church of the Assumption on the Marktplatz as well as the 13th-century hospital church of St. John.

The main reason for stopping off in Kehlheim, however, is

to see the Brobdingnagian **Befreiungshalle** (Liberation Hall; open daily) on the Michelsberg, a lush green mountain that rises above the town. The last of the many Greco-Roman–style monuments commissioned by Bavaria's flamboyant King Ludwig I, the Befreiungshalle commemorates the so-called Wars of Liberation waged by other European powers against Napoleon from 1813 to 1815.

With Friedrich von Gärtner, one of Ludwig's favorite Munich architects, in charge of the project, the cornerstone was laid in 1842. By 1847, only the huge circular terrace had been completed. Then Gärtner died of a heart attack, at which point Ludwig turned to an even greater favorite, Leo von Klenze. Klenze accepted the assignment on condition that Ludwig allow him to scrap Gärtner's somewhat eclectic plans and proceed with an "Antique Roman" monument. Ludwig agreed to the change, but a year later, after he was forced to abdicate because of his scandalous affair with the dancer Lola Montez, work on the project was halted.

Construction resumed in 1849, with Ludwig paying for much of it out of his own pocket, but it proceeded at a much slower pace and with considerable cost cutting, such as the use of brick instead of limestone blocks for the shell. The monument was finished and dedicated in 1863, on the 50th anniversary of the "Battle of the Nations" at Leipzig, in which Napoleon suffered his first decisive defeat in western Europe. The ex-king and Klenze, both 79 years old by then, were in attendance.

The rotunda Klenze wrought atop the Michelsberg is certainly vast—more than 160 feet in diameter and almost 200 feet high. Set in a circle around its perimeter, and holding hands as if they were playing "ring-around-the-rosie," are 34 twice-life-sized marble figures of Winged Victory, each representing one of the then-independent German kingdoms, principalities, duchies, and city-states. Between these 34 monumental statutes are 17 bronze shields inscribed with the names of the principal battles waged against Bonaparte, and above them 17 plaques inscribed with the names of the most important German and Austrian field marshals and generals.

Bombastic as the Liberation Hall may be, however, it pales in comparison to Ludwig's other great monument on the Danube, Walhalla, some 34 km (21 miles) farther downstream. But before driving that far, plan on spending a day or two in Regensburg, the greatest of the cities on our Danube route, just 24 km (15 miles) to the east.

# *REGENSBURG*

The city has had many names. To the Celts, who founded it around 500 B.C., it was Radaspona. To the Romans, who made it an impregnable fortress during the reign of Marcus Aurelius in the second century A.D., it was Castra Regina, meaning "camp on the Regen," a reference to the tributary that meets the Danube here. Then, four centuries later, came the Germanic Baiuoarii, ancestors of today's Bavarians, who called it Regenespurc, which seems close enough to its contemporary German name.

Its many names—there have been 75 others as well, including the seven coined by Goethe's Mephistopheles as he was flying toward it on his magic cloak with Dr. Faustus—speak volumes. The age of West Germany's cities is frequently in dispute and often the source of considerable rivalry between them, but Regensburg regards itself above such petty competition. By virtue of its documented past, most of the others are upstarts. Its past, moreover, has been remarkably well preserved.

Regensburg is how all German cities are expected to look—like a travel poster. Left virtually untouched during World War II, it is, with a population of 130,000, the largest and most perfectly preserved Medieval city in West Germany. Known for centuries as the German gateway to the Balkans and the Orient, it is an urban gem—a town for strolling, exploring, and soaking up history; for admiring the art and craftsmanship of past epochs; a city of narrow lanes, cobblestone streets, secluded courtyards, gabled burgher houses, imposing defensive walls and towers, splendid palaces, and majestic Romanesque and Gothic churches.

It is a city, morever, where the living past is treated with light-hearted humor. Amble through the town—and walking is not only the best but virtually the only way to master the mile-by-half-mile historic center that hugs the Danube's right bank—and you will come upon streets with such charming names as the Fröhliche-Türken-Strasse (Cheerful Turks Street), Zur Schönen Gelegenheit (roughly translatable as Good Opportunity Corner), the Entengang (Ducks' Way), the Gässchen Ohne End (Alley Without End), or the Hundsumkehr (Dogs' Turnaround Lane). Human foibles are as much the theme of the murals and bas-reliefs that grace the city's ancient buildings as are great deeds.

Regensburg's Roman military contingent numbered 6,000, and with the usual codicil of families, camp followers, merchants, and other hangers-on, it was a fortified town of 12,000, replete with forum, temples, pottery workshops, and a mint, which struck the last Roman coin in A.D. 408. The wall surrounding old Regensburg, more than a mile long and 23 feet high, was built of huge limestone blocks fitted so exactly without mortar that even today a razor blade cannot be squeezed between them. Massive gateways to the fortress, such as the **Porta Praetoria**, guard towers, and other sections of the wall remain visible today, integrated into churches, hotels, shops, and a parking garage. In Regensburg the Roman heritage is very much alive.

Unlike other frontier towns of the Roman empire, Regensburg was not abandoned when Rome itself collapsed and the Baiuoarii invaded in the fifth and sixth centuries. Somehow, it just absorbed them, turning those proto-Bavarians into Christians long before Christianity took root elsewhere in Germany. In fact, the oldest Christian tombstones found in the city date from the late fourth and early fifth centuries; its first abbey was founded 1,300 years ago; and by the time Saint Boniface, the Irish missionary known as the Apostle of the Germans, arrived in 739, Regensburg was, by the standards of the times, a surprisingly civilized place. Charlemagne then made it the most important town in southern Germany, and from the tenth through the 18th centuries it ranked as one of the great centers of the German Holy Roman Empire.

## The Rathaus Area

Within the empire Regensburg enjoyed a privileged position, not only as an independent city-state but as the seat of the *Reichstag,* the Imperial Diet. Throughout the Middle Ages this parliament of nobles met periodically in the ornate chambers and council halls of Regensburg's beautifully preserved 14th-century **Rathaus** (City Hall), on the Rathausplatz, and had its permanent home there from 1663 until 1806, when Napoleon disbanded the diet and abolished the empire. There are numerous daily guided tours of the building (in which the mayor still has his office); these include its lavishly appointed *Reichssaal* (Imperial Hall), the *Kurfürstenkollegium* (Electors' Chamber), *Fürstenkollegium* (Princes' Chamber), and the bloodcurdling *Fragstatt* (torture dungeon). Regensburg's municipal tourist office, the *Verkehrsamt,* is on the ground floor of the Rathaus.

Be sure, before or after your tour of the city hall, to have coffee and pastry at the **Café Prinzess**, Rathausplatz 2, which has been open for business since 1686, making it Germany's oldest coffeehouse.

For all of Regensburg's historic role as a political center, its real power and influence derived from its advantageous location on the Danube, and its famous **Steinerne Brücke** (Stone Bridge) across the river, unaltered in appearance and still very much in use today. Completed in 1146 after only 11 years of construction, it was one of the engineering marvels of the Middle Ages, and for hundreds of years virtually the only bridge across Europe's chief transportation artery. So large did it loom in the affairs of its day, in fact, that two Crusades—the second, led by Holy Roman Emperor Conrad III in 1147, and the third, begun by Emperor Frederick Barbarossa in 1189—set out from this bridge in Regensburg.

At its southern end, right on the Danube embankment, is the **Alte Wurstküche** (Old Sausage Kitchen), Thundorferstrasse 3, famed precisely for what its name suggests: sausages. They are pork, four inches long, half an inch in diameter, and charcoal broiled; come in portions of four, six, eight, or twelve; and are accompanied by sauerkraut. Other than potato soup, there is little else on the menu. The Wurstküche has only a half-dozen plain wooden tables, but what it lacks in elegance is more than compensated for by venerability: It has been in business continuously for more than 800 years, having been started in the late 1130s as a canteen serving the masons and construction workers who built the Stone Bridge. (Right in front of the building is the landing for the excursion steamers that take travellers to Regensburg's barge harbor, through the locks of the Rhine-Main-Danube canal, and on longer trips on the river.)

The Stone Bridge bolstered Regensburg's position as the principal trade crossroads between southern Europe and Scandinavia, as well as between the Orient and Middle East and France and the Netherlands. In time, the city's merchants amassed fabulous wealth, and its coinage was considered so solid that it was accepted as legal tender throughout Europe. For centuries its only serious commercial rival was Venice, and some Regensburg merchants were even entrenched in that fair city. Its ties to other Italian city-states—Florence and Siena—were close as well, and it was from these that rich Regensburgers imported an architectural style that became peculiar to the city: fortresslike tower houses, some 12 stories high. The higher the house, the richer its owner was presumed to be. While 60 of these

Medieval skyscrapers once punctuated the city's skyline, making Regensburg a kind of Manhattan of the Middle Ages, only 20 have survived, most of them in use today as studio-apartment houses much sought-after by local university students and artists. The two that are best preserved, both dating to the 13th century, are the **Baumburger Turm**, on the Watmarkt, seven stories and 92 feet tall, and the **Goldener Turm**, also called *Haymohaus,* Wahlenstrasse 16, nearly 139 feet high.

Equally impressive is the **House of the Golden Cross**, at Haidplatz 7. From the 16th through the 19th centuries the Goldenes Kreuz served as Regensburg's imperial inn, a sort of grand hotel for visiting emperors, kings, electors, princes, foreign emissaries, and other potentates. And, like any hotel, it had its share of scandal and hanky-panky in the bedrooms. Perhaps the most famous affair was the 1546 tryst between Emperor Charles V (grandson of Spain's Ferdinand and Isabella) and 18-year-old Barbara Blomberg, a Regensburg saddlemaker's daughter 28 years his junior. The young lady, renowned for her beauty, bore the emperor a son as the result of their meeting. He was born February 24, 1547, Charles's own birthday, in the 13th-century **Weinstube zur Stritzelbäckerin**, Watmarkt 6, near the Baumburger Turm, renowned then and now as an inn thanks to its wine cellar, good food, and salty rolls known as *Stritzel.*

The emperor's illegitimate offspring, Don Juan de Austria, grew up to become an important figure in his own right. As admiral of the Holy League's fleet, he was said to have saved Christian Europe and the Occident from conquest by the Ottoman Turks in 1571 by winning the murderous Battle of Lepanto against Uluc Ali Pasha. Shortly after the victory, the grateful citizens of Sicily, which had provided a good part of Don Juan's fleet, erected a bronze monument to him in Messina. In 1971, some 400 years later, a copy of it was cast and brought to Regensburg, where it now stands on the Zieroldsplatz, a tiny square near the Rathaus. The tale of Emperor Charles V's liaison with Barbara Blomberg is told in a mural that graces the façade of the House at the Golden Cross. Another reminder of the scandalous affair are the delectable chocolate pralines, called "Barbara's Kisses," made by the Café Prinzess.

For elegant evening dining in a beautifully restored Medieval house, there is the **Restaurant zum Krebs**, Krebsgasse 6, at the corner of the Haidplatz near the Goldenes Kreuz; Tel: (94) 15-58-03.

# South of the Rathaus Area

Don Juan was by no means Regensburg's only famous native son. Albertus Magnus, the "universal doctor," also known as St. Albert the Great, taught in the city from 1236 to 1240, and was its bishop from 1260 to 1262. Albrecht Altdorfer, the first German landscape painter and founder of the Danubian school, was born in Regensburg in 1480 and died here in 1538. For a while he was the city's chief architect, served two terms as a town councilor, and was even nominated as mayor, an honor he rejected because he feared it would take too much time from his art. The house in which he lived and worked from 1513 to 1538 is at Obere-Bach-Gasse 7, about a ten-minute walk due south of the Rathaus. Though Altdorfer's most prized paintings are in galleries elsewhere, the **Regensburg municipal museum** (Museum der Stadt Regensburg), Dachauplatz 2-4, exhibits a number of his important pictures.

Johannes Kepler, the mathematician and astronomer whose description of the elliptical movement of the planets is still the basis of modern astronomical studies, had numerous ties to Regensburg, where he died in 1630. His first long stay in town began in 1613, and he was often a guest at the **Walderbacher Hof,** an inn at Georgenplatz 6, now a tavern oddly called the Old Vienna. While some of his visits were to see friends and relatives, others were strictly business—to collect the 12,000 guilders in back pay that a succession of Holy Roman emperors, his nominal employers, owed him. In the late 1620s Kepler used the city as a base for travelling to other centers of science, leaving his wife and children in a rented house at what is today Keplerstrasse 2, a picturesque street that runs parallel to the Danube just two blocks north of the Rathaus. He died in the building across the street, Keplerstrasse 5. The latter, today, is the **Kepler Gedächtnishaus** (Kepler Memorial House), a museum containing many of his original scientific instruments and manuscripts; guided tours four times daily, and two on Sunday.

If you're on the lookout for a place to have dinner, then the rustic **Restaurant Gänsbauer,** Keplerstrasse 10, just across from the Kepler house, is both convenient and good, and specializes in regional cuisine prepared in the nouvelle style. Open evenings only; reservations recommended. Tel: (94) 15-78-58.

# The Dom St. Peter Area

Regensburg's wealth was directly responsible for its profusion of magnificent Romanesque and Gothic churches—26 in all—of which the Dom St. Peter (St. Peter's Cathedral), on the Domplatz, about a ten-minute walk east of the Rathaus, is actually the newest, not having been completed (despite the fact that it was begun in 1250) until 1525. It is one of Europe's most impressive and harmonious Gothic cathedrals, ranking with those of Chartres, Cologne, Reims, Strasbourg, and Ulm for its sheer size and splendor. In addition to its impressive exterior stonework and sculpture, especially the west portal, you'll want to go inside to see its stained-glass windows and fine altars from the 13th and 14th centuries. The cathedral is part of a larger complex called the *Domstadt* (Cathedral City), much of it considerably older than the Dom itself, which includes the 12th-century **Allerheiligenkapelle** (All Saints' Chapel) and the adjacent **St. Ulrich's church**, which was built between 1230 and 1250.

One of the cathedral's greatest "treasures" is more audible than visible, and is best heard not in the Dom itself but in the 12th-century **Niedermünster**, adjacent to the bishop's palace, about 300 feet east of St. Peter's: the **Regensburger Domspatzen** (Cathedral Sparrows), a 60-member boys' choir, has been getting rave reviews for over 1,000 years. Founded by Bishop Wolfgang in 975, the choir is part of the cathedral school. Although the performance of liturgical music remains the choir's primary charge, over the centuries it has turned its attention increasingly to secular works. The proceeds from these concerts, as well as its radio and television performances and commercial recordings, go toward the running of the school. The Domspatzen can be heard most Sundays and holidays at the 9:00 A.M. mass; their performances of secular music take place throughout the concert season.

The **Domschatzmuseum** (Cathedral Treasury Museum), entrance via the cathedral garden, is a stunning collection of ecclesiastical art from the Middle Ages and the Renaissance, including a 13th-century gem-and-pearl–studded crucifix that belonged to Bohemia's King Óttokar III.

The Domplatz and the Domstadt are convenient to some of Regensburg's more commendable "old city" hotels. The **Bischofshof**, Krauterer Markt 3, tucked into a section of the Roman wall and the Porta Praetoria, has all the modern comforts in a centuries-old environment. Run by Monika and Herbert Schmalhofer, the hotel also has a fine restaurant. The **Hotel Kaiserhof am Dom**, Kramgasse 10, located in a 16th-century mansion that faces the west portal of St. Peter's, is moderately priced and rich in atmosphere. Its restaurant, hidden away in a vaulted cellar of the building, serves Bavarian regional specialties and German dishes. The **Hotel Karmeliten**, Dachauplatz 1, about a quarter-mile southeast of the Domplatz, across from the Regensburg city museum, is located in a 150-year-old house that sits on Roman foundations (which proprietor Emil Seidl eagerly shows to all guests), and is also moderately priced.

The old city's most fashionable inn is the **Parkhotel Maximilian**, Maximilianstrasse 28. A grand 19th-century neo-Baroque hotel that was completely renovated in 1985, the Maximilian offers touches of real luxury and elegance at remarkably reasonable prices.

## St. Emmeram's

From the Maximilian it is a ten- to fifteen-minute walk west along the Sankt-Peters-Weg to the most remarkable of Regensburg's churches, St. Emmeramskirche, as well as the Thurn-und-Taxis palace.

St. Emmeram's is the oldest center of Christianity in Regensburg, having been founded in the fifth century by Christianized Romans and Baiuoarii. It is named for a missionary monk, St. Emmeram, who was martyred in southern Bavaria and entombed in the church in 685. A Benedictine abbey was built adjacent to the church soon after, and by the tenth century it was known as one of the greatest centers of learning in Europe. The abbey **library**, with more than 200,000 books, includes numerous illuminated manuscripts; a number of the sculptures and tombs in the church itself, some dating to the ninth and tenth centuries, are of inestimable value to art historians. Also of interest are the **cloisters**, among the largest and most beautiful in Germany, and the Romanesque nave of the **church**, which was redecorated with a dazzling splash of stucco, trompe l'oeil frescoes, and magnificent sculptures by the Asams in the 18th century.

The immense monastery is now the gaudy neo-Renaissance-style **Thurn-und-Taxis Schloss**, the palace of the Thurn-und-Taxis family, who acquired the abbey in 1812. The Thurn-und-Taxis family traces its origins to northern Italy and the southern Tyrol, where the ancestral name was Daxis, to which they later added the "de la Torre" that became today's "Thurn." Their business in the Middle Ages,

as Prince Johannes, the reigning head of the family, con-
cedes, was robber barony, or, to be more precise, piracy.
Then, in the 15th century, the Daxis barons became mailmen. That is, they invented—and eventually gained a
Europe-wide monopoly on—postal services. By the 17th
century their network of stage coaches, dispatch riders, and
postal relay stations spanned the continent. Legend has it
that, in addition to delivering the mail, they also read it. This
made their services doubly valuable to scheming dukes,
kings, emperors, and popes, all of whom rewarded—or in
some cases paid off—these clever postmen. The "postage,"
in many cases, amounted to titles of nobility as well as
land—lots of land. The latter is one reason why Prince
Johannes, with assets conservatively estimated at $4 billion,
rates as probably the richest man in Germany.

The Thurn-und-Taxis clan moved to Regensburg in 1790,
and when Saint Emmeram's was secularized by an edict of
Napoleon they bought the monastery and turned it into their
palatial digs. Today Prince Johannes and his family live in a
resplendent third-floor "apartment" surrounded by servants
who, on formal occasions, wear 18th-century livery. When he
does not need them, the lavishly decorated formal rooms of
the palace, all crammed with priceless art, are open to the
public. So are the cloisters of St. Emmeram's, which connect
the church to the abbey/palace, and the **Marstall** (Stables)
**museum**, with its scores of 19th-century coaches and carriages, silver and gold harnesses, and equestrian paintings.

Across the square from the church and the entrance to the
palace is another worthwhile museum, the **Diözesan** (Dioce-
san) **Museum**, Emmeramsplatz 1, which has a fine collection
of ecclesiastical art that spans a period of some ten centuries.

On your way back toward the river and the area around the
Rathaus and Dom, you may want to stop for a look at two
other interesting churches. The **Dominikanerkirche** (Dominican church), on the Beraiterweg, was consecrated in
1300, and is one of the earliest Gothic structures in Germany. **St. Jakob** (St. James), on the Jakobstrasse off the
Bismarckplatz, was completed in 1195, and was once the
chapel of an Irish-Scottish missionary monastery, which is
why it is also called the *Schottenkirche* (Scottish Church). Its
most remarkable feature is its main portal, a dazzling example of Romanesque sculpture and stonework that blends
Roman and Celto-German influences with Christian symbols
and imagery.

Even if you decide not to continue along our Danube

route, choosing, instead, to drive northwest 90 km (56 miles) to Nürnberg, no visit to Regensburg would be complete without a visit to Donaustauf and the Walhalla there, 10 km (6 miles) downstream.

# WALHALLA

Walhalla is an almost perfect replica of the Parthenon, and has virtually the same dimensions. But instead of being sited on the Acropolis, it rises from a nondescript mound called the Breuberg, near the bucolic village of Donaustauf on the left bank of the Danube, where it has stood for a century and a half—a temple to Germanic greatness as well as a symbol of imperial dreams gone awry.

This huge edifice is quite literally a "hall of fame" containing busts of and memorial plaques to more than 200 German luminaries. That not all enshrined here were Germans in the strictest sense of the word, and that some defy the dogged efforts of historians and encyclopaedists to attribute to them even a modicum of greatness, hardly seems to matter to the almost one million people who visit the monument annually.

The idea for Walhalla began to germinate in the future King Ludwig I's head in 1807, when, as Bavaria's 21-year-old crown prince, he was dispatched to Berlin to attend Napoleon's galling celebration of victory over Prussia at the tomb of Frederick the Great. Young Ludwig, who had been less than enthusiastic about Bavaria's alliance with France, became even more disenchanted as he witnessed Bonaparte's triumphant prancing in Berlin. On his return to Munich he decided he would avenge the Corsican's performance by building a monument to Frederick and other great Germans once he was king.

Ludwig's day was a while in coming. In fact, his father Maximilian I remained on the throne for another 18 years. In the meantime, Ludwig began ordering busts. He also began to search for an appropriate site, finally persuading Regensburg's Prince von Thurn-und-Taxis to donate a portion of his vineyards on the Breuberg slope near Donaustauf. Within a year of becoming king, Ludwig commissioned his then-favorite architect, Leo von Klenze, to start drawing up plans for the pantheon, telling him, "I want it to be great, not just colossal in size, but great in concept and design."

Klenze, who was deeply involved in turning Munich, Ludwig's capital, into a "new Athens," drew up his plans and began ordering marble for the project: 6,000 blocks of the finest available from Italy, hauled over the Alps by ox-drawn wagons. The ceiling was to be made of plates of bronze, gilded with gold leaf and inset with stars of platinum. The iron portals were designed to be—and are—28 feet high and weigh two tons each.

The cornerstone was laid in 1830; the monument opened officially 12 years later. To avoid antagonizing Bavaria's parliament, Ludwig financed virtually all his building projects from his civil list of four million guilders annually.

The placement of people along the walls of Walhalla always was, and remains, a puzzle. Thus the watchmaker Henlein has a niche above Charlemagne; Erasmus of Holland sits next to Philippus Paracelsus, whose next-door neighbor is Copernicus (considered a Pole in Poland). The Holy Roman Emperor Charles V is in a row with a barely known duke of Württemberg, who shares his billing with Goethe and Austria's Count Joseph Radetzky (in whose honor Vienna's Johann Strauss composed the famous "Radetzky March"). Strauss himself has yet to make it into Walhalla, though his Munich-born namesake and fellow composer Richard is duly enshrined. Painter Hans Holbein the Younger is there, his father is not. Likewise, the composer Anton Bruckner is represented, but not Johannes Brahms.

If you're not ready to turn back to Nürnberg and Franconia after your visit to Walhalla, continue along the Danube for approximately 40 km (25 miles) to Straubing.


# *STRAUBING*

Straubing, like Regensburg, can trace its origins to Roman times, when it was a military camp called Sorviodurum, out of which the sixth-century Baiuoarii came up with "Strupinga." Although it is mentioned as early as A.D. 900, the town you see today began as a planned city of the early 13th century, and its Medieval character has been almost perfectly preserved. Indeed, a 16th-century model of the town, made by a local carpenter and on permanent exhibit at the Bavarian national museum in Munich, shows Straubing 400 years ago pretty much as it appears today.

The most striking feature of the town is its main street, a vast half-mile long market square—which, in fact, is exactly what it was; Straubing has been the principal market town of Bavaria's richest agricultural region for centuries. No less striking is the 14th-century **Rathaus**, which stands right in

the center of this elongated plaza, one end of which is now
called the Ludwigsplatz, the other the Theresienplatz (in
honor of Bavaria's King Ludwig I and his Queen Theresa).
The building's square tower, one of the tallest of the many in
town, is unusual for the four oriels on its corners—Medieval
lookout posts for vigilant watchmen.

The Asam brothers twice left their characteristically exu-
berant mark on Straubing: with a side altar in the **Stifts und
Pfarrkirche St. Jakob** (Collegiate and Parish Church of St.
James), Pfarrplatz 7, a 15th-century basilica whose red-brick
Gothic exterior has been preserved despite the Baroque
restyling of its interior; and with the 18th-century **Ursu-
linenkirche**, the convent church of the Ursuline Order, at
Burggasse 9. One of their chief rivals, Johann Wolfgang
Dientzenhofer, was the architect and master builder who
contributed all the Baroque interiors to the 14th-century
**Karmelitenkirche** (Carmelite Church), Albrechtgasse 20.
You can get a welcome break from all this Baroque extrava-
gance at the **Pfarrkirche St. Peter** (Parish Church of St.
Peter), a refreshingly simple, triple-naved Romanesque basil-
ica that was completed in 1200.

In the little cemetery surrounding St. Peter's you'll find
the tomb of Agnes Bernauer, Bavaria's best-loved tragic folk
heroine. Agnes was the daughter of a bathhouse proprietor
in Augsburg, where, during the 1428 carnival season, Albrecht III, heir apparent to the Bavarian throne and son of
Duke Ernst, first met her. Only 16 at the time, Agnes was
considered one of the great beauties of the age, and the
young nobleman fell in love with her after their first bath
together—a not uncommon practice in those days. It was the
beginning of a torrid love affair. In 1432 the two were
secretly married in a village church, and a year later Agnes
bore the future duke of Bavaria a daughter. Her Cinderella
story might have had a happy ending had it not been for all
the gossip and Papa Ernst's indignation. The duke had Agnes
arrested, imprisoned in the ducal castle at Straubing, and put
on trial as a witch. The trial consisted of tying her hands and
feet and tossing her into the Danube; her guilt would be
proven if she floated, her innocence if she drowned. Alas,
poor Agnes was innocent. Her tragic story is re-enacted
every four years in the courtyard of Straubing's castle during
the quadrennial "Agnes Bernauer Festival," which will next
be held in June of 1992.

The best and most historic place to stay, or to have lunch
or dinner in town, is the 500-year-old **Hotel Seethaler**,
Theresienplatz 25.

# DEGGENDORF AND THE BAYERISCHER WALD

Deggendorf, on the opposite (left) bank of the river, some 28 km (17 miles) downstream from Straubing by way of country roads, is not only a charming little city worth exploring but also the gateway to the Bayerischer Wald, the Bavarian Forest.

Somewhat smaller than Straubing, Deggendorf has been an important transfer point of Danube shipping for some 1,000 years. It was fortified in 1242 when it became Bavarian ducal property, and today boasts one of the area's most beautiful city squares, in the middle of which stands a Gothic Rathaus.

## Metten

Five km (3 miles) west and back upstream from Deggendorf's Marktplatz is the village of Metten, site of the Benedictine **monastery church of Saint Michael**, one of the "musts" on our Danube route. The church, which was completed in 1720, has a high altar with Cosmas Damian Asam's painting *Lucifer Destroyed by St. Michael*. Even more important are the 17th-century monastery buildings, and most important of all is the **Klosterbibliothek** (Monastery Library), built and stocked between 1706 and 1720. Wherever there's a spare inch inside the library there is Rococo stucco work, and where there's a surface, there is an elaborately decorated panel—which means there's not much space for books. The ten carved figures that surround the columns supporting the library's gallery depict the trades involved in producing and publishing books. Perhaps not surprisingly, the critic fares the worst, here being pinched on the nose by a crane.

From Deggendorf two scenic highways—B 11 and an unnumbered state road—both lead north into the Bayerischer Wald.

## The Bayerischer Wald

This mountainous, densely wooded region stretches in a broad band some 50 km (31 miles) wide and nearly 150 km (93 miles) long from the German-Austrian-Czechoslovak border north and west along the frontier with Czechoslovakia. Within its confines are two nature preserves and a national park.

Settlement of the region goes back to the Stone and Bronze ages: Its first known inhabitants were Celts and Marcovinians, who were displaced by Slavic tribes in the fifth century. The Slavs in turn were overrun in the sixth century by the Baiuoarii. Yet measurable settlement did not really begin until the 13th century, with small villages slowly growing up around monasteries and churches. As a result of this pattern, the entire region remains one of the least populated and least industrialized in southern Germany. Even modern mass tourism remains in its infancy here, which is perhaps a blessing, although the potential for summer recreation and winter sports is great. Only a few isolated spots have been turned into ski resorts, and they are mostly of the cross-country variety. Resorts that draw summer visitors emphasize the clean air, the pristine environment, and the wonders of nature.

It is possible to drive for miles in the Bayerischer Wald without seeing signs of human habitation. In the minds of most Germans, however, the region has an aura of hokey backwoodsiness about it, no doubt reinforced by sensational media stories in the 1960s and 1970s about village women from the forest who were ostracized by their neighbors for practicing witchcraft.

Although a number of clean, high-tech industries have struck roots in some of the larger towns in recent years, the crafts and cottage industries such as wood carving, glass blowing, and the production of snuff jars called Schmalzler bottles remain the most important components of the local economy. And so it is to two of the glass-blowing centers—Frauenau and Zwiesel—that we want to direct you in particular.

The glass-blowing tradition in the forest is some 650 years old, and no doubt owes its origins to the abundance of quartz in the region. The original *Glashütten,* or glass smelters and factories, were small family-run enterprises—many of which have become fairly large operations. A specialty—actually an art—developed through the centuries was the blowing of the so-called *Schmalzlerglas,* the clear-glass stoppered flagons bearing tantalizing spiral decorations, swirls of color, and even lettering. They were, and are, used for snuff, which is popular in Bavaria. To prevent the glass-blowing art from dying out, a number of communities have started trade schools to teach their youngsters the secrets of the craft.

**Zwiesel**, 35 km (22 miles) northeast of Deggendorf by way of the unnumbered road that takes you through the town of Regen, has been a glass-blowing center since the 14th century. A town of 10,000 inhabitants, it has a state-run school for apprentice glassmakers, and a very fine **Glasmuseum** located right behind the city hall on the Stadtplatz, the main square. The town is also a summer hiking and winter ski resort, and has a number of commendable hotels, inns, and restaurants. The best is the **Kurhotel Sonnenberg**, Augustinerstrasse 9.

**Frauenau**, just 6 km (4 miles) south of Zwiesel along the scenic road that leads into the Nationalpark Bayerischer Wald and then on to Passau, also has a fine **Glasmuseum** located right on its Rathausplatz; it's also the best place to pick up information on factories that are open to the public.

Though only a third the size of Zwiesel, Frauenau also banks on summer recreation and winter sports, including downhill skiing on the 4,790-foot-high Rachel peak that looms above the town. There is a range of accommodations in moderately priced country inns as well; the coziest, right in the center of town, is the **Gasthaus Eibl-Brunner**, Hauptstrasse 18.

From Frauenau you have a choice of two routes that continue on to Passau, our last destination on the Danube. If you'd like to stay close to the river, return to Deggendorf the way you came (by way of Zwiesel and Regen), and then follow it downstream for another 65 km (40 miles). The alternative is to drive south for about 60 km (37 miles) through the national park and the southeastern corner of the Bayerischer Wald. This route will take you first to the town of **Grafenau**, where there is an especially fine and renowned restaurant (which we recommend as a gastronomic side trip from Passau in our discussion of that city). From Grafenau, B 85 takes you directly into Passau.

## PASSAU

The Celts had a sense of location that was uncanny, in terms of both defense and aesthetic appeal. They outdid even themselves when they chose to settle on the site of what is now Passau, population 50,000, some 2,500 years ago.

The little city is situated on a tongue of land at the confluence of two rivers, the Inn and the Ilz, with the Danube. The Inn flows into the Danube after its long, twisting course from the Alps through Switzerland, Austria, and southern Bavaria. The Ilz arrives after a short but turbulent journey through the Bayerischer Wald, where it rises. In addition to the almost impregnable natural barrier it poses for would-be attackers, the meeting of the three rivers creates one of the most memorable spectacles of nature, which you can observe from a cliff towering high above the bank of the Danube: The Inn is a chalky green on arrival, the Ilz almost turquoise, and the Danube, contrary to song and legend, a rather muddy brown; spread out beneath you on nature's canvas, the colors are blended magically.

The Celts called their settlement Boiodurum; the Romans, who, here as elsewhere along the Danube, built one of their forts, named it Castra Batava, or just Batavis, for the ninth Batavian Cohort, which was stationed here. Then, in the fifth century, came the Baiuoarii, who called it Bazzawa, which eventually became Passau. Some 1,400 years later the German naturalist Alexander von Humboldt arrived, took one look, and declared Passau "one of the seven most beautiful cities in the world."

It was Saint Boniface who established Passau as a bishopric in 739 (though there is evidence that the first Christian church here was built as early as 460). The bishops of the day were also temporal rulers, and they turned Passau into one of the most powerful church city-states of southern Germany. Among them were many learned men, and one of the most learned was Bishop Pilgrim, who during his rule (970–991) had the *Nibelungenlied* (Song of the Nibelungs), one of the old Germanic sagas, set down on parchment in Middle-High German. Elsewhere in town, a large-scale mural in the great hall of the 17th-century Rathaus, on the right bank of the Danube, depicts the arrival of the Nibelungs in Passau. Of course, it was left to Richard Wagner, in the 19th century, to move the Nibelung legend from the Danube to the Rhine, turning what must have been originally "Danube maidens" into Rhine maidens.

# The Stephansdom Area

Passau, on the Danube, is dominated by **St. Stephansdom** (St. Stephen's Cathedral), its immense octagonal dome a familiar landmark visible for miles around. Begun in late-Gothic style in 1407, the cathedral wasn't completed until 1530, by which time a number of Renaissance elements had been added. Then, in the late 17th century, after a devastating fire, some of the restoration work was done in Italian Baroque style. The result is a church that is overwhelming both in its size and in the richness of its decoration. It is also downright overpowering acoustically, for it contains the world's largest organ. The instrument, with 17,388 pipes and 231 registers, is played at noon every day of summer; an additional recital is added at 6:00 P.M. during July and August.

The bishops of Passau commissioned several palaces in and around town. Adjacent to the cathedral, on the Residenz-platz, are the **old and new residences**, the former a largely Renaissance creation, the latter Baroque. More important are the **Veste Oberhaus** (Upper Citadel) and **Veste Niederhaus** (Lower Citadel) on the left bank where an escarpment is all that stands between the Danube and the Ilz. Built in the 13th century (though added on to for the next few centuries), the Veste Oberhaus was designed to keep the bishops in firm control of Passau's burghers. The Veste Niederhaus, which dates to the 14th century, had pretty much the same purpose. The complex, which is reached by crossing the Luitpold bridge across the Danube, today houses three museums, including the **historical city museum** and a branch of the **Bavarian state pictures collection**.

Other worthwhile museums in Passau are the **Spielzeug-museum** (Toy Museum), on the Residenzplatz, and the **Passau Glasmuseum** (Glass Museum), with a fine collection of the Bavarian, Bohemian, and Austrian glassblowers' art, on the Rathausplatz.

## Exploring Passau

Above all, Passau is a town for strolling, and a day of window shopping along its cobblestone streets will barely do it justice. Like Deggendorf, the city is also a gateway to the Bavarian Forest, as well as to neighboring Austria and Czechoslovakia. Last but certainly not least, Passau is the main passenger port for Danube cruises, its main quay lined end to end during the summer months with German, Austrian, Hungarian, Romanian, and Soviet river steamers about to embark on their week-long trips to the Black Sea.

The most romantic and historic place in town to have lunch is the **Heilig-Geist-Stift-Schenke**, Heiliggeistgasse 4, less than half a mile east of St. Stephen's cathedral. Its vaulted cellar tavern has been in operation since 1358, and the wines served are from the Holy Ghost Monastery's own vineyards in Austria's Wachau district. For a special treat, order one of the meat dishes, which here are skewered and grilled over the open hearth.

Passau's two most highly rated restaurants are in the **Hotel Wilder Mann**, Schrottgasse 2 on the Rathausplatz, and in the

**Hotel Passauer Wolf**, Rindermarkt 6. Both serve nouvelle cuisine as well as regional specialties. Both hotels are also ideal for spending a night or two in Passau. The Wilder Mann, with 60 rooms, is a modernized patrician's house, and has entertained such notables as Goethe, Napoleon, Tolstoy, and Austria's Empress Elizabeth. The Hotel Passauer Wolf, with 40 rooms, is located in an elaborate Baroque building.

For the ultimate in dining pleasure along the Danube, make a special trip back north into the Bayerischer Wald to **Grafenau** for dinner or lunch (Thursday through Sunday only) at the **Säumerhof**, Steinberg 32; Tel: (8852) 24-01. Proprietor-chef Gebhard Endl, ably assisted by his wife, Renate, who acts as hostess, was an understudy of Munich's Eckart Witzigmann, Germany's greatest chef, before opening the Säumerhof some years ago. On his own now, he approaches regional Bavarian and Austrian specialties with an adept touch. Every meal here is a celebration of food and the culinary art, and well worth the 37-km (23-mile) drive each way. The chalet-style inn also has 11 rooms.

From Passau, you can wind your way in a northwesterly direction through the Bayerischer Wald and its extensions to reach the heart of Franconia, the focus of our next section. But if you really want to understand Franconia, you should start your tour of the region by visiting its capital, Nürnberg, first. The quickest way to do that is to take the A 3 Autobahn directly from Passau. The distance to Nürnberg is 220 km (136 miles), about a two-and-one-half-hour drive.

# FRANCONIA

Our proposed Franconia route loops around the northeastern corner of northern Bavaria in a counterclockwise direction from Nürnberg to Bayreuth to Coburg to Bamberg. It is a restful and relaxing itinerary, and at the same time a stimulating one. It includes the Bier und Burgenstrasse (Beer and Fortress Road) in the Fränkischer Wald (Franconian Forest), with stops at some of the remarkable castles in the area, as well as a taste of Kulmbach's and Bamberg's strong and excellent beer. From there it is on to the

Porzellanstrasse (Porcelain Road), along which some of West Germany's best-known chinaware factories are located, and where Richard Wagner came to build his opera house. And, finally, it is the land that sent Albert, Prince of Saches-Coburg-Gotha, to marry his cousin Victoria in London.

Franconia is a land rich in churches and cathedrals, in castles, and in palaces and residences built by powerful prince-bishops, who ruled in the region from the Middle Ages until the great secularization imposed by Napoleon. But in spite of all its manmade splendors and riches, the landscape itself is unpretentious, the towns, half-timbered houses, and well-tended fields endearing. There is a toylike quality to its villages and barnyards, and a naiveté and sweetness in the scenery.

Whichever way you decide to do the loop, ending at Bamberg, as we suggest, or ending at Nürnberg, the route to Würzburg, which is at the beginning of the Romantic Road and the start of our next chapter, is short and direct.

# *NÜRNBERG*

Glowing testimonials to Nürnberg abound, but so do the harshest judgments. Martin Luther said it shone "forth throughout Germany like a sun among the moon and stars." Goethe lavished praise on it. Hans Christian Andersen, who visited Nürnberg in the 19th century, spoke of its "royal dignity" and saw it as the "quintessence of Medieval culture." Mozart, on the other hand, was deeply depressed by its Gothic severity. "An ugly city," he wrote tersely in 1790 in a letter to a friend.

Nürnberg, with a population of 480,000, making it the second-largest city in Bavaria after Munich, evokes mixed emotions precisely because it embodies like almost no other city in Germany the contradictions of the German soul: the spirit of both Christmas and the Holocaust; the artistic achievements of Medieval craftsmen as well as the architectural braggadocio of a murderously criminal regime; the forces of light and darkness locked in perpetual conflict but also in perennial symbiosis.

It is the city of Albrecht Dürer, Veit Stoss, Peter Vischer, and Adam Kraft, artists whose inimitable legacy endures, but also of Albert Speer, whose bombastic temples to Nazism have doggedly defied the demolition teams. It is the city of Hans Sachs, the master cobbler turned mastersinger of thousands of poems and fables, but also of Julius Streicher, the

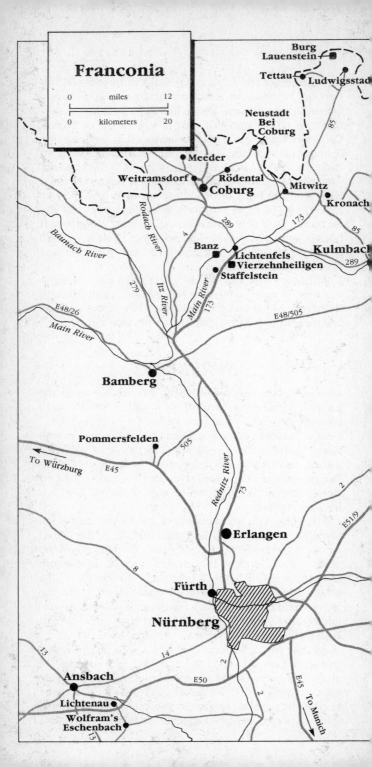

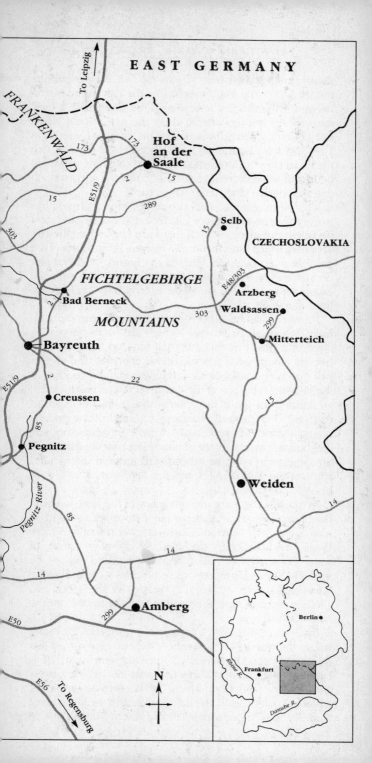

sadistic anti-Semite whose vicious rag *Der Stürmer* became the gazette of the Third Reich. It is the city where Martin Behaim made the first terrestrial globe, and where a local astronomer, Regiomontanus, drew the navigational charts that Columbus carried with him on his voyage to America in 1492. But it is also the city where Adolf Hitler promulgated the racial laws that unleashed the "final solution," as well as of the historic war-crimes trials that closed the era of a Reich that was to have lasted a thousand years.

What Nürnberg was, and once represented, collapsed in a storm of fire on the night of January 2, 1945, during the most destructive of many air raids that were targeted on the city. That raid, which lasted a mere 53 minutes, left a fourth of the population homeless and turned the historic Medieval part of Nürnberg into a rubble heap. No other city, with the exception of Dresden six weeks later, was so totally devastated in a single raid.

Nürnberg has since been completely and splendidly rebuilt. Proposals for an entirely new city were rejected in favor of a plan that called for patching up as many of its historic monuments, majestic Gothic churches, and elegant patrician houses as could be salvaged from the wreckage. At the same time, the rest of the Old Town was reconstructed in an updated version of the original style, using the materials that had characterized Nürnberg for centuries, especially red sandstone. Wherever walls, towers, fountains, bridges, and burgher mansions could not be put back together, new buildings expressing the steep-roofed, turreted architectural spirit of the Middle Ages and the Renaissance took their place.

As a result, there are mercifully few of the steel-and-glass boxes or plastic-façaded department stores one sees in so many other West German cities. And fewer still of the cutesy Disneyland-like copies that mar the downtown areas of some cities. Neither has it been scarred and slashed by throughways and turnpikes, as some cities were during the Wirtschaftswunder (Economic Miracle) of the 1950s and 1960s in order to make them *autogerecht,* or suitable for the new automotive age.

By German standards, Nürnberg is a comparatively young city. In the year 1050, "Nourenberc" was first mentioned in a document signed by the Holy Roman Emperor Henry III. It had probably gotten its start a few years earlier as a fortress and military base from which the imperial territories of eastern Franconia could be defended against the kingdom of Hungary and the duchy of Poland. In time, a hamlet grew on the hill that sloped down from the castle to the Pegnitz river, and it soon became a favorite stopping point for the then-peripatetic imperial court.

Royal favor brought wealth, and the hamlet grew into a town. By the early 13th century, under Emperor Barbarossa, it had become a *Freie Reichsstadt,* entitled to collect taxes and levy duties, and virtually self-governing through a council of patricians who rotated the burgomastership among themselves. Thanks to the Golden Bull of 1356, which established the imperial succession on the basis of majority vote among the seven most powerful princes, or *Kurfürsten* (electors), the city became the de facto capital of the Holy Roman German Empire, for that document also specified that each newly elected emperor had to convoke his first diet—the *Reichstag*—in Nürnberg.

Moreover, the city soon became the permanent repository of the imperial insignia—the ball and scepter as well as the crown of Charlemagne—which were kept in the sacristy of Heiliggeistkirche (Holy Ghost Church). There they remained from 1424 to 1796, when they were finally transferred to Vienna, seat of the Hapsburgs, who had long been, for all intents and purposes, the hereditary emperors. (After Hitler annexed Austria in 1938 he forced the return of the crown to Nürnberg, where it was hidden during the last year of World War II. The American-appointed mayor of the city revealed its hiding place to U.S. authorities in 1945, and the crown was repatriated to Vienna.)

But Nürnberg's role as the capital of the empire was only one factor in its rise to fame, wealth, and power. Far more important were the industriousness of its burghers, who benefitted greatly from its fortuitous location at the crossroads of the four major European trade routes: from the Orient and Balkans to the Low Countries; from Venice to Hamburg; from Strasbourg to Prague; and from Switzerland to Poland. Together, they combined to make the city one of the principal commercial and manufacturing centers of the Middle Ages and early Renaissance.

Ironically, it was Nürnburg's contributions to the science of navigation that precipitated its decline, for the discovery of the New World and sea passages to Asia soon led to the overshadowing of the old overland trade routes that passed through the city. The Thirty Years War and the decline of the old German empire accomplished the rest. By 1806, when Napoleon elevated the duchy of Bavaria to a kingdom and gave it Nürnberg with surrounding Franconia as a colonial prize, the city was a sleepy provincial backwater with 25,000 inhabitants—about half the number it had had 300 years earlier. The Bavarians and their kings treated it as such, though in 1835, under the aegis of Ludwig I, they built Europe's first railroad line between Nürnberg and nearby Fürth. Nürnberg did not regain its importance until the end of the 19th century, and, much to the chagrin of Nürnbergers, it was only because of Hitler that it again made its mark on history.

To Hitler, Nürnberg's architecture, appearance, and role in the Holy Roman Empire represented the quintessence of everything German and of the Third Reich he envisioned in particular. To that one must add the special role of Julius Streicher, the virulently anti-Semitic Franconian Nazi party leader to whom Hitler owed much as a result of the key role that Streicher had played as agitator and propagandist during the abortive 1923 "beerhall putsch" in Munich.

Hitler's cult in Nürnberg had actually begun a couple of months before the putsch when his National Socialists and other radical rightist organizations staged a so-called "German Day" in the city, the high point of which was a review of their private armies on the picturesque Hauptmarkt, the market square. In 1927 and 1929 the Nazis held their party conventions in Nürnberg, and after taking power in 1933 Hitler made the city the party's permanent convention and rally site. It was during the 1935 convention that he also convened a special session of the Reichstag to enact the so-called "Nürnberg Racial Laws," which heralded the Holocaust.

It was to stage these frightening displays of political power and hysteria that Hitler commissioned Albert Speer to build the various temples to Nazism on a 1,500-acre plot at the southeastern edge of the city. The plans were megalomaniacal: a congress hall that would accommodate 50,000 people; a stadium with a seating capacity of 400,000; marching and rally arenas where hundreds of thousands of stormtroopers could goosestep in review. Only some of these monstrosities were completed by 1939, at which point the invasion of Poland and the subsequent demands of the war put an end to the annual rallies and construction effort.

How Nürnbergers feel today about the Nazi past is perhaps best reflected by what has happened to Speer's concrete mecca. Most of the huge parcel of land has been turned into a park dotted by ponds and wooded glens. Apartment blocks, the ultramodern Meistersingerhalle (a concert hall and convention center), and the Messe, Nürnberg's trade fair grounds, occupy another chunk of it. Speer's horseshoe-shaped Kongresshalle, larger than

Rome's Colosseum, and completed except for its central auditorium roof, now serves as a warehouse for a mail-order company and as the recording studio for the Nürnberg Philharmonic orchestra. The grand avenue, a mile and a half long and 200 feet wide, has been turned into a gigantic parking lot. The Zeppelinfeld arena, in which half a million jack-booted SA and SS troopers used to stand hoarsely shouting allegiance to their Führer, does double duty: as a site for rock and pop festivals and as an athletic field for the U.S. Army units stationed in Nürnberg. For those with an inclination for the macabre, the Nazi relics are there to ogle. Fortunately, Nürnberg has more and better things to offer.

## Exploring the Altstadt

Nürnberg is a city that must be walked; no tour on wheels will do it justice. Moreover, much of it has been turned into a pedestrian mall. But because of the size of its Medieval center, strong legs and sturdy shoes are a must. The defensive **wall** alone is 3 miles long. With 120 sentry towers, 12 fortified gates, numerous bastions, and a 60-foot moat, the wall is also the perfect place from which to get your bearings and a feeling for the geographical layout of the city.

Huddled inside the wall at the Königstor (King's Gate), near the southern periphery of the Old Town and the railway station, is the **Handwerker Hof** (Crafts Court), an enclave of half-timbered shops and stalls that conjures up images of life in the Middle Ages. The wares made and sold here range from wooden toys and stained glass to *Nürnberger Bratwürste* and *Lebkuchen,* the city's most renowned comestibles. Although it may be too early in the day to think about eating, their mention in connection with the Handwerker Hof is reason enough to pause and talk briefly about Bratwürste and Lebkuchen.

Finger-sized Nürnberger Bratwürste are made of pork and various spices, and are charcoal broiled on grills in open booths like the ones in the Handwerker Hof. The sausage man stands high above the action shouting, "One, two, three, four . . ." and so on. You'll feel as if you're at an auction, until you realize you are expected to shout back the number of sausages you want. Less than six makes a snack, 14 will do for lunch. You also have the option of consuming them with sauerkraut or a slab of rye bread. The mustard is very hot.

Lebkuchen, which are sometimes called gingerbread cookies, though traditional recipes do not call for ginger, is to Nürnberg what marzipan is to Lübeck: The city is the Lebkuchen capital of the world, and has been since at least 1409, when the baking of the sweet little confections was first mentioned in municipal records as an independent craft, subject to taxation. Each year, 50 million pounds of Lebkuchen are produced by Nürnberg's bakeries. The oldest Lebkuchen maker has been in business since 1598.

Though these honey-and-spice cakes have been considered delicacies for almost 4,000 years, there seems to be no disputing the fact that it was really in Medieval Nürnberg where they evolved their classical form—round, generally four to five inches in diameter, a half-inch thick, and stuck on a wafer-thin sheet of unleavened and unsweetened dough that is somewhat reminiscent—in taste, consistency, and appearance—to parchment paper. Today, Lebkuchen can be made oblong, square, bite-sized, or heart-shaped. They can come sugar-coated, chocolate-coated, sugar-glazed, or plain. In fact, there are probably as many recipes as there are commercial bakers, and each is a closely guarded secret. The crème de la crème, however, is the *Elisen*-Lebkuchen, so named, legend has it, for Franconia's Countess Elisa, whose husband became one of the dukes of Brandenburg.

Whether or not you've fortified yourself with Bratwürste and Lebkuchen, you will find food for the eyes and intellect about two blocks west of the Handwerker Hof at the **Germanisches Nationalmuseum** (Germanic National Museum), Kornmarkt 1. Founded in 1852 amid the prevailing Romantic-era enthusiasm for things old and German, this huge complex, which includes a 600-year-old Carthusian monastery, is dedicated to exhibiting and preserving the art, culture, handicrafts, and technology of the Germanic lands and tribes, from the earliest times through the 19th century. Its art collection includes some of the finest paintings by Altdorfer, Hans Baldung-Grien, Hans Burgkmair, the Cranachs, Dürer, and the Holbeins, as well as sculptures by Adam Kraft, Tilman Riemenschneider, Veit Stoss, and Peter Vischer. There are, in addition, more than 1,000 antique musical instruments, countless pieces of Medieval armor, the original score of Wagner's *Die Meistersinger,* and Behaim's famous globe.

The **Verkehrsmuseum** (Transport and Communications Museum), Lessingstrasse 6, two blocks south of the Nationalmuseum, and just outside the wall, is just as overwhelming. Here, among many other exhibits, you'll find one of the world's largest postage stamp collections, antique coaches, early railroad cars, and a working replica of the "Adler," the 1835 train that ran between Nürnberg and Fürth.

To reach the main sights of the inner city, walk north from the Handwerker Hof along the Königstrasse. At the corner of the Königstrasse and the Lorenzerplatz stands the **Pfarr-kirche St. Lorenz** (Parish Church of St. Laurence). Begun in the 13th century and completed in the 15th, this twin-spired church is generally regarded as the most beautiful in the city, and contains three prized works of art: a magnificent stained-glass rosette window above the organ at the west end of the nave; the "Angelic Salutation," an intricate wood-carving by Veit Stoss that is suspended from the cross-vaulted ceiling over the entrance to the choir; and Adam Kraft's remarkable tabernacle, chiseled from stone and sup-ported by a kneeling self-portrait of the sculptor and like-nesses of two of his apprentices.

Farther up the Königstrasse is the Pegnitz river, which bisects the inner city on an east-west axis. To call it a river, however, is being generous: "creek" would be a more appro-priate term, for nowhere is it more than 50 feet wide. Still, it gives Nürnberg a verdant and picturesque charm, and a walk along its banks is like strolling into a fairy-tale world. The most memorable views are of the **Heiliggeistspital** (Holy Ghost Hospital), Spitalgasse 12, whose foundations spill into the streambed, and which now serves as a moderately priced restaurant; the half-timbered **Weinstadel**, a 15th-century wine warehouse; and the **Henkersteg** (Hangman's Bridge), which is surrounded, fittingly, by weeping willows.

## The Hauptmarkt

Nürnberg's heart—geographically as well as figuratively—is the cobblestone Hauptmarkt, the main market square, just north of the river at the northern end of the Königstrasse. Eleven months of the year it teems with flower, fruit, and vegetable sellers hawking their produce, but during the four weeks from Advent Sunday until December 24 it is trans-formed into a small town of wood-and-cloth stalls that is the scene of one of the city's most popular and colorful attractions—the *Christkindlmarkt* (Christ Child Market).

In addition to being the world's oldest Christmas fair, having been held on the same spot for more than 400 years now, it is by far the most dazzling—a kaleidoscope of stands selling toys, tree ornaments, tinsel, handicrafts, candles, candy, Lebkuchen, fruitcakes, and *Glühwein* (hot red wine spiced with cinnamon and cloves). There are daily carol and trombone concerts, as well as performances by theater, dance, and puppet groups. The setting for all this is as spectacular as the month-long event itself, for the Hauptmarkt is squeezed between the Rathaus, with its filigreelike façade, the red sandstone front of the Frauenkirche, and the Schöner Brunnen, a gilded 60-foot spirelike Gothic fountain. The best time to visit the Christkindlmarkt is at night, when everything is floodlit and the square is suffused with the magic that is so much a part of Christmas.

The **Frauenkirche** (Church of Our Lady), on the eastern edge of the Hauptmarkt, is situated on the site of a Jewish synagogue that was destroyed, along with the entire Jewish quarter, in an early-14th-century pogrom. The gilded 16th-century mechanical clock on the façade depicts the pageant of the seven electors of the Holy Roman Empire paying homage to the emperor. The **Altes Rathaus**, on the Rathausplatz, just off the market square, combines late Gothic and early Renaissance elements in its design. The **Schöner Brunnen** (Beautiful Fountain), on the northwest corner of the Hauptmarkt, was completed in 1396, and is the finest example of Gothic fountain architecture anywhere. Unfortunately, the many figures on it are copies. Fragments of the originals are on exhibit at the Germanisches Nationalmuseum.

Wherever you walk in Nürnberg, the **Kaiserburg** (Imperial Castle) is in view, but the view is most beckoning from the Hauptmarkt, so start your climb up the steep, narrow cobblestone streets from there. The Kaiserburg was one of Europe's largest fortified castles, though unique in the sense that it was never really any sovereign's permanent home but rather a kind of hotel in which the emperor, the electors, princes, and dukes lived when the Reichstag was in session. There are guided tours of its knights' hall, chapel, apartments, and council chambers.

Heading back downhill after your tour of the castle, stop first on the picturesque little square below the Kaiserburg's western bastion for a visit to the **Albrecht Dürer Haus**, Albrecht-Dürer-Strasse 39. Dürer bought this magnificent burgher house in 1509 and used it as his home and studio until his death in 1528. It contains period furnishings and interiors, as well as originals and copies of his work.

Three steep blocks downhill from Dürer's house is the **Stadtpfarrkirche St. Sebaldus** (Parish Church of St. Sebald), Winklerstrasse 26. Named for Nürnberg's patron saint, it was built in the 13th century and represents the stylistic transition from late Romanesque to early Gothic. It is also filled with works by Nürnberg artists, including Veit Stoss and Adam Kraft, but its greatest masterpiece is the elaborate bronze tomb created by Peter Vischer in 1519 for St. Sebald's remains. One of the newest additions to the church, which was heavily damaged during the war, is its organ, a magnificent instrument with 84 registers that was completed by a Nürnberg craftsman in 1975.

From St. Sebald's it is a two-minute stroll to the charming **Spielzeugmuseum** (Toy Museum), Karlstrasse 13, a dazzling collection of dolls, dollhouses, miniature trains, tin figures, and children's books from Medieval times to the present.

Returning to the Hauptmarkt, take another stroll down the Königstrasse and stop in briefly at little **St. Martha's Church**, Königstrasse 77, which is noted both for its stained-glass windows and for the fact that it is where the Meistersinger had their school in the 16th and 17th centuries.

# Dining and Staying in Nürnberg

You will, of course, find more to eat in Nürnberg than Bratwürste and Lebkuchen, though, alas, the few culinary stars that once shone in the center of town flickered out a number of years ago. Nonetheless, you will eat well at the **Goldenes Posthorn**, Glöckleingasse 2, just north of St. Sebald's. One of Nürnberg's oldest restaurants, it has a dining room filled with historic artifacts, and emphasizes the nouvelle approach to Franconian specialties. Reservations are recommended; Tel: 22-51-53. **Zum Waffenschmied**, Obere Schmiedgasse 22, at the foot of the Kaiserburg, is historic, rustic, and more traditional in its approach. Reservations for dinner are essential; Tel: 22-58-59. **Böhm's Herrenkeller**, Theatergasse 19, just off the Königstrasse, has a pedigree that goes back to 1499, and is recommended by Nürnbergers for its excellent selection of Franconian wines.

When it comes to hotels, the choice is complicated by the necessity of making a decision on whether to try for a spot within the Altstadt, where establishments are generally less expensive and sometimes hard to reach because of the pedestrians-only areas, or settle for the posher spots outside the wall. Of the latter the ultra-modern **Maritim**, Frauentorgraben 11, ranks highest and is the most expensive, despite the fact that it is part of a chain operation and rather faceless. Not so the **Grand Hotel**, Bahnhofstrasse 1, directly across the square from the railway station and virtually adjacent to the Königstor gate. A grand hotel in every sense, each room is decorated differently.

Within the wall, you will find the **Victoria**, Königstrasse 80, located in a 19th-century burgher house, very comfortable and within easy walking distance of all the important sights. The most picturesquely located establishment, just below the Kaiserburg, is the **Burghotel-Grosses Haus**, Lammsgasse 3, at the corner of the Albrecht-Dürer-Strasse. There is a *dependence* of it about a block away at Schildgasse 16. In either house you can ask for a room looking out on the cobblestone streets, which may get a bit noisy but gives you the feeling of being back in the Middle Ages.

# *NORTH TO BAYREUTH*

To head north from Nürnberg, you can of course take the Nürnberg-to-Berlin Autobahn. It is more interesting, instead, to take the B 2 (follow the signs to the Nürnberg airport to get out of the city), which runs through picturesque Franconian villages to Pegnitz, Creussen, and Bayreuth, our next three destinations.

**Pegnitz**, 60 km (37 miles) northeast of Nürnberg, is on our route not for its cultural attractions, of which there really are none, but for its earthly pleasures, especially the marvelously memorable **Pflaum's Posthotel**, Nürnberger Strasse 14.

This luxury establishment, with its outstanding restaurant, has been a country inn, brewery, and postal relay station belonging to the Pflaum family for more than 280 years. Two Pflaum brothers, educated and trained in New York, Paris, and London, have been operating it as a resort hotel and restaurant catering to the silk-stocking Bayreuth festival crowd since the early 1970s. Andreas, the younger of the two, is the manager; Hermann is the chef—and he cooks sublimely. Using local produce and livestock, as well as the freshest local fish, and accompanying his creations with the finest wines Franconia has to offer, he has managed to synthesize the best of gourmet and local peasant cuisine. Try, for example, the brook trout soufflé with wine sauce and sorrel, the fresh spinach soup, the roast quail in morel sauce, and the pear sherbet as dessert. The Pflaums also run a bus to and from Bayreuth for performances during the festival season.

## Creussen

You will pass through this charming hamlet, 14 km (8.5 miles) north of Pegnitz, on your way to Bayreuth; be sure to stop. The town grew up around a fortress that dates back to the year 1000, and still has a well-preserved (in parts) 15th-century defensive **wall**. Be sure also to visit the **Städtisches Krügemuseum**, Rennsteig 36, with its fine collection of Creussen's best-known product—stoneware jugs and beer steins—as well as a good collection of Bayreuth faïence. No less interesting is the 16th-century church in the town district of Lindenhardt, which features an altar painting by Matthias Grünewald, the last of the great German Gothic masters.

From Creussen it is a leisurely 12 km (7 miles) to Bayreuth.

## *BAYREUTH*

This city of 71,000 owes its international fame in part to two extreme personalities and two opera houses. Initially, there was, and still is, the **Markgräfliches Opernhaus**, built from 1745 to 1748 for the Margravine Wilhelmine, a Prussian princess who was the older sister of Frederick the Great. Inside, it is a riot of wreathed columns, gilded cupids, and Rococo shells. The second theater, Wagner's Festspielhaus, completed in 1876, represents the opposite extreme, in which nothing architectural or ornamental was, or is, allowed to distract from the stage or Wagner's music.

The earliest documents referring to Bayreuth date back to 1194. In the 13th century it became the property of the margraves of Kulmbach, cousins of the Hohenzollerns, who became the rulers of Brandenburg, Prussia, and eventually all of Germany. The margraves first ruled their little fief from the mighty Plassenburg fortress in Kulmbach, north of Bayreuth (see below), but in 1542 decided that the latter would make a far nicer capital. So, they built a little palace, the Altes Schloss, to which they kept adding, and in the 18th century Margrave Frederick and his wife Wilhelmine built an even more splendid château, the Neues Schloss. In time, Wilhelmine, envious of what her brother Frederick, the king of Prussia, was doing in Berlin and Potsdam, decided that she, too, needed an opera house, and so had the Markgräfliches Opernhaus built, with the result that by 1750 little Bayreuth was one of the most splendid residence cities in Germany. Its golden age came to a rather sudden end in 1806 when Napoleon invaded, occupied the town, dissolved the independent and sovereign Margraviate of Kulmbach, and then, four years later, sold it and the principality to his ally, Bavaria's King Maximilian I.

Enter, some 60 years later, Richard Wagner and his bride Cosima, daughter of the composer Franz Liszt and for 13 years wife of the Munich opera conductor Hans von Bülow, from whom Wagner had stolen her in one of the most scandalous affairs of the 19th century. By 1848, when he participated in the anti-monarchist, nationalist revolution, Wagner was one of the most celebrated personalities in the European music world. Because of his role in the abortive revolution, however, he was forced to flee to Switzerland. There followed a number of peripatetic and impecunious years, including a season as the conductor of the London Philharmonic. Then, in 1864, Bavaria's 18-year-old "Dream King," Ludwig II, a gushing fan, invited him to settle in Munich.

Wagner's stay in Munich certainly started out promisingly enough. *Tristan und Isolde* premiered (with Hans von Bülow conducting), and Wagner, having finished *Die Meistersinger von Nürnberg,* resumed writing *Siegfried* and *Götterdämmerung,* the last two operas of "The Ring" cycle, and began *Parsifal.* But his affair with Cosima, whom he had known as a child, and Ludwig II's outlay of public funds for the composer's productions and to support his lavish lifestyle, soon won Wagner more enemies than friends in the Bavarian capital. In 1867 he was asked to leave town. Together with Cosima, who was still legally married to von Bülow, he returned to Switzerland and settled at Triebschen near Lucerne. Restless and ambitious as ever, he began to look for an opera house in which to stage "The Ring"—a dream that was fulfilled by Bayreuth in 1871.

The city offered Wagner Margravine Wilhelmine's Baroque theater. After he and Cosima visited Bayreuth, however, Wagner turned down the offer on the grounds that the margravine's opera house was too small for "The Ring." Turning to his erstwhile sponsor, Ludwig II, Wagner proposed building a new festival opera house in Bayreuth, and asked for money. Ludwig, no doubt figuring that the cost of an opera house would be piddling compared to what he was already spending on his fairy-tale castles in the Bavarian Alps, coughed up the needed funds. The cornerstone for the Festspielhaus, which was to rise on a hill at the northern end of Bayreuth at the end of a mile-long boulevard now called the Nibelungenstrasse, was laid on May 22, 1872. Designed by Gottfried Semper, who had also built the Dresden opera house, the theater opened with the first complete performance of "The Ring" four years later.

The Wagner **Bayreuth Festival** usually takes place from the last week of July through the last week of August. Tickets are very hard to get in Germany, so it's best to order them through your travel agent at home. (The ticket office in Bayreuth is Kartenbüro, Festspielleitung Bayreuth, Postfach 100262, D-8580 Bayreuth 1, Germany.) The **Festspielhaus** should be seen even if it is empty, however.

For festival-goers, elaborate and mysterious dinner arrangements at hotels and restaurants in and around Bayreuth—whereby you leave your soup after the first intermission and find your place at the same table in the second intermission, with your next course ready and waiting—seem to be the rule. In addition, the audience is always summoned back to the auditorium by a fanfare of trumpets that ties in with the leitmotif of the next act. Though Bayreuthers are perfectly normal people living in a normal city, during the Wagner Festspiel they go quite mad. Many of them dress in costumes to match the work being performed. And there is usually one elderly couple in lace shawl and black velvet tam-o'-shanter playing the part of Richard and Cosima.

Another important Bayreuth sight is the composer's mansion **Villa Wahnfried**, the large Neoclassical cube at Richard-Wagner-Strasse 48. The giant bronze head that rests on a polished marble pedestal in front of the house is King Ludwig II as he looked in the 1860s. There is a Wagner kitsch show put on in the villa.

Though it is Wagner who occupies center stage in Bayreuth, he does not totally monopolize it. The Margravial opera house, on the Opernstrasse, is still very much used during the annual Franconian Rococo festival (Musica Bavaria; the first two weeks of May), as well as for concerts. Stop in at the **Café Zellinger**, in the corner of the building, for coffee and pastry while waiting for a guided tour of the theater. All Bayreuthers and most visitors seem to congregate there sooner or later for a second breakfast, afternoon coffee, or assorted delicacies at intermission.

The **Altes Schloss** (Old Palace), on the Maximilianstrasse, just a few steps west of the opera house, should be seen, as should the **Schlosskirche** (Palace Church), which was added to the complex in the 1750s.

The **Neues Schloss** (New Palace), at Ludwigstrasse 21, commissioned by Wilhelmine and built from 1753 to 1754, expresses her fondness for nature and the East-Asian motifs. The New Palace is now a museum, rich in artifacts from Bavaria's past, and also has a branch of the **Bavarian state pictures collection**.

For in-town dining in rustic country-style surroundings, try the **Gasthof zur Lohmühle**, Badstrasse 37, near the Margravial opera house. The emphasis here is on fish dishes from the region and game in season. The inn also has 12 comfortable, moderately priced rooms. For dinner, reservations are recommended; Tel: (921) 630-31.

Bayreuth's three other major hotels are all close to the railway station, about halfway between the Festival Theater and the Old Palace. The **Hotel Bayerischer Hof**, Bahnhofstrasse 14, has 62 pricey rooms, all decorated in neo-Baroque style, and have had as guests Konrad Adenauer and boxing champion Floyd Patterson. The **Hotel Königshof**, Bahnhofstrasse 23, also in the first-class category, has 44 rooms and was totally renovated and redecorated in 1980. The somewhat more moderately priced **Hotel Goldener Hirsch**, Bahnhofstrasse 13, has a pedigree as an inn going back 300 years.

# Outside Bayreuth

The **Eremitage**, 4 km (2 miles) east of the city on B 22, offers a glimpse of how 16th- and 17th-century royalty escaped the responsibilities of their position. At the Hermitage outside of Bayreuth the margraviate court would come dressed as shepherds and shepherdesses to lead the simple life, with the margrave himself dressed in religious habit and acting as a kind of abbot. The era was also one of preoccupation with landscaping, and there is a fine park around the Hermitage. In it, you will find a Sun Temple, considered one of the finest rotunda structures of the late Rococo period, as well as a Dragon's Den, a Hermit Chapel, fountains, cascades, and the tomb of Margravine Wilhelmine's dog Folichon, which was built to resemble an ancient ruin. On the grounds there is also a small (ten rooms) moderately priced hotel, the **Eremitage**, Eremitage 42; Tel: (921) 992-87.

Just 6 km (4 miles) south of Bayreuth, in the suburb of Thiergarten back toward Creussen on B 2, is the Schloss Thiergarten, built in 1753 by Wilhelmine's son, Margrave Georg Wilhelm, as a hunting château. An armchair sportsman if ever there was one, Georg Wilhelm was the envy of crowned and coroneted Europe for his hunting lodge. It had one room so large that servants could drive deer through it while the royal hunters, seated on balconies along the wall, could shoot the bewildered animals without sacrificing their comfort. The château is now the **Schlosshotel Thiergarten** (12 rooms), with a restaurant highly rated for its nouvelle cuisine and Franconian dishes.

## *NORTH TOWARD COBURG*

Though the next destination, Kulmbach, is only 20 km (12 miles) north of Bayreuth by way of B 85, you might consider using either Bayreuth or Kulmbach as a base for travelling eastward toward the border with Czechoslovakia and into the **Fichtelgebirge** (Fichtel Mountains), or for a drive along the **Porzellanstrasse** (Porcelain Road), with stops in some of its porcelain manufacturing towns such as **Arzberg** or **Selb**. The easiest and fastest way to do the latter is to get on the Nürnberg-Berlin Autobahn, head north in the direction of Berlin, get off after only 8 km (5 miles) at the "Bad Berneck" exit, swing onto B 303 in the direction of the resort town of Bad Berneck, and then continue on B 303 some 33 km (20 miles) to its junction with B 15. The latter is the so-called Porcelain Road. Selb is 20 km (12 miles) north of the intersection, right on the highway. To get to Arzberg continue east on B 303 for another 9 km (5 miles). (For more information on the Porcelain Road contact the German National Tourist Office.)

## Kulmbach

The picturesque smallish town of Kulmbach, 7.5 km (12 miles) north of Bayreuth, is famous for three things: its beer, Plassenburg Fortress, and the German Tin Figures Museum.

Start with the beer, the richest and strongest in the world, called *Kulmbacher Eisbock* (ice bock), which came into being a child of coincidence. According to local legend, on a bitterly cold winter afternoon in the year 1890 a brewery worker at the **Reichelbräu**, one of two breweries in Kulmbach, was told to move several barrels of regular bock beer from the courtyard into the cellar. However, it was late in the day, and he was tired and wanted to go home—which he did, leaving the beer to stand outside overnight. The next morning the barrels of beer were frozen solid, their staves and hoops burst, but in the middle of each block of ice was a core of concentrated beer. Naturally, the brewmaster was furious and, to punish the worker, ordered him to drink the liquid. The young employee did as told, fully expecting to get sick. But after just one sip, he smiled. Never before, he exclaimed, had he tasted anything as delicious. Somewhat reluctantly, his boss tried it too, and agreed. The two hurried off to get the brewery director, who, after having a taste, decided on the spot to call it Eisbock and to mass produce and market it. To this day both the Reichelbräu and its chief competitor, Erste Kulmbacher Actien Exportbierbrauerei (EKU), produce Eisbock and sell it all over Germany. EKU's is even stronger than Reichel's—a syrupy honey-blond concoction with an alcohol content of 8 to 9 percent. To try it, stop in at the **EKU-Inn**, the brewery's tavern at Klostergasse 7, right in the center of town at the foot of the Buchsberg, the hill crowned by the Plassenburg.

**Veste Plassenburg**, visible for miles, is one of the longest, most elaborate, and most impressive Renaissance castle-fortresses in Germany, an impregnable walled city sitting atop the Buchsberg. The first references to it date back to the early 12th century. To visit it, head up the steep incline from the center of Kulmbach to the Kommandantenhaus (Commandant's House), go on through the main gate and into the **Schöner Hof** (Beautiful Courtyard).

The mammoth structure was designed by Caspar Vischer, who knew all there was to know about making walls impregnable. But the Plassenburg's builders also took pains to beautify the castle, especially its inner courtyard, which blooms with more than a hundred carved portrait medallions, *putti* and monsters, wreaths and delicate tracery, birds and flowers, and every now and then an intricate interweaving of mermaids and garlands.

Today the Plassenburg **apartments** are open to the public as a museum containing rare collections of arms and silver, furniture and paintings. But within the huge complex is another museum, the **Deutsches Zinnfigurenmuseum** (German Tin Figures Museum), the largest museum of tin soldiers and tiny metal figures in the world. For the sheer beauty, diversity, and artistic perfection of its figures it is also, by far, the most spectacular and impressive collection in the world.

Every two years in August, Kulmbach and the Plassenburg are the scene of the **International Tin Figures Bourse**, a trade fair that brings in collectors and dealers from nearly three dozen countries. (The next fair will be in 1991.)

Where these visitors stay is a bit of a mystery, however.

Kulmbach has only five or six moderately priced hotels, and none of them is in the historic center of town. Your best bet is the **Hansa-Hotel**, Weltrichstrasse 2a, at the southwestern end of town.

Kulmbach also marks the start of the **Bier und Burgenstrasse** (Beer and Fortress Road), a promotional term for B 85, along which it is a mere 29 km (18 miles) to Kronach and its fortress castle, Veste (fortress) Rosenberg.

# Kronach

Though there is not much evidence of it besides a plaque, the painter Lucas Cranach the Elder was born in Kronach, and locals still dispute whether it was in the house at Zum Marktplatz 1, or at the Haus zum Scharfen Eck. Either way, Cranach, intimately connected with Martin Luther and the Reformation, was one of the greatest German artists of the late 15th and early 16th centuries, and his home town is justly proud of him.

The artist was actually born Lucas Sunder in 1472, but subsequently adopted the town's name and changed the spelling on numerous occasions in his long career. Eventually he became court painter to the Elector Frederick the Wise, duke of Saxony, who was the chief protector of Luther and founder of the university of Wittenberg, where Luther taught and first posted the theses that triggered the Reformation. Cranach did much of his best work in Wittenberg, including portraits of the various leaders of the Reformation and of most of the university's faculty members. His son, Lucas Cranach the Younger, was almost his equal, and you will find some fine paintings of his in the Veste Rosenberg, the mighty fortress that sits high above Kronach.

**Veste Rosenberg** was built in the early 12th century by a prince-bishop of Bamberg, enlarged several times in the Middle Ages, became a residence of the Bamberg prince-bishops in the 16th century, and played a key role in the Thirty Years War. In 1730 Balthasar Neumann, one of Germany's greatest and most imaginative Baroque architects, redesigned it to its present appearance. It now serves as a youth hostel, as well as the home of the **Frankenwald Museum**, which has Cranach the Younger paintings in its collection.

For a look at an even more impressive castle, drive 35 km (22 miles) north along B 85, the Beer and Fortress Road, to Ludwigsstadt and Burg Lauenstein.

The trip takes you through hilly, wooded countryside, the **Naturpark Frankenwald** (Franconian Forest Nature Preserve), which, because of the abundance of blue-black slate, takes on a somewhat mysterious character. In the towns and villages along the way you'll notice that all the buildings are covered with small slate shingles, walls as well as roofs. In sunlight they reflect a striking sea-blue color; in shade they appear almost black. In contrast, window frames are always a gleaming white, and foundations and ground floors painted a pale yellow or white. It should come as no surprise that there are still teams of itinerant slaters in this country, artisans who can slate-shingle around curves, corners, and even onion-domed church spires.

**Ludwigsstadt**, near the end of the route, is a small town that saw better times during its mining days, and has now become a health resort. Its chief attractions are a 12th-century Romanesque church and the nearby Lauenstein Fortress (*Burg*).

**Burg Lauenstein** has, since the 14th century, stood on a rock looking out across pine-wooded hills into a wild landscape that matches its blue–greenish slate roofs and turrets. As a castle site it dates back to the year 915, when the Holy Roman Emperor Conrad I had it built as an outpost, but Lauenstein was frequently rebuilt and enlarged, and just as frequently changed hands. It now belongs to the State of Bavaria, which financed its restoration in the 1960s and 1970s.

Inside, the castle is beautifully furnished, and contains many interesting and curious collections, among them one of rare locks and door hardware, another of lighting fixtures. In fact, it lacks nothing that a Medieval castle should have, not even a ghost. The "white lady" is condemned forever to walk the ramparts of Lauenstein because of a fatal misunderstanding. Legend has it she was a widowed countess of Orlamünde who desperately wanted to marry Albrecht the Handsome of Nürnberg. He turned her down on the grounds that there were "four eyes in the way." She misunderstood this to mean her two children and, tragically, killed them (Albrecht had actually meant his own aged parents).

You can spend a night like a knight right in Lauenstein. The **Burghotel Lauenstein** here has 22 rooms at moderate prices, and its rustic restaurant is justly famous for stick-to-the-ribs Franconian dishes; Tel: (9263) 256.

From the castle it is 62 km (38 miles) south on B 85 as far as Kronach, then west on B 303, to Coburg.

# COBURG

For nearly 400 years this little city of 45,000 inhabitants just south of the state of Thuringia was the residence and capital of the dukes of Sachse-Coburg-Gotha, a dynasty whose major impact on world history lies in the fact that one of its scions, Prince Albert, married his first cousin, Queen Victoria of England, in 1840.

The town is idyllically situated astride the little Itz river, a tributary of the Main, amid the rolling foothills of the Thüringer Wald (Thuringian Forest). Among its most important sights and attractions are the Veste Coburg, the huge fortress that towers over the city; Ehrenburg Palace; the 16th-century Rathaus; and a market square lined by beautiful burgher houses.

**Veste Coburg** (Coburg Fortress), the "Crown of Franconia," literally dominates the town, an enormous, intimidating complex that had become impractical and virtually uninhabitable long before the ruling dukes moved out in the 16th century. The fortress does command sweeping views over much of Franconia and parts of Thuringia to the north (on a clear day, it can itself be seen for miles around), and three sides of it overhang the practically unscalable rocks on which it sits (the fourth—or southern side—was protected by two drawbridges and entry courtyards). It wasn't until our own century, in fact, that the advent of new weapons and flying machines made the castle vulnerable.

This stupendous stronghold was begun in the 11th century, and expanded and strengthened over the next two hundred years. The ruling family of Sachse-Coburg-Gotha inhabited it continuously from 1056 until 1547, when its discomforts persuaded the then-reigning duke, Johann Ernst, to move his family and entourage into the relative comfort of Ehrenburg Palace, in the center of town. (Only the rats, they say, were comfortable in the fortress.)

Yet it is well worth a visit. Among the famous people who have stayed in it were the elder Lucas Cranach, Goethe (who allegedly could bear it for only three days), Queen Victoria, and Martin Luther, who, rather involuntarily, remained here for five months in 1530 while awaiting an opportunity to present his arguments to a papal emissary in Augsburg. During that time he continued to work on his translation of the Bible into German. The **Luther room** in the fortress still holds the table at which he wrote. Among the castle's other treasures are a fine selection of Cranach paintings, a library of 450,000 volumes, a collection of Medieval coins, engravings and etchings, a glass collection, and Germany's largest collection of antique firearms and hunting weapons.

Given the disadvantages of living in the fortress, it is small wonder that Johann Ernst moved into the more comfortable and elegant environs of **Schloss Ehrenburg**, a former Franciscan monastery on Coburg's Schlossstrasse. Its curious name—it means "Honor Castle" in German—is owed to the honor of a visit paid it in 1547 by the Holy Roman Emperor Charles V. The palace in its present form is an extensive 17th- and 18th-century renovation of the Renaissance original. Most of it is now a museum, which makes it possible to see the Giants' Hall, so named for its 28 stucco figures of giants; the ornately decorated Gobelin Room; and the lavish throne room, which is very properly decked out in red velvet, crystal, and gold. The room is unusual, however, in that it does not contain a throne at all; instead, there is a long, cushioned sofa from which the dukes of Sachse-Coburg-Gotha apparently ruled in a kind of semi-reclining position. The museum also includes the bedroom that Victoria and Albert used on their various visits to his family in Coburg. In the left back corner of the bed-niche, partly hidden by a curtain, is what appears to be a telephone booth. In fact, it was, in its day, an unprecedented sensation and the first of its kind in the region: an English water closet.

Albert's early death left Victoria bereft the rest of her life. It was she who gave Coburg the tall statue of Prince Albert that stands in the center of the Marktplatz amid the people and activities of the city he loved. He is portrayed as wonderfully handsome, in the full regalia of his office, extending a shapely leg adorned with the Order of the Garter.

Traffic, which ill suits the magnificently orieled and gabled Medieval **Rathaus** and the half-timbered burgher houses lining the Marktplatz, moves slowly around the statue of Prince Albert, while pigeons flutter about his head and market women screech at his feet. Coburg's characteristic olfactory sensation, the scent of Bratwürste broiling over charcoal fires, drifts across the square and rouses hundreds of Coburgers to their accustomed morning snack. Be advised, however, that Coburg Bratwürste are unlike those you may have tasted in Nürnberg and Regensburg. None of that finger-long, finger-thick stuff here. A Coburg sausage is precisely 31 centimeters (about 12 inches) long—a measure determined by the length of the marshal's staff in the hand of Coburg's patron Saint

Mauritius, who stands high atop the Rathaus gable—thumb-thick, and is consumed between the halves of a small crisply crusted roll.

# Dining and Staying
# in Coburg

For more substantial lunching or dining, saunter a block west of the Marktplatz to the **Goldene Traube**, Am Viktoriabrunnen 2, where the menu lists a variety of international dishes as well as Franconian specialties, not to mention a fine selection of Franconian wines. The Goldene Traube is also a hotel, with 88 rooms in the moderate-price category. An alternative just south of the Rathaus that is popular with the Coburg business community is the **Goldener Anker**, Rosengasse 14, which has been run by the same family for more than 85 years. The cuisine is solid and unpretentious, the service friendly. The Goldener Anker too is a hotel, with 63 moderately priced rooms. For the ultimate in fine dining and accommodations in Coburg, you will, however, have to travel a little beyond the confines of the picturesque Old City, about half a mile south of the Marktplatz along the Ketschendorfer Strasse, to the **Restaurant Schaller** in the **Hotel Coburger Tor**, Ketschendorfer Strasse 22. Proprietor-chef Ulrich Schaller deserves the recognition he has won since turning the dining room of this small (20 rooms), moderately priced hotel into Coburg's most elegant and dignified eatery. The decor is subdued and elegant, the cuisine memorable. The menu changes daily according to season and the availability of the best and freshest products. Schaller is a master at putting a light, nouvelle touch to regional specialties such as quenelles of Main river pike or wild duck in a morel sauce. Reservations are recommended, as there is seating for only 50; Tel: (9561) 250-74. No credit cards are accepted, which also goes for the hotel. The restaurant is closed Friday and for lunch Saturday, as well as from July 20 to 27.

# *BETWEEN COBURG*
# *AND BAMBERG*

From Coburg our route heads south again, towards Bamberg, by way of two of Franconia's most stunning Baroque churches—the Banz Monastery and Vierzehnheiligen church—situated on opposite sides of the road just south of the basket-weaving town of **Lichtenfels**. The best way to get there is to take B 4 south out of Coburg for 9 km (5 miles) to the junction with B 289. Follow B 289 for another 10 km (6 miles) to Lichtenfels. Just past Lichtenfels, you'll come to the junction with B 173. Take it south (follow the signs to Bamberg), and you will see Banz and Vierzehnheiligen after about half a mile. The highway follows the left bank of the Main River.

# Banz and Vierzehnheiligen

These two churches are breathtaking examples of Baroque architecture and craftsmanship. Here, rising unexpectedly against wooded hills on opposite banks of the Main river, they are exalting. As you approach them from the north, you'll see Vierzehnheiligen towering on the hill to your left, Banz across the valley to your right.

**Banz** began as a fortress castle belonging to Countess Alberada of Schweinfurt, who, in 1065, donated her property to the Benedictine order for conversion into a monastery. In 1071 the abbey came under the supervision of the prince-bishop of Bamberg. An abbey church, consecrated in 1114, was destroyed during the Thirty Years War. Nearly half a century later, the architect Johann Leonhard Dientzenhofer drew up plans for a new church. Work, largely by lay brothers, began in 1695 and continued through the first half of the 18th century, with other members of the Dientzenhofer family as well as Balthasar Neumann contributing, not only to the church itself but to the reconstruction of the entire monastery complex.

The result was two long structures, each with 27 bays, running parallel to the mountain and looking out over the Main river. These structures, connected by wings, contained an enormous library, a number of schools, and the friars' quarters. But the most important part of the complex was the church dedicated to St. Dionysius, with its magnificent ceiling frescoes, choir stalls, high altar, and pulpit. The abbey was secularized in 1806, and is used today as an old people's home, but the church, the abbot's chapel, and the Kaisersaal (Imperial Hall) are open to visitors.

**Vierzehnheiligen** (Church of the Fourteen Saints of the Intercession) is a pilgrimage church that owes its origins to a 15th-century vision. According to the legend, a shepherd boy, Hermann Leicht, saw a vision of the Christ child and the 14 Auxiliary Saints on several occasions between 1445 and

1446 and told the abbot of Banz about the appearances; eventually, the abbot ordered the construction of a small chapel on the spot. The chapel became the object of many pilgrimages, and by the early 18th century was clearly too small to accommodate all its visitors. Balthasar Neumann was commissioned to build a new church. Work began in 1743 and continued through 1772. Some of the greatest artists of the time—Johann Michael Küchel, Franz Xavier Feuchtmayer, and the Italian fresco painter J. I. Appiani— contributed to the project. The result is one of the most harmonious and dazzling examples of Baroque artisanship, a beautiful blend of marble and stucco, painting, and elegant, albeit exuberant, interior design.

Should you be ready for a lunch break after seeing Vierzehnheiligen and Banz, drive 5 km (3 miles) south to the charming town of Staffelstein and turn in at the **Gasthaus Rödiger**, zur Hergottsmühle 2, where the cooking is unpretentiously Franconian. The restaurant is closed on Friday and during the month of August. From here it is another 26 km (16 miles) south along B 173 to Bamberg.

# BAMBERG

Nestled in the rolling hill country of Franconia, at the confluence of the Regnitz and Itz rivers with the Main, this town of 70,000 (plus 12,000 U.S. servicemen and their families) is billed as "the gift of a thousand years," which is how long it has been making its mark on history. Probably no other city in Germany evokes the essence of the country more effectively, and many Germans simply say, "We may not have Florence or Venice, but we do have Bamberg, which is even greater."

To be sure, Germany has numerous other picturesque and historic spots—but most of them are either living museums of the past or situated so squarely on well-trodden tourist trails that visitors to them invariably photograph each other. Bamberg is a refreshing exception to the clichés. Although it also welcomes, and gets, plenty of tourists, it does not depend on them. And although its architectural masterpieces are in mint condition, it is neither frozen in time nor mired in its once-great past. As one of its burgomasters once put it, "Our city is the house in which we live, but because it is so unique and beautiful, we live like the gods."

Bamberg is a radiant assemblage of Europe's greatest

architectural styles—Romanesque, Gothic, Renaissance, and Baroque—as well as a treasure trove of some of Germany's finest art. It abounds with majestic churches, lavish palaces, and dazzlingly ornate mansions. The town itself is an engaging maze of narrow, winding cobblestone streets and an oasis of sparkling little streams, dreamy canals, old bridges, and vibrant colorful market squares.

For 800 of its 1,000 years Bamberg was the capital of an independent prince-bishopric whose properties included substantial chunks of real estate as far afield as present-day Austria, Italy, and Switzerland, and whose affluent art-loving rulers, usually more princely than pious, exercised both secular and ecclesiastical powers. That is why there are actually two towns—the Bischofstadt (Bishops' City) and the Bürgerstadt (Burghers' City)—each strikingly different.

They are separated by the Regnitz river, in the middle of which sits Bamberg's most photogenic edifice, the ornately embellished and fresco-painted **Altes Rathaus**. Built on an artificial island in 1450 as a compromise between the bishop and the burgomaster, each of whom wanted the city hall on his side of the Regnitz, it was redecorated in its present Baroque style in the 1750s. The Medieval Obere Brücke (Upper Bridge) links it to either bank of the river.

There is also a **Neues Rathaus** (New City Hall) about half a kilometer north on the Maximiliansplatz, in the Bürgerstadt, designed in 1732 by Balthasar Neumann.

The officially celebrated date of Bamberg's founding is 973, when it became the property of a litigious and cantankerous duke of Bavaria named Henry the Squabbler. His son, the Holy Roman Emperor Henry II, briefly made Bamberg the capital of the German Holy Roman Empire, which in those days stretched from the North Sea and Baltic to the Mediterranean and Adriatic.

# The Cathedral Area

Like Rome, Bamberg is built on seven hills, and the only practical way to explore it is on foot. Almost every hill is crowned by a church, of which the **Dom** (Cathedral), commissioned by Henry II in 1004 and completed in its present form in 1237, ranks as one of the finest and most harmonious examples of late Romanesque and early Gothic architecture in Europe. With its four massive spires, it towers above the city and is visible from miles away. (As the crow flies, it is no more than 500 yards southeast of the Altes

Rathaus, but because the way up is through steep, winding streets, figure on a 15-minute climb.)

On your way to the Dom, if you haven't reserved elsewhere, you might consider checking in at the **Barock-Hotel am Dom**, Vorderer Bach 4, a small (19 rooms), charming, moderately priced hotel tucked into an 18th-century town house. Breakfast is served in its cross-vaulted cellar.

Although the Dom's exterior is surprisingly austere, the main embellishment being a few gargoyles and a vividly sculpted scene of the "Last Judgment" in the tympanum of the Prince's Portal, the cathedral is crammed with art treasures. The most famous is the **Bamberger Reiter** (Bamberg Rider), which was sculpted by an unknown master in 1235. The identity of the rider is as anonymous as that of the artist. A number of other statutes in the cathedral, as well as the Tomb of Clement II, the only pope buried north of the Alps, are believed to be works by the same artist.

There is no mystery, on the other hand, about the **sarcophagus of Henry II and Kunigunde** (his wife), which was sculpted out of Italian marble by the Würzburg master Tilman Riemenschneider in 1513, or the **Nativity Altar**, carved from linden wood in 1523 by Veit Stoss. The tomb of Henry and Kunigunde depicts many of the legends surrounding their lives, including the one in which she walked barefoot, without suffering so much as a blister, over red-hot plowshares in order to prove she had remained faithful to Henry during one of his sojourns through the empire.

North of and adjacent to the Dom is the soaring Renaissance façade of the **Kanzleibau**, the Episcopal Chancellory, which leads to the **Alte Hofhaltung** (Old Court), a large, gabled, half-timbered Gothic palace that served emperors and, later, the prince-bishops as a palace and residence until the bishops, in 1703, moved into the Neue Residenz diagonally across the square from the cathedral.

In the minds of many people there are striking similarities between Bamberg and Prague, in part because the layout of both cities encourages that impression. But there are also very tangible links, and one is the **Neue Residenz**, designed in 1697 by Johann Dientzenhofer. The Dientzenhofers were to Baroque architecture what the Bachs were to music: an entire family—five brothers plus a nephew—who devoted their lives to building churches, monasteries, palaces, and mansions throughout northern Bavaria, Franconia, and neighboring Bohemia. In fact, half the Baroque buildings in Prague, and nearly all of them in Bamberg, are their work.

Today the Neue Residenz, crammed with works by the

Cranachs, Hans Baldung Grien, and other German Old Masters, serves as Bamberg's main art gallery. Its richly decorated imperial hall is also used for chamber concerts by members of the Bamberger Symphoniker. This internationally acclaimed orchestra, established in 1946, is another link to Prague: All its founding musicians were members of the Prague German Philharmonic who fled Czechoslovakia in May 1945 and settled in Bamberg and the surrounding region.

## Exploring Bamberg

Bamberg is a music center thanks also to E. T. A. Hoffmann, the early-19th-century novelist, illustrator, and composer (though a lawyer and judge by profession), who spent the five most productive years of his life as director and conductor of Bamberg's municipal theater. Hoffmann was not only a highly talented musician, greatly influenced by Robert Schumann and Johannes Brahms, but also a master teller of stories of madness and horror (many of which reputedly were written in an alcoholic delirium). At night the winding streets that climb the hill between the cathedral and the Regnitz evoke visions of his "Devil's Elixir," "Educated Cat," and the grotesque tales that composer Jacques Offenbach later turned into the opera *The Tales of Hoffmann*. The modest house in which Hoffman lived, the **E. T. A. Hoffmann-Haus**, at Schillerplatz 26, across the street from the theater that bears his name (and around the corner from the taverns where he drank to fatal excess), is now a museum devoted to him.

For all of Bamberg's fine examples of Romanesque, Gothic, and Renaissance architecture, however, its showiest architectural style is Baroque, and the most ostentatious display of it is the **Böttingerhaus**, Judenstrasse 14, tucked into a narrow street on the left bank of the Regnitz. A cornucopia of stone and stucco cupids, gods, goddesses, mythical fauna, and swirls of flora, it was built between 1706 and 1713 as a private mansion for Johann Ignaz Tobias Böttinger, a commoner who became one of 18th-century Germany's richest men by playing at politics. The house today belongs to an architect who restored it, and whose daughter and French son-in-law, Victor and Maria Orsenne, have turned it into Bamberg's priciest and most elegant restaurant. Orsenne is a highly talented chef who presents French nouvelle cuisine as well as regional Franconian dishes cooked in a light, nouvelle style. The most ornate dining rooms are only open evenings; the gallery overlooking the Böttingerhaus courtyard for lunch only. Reservations are recommended; Tel: (951) 540-74.

The Regnitz was dotted with mills in the days when it was Bamberg's chief source of energy, and in one of these, just a block northeast of the Böttingerhaus, you will find a pleasant, more moderately priced eatery, **St. Nepomuk**, Obere Mühlbrücke 9; Tel: (951) 251-83, whose windows offer breathtaking views of the Altes Rathaus and the old fishermen's district, Klein Venedig (Little Venice). St. Nepomuk is also a moderately priced hotel, with only 12 rooms.

From this cheerful inn it is a short walk to the charming row of fishermen's houses known as **Klein Venedig**. You can get a good view of it from the Untere Brücke, the bridge just downstream from the Altes Rathaus.

Though Bamberg is just a few miles east of the Franconian wine region, *the* beverage of Bamberg is beer, of which more is consumed here than anywhere else in Germany. The city's 11 independent breweries—actually a drop in the keg compared to the 1,500 that operated in the 16th century—all produce a unique local specialty: *Rauchbier* (smoked beer), which is made by drying barley malt over logs of smouldering beech wood. *Rauchbier* dates from the Middle Ages when, so the story goes, a fire broke out in one of the abbey breweries. The monks liked the resulting beverage so much that they began to duplicate the process, although less pyrotechnically. Dark, somewhat bitter and tangy, and not as strong as most German beer, it takes some getting used to. It's especially good when used to wash down regional specialties such as baked carp, sauerbraten, bratwurst, and an aspic of sausage meats called *Wurstsülze*.

In the warm months *Rauchbier* is best in any of the dozens of beer gardens that dot Bamberg's seven hills; during the rest of the year you'll find it in the many taverns operated by the breweries, of which the **Schenkerla**, Dominikanerstrasse 6, is the most famous. Located in the vaulted halls of a 13th-century Dominican monastery, it has been in operation since 1678. Though you can also order a hearty meal here, the Schenkerla is unique in that, except between noon and 2:00 P.M., you can bring your own food and will be given a plate and cutlery with which to eat it, provided you order beer.

Those who seek more elegant dining than the rustic fare served up by the Schenkerla and other beer halls, with their cavernous rooms and bare wood tables, will find a number of restaurants in Bamberg in a category just a notch below a Michelin star or a Gault-Millau toque. Besides the Böttingerhaus, already mentioned, there is the **Würzburger**

**Weinstube**, Zinkenwörthstrasse 6, one of E. T. A. Hoffmann's favorite watering places, and just around the corner from his house on the Schillerplatz. If you're looking for first-class accommodations, the **Hotel Bamberger Hof-Bellevue**, Schönleinsplatz 4, is a scant block away. Bamberg's most historic eatery is the **Weinhaus Messerschmitt**, Lange Strasse 41, just a few steps from the Schönleinsplatz. It has been run by the same family since 1832 and is a jewelbox of antique furnishings and bric-a-brac amassed by six generations.

Just 21 km (12 miles) south of Bamberg, along B 505 near its junction with the Autobahn south to Nürnberg or west to Würzburg, is the last destination on our route, the hamlet of Pommersfelden, worth a detour if not a special trip for its magnificent Baroque palace.

# POMMERSFELDEN

Although you may think you have seen Baroque splendor, you really haven't until you see **Schloss Weissenstein** in Pommersfelden. In 1711 Lothar Franz von Schönborn, ecclesiastic and temporal ruler of Würzburg, and also archchancellor of the Holy Roman Empire, commissioned three of Europe's leading architects to build these palatial digs: Balthasar Neumann, Maximilian von Welsch, and Lukas von Hildebrandt, court architect to the Hapsburgs in Vienna. However, legend has it that Schönborn, a hands-on ruler born with a draftsman's compass in his hand, acted as foreman throughout.

He placed Schloss Weissenstein on open ground in a vast park southeast of Pommersfelden, so that it could be seen from all directions—and so that it could grow in all directions as well. The central building was flanked by two projecting side wings, an arrangement that created the huge courtyard called the Ehrenhof. Opposite this "court of honor" was—and is—the *Marstall* building, the stable, which housed equipages, carriages, coaches, and sleighs.

Oddly enough, the exterior of the palace has none of the lavish ornamentation or joyfulness that one finds in other Baroque buildings. It might, instead, better be called German Renaissance. The interior, on the other hand, is an eye-popper.

Weissenstein is still the private property of the Schönborn family, who live in it part of the year, keep it in mint condition, and allow it to be used for summer musicals and chamber concerts. As a result, it is not the sort of place where visitors can just roam. In fact, guided tours are taken through in rather quick succession. Still, it is the first look through the main door that impresses most. An arched passageway under the grand staircase leads to the oval Grotto Hall, which opens, in turn, onto the garden beyond. The grotto is lined with stucco sea shells, leaves, and sea creatures. The tour will also take you through the Marble Hall, five stories high, an audience room, a great gallery where some of the Schönborn art treasures are on exhibit, and a lavishly ornamented dining room done all in pink.

Pommersfelden is one of the grand monuments to Europe's, and especially northern Bavaria's, past. And if you wish to relive a bit of that past, you will find the **Schloss Restaurant** in the palace itself, and the moderately priced **Schlosshotel** in a guesthouse just across the way.

Pommersfelden is only 40 km (25 miles) northwest of Nürnberg, where our tour of Franconia began, and 64 km (39 miles) east (by way of the same Nürnberg-Frankfurt Autobahn) of Würzburg, the beginning of the Romantic Road and the next chapter.

## GETTING AROUND

Major airline gateways to the Danube region are Stuttgart and Munich; for Franconia they are Nürnberg, Frankfurt, Munich, and Berlin. Major car rental agencies are represented at all these airports.

From Stuttgart to Ulm there are more than 50 trains daily, 22 of them InterCity (IC) expresses, which make the trip from Stuttgart to the Ulm main station in a little under an hour. Figure about 1.5 hours, depending on traffic conditions, from Stuttgart airport to Ulm by car, using the Stuttgart-to-Munich (A 8) Autobahn route. From Munich to Ulm there are 38 trains daily, 22 of them IC expresses; the trip on the express takes a little over an hour. By car it is approximately 1.5 hours on the Munich-to-Stuttgart (A 8) Autobahn.

If you fly to Nürnberg, you are at the start of the Franconia route. From Frankfurt to Nürnberg there are 27 trains daily, including 19 IC expresses, 17 of which can be boarded directly at Frankfurt airport. The trip from the Frankfurt station takes 2 hours and 23 minutes, from the Frankfurt airport 2 hours and 44 minutes. By car it's 2.5 to 3 hours, depending on traffic, from the Frankfurt airport to the center of Nürnberg, using the Frankfurt-Nürnberg (A 3) Autobahn. From Munich to Nürnberg there are 28 trains daily, including 14 IC expresses. The trip takes 1 hour 40 minutes. Depending on traffic, it may take you 1.5 to 2 hours by car from the Munich airport to the center of Nürnberg, using the A 9 Autobahn. Train connections from Berlin to Nürnberg were still few as we went to press, although improvements in service are promised for 1991 and 1992. Until then, the best way to get from Berlin to Nürnberg is to drive, using the A 9 (Berlin to Munich) Autobahn. The total distance is about 400 km (250 miles), and you should allow four to five hours for the trip, depending on traffic. A speed limit of 100-km (62-miles) an hour is posted within East Germany.

There are train connections between all the towns described on both the Danube and Franconia routes, though services between smaller communities is infrequent and slow. The only fast train connection on the Danube route is between Ulm and Regensburg, with 29 trains daily, 12 of these being IC expresses, which take just over 3 hours to make the trip. Should you be using trains, there are also good connections between Regensburg and Nürnberg, and vice versa, with 28 trains daily in both directions, five of them IC Expresses. The trip takes about 1 hour and 10 minutes. There are also regular train connections between Regensburg and Munich, with 23 trains daily in both directions, none of them express. It's a 1.5 hour journey.

Though bus connections (the buses of the Bundesbahn, the German railway system) do exist between towns and cities on both routes, they are infrequent (at best) and slow.

The best way of getting around and seeing the sights described above is to drive, and our itinerary is designed accordingly. We have intentionally given directions that will keep travellers off the Autobahns and, in the case of the Danube, as close to the river as possible (using unnumbered country roads where necessary). Do, however, carry along a detailed map or road atlas (the *Shell Atlas,* available in bookstores as well as Shell gas stations, is used by most Germans, though there are other good ones such as the *Aral Atlas* and the *V.A.G. Atlas*). You may also want to purchase the appropriate *H-B Bild Atlas* for these regions. Though they are published only in German, you will find the maps in them very detailed and useful. For the Danube route and the Bayerischer Wald, the two you'll want are number 36, "Niederbayern"; and number 6, "Bayerischer Wald." For Franconia, number 50, "Mainfranken," covers part of our route.

## ACCOMMODATIONS REFERENCE

### *Along the Danube*

► **Hotel Bischofshof.** Krauterermarkt 3, D-8400 **Regensburg.** Tel: (941) 590-86.

► **Gasthaus Eibl-Brunner.** Hauptstrasse 18, D-8377 **Frauenau.** Tel: (9926) 316.

► **Intercity Hotel.** Bahnhofsplatz 1, D-7900 **Ulm.** Tel: (731) 612-21; Telex: 712871; Fax: 62239.

► **Hotel Kaiserhof am Dom.** Kramgasse 10, D-8400 **Regensburg.** Tel: (941) 540-27; Fax: 54025.

► **Hotel Karmeliten.** Dachauplatz 1, D-8400 **Regensburg.** Tel: (941) 543-08; Telex: 65170; Fax: 791260 or 561751.

► **Kirchbaur-Hof.** Monheimer Strasse 119, D-8858 **Neuburg-Bittenbrunn.** Tel: (8431) 25-32.

► **Kurhotel Sonnenberg.** Augustinerstrasse 9, D-8372 Zwiesel, Ulm. Tel: (9922) 20-31.

► **Hotel Neutor-Hospiz.** Neuer Graben 23, D-7900 Ulm. Tel: (731) 15-16-00; Telex: 712401; Fax: 1516513.

► **Parkhotel Maximilian.** Maximilianstrasse 28, D-8400 **Regensburg.** Tel: (941) 510-42; Telex: 65181; Fax: 52942.

► **Hotel Passauer Wolf.** Rindermarkt 6, D-8390 **Passau.** Tel: (851) 340-46; Telex: 57817; Fax: 36757.

► **Hotel Rappensberger.** Harderstrasse 3, D-8070 **Ingolstadt.** Tel: (841) 31-40; Telex: 55834, Fax: 3142000.

► **Säumerhof.** Steinberg 32, D-8352 **Grafenau.** Tel: (8552) 24-01.

► **Hotel Seethaler.** Theresienplatz 25, D-8440 **Straubing.** Tel: (9421) 120-20.

► **Hotel Ulmer Spatz.** Münsterplatz 27, D-7900 **Ulm.** Tel: (731) 680-81.

► **Hotel Wilder Mann.** Schrottgasse 2, D-8390 **Passau.** Tel: (851) 350-71; Fax: 31712.

### *Franconia*

► **Hotel Bamberger Hof-Bellevue.** Schönleinsplatz 4, D-8600 **Bamberg.** Tel: (951) 12-22-16; Telex: 662867; Fax: 22219.

► **Barok-Hotel am Dom.** Vorderer Bach 4, D-8600 **Bamberg.** Tel: (951) 540-31.

► **Hotel Bayerischer Hof.** Bahnhofstrasse 14, D-8580 **Bayreuth.** Tel: (921) 220-81; Telex: 642737; Fax: 22085.

► **Burghotel-Grosses Haus.** Lammsgasse 3, D-8500 **Nürnberg.** Tel: (911) 20-44-14; Telex: 623567.

► **Burghotel Lauenstein.** Burgstrasse 4, D-8642 **Ludwigs-stadt-Lauenstein.** Tel: (9263) 256.

► **Hotel Coburger Tor.** Ketschendorfer Strasse 22, D-8630 **Coburg.** Tel: (9561) 250-74; Fax: 28874.

► **Hotel Eremitage.** Eremitage 42, D-8580 **Bayreuth.** Tel: (921) 992-87.

► **Hotel Gasthof zur Lohmühle.** Badstrasse 37, D-8580 **Bayreuth.** Tel: (921) 630-31; Fax: 58286.

► **Hotel Goldene Traube.** Am Viktoriabrunnen 2, D-8630 **Coburg.** Tel: (9561) 98-33; Fax: 92621.

► **Hotel Goldener Anker.** Rosengasse 14, D-8630 **Coburg.** Tel: (9561) 950-27; Fax: 92560.

► **Hotel Goldener Hirsch.** Bahnhofstrasse 13, D-8580 **Bayreuth.** Tel: (921) 230-46; Fax: 22483.

► **Grand Hotel.** Bahnhofstrasse 1, D-8500 **Nürnberg.** Tel: (911) 230-46; Telex: 622010; Fax: 2322444.

► **Hansa-Hotel.** Weltrichstrasse 2a, D-8650 **Kulmbach.** Tel: (9221) 179-95.

► **Hotel Königshof.** Bahnhofstrasse 23, D-8580 **Bayreuth.** Tel: (921) 240-94; Fax: 12264

► **Hotel Maritim.** Frauentorgraben 11, D-8500 **Nürnberg.** Tel: (911) 236-30; Telex: 622709; Fax: 2363823.

► **Pflaum's Posthotel.** Nürnberger Strasse 14, D-8570 **Peg-nitz.** Tel: (9241) 72-50; Telex: 642433; Fax: 404.

► **Hotel St. Nepomuk.** Obere Mühlbrücke 9, D-8600 **Bam-berg.** Tel: (951) 251-83.

► **Schlosshotel Pommersfelden.** Im Schloss Weissenstein, D-8602 **Pommersfelden.** Tel: (9548) 488.

► **Schlosshotel Thiergarten.** D-8580 **Bayreuth-Thier-garten.** Tel: (9209) 13-14; Telex: 642153.

► **Hotel Victoria.** Königstrasse 80, D-8500 **Nürnberg.** Tel: (911) 20-38-01; Fax: 227432.

# THE ROMANTIC ROAD

## WÜRZBURG, ROTHENBURG, AUGSBURG, NEUSCHWANSTEIN CASTLE

*By John Dornberg*

The Romantic Road—*Die Romantische Strasse*—is purely an invention, the promotional brainchild of some word-smith at the German National Tourist Board. It was coined in 1949, when the automobile age in West Germany was just dawning. Although the Romans used a part of it, calling it the Via Claudia, it is a route rather than a road, which, being a mere 220 miles long, you could drive in four to five hours, assuming you were in a hurry. But what a shame if you did, for the Romantic Road—from Würzburg on the Main river south across the Danube, through Augsburg in Bavaria to Füssen in Bavaria's Allgäu Alps—is a trail through Germany incarnate, a splendid pathway to the past, a glittering chain of majestic cities, storybook towns, and picture-postcard villages studded with gems of art and architecture that span more than two millennia of human creativity and history.

From the meandering, twisting Main river south to the Alpine border with Austria, the Romantische Strasse is a route through Germany at its most picturesque, a living travelogue of wooded hillocks, placid valleys, dark forests, formidably

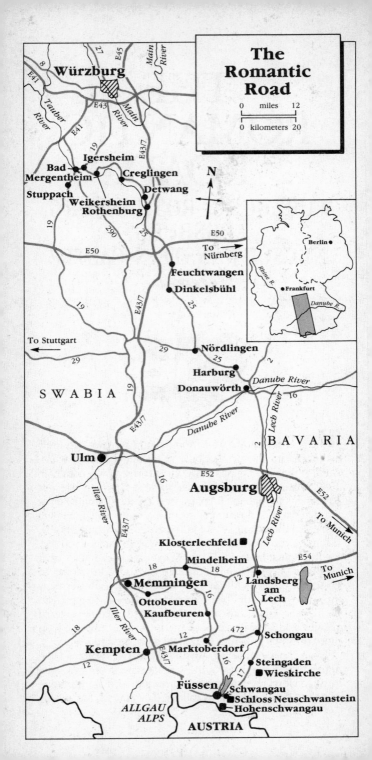

walled Medieval towns, graceful Gothic churches, elegant Renaissance town halls, dazzling Baroque palaces, and fanciful fairy-tale castles: a passageway to enclaves of half-timbered and cobblestone charm, to redoubts where time seems to have stood still and yesteryear comes alive.

MAJOR INTEREST

The Medieval, Baroque, and Rococo town of
    Würzburg
Rothenburg's 17th-century Altstadt
Medieval Dinkelsbühl
Nördlingen's meteor crater and walled Altstadt
Riemenschneider wooden altarpieces in Creglingen
    and Rothenburg
The historic Fugger city of Augsburg
Castles in Bad Mergentheim, Weikersheim, Harburg,
    and Hohenschwangau (where King Ludwig II's
    dream castle, Neuschwanstein, is located)
Side trips to the Romanesque and Baroque towns of
    Kempten and Memmingen
The Wieskirche at Steingaden

The north–south Romantic Road is, in effect—as our book is structured—a vertical band separating Stuttgart/Swabia to the west from Northern and Southern Bavaria to the east, except that the Danube coverage in the chapter about Northern Bavaria cuts across the band from Ulm in the west. The start of this chapter's journey is in Würzburg, 121 km (75 miles) southeast from Frankfurt, 110 km (69 miles) northwest of Nürnberg, and 75 km (47 miles) due west of Pommersfelden on the Autobahn. If you are coming from Pommersfelden, you will be travelling from one great Schönborn palace to another—right in the center of Würzburg.

# WÜRZBURG

It is called the "Jewel on the Main," and it gleams. Few other rivers in Germany are as gentle, few other valleys as romantic, picturesque, pastoral, and untrampled by the touring masses as the Main river and valley. And no town along it is as majestic or as rich in treasures of art and architecture as Würzburg.

Nestled among vineyards along the riverbank, this city of

130,000 is resplendent with architectural gems from a period of more than 1,000 years, and is itself a jewel among German Baroque and Rococo towns. Its history and monuments in stone date from the beginnings of Christianity in Germany, when Frankish dukes, converted by the Irish missionary monk Saint Kilian, settled on the site of the present town and built the massive Marienberg fortress on the crest of the highest of Würzburg's many terraced and vine-covered hills. One of the oldest churches in the country, the **Marienkirche**, built in 706, stands almost pristine in the citadel's courtyard.

Although it is the site of a 400-year-old university, Würzburg is merely a provincial capital, best known for its palaces and churches and white Franconian wines, inimitable in taste and distinctive for their *Bocksbeutel* bottles. But from the eighth century until 1806, when Napoleon reshaped the map of Europe, imposed secularization, and ceded the town to the newly created kingdom of Bavaria, it was an independent and influential prince-bishopric. Its rulers, who enjoyed both ecclesiastical and temporal powers, were nearly all great patrons of the arts. They attracted the services of some of the greatest masters of their times, and left an incomparable legacy.

It was in Würzburg that the painter Matthias Grünewald was born, in 1475, and did much of his work, and it was under Prince Bishop Rudolf von Scherenberg that Tilman Riemenschneider, arguably the greatest of the Medieval wood sculptors, came to the city and settled in 1483, ultimately becoming Würzburg's burgomaster. His work is richly represented in some of the city's churches and those of villages nearby. It was Prince Bishop Johann Philipp von Schönborn who commissioned the Residenz, a vast, ornate, 300-room château.

Much of Würzburg's Romanesque, Gothic, Renaissance, Baroque, and Rococo heritage was blasted to rubble during a single air raid in March 1945, with the result that nearly all its beautiful churches, magnificent bridges, patrician houses, and splendid hospices are reconstructions—stone by stone, gargoyle by gargoyle, cupid by cupid. Amazingly, the Residenz escaped with relatively little damage.

Besides all the art and architecture, the town is the epitome of romantic ambience and Old World charm. The two largest hospices, the Bürgerspital and the Juliusspital, are both famed for their wine taverns, serving vintages from their own vineyards.

# Marienberg Citadel

The former fortified residence of the prince bishops, now the home of the Mainfränkisches Museum, is Würzburg's distinctive landmark, visible from far away. Warlike as the citadel may once have been, its appearance is softened by the vineyards on the hill it crowns. Situated on the left bank of the Main, it is the ideal place to start your tour—for the magnificent view from its ramparts, which will help orient you, and for a sense of the city's history.

The oldest walls and buildings of the complex date from the early 13th century; the Marienkirche, part of the fortress, has sections going back to its consecration in 706.

The **Mainfränkisches Museum** contains the world's most complete collection of Riemenschneider sculptures and wood carvings. These are the originals of copies you will find in churches elsewhere in Würzburg and Franconia. One of its greatest art treasures is Tiepolo's canvas *The Appointment of Cincinnatus,* and there are some fine paintings by both Cranachs. The collection also includes a complete 18th-century apothecary shop, some excellent Bayreuth faïence, old toys, a great many 16th- through 18th-century wine presses, and a huge lode of local and regional applied art.

# The Old City

A walk downhill and north of the Marienberg will lead you to one of Würzburg's oldest inns, the **Wein und Fischhaus Schiffbäuerin**, Katzengasse 7, where you may want to stop for lunch after exploring the citadel. The *Schiffbäuerinnen* (ship peasant women) were two women who presided over a lovely half-timbered house to which the Main fishermen brought their choicest catch straight from the river—as they still do today. The daily menu changes according to the catch and the season. Some of the wines served are right from the Marienberg above the inn.

The nearby Alte Mainbrücke will lead you into the center of the Altstadt. The bridge was completed in its present form in 1543, after 70 years of construction work, and ranked as one of the engineering marvels of its time. The 12 statues of mitered, sword-bearing, and rather belligerent-looking bishops that adorn it are additions of the Baroque period.

Just north of the bridge, on the river's right bank, is the **Alter Kran**, a Würzburg landmark constructed in 1773 by the son of the great Baroque architect Balthasar Neumann. Once essential equipment to the city's river port, the old loading crane bears a Latin inscription that translates: "I receive transport and dispatch anything you like."

The **Marktplatz**, Würzburg's main square, is just a couple of blocks east. On your way you will pass the Rathaus, much of it dating from around 1200, with upper stories added in the 15th and 16th centuries, making it a fine example of Renaissance architecture. The **Marienkapelle** (St. Mary's Chapel) on the Marktplatz was built on the site of a synagogue destroyed in a 14th-century pogrom. Construction began in 1377 and continued for almost 100 years. A number of the exterior statues are copies of works by Riemenschneider, who was as skilled a carver in stone as he was in wood. The originals are in the Mainfränkisches Museum.

The **Neumünster**, on St.-Kilians-Platz, just a little east of the market square, was the original bishops' church, built in the eighth century on the spot where Saint Kilian and his brother missionaries were murdered by heathen Franks in 689. Though redesigned in Baroque style in the 18th century, the present church is mostly of 13th-century construction. The exterior is a meticulous reconstruction done after the 1945 air raid, but the interior is disappointing.

Würzburg's **Dom** (Cathedral), on the Domplatz just south of St.-Kilians-Platz, is a classic example of Romanesque style on its exterior, but the interior was transformed into Baroque decor with stuccowork in the 18th century. Construction of this cruciform pillared basilica began in 1050 and was completed about a century later. There were some major additions, including the east tower, in the 13th century. Among the most important works of art are the numerous tombstones, covering 700 years of stylistic development, placed between the pillars of the nave. Two of them, depicting prince bishops Rudolf von Scherenberg and Lorenz von Bibra, are magnificent original works by Riemenschneider. The Dom is also a kind of pantheon, harboring the tombs of some of Würzburg's most famous burghers, among them Matthias Grünewald, Wilhelm Conrad Röntgen, the Nobel Prize–winning physicist who discovered the X-ray and who taught for many years at Würzburg University, and not least, Riemenschneider himself, who was tortured and slain because of his participation in the 1526 Peasants' War.

A stroll back north along the **Schönbornstrasse**, Würzburg's main pedestrian and shopping mall, will take you to the **Juliusspital**, at Juliuspromenade 19. The hospital and the vineyard that supported it date back to 1586 and were founded by Prince Bishop Julius Echter, from whom it draws its name. The original hospital complex was often modified over the centuries, then almost completely destroyed in World War II. Among the buildings restored is the central **Fürstenpavillon** (Prince's Pavilion), which includes a magnificent 18th-century pharmacy. Beneath the building are the cavernous wine cellars, with huge oak casks where the premium vintages from the Julius Echter Berg and other hospital-owned vineyards are matured to be sold to the public—by the glass, by the carafe, and by the *Bocksbeutel*. Go there for a *Frühschoppen* (an early glass), served before noon, imbibed with a small snack of Franconian cold cuts.

You may even find one of Würzburg's local specialties— *Meefischli. Mee* is local dialect for the Main, and *fischli* are small fish—so small, in fact, that they are about the length of your little finger and no thicker than your thumb, and are plunged into deep hot fat without being drawn. Würzburgers say they swim three times: once in the Main, once in deep fat, and once in golden Franconian wine, which is the perfect beverage to accompany them. Your concierge will be able to tell you in which restaurant the catch is best that particular day. The real secret of Meefischli is to add a pinch of cinnamon to the flour in which they are dredged. A meal-size portion can be up to a dozen, served with lemon wedges and potato salad.

The Juliusspital's principal competition for Würzburg and Franconian wine is the **Bürgerspital**, Theaterstrasse 19, at the corner of the Semmelstrasse, about 500 feet south of the Juliusspital. Founded in 1371 and endowed by a bourgeois family, this infirmary was also supported by the sale of wine from its own vineyards. More than 30 of them are dispensed by shirt-sleeved, leather-aproned cellar masters who dart among the scores of tables in ten different rooms.

From the Bürgerspital, continue south for another 1,000 feet along the Theaterstrasse to the Residenzplatz and the Residenz, Würzburg's most magnificent Baroque jewel.

# The Residenz

Johann Philipp Franz von Schönborn was the first prince bishop of Würzburg who wanted to move from the Medieval digs in Marienberg fortress down into the city, right after being elected Würzburg's ruler in 1719.

Schönborn found the available city palace inadequate, so plans for a new one were drawn up. He finally approved a château with about 300 rooms—plus large reception and official state halls, a court church, gardens, parade halls, a gallery for his paintings, and a magnificent *Treppenhaus* (stair-well), all shielded from the rest of Würzburg by a huge square, the Residenzplatz. It was said at the time that the Schönborns built their palace behind the plaza to avoid contact with non-Schönborn people. This exclusivity is now seen as a blessing, as it provides the tourist throngs with an enormous parking lot. Be all that as it may, the Residenz is today one of the largest, most grandiose—and harmonious—Baroque palaces in Central Europe.

Schönborn retained his favorite builder, Balthasar Neumann, who was soon joined in the project by Vienna's Lucas von Hildebrandt and Maximilian von Welsch, who had done most of Schönborn's work in the bishopric city of Mainz. The joint project went well, although there were disagreements. Hildebrandt did not believe that Neumann's unsupported ceiling over the stairwell would hold. Neumann offered, at his own expense, to bring in heavy artillery to create vibrations and prove that it could. He was again proven right in 1945, when the bombs that destroyed 85 percent of Würzburg and took the lives of 5,000 people left the staircase intact.

Schönborn could hardly wait to move into his Residenz and drove his artists and workmen mercilessly. But he didn't live to see moving day: He died while out hunting one morning, so suddenly that poison was suspected. His family and successors carried on, and in December 1744, 24 years after the cornerstone had been laid, the basic building was completed.

As was common in Baroque architecture, the grand central staircase forms the centerpiece of the palace. This was not only where the stucco masters and sculptors were supposed to do their greatest and most representational work, but where the ceiling space was intended as one of the most important elements. Its master was none less than the Venetian painter Giovanni Battista Tiepolo, assisted by his sons, Domenico and Lorenzo.

The Tiepolos stayed in Würzburg for more than three years, as the job eventually entailed far more than the banquet hall (nowadays the scene of Würzburg's annual Mozart Festival). The **stairwell ceiling**, allegorically depicting Earth's then-known four continents, was not only Tiepolo's crowning work but so monumental that in size alone it is unique in the history of art. You will be amazed by its exuberance, and amused by the self-portrait of the master, with his dog, near the top. One of Tiepolo's original sketches for the ceiling fresco is at the Metropolitan Museum of Art in New

York; an original sketch for the Kaisersaal (the banquet hall)
ceiling is in the Mainfränkisches Museum.

The central building of the palace complex is situated
atop the prince bishops' wine cellars, with storage space for
1.4 million bottles. Also not to be missed are the Hofkirche,
the court church; the Gartensaal (a banquet hall facing the
court garden); and the geometrical, meticulously manicured
Hofgarten itself, where the highlights are the splendid
wrought-iron gates designed by Balthasar Neumann and
sculptures by Martin von Wagner. The south wing of the
Residenz houses the **Martin von Wagner Museum**, an exquisite collection of Greek vases, Roman sculptures, and 14th-
through 19th-century European and German paintings.

# Other Sights in Würzburg

A two-minute walk southwest from the Residenz, along
Balthasar-Neumann-Promenade, will take you to the **University**, founded in 1582 by Prince Bishop Julius Echter (of
Juliusspital fame). Be sure to take in the courtyard side of
this extensive Renaissance complex. **St. Peter's church**, on
the nearby Petersplatz, is a Romanesque basilica, rebuilt in
the 18th century in Baroque style. Its western towers, however, remain unchanged.

From the Petersplatz it is just a few steps north along the
Münzstrasse to the **Hotel Rebstock**, at Neubaustrasse 7. An
inn since 1408, it is as notable for its comfortable rooms as
for its magnificent Rococo façade, dating from 1737. Its
Franconian Weinstube is good for unpretentious dining. The
main dining room, where chef Franz Frankenberger offers a
daily changing six-course gourmet menu as well as a vast
array of nouvelle cuisine à la carte selections, ranks as
Würzburg's best eatery.

For a more modern hotel you might consider the **Maritim
Hotel Würzburg**, at Pleichtorstrasse 5, near the northern tip
of the Altstadt. A swimming pool is among the amenities. Its
**Palais Grill** is another first-rate restaurant.

The best accommodations out of town, in the environs, are
at the **Wittelsbacher Höh**, Hexenbruchweg 10, in Würzburg-
Zellerau, 2 km (1.2 miles) northwest of the city center. A
Victorian-style inn with a modern annex, it includes a restaurant in rustic Franconian decor that features solid regional
dishes as well as a wide selection of local Franconian wines.
To go there you must cross the Main to the Marienberg side,
where you can swing onto B 19, which you follow 45 km (28

miles) south for the next destination on the Romantic Road, Bad Mergentheim.

## BAD MERGENTHEIM

Nearly 160 West German towns are legally permitted to precede their names with the word *Bad* (bath). They are spas—and the definition of a bath is rather flexible. In some you do actually bathe in various healing mineral waters, guaranteed to cure whatever you think ails you, or in various kinds of mud; in others you merely drink the water, and in some where there is no mineral water at all you breathe the air until you are dizzy. Germans call this kind of activity a *Kur,* and for millions of them it is a way of life.

Bad Mergentheim has been part of the cure circuit since 1826, when healing bitter salt springs were discovered and doctors began sending patients here to take the waters. The town was then some 600 years old and already rather famous.

The fame derives from its role as the residence, or capital, of the Deutschordens-Ritter, the Order of Teutonic Knights. Founded in 1190, during the Third Crusade, this German military religious order of nobles and knights, dedicated to poverty, chastity, and obedience, played a key role in German expansion into Eastern Europe and eventually colonization of vast areas of Poland, today's Baltic republics, and Russia itself. Wherever they went and conquered, German-speaking peoples soon followed as settlers. (In 1263 the pope allowed the knights to engage in trade, a privilege they increasingly abused.) The knights' era was from the mid-13th through the early 16th century, until the Protestant Reformation broke their power, a demise effected in part in 1525 when their own grand master, Albert of Brandenburg, accepted the Reformation. After that the order continued only in predominantly Catholic southern and western Germany, which is how Bad Mergentheim entered the history of the Teutonic Knights. It was in the town's moated castle that the order's grand masters who remained Catholic and loyal to the pope established their residence, in 1527.

The **Deutschordens Schloss** (Castle of the Teutonic Order) had been property of the knights since the 13th century, but owes its present appearance to extensive enlargement and modification in the years 1565 to 1570, after it had become the grand master's palace. Most of the various Renaissance-style towers were added about 50 years later. The **Deutschordens Museum** and a museum of local history and handicrafts now occupy most of the rooms in the large complex. The **Schlosskirche**, nowadays Protestant, is a collaboration between two of Europe's greatest Baroque architects: Balthasar Neumann and the French Walloon François de Cuvilliés, who made his mark originally in Munich.

**St. Johanneskirche**, on the Kirchstrasse, built from 1250 to 1270 by the Knights of St. John of Jerusalem and taken over by the Teutonic Order in 1554, is a fine example of Gothic style with Renaissance additions. Neo-Gothic restoration in the late 19th century unfortunately reduced the appeal of the Dominican **church of St. Mary** on the Hans-Heinrich-Ehrler-Platz, though the building itself was completed in 1388. Be sure, however, to see the bronze epitaph of Walther von Cronberg, a Teutonic Order grand master. It is a work by the Nürnberg bronze caster Hans Vischer. Mergentheim's **Marktplatz**, with its 16th-century Rathaus, is an almost perfect ensemble of Renaissance buildings. Be sure to see the Engelsapotheke (Engels Pharmacy) and the old Gasthaus Straussen (Ostrich Inn), now occupied by a bank.

Like all spa towns, Bad Mergentheim has a profusion of comfortable hotels. The **Victoria**, Poststrasse 2, has its own mineral baths and massage department, a pool, and a sauna, and even rents bicycles. The dining room is distinguished and has a prodigious wine cellar. Wines in carafes and by the glass are all from the Tauber river valley, one of Germany's smallest growing areas—so small that most of its excellent wine is consumed by locals. If you're looking for something super modern in accommodations, consider the **Parkhotel Maritim**, Lothar-Daiker-Strasse 6. Many of the rooms have glass-enclosed loggias with views of the lovely Tauber valley. There is a medicinal bath, an in-house spa doctor, a swimming pool, and a beauty farm, and you can rent bikes for the duration of your stay.

No visit to Bad Mergentheim would be complete without a brief 6-km (4-mile) side trip father south on B 19 to the village of **Stuppach** and a visit to its **Pfarrkirche**, the repository of Matthias Grünewald's 1517–1519 painting of the Virgin Mary. It is one of the greatest masterpieces of Old German painting.

To continue on the Romantic Road, head back north through Bad Mergentheim on B 19, and drive on another 4 km (2.5 miles) to the intersection just past the village of Igersheim. There, take a right turn, following the signs to Weikersheim, your next destination. You will be driving on an unnumbered road that follows the right bank of the Tauber upstream for about 6 km (4 miles).

# SOUTHEAST TO ROTHENBURG
## Weikersheim

Called "The Heart of the Tauber Valley," this town of 6,500 should be visited if for no other reason than to see the **Hohenlohe Castle** and its stupendous **Rittersaal** (Knights' Hall), a former residence of the princes of Hohenlohe and rich in its untouched Renaissance, Baroque, and Rococo interiors. The Hohenlohes, a German noble dynasty dating back to the 12th century, once owned so many castles and châteaux here that the area around Weikersheim is called the Hohenlohe Land. In its heyday it was an independent and sovereign state.

The dimensions of the castle are overwhelming, for when Count Wolfgang von Hohenlohe built it, from 1586 to 1603, he wanted his residence to be second to none. The Knights' Hall is an overwhelming 115 by 39 feet and a cavernous three stories from floor to ceiling. Its fireplace, too, is three stories tall. Life-size carved animals, including an elephant, project from the upper walls among the antlered heads of hunting trophies. Family portraits are hung at an angle outward from the walls, the better to see them. One of Europe's deepest coffered ceilings crowns the whole thing. It has been said that knights rode their mounts up the wide, shallow stairs leading to the hall, and there is no question that a few horses would be inconspicuous in this space.

Other rooms in the castle are on a slightly more normal scale, although one contains a bed that called for a ladder to scale the carved enclosure and reach the top of the mattresses. There are angels at its corners, a ceiling-high headboard, and a baldachin that would, if it collapsed, wipe out the bed's occupants.

The beautifully laid-out castle gardens face south and end in an architectural composition of obelisks, statuary, and an amusing dwarf's gallery. The castle is entered from town at the bottom of the fountained Marktplatz, through an arcade, a gate, and a second courtyard; the castle tower ahead will guide you.

In keeping with such stupendous princely digs in Weikersheim, a luxury hotel with a fabulous restaurant might be welcome, but the best in town is only a (very) comfortable inn, the **Laurentius**, Marktplatz 5. Its restaurant, presided over by proprietor-chef Heinrich Koch, offers exquisitely prepared nouvelle German dishes.

A drive farther east of 18 km (11 miles) will take you to Creglingen.

# Creglingen

It is said that two miracles happened in this town of 5,000. The first was on August 10, 1384, on the eve of the feast of Saint Laurentius, when a local peasant found the Sacred Host in a newly plowed furrow in his field. Numerous healings ensued; prayers were answered. Finally a small chapel was built over the sacred spot. With time, the chapel proved too small to hold all the pilgrims who came to Creglingen, and the **Herrgottskirche** was built. It was completed in 1505 and is situated on land donated by the brothers Konrad and Gottfried Hohenlohe-Brauneck, a bit south of Creglingen's center.

The two noblemen commissioned Tilman Riemenschneider to create an altar, dedicated to the life of Mary, to stand in the center of the small church right over the spot where the Host had been found. It is one of Riemenschneider's most sensitive and elaborate pieces of wood carving. The doors to the altar, however, remained uncarved because Creglingers could not afford to pay for more work, with the result that when the altar was closed, it looked like a plain wooden box. With passing time, according to custom, funeral wreaths were hung against it, and, as they dried, others were hung over them, creating a pyramid of dried wreaths in the center of the church. For nearly 300 years no one ever asked what was under them. Then, in 1832, Creglingen experienced its second miracle. Curious parishioners opened the box and discovered one of Germany's most important missing works of art.

Continue upstream along the Tauber for another 14 km (8.5 miles) to Detwang, the next destination.

# Detwang

This is probably the smallest and most bucolic village on the Romantic Road. It rates a stop for its carefully guarded masterpiece: Riemenschneider's magnificent 1510 **Holy Cross Altar**, installed in the tenth-century Romanesque **Peter-und-Paul-Kirche**.

There is room for two cars in the space in front of the church, and as soon as you drive into one of them, the guardian pops up, as if by magic, to sell you a ticket and unlock the door. Given the vast amount of ecclesiastical art that has been stolen in Germany during the past three decades, including some fine Riemenschneider carvings from village churches near Würzburg, the security is hardly excessive.

From Detwang it is a mere 3 km (2 miles) farther south along the river to Rothenburg-ob-der-Tauber, the very embodiment of what is called "Romantic Germany" and one of the most visited spots on the Romantische Strasse.

# *ROTHENBURG*

Rothenburg is a child's dream of knighthood, shining armor, and Medieval chivalry come true: a walled and gate-towered city that stands today exactly as it stood in the 11th century, with steeply roofed, step-gabled houses, soaring spires, narrow cobblestone streets, and fortified ramparts. No one has ever put up a neon sign or taken down an old street lantern here. Its visitors (and on weekends and public holidays it is crowded to bursting) are more like pilgrims who come to see a relic of the Middle Ages than conventional sightseers. It has been one of Germany's major attractions since modern mass tourism began, in the second half of the 19th century. It is also the incarnation of Romanticism: Thousands are the middle-aged to elderly German couples who will tell you with a blush that they honeymooned in Rothenburg, adding, "So did our parents and grandparents." Rothenburgers themselves—of whom 8,000 live within the old walls, 12,000 in new districts around the historic quarter—all seem to be engaged in preserving its image. Odd vicissitudes of history helped to create the Medieval appearance, and to maintain it.

Though mentions of Rothenburg go back to the year 700, it was not until the 11th century that it began to flourish, when it became the property of the Hohenstaufen dynasty and Holy Roman Emperor Conrad began enlarging the tenth-century castle on the hill overlooking the Tauber. The town became a *freie Reichsstadt,* a Free Imperial City, in 1274, by decree of Emperor Rudolf, the first Hapsburg on the Holy Roman throne. What this meant was that Rothenburg was not subordinate to any baron, count, prince, or duke, but only to the emperor himself. It had its own judicial jurisdiction and the right of coinage, paid taxes only to the emperor, and needed to grease his palm and no one else's to obtain the trade and crafts privileges that were the keys to Medieval prosperity and wealth.

By the mid-14th century, thanks to its location at the junction of major south–north and west–east trade routes, to milling and textile production, and to the energetic promotional activities of its then mayor Heinrich Toppler, Rothenburg had become one of the most prosperous free cities in the empire. The wealth is evident in its richly furnished and endowed churches, magnificent public buildings, and great burgher houses.

But weren't there many such towns in the German realm? Why and how was Rothenburg preserved? The answer is "two miracles"—and commercial decline.

The first miracle was in October 1631 during the Thirty Years War when, after bitter, stubborn resistance, the town was conquered by the troops of Count Johannes von Tilly, the imperial field marshal. Tilly was so angry about the costly defense that Rothenburg's militia had put up that he announced he would immediately execute the four town councillors who had ordered the resistance, and then destroy Rothenburg. The niece of one of the councillors, accompanied by two other small children, implored Tilly to spare the men's lives. The general refused. Then the daughter of the town's cellar master arrived, offering refreshments while everyone waited for the executioner, and praised Rothenburg's fine Tauber valley wine. Tilly, so the story goes, agreed to try the wine, which was brought to him in a huge three-quart tankard. He tasted it, and humorously suggested, because the goblet was so enormous, that he would pardon the four councillors and spare the town if one of Rothenburg's men could empty the tankard in one swallow. Hastily a former mayor, Herr Nusch, known more for his drinking prowess than governing skills, was brought to the square, and drank off the wine in one draught without so much as taking a breath. Tilly, amazed, kept his word, and Rothenburg as well as its councillors were saved. Nusch himself, after sleeping straight through for three days, also survived and lived on for another 37 years. The *Meistertrunk* (master draught) is reenacted in a folk play by Rothenburgers wearing 17th-century costume every Whitsuntide weekend and the second Sunday in July. The pageant draws visitors by the tens of thousands.

The second "miracle" is of more recent origin—April 15, 1945. Credit for it goes to the late John J. McCloy, then the U.S. assistant secretary of war, later the American high commissioner for occupied Germany. Rothenburg was about to be subjected to a U.S. Army artillery barrage when McCloy flew to the front near Rothenburg and dispatched an armistice commission promising that no shot would be fired if the German defenders surrendered unconditionally. They did.

Through an ironic twist of history, there probably would have been little of Medieval Rothenburg to spare in 1945 had not the town gone into economic decline in the 17th through 19th century, due to the shift of commerce and trade routes to elsewhere. Lack of money hindered Rothenburgers from modernizing as many other communities did, forcing them to preserve the old town to a degree found nowhere else in the country.

Rothenburg is situated on the flat top of a hill some 180 feet above a 14th-century viaduct over the Tauber. Its full name, Rothenburg-ob-der-Tauber, means "Red Fortress over the Tauber." Nothing of that original tenth-century castle remains, but there is so much else to see and do that you could easily spend a couple of days here and still not scratch the surface. The best initiation and orientation is to start with a walk around the wall and ramparts.

# The Wall

The fortifying of Rothenburg began in the 12th century. As the town grew and expanded through the 15th century, the wall assumed an ever greater circumference. You can still circle most of the city on the roofed-over ramparts from which burgher militiamen shot their arrows from crossbows and poured boiling oil on attackers. It is a walk of about 3 km (1.8 miles) that will include exploring 16 towers, five of them with gates to the city. While all the gates and towers are worth seeing, you would soon wear yourself out if you tried to climb to the tops of all of them. The **Klingenturm**, which protected Rothenburg from the north, has an especially fine view of the city and the valley.

# In the Town

Rothenburg's most important ecclesiastical structure, the **Jakobskirche** (Church of St. James), on the Kirchplatz, was begun in 1300 and consecrated in 1448. It is somewhat austere on the exterior, but its interior is a splendid example of Gothic design and appointment. The greatest treasure is the **Heiliges-Blut-Altar** (Altar of the Holy Blood), one of Riemenschneider's finest works. Another of his pieces is the Altar of St. Francis. Be sure also to see the Altar of the Twelve Apostles, with its paintings by Nördlingen artist Friedrich

Herlin. On one of the panels, completed in 1466, he depicted Rothenburg's market square and Rathaus almost as they look today. The stained glass in the three choir windows dates from the late 14th through mid-15th century.

The **Marktplatz**, with its magnificent Rathaus, is just a block south of the Jakobskirche. The town hall was built in two stages. The older section, dating from the 13th century, is graced by a tall, slender belfry that in the Middle Ages also served as a watchtower. The newer portion, though refaced later with Renaissance elements, was completed in the 15th century. Compare what you see with Herlin's altar painting in the Jakobskirche, and you will notice the exterior changes made about a century after the whole complex was completed.

Adjacent to the Rathaus is the **Ratsherrntrinkstube**, the Councillors' Tavern. On its gable are three clocks. The bottom one gives the correct time, the middle instrument is a calendar clock, and above it is a sundial, which is accurate when there is sun and daylight savings time is not in effect. Seven times daily the two little windows on either side of the the lower clocks open to reveal figures of General Tilly and Burgomaster Nusch reenacting the Meistertrunk.

The original tankard, made of pewter and dated 1616, is on exhibit in the **Reichsstadtmuseum** (City Museum), at Klosterhof 5, just north of the Jakobskirche, which is housed in Rothenburg's 700-year-old **Dominican convent**. The structure ranks, together with St. James's and the Rathaus, as one of the town's oldest and most important architectural sights. The original convent kitchen is still intact, even to its utensils. Besides the huge pewter tankard, the collection includes craftsmen's tools, furnishings, and artifacts reflecting life and the decorative arts in Rothenburg over a period of nearly a millennium. The most important works of art are the 12 panel paintings of the *Rothenburg Passion,* by Martinus Schwarz, dated 1494.

You will also find a **Puppen und Spielzeugmuseum** (Doll and Toy Museum), at Hofbrunnengasse 5, and—a bit on the macabre side—the **Mittelalterliches Kriminalmuseum** (Medieval Crime Museum), at Burggasse 3, which illustrates a thousand years of the history of crime and punishment. Among the torture instruments on exhibit are a spiked cane chair, an iron maiden, and a dipping basket.

The chief experience in Rothenburg, however, is simply walking the town's ancient streets, admiring the beautiful old patrician and burgher houses on the **Herrengasse**, and soaking up the atmosphere of being in one of Europe's best-preserved Medieval cities—a city, moreover, that is very much alive. Interrupt your walking with a Rothenburg specialty—*Schneeballen* (snowballs), crisp round pastries powdered with sugar, sold in most of the bakeries and pastry shops. And after looking at the Middle Ages, move *into* them at the Hotel Eisenhut.

## Staying and Dining in Rothenburg

There are 19 hotels in Rothenburg, which is Germany's most visited city. The **Hotel Eisenhut**, Herrengasse 3–7, located in four 15th- and 16th-century patrician houses, is as famous as Rothenburg itself. It belongs to Frau Georg Perner, née Eisenhut. *Eisenhut* means an "iron, armored hat," or casque, and a large one hangs over the hotel's entrance. You will find living in the Middle Ages both fascinating and comfortable. The Eisenhut combines old walls, beautiful antique furnishings, impeccable service, modern amenities, and a master chef to create near perfection. No matter how many visitors may be swarming in Rothenburg, the Eisenhut remains quiet, serene, and the personification of hospitality.

For comfortable accommodations behind even older walls, consider the **Goldener Hirsch**, at Untere Schmiedgasse 16, located in two adjacent 500-year-old houses. The interior decor may at first seem a bit incongruous—Chippendale cheek by jowl with Germanic wrought iron—but the incongruity is more than compensated for by the hotel's location adjacent to the fortification wall and the view of the romantic Tauber valley from the terrace restaurant.

The **Romantik-Hotel Markusturm**, Rödergasse 1, almost next to the Rödertor, the city's eastern gate, is a family hotel popular with honeymooners and tourists alike, run by Marianne Berger assisted by her schoolmaster husband, who gives a helping hand when not busy with his pupils. Specialties of the hotel's kitchen are trout fresh from the Tauber, chanterelles from the nearby forests during August, September, and October, and game dishes from November through January.

Two other establishments that combine Medieval ambience with modern comforts and amenities are the **Tilman Riemenschneider**, Georgengasse 11, and the **Prinzhotel**, An der Hofstatt 3.

The best eating in town is in the hotels, all of whose dining rooms (except the Prinzhotel's) are open to transients.

In planning your trip along the Romantic Road, Rothenburg is a perfect base. Bad Mergentheim is only 45 km (28 miles) away, and your next destination, Feuchtwangen, is a mere 32 km (20 miles) farther south. B 25 will take you there.

## Feuchtwangen

This picturesque town of 10,000 had its origins in its eighth-century Benedictine monastery, and one of the main attractions is the 13th-century **Stiftskirche** on the Marktplatz, where the friars once prayed. Major works of art in the church are the high altar, completed in 1483 by a Nürnberg master, and the early 16th-century choir stalls.

The Stiftskirche's 800-year-old **Kreuzgang** (Cloister) is the site of a June and July repertory theater festival. The cast is good, the seats are comfortable, and the performances are in German (although Shakespeare can be hard to sit through if you don't understand the language).

Your entire time in Feuchtwangen can be happily spent in the Stiftskirche and its cloister without going to the theater, because the secularized complex now houses half a dozen perfectly reproduced crafts shops where artisans work at weaving, cobbling, pewter smithing, pottery making, and baking. There is also an excellent café, bakery, and pastry shop in the corner of the building.

The nearby **Fränkisches Museum** houses a fine collection of Franconian folk and applied art.

No less an attraction in town, and almost as old as the Stiftskirche, is the **Romantik-Hotel Greifen-Post,** Marktplatz 8. Actually once two rival adjacent inns, both in business for more than 500 years, the Post is the older, dating from 1369. The register over the centuries has included such notables as Holy Roman Emperor Maximilian I and Lola Montez, the Irish dancer with the Spanish stage name whose torrid liaison with Bavaria's King Ludwig I led to his abdication. You can rent bicycles here to explore Feuchtwangen and the countryside. Among the other amenities are rooms with Biedermeier furnishings and one suite where you can slumber peacefully in a baldachin bed with eiderdown covers. Like all hotels in the "Romantik" association, the Greifen-Post is both historic and family run, and it has been maintained by the Lorentz family for four generations. The restaurant, one of the best along the Romantische Strasse, emphasizes a nouvelle approach to regional dishes—lighter, smaller portions and the best, freshest ingredients available on the market. Like Rothenburg, Feuchtwangen is a good base for a day or two if

you want to explore the Romantic Road without hotel hopping, and the Greifen-Post will make you feel at home.

Your next destination, Dinkelsbühl, is a mere 12 km (7.5
miles) farther south on highway 25.

# DINKELSBÜHL

What distinguished Dinkelsbühl from Rothenburg, according to the early 20th-century German novelist and essayist
Kasimir Edschmid, is that it "does not have the sound of
trumpets in the air, nor the bloody drama, nor the ghosts of
history." That may well be to its advantage, for although the
town of 11,000 is just as well preserved in its Medieval
appearance, it does not draw quite the crushing crowd of
visitors.

Driving south from Feuchtwangen, you will see two of
Dinkelsbühl's 20 gate and church towers rising out of the
woods to your right. They mark the turnoff that will lead you
through the Wörnitztor and on to the **Alt-Rathaus-Platz**,
where everything happens.

From late June until August, for example, the Alt-Rathaus-
Platz is the stage for an open-air theater festival with special
weekend performances for children. Children were to Dinkelsbühl what Burgomaster Nusch was to Rothenburg, with
the important difference that this time the conquerors were
the anti-Imperial and Protestant Swedes. It happened in
1632, and the Swedish siege was one of eight to which this
Medieval trade junction and weaving center was subjected
during the Thirty Years War.

According to the story, Dinkelsbühl's ill-equipped, under-
nourished citizens' militia held out long and valiantly against
a division of King Gustav Adolph's army, commanded by
Colonel Sperrent. They were hoping in vain for relief from
General Albrecht von Wallenstein, Tilly's successor as supreme commander of the Imperial armies. When Sperrent
threatened to level the entire town, its councillors threw
open the city gates and the mayor humbly presented
Sperrent with the keys to the arsenal and warehouses. But
the Swedish commander seemed bent on revenge.

Suddenly the town's children, led by Lore, the gate-
keeper's daughter, approached Sperrent singing and pray-
ing. Falling on their knees, they implored the colonel to
spare their beloved town. Sperrent, so a slightly embellished
history tells it, had recently lost his only son, and wept when
a little boy his child's age was handed up to him on his

horse. For the children's sake, he decreed that Dinkelsbühl should be spared.

On and around the third Monday of July, Dinkelsbühl stages its annual *Kinderzeche* festival for children. The highlight is a colorful pageant parade in which youngsters and town fathers wear 17th-century costumes to reenact the 1632 event. All of it takes place on and around the Old Town Hall Square, and not a room or even a window looking down on the plaza can be had.

Though the date of Dinkelsbühl's actual founding is uncertain, the town's name first appeared in documents as long ago as the year 928. The origin of the name is in dispute. One version holds that an Alemannic settler called *der Dinkelbauer* led his herds to the banks of the Wörnitz river (a Danube tributary that flows through the town) about 1,500 years ago, and there planted seeds of *Dinkel* (spelt wheat). He offered hospitality to a group of wandering monks, who established a monastery on a hill—a *Bühl,* in southern and Alemannic German dialect—and eventually people began settling around it. Ergo, Dinkelsbühl. Another version says the name derives from *Ding,* Old German for "court" or "assembly."

The point on which everyone agrees is that the location was vital to the town's growth in the Middle Ages, for it was sited at the intersection of major Medieval trade routes. Walls to protect it were first built in the tenth century, but as the town grew in population and importance the defensive perimeter was enlarged, with new walls going up in the 12th and 14th centuries.

Spared in the Thirty Years War and in World War II, Dinkelsbühl today looks much as it did in the Middle Ages. Its ramparts and fortifications are still intact, including 16 wall and gate towers, of which the 13th-century **Wörnitztor** and the 14th-century **Rothenburger Tor** are the oldest.

Within the wall every street offers flower-decked, steeply gabled burgher houses, many of which now contain attractive shops. The most famous half-timbered house in Dinkelsbühl (perhaps in all Southern Germany) is the **Deutsches Haus,** Weinmarkt 3, just opposite the Marktplatz. Built in 1440, it was originally the town house of the counts of Drechsel-Deufstetten, and presents a flower-boxed seven-story façade that outshines all the others. The Deutsches Haus is also a hotel, so you can see the interior and sleep under its steep roof, or have lunch or dinner in its **Altdeutsches Restaurant**. Because it has only 11 rooms for overnight guests, a spur-of-the-moment decision to stay there might backfire. An alternative is the **Eisenkrug**, Martin-Luther-Strasse 1, which has a good historic restaurant in its vaulted cellar. The **Hotel Blauer Hecht**, Schweinemarkt 1, with 30 rooms, is another establishment in the moderate category.

Be sure to visit the **Stadtpfarrkirche St. Georg** on the Marktplatz. The 15th-century Gothic church contains a number of objects from the time of its construction, including the tabernacle, the pulpit, and a baptismal font. The **Historisches Museum**, Martin-Luther-Strasse 6, across the street from the Hotel Eisenkrug, has a collection of exhibits devoted to the town's history and local arts and crafts.

Change has come slowly to Dinkelsbühl, and in some respects has not come at all. It is one of Germany's few towns that still has a salaried, lantern-carrying town crier, who makes his rounds every night calling out "All is well!"

From Dinkelsbühl continue 31 km (19 miles) south on B 25 to the Romantic Road's third pristinely walled Medieval town, Nördlingen. But be prepared for a change in pace, for this town of 20,000 is a former Roman settlement, and the center of a great deal of old culture and architecture and also of a natural wonder that literally shook the world nearly 15 million years ago.

## *SOUTH TO THE DANUBE*
### Nördlingen

For one way to appreciate what Nördlingen is all about, climb 350 steps to the top of the Daniel, as the belfry tower of its 15th-century Stadtpfarrkirche St. Georg, on the Marktplatz, is called. First you will see how perfectly this Medieval town, with its maze of cobblestone streets and steeply roofed houses, has been preserved, and how it is totally enclosed by its massive 16th-century fortification wall. And on a clear day you will see that Nördlingen is surrounded by yet another, far more distant ring, the Ries, made up of sparsely wooded hills that vaguely resemble the raised edge of a dinner plate.

The "plate," some 25 km (16 miles) in diameter, is dotted by nearly 100 small villages, and until as recently as 1960 was one of the great unsolved mysteries of geological science. Two Americans—Dr. Eugene C. Shoemaker and Dr. Edward T. C. Chao, both of the U.S. Department of Interior's Geological Survey—finally solved it. The "plate" and the hilly "ring" surrounding it are what remain of a crater caused by one of the largest meteorites to strike our planet in recent times ("recent" being 14.8 million years ago).

Knowledge that the Nördlinger Ries was a crater formation goes back to at least the mid-18th century, but for more than 200 years scientists speculated that it had been caused by something else: a now-extinct volcano—although there is not even a trace of magma in the soil and rocks surrounding Nördlingen—or, according to another theory, a massive underground explosion of water vapor or subterranean gases like the one that blew up most of the Indonesian island of Krakatoa in 1883. Neither theory accounted for the strange deposits of crushed rock, called suevite, found all around Nördlingen (of which St. Georg's parish church is built) or the odd fact that all the stone formations in the area look as if some huge Brobdingnagian hand had grabbed up a fistful of earth and let it fall again, leaving much older stone strata piled atop much younger ones. Not until Shoemaker and Chao found the telltale signs of meteor impact, of a type that they had already discovered at Meteor Crater in Arizona, was the "Ries Mystery" solved.

It was an asteroid from the belt between Mars and Jupiter that struck here so long ago. The missile from space had a diameter of half a mile and crashed with the force of 250,000 Hiroshima-type atomic bombs. As it bored into the ground it totally vaporized five cubic km of stone into steam, melted and pulverized another 250 billion tons of rock, and caused a mushroom cloud of gas and dust at least 12 miles high. Pellets of melted stone-turned-into-glass jetted 250 miles eastward, as far as Brno in today's Czechoslovakia. Huge boulders of Jurassic and crystalline bedrock from the Earth's crust were catapulted up to 37 miles away. All animal and plant life within a radius of 310 miles was killed, and there may have been a kind of "nuclear winter" that lasted for decades. And it all happened within seconds.

Ever since Shoemaker and Chao proved their theory 30 years ago, Nördlingen has been the center of some of the world's most important astrogeological research. Thousands of scientific papers have been written about the Ries. In 1970 U.S. astronauts spent several weeks in Nördlingen to learn the kinds of rocks they should be looking for when their Apollo capsules landed on the Moon.

The crowning event was in May 1990: the opening of Nördlingen's fabulous **Ries Crater Museum**, Vordere Gerbergasse 1, located in a 16th-century warehouse right in the center of this picturesque Medieval town. The centerpiece of the many scientific and geological exhibits devoted to meteorite, crater, impact, and solar system phenomena is a 5.5-ounce piece of moon rock, on permanent loan from the U.S. National Aeronautics and Space Administration.

Nördlingen grew originally from a Roman settlement, became a king's court under the Carolingian Stauffens, and waxed prosperous in the 12th century. You can walk around the completely preserved **Wehrgang** (covered ramparts) of the fortification wall and see the city from every angle. Visible from every angle too is St. Georg's 297-foot-high Daniel tower.

**St. Georg's**, begun in 1444 and completed in 1508, with nine different architects in charge, has a high altar with some fine 15th-century wood carvings depicting the crucified Christ between the mourning figures of Mary, John the Baptist, Mary Magdalene, and Saint George.

**St. Salvator**, Salvatorgasse 15, was the church of a Carmelite convent and is noteworthy for its well-preserved 15th-century wall frescoes and a high altar attributed to the Bamberg master Hans Nussbaum.

The Rathaus, on the Marktplatz, was built in the 14th century and, except for the early 17th-century Renaissance-style open-air staircase on its façade, exhibits classic Gothic design and decoration. There are numerous fine old public and burgher houses on the Marktplatz, on the Weinmarkt, and along the Rübenmarkt, Nonnengasse, and Kämpelgasse.

The **Stadtmuseum**, just across the street from the Ries Crater Museum, has a fine collection of Roman, Carolingian, and Medieval artifacts and applied art.

Indeed, the only thing missing in this otherwise captivating and charming town is a suitable hotel. So either overnight in Dinkelsbühl or head on to the next destinations: Harburg and Donauwörth.

# Harburg

Just 16 km (10 miles) southeast of Nördlingen on B 25, Harburg is notable primarily for its huge fortress-castle, visible from miles away, which guards the highway, once an old trade route, between Nördlingen and Donauwörth.

No one knows for sure when **Harburg castle** was built, but it was already around in 1150 when Emperor Conrad III, first of the Hohenstaufen dynasty and uncle of Barbarossa, had title to it. In 1295 it became the property of the counts of Oettingen, whose descendants still own it. It was never conquered and is one of the best-preserved castle complexes in West Germany. Among its highlights are the

**Schlosskirche St. Michael**, the castle church dedicated to Saint Michael. Although it was enlarged in the 14th century and then reworked with Baroque stucco elements in the 18th, its earliest parts are austerely and quietly Romanesque.

The castle's **Fürstenbau** (Prince's Building) contains the Oettingen clan's prodigious art collection, including the side wings of a Tilman Riemenschneider altar and an exquisite 12th-century ivory crucifix.

If you want to spend a night like a prince, then opt for one of the nine rooms in the **Fürstliche Burgschenke**, the castle tavern, right within the fortress complex, which provides not only accommodations but a magnificent view, and serves a good lunch.

From Harburg it is 12 km (7.5 miles) along B 25 to Donauwörth, the last stop on the northern half of the Romantic Road, where you can make an important choice: Either continue south on this route or follow our Danube river itinerary, going west to Ulm or heading east to Passau, the river's last point and port in Germany.

# DONAUWÖRTH

*Donau* is the German term for Danube, and Donauwörth, as the name indicates, is situated on the Danube at its confluence with the little Wörnitz river. It is not a very dramatic meeting of rivers in the geological-geographic sense, but in historical terms, this is where Medieval river routes intersected and where the Reichsstrasse, the old imperial trade route between Nürnberg and Augsburg, crossed the most important commercial artery between Füssen in the Alps and Würzburg, where the road continued into Northern Germany.

Considering Donauwörth's advantageous location on this crossroads, its nearly 18,000 inhabitants, and the fact that the Danube is still quite navigable this far upstream, it is surprising that it has neither a starred restaurant nor a luxury hotel. But never mind, it does have two comfortable small hotels, each with fewer than 40 rooms: the **Drei Kronen**, Bahnhofstrasse 25, and the **Traube**, Kapellstrasse 14, with a slightly richer menu.

More sumptuous, though a bit out of the center, is the **Parkcafé**, Sternschanzenstrasse 1, in the district of Donauwörth-Parkstadt. The best dining right in town is at the **Tanzhaus**, Reichsstrasse 34, in a building that has stood here since 1400. The eatery is on its second floor, and if you're too weary to walk up, an elevator will take you there.

Visible from everywhere in the little city, because of its massive spire, is the **Pfarrkirche Maria Himmelfahrt** (Parish Church of the Assumption), on the Reichsstrasse, built between 1444 and 1461. Among its rich furnishings and appointments are 15th-century frescoes and stained-glass windows, a tabernacle from the year 1500, ascribed to Augsburg stonemasons, and 16th-century paintings. The **Heilig Kreuz Kirche** (Church of the Holy Cross), on Heilig-Kreuz-Strasse, is a Baroque edifice, part of a former Benedictine monastery, built between 1717 and 1720 on the site of a 12th-century church, of which the lower stories of the tower remain.

The **Fuggerhaus**, also on the Reichsstrasse (not far from the church of the Assumption and the Tanzhaus restaurant), was built in 1543 by the fabulously wealthy Fugger family of Augsburg. A stunning Renaissance building, it served as a guest house for nobility for nearly two centuries after its construction and well after the Fuggers themselves had lost their position as Europe's richest commercial and banking dynasty. King Gustav Adolph used it as his headquarters and temporary residence in 1632 during the Thirty Years War, and Holy Roman Emperor Charles VI was a guest in 1711.

The 15th-century half-timbered **Gerberhaus** (Tanners' House), Im Ried 103, is now the home of the **Heimatmuseum**, the local history museum, with an interesting collection of folk and applied art, including votive tablets and *Hinterglas*—behind-glass—paintings, a southern German and Alpine art that entails building up the picture in reverse order (the last touches first) directly on a sheet of glass.

Portions of Donauwörth's fortification wall remain to be seen, as do two of the old town gates.

After Donauwörth, and across the Danube, the Romantic Road follows B 2 south along the Lech river, a Danube tributary, for 34 km (21 miles) to Germany's second-oldest, and Bavaria's third-largest, city, Augsburg (population 250,000).

# AUGSBURG

The official reading is that Augsburg, set astride what used to be known as the Claudian Road, the trade artery linking the Adriatic with the North Sea, was founded in 15 B.C. as a fortified encampment by two famous Roman generals, Drusus and Tiberius, both stepsons of Augustus Caesar. They called it Augusta Vindelicorum—the citadel of Augustus in the land of the Vindelicians (the Celtic tribe they had subjugated). A heroic statue of Augustus, cast in 1594, tops the elaborate fountain, one of more than a hundred in town, in front of the Rathaus. There is no written record of the founding, but there is no doubt that by the early first century the military camp had blossomed into the capital of the Roman province of Raetia. In A.D. 98 Tacitus referred to this "City of Augustus" as "exceedingly splendid," and since then there has been no dearth of other testimonials.

Holy Roman Emperor Maximilian I was so fond of the town and spent so much of his time within its walls in the late 15th and early 16th centuries that he was known, among other titles and honors, as "Augsburg's other burgomaster." The Maximilianstrasse, one of the grandest boulevards of the Renaissance, is named for him.

Michel de Montaigne, who spent the winter of 1580 in the city, called it "the most beautiful in Germany" and "the cleanest." The latter reference was inspired by an experience at his inn, the Gasthaus zur Linde. Each time he entered after the steps had been scrubbed—which seemed to be several times weekly—he found them covered with strips of fustian to protect them from guests' dirty boots. (This fabric of cotton and flax was Augsburg's biggest export item and the source of much of its fabulous wealth in the 15th through 17th century.)

The Chevalier de Seingalt, better known as Casanova, considered Augsburg "the freest, most illustrious town in the world." In 1761 he spent six months carousing and shocking the local burghers as Portugal's delegate to the peace parley that ended the Seven Years War between Austria and Prussia. He had intended to reside in the **Hotel Drei Mohren**, a splendid Renaissance hostelry, but the French ambassador had already booked the entire establishment for his own entourage. An accommodating banker provided Casanova with a nicely furnished private villa. Alas, neither that house nor the original Drei Mohren survived a 1944 air raid, but the hotel, although a modern postwar shadow of its erstwhile splendor, is still Augsburg's best.

Fifteen-year-old Marie Antoinette, on her sojourn from Vienna to Paris in 1770 to marry the French dauphin who was to became Louis XVI, was so enamored with Augsburg and stayed so long that the groom sent a courier with an urgent note asking her to stop dallying. During her visit she inaugurated the magnificent **Schaezler Palais** on the Maximilianstrasse—a banker's mansion that now houses the Municipal Art Museum, the Baroque Gallery, and the State Gallery—by dancing all night in its opulent gilded banquet hall, where candlelit Mozart concerts are now held in the summer months. She also went antique-hunting, and tried to buy a 17th-century portrait of a barechested, musclebound man wielding a huge sword—an executioner. The local dealer refused to sell it to her.

Augsburg lore abounds with such anecdotes, as it does with tales of famous native sons. Among them are the master painters Hans Burgkmair and both Holbeins (Elder and Younger); Elias Holl, Germany's leading Renaissance architect, who created most of the city's splendid buildings; Mozart's father, Leopold, who got his musical training at St. Salvator Gymnasium and remained an Augsburg citizen all his life despite moving to Salzburg in 1737; Rudolf Diesel, inventor of the engine that bears his name; Willi Messerschmitt, the aircraft designer and builder; and the playwright Bertolt Brecht, whose sharp-tongued irreverence and Marxist proclivities Augsburg citizens did not really forgive until early 1985, when his birth house, at number 7 Auf der Rain, bought and renovated by the city, was opened as a museum.

Though their town is only 60 km (37.5 miles) northwest of Munich, a half-hour train ride, and administratively part of Bavaria, Augsburgers emphasize that they are Swabians, not Bavarians—with important differences in dialect, cuisine, architecture, customs, and costume. In fact, it was not until 1806, by decree of Napoleon, whose armies were occupying that area of Germany, that Augsburg and the southeastern Swabian lands were ceded to Bavaria. Augsburgers are quick to point out that there might never have been a Munich had it not been for a conference in 1158 in Augsburg between Emperor Frederick Barbarossa and his cousin Henry the Lion, duke of Saxony and Bavaria, at which Barbarossa chartered Munich, where Henry had built a bridge to levy duty on the salt trade, as a town.

Little remains of Augsburg's role in Roman times except for a substantial collection of artifacts, tools, coins, statues, sarcophagi, tombstones, and other archaeological finds, most of which are on exhibit at the Roman Museum, located in a former Dominican monastery church at number 15 Dominikanergasse.

Christianity had a comparatively early impact. The city's patron saint, Afra, was a local maiden martyred in 304 during the persecution under Roman co-emperors Diocletian and Maximian. The town was already a bishopric in 400, and the names of all its bishops, who were both spiritual and temporal rulers, are known since 596. Their portraits hang on a wall of the Dom, construction of which began in 944 by incorporating foundations and elements of a sixth-century church.

The most famous of those early prince-bishops was Count Ulrich von Dillingen, who reigned from 924 to 973. He played a key role in helping Holy Roman Emperor Otto I defeat the Magyars at the battle of the Lechfeld in 955, thus ending their incursions into Western Europe and driving them back into Hungary, where they have remained ever since. The battle was on a plain along the Lech river, whose branches lace Augsburg as romantically as the canals do Venice.

By this time Augsburg was already one of Europe's most important cities. A scant century later it was given its own coinage privileges, and in 1156 Barbarossa confirmed its status as a *freie Reichsstadt,* a free city of the realm, subject to no other overlord save the emperor himself.

But its golden age was undeniably the 15th through 17th centuries, when it was one of the richest and most prosperous towns on the Continent, due to its role as a center of weaving and gold- and silver-smithing, and thanks to its two leading families, the Fuggers and the Welsers. In 1500 Augsburg had 50,000 inhabitants, more than Paris or London, with 2,500 weaving shops, and was exporting a staggering quantity of linen and fustian annually.

Merchants and bankers, the Midas-like Fuggers and Welsers financed many of Europe's wars and pulled quite a few of the strings that determined the course of history. They virtually owned the house of Hapsburg, which borrowed more than four million ducats from the Fuggers alone—an amount never repaid. The Fuggers were richer than the Medicis. One Welser, Bartholomäus, who lived from 1488 to 1561, once owned all of Venezuela, having obtained the territory from Holy Roman Emperor Charles V, grandson of Spain's Queen Isabella, as an unredeemed pledge on a loan.

The foundation for the Fugger fortune was laid by Johann Fugger, a weaver who had moved to Augsburg from a small Swabian village in 1370. During the Renaissance they owned merchant fleets, had a monopoly on the Continent's silver, copper, and mercury mining, and enjoyed the right to coin their own money. The most powerful of all the Fuggers was Jacob the Rich (1459–1525), who in 1519 actually bought the election of the great Charles V by bribing the seven Holy Roman electors.

The Fuggers are still one of Germany's richest families,

with vast real-estate and forestry holdings. The Fugger and Welser legacy is architecturally omnipresent in Augsburg as well. It begins with the huge **Fugger palace** at Maximilianstrasse 36, the main street, which houses not only the Fuggerkeller restaurant and a branch of the Fugger Bank (assets over $100 million) but, appropriately, the offices of tax lawyers and consultants. It continues with a whole array of Fugger and Welser mansions dotted around town, culminating with the picturesque Fuggerei, the world's oldest welfare housing project, where an indigent family can still live in dignity for the equivalent of 50 cents a year.

Of the many famous visitors to Augsburg during its 20 centuries, one of the most renowned was Martin Luther, summoned here in 1518 to recant his 95 Theses before the papal legate, Cardinal Thomas de Vio, known as Cajetan (not to be confused with Saint Cajetan, a fellow Italian and contemporary who was a Catholic Church reformer). Luther stayed in the Carmelite **monastery of St. Anne** on **Annagasse**, now the city's main pedestrian and shopping street. The monastery's prior was a friend of his from student days in Erfurt. The cardinal was a guest of the Fugger family in their Maximilianstrasse palace, where the days-long dispute took place. When the debate reached an impasse, Luther, warned not to trust an imperial letter of safe conduct he carried, hurriedly left town by night through a small door in the city wall, opened by sympathizers.

Augsburg was as much a hotbed of the Reformation as Luther's native Saxony. St. Anne's became Protestant a mere seven years after his visit. His book-lined cell on the second floor of the cloister, where he lived during the debate with Cajetan, is one of its treasures, along with portraits of him and Saxon Duke Johann Friedrich by Lucas Cranach the Elder. In addition, this church, less than five minutes' walk northeast of the railway station, contains the private burial chapel of the Fuggers. Two of the reliefs on their sepulcher were designed by Albrecht Dürer.

The city played a key role in the Reformation. There was the Augsburg Confession of 1530, the official statement of creed by the Lutheran churches. The 1555 Peace of Augsburg, a temporary settlement of the religious conflict in the Holy Roman Empire, established the principle of *cuius regio, eius religio,* which allowed each prince and duke of the realm to determine whether Protestantism or Catholicism was to prevail in his lands and to force subjects of a different mind to emigrate.

The Peace of Augsburg was short-lived, interrupted in 1618 by the Thirty Years War. Miraculously, the city escaped that murderous conflict virtually unscathed. It was less fortunate in World War II. The big February 1944 air raid, aimed at the Messerschmitt plant and at Maschinenfabrik-Augsburg-Nürnberg (M-A-N), where Rudolf Diesel had developed his engine, left some ugly rents in the historic fabric. A few remain and others have been mended with patches of challengeable aesthetic value. Nonetheless, few other large German cities have as much to offer visitors in terms of architectural splendors, art treasures, living history, or Medieval and Renaissance patina. The gems were all brightly polished in 1985, Augsburg's 2,000th anniversary year, and the best way to see them is to walk. Sturdy shoes are recommended because most of the historic streets are paved with cobblestones, over which, legend has it, Napoleon tripped on visits in 1805 and 1809.

## Rathaus and Rathausplatz

Augsburg's epicenter is the Rathausplatz, with its 16th-century fountain and statue of Augustus Caesar. The greatest showpiece there is the Rathaus, built between 1615 and 1620 to replace a Gothic town hall that had stood there for 300 years. A palatial eight-story structure that towers over the square, it is the most dazzling example of secular Renaissance architecture north of the Alps. Next to it stands the **Perlachturm**, once an 11th-century watchman's turret, then a church belfry, and now a largely decorative campanile raised to its present height of 230 feet strictly for eye appeal in 1616. The 35-bell carillon chimes every day at noon.

The air raid left the Rathaus a gutted shell, the greatest interior loss being that of its magnificent **Golden Chamber**, a 6,000-square-foot, three-story reception hall with painted cedar wood ceiling, frescoes, intricately carved paneling, and lavish gold-leaf decor. The building was patched up hurriedly by 1947, but it was not until 1980 that Augsburgers set out in earnest to raise the money and restore the Golden Chamber to its former splendor. It reopened in 1985.

**Die Ecke**, just behind the Rathaus at Elias-Holl-Platz 2, began as a tavern in 1492 and claims such local luminaries as Hans Holbein the Elder, Hans Burgkmair, Leopold and Wolfgang Amadeus Mozart, Diesel, and Brecht as former guests. It is now one of Augsburg's better eateries, especially for game dishes.

# The Dom and the Mozart Museum

A walk north from the city hall along the Karolinenstrasse, which changes its name to Hoher Weg, leads to the Dom and the former bishops' palace, a complex of Baroque buildings that now accommodate various government offices. The tree-shaded square in front of the cathedral, the **Fronhof**, was the Roman Forum. The five-naved church, much of it Romanesque with Gothic additions, is a treasure trove of masterworks, including four altarpieces by Holbein the Elder and the world's oldest examples of stained glass, five 12th-century windows. The huge bronze portal, with scenes from the Old Testament, was cast in the 11th century.

Mozart buffs will find Papa Leopold's birth house just north of the cathedral at Frauentorstrasse 30. The austere magenta-colored building is now the **Mozart Museum**, covering the family's history. Among the furnishings and various artifacts is a 1785 pianoforte made by Johann Andreas Stein, an Augsburg organ and piano builder whose instruments were favored by Mozart and Beethoven. It is still used for recitals in the house. Besides documents dealing with Leopold's own career as a composer, conductor, and virtuoso violinist, the collection also includes some of 21-year-old Wolfgang's pornographic letters to his young Augsburg cousin Maria, with whom he once had a torrid affair. But the most interesting exhibits are those tracing the origins of the family name: It is linked to a village 19 miles west of Augsburg that in 13th-century Middle High German was called Mothardishouen. Historians and philologists believe that Mutzharts, Mutzerts, Motzets, and Motzardts came from there, and that some of the latter eventually simplified the spelling to Mozart. Suffice it to say, by 1597 there were 19 Mozarts registered in Augsburg, and the current phone book still lists eight.

The Jesuitengasse, a street that intersects with the Frauentorstrasse near the Mozart Museum, leads past the Jesuit school where Leopold got his primary and high school education and ends at **Holy Cross church** (Heilig Kreuz), where he sang in the choir and played the organ. An altar picture, *The Assumption of Mary* by Peter Paul Rubens, is one of its treasures.

The **Hotel Fischertor**, Pfärrle 16, just north of the Mozart house on the Frauentorstrasse, then around the corner, is a pleasant, moderately priced inn in quiet, historic surroundings. The adjacent restaurant **Zum Alten Fischertor**, Pfärrle 14, while hardly moderate in price, is Augsburg's temple of haute cuisine. A local scribe not long ago declared its owner Albert Oblinger to be the "Boris Becker of German nouvelle chefs."

# Maximilianstrasse

Augsburg's grand boulevard, the Maximilianstrasse, runs uphill and south from the town hall and the Rathausplatz. The cobblestone avenue, nearly a mile long and as broad as a market square, is interrupted in its path only by two magnificent Renaissance fountains. Many historians maintain that it follows the axis of the Roman Via Claudia. Be that as it may, it was a road travelled by some of the most illustrious figures of European history and is lined on both sides by the palaces of the rich merchants and bankers of the Renaissance.

The **Fugger Palais**, at number 36, is actually a whole complex of adjoining houses and wings, connected by four Italianate courtyards. The best preserved of these, the Damenhof, is where the Fugger ladies entertained guests and played badminton in summer. A bit of exploration through the courtyards will take you to the back of the building and the Zeughausplatz, where Elias Holls's first civic structure, the Armory, stands. Long neglected after being damaged in World War II, it has been rebuilt and serves now as a community center, adult education facility, and gallery for visiting art exhibits.

The **Fugger Keller**, at number 38, in the cellar of the palace, serves solid Swabian and Bavarian food in rustic beer-hall surroundings.

The **Schaezler Palais**, at number 46, where Marie Antoinette danced the night through on April 28–29, 1770, was built between 1765 and 1770 as a 60-room mansion for an Augsburg banker, Benedikt von Liebert, whose descendants willed it to the city after World War II. Today it houses the **Städtische Galerie** and the **Deutsche Barockgalerie**, the municipal and the German Baroque galleries of art, which include works by German masters as well as by Rubens, Van Dyck, Rembrandt, Veronese, and Tiepolo. A passageway from the extravagant, richly ornamented festival chamber on the mansion's second floor leads directly to an adjacent former convent, secularized in 1807, that now holds a stunning collection of old German masters, including works by Holbein the Elder, Burgkmair, Lucas Cranach the Elder, and Albrecht Dürer, belonging to the **Staatsgalerie**, a Bavarian state gallery.

Brass plaques on the houses along the Maximilianstrasse

briefly tell the histories of the most important edifices. More often than not, the courtyards and interiors are as interesting as the façades, such as the arcaded courts of numbers 48 and 58, which was the home of Philipp Fugger, or the beautifully frescoed staircase at number 51.

Augsburg's most colorful and unusual gustatory pleasure is offered at the **Welser Küche**, Maximilianstrasse 83, a Medieval cellar where you dine as Augsburgers did 450 years ago, sitting at large, rough wooden tables, using only a dagger and your fingers as utensils. The gargantuan, eight-course meals are served by "knaves" and "wenches" in 16th-century costumes. Unlike some similar establishments elsewhere in Europe, this one is more than just a show. The food is as genuine as the ambience, prepared strictly according to recipes in the cookbook of Philippine Welser (1527–1580), who was married to Hapsburg Archduke Ferdinand. A typical repast in this unique spot consists of a pre-dinner drink of mead served in a bull's-horn cup, dark flatbread with lard, pike fritters with a saffron sauce, lamb broth, capon pie with plum sauce, roast ribs of beef, air-cured cheese from the Allgäu, sage cake, and apple fritters. For those who cannot decipher the menu, printed in Old German, or the accompanying ceremony in 16th-century Swabian dialect, a translation in impeccable Shakespearean English is furnished.

The Maximilianstrasse culminates in what is Augsburg's largest and most impressive church, visible from miles around and even more impressive than the cathedral: the **basilica of Sts. Ulrich and Afra** (the Augsburg bishop who helped Otto defeat the Magyars, and a Roman girl killed for refusing to recant her Christian faith). Built between 1476 and 1500 on the site of a Roman temple, the basilica holds the remains of both saints. The sepulcher of Ulrich is a masterpiece of Rococo sculpture. Of the many art treasures, one of the finest is the intricate wrought-iron fence that separates the nave from the vestibule. Cast in 1712, this trelliswork uses optical tricks to create three-dimensional illusion.

The smaller church in front of the basilica, also named for St. Ulrich, is Protestant, a testimony to the coexistence of both faiths in the city. In the 14th century it was a market hall, and did not become a house of worship until 1457. Its present interior, a dazzling example of stuccowork, dates from the 18th century.

# The Lower Town

The narrow, hilly streets sloping down north and east from the Maximilianstrasse lead to the Untere Stadt, Augsburg's lower town, where the weavers, goldsmiths, and craftsmen had their shops, where the first textile and calico printing plants were started, and where the artisans, workers, and artists lived. Here you will find the **Holbeinhaus**, the home of both Holbeins, at Vorderer Lech 20, rebuilt after World War II damage and now a gallery of changing contemporary art exhibitions; the **Brechthaus**, Auf der Rain 7, with documents and photographs pertaining to Brecht's life in Augsburg; and the **Römisches Museum**, Dominikanergasse 15, with exhibits of prehistoric, Roman, and early Germanic artifacts, art, sculpture, jewelry, coins, glass, and pottery.

The Untere Stadt is a quarter of small Medieval buildings, narrow lanes, cobblestone alleys, dimly lit courtyards, and a labyrinthine network of little canals and offshoots of the Lech. Their names are often as colorful as the streets: Bauerntanzgasse, Findelgasse, Waisengasse, Katzhof, and Im Sack, which translate as Peasant Dance Alley, Foundlings' Alley, Orphans' Lane, Cat's Court, and In-the-Sack. Recently gentrified and abounding with boutiques and antiques shops, this is a district for strolling, exploring, and soaking up atmosphere.

# The Fuggerei

From the Untere Stadt it is just a couple of blocks eastward to the Fuggerei section, founded in 1519 by Jakob Fugger (Jakob the Rich), the most flamboyant and wealthiest of all the Fuggers. According to popular local legend, his immense riches caused this Croesus pangs of conscience. To soothe them, he decided on a grand philanthropic act: building the world's first low-rent housing project for the poor. Historians who are not as convinced of Jakob's generosity and altruism tell a different version: According to them the Fuggerei was a Renaissance tax shelter. The most disrespectful chroniclers even describe it as a kind of "laundry" for money that Fugger had earned by violating, or at least ignoring, the antitrust laws of his day.

Whatever Jakob's motives, the Fuggerei was a revolutionary concept, a unique approach to 16th-century social problems: a refuge for Augsburgers who had become impoverished through no fault of their own. Unlike the simple hospices and almshouses that then existed elsewhere in Europe, it was built as a town-within-a-town, consisting of

106 gabled cottages lining ruler-straight streets. It did not just dispense charity and welfare, but was based on the principles of self-help, human dignity, and thrift—and is still in operation.

Each little house has a ground-level shop for indigent craftsmen, with dwelling space for their families on the second floor. Tenants had to pay a nominal annual rent of one guilder: a pittance, but enough to give them a sense of self-reliance and self-worth. A woman whose husband had died was given a smaller "widow's home" for an even lower rent. The compound had a resident nurse and was visited by a doctor once a week. Walled and protected against thieves and marauders, the settlement included a chapel and church and a small hospital, and was granted some self-management.

Among its residents over the centuries were many a former petit bourgeois Augsburger who had fallen on hard times, including a once-respected master mason named Franz Mozart, Wolfgang Amadeus's great-grandfather, who lived at Mittlere Gasse 14 from 1681 until his death in 1683.

The Fuggerei today is almost pristine, an idyllic enclave within the city. It is still owned and operated by the Fugger family and is financed from the family foundation's private forest holdings. Moreover, it operates on the same principles set down more than 470 years ago. Even the symbolic rent remains unchanged—one Rhineland guilder per year, which the Fugger foundation equates at DM 1.72 (though today's residents do pay a DM 25 annual surcharge for such modern public services as refuse disposal, sewage, running water, and street cleaning).

Granted, there have been some changes. About one third of the Fuggerei's houses were destroyed or severely damaged during the 1944 air raid. Those that were rebuilt, as well as those that remained undamaged, have all been modernized and renovated. Gone is the Fuggerei's own hospital and the 18th-century school.

The house at **Mittlere Gasse 13** is a museum. Its rough-hewn 16th- and 17th-century furnishings, utensils, and artifacts are original. Its wood-paneled walls and ceilings, the cast-iron heating stove, stoked from the kitchen, and the objects in the rooms give some idea of what life was like four centuries ago. It is open daily from 9:00 A.M. until 6:00 P.M., between March 1 and October 31.

The Fuggerei and its lifestyle have remained remarkably untouched by time. An oasis of six quiet and impeccably clean streets within the city, its gates are closed at 10:00 P.M. each day and reopen at 5:00 A.M. It is a compact little world made up largely of old-age pensioners and cheerful grandmothers. But it is also a little world with strict regulations and tough entry requirements. Occupants must be Catholic and either natives or long-time residents of Augsburg. They must be "poor but industrious." Cleanliness and a pious and honorable lifestyle rank at the top of the community's regulations. Residents are not allowed to have dogs or to dirty the premises by feeding birds. They may not park cars within the Fuggerei or install outside television antennae. They are also forbidden to bleach and dry laundry in the front yard, to chop wood indoors, and to play radios above normal speaking-voice levels at night. Each resident must attend mass daily in the Fuggerei's wood-ceilinged, elegantly restored St. Marcus church, say one Our Father and one Hail Mary, and pray for the souls of the Fuggers. The foundation has the right to evict anybody, and failure to move out within three days after receipt of an eviction notice can be followed by forcible dispossession.

Most important, perhaps, the Fuggerei tries to show that poverty need not be degrading. A pamphlet in the museum says: "What you see here is not intended for your amusement but to convey an impression of the life of the poor centuries ago." Thanks to the Fugger family, it was at least a life with some comforts and dignity.

# SOUTH OF AUGSBURG
## Kloster am Lechfeld

After Augsburg you continue on the Romantic Road south along the Lech by following B 17 out of the city. The first point of interest is at Klosterlechfeld, 22 km (14 miles) south of Augsburg, the site of the battle of the Lechfeld, a bloody conflict in 955 in which Holy Roman Emperor Otto I defeated the Magyars, forebears of today's Hungarians.

Historians really aren't sure where the famous battle took place. According to some it was on a plain north of Augsburg, according to others south of the city. But this did not deter Regina Imhoff, the widow of a wealthy Augsburg patrician, from commissioning Elias Holl some six centuries later to build a votive chapel on what she believed was the right spot. Holl based the cylindrical design and the half dome on the Pantheon in Rome, and completed his work in 1603. A nave was added in 1656 to 1659, and two little chapels in 1691. All the towers have onion domes. Franciscans built a monastery adjacent to the church in the late

1660s. While there are no signs of the famous battle, the whole complex is worth a short visit, especially for a view of the ornate stucco-and-gilt Rococo interior of the church.

From here it is another 16 km (10 miles) south along the Lech valley, which narrows and becomes more verdant, to Landsberg.

## Landsberg am Lech

A town of 20,000, and one of the most picturesque and idyllically situated on the Romantic Road, Landsberg looks like the stage set for a fairy tale, though the name also evokes more recent history: It was in the **fortress prison** here that Adolf Hitler was incarcerated after his abortive 1923 Beer Hall Putsch and wrote *Mein Kampf,* his blueprint for world conquest and genocide. Ironically, after World War II the jail was taken over by the U.S. Army, and scores of convicted Nazi criminals were executed and interned here. The prison still stands, serving its intended purpose as a Bavarian state penitentiary.

Situated on the old tribal boundary line between Bavarians and Swabians, Landsberg owes its origins to Henry the Lion, who, in 1160, four years after Emperor Frederick Barbarossa had deeded him the duchy of Bavaria, built a fortress castle on the hill above the swiftly flowing Lech, to serve as a border post and customs station where his agents levied duty on the east-west salt trade. A market community soon sprouted around the castle, and grew so fast that by 1260 it was a little city with municipal rights.

To this day Landsberg is still partially surrounded by a 13th- to 15th-century defensive wall with mighty towers and fortified gates. The town expanded so rapidly in the Middle Ages that its fortifications had to be expanded several times, but the eastern **Bayertor** (Bavarian Gate), constructed in 1425, is one of the best preserved in all Germany, and with its carved and painted coats-of-arms and a crucifixion scene is also one of the most photogenic.

Landsberg's market square, lined by colorfully painted and stuccoed Renaissance and Baroque town houses, is among the most beautiful in the country. It is dominated by the late 17th- to early 18th-century **Rathaus**, whose exterior and interior stuccowork was executed by Dominikus Zimmermann. Zimmermann, one of the great master architects of the Baroque and Rococo periods in southern Germany, served as the mayor of Landsberg from 1759 to 1764. He also designed the **St. Johannes Kirche** on the Vorderanger and did the stuccowork in the **sacristy of the Heilig Kreuzkirche** on the Helfsteingasse, almost undecorated on the outside but resplendent with embellishment on the interior. The most impressive building in town is the **Pfarrkirche Maria Himmelfahrt** (parish church of the Assumption), a 15th-century basilica on the Georg-Hellmair-Platz that has been "*barockiziert*"—baroquized—with blinding splendor.

The traditional spot to stay is the **Hotel Goggl**. The original 17th-century building was razed some time ago, but its replacement successfully maintains its traditions.

Landsberg is the departure point for a detour from the Romantic Road that you may well want to consider: a trip due west to Memmingen and then south from Memmingen to Kempten. The highway leading out of Landsberg heading west combines B 12 and B 18. About 20 km (12.5 miles) out of town it divides, with the B 18 continuing straight for about 50 km via Mindelheim to Memmingen. The B 12 fork runs generally southwest for about 60 km (37.5 miles) by way of Kaufbeuren to Kempten. Memmingen and Kempten in turn are linked by a 38-km (24-mile) stretch of north–south Autobahn (the A 7).

# Memmingen

Founded in 1160, Memmingen (population 38,000) has been a prosperous trading town for some eight centuries, and the prosperity shows in its public buildings and richly appointed churches. Of the latter the most interesting are the 15th-century **Martinskirche** on the Martin-Luther-Platz and the **Frauenkirche** on the Frauenkirchplatz, famous for its 15th-century frescoes, which had been painted over and were rediscovered during restoration work in the 1890s. The town's secular landmark is the half-timbered **Siebendächerhaus**, with seven roofs—four on one side, three on the other—each overlapping the next. Dating from 1601, it was the tanners' guild hall, and the roofs had a very practical purpose: Skins were hung to dry on them, and the more roofs the more drying space. The **Rathaus**, on the Marktplatz, is a classic Southern German Renaissance structure of the late 16th century, whose 18th-century façade is a fine example of Rococo stuccowork.

From the center of Memmingen it is 11 km (7 miles) southeast by unnumbered country road to **Ottobeuren**, site of one of Germany's most magnificent Baroque monasteries and monastery churches. The Benedictine abbey with its **Klosterkirche zur Heiligen Dreifältigkeit** (Trinity Church) was founded in 764. Various buildings dating from the 11th through 16th centuries burned down before work on the present complex began in the early 1700s. The most noted architects and artists of the time, including Dominikus Zimmermann, competed for the commission, with the nod finally going to Johann-Michael Fischer, who is responsible for church buildings all over Bavaria and Swabia. The 290-foot nave is an incomparable splash of stucco and gilded Baroque decoration, with gloriously colorful ceiling frescoes. A bit more subdued, though no less interesting, are the monastery's chapterhouse, library, and theater.

## Kempten

A journey to this architecturally rich little city of 58,000 astride the swift, chalky Iller river will take you to the verdant doorstep of the Allgäu Alps, Germany's largest cheese-producing region, and back in history to Roman times. Exactly when the Oppidum Cambodunum was founded as a military camp by Roman legionaries is unknown, but it must already have been a substantial town when first mentioned in A.D. 18. Excavations have uncovered a basilica, baths, a forum, and countless artifacts that are on exhibit at the **Römische Sammlung**, on the Residenzplatz.

In the Middle Ages Kempten began a kind of two-track, split-personality existence that continued into modern times. On the one hand, in 752, it became the site of a Benedictine monastery whose abbots were also temporal rulers. On the west bank of the Iller a trading town developed that by the year 1289 was already a Free Imperial City. During the Reformation the city turned Protestant, but the area around the abbey remained Catholic, and the division has, in a sense, never ended. When the first railroad line came in around 1850, local burghers thought seriously of erecting two stations: one Catholic, the other Protestant.

During the Thirty Years War the Swedes, supported by Protestant burghers, destroyed most of the monastery and its surrounding area. The Catholic Imperial troops paid back in kind by demolishing the Protestant city. As a result, nearly everything you see in Kempten today is reconstruction dating from the middle of the 17th century. That includes both the **Stiftskirche St. Lorenz** (Collegiate church of St. Lawrence) on the Stiftsplatz, and the former **Prince-Abbot's Residence**, on the Residenzplatz.

The Stiftskirche St. Lorenz was the first large ecclesiastical construction of any kind in Germany after the Thirty Years War. Begun in 1651 and completed in 1654, it is in North Italian style. The interior stucco decoration was the work of Giovanni Zucalli, a Swiss architect and plasterer whose uncle, Enrico, was busy in a similar role, and working in a similarly grand manner, at about the same time in Munich. Work on building a new palace for the prince bishop also began in 1651, but as it took longer and extended into the Rococo era, the Residenz, with its ostentatious state and guest rooms, is even richer. Its architects borrowed many ideas from the French master François de Cuvilliés, then working in Munich, and from the brothers Dominikus and Johann-Baptist Zimmermann, who were among the most flamboyant builders of their era.

There is much else to see in town, especially on and around the Rathausplatz, including the **Rathaus** itself, one of the few survivors of the Thirty Years War, though reconstructed afterward; the **Weberzunfthaus** (Guild House of the Weavers); and numerous patrician mansions such as the Ponikauhaus and the Londoner Hof, where foreign merchants stayed.

Have lunch or supper at **Zum Strittigen Winkel**, Fischersteige 9, an 18th-century tavern furnished with Gothic, Renaissance, and Biedermeier antiques, countless historic artifacts, and the closest thing you are likely to find to *Gemütlichkeit*. The food is solid Swabian, without nouvelle cuisine pretensions. If you wish to spend the night in Kempten, the top address, though moderately priced, is the **Hotel Fürstenhof**, on the Rathausplatz. Most of the rooms and suites are paneled with inlay root wood.

To return to the Romantic Road without retracing your steps, take B 147 east out of Kempten for 25 km (16 miles) to the town of Markt-Oberdorf, and there get on the B 472 for a very scenic 29-km (18-mile) drive east to Schongau, where the road intersects with the B 17, the Romantic Road, for the next leg southward, 12 km (7.5 miles) to Steingaden and the Wieskirche, the Church in the Meadow.

## Steingaden

This region is called the Pfaffenwinkel, or Parsons' Corner, an allusion to its profusion of Baroque chapels, churches, and monasteries whose spires are all capped by those distinctive onion domes that make you wonder whether you are in Bavaria or Russia. It is an area of gloriously stunning ecclesiastical architecture and art, the most elaborate examples of which are found in and around the village of Steingaden. Its 12th-century minster, **St. Johann Baptist**, has changed little on the outside during the past 800 years, but its interior is a breathtaking splash of gilded Rococo sculpture and stuccowork. Even more spectacular, about 6 km (4 miles) southeast, is the **Wieskirche**, known as the "Miracle in the Meadow church." Considered the most beautiful Rococo church in the world, it was built between 1746 and 1754 by Dominikus Zimmermann, the Landsberg master (and onetime mayor) who also designed the Steingaden minster.

What is such a building doing by itself in the middle of a meadow? The carved figure showing the scourging of Christ in the Wieskirche's high altar was the impetus. The wayside carving belonged to a local farmer, who reported one day in 1730 that it had suddenly begun to shed tears. He persuaded the abbot of Steingaden to build a chapel for it in the meadow where he had observed the miracle. It became the object of pilgrimages, so that a larger church had to be built, and Zimmermann was given the commission.

The Wieskirche was his crowning achievement. He led a team of the best artists of his time to do the interior decoration, stressing the concept of harmony between architectural shape and color. His brother, Johann-Baptist, was responsible for most of the fresco and stuccowork. There is probably no other building with such unity of Rococo style.

The Wieskirche has been closed for repair and renovation since 1986, when its magnificent ceiling showed structural cracks and proved to be in danger of collapsing. The cause: vibrations from low-flying supersonic German air force jets stationed at Memmingen. To be sure, the church has had to be renovated before, in 1903, 1950, and 1970. But never has so much work been necessary or the cost so high—about DM 7 million—and never has the danger to the church been as great. A team of 30 architects, restorers, and stucco masters has been at it for nearly five years. Whether they will finish so that the Wieskirche can be reopened for the public in 1991 was still in doubt when we went to press.

Steingaden and the Wieskirche will occupy you for at most an hour or two each. Consider Füssen and Schwangau, the southern terminus of the Romantic Road, destinations in themselves. From Steingaden it is about 20 km (12.5 miles) southwest along highway B 17 through steadily rising countryside to the base of the jagged, snow-capped Allgäu Alpine range, the Medieval town of Füssen, and what is surely the gaudiest example of Romanticism on the Romantic Road: King Ludwig II's fairy-tale castle, Neuschwanstein.

## SCHWANGAU AND FÜSSEN

Bavaria was a full-fledged kingdom for only 112 of its 1,100 years of recorded history, from 1806 until 1918, when the monarchy was replaced by a republic. Brief as it was, Bavarians regard the era as their greatest and grandest, and many still yearn for it. But when they speak wistfully and longingly about "the king," they mean only one: Ludwig II, the lonely "dream king" and patron of Richard Wagner.

His reign and indeed his life were short. He ascended the throne at age 19 in 1864, was deposed on charges of mental incompetence on June 9, 1886, and four days later drowned mysteriously, together with the psychiatrist who had ruled him insane, in Starnberg lake south of Munich. He was a legend in his lifetime, and has remained one since. No monarch since Louis XIV of France—whom he idolized and tried to emulate—captured the imagination of Europe more thoroughly than this Louis of Bavaria, the "Sun King of the 19th century." Paul Verlaine called him "a poet, a soldier, the only real king of this century of impotent kings." Wagner described him as "outstandingly talented, a ruler of prodigious capabilities." More than 200 biographies have been written about him, and five full-length feature films have been made about his enigmatic life.

A magnificent figure—six feet four, blue-eyed with carefully coiffed brunette locks—he was the idol of his time and the quarry of artful women and scheming mothers who haunted Munich's Residenz, the royal palace, with but a single thought: to meet him alone—just once. But with the notable exception of his first cousin, Sissy, who became Empress Elizabeth of Austria and met a fate as tragic as his own, Ludwig had little, indeed no, interest in women. Nor did he have much interest in governing his country, and he found escape in fantasy.

Ludwig had many eccentricities—all of them expensive. On the roof of the royal palace in Munich he built a winter garden with exotic trees, a painted Himalayan backdrop, and an artificial lake on which a hidden millwheel created waves and into which servants poured gallons of copper sulfate each day to make it look marine blue. He spent hours, dressed as Lohengrin, riding in a swan-shaped boat in the

Venus Grotto he had installed behind one of his mansions. But of all his eccentricities, the greatest was undoubtedly his mania for building dream castles. They were also his undoing, for they put him 20 million gold marks into debt. Bismarck helped him out with a loan, in exchange for which Ludwig agreed in 1871 to the creation of the German Reich, with Prussia's King Wilhelm I as the first kaiser.

On an island in the Chiemsee in southeastern Bavaria he created a replica of Versailles; on the steep slope of a craggy Alp he put up a hunting lodge in Moorish style; at Linderhof, deep in rugged mountain country, he created a gaudy, ostentatious imitation of a Baroque French château. And he was planning a full-scale copy of Peking's Forbidden City. His most outlandish concoction of all was Neuschwanstein, a fantasy castle of romantic fairy tales, a 19th-century adumbration of Disneyland, perched dizzily on a peak overlooking the village of **Schwangau.**

Before walking or taking a carriage ride up to it, a visit to another castle in this hamlet, **Hohenschwangau,** may give you some insights into the reclusive, enigmatic character of Ludwig II.

Like five other castles on peaks around Füssen, all once owned by the lords of Schwangau (a family that died out in the 16th century), Hohenschwangau was a ruin when Ludwig's father, Maximilian II, then Bavaria's crown prince, bought it in 1832. On the ruins he built a neo-Gothic palace that he used as a summer holiday residence. Completed in 1837 (and now open to the public from 9:00 A.M. to 5:00 P.M. daily), it was where he took his family on vacation every year and where Ludwig II spent a good deal of his joyless childhood. Maximilian was as straitlaced as his own father, Ludwig I, was flamboyant. He used to say that had he not been king he would have become a university professor. He had a love of Germanic legends, and had them painted on the walls of Hohenschwangau: the tale of the Holy Grail, of the Minnesinger (lyrical poet) Tannhäuser, and of Lohengrin, who, according to 19th-century lore, once lived in the old Hohenschwangau fortress. It was in this summer residence, and through the one and only frivolous passion of his father, that Ludwig II acquired his own love for the myths and for the solitude of the Bavarian Alps.

Hohenschwangau was the capital of the Swan Country (*Schwangau*). There were swans everywhere: on the lakes such as the Forggensee, Alpsee, and Schwansee; painted on the walls of the royal apartments; carved in the form of knickknacks. The swans fascinated father and son, and for the son they later became a near obsession.

A couple of years after his coronation, Ludwig II again spent part of a summer at Hohenschwangau and decided to buy property almost adjacent to it: the castle ruin of Vorder-hohenschwangau, on a peak overlooking the summer residence and perched precipitously at the edge of a gorge with a waterfall. In May 1868 he wrote Richard Wagner of his plans to build a castle on the ruins "in the style of the old German knights' castles." A year before, he happened to have visited the Wartburg above Eisenach (now in East Germany), scene of the Tannhäuser legend and of Medieval minstrel competitions, and it was a romanticized version of this fortress he wanted. Thus **Schloss Neuschwanstein** was born.

The court architect, Eduard Riedel, and Christian Jank, the chief set designer of the Bavarian State Opera, drew up the plans, which looked like stone stage sets for *Tannhäuser*. Work began in 1869 and was not even quite finished when, 17 years later, on June 10, 1886, a day after he had been declared incompetent by a royal commission of doctors, Ludwig II was arrested in his dream castle and taken to Schloss Berg on the shore of the Starnbergersee, where he was interned.

To describe Neuschwanstein's appearance and its interior decoration as opulent and like a fairy tale is probably the all-time understatement. The rich ornamentation had an influence on the later Jugendstil, the German form of Art Nouveau. The most important chambers in this dream castle are the Throne Room (without throne), patterned on a Romanesque basilica, and the Sängerhalle (Singers' Hall), its dark, heavy, wooden ceiling and murals depicting the Parsifal saga. The king's study, with pictures of the Tannhäuser legend, adjoins an artificial grotto with artificial waterfall and electric light effects.

Neuschwanstein was the least expensive of Ludwig II's castles (costing only 6.2 million gold marks to build, compared to 8.5 million for Linderhof and 16.6 million for Herrenchiemsee), yet it is not only the most visited—on average about 950,000 people a year—but the most photographed building in all Germany. Ironically, although Ludwig II was deposed for spending so recklessly on his make-believe palaces, admissions revenues from them alone pay for nearly the entire upkeep and maintenance of *all* the old Wittelsbach family castles now owned and administered by the state of Bavaria. (Hours at Neuschwanstein are 9:00 A.M. to 5:30 P.M. daily April through October, 10:00 A.M. to 4:00 P.M. November through March.)

Although the town of Füssen is only 7 km (4 miles) from Hohenschwangau and Neuschwanstein castles—a five-minute drive and 15-minute walk by a back road—you may want to spend the night in Schwangau itself, surrounded by the romanticism of the Dream King. The **Hotel Lisl-Jägerhaus**, built in the style of a hunting château, has 62 rooms and its dining room features trout from the lakes in and around Schwangau. The **Hotel König Ludwig**, on a quiet side street just 300 yards from the Forggensee, largest of the area's lakes, is built and decorated in Alpine chalet style with lots of natural pine paneling and furniture.

# Füssen

Nearby Füssen, romantically divided by the Lech river and just 4 km (2.5 miles) from the Austrian border, is a dramatic change of pace from the 19th-century artificiality of Maximilian's and Ludwig's castles. This town of 15,000, at an altitude of more than 2,600 feet, is genuine, as picturesquely Medieval as can be. More than Medieval, in fact, for like other spots along the Via Claudia, it goes back to Roman times, when it was known as Foetibus.

Of course there's a castle. The **Hohes Schloss**, on the Magnusplatz, dates back to the early 14th century, when Bavaria's Duke Ludwig built it as a fortress and occasional residence, though most of the structure was completed a century later. The interior, containing a division of the Bavarian state pictures collection, is largely 17th century.

Post-Roman Füssen owes its origins to an Irish missionary monk, Saint Magnus, known as the "Apostle of the Allgäu," who established a chapel here in the eighth century. A Benedictine abbey was built adjacent to it some years later, and enlarged in Romanesque style in the 12th century. Little of that remains, for in the early 18th century a local architect, Johann-Jakob Herkomer, who had studied in Venice, got a commission to build a new monastery and church around the old tower. What he created is a perfect Baroque gem with strong Venetian influence.

Above all, Füssen, tucked into the Lech valley and surrounded by 6,000- to 7,000-foot peaks, is perfect for soaking up atmosphere and strolling its narrow, cobblestone streets. You may want to take lunch in the **Gasthof zum Schwanen**,

Brotmarkt 4, a colorful old inn in a Gothic town house, perfect for sampling either Bavarian dishes such as pork roast with potato dumplings, or Allgäu-Swabian cuisine, among it such specialties as *Maultaschen,* a kind of ravioli, and Spätzle. The area around Füssen is a popular summer and winter holiday resort and abounds with inns and hotels, all of them modern. For Altstadt atmosphere at moderate prices right in Füssen, the best is the **Hotel Hirsch**.

## GETTING AROUND
To drive the entire Romantische Strasse from Würzburg to Füssen, leave Würzburg southward on B 19 to Bad Mergentheim. At Mergentheim double back 4 km (2.5 miles) on B 19 to the village of Igersheim, where, just north of the town limit, you will find an unnumbered road to the right (east) leading to Weikersheim, then Creglingen, then Detwang, and finally Rothenburg-ob-der-Tauber. This unnumbered country road follows the Tauber river valley all the way, so it is almost impossible to become lost.

To continue from Rothenburg, take B 25 south to Feucht-wangen, then Dinkelsbühl, Nördlingen, Harburg, and finally Donauwörth. On the German Shell map or atlas, the B 25 is colored yellow from Rothenburg to Nördlingen, and red from Nördlingen to Donauwörth. Don't let it confuse you. It is the same Bundesstrasse. The yellow marking indicates it is narrower and perhaps not in as good condition as the southern portion.

From Donauwörth follow B 2 to Augsburg. From Augsburg south the rest of the Romantic Road is along B 17, which terminates in Füssen.

To make the detour to Memmingen, Ottobeuren, and Kempten from Landsberg-am-Lech, leave Landsberg on B 12/18. About 20 km (12 miles) out of town, the B 12 and B 18 divide. It is a tricky junction, but mercifully the sign to Memmingen is in larger letters than the one to Kempten. Memmingen is via the B 18. In Memmingen an unnumbered road southeast (but there will be directional signs) takes you to Ottobeuren. From Ottobeuren it is best to retrace your route back north until you find a blue Autobahn sign, then take the A 7 south to Kempten. From Kempten, to return to the Romantische Strasse, take the B 147 as far as Markt Oberdorf, where it joins the B 472, which you follow east to where it intersects the B 17 at Schongau, and then continue south on the Romantic Road.

Steingaden is just off the B 17. To get to the Wieskirche (it is well marked), follow the unnumbered country road for 3 km (2 miles) east, then 3 km south. The only way to return to the B 17 is by doubling back.

In Schwangau there is a marked but unnumbered cutoff to Hohenschwangau and Neuschwanstein.

If you do not want to drive into Füssen, where parking is sometimes difficult, there is a footpath from Hohenschwangau into the center, a distance of about 1.5 km (less than a mile).

## ACCOMMODATIONS REFERENCE

▶ **Hotel Blauer Hecht**. Schweinemarkt 1, D-8804 **Dinkelsbühl**. Tel: (9851) 811.

▶ **Hotel Deutsches Haus**. Weinmarkt 3, D-8804 **Dinkelsbühl**. Tel: (9851) 23-46.

▶ **Donauwörther Hof**. Teutonenweg 16, D-8850 **Donauwörth-Nordheim**. Tel: (906) 59-50.

▶ **Drei Kronen**. Bahnhofstrasse 25, D-8850 **Donauworth**. Tel: (906) 2-10-77.

▶ **Hotel Drei Mohren**. Maximilianstrasse 40, D-8900 **Augsburg**. Tel: (821) 51-00-31.

▶ **Hotel Eisenhut**. Herrengasse 3–7, D-8803 **Rothenburg**. Tel: (9861) 10-41.

▶ **Hotel Fischertor**. Pfärrle 16, D-8900 **Augsburg**. Tel: (821) 15-60-51.

▶ **Fürstenhof**. Rathausplatz 8, D-8960 **Kempten**. Tel: 2-53-60.

▶ **Fürstliche Burgschenke**. Auf Schloss Harburg, D-8856 **Harburg**. Tel: (09003) 15-04.

▶ **Hotel Goggl**. Herkomerstrasse 19, D-8910 **Landsberg**. Tel: (8191) 20-81.

▶ **Hotel Goldener Hirsch**. Untere Schmiedgasse 16, D-8803 **Rothenburg**. Tel: (9861) 20-51.

▶ **Hotel Hirsch**. Schulhausstrasse 4, D-8958 **Füssen**. Tel: (8362) 60-55.

▶ **Hotel König Ludwig**. Kreuzweg 11, D-8959 **Schwangau**. Tel: (8362) 810-81.

▶ **Hotel Laurentius**. Marktplatz 5, D-6992 **Weikersheim**. Tel: (7934) 70-07.

▶ **Hotel Lisl-Jägerhaus**. Neuschwansteiner Strasse 1, D-8959 **Schwangau**. Tel: (8362) 810-06.

▶ **Maritim Hotel Würzburg**. Pleichtorstrasse 5, D-8700 **Würzburg**. Tel: (931) 508-31.

▶ **Parkhotel Maritim**. Lothar-Daiker-Strasse 6, D-6990 **Bad Mergentheim**. Tel: (7931) 61-00.

► **Prinzhotel Rothenburg.** An der Hofstatt 3, D-8803 **Rothenburg.** Tel: (9861) 60-51.

► **Hotel Rebstock.** Neubaustrasse 7, D-8700 **Würzburg.** Tel: (931) 309-30.

► **Romantik-Hotel Greifen-Post.** Marktplatz 8, D-8805 **Feuchtwangen.** Tel: (9852) 20-02.

► **Romantik-Hotel Markusturm.** Rödergasse 1, D-8803 **Rothenburg.** Tel: (9861) 23-70.

► **Tilman Riemenschneider.** Georgengasse 11, D-8803 **Rothenburg.** Tel: (9861) 20-86.

► **Hotel Traube.** Kapellstrasse 14, D-8850 **Donauwörth.** Tel: (906) 60-96.

► **Hotel Victoria.** Poststrasse 2, D-6990 **Bad Mergentheim.** Tel: (7931) 59-30.

► **Wittelsbacher Höh.** Hexenbruchweg 10, D-8700 **Würzburg-Zellerau.** Tel: (931) 420-85.

# MUNICH
## (MÜNCHEN)

*By John Dornberg*

Thomas Mann, who spent 40 of the most productive years of his life in Munich, wrote a singular tribute to it in his *Gladius Dei:* "Munich shines forth, a heaven of blue silk radiates over her festive squares and columned white temples, her Neoclassical monuments and Baroque churches, her playing fountains, her palaces and her parks. Art blooms, art reigns, art stretches her rose clad sceptre over this city and smiles." For Wassily Kandinsky, who began painting in the abstract during his nearly two decades in Munich, the city was "a unique intellectual island, an island of beauty that stimulated the world." Henrik Ibsen, who wrote some of his greatest plays during the 15 years he resided here, declared shortly after arriving in 1874: "There are but two cities in which one can really live—Rome and Munich. But in Munich even reality is beautiful." And Thomas Wolfe, who visited in 1925, said in *The Web and the Rock:* "How can one speak of Munich but to say it is a kind of German heaven? Some people sleep and dream they are in paradise, but all over Germany people sometimes dream that they have gone to Munich, a Germanic dream translated into life."

No other German city has contributed as much to the arts, literature, or music as this former capital of a former kingdom. The remarkable thing, after the dozen years of Hitler and Nazism, the wartime air raids that destroyed two-thirds of the city, and the four and a half postwar decades that have seen much of Germany change beyond recognition, is that Munich remains—or is again—what it was in the days of Mann, Kandinsky, Ibsen, and Wolfe: a stimulating intellectual island, "a Germanic dream." Though today merely the capital of one of the German Federal Republic's eleven states, Munich is Germany's "secret capital," the city where most Germans would live if they could, and on which 1.7 million of them—and an additional 1.3 million foreigners—converge as visitors each year.

Munich is a city of superlatives, offering *more* of just about everything. It is, for example, the most expensive city in Germany in which to live. It has more glitter, fashion, chic, and conspicuous consumption; more restaurants (one per 240 inhabitants), as well as more with Michelin stars; more fine-food shops and open-air markets; and also more privately owned Rolls-Royces, Jaguars, Lamborghinis, Ferraris, and Maserattis than any other city in Germany. (BMWs do not really count, because they are made in Munich, and neither do Porsches or Mercedeses, because they are not.) It also counts more movie stars and filmmakers, thanks to having Europe's largest studio and Germany's greatest number of production houses.

Munich also has more art, music, and culture than any other German city, in the form of 32 museums, 230 commercial galleries, 42 repertory theaters, two opera houses, five concert halls, and four symphony orchestras; more students—96,000—attending Germany's two largest universities; more scientific institutes and high-tech industries; and more trade fairs, congresses, and conventions. The city boasts the world's oldest and largest public park; Europe's biggest and bawdiest folk festival, the Oktoberfest; the Continent's cleanest, safest, and most efficient public-transit system (but also Germany's densest motor traffic); and the country's best soccer team, FC Bayern.

**MAJOR INTEREST**

**Museums**
Alte and Neue Pinakotheken (Old Masters and 19th-century art)
Antikensammlung (Celtic, Greek, Etruscan, Roman applied art)
Glyptothek (Greek and Roman sculpture)
Städtische Galerie am Lenbachhaus (modern art)
Haus der Kunst (modern and contemporary art)
Bayerisches Nationalmuseum (eighth- through 19th-century Bavarian and applied art)
Villa Stuck (Art Nouveau)
Hypo Kunsthalle
Residenzmuseum

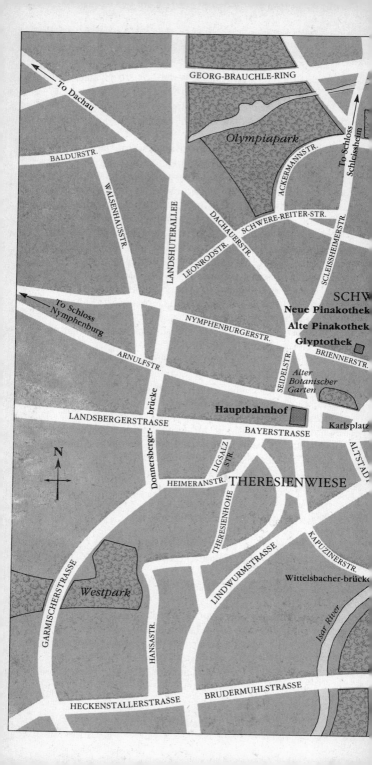

# Munich

| | | |
|---|---|---|
| 0 | yards | 1,100 |
| 0 | meters | 1,000 |

PETUELRING

LEOPOLDSTRASSE

UNGERERSTRASSE

*Luitpoldpark*

JOHANN-FICHTE-STR.

KARL-THEODOR-STR.

BELGRADSTR.

*Isar River*

OBERFÖHRINGERSTR.

ISARRING

ELISABETH STR.

*Englischer Garten*

IFFLANDSTR.

ABING

LEOPOLDSTRASSE

Max-Joseph Brücke

MONTGELASSTR.

ISMANINGERSTR.

R. STRAUSSTRASSE

BARERSTR.

**Universität**

RING-VON-DER-TANN-STR.

**Bayerisches Nationalmuseum**

BOGENHAUSEN

Karolinenplatz

Prinzregenten-brücke

**Friedensengel**

THEATERIN-STR.

DIENERSTR.

HOFGARTEN STR.

PRINZREGENTENSTRASSE

Prinzregenten-platz

WEINSTR.

**Residenz**

WIDENMAYER STR.

**Villa Stuck**

TROGER STR.

KAUFINGER STR.

Marienplatz

MAXIMILIANSTRASSE

EINSTEINSTRASSE

**Prinzregententheater**

INNENSTADT

Maximilians-brücke

**Maximilianeum**

OBERANGER RINDERMARKT

ZWEIBRÜCKENSTR.

INNERE-WIENER-STR.

KIRCHENSTR.

GRILLPARZER STR

RING

Zweibrücke

PREYSINGSTR.

HANS-SACHS-STR.

**Deutsches Museum**

ROSENHEIMERSTR.

HAIDHAUSEN

INNSBRÜCKER RING

WITTELSBACHER STR.

FRAUNHOFFERSTR.

Reichenbach-brücke

HOCHSTR.

HUMBOLDTSTR.

WELFENSTR.

LANDSTR.

WERINHERSTR.

GIESING

CHIEMGAUSTRASSE

Schatzkammer der Residenz (Royal Treasury)
Deutsches Museum (science and technology)

**Churches**
Frauenkirche
Michaelskirche
Asamkirche
Peterskirche
Theatinerkirche

**Neighborhoods**
Innenstadt
Schwabing
Haidhausen

**Environs**
Schloss Schleissheim

By German standards Munich is not old. It was founded officially on June 14, 1158, by decree of Frederick Barbarossa, the Hohenstaufen emperor, under duress from his cousin Henry the Lion, the Guelph duke of Saxony, to whom two years earlier Frederick had given the duchy of Bavaria. The city's beginnings lay in a crude act of extortion. Henry wanted to get the most out of his new Bavarian properties, including the lucrative customs revenues on the salt trade between the Bavarian Alps and the rest of the empire that Bishop Adalbert of Freising was collecting at the only bridge over the swift Isar river, located in the village of Föhring. Henry and a force of knights destroyed the bishop's bridge, then built a new one three and a half miles upstream at a tiny settlement called Zu den Munichen—"At the Monks"—which surrounded the church of a few mendicant friars. Of course, he made his bridge, which connected the banks of the Isar via an island (now the site of the Deutsches Museum), into a major toll station.

Bishop Adalbert, who also happened to be the emperor's uncle, was furious, and pressured his nephew to do something about Henry's act of piracy. Barbarossa, who probably considered the whole matter a storm in a schnapps glass, was powerless to act, however, counting as he was on Henry's military aid in the next invasion of Italy. On June 14, 1158, during a session of the Reichstag in Augsburg, Barbarossa proposed the compromise that led to the official birth of Munich: Henry could keep his bridge and levy duty, but he would have to pay the bishop of Freising a third of the customs revenues he collected.

The new town prospered. Henry was less fortunate. In 1176, after having refused to help in yet another of Barbarossa's interminable campaigns against the Pope and the city-states of Italy, the cousins went to war against each other. Henry lost, was stripped not only of his Saxon but also his Bavarian holdings, and then was exiled to England. After a period of penance, he returned to German soil as ruler of the insignificant, pocket-size duchy of Braunschweig. Four years later, in 1180, Barbarossa deeded Bavaria to Count Otto von Wittelsbach, a minor nobleman, whose descendants were to rule it as dukes, electors, and finally kings for more than 700 years. Munich became their capital in 1255.

To be sure, the Wittelsbachs quarreled a great deal among themselves. But no other dynasty in Europe ruled as long, gave its realm as great a sense of identity, or left as indelible an imprint on its capital. Granted, some of them were downright eccentric, and all were unusual in one sense: Unlike the Hapsburgs of Austria or the Hohenzollerns of Prussia, the Wittelsbachs were more drawn to the fine arts than the art of war. It was they who laid the foundations of Munich's magnificent art collections; they who patronized musicians from Orlando di Lasso to Richard Wagner; and they who created the city's splendid parks, subsidized its great libraries and educational institutions, and created a fertile environment for writers, thinkers, and scientists.

At the same time, nearly all the Wittelsbachs were dogged builders who left monuments and boulevards, theaters and museums, and castles and palaces. Among the latter are the Residenz, the "winter palace," in the center of the city; Schloss Nymphenburg, one of Germany's most dazzling Baroque-Rococo digs; and the Alte and Neue Schlösser at Schleissheim, built as additional summer retreats in the 17th and 18th centuries respectively. The greatest builder of them all—if you exclude his grandson King Ludwig II, who put up all those fairy-tale castles in the Alps south of Munich—was Ludwig I.

Ludwig reigned from 1825 to 1848, when, at the age of 62, he was forced to abdicate in favor of his son Maximilian II because of his scandalous love affair with the Irish dancer Lola Montez. He was both a Germanophile (at a time when a united Germany was but a distant dream) and a Grecophile (at a time when Greece was still under the yoke of the Ottoman Turks). Well before taking the throne he had vowed to make Munich a stately metropolis that would "do honor to all Germany" and become a "new Athens, a center of learning and culture." In order to carry out his vow he retained the services of two of the greatest architects of his time, Leo von Klenze and Friedrich von Gärtner, as well as the sculptor Ludwig Schwanthaler and the Nazarene painter Peter Cornelius. Subsequent Wittelsbachs also contributed lavishly to this dream, especially Maximilian II and a nephew, Prince Regent Luitpold, who reigned from 1886 to 1912.

## THE INNENSTADT

What Müncheners call the Innenstadt (Inner City) is an oval-shaped district about a mile by half a mile on the left (west) bank of the Isar river, which flows into the Danube near Deggendorf. It is belted by a piece of postwar madness called the *Altstadtring,* a four- to six-lane superhighway on which traffic is usually choked to a standstill. The ring more or less follows the city's Medieval fortifications, all of which, with the exception of three town gates—the Isartor, Send-linger Tor, and Karlstor—were razed in the late 18th and early 19th centuries. The Innenstadt can easily be explored on foot. In fact, there is no other option, as most of the area has been turned into a pedestrian zone.

Marienplatz is the Innenstadt's—and Munich's—epicenter.

## The Marienplatz

*Marienplatz* means "St. Mary's Square"—a name that this plaza, which has been the political, social, and commercial heart of Munich since the 13th century, has borne only since 1854. The renaming of the square was a belated tribute to the gilded bronze figure of Mary, Bavaria's patron saint, which had stood atop a red marble Corinthian column in the middle of the square since 1638—and was also a public prayer that the city fathers hoped would spare Munich from a cholera epidemic. (Before that it had been called Schrannenplatz—Grain Market Square.)

Over the centuries the square has been the site of festivals, imperial receptions, ducal weddings, political rallies, public executions, riots, rebellions, revolutions, and mayhem.

The biggest bash on the Marienplatz was the eight-day celebration of the marriage of Duke Wilhelm V to Renate of Lorraine in 1586, a party that cost millions and that brought the crowned heads of Europe to Munich as wedding guests. In 1683, as a gesture of gratitude for the end of the plague, the plaza was the scene of the first *Schäfflertanz* (Dance of the Coopers), a colorful folk ritual that the members of the barrelmakers' guild continue to stage every seven years in accordance with their 300-year-old pledge.

And then there was the "invention" of the *Weisswurst,* a deed ascribed to Sepp Moser, butcher and then keeper of the Marienplatz inn called the Tavern to the Eternal Light, now the **Peterhof**. On the morning of February 22, 1857, so the story goes, Moser went into his kitchen to make the day's usual batch of *Bratwürste*. He proceeded to reach for the wrong spice containers, ground up more veal than pork, miscalculated a few other ingredients, and overcooked the whole forcemeat mixture, thus accidentally coming up with a new sausage concoction. When he realized what he had done, Moser was horrified. Fearing the sausages would taste terrible, he decided to steam them in a tureen rather than broil them over charcoal. His guests were delighted, and news of the new delicacy spread through town within hours, winning Moser the eternal gratitude of sausage lovers everywhere. Today, though hundreds of Munich inns, restaurants, and butcher shops serve and sell Weisswürste, those at the Peterhof are still the best.

The Marienplatz is still where everything happens. When cars were banned and the maze of streetcar tracks removed from the inner city in 1971, the Marienplatz became the underground transportation hub of Munich, with two subway and seven interurban rapid train lines intersecting on three subterranean levels. Above ground it is the focal point of the city's shopping district, with a dizzying rush of humanity hurrying into stores and dashing into the streets that radiate from it.

The scene changes with the seasons. In balmy weather street musicians perform, agitators orate, Müncheners quaff beer and wolf down Weisswürste or creamy pastries at the many sidewalk restaurants and cafés, and foot-weary shoppers relax on chairs scattered among the planter boxes. From late November through December the plaza overflows with Christmas Market stalls selling handicrafts, toys, tree ornaments, and a cornucopia of traditional snacks and sweets, including sugar-coated toasted almonds, fruitcakes, gingerbread cookies, smoked meats and hams, and *Glüh-wein,* a spiced red wine served piping hot.

The Marienplatz is also the political and administrative heart of Munich, where election campaigns climax, demonstrations are staged, and the burgomaster and city councilors preside. The latter conduct business in the Neues Rathaus

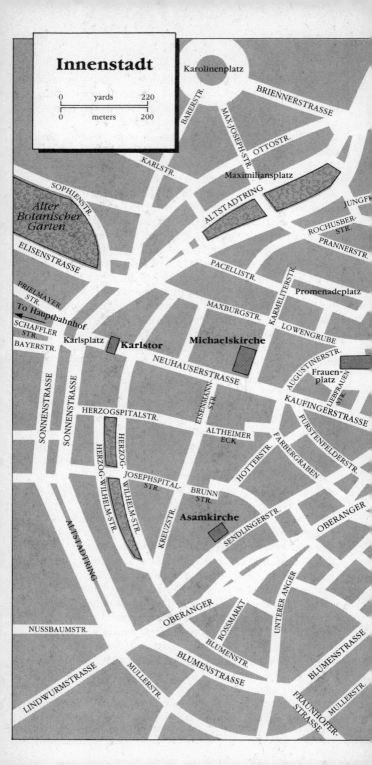

# Innenstadt

| 0 | yards | 220 |
| 0 | meters | 200 |

Karolinenplatz

BRIENNERSTRASSE

BAKERSTR.

MAX-JOSEPH-STR.

OTTOSTR.

KARLSTR.

Maximiliansplatz

SOPHIENSTR.

*Alter Botanischer Garten*

ALTSTADTRING

JUNGF

ELISENSTRASSE

ROCHUSBER-STR.

PRANNERSTR.

PACELLISTR.

KARMELITERSTR.

Promenadeplatz

PRIELMAYER STR.

To Hauptbahnhof

MAXBURGSTR.

LOWENGRUBE

SCHAFFLER STR.

BAYERSTR.

Karlsplatz

**Karlstor**

**Michaelskirche**

AUGUSTINERSTR.

Frauen-platz

NEUHAUSERSTRASSE

EISENMANN-STR.

LIEBFRAUEN STR.

KAUFINGERSTRASSE

SONNENSTRASSE

SONNENSTRASSE

HERZOGSPITALSTR.

ALTHEIMER ECK

FÜRSTENFELDERSTR.

HOTTERSTR.

FARBERGRABEN

HERZOG-WILHELM-STR.

HERZOG-WILHELM-STR.

JOSEPHSPITAL-STR.

BRUNN STR.

**Asamkirche**

SENDLINGERSTR.

OBERANGER

KREUZSTR.

ALTSTADTRING

NUSSBAUMSTR.

OBERANGER

ROSSMARKT

UNTERER ANGER

BLUMENSTRASSE

BLUMENSTR.

BLUMENSTR.

BLUMENSTRASSE

LINDWURMSTRASSE

MULLERSTR.

MULLERSTR.

FRAUNHOFER-STRASSE

(New City Hall) the largest building on the square. It looks old, but don't let the gargoyles and stone demons, statues of Guelph and Wittelsbach rulers, and filigreed façade fool you: This is a neo-Gothic structure, built in three stages between 1867 and 1909 after the Altes Rathaus (Old City Hall), off to the right at the plaza's eastern end, had become too small. The **Altes Rathaus** was built in the 15th century, but was almost totally destroyed during World War II. The building, with its elaborate Gothic council chamber, was reconstructed in the 1950s. The adjacent tower, on the other hand, is a 1974 replica of the late-15th-century original, which had to be razed after the air raids for safety reasons.

If all those shops along the ground-floor façade of the Neues Rathaus, including the city's oldest and priciest sporting-goods store at the corner, seem oddly out of place, chalk it up to Henry the Lion, who initiated the symbiosis of politics and commerce in Munich.

The best show on the Marienplatz—11:00 A.M. and 9:00 P.M. daily, as well as noon and 5:00 P.M. during the high season and pre-Christmas month—is the 43-bell glockenspiel on the 280-foot central spire of the Neues Rathaus. The brightly painted mechanical figures re-enact two of the most famous pageants from Munich history: the knights' tournament during the 1586 wedding feast of Wilhelm V and Renate of Lorraine and, on the level below, the Coopers' Dance. An elevator will take you to the spire's first balustrade, above the carillon, and stairs lead to the second and third tiers over that. From each tier the view of central Munich can be spectacular.

For an even loftier view—303 feet high—try the Alter Peter, the spire of the **Peterskirche**, which rises just south of the Marienplatz. St. Peter's is Munich's oldest church, older indeed than the city itself. Excavations during its postwar reconstruction—like everything else in the Innenstadt it was then a bomb-gutted ruin—turned up the foundations of an 11th-century Romanesque basilica that was probably the monastery church of the Benedictines for whose abbey the original settlement was named. That church was replaced in the late 13th century by a Gothic building, which was, in turn, destroyed by fire in 1327 and reconsecrated in its present, larger form in 1368. The spire is just as old. Virtually all of the leading artists and artisans who worked in Munich from the 15th through 18th centuries contributed to the interior furnishing and decoration of St. Peter's, among them the wood carver Erasmus Grasser, the painter Jan Polack, the sculptor and stucco master Egid Quirin Asam, the architect Andreas Faistenberger, and the muralist Johann Baptist Zimmermann.

A stroll down either side of the Petersplatz, the square on which St. Peter's is situated, will lead you directly from the heart of Munich to its belly, the Viktualienmarkt.

## The Viktualienmarkt

For Thomas Wolfe, Munich was not only a kind of German heaven, a "Germanic dream translated into life," but "an enchanted land where one ate and drank forever . . . a city fairly groaning with little fat, luxurious food, pastry or sweet shops." It still does, and the best action is in the Viktualienmarkt.

Located on the square of the same name, the Viktualienmarkt has been serving Müncheners for more than 180 years. Picture two dozen butcher shops, five cheese sellers (including one who offers a choice of 350 varieties), a whole section of bakeries (each stocked with dozens of kinds of Bavarian breads and rolls made fresh several times a day), fishmongers, wine merchants, and a virtual sea of produce stalls—each more tempting and colorful than the next and all of it squeezed into an area the size of a city block. Farmers come in very early with produce, poultry, eggs, and flowers, and most of the permanent stands open for business at 6:00 A.M. (which is also when the chefs of Munich's finest restaurants arrive to do their shopping) and stay open until 6:00 P.M. weekdays, 1:00 P.M. Saturday. The vegetables here are always the best in town, and several stalls feature only herbs. One sells only potatoes—dozens of different kinds. Another features honeys from all over the world.

While you need facility in neither German nor Bavarian to enjoy the Viktualienmarkt, it helps to remember two points. Don't touch the merchandise until it's yours. Feeling tomatoes for ripeness or lettuce for firmness is a mortal insult as well as a violation of German food laws. Moreover, unlike other open-air markets, the Viktualienmarkt is not the place to try out your bargaining skills. On the contrary, prices are equal to, sometimes even higher than, those at the finest gourmet emporiums. Quality is what counts here, and you'll pay accordingly.

## Munich's Major Churches

In addition to St. Peter's, Munich's four other major churches—the Frauenkirche, Michaelskirche, Asamkirche, and Theatinerkirche—are all within a few minutes' walk of the Marienplatz.

From the square it is about 250 yards down the **Kaufinger- strasse**, the main shopping mall, to the Liebfrauenstrasse and the **Frauenkirche**, officially known as Domkirche zu Unserer Lieben Frau, Munich's cathedral. Its 325-foot twin towers, each topped with an onion dome, are *the* landmark of the city.

This huge 15th-century Gothic structure, more than 300 feet long and 132 feet wide, is austere on the outside—a striking contrast to the rich façades of downtown Munich. Despite losses and thefts over the centuries the interior furnishings still include some major art treasures, among them the 15th- to 16th-century stained-glass windows of the chancel, the carved figures of Erasmus Grasser on the choir stalls, and the tomb of Ludwig the Bavarian, one of two Wittelsbachs elected Holy Roman Emperor.

From the Liebfrauenstrasse it is a couple hundred yards more along the Kaufingerstrasse to the Neuhauser Strasse and the **Michaelskirche**, the Jesuit Church of St. Michael, built in the late 16th century as a spiritual center of the Counter Reformation by Duke Wilhelm V of wedding feast and glock- enspiel fame. Like most of the Wittelsbachs, he thought in grand terms and was a builder on an even grander scale.

For St. Michael's, which Wilhelm V commissioned in the 1580s, he hired architects, artisans, and artists from Italy and the Netherlands. When a tower collapsed during the work in 1590, damaging much of the building and destroying the finished choir area, he saw it as a sign from the Archangel Michael to expand the project and build an even larger tower, which was completed in 1597. Wilhelm V's building boom took its toll on Bavaria's treasury, however, and brought the duchy to the brink of bankruptcy, forcing the duke to abdicate in favor of his son. Undeterred, he paid for completion of the Michaelskirche out of his own pocket.

Lavish in its exterior embellishment and interior furnish- ings, St. Michael's ranks as the prototype of Renaissance ecclesiastical architecture in southern Germany. It is also one of the churches where the Wittelsbachs are buried. The elaborate tombs and sarcophagi of 30 Bavarian rulers (Wil- helm V included) are in the Fürstengruft (Princes' Crypt) under the choir.

From the Marienplatz, another busy shopping street, the **Sendlinger Strasse**, leads to the **Asamkirche**. Its official name is Kirche St. Johann Nepomuk—church of St. John of Nepo- muk, the patron saint of Bohemia, who was tortured and

drowned in Prague in 1393 on orders of King Wenceslaus IV,
allegedly for refusing to disclose the queen's confessional
secrets. But Asamkirche is the Munich name, and it will do,
because the brothers Egid Quirin and Cosmas Damian Asam
built it for themselves.

Born in the latter stages of the 17th century, the Asams
were multitalented men who left their imprint—churches,
chapels, monasteries, palaces, mansions—all over Bavaria,
as well as Bohemia, Swabia, Switzerland, and the Tyrol.
Cosmas, the elder of the two, was a painter and muralist;
Egid was a sculptor and stucco master. Both were also
architects. After studying in Rome, where they were much
influenced by Bernini, they were instrumental in bringing
the Italian Late Baroque style north of the Alps, where they
developed it into a trademark style that was opulent in its
use of color, and perfect in its structural harmony.

In 1733 the brothers bought two adjacent lots on the
Sendlinger Strasse. On one they built a town house (the
Asamhaus) to serve as a studio and workshop, and on the
other the small church dedicated to St. John of Nepomuk.
They paid for the latter themselves in order to implement
their artistic and architectural concepts unhampered by the
wishes or strictures of a patron. Cosmas died in 1739,
seven years before the church was finished, so Egid gets
most of the credit. The Asamkirche is a dazzle of ecclesiastical theater, with silky blue-and-gold draperies of stucco,
walls with red stucco marble, and a profusion of medallions, cupids, elaborate columns, and porticos.

The Theatinerkirche lies in the opposite direction, north of
the Marienplatz via the Weinstrasse, which changes its name
to the Theatinerstrasse. As you stroll along these two streets—
now pedestrian zones lined by pricey stores—you may want
to visit a current exhibition at the **Hypo-Kunsthalle**, the newest addition to Munich's vibrant art scene. Sponsored by a
bank, it hosts a variety of visiting exhibitions—including
recent theme shows such as "Egyptian Art in Cleopatra's
Time" and retrospectives of the work of Magritte, Léger, and
Egon Schiele.

The saffron-yellow **Theatinerkirche**—its official name is
St. Cajetan's—is visible from miles around thanks to its two
elegant towers and immense central dome. To call it Italianate is an understatement: not only was it commissioned
by an Italian princess, who donated it to the Theatines, a
community of priests founded by the Italian churchman and
reformer Saint Cajetan, it is also the work of Italian architects, artisans, and artists.

Its story begins with the marriage in 1650 of Duke Ferdinand Maria, grandson of Wilhelm V and the second Wittelsbach to hold the title of elector of the Holy Roman Empire, to Princess Henrietta Adelaide of Savoy. When, in 1662 Adelaide fulfilled the duke's most fervent hope, providing him with an heir, the happy couple gave thanks by commissioning the church.

Adelaide hired the Bolognese architect Agostino Barelli for the church and Nicolo Petri of Como to build the adjacent Theatine abbey, which has served as a Dominican monastery since its postwar reconstruction. Barelli designed a building reminiscent of Rome's San Andrea della Valle, the mother church of the Theatine order, and construction began in 1663. He and the impetuous duchess had a falling out, however, and in 1669 he was replaced by Enrico Zucalli, a Swiss from the Grissons, who changed the plans by adding the 230-foot central dome and the two spires that emulate those of the church of Santa Maria della Salute in Venice. By 1688—twelve years after Adelaide's death and nine years after Ferdinand Maria's—St. Cajetan's was more or less completed—"more or less" because the façades were still bare and just roughly plastered over. It took another foreigner, François Cuvilliés, and some 80 years to solve that problem; the Frenchman added the Rococo embellishments and structural elements the visitor sees today. Despite the various architects who had a hand, the Theatinerkirche is enticingly harmonious, and one of the city's architectural jewels.

Like St. Michael's, it is also a burial church for Wittelsbachs. Among those interred in its royal crypt are Adelaide and Ferdinand Maria and their son Maximilian Emmanuel.

## The Hofbräuhaus

No foreigner was a more literate connoisseur of Munich beer than Thomas Wolfe, In fact, the American glowingly wrote that "the best beer in Germany, in the world, is made in Munich"—despite getting clobbered with a one-liter stein during a brawl at the 1925 Oktoberfest.

Today, the most renowned beer cellar in Munich is the Hofbräuhaus, located on a little square called Am Platzl, only three minutes' walk northeast of the Marienplatz. The Hofbräuhaus (Court Brewery) is more than just a beer hall, however. It is an institution—and one that is immortalized in history, legend, and raucous drinking songs. Again it is Duke Wilhelm V who gets the credit. In 1589 the duke decided to build *ein aigen Preuhaus* (a personal brewing house) in order to halt expensive imports of "foreign" beer, meaning from Einbeck, 400 miles north of Munich. Though it took until 1613 for Munich brewmasters to get the knack of making the light, golden Einbeck suds (from which, incidentally, the name "bock beer" derives), the original Hofbräuhaus started operating in 1592.

The present building, in place since 1644, was extensively reconstructed in 1896. Beer has actually not been produced on the premises since 1890, when a huge new brewery opened on the right bank of the Isar in the Haidhausen district. But otherwise little has changed, especially the fact that Müncheners still regard beer as a food, not a beverage, and it must be made in strict accordance with the pure-food laws promulgated in 1516 by Wilhelm V's grandfather, Duke Wilhelm IV.

History has been written here as well. It was in the Hofbräuhaus in 1844, that King Ludwig I first encountered the public disenchantment with his reign, a sentiment that culminated in his abdication four years later; he had raised the price of a *Mass*—a liter of beer—from 6 to 6.5 kroner. And it was in the Festsaal, the ballroom, on February 24, 1920, that Adolf Hitler, then a little-known political agitator who only a few months earlier had joined an obscure radical party, delivered his first speech to a large audience. Political speeches and rallies are still held in the Hofbräuhaus, as they are in the ballrooms of Munich's other big brewery-connected beer halls, such as the Löwenbräukeller on the Stiglmaierplatz.

Although the Hofbräuhaus has various side rooms and upstairs dining chambers where solid Bavarian food at moderate prices is dished out in relatively quiet, rustic surroundings, the real action and local color are concentrated in the cavernous street-level *Schwemme* (Trough), with its rows of long wooden tables, rough benches, oompah-pah band, and assemblage of bearded lederhosen-garbed regulars who arrive for their breakfast suds when the place opens at 9:00 A.M., and often remain all day. The noise is usually deafening—never more so than when imbibers, many of whom seem to be non-Bavarians and non-Müncheners, rise up to belt out drinking songs. The liter-size steins—a *Mass* actually means a "measure"—seem at first awesomely daunting, but rare is the first-time visitor who doesn't down one to the last drop.

# The Maximilianstrasse

Given their proclivity for seeking immortality in stone, it should come as no surprise that the Wittelsbachs commissioned entire avenues and boulevards. Thus there is Ludwig I's Ludwigstrasse and Prince Regent Luitpold's Prinzregentenstrasse. King Maximilian II, Ludwig I's son, who reigned from 1848 to 1864, is commemorated by the Maximilianstrasse, which starts two blocks north of the Marienplatz and runs in a straight line east for nearly 2 km (1.2 miles), crossing the Isar by way of the graceful Maximiliansbrücke and continuing up the verdant hill of the river's right bank to the Maximilianeum, a neo-Renaissance structure originally built as a picture gallery and boarding school for gifted offspring of the nobility, and now the Bavarian state parliament building.

Maximilian II, who became king in 1848, began making plans for the street as early as 1832, when he was merely the 21-year-old crown prince. A romanticist of the first order, he envisioned a boulevard lined by a mix of government buildings, private homes, hotels, and shops that would connect the inner city and the Residenz (the Royal Palace) with Munich's outlying districts on the Isar's right bank. The resulting style combines elements of English and Flemish Gothic Revival with Italian Late Renaissance and the odd bit of eclecticism. Whatever its provenance, however, it would be hard to find another avenue of comparable length anywhere in Europe with such stylistic unity. Undoubtedly, this unity owes much to the brevity of its construction period, which began in 1854 and was more or less over by 1875. (Though there were some later additions, all are reasonably faithful to the original concept.)

In fact, the only blemish on this masterpiece of 19th-century urban planning was a postwar abomination—the six-lane Altstadtring, which intersects the avenue at midpoint and destroyed the original "Roman Forum" arrangement there. Müncheners began howling about this disruption of the Maximilianstrasse's architectural unity as soon as the deed was done in 1969, and finally won a small victory by getting the highway reduced to four lanes in 1984. Still, the Altstadtring is a classic example of the way in which possibly more damage was done to Germany's architectural heritage by postwar "urban renewal" than by wartime air raids. (Rather miraculously, very few buildings along the Maximilianstrasse were bombed beyond repair during World War II.

To this day, unfortunately, some gaps remain, filled by temporary one-story shops.)

As soon as the street had begun taking shape in the 1850s
it became popular among actors, artists, and authors. Henrik
Ibsen had an apartment at Maximilianstrasse 32, and was
seen every afternoon at the Café Maximilian, meeting place
of Munich's literati, where he had a permanently reserved
marble table on which a stein of beer and a glass of cognac
awaited him as he entered.

From early on it was also a street of playhouses (*Hedda
Gabler* had its world premiere at the Residenz-theater in
January of 1891), and still is: the Kammerspiele, Kleine
Komödie am Max II Denkmal, and Theater Kleine Freiheit
make it a kind of off-off-Broadway. Museums, too, are part of
the scene: the **Museum für Völkerkunde** (Ethnology Museum) at Maximilianstrasse 42, and the recently opened
**Jüdisches Museum** (Jewish Museum), at Maximilianstrasse
36 (Open Thursday and Friday, 2:00 to 6:00 P.M., Saturday
from 10:00 A.M. to 2:00 P.M.)

Ever since the 1857 opening of the luxurious **Hotel Vier
Jahreszeiten** at number 17, the Maximilianstrasse has also
been a boulevard favored by the rich and powerful. Over
the nearly 140 years that the "Four Seasons" has been Munich's classiest address, this often renovated and enlarged
grand hotel has been home away from home to hundreds of
globe-trotting VIPs and royalty, among them the king of
Siam, who arrived in July of 1934 with 1,320 pieces of
luggage.

The Maximilianstrasse is a kind of "miracle mile", lined
with the top names in fashion, jewelry, leather goods, footwear, and furnishings, all of it further proof that Munich has
more money looking to be spent—and places to spend it—
than any other city in Germany. It is also the home of more
than two dozen commercial galleries, most of them dealing
in modern and contemporary work.

## The Nationaltheater

Maximilian I, the first Wittelsbach king, was a Francophile
who allied himself with Napoleon, who elevated the duchy
of Bavaria to a kingdom. Though their partnership resulted
in a doubling of Bavaria's size, it also cost Bavaria the lives of
30,000 of its finest men in Napoleon's ill-fated Russian campaign. Shortly before that disaster Maximilian I had visited
Paris and been greatly impressed with the Théâtre de

l'Odéon, and he returned home eager to have a similar drama and opera house in Munich.

As the site for what is today called the Nationaltheater, the home of the Bayerische Staatsoper (Bavarian State Opera), he selected a plot adjacent to the royal Residenz (see below) at what is now the beginning of the Maximilianstrasse. Work on this huge Neoclassical temple of the performing arts began in 1811 and was completed in 1818. Twice destroyed—by a fire in 1823 and an air raid in 1943—and each time rebuilt exactly as before, it was and still is one of the largest opera houses in Europe. It was here, for example, that Richard Wagner, lavishly subsidized by Ludwig II, staged the world premieres of *Tristan und Isolde, Die Meistersinger von Nürnberg, Das Rheingold,* and *Die Walküre,* as well as where some of the greatest conductors of the 20th century, among them Bruno Walter, Hans Knappertsbusch, Joseph Keilberth, Sir Georg Solti, and Karl Böhm, have worked as musical directors and general managers.

If you are in Munich during the season—year round except for a six-week break in August and September—a night at the opera is a must, and not just for the performance or a glimpse of the ornate marble foyers and the red-and-gold auditorium with its statuary and Corinthian columns. The audience can be just as entertaining, with the preferred attire ranging from white and black tie to lederhosen. Tickets are always hard to track down, however. For performances several days ahead they can be purchased at the Vorverkauf office in one of those single-story shops at Maximilianstrasse 11 (Tel: 22-13-16); open weekdays 10:00 A.M. to 1:00 P.M. and 3:30 to 5:30 P.M., Saturday from 10:00 to 12:30). The evening box office, on the Maximilianstrasse side of the theater itself, opens one hour before the curtain is raised, which can be at 7:00, 7:30, or 8:00 P.M., depending on the length of the opera.

# The Residenz

Though you wouldn't notice it today, given all its Renaissance, Baroque, Rococo, and Neoclassical additions, the Residenz, Munich's sprawling royal palace just north of the Max-Joseph-Platz, was actually begun in 1385 as a Gothic-style castle called the Neuveste (New Fortress). Until then the dukes had resided closer to the Marienplatz in the Alte Hof (Old Court), a Medieval structure of which little remains.

The reason for the 14th-century exodus from the Alte Hof was an uprising on the Marienplatz that culminated in the beheading of Hans Impler, a cloth merchant who was a friend of the ducal family and whom angry Müncheners wrongly accused of fraud. Figuring that the old digs were no longer safe for nobility, Duke Stephan III started construction of the Neuveste, a fortified palace a full third of a mile, quite a distance in the Middle Ages, from the town's unruly burghers.

By the mid-16th century the Neuveste was a walled and moated castle with practically impregnable defense towers, a ducal chapel, a knights' hall, residential apartments, servants' quarters, an apothecary, an alchemist laboratory, stables, and a central keep to which everyone could retreat. Then various Wittelsbachs began to commission additions to the castle in Renaissance style—a ballroom tract here, an Antiquarium to display Greek and Roman sculptures there, a palace for the crown prince, a mansion for ducal widows—and they continued adding on in various architectural styles until the entire complex had become the vast maze that it is today. One of the last additions was a huge winter garden, with a menagerie of parrots and peacocks, stuffed lions and carved marble elephants, Moorish fountains, opera house sets, and artificial lake—all of which King Ludwig II had installed on the roof of one of the buildings in 1865. The Neuveste itself, meanwhile, dwarfed and surrounded by the other structures and wings, fell victim to a fire in 1750 (and Ludwig's gaudy winter garden was destroyed by a bomb during World War II).

The Wittelsbachs did more than enlarge and embellish the palace, however; with the exception of Ludwig II, who preferred his fairy-tale castles in the Alps, all of them resided in and governed from the Residenz until November 7, 1918.

That was the day when thousands of Müncheners rallied on the Theresienwiese, site of the annual Oktoberfest, to demonstrate for peace and an end to World War I. The main speaker was Kurt Eisner, leader of the Independent Socialist Party. The demonstration was just about to culminate in a silent march through the city when one of Eisner's followers, brandishing a red flag, leaped on the platform and shouted, "Long live the Revolution!" Within a few hours Eisner's group had occupied the military and police barracks, the government ministries, and the Bavarian parliament building. There Eisner was proclaimed head of a workers' and soldiers' soviet and named himself provisional president and prime minister of the People's Republic of Bavaria. A few hours later, under cover of darkness, and without formally abdicating, 73-year-old Ludwig III, Bavaria's last king, fled the Residenz through a side entrance and headed, by car, into exile at his Berchtesgaden castle.

Ever since that revolution, the Residenz has harbored a potpourri of government offices, scientific institutions, theaters, concert halls, and museums. However, the museums require sturdy legs, comfortable shoes, and a strategy.

The **Residenzmuseum** itself comprises more or less the entire palace. Only portions of it are open at specific times: some sections in the morning, some in the afternoon, still others morning *and* afternoon. There are two tours, one in the morning (Tuesday through Saturday, 10:00 A.M. to 12:30 P.M.; Sunday until 1:00 P.M.), the other in the afternoon (Tuesday through Saturday, 12:30 to 4:30 P.M.; closed Sunday and Monday). Doing them both is a marathon that will take you through more than 120 richly appointed rooms, chambers, and halls spread over a dozen buildings and wings. The morning tour includes the **Antiquarium**, the largest secular Renaissance building north of the Alps, and one that is not only crammed with ancient sculpture but is still used for formal state occasions such as the Bavarian prime minister's New Year's reception for the press and banquets for foreign dignitaries; the **Porzellankammern**, which is filled with East Asian and 19th-century European china; and the opulent **Ahnengalerie** (Ancestors' Gallery), a collection of dozens of amusing portraits and Wittelsbach family trees framed by an overwhelming splash of gilded Rococo stuccowork. Among the sights on the afternoon tour are the throne room and the spectacular apartments of Ludwig I and his queen, as well as more than a dozen chambers filled with 18th-century porcelain.

The **Schatzkammer** (Treasury) is a separate museum within the Residenz (Tuesday through Saturday, open 10:00 A.M. to 4:30 P.M., Sunday until 1:00 P.M.). Its ten rooms harbor the dazzling collection of jewelry, gold and silver artifacts, and crystal bibelots amassed by the Wittelsbachs over a period of a thousand years, including the royal insignia and crown jewels. The standouts in this collection are a miniature golden ciborium made around 890 for the Frankish King Arnulf, an 11th-century gold crucifix, the 11th-century crown of the Holy Roman Empress Kunigunde, and a 16th-century reliquary on which a bejeweled St. George slays a ruby-encrusted dragon.

The **Staatliche Münzsammlung** (State Numismatic Collection), to which the entrance is not from the Max-Joseph-Platz but at Residenzstrasse 1, is open daily except Monday. The collection, begun by Duke Albrecht V, the father of Wilhelm

V and builder of the Antiquarium, contains more than 250,000 coins and medallions, from Roman times to the present.

The **Altes Residenztheater**, popularly called the Cuvilliés-Theater (open Monday through Saturday, 2:00 to 5:00 P.M.; Sunday, 10:00 A.M. to 5:00 P.M.; entrance also by way of the Residenzstrasse 1 portal), is not truly a museum, as it is used regularly for concerts, plays, and chamber opera performances. But don't let a semantic technicality deter you. Designed by François de Cuvilliés in 1750 and opened in 1753, it is the epitome of the floriated, gilded, cupid-rich Rococo style. Seeing it is one thing, but nothing equals sitting in it for an evening performance of, say, Mozart's *Marriage of Figaro*.

The **Staatliche Sammlung Egyptischer Kunst** (State Collection of Egyptian Art) is accessible from the Hofgarten (Palace Garden) side of the Residenz at Hofgartenstrasse 1 (open Tuesday through Sunday, 9:30 A.M. to 4:00 P.M., and Tuesday evening from 7:00 to 9:00). It contains a rich yield from the tombs of the pharaohs as well as some gems of Assyrian and Egyptian craftsmanship, covering the spectrum from shipbuilding to weaving.

# OUTSIDE THE ALTSTADTRING

Vexing as the Altstadtring may be, it has the advantage of compartmentalizing the inner city, making it easy to explore. But what lies beyond it in all directions is of no less importance to appreciating Munich.

## Ludwigstrasse

Ludwig I's dream of making Munich a world capital and the "new Athens" is expressed in the grand boulevard that bears his name and connects the Innenstadt with the former suburb of Schwabing to the north. Straight as a ruler, exactly one kilometer long, and grandiosely wide, it begins with the Feldherrnhalle on the Odeonsplatz, at the northwestern corner of the Residenz, and culminates in the triumphal arch of the Siegestor. Construction began in 1817 under the supervision of Ludwig I's then-favorite architect, Leo von Klenze, and was completed by Klenze's rival and successor, Friedrich von Gärtner, in 1850.

Ludwig supervised much of the work, often badgering Klenze and Gärtner about the slightest deviation from his original concept, and issued his instructions not from the Residenz but from the scaffolding erected at the various construction sites, where laborers referred to him as *der königliche Oberpalier,* the royal foreman. From the time work started on his boulevard until his coronation in 1825, it was his private enterprise—and became so again after his abdication in 1848, when he financed the rest of the project out of his own pocket (and reaped a tidy profit from property sales and rentals).

When he and Klenze first started planning the boulevard in 1816 they were of one mind. Both, after all, were Greco-Roman buffs—Ludwig so much so that in 1833 he dispatched his younger son, Otto, then 18, to Athens to become the first modern king of Greece. Given their tastes, Ludwig and Klenze envisioned an avenue in Neoclassical style. By the late 1820s and early 1830s, however, Ludwig had become enamored of the neo-Romanesque, neo-Renaissance, and Italianate fashion sweeping Europe—a style Klenze abhorred. As a result, Ludwig turned more and more to Gärtner, who in turn imparted the cold and haunting look that the upper end of Ludwigstrasse has to this day.

The most obvious monument between the Residenz and the Theatinerkirche, right where the Residenzstrasse and the Theatinerstrasse merge to become the Odeonsplatz, is the **Feldherrnhalle** (Hall of the Field Marshals). Begun in 1841, the Feldherrnhalle was completed in 1844.

The bronze field marshals who stand in it are Count Johannes von Tilly, the bloodthirsty but luckless Bavarian hero of the Thirty Years War, and Karl Philipp von Wrede, the general who led the Bavarian corps that aided Napoleon's victory at Wagram in 1809 and later accompanied Bonaparte's Grande Armée into Russia but who, just before the 1813 "Battle of the Nations" at Leipzig, turned against Napoleon and joined the allies. The bronze memorial between and behind the two is supposed to honor the Bavarian army for its role—actually small—during the Franco-Prussian War of 1870–71.

The Feldherrnhalle was also where Hitler's "Beerhall Putsch," his first grab for power, ended in a bloodbath on November 9, 1923. The previous evening he and his armed followers had attempted, and failed, to topple the Bavarian government by taking hostage its key officials, who were attending a political rally at the Bürgerbräukeller, a beer hall in Haidhausen on the Isar's right bank. Shortly before noon the next day, Hitler and his closest aides led their ragtag army of 3,000 storm troopers on a demonstration march through the Innenstadt. When they reached the Feldherrnhalle and the Odeonsplatz they were stopped by a company of state police. After a wild, one-minute gun fight, 14 Nazis and four policemen lay dead or dying on the square, and scores of others were critically wounded. Hitler was subsequently imprisoned at Landsberg Fortress, where he wrote his blueprint for world conquest, *Mein Kampf.*

During the 12 years of the Third Reich the Nazis annually reenacted the march, and the Feldherrnhalle became a temple of Nazi martyrdom. A bronze plaque on its Residenzstrasse side, guarded round the clock by two black-uniformed SS men, commemorated the putsch, and everyone who passed by had to stop and salute. Those Müncheners who opposed the Führer would make a detour behind the Feldherrnhalle by dashing from the Residenzstrasse to the Theatinerstrasse via narrow little Viscardigasse, which soon became known as the Drückebergergasse—"Bugout Alley."

The vicissitudes of history are also embodied in the monument at the Ludwigstrasse's northern end, the **Siegestor** (Victory Gate). A triumphal arch, it was begun in 1843 to honor the Bavarian army's role during the "Wars of Liberation" against Napoleon. Badly damaged during World War II but rebuilt, the inscription on it now reads *Dem Sieg geweiht, im Krieg zerstört, zum Frieden mahnend*—"Dedicated to victory, destroyed in war, an admonishment to peace."

Ludwig's avenue of government, learning, and banking is still evident between the two monuments. Since Bavaria no longer has its own army, the former war ministry building at Ludwigstrasse 14 is now the Bavarian state archives. The ministry of agriculture occupies the building at number 2, and on the Odeonsplatz are the ministries of interior (number 3) and finance (number 4). Gärtner's **Bayerische Staatsbibliothek** (Bavarian State Library), one of the world's largest with 5.5 million volumes, is at number 16. The four seated figures on its steps are Aristotle, Hippocrates, Homer, and Thucydides. The Ludwigskirche (church of Saint Louis), at number 20, an eclectic Romantic-Christian-Italian-style building, was Gärtner's first effort on the boulevard, and was begun in 1829 and completed in 1844. His contributions to **Munich Universität**, formally called Ludwig-Maximilian-Universität, Germany's largest with 65,000 students, flank both sides of the street. The forumlike circle between them is now called Geschwister-Scholl-Platz, in honor of Hans and Sophie Scholl, the brother and sister who, as students in 1943, launched the anti-Nazi resistance group called the "White Rose." (They were later executed at Munich's Stadelheim prison.)

# Königsplatz and the Museums

Munich's Königsplatz (King's Plaza), a mile-long walk straight down the Brienner Strasse northwest from the Odeonsplatz, is the finest example of Leo von Klenze's talent for translating Greco-Roman dreams into reality.

The idea of creating a Bavarian Acropolis on what in those days was a virtual wasteland was germinated in 1808. Construction began in 1816 with the laying of the cornerstone for the templelike Glyptothek, which was intended to house the collection of Greek and Roman sculpture that Ludwig I was amassing. That marble building, with its Ionic columns, was completed in 1830, and was merely the beginning. Across from it Ludwig wanted an exhibition hall in Roman style with Corinthian columns, which now houses the Staatliche Antikensammlung (State Collection of Antiquities). Then Klenze proposed closing off the area at its far end with a huge Propylaeum. In all, work on the complex went on for more than 45 years. When it was completed, Ludwig I had one more brilliant thought: With the exception of a cobblestone main street through the plaza, the rest of the area would remain covered with grass in order to create an urban version of the Elysian Fields.

So it was until 1934, when Hitler decided that the Königsplatz was an ideal site for Nazi rallies. Out went the grass and in went slabs of stone, which gave the jackboots of marching storm troopers just the right resonance. One might have expected Müncheners to get rid of those stones as soon as they were rid of Hitler. But in the postwar years the Königsplatz was turned into Munich's largest parking lot. Given that no other German city has so many cars, resistance to relinquishing so convenient an area was great. Only in 1988 did traditionalists on the city council triumph, with the happy result that the Königsplatz, replete with replicas of 19th-century streetlamps, now looks almost as grassy as it did in the days of Ludwig I and Leo von Klenze.

It is unlikely, however, that two other nearby architectural relics of the Third Reich will ever disappear: Albert Speer's massively grim Führerbauten, the headquarters and administrative buildings of the Nazi party. While Speer, Hitler's architect and minister of armaments, built them to last the 1,000 years that the Führer envisioned for his new Reich, they now serve a useful, peaceful, and democratic purpose: The one on the Arcisstrasse is the state music conservatory; its horrid twin on the Meiserstrasse houses various institutes of the academy of art and departments of the ministry of culture.

The Königsplatz (the foot-weary will be happy to know there's a glossy U-Bahn station of the U-2 line right underneath it) is more than just a remarkable architectural ensemble. It is also the gateway to Munich's most rewarding museum area.

The **Glyptothek** (open Tuesday and Wednesday, and Friday through Sunday, 10:00 A.M. to 4:30 P.M.; Thursday, 12 noon to 8:30 P.M.) contains the Greek and Roman sculpture that Ludwig I assembled on his many buying sprees, plus much more that has been added since.

The **Antikensammlung**, across the Königsplatz at number 1 (open Tuesdays and Thursday through Sunday, 10:00 A.M. to 4:30 P.M.; Wednesday, noon to 8:30 P.M.), contains a wonderful collection of classical craftsmanship: Greek vases and pottery; Greek, Celtic, Etruscan, and Roman jewelry; glass, miniature sculptures, and applied art.

From the Königsplatz a walk of two blocks up the Arcisstrasse will take you to the Alte and Neue Pinakotheken.

The **Alte Pinakothek** (Old Picture Gallery), Barerstrasse 27 (open Tuesday through Sunday, 9:00 A.M. to 4:30 P.M.; Tuesday and Thursday, 7:00 to 9:00 P.M.), was designed by Klenze and opened in 1836. In addition to later purchases, donations, and permanent loans, it houses the entire collection of paintings amassed by various branches of the Wittelsbach family, starting with Duke Wilhelm IV, who began buying art in 1530.

Because of the building's comparatively small size, only a fraction of the collection can be shown at any one time. Still, that is usually an amazing display of hundreds of paintings, including Rubenses, Brueghels, van Dycks, Rembrandts, Dürers, Tintorettos, and Titians. While the Alte Pinakothek's reputation is based to a considerable extent on its early German masters, it is also a stunning repository of Flemish, Dutch, Italian, Spanish, and French painting. Moreover, if there was ever a museum where you can be sure of authenticity, this is it. Virtually every painting has an unbroken pedigree of ownership—the Wittelsbachs.

The **Neue Pinakothek** (New Picture Gallery), directly across the Barerstrasse at number 29 (open Tuesday through Sunday, 9:00 A.M. to 4:30 P.M.; Tuesday evening, 7:00 to 9:00) is so named because of what Ludwig I intended it to be: a gallery of "new" painting from his own era, the 19th century. The building, designed by Gärtner, was so badly damaged during World War II that it was razed in 1949. The collection (which begins with Goya and Jacques-Louis David) was placed in storage and shown in part elsewhere around town while a debate raged for decades over whether to build another Neue Pinakothek. The debate was finally settled in 1975 when ground was broken on the site of the old Neue Pinakothek and work began on the present building.

The collection includes works by some major French Impressionists, including Manet's *Breakfast in the Studio,* Monet's *The Bridge,* and Degas's *Laundry Girl,* as well as Daumiers, Courbets, van Goghs, Goyas, some fine Turners, and sculptures by Maillol and Rodin. The main body of the collection, however, is German, in particular work by Bavarian and Munich artists, including Arnold Böcklin, and Franz von Lenbach, whose luxurious villa (site of the next museum) is just three blocks away, virtually adjacent to the Königsplatz.

The **Städtische Galerie im Lenbachhaus** (Municipal Gallery in the Lenbach House), Luisenstrasse 33 (open Tuesday through Saturday, 10:00 A.M. to 6:00 P.M.), is what its name implies: a city-owned museum and collection. (All the others are owned and maintained by the Free State of Bavaria, legal heir to the Wittelsbach riches.) The sprawling Italian Renaissance–style villa was built by Franz von Lenbach in the late 1880s when he was at the height of his fame as the portrait painter of everybody who was anybody in imperial Germany, and at the zenith of his power as the virtual dictator of art in Munich. In effect, the "Lenbach Circle" determined what was painted and how until the "Munich Secession," led by another "painter-prince," Franz von Stuck, the self-anointed prophet of *Jugendstil,* the Austro-German form of Art Nouveau, came along. The city of Munich acquired the Lenbach mansion and private collection in 1929, 25 years after his death, and turned it into a museum.

The collection as a whole covers Munich and other German art from the 15th century to the present. Its high point is the huge lode of works by Kandinsky, Klee, Franz Marc, August Macke, Alexej von Jawlensky, Marianne von Werefkin, Alfred Kubin, and Gabriele Münter. Nearly all of these works were donated by Münter, Kandinsky's mistress and collaborator for most of the 20 years (1894–1914) that he lived and worked in Munich or the nearby mountain town of Murnau (see the Southern Bavaria chapter).

Munich was where Kandinsky began painting in the abstract, and where in 1910 he, Münter, Marc, Jawlensky,

Werefkin, Klee, and Kubin founded the Neues Künstlerver-
einigung (New Artists' Association), which was dedicated to
breaking with genre painting and Jugendstil, and launched
the almanac *Der Blaue Reiter* (Blue Rider), heralding an
entirely new international art movement and style. In 1957,
Gabriele Münter donated 90 Kandinsky oils, 300 of his
watercolors and drawings, 29 sketchbooks, and numerous
other works of the Blaue Reiter circle, including her own, to
the Lenbachhaus.

For an even more vivid and concrete view of modern
art—and what the Nazis thought of it—visit the Haus der
Kunst on the Prinzregentenstrasse.

# Prinzregentenstrasse

From the Odeonsplatz and the Feldherrnhalle it's a five-
minute walk east—more pleasant if you go through the
Hofgarten of the Residenz—to the start of the Prinzregentenstrasse (Prince Regent Street). This newest of Munich's
grand avenues, begun in 1891 and completed in 1907, was
named for Luitpold, who ruled Bavaria as prince regent
from 1886 to 1912, between the reigns of his nephew,
Ludwig II, and his son, Ludwig III. A wide tree-shaded
boulevard that runs east for nearly one and one-half miles
from the edge of the Hofgarten to the Bogenhausen district,
it is one of the city's many examples of Belle Epoque and
Jugendstil architecture.

The starting point is the Neoclassical **Prinz Carl Palais**,
which since 1807 has served variously as the home of
Wittelsbach scions, the Austrian embassy, a Third Reich
guesthouse, and, since 1972, as the official seat of Bavaria's
prime minister.

Diagonally across from it is the **Haus der Kunst** (open
Tuesday through Sunday, 9:00 A.M. to 4:30 P.M., Thursday
evening 7:00 to 9:00). This colonnaded gray stone building
at the southern end of the Englischer Garten is the first of
various architectural monstrosities Hitler bequeathed to Munich. Designed by Paul Ludwig Troost in what was then
called Germanic Tectonic (now known as Third Reich bombastic) style, it opened on July 18, 1937, as the Haus der
Deutschen Kunst (House of German Art)—a pantheon for
the propagandizing kitsch the Nazis endorsed. That inaugu-
ral show coincided with one in the nearby Hofgarten gallery
called *Entartete Kunst* (Degenerate Art): an exhibition of 600
masterworks of Expressionism, Cubism, Abstractionism, and
Surrealism (of the thousands that had just been confiscated

from museums and private collections all over Germany)
mounted with the object of deriding them.

Today the Haus der Kunst is the home of the **Staatsgalerie
Moderner Kunst**, which shows paintings and sculptures by
20th-century artists the Nazis hounded or banned, including
Max Beckmann, Oskar Schlemmer, and Joseph Beuys. The
building is also used for visiting exhibitions and antique
fairs. Moreover, it houses **Piroschka**, one of Munich's better
Hungarian restaurants, and the city's hottest, most fashionable discothèque, **P-1**—which makes it the world's only
major art museum where pictures vibrate nightly (except
Monday) to the din of disco music.

The **Bayerisches Nationalmuseum**, Prinzregentenstrasse 3
(open Tuesday through Sunday, 9:30 A.M. to 5:00 P.M.), is an
architectural Disneyland: The east wing is Romanesque, the
west wing Rococo, the façade Renaissance, the central tower
Baroque—and all of that "neo." Müncheners call it "Bavaria's
Attic," and you're never sure whether they mean it benignly
or scornfully. But what an attic! The vast collection of fifth-
through 19th-century painting, sculpture, wood carving,
stained glass, porcelain, ceramics, tapestries, jewelry, gold-
smithing, furniture, armor, ecclesiastical art, and folk handicrafts covers 140,000 square feet of exhibit space spread
over three floors. Among its highlights are the chamber with
Medieval ivory carvings, the gallery with works by Erasmus
Grasser, the room with Tilman Riemenschneider wood
sculptures, and the section of porcelain figures designed by
Franz Anton Bustelli. A separate wing houses the **Neue
Sammlung** (New Collection), the museum of applied art.

The **Schackgalerie**, Prinzregentenstrasse 9 (open Wednesday through Monday, 9:00 A.M. to 4:30 P.M.), located in what
used to be the Prussian embassy, is a small but well-
appointed gallery of 19th-century German Romantic and
genre painting.

If your feet don't go on strike, continue east across the Isar
by way of the Prinzregentenbrücke, around the *Friedensengel*
(Angel of Peace) monument, to the silk-stocking and carriage-
trade section of the Prinzregentenstrasse in **Bogenhausen**.

The four reclining figures on the bridge, a gift to Luitpold
on his 70th birthday in 1891, represent the tribal areas of the
Wittelsbach realm when it stretched across southern Germany from the Rhine to Bohemia. The Angel of Peace
ensemble, with its gilded figure of Winged Victory atop a
Corinthian column, fountain, graceful steps, terrace, and
loggias where lovers tryst on balmy evenings, is a contradic-
tion in terms: Its cornerstone was laid in 1896 to mark the

25th anniversary of Germany's triumph in the Franco-Prussian War, and its bas-relief portraits of various generals, the three kaisers, Otto von Bismarck, and, naturally, Luitpold, do little to enhance the message of peace. But as a Munich landmark and an example of iconographic 19th-century architecture, it's a joy.

The **Villa Stuck**, Prinzregentenstrasse 60 (open daily, 10:00 A.M. to 5:00 P.M., Thursday evening to 7:00), is proof that artistic rebellion pays. Franz von Stuck, the leader of the Munich Secession, was soon so successful that he could afford to build a house with studio every bit as grand as Franz von Lenbach's, *and* on a hill above the Isar from where he could look down on his rival. This Roman-style villa, with its exterior motifs borrowed from antiquity and its interior blend of Classical, Baroque, and pre-Raphaelite decor, is a perfect example of Jugendstil. Villa Stuck is also a museum of 19th- and 20th-century art, in addition to housing the showrooms of several commercial galleries and—of all things—one of Munich's three dozen Chinese restaurants.

You will find a symbol of what late-20th-century Munich is about—money and conspicuous consumption—at Prinzregentenstrasse 73, the home of **Käfer's**, a resplendent fine-food emporium boasting more than 15,000 of the best and most expensive comestibles, as well as its own restaurant. The ornate Art Nouveau building, brightly illumninated at night, is one of the avenue's architectural gems.

Another gem is the **Prinzregententheater**, Prinzregentenstrasse 82. Virtually a copy of the Wagner Festival theater in Bayreuth, it was built for festival purposes in 1901 despite strong protests by the composer's widow, Cosima, who was still angry at Munich for having snubbed her Richard following their scandalous liaison. Because the Nationaltheater on the Maximilianstrasse was a bombed-out ruin at the end of World War II, the Bavarian state opera used the undamaged Prinzregententheater until 1963. After the reopening of the Staatsoper it was shut and became a warehouse for stage sets. In 1988, more splendid than ever, it reopened as a repertory drama theater and concert hall. The restoration uncovered the dazzling Art Nouveau interior frescoes and stucco reliefs that had been painted over and covered with panels on Hitler's orders in the 1930s because they depicted scenes of Bacchanalian debauchery.

Just as the Prinzregentenstrasse starts with a Hitler legacy, so in a sense it ends with one, for his erstwhile home stands where the avenue intersects with the Grillparzerstrasse and widens and changes its name to Prinzregentenplatz. In 1929, flush with royalties from *Mein Kampf,* Hitler rented a vast nine-room apartment on the third floor of the gray Jugendstil building at Prinzregentenplatz 16, retaining it as his legal residence until he committed suicide in the Berlin bunker on April 30, 1945. There he also lived in incestuous sin with his half-niece, Geli Raubal. On the morning of September 18, 1931, they had a lovers' quarrel that culminated in a shouting match—Geli standing on the third-floor corner balcony screeching down at Hitler, who was getting into an open-roof car on the street. After he drove off, she went to her room—so the official version goes—and shot herself. But according to rumors that still percolate, she may have been murdered by his henchmen. The apartment house today is an office building.

From the Prinzregentenplatz a convenient subway connection on the U-4 line provides a short ride back to within a couple of blocks of the Englischer Garten.

## The Englischer Garten

The Englischer Garten, on the west side of the river running north from the Prinzregentenstrasse, is not only the oldest—200 years—and largest—922 acres—public park in the world, it is also one of the oddest. The brainchild of an American, it was started in 1789, the year of the French Revolution, and is a natural garden, deliberately asymmetrical and unmanicured in the English style. It is dotted with a grab bag of seemingly displaced structures, among them a Chinese pagoda, a Japanese teahouse, a Greek temple, Roman-style statuary, and a Neoclassical château, and on any balmy summer day it is populated with hundreds of sunbathing nudists.

From the Prinzregentenstrasse the park runs for more than three miles along the left bank of the Isar to the northern edges of the city. In places it is one and one-half miles wide—an oasis of lawns, densely wooded glens, lakes, ponds, rippling brooks, waterfalls, recreational facilities, beer gardens, restaurants, and 45 miles of bridle paths, walkways, and trails. Its praises have been sung by some of Germany's greatest literary figures, from Bettina von Arnim to Arnold Zweig, and it even gave birth to a school of art—early-19th-century German Romantic landscape painting.

Credit for this vast green repose goes to Benjamin Thompson, commemorated by a stone monument just off the Prinzregentenstrasse between the Haus der Kunst and the Nationalmuseum. Franklin D. Roosevelt once put Thompson on a par with Benjamin Franklin and Thomas Jefferson as "the three greatest intellects America ever brought forth."

Born in Woburn, Massachusetts, in 1753 and buried in 1814 at Auteuil cemetery in Paris, Thompson was one of the most scintillating and enigmatic figures of his time. He was both a social reformer and an incorrigible social climber; a traitor and spy, but also an officer in several armies; a brilliant scientist, ingenious inventor, and successful entre-preneur; a philanthropist but also a miser; a humanitarian and at the same time a misanthrope; and, not least, a dashing ladies' man who behaved scurrilously toward women.

Largely a self-made, self-educated man, he was a Tory who spied for the British during the early years of the American Revolution. In March 1776, abandoning his wife and infant daughter in New Hampshire, he escaped to England, where he entered the service of George III, rising in the colonial office to become undersecretary for North America. He was eventually knighted, and in 1784, with the war over, a rest-less and ambitious Thompson headed for the Continent in search of adventure and a new job. By chance he met Bavaria's future King Maximilian I, who commended him to his uncle, Elector Karl Theodor. The duke was sufficiently impressed to give Thompson a colonel's commission in the Bavarian army, but suggested that before taking on specific duties he should learn German and study the country, with all expenses paid by the Bavarian treasury.

Thompson moved into a palais at what is today Theatiner-strasse 9, sharing the building with the Russian ambassador, who occupied the ground floor. He was given an entourage of military adjutants and house servants, and soon became a grandee of Munich society. For the next four years he fol-lowed Karl Theodor's advice, studying not only German but the duchy, and learning that it was one of the most backward in Europe, "its aristocracy, military caste, and civil administra-tion steeped in a morass of decadence, indolence, and corruption."

Finally, in 1788, he presented Karl Theodor with recom-mendations for sweeping reform, especially of the military. Though a force of only 18,000, it had several field marshals and even a couple of grand-admirals, who commanded a "navy" of three boats. Karl Theodor saw in the proposals of the 35-year-old American a way to build a reputation as an enlightened and progressive ruler. He promoted Thompson to major general, and made him Bavaria's minister of war and minister of police. Virtually overnight, he became the most powerful figure in the duchy, and immediately made use of his powers. For his services to Munich and Bavaria Karl Theodor appointed him "count of the Holy Roman Empire." As his title Thompson chose Rumford, the former name of Concord, New Hampshire, where he had met, married, and abandoned his wife.

Thompson's most lasting contribution to Munich was the Englischer Garten, which he proposed to Karl Theodor shortly after the storming of the Bastille in Paris, arguing that a people free to stroll, relax, and enjoy themselves in a public park would be disinclined to storm their monarch's palace. Thompson personally selected the site, the Isar Auen, a vast marshland along the river; commanded the regiments of soldiers who drained it and turned it into a garden; drew the plans; hired the landscape architect who implemented them; and provided most of the ideas for its bridges, monuments, and amusement facilities.

The transformation was close to miraculous. Thousands of nearly full-grown trees were planted; coach roads, bridle paths, and footpaths were laid out; and 11 charming stone and wrought-iron bridges were laid across brooks. There was a little wooden Apollo temple, precursor to today's Monopteros. A veterinary school in the park, now an institute of Munich university, opened its doors to 30 students and two professors. The high point, however, was the Chinesischer Turm, a Chinese pagoda modeled on a similar one in London's Kew Gardens.

Two centuries later the Chinesischer Turm is still the high point of a visit to the Englischer Garten, all the more so because it is surrounded by one of Munich's largest and most popular beer gardens, with seating for 7,000. Today's tower is an exact replica of the original pagoda, which burned to the ground in a World War II bombing attack.

## Schwabing

In Karl Theodor's time Schwabing was a nondescript village northwest of the Englischer Garten. After Ludwig I built the Ludwigstrasse it became an integrated district of Munich. Today it comprises, more or less, the entire area west of the Englischer Garten to Luisenstrasse, on which the Lenbachhaus is located, and from just beyond the Odeonsplatz and the Brienner Strasse in the south, to the area in the north where Munich begins to fray into industrial sites and highrise residential blocks.

But to describe Schwabing geographically misses the point. It is not so much a neighborhood as a state of mind—

*the* state of mind that made Munich the intellectual and cultural center of Germany from the time Wagner arrived in 1867, at Ludwig II's invitation, until 1919, when the title passed, for the 14 years of the Weimar Republic, to Berlin. Schwabing was to Munich what the Latin Quarter is to Paris or Greenwich Village once was to New York, an enclave of artists, musicians, writers, thinkers, and revolutionaries.

Not only was Schwabing the site of Ludwig-Maximilian university as well as Munich's technical university and the academy of art, it was also inexpensive. As a result, it attracted struggling students as well as impecunious poets, writers, musicians, artists, intellectuals, and low-budget publishers. It was the perfect soil for a counterculture that, given the unique Bavarian climate, rejected all things Prussian, including the new Wilhelminian era with its adoration of powerful captains of industry, swaggering militarists, and heraldic decor.

In Schwabing were found not only a mixture of scholarliness and skepticism, thanks to the universities and academies, but also the traditional Munich *Gemütlichkeit* of beer cellars, coffeehouses, and taverns. To list those who at one time or another lived and worked there is tantamount to name dropping: three chemistry and physics Nobel laureates, Adolph von Baeyer, Walter Wien, and Werner Heisenberg; writers, poets, and dramatists such as Bertolt Brecht, Oskar Maria Graf, Stefan George, Ibsen, Thomas and Heinrich Mann, Rainer Maria Rilke, and Frank Wedekind; all the Munich Secession and Blue Rider artists; and historians and philosophers such as Oswald Spengler, who wrote and published his *Decline of the West* during the 25 years he lived in Schwabing.

Countless satirical journals, critical reviews, and iconoclastic periodicals had their editorial offices in the district. Many abounded with stories and drawings of Bavarian mountain yokels and highland humor about the city slickers, invariably those from Berlin and northern Germany. It was a code language, and its message was anti-authoritarian and anti-establishment.

Schwabing bubbled with the enthusiasm of young talent and crackled with the tension of new ideas. Lenin, who lived here for two years at various addresses—Kaiserstrasse 53, Schleissheimer Strasse 106, Siegfriedstrasse 14—founded his revolutionary paper *Iskra* while living in Schwabing. Hitler lived in Schwabing only briefly before World War I, but was an habitué of the neighborhood afterward, especially from 1925 to 1931, when the Nazi party had its head-

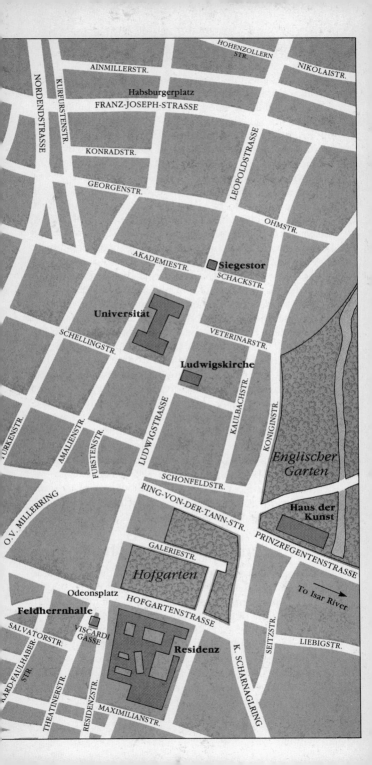

quarters at Schellingstrasse 50. (An eagle with its head and swastika chiseled away remains carved over the entrance-way.) The **Schelling Salon**, a popular café with billiard and card tables at Schellingstrasse 56, was one of his haunts until the proprietor cut off his credit. The **Osteria Italiana Lombardi**, Schellingstrasse 62, oldest of Munich's more than 320 Italian restaurants, then known as "Osteria Bavaria," was one of his favorite eating places.

Today, old-timers and nostalgic Müncheners say Schwabing isn't what it used to be. They bemoan the fast-food spots, pizzerias, pseudo-ethnic restaurants, heavy-metal discos, *schicki-micki* (jet-set) cafés, beautiful-people bars, overpriced boutiques, and usurious interior design shops. Schwabing, they say, has been *vermarktet*—commercialized.

Yes, Schwabing has changed and is changing, but not as fast as some of the critics would have you believe. The Leopoldstrasse (the northern continuation of the Ludwigstrasse after the Siegestor), its main boulevard, continues to shine as Munich's liveliest avenue, lined with sidewalk cafés, terrace restaurants, and, on balmy summer evenings, the stalls of artisans hawking their wares. Since neither the two universities nor the art academy have moved, it is more a student quarter than ever before. The Schellingstrasse and the Amalienstrasse are still lined with book shops. Artists continue to opt for studios in Schwabing, and for writers and publishers a Schwabing address continues to look good on their business cards. Traditional hangouts like **Alter Simpl**, Türkenstrasse 57, or the **Allotria**, Türkenstrasse 33, famed for the best jazz in town, are also still around.

In other words, a visit to Munich without soaking up some daytime and nighttime atmosphere in Schwabing is missing what the city was and is about.

# Museumsinsel and Haidhausen

The Museumsinsel (Museum Island) is the site of the **Deutsches Museum** (open daily 9:00 A.M. to 5:00 P.M.), the world's largest, most unusual museum of science and technology and one of the most popular, visited by two million people on average each year. A ten-minute walk southeast from the Marienplatz, along the Tal, past the Isartor gate, and up the Zweibrückenstrasse, or a one-stop ride on any S-Bahn to Isartorplatz station, will get you there. It was founded in 1906 by Oskar von Miller, a civil engineer and businessman who built the world's first long-distance high-voltage line.

Miller, born in Munich in 1855, was by avocation a kind of collecting Boswell to the towering figures of technical ingenuity and mechanical innovation. He created this museum to honor the great scientists and inventors by displaying originals, replicas, and models of their achievements. It is a huge institution, with some 80,000 objects plus a library, also open daily, containing nearly a million volumes on science and technology, manuscripts, letters and diaries by great inventors, and original sketches, drawings, and blueprints. He was also a moocher, as are his successor curators, with the result that the Deutsches Museum owns such treasures as an original 1895 Otto Lilienthal glider, the monoplane with which Bleriot crossed the English Channel in 1905, an 1839 camera of Louis Daguerre, a glass harmonica designed by Benjamin Franklin, and the laboratory table on which Otto Hahn and Lise Meitner split the uranium atom in 1938.

But Miller's aim was also to familiarize as many people as possible with the laws and phenomena of science, the methods and tools of technology, their historical development, and their practical uses. He built a museum that would unravel the secrets of science and technology for lay visitors, especially the young, by means of simple explanations, working models, and demonstrations. Wherever you go in the Deutsches Museum, things snap, crackle, and pop. An old James Watt steam engine still works. A turn of the crank would start the world's first motorcar, built by Carl Benz. An early Wright airplane remains flyable. A scaled-down model of the Montgolfier brothers' 1784 hot-air balloon takes off from its pad. A 1.1-million-volt generator sends lightning bolts into a group of doll-sized houses to show the benefits of proper grounding. It is a museum that comes alive at the touch of a button, and there are hundreds of buttons that visitors are encouraged to press.

Miller wanted people to go through his museum the way they go "to the sideshows at the Oktoberfest." While just as much fun, and far more enlightening, it could take you even longer. There are more than 13 miles of exhibit rooms and halls spread over five floors and several wings. It would take three to four hours just to walk through, without stopping to look at anything.

**Haidhausen**, the rapidly gentrifying neighborhood that begins on the hill of the Isar's right bank just beyond the Deutsches Museum, is touted as the "new Schwabing." That is premature, but it is worth a visit nonetheless for two things: the **Gasteig philharmonic hall and cultural center**, just a block from the Deutsches Museum, and the so-called *Franzosenviertel* (French Quarter), a planned neighborhood of the 1870s to 1890s.

The fortresslike Gasteig complex, incorporating the Philharmonie, a smaller concert hall, the public library, and the Volkshochschule, an adult-education facility, was completed in 1986. While Müncheners are gradually getting accustomed to the architecture, musicians remain up in arms over the hall's fickle acoustics—so fickle that after conducting the Munich Philharmonic in it for the first time Leonard Bernstein had only one comment: "Burn it!" Performing the Mendelssohn concerto recently, violinist Anne-Sophie Mutter, could not even be heard in some sections of the auditorium, though she and her Stradivarius are known for anything but a timid tone.

Haidhausen's **Franzosenviertel** is interesting not only for all the boutiques, fancy restaurants, art galleries, and artists' studios, but for the French neo-Baroque façades of the rows of 19th-century apartment houses and the names of its streets—Orléans, Metz, Bourdeaux, Paris, and others—that serve as reminders of the victory over France in 1871, when construction of the district began.

# THE OUTSKIRTS
## Theresienwiese

The Theresienwiese (Theresa's Meadow), west of the Innenstadt, easily reached by taking the U-4 subway line to the stop of the same name, is the site of the annual Oktoberfest, first staged in 1810 as part of the celebration for Ludwig I's wedding to Princess Thérèse. A meadow is all it is except during Oktoberfest time. A different matter is the neo-Greek temple with the huge statue of Bavaria on the hill, called Theresienhöhe, above the field—two more of Ludwig I's legacies.

The building, designed by Leo von Klenze, is the **Ruhmeshalle** (Hall of Fame), which contains the busts of famous Bavarians.

**Bavaria** is a lady weighing 171,600 pounds and standing 60 feet tall. She is made of cast bronze, and inside her head, to which some 50,000 people climb annually for a good view of Munich, there is room for 30 adults. To build her was a herculean artistic and technological achievement. Ludwig commissioned the monument in 1833 and chose Klenze, who did the initial sketches—the figure of a majestic woman with helmet, lance, and shield, remarkably similar to Athena. Details for creating the figure were left to Ludwig von Schwanthaler, then Munich's most prominent sculptor, who ultimately came up with something quite different: a very Germanic woman in a shirtlike garment, partly covered by a bearskin, a wreath of oak leaves in her left hand, a short sword in the right, and the Lion of Bavaria at her feet. It was a far cry from Greece, but King Ludwig nodded approval.

Because Ludwig insisted on the figure being cast in bronze, Schwanthaler began making a full-size gypsum model. It was not until 1844 that he had an acceptable model ready. The casting took six years, and when it was done, Ludwig was no longer king. Special wagons, drawn by 12 huge horses, had to be built to transport the various segments from the foundry to the Theresienwiese.

# Nymphenburg

**Schloss Nymphenburg**, the "summer palace" in the west end of Munich (open Tuesday through Sunday, 9:30 A.M. to 12:30 P.M. and 1:30 to 5:00 P.M.), reachable by tramway number 12, is how a royal palace should look. Its origins take you back to Duke Ferdinand Maria and his flamboyant Italian wife, Princess Henrietta Adelaide of Savoy on the occasion of the birth of their son Max Emmanuel in 1662. Ferdinand Maria ordered Nymphenburg as a little present for Henrietta Adelaide. When Henrietta Adelaide died, Ferdinand Maria lost interest in the château, but Max Emmanuel expanded it into a real summer palace in the early 18th century, adding courtiers' buildings and pavilions in its expansive park. His son and grandson contributed even more. By 1760 it was one of the largest and loveliest Baroque-Rococo palace complexes in Europe. It still is, and to see the parts open to the public (Wittelsbach duke Albrecht von Bayern still resides in one wing) takes the better part of a day.

Highpoints are the lavishly furnished and ornately decorated representational rooms and apartments in the main building; the **Marstall Museum** (Stable Museum), with its grand collection of richly carved and gilded royal coaches, carriages, sleighs, and silver equestrian equipment; the Badenburg, built as a little "bathing château" for Max Emmanuel; the Pagodenburg, designed for him as a "pleasure palace"; the Magdalenenklause, Max Emmanuel's "hermitage" in the form of an artificial Medieval castle ruin; and the enchanting **Amalienburg**, designed by Cuvilliés as a hunting château for Elector Karl Albrecht's wife, Maria Amalia. The

Badenburg, Pagodenburg, Magdalenenklause, and Amalienburg are all located in the 500-acre park, where you will also
encounter fountains, cascades, artificial lakes, numerous
sculptures of Greek gods, goddesses, and mythological figures, little temples, and flower gardens.

During the lunch break, when the palaces and museum
are closed, you may want to retire to the nearby **Königlicher
Hirschgarten** (Royal Deer Garden), Munich's largest beer
garden (seating for 10,000).

Like many other German and European rulers, the Wittelsbachs also had their own china and porcelain manufactory,
at Nymphenburg. The workshop was in one of the Rondel
buildings, the semicircle that faces the front of the palace.
**Nymphenburger Porzellanmanufaktur**, now owned by the
Free State of Bavaria, is still very much in business, making
not only modern and traditional chinaware but also copies
of Bustelli porcelain figurines. There is a sales and showroom in the same 18th-century building that housed the
original factory.

# Olympiapark

Olympiapark (final stop for the U-2 and U-3 subway lines
northwest of the Innenstadt), site of the 1972 Olympic
Games, is one of Munich's splashiest examples of modern
architecture. It is also of interest to modern history buffs.
Called the Oberwiesenfeld until construction started for the
stadium and other sports facilities, this was, until 1939,
Munich's airfield, where Neville Chamberlain arrived to sign
the Munich Accord with Hitler, sealing the fate of Czechoslovakia and setting the stage for World War II. The 200-foot-
high mountain in the park is artificial, constructed of the
rubble of Munich buildings bombed during World War II.

The things to see here are the Olympiastadion, the
Schwimmhalle, and the Olympiahalle, all accommodated
under the 82,000 square yards of a "tent" roof made of mesh
steel netting covered with translucent acrylic panels.

Not part of the park is the spectacular "four-cylinder" 20-
story headquarters building of Bavarian Motor Works, with
the adjacent silvery-gray **BMW Museum**, which looks like a
flying saucer. BMW, which started as a manufacturer of aircraft
engines and planes long before it got into the motorcycle and
automobile business for which it is now famed, has been at
this location since 1916. The museum is a retrospective of
aero-engine and motor vehicle manufacturing, with plenty of
exhibits and multilingual video presentations.

The 963-foot Fernsehturm (Television Tower) is not only Munich's tallest structure, but also, thanks to its observation platforms and rotating restaurant, the highest point from which to get a view of the entire city and the Alps beyond. You can see the Italian Dolomites and Switzerland's Bernese Oberland from its platforms.

# MUNICH'S ENVIRONS
## Dachau

**Dachau**, only nine S-Bahn stops northwest of the Marienplatz on the S-2 line, is not only a separate city of 35,000 people but also is considerably older than Munich itself. It was first mentioned in documents in 805. A branch of the Wittelsbach family built a fortified castle here in the 11th century, which fell into disuse a century later. In 1546 Duke Wilhelm IV began building a "country palace" on the ruins, to which his various descendants and successors, right through Max Emmanuel, kept adding.

The high points of **Schloss Dachau**, are the Festsaal (Festival Hall), with its magnificent coffered ceiling, and the stately early-18th-century staircase leading up to it.

But Dachau is no longer known in the world for its castle, of course. Instead, it is infamous as the site of the Nazis' first concentration camp, which is now a memorial. The **KZ-Gedenkstätte Dachau** is open Tuesday through Sunday, 9:00 A.M. to 5:00 P.M.. The central administration building, with photographic exhibits and twice-daily (11:30 A.M. and 3:30 P.M.) showings of a documentary film in English, has been preserved, as have two of the original barracks. The foundation outlines of the other barracks remain as well, as do guard towers and barbed-wire fences, to give visitors a feeling for this grim place where, between 1933 and 1945, more than 206,000 inmates were incarcerated and tortured, and nearly 32,000 died.

## Schleissheim

Though Müncheners generally speak of **Schloss Schleissheim**, in the suburb of Oberschleissheim (nine station stops north of the Marienplatz on the S-1 line), as one palace, there are actually three, and each can keep you busy.

The Altes Schloss, classically Renaissance, was built as a country retreat for Duke Wilhelm V. Work started in 1597, the year of his abdication, after Bavaria was declared bankrupt, and completed in 1616. Today, the Altes Schloss houses a collection of religious folk art (open daily from 10:00 A.M. to 5:00 P.M.).

The Neues Schloss, commissioned by Max Emmanuel, was never completed, though you would hardly notice. The first problems arose after the laying of the cornerstone: The entrance hall collapsed because Zucalli, the chief architect, had apparently made some miscalculations regarding the foundations. The problem was solved by reinforcement with earth, but this affected the proportions: The palace looks a bit as if it had sunk into the ground. When Max Emmanuel was forced into exile after the War of the Spanish Succession, work on the building came to a complete halt. Construction resumed in 1719, after Max Emmanuel's return and what the artists and artisans achieved is one of the finest works of German Baroque, in no small measure because some of the finest masters did the job. Cosmas Damian Asam did the fresco painting, Johann Baptist Zimmermann the stucco work. The frescoes depict mythological scenes alluding to Max Emmanuel's successful campaign against the Turks at Belgrade. Few palaces are as lavish. While you can visit the Neues Schloss Tuesday through Sunday from 10:00 A.M. to 12:30 P.M. and 1:30 to 5:00 P.M., it is at its most impressive if you can garner a ticket for a concert during the July and August music festivals here.

**Schloss Lustheim**, across the neatly manicured park from the Neues Schloss, was built as a hermitage for Max Emmanuel in 1687. Zucalli, who made no mistakes on this one, modeled it on Italian Baroque châteaux and created a jewel. Its great hall is vaulted with mirrors, decorated with frescoes, and supported by painted atlantes. Lustheim, open the same hours as the Neues Schloss, houses a vast collection of Meissen china.

## GETTING AROUND

Because of Munich's proximity to the Alps, its weather is fickle. A week of uninterrupted downpour can be followed by two weeks of glorious sunshine. There can be blizzards as late as mid-May and as early as mid-October. One real freeze, well below zero Fahrenheit, is guaranteed for a week to ten days in winter, as is a scorcher in the low 90°s for an equal duration once each summer.

Generally speaking, the weather in late May through October is best. But there are 12 to 15 major trade fairs each year, during which accommodations are at a premium, so booking well in advance is most advisable. The most difficult period is during the two-week Oktoberfest, from late September through the first week of October, which always ends on the day the fall *Modewochen* (a fashion trade fair, with exhibitors and buyers from all over Europe) begins.

### Arrival

In terms of passenger volume and landings and departures, Munich's Riem airport is Germany's second largest (after Frankfurt), and so close to the city that the cab ride to the Innenstadt takes less than 20 minutes, traffic jams included. A nonstop airport bus leaves for the Hauptbahnhof every 15 minutes between 4:15 A.M. and 9:00 P.M. In addition to Lufthansa, several American airlines (American, Delta, Pan Am, TWA) have direct flights from the United States to Munich, as do Air Canada from Toronto, British Airways and Dan Air from London, and Air France from Paris.

The Hauptbahnhof, about 15 minutes' walk from the Marienplatz and just outside the Altstadtring to the west, is served by Inter-City (IC) and Euro-City (EC) express trains, operating on an hourly schedule, from every major German city north of Munich. Connections from Austria, Italy, Switzerland, and France are far less frequent, however. Four U-Bahn (U-1, U-2, U-4, U-5) and all seven S-Bahn lines (discussed below) intersect on several underground levels of the Hauptbahnhof, and there is access to them from the main concourse. The tourist office has an information center (open 8:00 A.M. to 11:00 P.M.) on the main platform area, near the Bayerstrasse exit and across from the end of tracks 11–14.

Three Autobahn routes—from Stuttgart, Nürnberg, and Salzburg—converge on Munich and end at the city limits. On the Stuttgart and Salzburg routes there are information kiosks just before the last exit. At both there is also a *Lotsendienst,* a pilot service, whose guides will either give you directions or lead you in another car to your destination.

### In the City

A car is not merely a burden in Munich but a curse. Much of the inner city is a pedestrian zone, and where you are permitted to drive the traffic is either choking or parking is impossible. Fortunately, most of Munich can easily be walked, and the transit system is superb.

The whole network—U-Bahn (subway), S-Bahn (interurban trains), Strassenbahn (tramway), and buses—interconnects, with subways, trams, and buses running at ten-minute intervals most of the day and twice as frequently during morning and afternoon rush hours. A single ticket allows you to ride all conveyances as well as transfer among them. It is an honor system, backed by spot inspections, with a hefty fine if you violate it. You buy a ticket from the vending machines found at U-Bahn, S-Bahn, and tramway stops and validate it in the meters at the platform entrances or aboard trams and buses. Bus drivers also sell tickets. Multiple-ride tickets for DM15 or DM9.50, which require validating two strips for travel within the city limits (more on a zonal basis if you ride the S-Bahn to Dachau and Schleissheim), are cheaper per ride than single-ride tickets, and the best deal is a *Tageskarte* (one-day pass) for DM7.50 (within the city limits), good for unlimited rides and transfer from the time you validate it until 4:00 A.M. the next day.

Taxis, all cream colored, are usually plentiful and expensive. They also get stuck in traffic. There are plenty of taxicab stands around the city, and a cab can also be hailed on the street if its rooftop sign is illuminated, or called (Tel: 216-11).

One of the best and fastest ways of getting about is by bicycle. There are 680 miles of marked bike lanes, many with their own traffic signals, to accommodate the 400,000 bicycle owners (out of a total population of 1.3 million). Recently a reporter for the biggest Munich daily newspaper tested getting to his office by car, subway, and bicycle: It took him 27 minutes, 35 minutes, and 23 minutes respectively. A booklet (in German) with proposed bicycle sightseeing tours and maps is available from the tourist office information centers at the airport, main railway station, and in the Neues Rathaus on the Marienplatz. Bikes can be rented by the day or week all year around at **Lothar Borucki**, Hans-Sachs-Strasse 7 (Tel: 26-65-06); **Radl Gipp**, Kirchenstrasse 23 (Tel: 47-98-46); **Park & Ride**, Häberlstrasse 2 (Tel: 55-41-81); and, from mid-May through mid-October, from **Bayern Bike Tours**, which is operated by a couple of enterprising Americans who have their stand on the sidewalk at the Arnulfstrasse exit of the railway station (Tel: 59-61-63).

## ACCOMMODATIONS
Given that three million visitors converge on Munich annually, rooms are always scarce here and, regardless of category, more expensive than elsewhere in Germany. But the squeeze is easing gradually, thanks to the opening of a number of new hotels in the first-class and moderate categories; a 3 percent increase in available rooms was predicted for 1989.

All the major chains are represented, standardized in their service and decor, though not one of them has a hotel in the

Innenstadt or the railway station area. The telephone area code for Munich is 89.

## Innenstadt and Station Area

Merely to list the crowned heads, presidents, and prime ministers, the famous writers, opera singers, musicians, and stars of stage and screen who have called the **Vier Jahreszeiten** Kempinski a home away from home since it opened in 1858 would fill another book. Neither wartime destruction nor a 1970 expansion and renovation has deprived this *"beste Adresse Münchens"* of its genteel, mahogany-paneled elegance, and its appeal to an upscale clientele remains undiminished. What enhances the attraction is its location on Munich's most expensive street as well as its proximity to everything, especially the opera.

Maximilianstrasse 17, D-8000 München 22. Tel: 23-03-90; Fax: 23039693.

Competition in the luxury class opened nearby in 1989 in the form of the **Hotel Rafael**, with 74 grandly spacious rooms, 55 of them suites, in a neo-Renaissance building. The lobby is a splash of marble, cherry, and ebony. Each guest room is individually designed, and all feature opulent interiors decorated with period pieces. Several suites open onto terraces with spectacular views of the city.

Neuturmstrasse 1, D-8000 München 2. Tel: 29-09-80.

If price is an obstacle but gentility and elegance remain a goal, then the **Splendid** is splendid indeed. Each of its 40 rooms is appointed differently, and service is so friendly and personal that the feeling of being in a hotel soon dissipates.

Maximilianstrasse 54, D-8000 München 22. Tel: 29-66-06; Fax: 2913176.

Modern functional comfort, quiet surroundings, and personalized efficient service come together just off Maximilianstrasse at the **Hotel an der Oper**, which, with 17 singles and 38 doubles, is a kind of secret tip for the budget minded.

Falkenturmstrasse 10, D-8000 München 2. Tel: 29-00-270.

The **Continental** is within easy walking distance of the Königsplatz and the museums. The Baroque wood paneling in the public rooms is genuine, salvaged from a razed castle. The antiques in the public rooms, restaurants, and many of the 134 guest rooms and 15 suites are collector's pieces. Discretion and personal service remain the tradition, despite the recent acquisition of this quiet luxury-class establishment by a Swedish chain.

Max-Joseph-Strasse 5, D-8000 München 2. Tel: 55-15-70.

The pedigree of the **Königshof** reaches back to 1862,

when a baronial mansion in what was then still a verdant area between the Hauptbahnhof and the Karlstor, one of the city's old Medieval gates, was converted into a hotel. As the spot is now the city's busiest square, the Geisel family, which has owned the establishment for a generation, could have rested assured that its 120 rooms would always be filled. But in the late 1970s they decided to elevate it into the top category by retaining a prize-winning architect and interior designer, who gave it a total overhaul: a dining room of chalked oak panels and hand-wrought bronze chandeliers, a lobby of tinted mirrors and stucco, carpeting everywhere, opulent guest rooms with floor-to-ceiling marble bathrooms, and nine suites with silk wallpaper and period pieces. Lushness is not a strong enough word.

Karlsplatz 25, D-8000 München 2. Tel: 55-13-60; Fax: 55136113.

The same spirit and the same family—the Geisels—prevail a block away at the slightly less pricey **Excelsior**, conveniently located within shouting distance of the Hauptbahnhof. In an old though completely modernized and renovated building, it offers some pleasant surprises: high ceilings and some bathrooms with windows that face the courtyard, providing natural light.

Schützenstrasse 11, D-8000 München 2. Tel: 55-13-70; Fax: 55136113.

On the whole, the railway-station neighborhood is grim, but the reasonably priced **Drei Löwen** is a quiet, dignified oasis. The feeling of escape and relief overcomes you the minute you enter the lobby and get a friendly greeting. It is enhanced by the cozy comfort of the 130 modern but individually appointed rooms.

Schillerstrasse 8, D-8000 München 2. Tel: 59-10-40; Fax: 55104905.

The **King's Hotel**, just 200 yards from the station, is not a play on Munich's royal past. The proprietress of this medium-price establishment, opened in 1988, is Hanna King, and she oversees it personally. Besides the usual comforts and conveniences, each of the 72 rooms has a canopy bed.

Dachauer Strasse 13, D-8000 München 2. Tel: 55-18-70.

Not far from the Viktualienmarkt and Marienplatz is a bit of innkeeping history that is a boon for the budget minded, the **Blauer Bock**. A picturesque old *Gasthaus,* originally built as a church in 1300, it has been run by the same family since 1900. Of its 41 double rooms, however, only 24 have private baths.

Sebastiansplatz 9, D-8000 München 2. Tel: 260-80-43.

## Schwabing

Whether the **Carlton**, only a few minutes' walk north of Odeonsplatz, is already in Schwabing depends on where you draw the neighborhood's southern boundary. But this establishment, built in 1920, is a gem in the moderate bracket. Its light and airy 45 rooms, 17 of them doubles, are all exquisitely appointed in Baroque style and furnished with period pieces. The service is refreshingly personal.

Fürstenstrasse 12, D-8000 München 2. Tel: 28-20-61; Fax: 284391.

Relatively new and functional, the **König Ludwig**, just off the Leopoldstrasse north of the Siegestor, will give you the feeling of being in the middle of whatever Schwabing is about these days. The decor of its 60 rooms is vaguely postmodern.

Hohenzollernstrasse 3, D-8000 München 14. Tel: 33-59-95; Fax: 394658.

Also north of the Siegestor and equidistant from the Leopoldstrasse and the Englischer Garten, on one of Schwabing's old squares, the moderately priced **Astoria** will give you an even better sense of the district. A well-kept Jugendstil house, its 20 doubles and 10 singles are all furnished in ultramodern style and, along with the corridors, small lobby, and breakfast area, decorated with contemporary art, which changes frequently as in a commercial gallery. Ilona Leven, the proprietress, makes sure the service is friendly and personal—and that service includes bicycle rental.

Nikolaistrasse 9, D-8000 München 14. Tel: 39-50-91.

## Upper Prinzregentenstrasse

This carriage-trade neighborhood has become more accessible since the opening of the U-4 subway line, and with it new hotels have been sprouting up. The most luxurious, and accordingly priced, is the **Palace**, at the corner of Prinzregentenstrasse. All marble, stucco, deep pile, and plush, with period furnishings, it exudes elegance.

Trogerstrasse 21, D-8000 München 80. Tel: 4-70-50-91.

The bill will be a little more reasonable a block away at the **Prinzregent**, right around the corner from the Stuck Villa. Its lobby, bar, restaurant, and 68 rooms are all richly paneled with wood and have a rustic Bavarian country-style look. The service is exceptionally friendly and attentive.

Ismaninger Strasse 42–44, D-8000 München 80. Tel: 470-20-81; Fax: 4702392 and 41605466.

### Haidhausen

Here, too, new hotels are mushrooming, most of them branches of international chains. Though also located in a modern building, a welcome exception is the not-inexpensive **Preysing**, which is so close to the philharmonic hall that, given the hall's devious acoustics, you will probably hear the music better from one of the hotel's 60 plushly furnished rooms. For all its modernity, it sits atop a 14th-century vaulted cellar with one of the city's really fine restaurants, the **Preysing-Keller**.

Preysingstrasse 1, D-8000 München 80. Tel: 48-10-11.

## DINING

Thomas Wolfe described Munich as "an enchanted land where one ate and drank forever." Little has changed. It is not only Germany's secret capital but also its culinary capital. The statistics of its gastronomic wonders are positively staggering. It has more *Gourmettempel*—"temples of haute cuisine"—with more Michelin stars, Gault-Millau toques, and similar badges of culinary supremacy than any other German city. *Gasthäuser* and *Gaststätten* (eateries and beer halls serving rustic German and regional Bavarian food) number more than 2,000. To them add some 320 Italian, 200 Yugoslav, and 80 Greek spots: a natural consequence of all the resident foreigners and the fact that the Italian and Yugoslav borders are only a few hours away. Twenty McDonalds, in addition to the standard repertory, make a concession to local taste by serving beer. On top of all this, there are more than 300 Konditorei-Cafés, most of which make their own calorific tarts, cream cakes, petits fours, confectionery, and chocolates. To eat and drink your way through the city would be a tour de force.

### Haute Cuisine

Germany has been in the throes of a culinary revolution, aimed at changing the image of German food and cooking from rib-sticking but boring to artistic and creative since the early 1970s, and Munich has been the epicenter. Its leader, ironically, was not a German but an Austrian strongly influenced by French teachers: Eckart Witzigmann. He was working as sous chef at Washington's Jockey Club when a wealthy Munich real-estate developer invited him to preside over the kitchen of a new restaurant with a concept of haute cuisine the likes of which Germany and Munich had never seen before, the **Tantris**, Johann-Fichte-Strasse 7, in Schwabing. In less than a year Witzigmann parlayed it into the country's most celebrated eatery. For Witzigmann's taste, however, it was not only too large but too confining creatively. In 1978, having trained an equally talented fellow Austrian, Heinz Winkler, who has presided at the Tantris since then, Witzigmann left and opened his own exquisitely elegant 40-seat **Aubergine**, at the northwestern Altstadtring toward Königsplatz at Maximilianplatz 5, where his creativity (engraved in the cookbooks he has written) reaches seemingly unattainable new heights with each day's changing menu. To eat there is as close to culinary perfection as you can get, but it does require a very fat wallet as well as planning, for sometimes reservations several weeks in advance are necessary. The Tantris is closed Sunday and at lunchtime Saturday and Monday; Tel: 36-20-61. Aubergine is closed Sunday and public holidays; Tel: 59-81-71.

No less creative a genius in the kitchen is Otto Koch (the name means "cook"), proprietor and chef of the sumptuous little **Le Gourmet**, Ligsalzstrasse 46, near the trade-fair grounds and the Bavaria statue. Koch once aspired to be a psychologist, but his therapy at the table, resulting in total bliss, surely surpasses any he might have dispensed on the couch. The treatment is heavenly, all the more because he applies his skill and imagination to nouvelle-style transformation of traditional and long-forgotten Bavarian recipes. Open evenings only, closed Sunday. By reservation only; Tel: 50-35-97.

Two hotel restaurants are climbing the ladder to reach culinary stardom. One is the **Königshof**, where every dish is as much a feast for the eyes as for the palate. For reservations Tel: 55-13-61-42. The Preysing Hotel's **Preysing-Keller**, entrance at Innere-Wiener-Strasse 6, on an equal plane of perfection, offers the added pleasure of dining exquisitely in Medieval surroundings. Closed for lunch and on Sunday; for reservations Tel: 48-10-15.

Game has always ranked as a delicacy in Bavaria and elsewhere in Germany, in part because most of the forests belonged to nobles and hunting was a jealously guarded privilege of the nobility. But when a Witzigmann protégé prepares it, even the nobles bow. The master is Hans Mair, who owns and presides at **Halali**, Schönfeldstrasse 22, just off Ludwigstrasse. There you dine amid the regal splendor of candelabras, heavy silver, and precious china and crystal in a wood-paneled room filled with antlers and other hunting trophies. Closed Sunday and lunchtime Saturday; Tel: 28-59-09.

## Bistros

Munich's latest culinary vogue is the bistro, of which dozens have sprouted during recent years. The best are in and around Schwabing. Alas, what distinguishes them from their French models is that they are not exactly inexpensive.

At **Le Cézanne**, Konradstrasse 1, the proprietor-chef is from Marseilles, the cuisine is classically Provençale and usually impeccable, the choice limited to half a dozen entrees, and the wine list small but credibly honest and reasonable in price. Open evenings only, reservations recommended; Tel: 39-18-05.

**Bistro 33**, Feilitzschstrasse 33, in the heart of Schwabing's disco district, is an intimate, candelit establishment that successfully blends Italian and French cuisine. Open evenings only, reservations recommended; Tel: 34-25-28.

**Käthe's Küche**, Georgenstrasse 48, is on the ground floor of a 100-year-old Jugendstil apartment house in the heart of Schwabing. Owner Mike Maples and his wife, Barbara, are masters when working with lamb, hare, and salmon. Lunch and dinner served on weekdays; dinner only on weekends; Tel: 361-36-20.

## Bavarian Fare

Start with the caveat that it is regional, that such "German" dishes as *Wienerschnitzel* and *Sauerbraten* really aren't part of it, but that *Leberknödelsuppe* (liver dumpling bouillon), *Kalbshaxe* (roast leg of veal), *Schweinsbraten* (pork roast), *Weisswürste, Leberkäse* (a meat loaf), *Semmelknödel* (breadcrumb dumplings), and sauerkraut definitely are, though it is far more varied and richer than that. Go from that premise to the premise that most of the 2,000 Munich eateries purporting to serve it do not, and you have the picture.

The *Weisswürste,* which tradition dictates must be eaten before noon, as a midmorning snack rather than a meal, are by consensus still best where they were invented, the **Gaststätte Peterhof**, Marienplatz 22, open daily 9:00 A.M. to midnight; Tel: 260-80-97.

Because of the Francophile bias of Michelin inspectors, it will take a miracle for any real Bavarian Gasthaus to ever get a star, but if the miracle happens, it will be at the **Straubinger Hof**, Blumenstrasse 5, right by the Viktualienmarkt, where the daily menu includes not only the standard dishes mentioned above but also more esoteric Bavarian specialties such as *Züngerl* (tongue) and *Kutteln* (tripe). Closed Saturday evening and Sunday, otherwise open 9:00 A.M. to 11:00 P.M.; Tel: 260-84-44.

At the **Augustiner-Gaststätten**, Neuhauser Strasse 16, right along the main pedestrians-only shopping street that leads from the Marienplatz, the food is as genuine as the ambience is traditional and *gemütlich*. The building, dating from the early years of this century, was one of the few that suffered no wartime damage. There are a number of cavernous rooms, all rustic. The menu is voluminous and prices are moderate. Open daily 9:00 A.M. to 10:00 P.M.; Tel: 260-41-06.

Munich's oldest eatery, in operation since 1410, is the **Hundskugel**, Hotterstrasse 18, west of the Marienplatz, but it's gradually going up market and offering what is vaguely called "international cuisine." Closed Sunday, otherwise open 11:00 A.M. to 1:00 A.M.; Tel: 26-42-72.

A little mixed, too, is the **Spatenhaus**, Residenzstrasse 12, directly across the Max-Joseph-Platz from the opera house. But that's what makes it such an institution and a lot of fun, especially after performances, when you can see the white-tie and designer-gown crowd quaffing huge steins of beer to wash down mountains of Knödel. Open daily 10:00 A.M. to 1:00 A.M.; Tel: 22-78-41.

### Beer Halls and Gardens

These terms are expandable. Any large Gasthaus can be taken for a beer hall, if it is large enough, and any place with a few tables outside, shaded by trees, can be called a garden. The biggest and most colorful are, as previously mentioned, the **Hofbräuhaus**, **Chinesicher Turm** in the Englischer Garten, and the **Königlicher Hirschgarten** near the Nymphenburg palace.

Add two more, both virtually adjacent to and operated by the breweries whose beer they serve. The **Löwenbräukeller**, on the Stiglmaierplatz west of Königsplatz, can seat 7,000. The surrounding garden is, mercifully, somewhat smaller, but therefore crowded to bursting on a warm summer evening. The **Salvatorkeller** (Hochstrasse 49, close to Gasteig philharmonic hall), operated by the Paulaner-Thomas brewery, derives its name from *Starkbier* (strong beer), a potent, oily brew served for two weeks only during Lent. It was first brewed by the Franciscans of St. Paul's Abbey in the 17th century, with the idea that it would see them through the 40-day fast. They called it "Salvator"—"beer of the Savior"—though what kind of salvation was intended remains in doubt.

In all beer gardens, incidentally, it is perfectly acceptable to bring your own food.

## *Konditorei-Cafés*

Traditional *Kaffee und Kuchen* (coffee and cake) time is 3:00 to 5:00 P.M., and Müncheners certainly uphold the tradition, though most of these establishments open for Continental breakfast and serve all manner of other libations, and many remain open until 7:00 P.M. The best and most elegant, with deep upholstered chairs, sumptuous, carpeted, chintz-curtained surroundings, waitresses in black dresses with primly starched white aprons, and a mouth-watering selection of pastries at the counter are within a block or two of the Marienplatz. The ones to seek out are **Café Kreutzkamm**, Maffeistrasse 4, **Café Feldherrnhalle**, Theatinerstrasse 38, and **Café Hag**, Residenzstrasse 26, which was once confectionery shop by appointment to the Wittelsbach court.

## BARS AND NIGHTLIFE

Considering that every beer hall, Gasthaus, restaurant, café, and even ice-cream parlor serves alcoholic beverages, and that for many people going there to imbibe is as important as eating, bars and pubs in the Anglo-American sense are rare, but they are in vogue among the "fashionable people." The five most chic spots are **Harry's New York Bar**, Falken-turmstrasse 9 off the Maximilianstrasse south of the Residenz, open 4:00 P.M. to 3:00 A.M., closed Sunday; **Schumann's**, Maximilianstrasse 36, open 6:00 P.M. to 3:00 A.M., closed Saturday; **Odeon**, Brienner Strasse 10 in the Königsplatz area, open nightly 8:00 P.M. to 4:00 A.M.; **Bogey's**, Maximiliansplatz 5, a real American-style piano bar, open nightly 8:00 P.M. to 9:00 A.M.; and **Bourbon Club**, Herzog-Wilhelm-Strasse 7, just inside the western Altstadtring, daily from 10:00 P.M. to 7:00 A.M..

Nightlife in other forms—discothèques and nightclubs with shows—tend to have a patina of provincialism. The "in" discos of the moment—and moments are brief in Munich—are **P-1**, Prinzregentenstrasse 1, in the Haus der Kunst (closed Monday, otherwise open 9:30 to 4:00 A.M.); **Maximilians**, Maximiliansplatz 31 (also closed Monday, otherwise open 9:00 P.M. to 3:00 A.M.), preferred by the well-heeled *arrivée* crowd; and **Clip**, Leopoldstrasse 25 in Schwabing (open 9:00 P.M. to 4:00 A.M.), strictly for the young.

Of the striptease places, the most established and expensive is **Cabaret Eve**, Maximiliansplatz 5 (closed Sunday, otherwise open 10:00 P.M. to 4:00 A.M.). This venerable establishment, whose guests have included Robert Kennedy and Mick Jagger, used to be located two blocks away on Karolinenplatz in the little Neoclassical house where Ludwig I kept

Lola Montez. An indication of the clientele it attracts can be drawn from the fact that the day's stock market listings are posted at the coat-check area. The best shows and shapeliest dancers, on the whole, are to be found at **Maxim**, Färbergraben 33, just west of the Marienplatz, daily from 9:00 P.M. to 4:00 A.M.

## SHOPS AND SHOPPING

To ask where the most interesting shops are in Munich is like looking for the forest through the trees. The entire city is a shop, with purchasing power seemingly unlimited, and prices for everything juicily inflated to meet insatiable demand. If there is such a thing as a bargain we have yet to find it, and the chances are we never will.

The most gilt-edged tour begins on the Maximilianstrasse, where you will find every high-carat name from Bulgari to Yves St. Laurent. It has a little codicil called the Perusastrasse, where the action includes Tiffany's and Etienne Aigner. Then turn right up the Theatinerstrasse, where it's the millionaire instead of billionaire crowd, not forgetting, however, to dash through the passageways to the parallel Residenzstrasse. At the Odeonsplatz, turn left into the Brienner Strasse, where you again find yourself in the nine zeros bracket, and end up a couple of blocks down face to face with Cartier's. You will have walked perhaps one-and-a-half miles and encountered every glittering name of international haute couture, sartorial splendor, footwear and leather goods, and jewelry.

Dotted between these branch outlets of global fame are the names of some of Munich's own: **Rudolph Moshammer**, Maximilianstrasse 14, a tailor and haberdasher who caters to those who dare to be different and can plunk down several hundred dollars for a shirt or a couple of thousand for something like a cashmere-and-silk sport jacket; **Gebrüder Hemmerle**, also at Maximilianstrasse 14, purveyors of extravagant jewelry of their own design to royalty and cinema stars; the **Bognerhaus**, Residenzstrasse 15, home of Willy Bogner's line of sports and casual wear; **Max Dietl's**, Residenzstrasse 16, the five-story fashion palace of Munich's most renowned couturier and tailor for both women's and men's wear; **Eduard Meier**, Residenzstrasse 22, a shop that has been cobbling for Europe's rich, powerful, and pampered since the 16th century; **Kunstring München**, Brienner Strasse 4, porcelain shop filled with Meissen, new and antique; and **M. Lange & Co.**, Brienner Strasse 1, a fashion house that sells only its own designs and creations, made to order or ready to wear.

More in the mainstream are the streets leading directly off the Marienplatz: the Kaufingerstrasse and the **Neuhauser Strasse**, the main pedestrian mall, which leads all the way down to Karlstor and Karlsplatz; **the Tal**, which begins at the back side of the Altes Rathaus; the **Dienerstrasse** and the **Weinstrasse**, which parallel along the eastern and western sides of the Neues Rathaus; and the **Sendlinger Strasse**, which is perhaps affordable though rather trendy.

There are more than 300 antique and bric-a-brac dealers in Munich, by no means concentrated in any single area. The **Westenriederstrasse**, a long, narrow lane that extends from the Viktualienmarkt to the Isartor, is lined on both sides by bric-a-brac shops. The **Ottostrasse**, which extends in a south-westerly direction from the Brienner Strasse to the Karlsplatz, is a good place to browse if you are in the market for authentic—meaning expensive—antique furnishings and applied art. Along it, at number 11–13, is the Neuer Kunstblock, an entire building of dealers. The **Türkenstrasse** in Schwabing is good for both bric-a-brac hunters and less demanding collectors of antiques.

Auction houses, on the other hand, are not concentrated in any area. The local branch of Sotheby's is at Odeonsplatz 16, Christie's at Residenzstrasse 27. **Hartung & Karl**, good for old books, manuscripts, and autographs, is located at Karolinenplatz 5a. **Karl & Faber**, major players on the old master as well as modern art scene, are at Amiraplatz 3, just off Brienner Strasse. **Wolfgang Ketterer**, good for Jugendstil applied art as well as modern art, operates at Brienner Strasse 25. **Rudolf Neumeister,** whose auctions are strong on both 19th-century German and 20th-century art, has showrooms and auction facilities at Barerstrasse 37. **Hugo Ruef**, interesting for folk as well as old and modern art, is based at Gabelsbergerstrasse 28.

But here again, do not set your hopes too high if "finds" are what you are after. They have already been found. That for which Munich ought to be best known—Biedermeier art and decorative art, Jugendstil, German classical modern, Art Deco, and even the rustic Bavarian folk art and furnishings of the 18th and 19th centuries—was all gobbled up years ago, and when it does go on the market again, either for direct sale through dealers or at auctions, prices are at international levels.

What, then, can you find in Munich that you cannot find elsewhere, and at prices still in line?

## Loden Fashions, Trachten, Bavarian Handicrafts

Müncheners really do wear dirndls, Lederhosen, Loden togs, and other variations on the Bavarian folk costume theme, all of which fall under the generic term of *Trachten*. They even wear such apparel to the opera, for which gown-length dirndls and tuxedos tailored like traditional peasant garb are fashioned. Munich without Trachten would be like Texas without ten-gallon hats and cowboy boots, and nowhere in Germany or anywhere else in the world are such duds more easily acquired, and at still-reasonable prices, than in the Bavarian capital.

One of the best addresses for folk fashions, and also for genuine as well as replica folk artifacts and furnishings such as antique etched glasses, hand-painted schnapps flasks, lusterware jugs, pillows covered with old lace or embroidery, antique peasant furniture, and the like is **Wallach's**, Residenzstrasse 3, just a block up from the Marienplatz via the Dienerstrasse. **Loden-Frey**, Maffeistrasse 7–9 north of the Frauenplatz, though now an entire department store of top-of-the-line designer ready-to-wear for men and women, got its start in 1842 when Johannes G. Frey, then 21, set up a mill with ten looms to produce *Loden,* a thick, felted woolen cloth cherished by Bavarian highland farmers because it is both very warm and waterproof. Eleven years later he opened his first retail store, and today, under direction of his great-great-grandchildren, the company is a Munich institution known worldwide for its handsome, sturdy Loden fashions—men's jackets, women's skirts, overcoats—all cut to meet the latest styles. You will also do well in this genre at **Ludwig Beck am Rathauseck**, sometimes referred to as the "Bloomingdale's of Munich" for its imaginative merchandising techniques—not, however, in the main store at the corner of Marienplatz and Dienerstrasse, but right behind it in a special *Trachten* division on Burgstrasse. Lederhosen—a good pair made of the finest soft chamois can cost well over DM1,000, but will last a lifetime—are still hand made and embroidered to order at **Leder-Moser**, Herzogspital-strasse 7, and by **August Strauss**, Heiliggeiststrasse 2. The best place for *Gamsbärte,* tufts of chamois hair worn on Bavarian and Tyrolean highlanders' hats, and resembling giant shaving brushes, is **Johann Bösl**, Hochbrückenstrasse 4, a tiny Trachten shop near the Hofbräuhaus where, indeed, those regulars show up in all this garb at 9:00 A.M. for their first beer of the day.

# SOUTHERN BAVARIA

*By John Dornberg*

To many people, Southern Bavaria is Germany incarnate. It is made up of two regions that also happen to be political provinces, Oberbayern and Niederbayern. Oberbayern, or Upper (higher-in-altitude) Bavaria, takes in the Alpine highlands south of Munich, stretching more or less from the Lech river eastward to the little Salzach river that, from Salzburg north, divides Germany from Austria. Niederbayern, (Lower Bavaria) is lower country, mostly flats and gentle hills, located generally north and east of Munich between the Inn river and the Danube, again to the Austrian border.

By any name, Southern Bavaria is *the* vacationland of Germany, as the annual invasion of visitors, both foreign and German, attests: on average 15 million, more than the population of all Bavaria. The majority arrive with travelogue expectations of a land of fairy-tale castles and buxom dirndled maidens and bearded *Lederhosen*-clad peasants yodeling from snow-capped Alpine peaks.

Granted, some of the clichés are true, though primarily in Oberbayern, and where they aren't, Bavarians fulfill them artificially. Well aware that they have a touristic gold mine, they assume that travellers like nothing better than to have preconceived illusions affirmed. Many dress in *Trachten* (folk costume) that are about as genuine as American Western duds produced in New York's garment district. But there are also 18 regional folk-costume festivals each year, sponsored and arranged by the 130,000 Bavarians who belong to nearly 900 *Trachtenvereine* (folk-costume societies). These costumes are heirlooms or meticulously reconstructed replicas, often costing thousands of marks and as distinctively representative of a specific town or county as a Scottish kilt is of a clan. Unfortunately, many of Southern Bavaria's visitors see only the phony setups, missing out on the opportunity to see some of the region's genuine traditions and costumes. Also invisible to most travellers are the 4,000 village brass bands, more than 500 folk-music groups, and dozens of folk-dance ensembles, all doing their thing as it has been done for generations.

Most preconceptions about Southern Bavaria are part truth, part myth. Consider the notion that the region is a bucolic backwater. True, it does produce as much milk and cheese as Switzerland, but it is also the sun-belt region of Germany and home of the country's burgeoning aerospace industry. Leading electronics, electrical, machine-tool, automobile, heavy engineering, optical goods, and petrochemical companies have their headquarters here. Then there's the sausage-and-beer legend. Sausages are indeed consumed in vast quantities in Southern Bavaria, where, moreover, two-thirds of West Germany's 1,500 independent breweries are located. But you will also find inns and restaurants applying the principles of nouvelle cuisine to traditional Bavarian recipes in refined surroundings.

While our discussion of the region covers some of the well-beaten paths and the best-known Alpine resort areas, which are certainly more than worthwhile—and many of which can be explored in one- or two-day trips from Munich—we will also introduce you to Bavaria beyond the myths and legends, with a fascinating history, spectacular scenery, and a centuries-old culture.

### MAJOR INTEREST

Castles, fortresses, and churches
Folk festivals
Spectacular scenery
Summer and winter sports in the Alps
Spa towns
Gothic town of Landshut
Scenic beauty of Inn river towns
Ludwig II's reproduction of Versailles on the
    Chiemsee
Wassily Kandinsky and Franz Marc museums in
    Murnau and Kochel
Linderhof, Ludwig II's most elaborate palace
Passionsspiel at Oberammergau
Violin-making at Mittenwald

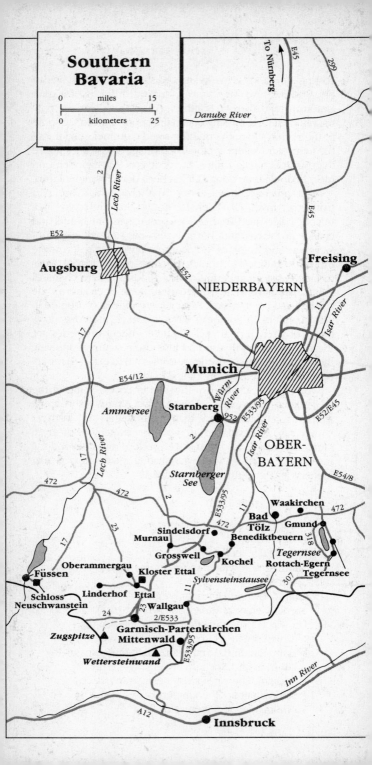

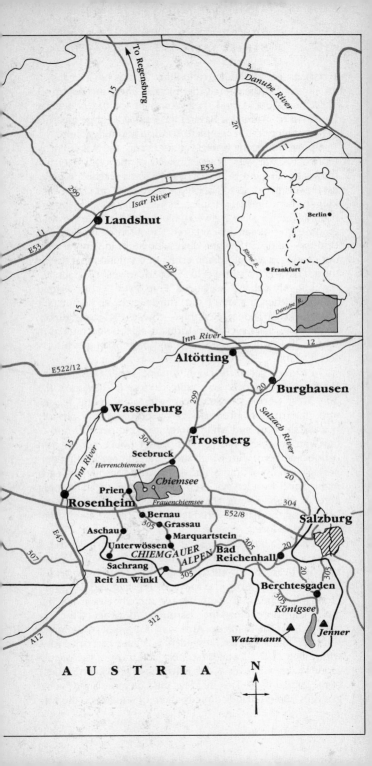

Bavarians are sometimes called the "Texans of Germany"—
an allusion to their territorial bigness, their inclination toward braggadocio, and their penchant for independence.
History is to blame, for Bavaria has enjoyed a large measure
of sovereignty, often complete, for nearly a millennium.

A powerful duchy whose ruling dynasty, the Wittelsbachs,
tended to side with France instead of the other German
mini-states in many European wars, Bavaria reached its greatest flowering thanks to Napoleon. In 1806 he proclaimed it a
kingdom and virtually tripled its territory, so as to have a
friendly buffer state between his realm and the Austrian
empire. The monarchy outlasted Napoleon by more than a
century—until 1918, when dukes and kings in general went
out of style in a Götterdämmerung of revolution that briefly
turned Bavaria into the world's second "soviet," or "council,"
republic. After that it became a "Free State" within Weimar
Germany, then a part of the Third Reich, and ultimately
joined today's Federal Republic—whose 1949 constitution,
incidentally, has never been formally signed and ratified in
Bavaria. It is still a "Free State," and more than just history
sets it apart.

"*In Bayern gehen die Uhren anders,*" other Germans say:
"In Bavaria the clocks go counterclockwise." Bavaria is the
only West German federal state with a bicameral legisla-
ture. Its frontiers are marked by border signs proudly
bearing the blue and white rhombuses and heraldic lion of
the Wittelsbachs. It has its own border police and its own
national anthem, with which the Bavarian broadcasting corporation signs off radio and television transmission each
night. Small wonder that even Germans feel they are going
abroad when visiting Bavaria, a sensation no doubt enhanced by the natives' predilection for regarding all non-
Bavarians as foreigners.

Munich is a perfect base for exploring Southern Bavaria. A
route generally northeast, along the Isar river, will take you
into the heartland of Altbayern and the administrative district of Niederbayern—the towns of Freising and Landshut.
From there, heading southeast (or directly east from Munich), you can explore the charming old towns of the Inn
river valley. The Bavarian Alps run in an east–west range
south of Munich—Berchtesgaden is at the eastern end—
with much of the loveliest scenery and most of the picturesque towns within an hour's drive (about 100 km/62 miles)
of the capital itself. This includes the Chiemsee and Chiemgau Alps, the highlands directly south of Munich on the way

to Garmisch-Partenkirchen, and the Zugspitze, Germany's highest peak.

## *FREISING AND LANDSHUT*

Freising, set on the banks of the Isar river, is so close to Munich (34 km/21 miles northeast) that you can take an S-Bahn there (15 stops on the S-1 from Munich's Marienplatz; see the Munich chapter). Originally called Frisinga, the town was first mentioned in documents in 744 and was one of the great spiritual and ecclesiastical centers of southern Germany in the Middle Ages. Not only was it the seat of the archdiocese that includes Munich, it was also the residence of the 12th-century bishop Adalbert, uncle of Holy Roman Emperor Frederick Barbarossa, whose bridge over the Isar was destroyed by Henry the Lion's knights in 1157: the act that led to the official founding of Munich a year later.

Freising was a cathedral town from the mid-eighth century until 1821, when the see and archbishop's residence were moved to Munich. Its cathedral, the **Dom St. Maria und St. Korbinian**, on the Domberg, a ridge high above the town and river, is in its exterior essentials still the same building consecrated in 1160. The interior, however, has undergone several transformations. The original flat ceiling was replaced by vaulting in the Late Gothic period. In the early 17th century it was redecorated in Renaissance style. A hundred years later, in 1723, Cosmas Damian Asam and Egid Quirin Asam, the two Munich brothers renowned for their work on churches, gave it the lavish Rococo stuccowork and extravagant frescoes that it has today. The high altar, installed in 1625, once contained Rubens's *Woman of the Apocalypse*. The original is now in Munich's Alte Pinakothek; what you see here is a copy.

Behind the Dom, connected to it by cloisters, is the **Benediktuskapelle** (Chapel of St. Benedict), also known as the Old Dom. Although it is a 14th-century work of the high Gothic style, its pillars and vault ribs were covered with Baroque stuccowork in the 1700s. More pure in its Gothic forms is the **Johanneskirche** (St. John's Church), on the west side of the Dom, built between 1319 and 1321. The **Bischöfliche Residenz** (Bishop's Residence) next door, now a school, has exterior and interior decoration by François de Cuvilliés and Johann-Baptist Zimmermann.

For more earthly pleasure in Freising you may want to

have a hearty lunch of warm *Leberkäs* (meat loaf) or *Haxen* (roast shank of veal or pork) at the **Bräustüberl Weihenstephan**, Weihenstephan 1, west of the Domberg. The restaurant is attached to the Weihenstephan brewery, the oldest in the world, founded in 1040. To this day it produces the cream of Bavarian beers—which is quite a claim, because in Upper Bavaria alone there are more than 600 independent breweries. There is a selection of 12 types on tap daily, including a tart, unfiltered Pilsner. The brewery is also a college-level training school for brewmasters.

**Landshut**, the first capital of Bavaria—38 km (about 23 miles) northeast of Freising by way of highway B 11 along the Isar or 72 km (45 miles) from Munich along the Autobahn—is one of the most beautiful and best-preserved Gothic towns in all of Germany. Its central area and two parallel main streets, Altstadt and Neustadt, have scarcely changed since the 16th century.

Like Munich, Landshut was created through an act of force, when an Isar river crossing with its lucrative toll and duty revenues was moved a short distance upstream under the menacing protection of a fortress built by Bavaria's second Wittelsbach ruler, Ludwig-der-Kehlheimer, in 1204. He called the stronghold Landes Hut. Known today as **Burg Trausnitz**, this massive, much-expanded castle is situated on a bluff overlooking the city and is visible from miles away. Defensive and residential buildings were added during the 14th, 15th, and 16th centuries, and Italian artists and craftsmen were hired in the 1570s to embellish it in Renaissance style, turning it into a *Lustschloss* (pleasure palace). Duke Wilhelm V and Renate of Lorraine (whose costly wedding bash is commemorated in the glockenspiel in Munich's Neues Rathaus) spent their honeymoon here. Wilhelm lived in the castle 11 years before becoming duke in 1579 and made it into an international meeting place for artists, actors, minstrels, and musicians. He hired artisans recommended to him by Hans Fugger, one of the rich Augsburg merchants and bankers, to decorate Trausnitz. The most dazzling legacy of the era is the *Narrentreppe* (Fools' Staircase), frescoed with vigorous *commedia dell'arte* figures.

For all its impressive majesty and visibility, Trausnitz is dwarfed by **St. Martin's**, Landshut's 14th-century parish church and collegiate minster. The majestic brick church stands in the very center of the town, on the Altstadt. The castle looms directly above it on the bluff south of the city. St. Martin's may well be the only Gothic church that was the

work of a single architect. Not only is his name known—
Hans von Burghausen—but on the south wall, between two
portals, there is a monument to him erected by his co-
workers and successors after his death in 1432. The church's
430-foot spire, completed in 1500, is the tallest brick church
tower in the world. St. Martin's is not only huge—the nave is
300 feet long and 95 feet high—but it is rich in 15th- and
16th-century sculpture and carved stone portals and altars.
The *Landshut Madonna,* a larger-than-life-size figure carved
in 1520, is the finest piece.

Landshut's two principal streets, Altstadt and Neustadt, run
south to north from the foot of the castle hill to the Isar. Both
are lined by richly decorated burgher and patrician houses.
The most impressive structure is the **Stadtresidenz**, at
Altstadt 79 (two blocks north of St. Martin's), a little city
palace that the Wittelsbachs used when they considered
Trausnitz castle too "suburban" for their mood. Duke Ludwig X admired the Palazzo del Té in Mantua during his visit
to Italy in 1563, and hired builders and craftsmen from
Padua to make him this replica in Landshut. Today the Italian
Renaissance palace is a dual museum, showing 18th-century
applied art (the **Stadt und Kreismuseum**) and 16th- to 18th-
century European painting (the **Staatliche Gemäldegalerie**).

A few yards south on a little side street, at Ländgasse 51, is
the former ducal chancellor's house, **Beim Vitztumb**, where
you can dine superbly in 15th-century surroundings. For a
substantial Bavarian lunch there is also the moderately
priced **Goldene Sonne**, at Neustadt 520, an old inn with 54
comfortable guest rooms. For more expensive, but romantic, overnight surroundings, consider the **Hotel Kaiserhof**,
Papiererstrasse 2, idyllically situated on the left embankment
of the Isar, just a two-minute walk from Landshut's historic
quarter.

The historic quarter was also the scene of the most famous event in Landshut history—the marriage in 1475 of
Duke George the Rich to Jadwiga, daughter of Poland's King
Casimir V. To celebrate, the duke invited all of Europe's
royalty and nobility and spent the equivalent of around
today's DM 20 million to stage a week-long orgy, during
which the guests and townsfolk consumed 333 roast oxen,
490 calves, 1,133 sheep, 1,537 lambs, 684 pigs, 11,500 geese,
40,000 chickens, and oceans of beer and wine. Every four
years (the last time was in 1989) some 1,300 Landshuters
don Medieval costumes and stage reenactments of the
"Landshuter Hochzeit." It is one of Bavaria's chief folk festi-

vals, and although the original wedding was on November 19, the reenactment is staged in June for the benefit of summer visitors.

## INN RIVER TOWNS

The Inn river rises in Switzerland's Graubünden canton, winds its way generally northeast through Austria's Tyrol, passes Innsbruck, enters Bavaria near Rosenheim, a Medieval mountain city some 56 km (35 miles) southeast of Munich, then continues its convoluted chalky-green course first through Oberbayern and then Niederbayern and along the Austrian border to spill into the Danube at Passau. It cuts a glistening, and often turbulently flooding, swath through Southern Bavaria and some of its oldest, most colorful towns.

The Inn valley is at its most breathtaking and dramatic at **Wasserburg**, where the river makes a hairpin bend so sharp that this 850-year-old town appears to be a fortified island with the river serving as a moat. Its name, in fact, means "water fortress."

Located 50 km (31 miles) east of Munich along highway B 12, then 16 km (10 miles) south on the B 15, the incomparably picturesque town of Wasserburg is perfect for half a day of wandering through streets that take you back to a time long past. Ironically, the little city owes its perfect Medieval appearance to economic decline. Founded in 1137, it became rich and powerful as a central junction on the vital salt-trade routes from the mines in the Bavarian and Tyrolean Alps to Bohemia and northern Germany. But in the 16th century the salt road was shifted southward to Rosenheim, and Wasserburg went into a recession that lasted for hundreds of years. Lack of money prevented burghers from redecorating their houses, public buildings, and churches in later architectural periods, a practice that turned many other Bavarian towns into kaleidoscopes of Gothic, Renaissance, Baroque, and Rococo styles. Though it is lively enough today, you will find Wasserburg a perfectly preserved Medieval gem.

On the Kirchplatz, in the heart of the old quarter, stands the **Pfarrkirche St. Jakob**, built by Hans von Burghausen, the same master responsible for Landshut's minster. This parish church is a classic example of 15th-century Gothic. Up the steep hill from St. Jakob in a westerly direction is Wasserburg's 12th-century fortress, rebuilt in 1526 by Duke Wilhelm IV—in part to compensate the town for its commercial troubles—who turned it into an occasional residence. Now used as an old-age home, the fortress is notable for its elaborately decorated reception hall. The Rathaus (City Hall), on the Marienplatz, a few blocks east and downhill from the Burg, will give you a sense of Wasserburg's pride and wealth in the 15th and 16th centuries. It was a typical practice of the time to combine the town council chamber, a public ballroom, and a granary under one roof, and this curious trifold purpose has been preserved here. The councillors' chamber on the upper floor is richly decorated with intricately carved oak ceiling panels and allegorical murals.

**Altötting**, 60 km (37 miles) downstream and northeast of Wasserburg by way of highways B 15 and B 12, is a world unto itself, due to its centuries-long role as a kind of German Lourdes. The **Heilige Kapelle** (Holy Chapel) on the Kapellplatz, the center of the town, draws up to 600,000 faithful each year. First mentioned in 877, the little church may well have existed much earlier: One legend has it that a seventh-century Bavarian count was baptized in it by Saint Rupert, a missionary monk. Until 1491 the round church was just a simple chapel in the Carolingian style. But then it became the repository of the *Black Madonna*—so-named because it is blackened with soot—a two-foot-high 13th-century wood carving of Mary, thought to have come from Alsace and believed to have all kinds of miraculous powers. The figure has been kept in a richly decorated silver tabernacle since the 17th century. An almost-life-size solid-silver sculpture of Bavaria's Duke Max III Joseph, depicted as a ten-year-old, kneels before the shrine. It was an offering of thanks to the Madonna from his father, Elector Karl Albrecht, for the deliverance of the young duke from a serious illness in 1737.

Bavaria's Wittelsbach rulers have long been associated with the Heilige Kapelle, which is in effect a national shrine. The hearts of six Bavarian dukes and kings, two queens, two electors, and Field Marshal Tilly, the Bavarian hero of the Thirty Years War, are kept in silver urns in wall compartments opposite the shrine. The most famous pilgrim of modern times was Pope John Paul II, who visited Altötting in 1980.

The exterior and interior walls of the chapel, as well as the sacristy of the adjacent 16th-century **Stiftskirche St. Philipp und St. Jakob** (Collegiate Church of St. Philip and St. James), are covered with offerings of thanks for deliverance from sickness and danger. Among them are hundreds of

*Votiftafeln* (votive tablets), some of them five centuries old, which are fine examples of folk and primitive art.

Given its role as a place of pilgrimage, Altötting hardly lacks for hotels and inns. The top spot is the moderately priced **Hotel zur Post**, Kapellplatz 2, directly across the square from the Heilige Kapelle. It is owned, though not actively run, by Bavaria's minister of finance, Gerold Tandler.

Sixteen km (10 miles) southeast of Altötting, by way of an unnumbered country road, is **Burghausen**, a town in its own way as spectacular and photogenic as Wasserburg. Located on the left bank of the Salzach river, a tributary to the Inn, across from Austria, this 1,000-year-old town is crowned on the cliff above it by the largest Medieval fortress complex in Germany.

More than 1,200 yards long and almost a town in itself, the **Burg** is located atop a ridge between the Salzach and a little lake. Built over a period of epochs, starting in the 11th century, the castle served a succession of Bavarian dukes who at one time or another held court there, as did Holy Roman Emperor Henry II. Most of the remaining buildings, one of which contains a division of the Bayerische Staatsgemäldesammlung (Bavarian State Pictures Collection), date from the 13th to the 15th centuries. The castle, with its numerous buildings, could occupy an entire day, and since there is even more to see and do in Burghausen you may want to spend a night in the moderately priced **Hotel zur Post**, Stadtplatz 39, right in the center of the Altstadt, or the even more economical **Hotel Glöcklhofer**, Ludwigsberg 4, located on the castle hill directly at the entrance to the fortress.

Also on the Stadtplatz is the 14th-century Rathaus. Fifty yards away is the Pfarrkirche St. Jakob, and 150 yards farther south is the 16th-century Spitalkirche Heilig Geist (Church of the Holy Ghost). The narrow, winding, cobblestone streets of the quarter are lined by arcades and 16th- to 17th-century burgher houses. Thanks to the modern world of electronics and its own vast resources of silicon, Burghausen has become a major center of microchip manufacturing and is in the midst of an unprecedented period of prosperity that in turn is benefiting its abundance of old architecture with costly restoration and preservation. The renovated town now looks much the way it must have centuries ago.

# THE CHIEMSEE AND THE CHIEMGAU ALPS

A leisurely and scenic 35-km (22-mile) drive along sign-posted country roads southwest from Burghausen will lead you, via Trostberg, to Seebruck, on the northern tip of the **Chiemsee**, the largest of the Bavarian lakes. Because it covers nearly 33 square miles, it is often referred to as the Bavarian Ocean. The duchy did indeed once have a navy and even a couple of grand admirals before Benjamin Thompson, a.k.a. Count Rumford, the American who became Bavaria's minister of war, reorganized the ducal forces in 1788. But they sailed their boats on the Rhine; the Chiemsee was too shallow. Its shallowness, however, does not deter thousands of summer and weekend sailors and windsurfers. The shore from Seebruck to Prien, on the southwestern side, is lined with inviting little holiday towns and villages.

As spectacular as the lake itself are Frauenchiemsee and Herrenchiemsee, both islands reached by excursion boats, one of them a 1920s sidewheeler, from Prien.

**Frauenchiemsee** is so named for its 1,200-year-old Bene-dictine nunnery, one of the best-preserved Medieval con-vents in Germany, still active today. Saint Irmengard, a great-granddaughter of Charlemagne, was its abbess in the ninth century. Though much of the original eighth-century complex was destroyed in the tenth century by the Hungari-ans during their raids into Bavaria, reconstruction began not much later, and the convent church as well as surround-ing buildings, which are Romanesque in style, date from the 11th century. Renovations and excavations in the 1960s exposed portions of the earliest structures and some mag-nificent 12th-century frescoes that had been painted over.

Frauenchiemsee is also the name of the island's small fishing village, which became a favorite summer hangout of Munich painters and writers in the 19th century. They con-gregated to dine on *Renken,* a member of the trout family indigenous to the lake, and other charcoal-broiled fish at the colorful, cozy **Inselwirt,** a 200-year-old inn with a small beer garden, where you may well want to have lunch or supper in incomparably idyllic surroundings.

**Herrenchiemsee**, the larger of the two islands, derives its name from the Benedictine monks and canons who inhab-ited its monastery from the early eighth century until the Magyars laid waste to it in the tenth. Rebuilt in 1130, it became an Augustinian abbey and was later secularized, in 1803. Only a few of its buildings survive, among them the Gothic Pfarrkirche and the 19th-century Altes Schloss, which has a lavishly decorated Imperial hall and a richly endowed library.

But what really draws the steamboat crowds to Herren-chiemsee is the **Neues Schloss**, Ludwig II's extravagant replica of Versailles. Whatever the Dream King's romantic, fairy-tale motivations for building his other castles, this one seems to have had a pragmatic purpose. Since his first visit to Versailles in 1867 Ludwig had dreamed of building something equally grand in Bavaria. He bought the island in 1873 to prevent its falling into the hands of real-estate speculators and five years later began his copy of Versailles, complete with a Hall of Mirrors, a staircase that is almost an exact facsimile of Louis Le Vau's and Charles Le Brun's Escalier des Ambassadeurs, a suite of private rooms corresponding to the apartments of Louis XV, and a fountain of Apollo and a Latona fountain.

Ludwig II occupied the Herrenchiemsee palace on only one occasion, for ten nights in the fall of 1885—and when he was removed from the throne and died, in 1886, only the central block and one of the wings, since taken down, had been completed. But already the cost was more than that of Neuschwanstein (see the Romantic Road chapter) and Lin-derhof (see below) put together. To see what else was planned on Herrenchiemsee, visit the adjacent **King Ludwig II museum**, with its exhibits of construction drawings and models, and you may be inclined to ponder long about this enigmatic monarch.

In the Chiemsee region nearly every little *Gasthaus* has a portrait of Ludwig. But considering his eccentricities, the vast sums he spent on building his dreams, and his notions of absolutism in an age of constitutional monarchy, one would expect him to be regarded as anything but the folk hero he is. The explanation is that he really did care for the people. His castle projects provided a great deal of employment in Bavaria's most remote areas, and records show that he spent vast sums on charity. His eccentricity was just the kind that the mountain people understood.

Back on the mainland you are not far from the mountains. South of the lake are a number of spectacular routes and pretty villages that entail less than an hour or two of driving. But you may wish to rest for a night in the Chiemsee area before venturing into them. Take the unnumbered country road south from Prien on the Chiemsee to **Bernau**, a distance of only 6 km (less than 4 miles). Prien abounds with hotels, inns, and pensions, and is a very busy lakeside and boating resort. Bernau is a better choice to spend a night, and its best accommodations are at the **Alter Wirt-Bonnschloss**, Kirchplatz 9, a dignified, moderately priced 19th-century inn with rustic, wood-paneled decor, cozy guest rooms, and friendly hospitality.

Bernau is a good jumping-off point for the year-round attractions of the Chiemgau Alps. In summer, when the highland pastures, laced with stands of dark pine and spruce, are a velvety emerald green and the higher peaks rise chalky gray against the azure sky, the Chiemgau region attracts droves of hikers and climbers. Bernau, a mere 80 km (50 miles) from Munich, can be crowded on weekends, summer and winter alike. From December through February, sometimes March, it is a winter resort area with an abundance of downhill and cross-country skiing facilities. These are Munich's *Hausberge* (backyard mountains) and they attract the multitudes who don't want to drive farther afield, although the time they save on the road they lose by standing in lift lines.

Nevertheless, the beauty of the area outweighs any inconvenience caused by the crowds. One short and splendidly scenic itinerary leads from Bernau through Aschau, past the dramatic Kampenwand massif, to the hamlet of Sachrang at the Austrian border. The entire drive is only 20 km (12 miles), but you could easily spend a day or two along the way. Though **Aschau** is a mere 5 km (3 miles) southwest of Bernau, you may want to spend the night there, for its 17th-century **Hotel zur Post**, Kirchplatz 1, is as historic as it is charming. Post hotels in Bavaria and elsewhere in southern Germany go back to the 15th and 16th centuries, when local butchers, who were also the village innkeepers, did double duty as "mailmen" by carrying letters and information as they made the rounds to buy livestock for slaughter. In the 17th century, when the South Tyrolean princes of Thurn-und-Taxis started Europe's first postal service with express riders and stagecoaches that carried passengers and mail, the butcher-innkeepers became the local postmasters. Their inns became the relay stations along the rapidly expanded Thurn-und-Taxis routes, and these postal inns soon spread over the countryside and established reputations as the most comfortable places to stay.

On a cliff high above the town is **Burg Hohenaschau**, mightiest of the fortresses in the Chiemgau. The castle, first mentioned in 927, passed through various baronial hands, including those of the counts of Freyberg, one of whom transformed the uncomfortable digs into a Renaissance-style palace. The counts of Freyberg sold the property to the counts of Preysing, who lived in it from 1608 to 1853, at one point undoing the Renaissance decoration and replacing it with Baroque. Still private property, it now belongs to the baronial family Cramer-Klett, who also operate a small brewery at the foot of the cliff, but it can be visited during the summer months. Among the things to see on the guided tour is the monumental gallery of ancestors in the state ballroom of the main castle. It displays 12 larger-than-life statues on pedestals in ornately decorated surroundings. The chapel's Rococo interior, dating from the 18th century, is partly the work of Johann-Baptist Zimmermann.

Just beyond the castle the road passes the base station of the gondola up the **Kampenwand**, a 5,500-foot-high crenelated stone massif that is the landmark of the Chiemgau Alps. At the top of the gondola system there are numerous smaller chair lifts and T-bars that accommodate visitors to one of the area's most popular ski slopes. The gondolas operate in summer as well to transport climbers and hikers, but beware: This is no mountain for amateurs. The sheer cliffs that face north toward the Chiemsee can be negotiated only by experienced, fully equipped alpinists.

From the Kampenwand the road winds and climbs steeply through picture-postcard hamlets and dark evergreen forests to the Austrian border and the little town of **Sachrang**, whose main attractions are a Baroque parish church, winter lifts for nondemanding skiing, a maze of cross-country tracks, and well-marked hiking trails.

The same road takes you back to the starting point at Bernau, a half-hour drive—unless you get caught in weekend traffic.

From Bernau there is an even more dramatic and scenic journey (26 km/16 miles) south through a different valley to the winter-and-summer resort town of **Reit im Winkl**. Everything is well posted, but for guidance it may help to know that the road (B 305, the Deutsche Alpenstrasse) passes through Grassau, Marquartstein, and Unterwössen, then rises steeply, with grades of up to 15 percent and many hairpin curves, for the final lap to Reit im Winkl.

Reit im Winkl is a summer hiker's joy and a winter skier's paradise, with miles and miles of cross-country *Loipen* as well as downhill trails. Because of its altitude and enclosure by craggy peaks up to 7,000 feet high, the **Winklmoosalm** (10 km/6 miles east of the center of town) is one of the best ski areas in Bavaria. It has an exceptionally long season, and with luck you will find good snow as early as November and as late as April. Because there are nearly two dozen chair lifts and T-bars, waiting lines are tolerably short, even on Saturdays and Sundays. The road up to the Winklmoosalm is open in summer, but during the skiing season you must leave your car at the Seegatterl parking lot and take a shuttle bus up. Purchase of a pass to all the lifts includes the bus fare, and at the end of the day you can ski back down to the parking lot—a spectacular six-mile run that all but rank beginners can easily negotiate. Always popular, the Winklmoosalm became famous thanks to the daughter of a local innkeeper and ski-school operator, Rosi Mittermaier, who won two gold medals during the Winter Olympics and the World Cup in 1976. The area straddles Germany and Austria, and many of the lifts and trails crisscross the border. If you want to spend a night on top, the best spot is the **Alpengasthof Winklmoosalm**, Dünbachhornweg 6. In Reit im Winkl itself you will find very comfortable rooms and solid stick-to-the-ribs Bavarian food at the **Hotel Unterwirt**, Kirchplatz 2, adjacent to the parish church. There is less traffic and more fresh air and nature, as well as more sophisticated cuisine, at the **Hotel Steinbacher Hof**, Steinbachweg 10, at the foot of the *Sprungschanze* (ski jump).

From Reit im Winkl the **Deutsche Alpenstrasse** (German Alpine Road), one of Germany's more than 140 named scenic driving routes, leads generally east through gorgeous mountain country to Berchtesgaden. It is a drive of 61 km (38 miles), all of it along B 305.

# BERCHTESGADEN

Today, the name of this idyllically situated town, tucked into the southeasternmost corner of Germany and practically within shouting distance of Salzburg, conjures immediate recollections of Hitler. It was on the **Obersalzberg**, one of many high peaks surrounding Berchtesgaden, that Hitler had his vacation retreat and received foreign heads of state and government at the "Eagle's Nest," where so much of Third Reich and World War II history was made. You can still see the ruins of the complex, with its guesthouses, underground bunker system, and the barracks of Hitler's SS bodyguard detachment.

Berchtesgaden's history predates that dark period by nearly 850 years, and the town, rich in art and architecture as well as glorious Alpine scenery, offers far more than the legacy of Hitler's residence. It began around 1100 with an Augustinian priory and came to riches through the mining and export of salt, the "white gold" of the Middle Ages. Today, Berchtesgaden preserves its prosperity as a summer and winter resort.

Much of the monastery remains, including the former **Stiftskirche St. Peter und Johannes** (Collegiate Church of St. Peter and St. John the Baptist), a Romanesque and Gothic structure in the center of town, at the Schlossplatz. Built and decorated in stages from the late 12th through 16th centuries, its treasures include the sculpted tombstones of a number of the priors, who were also princes and secular rulers, and the richly carved 15th-century choir stalls. The *Stift* (Canonry), adjacent to the church, is now called the *Schloss,* because after secularization Bavaria's Wittelsbach rulers took it over and turned it into a summer palace in 1818. Exactly a century later the last king, Ludwig III, fled there from revolutionary Munich, and his son, Crown Prince Rupprecht, made it into his permanent home, filling it with treasures of art and applied art. It is still owned by the Wittelsbach family.

The **Schlossmuseum** inside the palace is the vaulted 14th-century dormitory of the abbey's canons and shows the excellent art collection assembled by Rupprecht—who, it should be added, lived until 1952, and shortly after World War II reputedly rejected an offer by General George S. Patton, then U.S. military governor of Bavaria, to restore the monarchy.

Also worth seeing are St. Andreas, a 14th-century parish Church with late 17th-century embellishments, on the Schlossplatz, and the early-16th-century Frauenkirche (Church of Our Lady) on the river Anger.

Typical of Bavarian mountain towns are the painted façades of the burgher houses around the **Marktplatz** and on **Metzgerstrasse**, the two central shopping streets, which are pedestrian zones. This *Lüftlmalerei* (roughly, "open-air painting") uses trompe l'oeil to create three-dimensional effects and often transcends pure folk art: The scenes of monkeys parodying human passions and frailties around the windows of the Gasthaus zum Hirschen are masterpieces.

Salt is still mined in Berchtesgaden today; to see how it was done centuries ago, visit the **Salzmuseum**, Bergwerkstrasse 83 (east of the center), operated by the mining company. Part of the fun is donning traditional miners' garb, sliding down wooden chutes into the shafts and tunnels, and seeing exhibits of old equipment. No less interesting is the

**Heimatmuseum** (Museum of Local History), on the Salzburger Strasse near the northern edge of town, with its rich displays of local craftsmanship, especially the intricate filigreelike wood carving and the brightly painted wooden boxes that are a local specialty. The **Berchtesgadener Handwerkskunst**, in the Heimatmuseum, is the best shop at which to buy them.

The landscape around Berchtesgaden, situated at the base of the 9,000-foot **Watzmann**, Germany's second-highest mountain, is spectacular, but nature seems to have outdone herself at the **Königssee**, 5 km (3 miles) south of the town. This crystal-clear mountain lake, surrounded by the steep cliffs of the Watzmann, Jenner, and Götzenberg peaks, is a three-dimensional picture of dramatic Alpine scenery. Nonpolluting electric-powered boats make excursions along the five-mile-long Königssee, stopping off at St. Bartholomä, a little Baroque church on the western shore. For winter sports, **Jenner mountain**, with an aerial cable car and an abundance of chair lifts and T-bars higher up, is the best place.

Hotels and inns in every category abound in Berchtesgaden. For royal accommodations at moderate prices, it is hard to top the **Königliche Villa**, Am Luitpoldpark. This erstwhile country mansion of the Wittelsbachs features marble bathrooms, parquet flooring, stucco ceilings, and a delightful wine and beer cellar. Closer to the center of town are the **Hotel Wittelsbach**, a recently renovated turn-of-the-century establishment, and the **Vier Jahreszeiten**, Maximilianstrasse 20, a more modern hotel with rustic Alpine decor.

Accommodations are even more plentiful, and range from moderate to pampered luxury, in Bad Reichenhall, one of Germany's oldest and most famous spa towns, 12 km (7.5 miles) northwest of Berchtesgaden by way of B 20.

# Bad Reichenhall

Legend holds that this gold-plated, gilt-edged health resort was an Illyrian settlement long before the Romans arrived in southern Germany. While there is little physical evidence of either Illyrians or Romans, it is a fact that *hall* was the Illyrian word for salt, and here, as in nearby Berchtesgaden, salt has been, if not the spice of life, then certainly the resource that gave (and still gives) Bad Reichenhall its riches and prosperity. The salinic mineral waters, guaranteed to cure whatever you think ails you, and the splendid mountain scenery attract the multitudes and also account for Bad Reichenhall's ornate Belle Epoque architectural look.

For all the salty spa atmosphere, the little city's Medieval beginnings, like Berchtesgaden's, were as a priory. **St. Zeno**, the church built here by the Augustinian canons and completed in 1228, is the largest Romanesque structure in Upper Bavaria. Though damaged by a fire in 1412, which resulted in reconstruction of its interior in Late Gothic style, the outside is classically Romanesque. The west portal is a remarkable piece of masonry in red and gray marble, strongly influenced by the style then prevailing in northern Italy. Be sure to see the Romanesque **cloisters** in the adjacent monastery building. On one of the columns there is a bas-relief of Emperor Frederick Barbarossa, a patron of the abbey. Bad Reichenhall's parish church, St. Nikolai—at the south edge of town, on a square between the Innsbrucker Strasse and the Tiroler Strasse—is older, dating from 1181, and also worthy of a visit.

Fortunately, not all of Bad Reichenhall is taking the waters and worrying about aches and pains. As in all German spa towns, there is a well-tended, neatly manicured Kurpark, a Kurhaus with auditorium for concerts and plays, and a plush **casino**, where the major attractions are roulette and baccarat.

For a hefty Bavarian lunch in a rustic environment stop in at **Gasthaus Hofwirt**, Salzburger Strasse 21, a pedestrian zone in the center of town. If your taste is for something more sophisticated, though not necessarily local, try the **Schweizer Stuben** at Thumseestrasse 11, on the west bank of the Saalach river at the south edge of town, where the fare is a mixture of Swiss and Swabian.

The hotel scene is abundant in Bad Reichenhall, though comparatively pricey in every category. For grand-hotel elegance, the top address is the venerable **Steigenberger-Hotel Axelmannstein**, Salzburger Strasse 4, surrounded by its own 300,000-square-foot park. Nearly directly across the street, just below where the Salzburger Strasse becomes the Ludwigstrasse, is the **Kurhotel Luisenbad**. The Hofwirt offers more moderately priced accommodations in the same Bavarian-inn style as its restaurant (see above).

Unless you want to retrace your route or see more of the countryside, the fastest return route to Munich is the Salzburg–Munich Autobahn. Access to the highway is only 3 km (less than 2 miles) from the center of Bad Reichenhall, and the distance from there is 136 km (85 miles).

# THE HIGHLANDS
# SOUTH OF MUNICH

Upper Bavaria is at its loveliest and most historic south of
Munich, where the countryside, dotted with lakes, rises
gently through foothills covered with verdant pastures and
groves of evergreens, and farther south reaches dramatic
heights in the Alpine ranges that divide Germany and western Austria.

A round-trip itinerary from Munich would entail little
more than 150 miles of driving, detours included. It is
possible to take in the scenery and charming towns along
the way in only a day or a weekend—but the area could also
easily occupy you for a week, or even two.

The journey we suggest begins at Starnberg, 27 km (17
miles) south of Munich, and leads south through Murnau
(on the Staffelsee), Kochel (on the Kochelsee), Oberammergau, Ettal monastery, King Ludwig II's Linderhof château, and
Garmisch-Partenkirchen, at the foot of the Zugspitze, then
east to Mittenwald, and northeast to Tegernsee and the little
mountain city of Bad Tölz.

**Starnberg**, best reached by taking the Munich-to-Garmisch-
Partenkirchen Autobahn, is practically a suburb of Munich,
and so are many of the other little towns around the
**Starnbergersee**, Bavaria's second-largest lake, which on a
wintry night can become as stormy as the Atlantic. Excursion
steamers ply it from April through October, and like the
Chiemsee, it is a popular weekend sailing and windsurfing
spot.

It was in this lake that Ludwig II, accompanied by his
psychiatrist-keeper Dr. Bernhard von Gudden, drowned mysteriously three days after his arrest at his castle, Neuschwanstein. The scene was at **Schloss Berg**, 6 km (less than 4
miles) south of Starnberg on the lake's eastern shore.

To call Berg a castle stretches the term; manor house is
more exact. Ferdinand Maria, the first Wittelsbach duke to
become an elector of the Holy Roman Empire, bought it in
1676, surrounded it with a lovely park, and used it as a base
for outings on the lake aboard an ornate ship called the
*Buccentaur*. More than a century and a half later King
Maximilian II rebuilt the mansion in neo-Gothic Tudor style.
It is still Wittelsbach property—octogenarian Herzog Albrecht von Bayern lives in it a great deal of the time. But

Berg is more than just a footnote to Bavarian and Wittelsbach history, because of the mysterious death of Ludwig II.

A first attempt to arrest the Dream King had been made the night of June 9, 1886, shortly after a commission of psychiatrists had ruled him incompetent. The doctors and some cabinet ministers and keepers arrived at Neuschwanstein but were themselves arrested by armed and angry highland peasants who had rallied to the king's defense. Ludwig decided to release them, but the next night they were back, and he surrendered. He was taken to Berg, where a royal prison was already being constructed for him; he was apparently to be locked up there forever, and the government of Bavaria was to go to his uncle, Luitpold. Three days after his arrival at Berg, Ludwig succeeded in being let out for a walk on the lakeshore, accompanied by Dr. von Gudden, the psychiatrist who had compiled the dossier and declared him insane. Several hours later both men were found floating dead in the water near the shoreline: Ludwig in shirt-sleeves, Gudden fully dressed and with strangulation marks and other bruises suggesting that he had died in a struggle.

To this day speculation as to what really happened has not subsided—not even the rumor that the fishermen who pulled the bodies out of the lake had actually hauled out wax dummies, and that the king had escaped to lead his dream life incognito for many more years, in Italy or Switzerland.

The memorial cross, just offshore at the site where the bodies were found, was erected almost immediately and is the scene of annual pilgrimages by Ludwig devotees, as is the memorial chapel on the shore. The chapel is a neo-Romanesque structure dedicated in 1896, built by Julius Hofmann, Ludwig's favorite architect. Flowers and wreaths from Ludvicophiles grace its altar every day.

A good place to contemplate the mystery and view the scene of the Dream King's demise is from the terrace restaurant of the **Strandhotel Schloss Berg**, at Seestrasse 17, virtually adjacent to the chapel. With its rustic public rooms and 27 bedrooms in period furnishings, it's an enjoyable place to spend a night or two.

For a different slice of Bavarian life, continue south on B 2 out of Starnberg in the direction of Garmisch-Partenkirchen, to **Murnau** and **Kochel**, where Wassily Kandinsky and Franz Marc founded the *Blaue Reiter* (Blue Rider) artists' circle. It is a drive of 46 km (28 miles) from Starnberg to Murnau, and from there about 15 km (9 miles) to Kochel, east on an unnumbered side road.

The skylines of both towns are punctuated with onion domes and the steep saddle roofs of chalets. Tourism and highland dairy farming are their primary sources of income and they are so studiedly picturesque that they seem to give a new dimension to the word *kitsch*. But there is nothing kitschy about the epochal art movement that began here.

The story begins in 1902 in Munich, where Kandinsky, then 36, having left a wife and a law practice behind in Moscow, had been living and trying to make his way as an artist since 1896. He was teaching at an art school and had befriended one of his students, Gabriele Münter. In 1908 the couple settled in bucolic Murnau, where Münter had bought a cozy three-story country house. Kandinsky painted their rustic furniture with peasant motifs and embellished the staircase with folkloric images of little horses and riders galloping up to the second floor, where he and Münter had their studios and bedroom. It was in Murnau that Kandinsky began nonrepresentational painting. His 1910 *Church in Murnau,* a brightly colored, abstract view of the town's 18th-century parish church of St. Nikolaus, was painted from the bedroom window of the house.

Also in 1910, Franz Marc, then 30, moved with his second wife, Maria, to the farming hamlet of Sindelsdorf, a cowbell's ring away from (and today a part of) the town of Kochel. Marc, a native Münchener, was already a member of the new artists federation that Kandinsky, Münter, Paul Klee, Alexej von Jawlensky, Marianne von Werefkin, Alfred Kubin, and others had launched as an association committed to breaking away from the genre painting then admired in Munich.

Marc and Kandinsky became close friends, and with Murnau and Kochel less than an hour away by bicycle, visited each other almost daily. In March 1911 they forged plans to publish a yearly almanac for the circle, to be called *Der Blaue Reiter.* Many years later Kandinsky explained how the name came about: "Marc and I chose the name as we were having coffee on the shady terrace of his house. Both of us liked blue, Marc for horses, I for riders. So the name came by itself." The first and only edition was published in May 1912, with most of the preparatory work done in Murnau and Kochel.

The artistic idyll in the two villages might well have continued had World War I not intervened. Marc, a reserve lieutenant in the Bavarian army, was killed in action at Verdun in March 1916. His remains were brought from a battlefield cemetery for reburial in the Kochel village graveyard after the war. Kandinsky, fearing internment as an enemy alien, had fled to his native Russia. He and Gabriele Münter met once in Stockholm, in 1915, but then never saw each other again. In 1931 Münter moved back into the Murnau house and preserved it almost exactly as she and Kandinsky had left it. When the Nazis came to power and declared all the avant-garde artists degenerate, some 130 of Marc's pictures were confiscated and destroyed. Kandinsky had left Münter a substantial lode, and to protect it she built a brick vault around the paintings in the basement of the Murnau house. In 1957 she donated this priceless collection—90 oils, 300 watercolors and drawings, 29 complete sketchbooks, four dozen of her own pictures, and numerous works by other Blue Rider artists—to the Städtische Galerie in Lenbachhaus, in Munich, which got title to the house after Münter's death in 1962.

The **Münter house**, at Kottmüllerallee 6, has been turned into a small museum. The entry hall, staircase, and second-floor rooms look almost the way they did when the two lived there, with all the furniture, personal belongings, and Kandinsky's collection of Bavarian clay pipes in place. In 1986 the **Franz Marc Museum** opened in Kochel. It features a collection of memorabilia; paintings by Marc's father, a Munich landscape artist; several early works of the artist as well as some of the fine abstract paintings he did between 1910 and 1914 and that his widow preserved; and even some of his original woodcuts and proofs of the *Blaue Reiter* almanac. There is also a fascinating collection of paintings by Münter, Jawlensky, Werefkin, Klee, and other members of the Munich avant garde, and Kandinsky's oil-on-cardboard study for that topsy-turvy view of Murnau's St. Nikolaus church from the bedroom window. The museum is just off highway B 11 on the way out of Kochel in the direction of Urfeld (large signs point to it).

Because you cannot live on art alone, have lunch—or have dinner and spend the night—at the **Hotel Schmied von Kochel** at Schlehdorfer Strasse 6 in Kochel. This pleasant inn has historical significance for Bavarians. The *Schmied* (blacksmith) of Kochel was Balthasar Mayer, a well-loved Bavarian hero. He led a bloody albeit unsuccessful peasant rebellion against the Austrians, who had occupied Munich during the War of the Spanish Succession in 1705. The hotel was his smithy, and his forge and anvil remain in place in the vaulted tavern room. A huge mural in the lobby tells the story of the uprising and its tragic defeat, which resulted in the death of every man.

If you prefer to stay instead in Murnau, you will find delightful accommodations, with breathtaking views of the

Alps from your room, and exquisite nouvelle Bavarian cuisine, at the **Hotel Alpenhof Murnau**, Ramsachstrasse 8.

Two short side trips from both Murnau and Kochel open up yet another dimension of this area. Near Grossweil, off the road between Murnau and Kochel, is the open-air **Dorfmuseum** (Village Museum), with 90 historic chalets and Alpine farmhouses, where local people demonstrate handicrafts and depict Bavarian countryside life in the 17th through the 19th centuries. It is open from spring through fall.

An 8-km (5-mile) drive north from Kochel, on B 11, will take you to **Benediktbeuern**, site of the oldest Benedictine monastery in Upper Bavaria. Though founded around 747, the complex, which includes the church of St. Benedict, is largely 17th- and 18th-century Baroque, featuring frescoes, stuccowork, and embellishment by such masters as the Asam brothers and Johann-Baptist Zimmermann. The text of *Carmina Burana,* set to music by Munich composer Carl Orff in 1937, written here in the 12th to 13th century, was found in the monastery library.

To continue your journey through the highlands, drive south on B 2 from Murnau for 12 km (7.5 miles), then turn right at the junction with B 23 to make the steep, winding climb up to the Ettal monastery, Linderhof, and Oberammergau.

**Kloster Ettal**, 7 winding km (4.5 miles) from the highway junction, is known as the Bavarian Temple of the Grail. The Benedictine monastery was founded in 1330 by Bavarian duke and Holy Roman Emperor Ludwig-der-Bayer to house 22 monks, 13 knights and their wives, and several widows. An Italian painting of the Madonna, brought to the monastery church soon after its completion in 1370, made it the most important center of pilgrimages in the Bavarian Alps. The church, originally Gothic in style, was a 12-sided building modeled on the church of the Holy Sepulcher in Jerusalem. In 1710 Enrico Zucalli, the Swiss master architect set to work remodeling the building in Baroque style. Later work by other masters, including Zimmermann, turned the huge domed minster into one of the finest examples of Rococo in Germany.

A scenic drive through a valley flanked by 5,000- to 6,000-foot peaks will take you to **Linderhof**, 13 km (8 miles) west of Ettal on B 23. This most elaborate of King Ludwig II's palaces, built in the 1870s, is the full expression of his love for the solitude of the mountains. It is open for visits during the summer.

Designed vaguely to resemble the Petit Trianon at Versailles, Linderhof is a compact, dazzling white château in such a variety of Baroque derivatives from various periods and countries that it is hard to find a common denominator or pin down a model for it. Though the exterior, with its mass of sculptures and bas-reliefs, seems blindingly ornate, by comparison with the interior it is actually restrained. The inside is a riot of Rococo, a flash of mirrors, the glitter of gold, a bewildering mix of rich tapestries and crystal chandeliers. The most impressive chambers are the mirror room and the king's bedroom. In the oval dining room there is a Grimm's fairy tale come true: a "magic table." Those who remember the story will recall the command, "Little table, serve dinner." Ludwig's table could be lowered through the floor to the kitchen and pantry below and there reset with dishes, thus allowing the reclusive monarch to dine without the intrusive presence of servants.

For all its ostentatiousness, Linderhof is not without charm, thanks to the beauty of its natural setting in the Ammerberge range and the fine formal French gardens surrounding it.

After the dining room, the greatest attractions are the Moorish kiosk, a cast-iron pavilion walled with zinc plaques stamped in relief, and the Venus grotto, inspired by the Blue Grotto at Capri and containing an artificial lake fed by an artificial waterfall and a stage hung with a backdrop scene of the first act of *Tannhäuser*.

Equipped with hypocaustal heating, which can turn it into a sauna bath, and the first full electrical installation in 19th-century Bavaria, the room can be illuminated with changing colors. On the lake, which had artificial waves, Ludwig kept two swans and a gilded boat, in which he was frequently rowed by a servant. Legend has it that he once attempted to stage the first act of *Tannhäuser* in the grotto, but the roar of the waterfall and the fickle acoustics of the place turned the orchestra into a cacophony of sound and left the singers inaudible.

To get to **Oberammergau**, 17 km (11 miles) north of Linderhof, drive back toward Ettal, take a left turn at the fork in the road about 10 km (6 miles) past the castle, and follow the signs into the center of the "Passion Play town."

Oberammergau, a summer and winter resort with excellent downhill and cross-country skiing facilities, also famed for its woodcarvers and *Hinterglassgemälde* artists, is worth a detour any time, but in a festival year it becomes a magnet for the entire world. (*Hinterglassgemälde,* an art form unique to Bavaria, Croatia, and parts of Austria, is painting done directly on glass, and in reverse.)

The origins of the *Passionsspiel* (Passion Play) in Oberammergau go back to the year 1633, when townsfolk, in gratitude for the ending of the plague, first staged the play with amateur actors as an expression of thanks and as a hedge against a new outbreak of the plague. Since 1680 the drama of Christ's Passion has been performed by locals every year divisible by ten. A presentation with a cast of hundreds, the play depicts Christ's journey to the Cross in 16 acts and is staged in a special festival house, the **Passionsspielhaus** on the Theaterstrasse, which was built for the 1930 performance. During each season there are 102 performances, each lasting five and a half hours, with a two-hour lunch interval. Actors must either be Oberammergau natives or have lived in the town for at least 20 years. The text has often stirred controversy for its anti-Jewish lines.

Because of the multitudes who converge on Oberammergau, tickets are at a premium—and so are accommodations during the summer festival season. Choices are few, but if you are lucky enough to get tickets, select the chalet-style **Hotel Alois Lang**, St.-Lukas-Strasse 15, quietly located on the western edge of town. A bit more moderately priced is the **Hotel Alte Post**, Dorfstrasse 19, right in the center.

To leave town, B 23 will take you back down the valley to the junction with B 2, where you turn right (south) for the remaining drive (10 km/6 miles) to **Garmisch-Partenkirchen**.

This bustling, highly popular holiday town, the scene of the 1936 Winter Olympics, was once two separate communities, now incorporated into one. Located at the base of the 9,800-foot **Zugspitze**, Germany's highest point, this is a spot where nature outdoes herself. That is one reason why Garmisch-Partenkirchen is hopelessly overrun with visitors at all times of the year. Other attractions are folk theater and folk-costume festivals, central to the local tradition, and some surprisingly romantic nooks and crannies where you can wander to forget that one of the loveliest painted Baroque houses on Garmisch's main square now houses a McDonald's.

One of Europe's oldest and most scenic cog railways will take you up to the Zugspitze, as will a dramatic aerial cable car. There are ski lifts at the top and usually enough snow to last through the entire summer.

Because it was once two separate towns, Garmisch-Partenkirchen has two postal inns, and in the summer

months a 19th-century stagecoach still operates between
them (and on excursions beyond). The **Posthotel Partenkirchen**, at Ludwigstrasse 49, is the more venerable of the two.
It was registered as a monastery tavern in 1542, and the
building itself is at least a century older. It is a jewel of
*Gemütlichkeit* (coziness) with *Lüftlmalerei* (trompe l'oeil)
frescoes on its façade; wood-paneled, beam-ceilinged lobby
and dining rooms; and an array of Baroque art and peasant
handicrafts on display. Proprietor Otto Stahl serves sophisticated Bavarian food with a nouvelle touch. **Clausings Post-
Romantik-Hotel**, at Marienplatz 12 on Garmisch's main
square, is even more overwhelming architecturally—it is a
squat, three-story house with a huge overhanging Alpine
roof and a façade emblazoned with statues of various saints.
From the terrace, heated and glass enclosed in winter, you
will have a perfect view of the Zugspitze. The dining rooms
are invitingly cozy with mahogany paneling, soft Oriental
carpeting, and an assemblage of art and heirlooms collected
over the more than three centuries it has been serving
travellers.

# Mittenwald

One of Upper Bavaria's most scenic journeys is the 18-km
(11-mile) drive east along B 2 to Mittenwald, nestled in a
valley at the foot of the Wetterstein range, just 32 km (20
miles) north of Innsbruck, Austria.

A summer resort and winter sports center, though bliss-
fully less crowded than Garmisch-Partenkirchen, this town of
8,000 (whose name means "in the middle of the forest")
played an important role in the Middle Ages as a market
center on the treacherous mountain trade route from Venice
and the Adriatic to central and northern Europe. Its fame rests
even more on violin making, a local industry since 1683,
when native son Matthias Klotz, whose statue stands on the
main square, returned home from studies with Nicolo Amati
in Cremona, Italy, to open a workshop in his hometown.

Today Mittenwald is known not only as the source of
some of the finest stringed instruments made in the world
but also as the site of the world's oldest, largest, most
stringently demanding school for violin makers, the state-
run Staatliche Geigenbauschule. Its graduates ply their trade
in 40 countries on six continents.

Most people associate fine stringed instruments with Cremona, and Germany does not necessarily come to mind. But

there is persuasive evidence that the first makers of violins and of a related, somewhat earlier group of instruments known as viols or viola da gambas were actually Germans with Italianized names working in northern Italy. They were second- and third-generation descendants and pupils of 15th-century lute makers from Füssen, near Neuschwanstein. When viol- and violin-type instruments—both played with bows instead of plucked with the fingers—made their debut in the Renaissance music world of the early 16th century, they were produced at first by these German lute makers, who, in turn, taught their craft to Italian craftsmen.

Mittenwald's role in this began with Matthias Klotz. Born in 1653, the son of a well-to-do Mittenwald tailor, he was dispatched to Italy to learn the lute- and violin-making trade at the age of ten. The boy was accepted as an apprentice by Nicolo Amati in Cremona—two fellow students were Antonio Stradivari and Andrea Guarneri. Young Klotz spent two decades in Italy learning the craft from Amati and working for other masters, including Johann Railich in Padua. He also worked for a Tyrolean master, Jakob Steiner, at Absam, a town near Innsbruck. In those years Steiner's reputation equaled, and sometimes surpassed, that of Amati.

In 1683 Klotz returned to Mittenwald, married the daughter of a local weaver, and opened his own lute- and violin-making shop. He founded a family dynasty and started a local industry that has become an unbroken tradition and has borne Mittenwald's name to almost every country on earth. Klotz taught the craft not only to his own two sons, Georg and Sebastian, whose instruments were reputed to be of even higher quality than his own, but also to seven other Mittenwald youngsters. When he died, at age 90, in 1743, there were a dozen other master violin makers in the town, and by 1800 the number had swollen to 80. There were also ten bow makers and any number of journeymen and amateurs who made instruments or parts for them, often as a winter vocation and as home- and pieceworkers.

In the early years after Klotz had started the industry, the masters were also their own salesmen, travelling and selling their instruments as far as feet or horse could carry them. But by the middle of the 19th century, Mittenwald was producing thousands of stringed instruments for ultimate resale in places as far away as St. Petersburg and Cincinnati. The more this mass trade flourished, the more quality declined, along with the earnings of violin makers, who were now little more than assembly-line laborers. With the cheapest violins selling for as little as the equivalent of DM3, Mittenwald gained a reputation for inferior, mass-produced instruments, which lasted well into the early 1950s.

The bad reputation, along with the abominable pay, working conditions, and the deteriorating skills of the local craftsmen, was a source of concern to Bavaria's King Maximilian II. It was at his behest that the **Staatliche Geigenbauschule** was established in 1858. Now located in a three-story building on the Partenkirchner Strasse, it is the oldest violin-making school in the world and by far the leading one. A state institution with free tuition, its students come from all over the world. Two graduates, a Korean and a German, have started private schools in Chicago and Salt Lake City. At no time does the student body exceed 50 to 60, and since it is a three-and-a-half-year course, only 12 new students are accepted each year, though there are usually 1,500 to 2,000 applicants annually.

Thanks to the school's success, Mittenwald's violin makers now rank again among the best in the world, with their instruments fetching gold and silver medals at all major international competitions, not to mention prices of $10,000 and more. Although the school and the workshops of Mittenwald's top masters are usually not open to visitors, the **Geigenbaumuseum** (Violin-Making Museum), at Ballenhausgasse 3, is. The museum is devoted to the local instrument-making craft and has a fine collection of old violins, violas, and cellos as well as lutes and other stringed instruments.

From Mittenwald our journey leads northeast again to another popular beautiful lake, the Tegernsee. Drive north 12 km (7.5 miles) from Mittenwald on B 2 and then take B 11 (B 2 forks left and leads back to Garmisch-Partenkirchen) to Wallgau. There you might stop to have lunch or even spend a night at the **Hotel Post**, Dorfstrasse 6, a postal inn since 1621, run by the Neuner family for more than 350 years. Goethe stayed here, as did Elizabeth Taylor and Richard Burton. From Wallgau a memorably scenic toll road follows the Isar river eastward for some 20 km (12 miles) to the Sylvenstein Stausee, an artificial lake created as a reservoir. From there it is 27 km (about 17 miles) generally (and windingly) northeastward along B 307 to **Rottach-Egern**, the southernmost town on the shores of the **Tegernsee**, and the plushest.

The "developer" of the Tegernsee region was none less than Bavaria's first king, Maximilian I, who in 1817 bought the secularized Benedictine monastery in the town of Tegernsee, on the eastern shore of the lake, and commissioned Leo von Klenze to convert it into a summer vacation palace. Munich's and Bavaria's nobility followed suit, building mansions and chalets. For Müncheners the Tegernsee is one of the most popular mountain recreation areas, with boating and surfing in summer and skiing in winter.

Of Rottach-Egern's profusion of luxury and first-class hotels, the most luxurious is the **Bachmair-am-See**, Seestrasse 47. It is also the oldest, founded in the early 19th century as a village tavern. It has been owned and managed by the Bachmair family for nearly 150 years. Beamed ceilings, paintings, old etchings, ecclesiastical art, and wide fireplaces lend this hotel an atmosphere of deep tradition and comfort.

**Bad Tölz**, the last destination, is 12 km (7.5 miles) northwest of the Tegernsee by way of an unnumbered road from the lake's northernmost village, Gmund, to Waakirchen, then due west on B 472. Tucked into the Isar river valley and surrounded by peaks going up to 5,000 feet, the town is a popular spa and summer and winter resort, thanks to its iodine springs. The Marktstrasse, lined by 18th- and 19th-century houses with steep, protruding saddle roofs and painted façades, is one of the most picturesque main streets in Upper Bavaria.

Should you happen to be in the area on November 6, be sure to visit Bad Tölz for the annual **Leonhardifahrt**. Pilgrimage processions in honor of Saint Leonard, patron saint of livestock, are held in various parts of Bavaria, but none provides as much folkloristic color as this one. Farm women, dressed in their finest local *Trachten* (folk costumes), ride in elaborately carved and painted peasant carts, each drawn by a team of four garlanded horses, followed by drummers, trumpeters, hundreds of highland farmers on horseback, Lederhosen-wearing mountain rifle squads, and brass bands in all their finery. The parade follows a traditional route and ritual dating from the 18th century, passing through the main streets of the town and up to St. Leonhard chapel on the **Kalvarienberg** (Calvary Mountain). The fencing around this little church is made of chains from barns and stables, presented as devotional gifts by farmers whose cattle have been saved from disease or accidents. Before heading back to town, the procession encircles the church three times. On the way downhill the horseback riders snap huge 12- to 15-foot whips, called *Goaslschnalzen,* over the heads of the women and children in the carts, to protect them against demons and evil spirits.

Hotel accommodations are always hard to find during the Leonhardifahrt festival, so book well in advance. Try the

**Hotel Jodquellenhof,** Ludwigstrasse 13–15, on the left bank of the Isar. Though pricey, it's the best spa hotel in town.

From Bad Tölz it is a quick 53-km (33-mile) drive due north on B 13 back to Munich.

## GETTING AROUND
Though there are trains and buses, operated by the Bundes-bahn (maroon) as well as Bundespost (yellow), to all the destinations in Southern Bavaria, service tends to be a bit slow and infrequent and costs a great deal of time. Two exceptions are Freising and Starnberg: Freising is served by S-Bahn (number S-1) from Munich's Marienplatz every 20 minutes during the daytime, and is the last stop on that line; Starnberg can be reached by the S-6 and is the 14th stop on the line after Marienplatz.

The best way to get around Southern Bavaria is to rent a car in Munich. Stick to the roads given here, and take along a detailed road map or, before setting out from Munich, purchase in virtually any bookstore the *H-B Bildatlas:* number 7 for Oberbayern and number 36 for Niederbayern. Even if you speak or read no German, these picture atlases are useful, as they contain very detailed maps that show all the little side roads and unnumbered highways of the areas described.

Although there are Autobahn expressways from Munich to Landshut, from Munich past the Chiemsee to Berchtesgaden, and to Murnau (the stretch into Garmisch-Partenkirchen is incomplete), they tend to be heavily travelled and are no way to see the countryside, as they bypass the most interesting towns and the best scenery.

## ACCOMMODATIONS REFERENCE
▶ **Hotel Alois Lang.** St.-Lukas-Strasse 15, D-8103 **Oberam-mergau.** Tel: (8822) 41-41/10-41; Telex: 59623.

▶ **Hotel Alpenhof Murnau.** Ramsachstrasse 8, D-8110 **Mur-nau.** Tel: (8841) 10-45.

▶ **Hotel Alte Post.** Dorfstrasse 19, D-8103 **Oberammergau.** Tel: (8822) 66-91.

▶ **Alpengasthof Winklmoosalm.** Dürrnbachhornweg 6, D-8216 **Reit im Winkl.** Tel: (8640) 10-97.

▶ **Alter Wirt-Bonnschloss.** Kirchplatz 9, D-8214 **Bernau am Chiemsee.** Tel: (8051) 890-11.

▶ **Hotel Bachmair-am-See.** Seestrasse 47, D-8183 **Rottach-Egern.** Tel: (8022) 27-20; Telex: 526920.

▶ **Clausings Post-Romantik-Hotel.** Marienplatz 12, D-8100

Garmisch-Partenkirchen. Tel: (8821) 70-90; Telex: 59679; Fax: 709205.

▶ **Hotel Glöcklhofer.** Ludwigsberg 4, D-8263 **Burghausen.** Tel: (8677) 70-24.

▶ **Goldene Sonne.** Neustadt 520, D-8300 **Landshut.** Tel: (871) 230-87.

▶ **Gasthaus Hofwirt.** Salzburger Strasse 21, D-8234 **Bad Reichenhall.** Tel: (8651) 20-21.

▶ **Hotel Jodquellenhof.** Ludwigstrasse 13-15, D-8170 **Bad Tölz.** Tel: (8041) 50-91.

▶ **Hotel Kaiserhof.** Papiererstrasse 2, D-8300 **Landshut.** Tel: (871) 68-70; Telex: 58440; Fax: 687403.

▶ **Königliche Villa.** Am Luitpoldpark, D-8240 **Berchtesgaden.** Tel: (8652) 50-97.

▶ **Kurhotel Luisenbad.** Ludwigstrasse 33, D-8234 **Bad Reichenhall.** Tel: (8651) 50-11; Telex: 56131.

▶ **Hotel zur Post.** Kapellplatz 2, D-8262 **Altötting.** Tel: (8671) 50-40; Telex: 56962; Fax: 6214.

▶ **Hotel zur Post.** Kirchplatz 1, D-8213 **Aschau im Chiemgau.** Tel: (8052) 41-21.

▶ **Hotel zur Post.** Stadtplatz 39, D-8263 **Burghausen.** Tel: (8677) 30-44.

▶ **Hotel Post.** Dorfstrasse 6, D-8109 **Wallgau.** Tel: (8825) 10-11.

▶ **Posthotel Partenkirchen.** Ludwigstrasse 49, D-8100 **Garmisch-Partenkirchen.** Tel: (8821) 510-67; Telex: 59611.

▶ **Hotel Schmied von Kochel.** Schlehdorfer Strasse 6, D-8113 **Kochel am See.** Tel: (8851) 216.

▶ **Strandhotel Schloss Berg.** Seestrasse 17, D-8137 **Starnberg (Berg).** Tel: (8151) 501-06.

▶ **Hotel Steinbacher Hof.** Steinbachweg 10, D-8216 **Reit im Winkl.** Tel: (8640) 84-10.

▶ **Steigenberger-Hotel Axelmannstein.** Salzburger Strasse 4, D-8234 **Bad Reichenhall.** Tel: (8651) 40-01; Telex: 56112.

▶ **Hotel Unterwirt.** Kirchplatz 2, D-8216 **Reit im Winkl.** Tel: (8640) 88-11.

▶ **Vier Jahreszeiten.** Maximilianstrasse 20, D-8240 **Berchtesgaden.** Tel: (8652) 50-26.

▶ **Hotel Wittelsbach.** Maximilianstrasse 16, D-8240 **Berchtesgaden.** Tel: (8652) 50-61.

# STUTTGART AND THE SWABIAN HEARTLAND

*By Peter Hays*

**E**arly on most weekday mornings the whole of Swabia shifts relentlessly into high gear. By 2:00 A.M. towns, streets, and Autobahns are buzzing with traffic. Up in the hill country, schoolbuses thread their way through bustling villages. The region's overall mood of urgency is captured in the blur of cyclists swooping past the pedestrians in Stuttgart's Schlossgarten, legs pumping like well-tuned pistons.

For decades Swabia, the industrial heartland of the federal state of Baden-Württemberg, was a leader among even the pacesetters of the fabled "economic miracle." Its automobile industry, which owes much to Swabian inventors Gottlieb Wilhelm Daimler and Karl Friedrich Benz, led the way. The pace of industry has been stepped up of late and the state can now pride itself on the lowest rate of unemployment in the republic's *Länder*.

Swabians are also blessed with a natural environment that offers all manner of escape. A web of signposted hiking trails, which total some 12,500 miles, threads through vast forests, this landscape's recurring theme. The forests sweep south to the northern shore of palm-fringed Lake Constance on the border with Switzerland, popular among Central European vacationers from spring to autumn. In the west, the forests follow the meandering Danube as the river begins its course to the Black Sea. The more provincial Neckar, inspiration for Swabian poets including Friedrich Schiller, Eduard Mörike, and Friedrich Hölderlin, flows here, too. To the southeast, roughly between Biberach, Isny, Friedrichshafen, and Ravensburg, the coniferous and deciduous forest thins into coppice dotted with Baroque monasteries, churches, and palaces.

One of the biggest wood areas in the north, the **Schwäbische Wald** has sun-dappled trails and glades that easily match those of the Black Forest. It stretches to the **Schwäbische Alb**, a corrugated Jurassic limestone wedge of upland south of Stuttgart. This is the region's almost diagonal backbone, undulating northeast to southwest with peaks between 1,500 and 2,700 feet high.

Scores of subterranean streams and rivers percolate through the Alb's porous interior and well up in countless valleys, glades, and hollows, most spectacularly in the **Blautopf**, an azure pool in the monastery village of Blaubeuren. The huge ridge also generates thermal currents suited to the many model-airplane and glider enthusiasts here. Hang-glider pilots regularly plunge from limestone pinnacles, near Neuffen, for instance, that tower up along the Alb's westerly rim.

You may prefer to join in some of the less hazardous activities in the region. Recently, many municipal councils have gone to great expense to refurbish their Altstadt areas. To walk the newly recobbled alleys is to step back into a Medieval world. Towns like Schwäbisch Gmünd were granted charters in the 12th century by the local Hohenstaufen dynasty, which produced several Holy Roman emperors, including Frederick Barbarossa. The battlements and moats still existing in the region are evidence of a protracted territorial tussle among hundreds of rival principalities, duchies, prince-bishoprics, counties, palatinates, city-states, and tiny independent farming communities owing allegiance only to the Holy Roman Emperor. After the fall of the Hohenstaufen rulers in 1268, major and minor potentates spent centuries jockeying or fighting for supremacy. Unification was forced upon them in 1806, when Napoleon declared the then-dominant Swabian duchy the kingdom of Württemberg.

Despite the picturesque remains of the distant past, these were not exactly the good old days. Two centuries ago witches were still burned at the stake in many town squares, and Tübingen used its *Karzer,* a tiny cell, to punish university students for minor misdemeanors.

MAJOR INTEREST

Medieval towns of Schwäbisch Hall and Schwäbisch Gmünd

**Stuttgart**
Altstadt and Markthalle
Artifacts of Roman occupation in Römisches Lapidarium
Daimler-Benz Museum
Staatsgaleries, with German Old Masters and contemporary art

**Tübingen**
University and Altstadt
Hölderlinturm, where Hölderlin languished in the grip of schizophrenia for 40 years

**Schwäbische Alb Region**
Wimsener Höhle (aquatic cave)

**Hohenzollern Country**
Castles in Hechingen and Sigmaringen
Ancient Roman artifacts in Rottweil
Source of the Danube at Donaueschingen

**Lake Constance (Bodensee) Region**
Konstanz
Islands of Reichenau and Mainau
Überlingen
Stone Age village in Unteruhldingen

**The Baroque Road**

# Schwäbisch Hall

Do not be put off by the unprepossessing outskirts of this town, 68 km (42 miles) northeast of Stuttgart on B 14. A business belt is a postwar phenomenon around most Swabian towns. The Altstadt proper is on the bank of the river Kocher; enter it along the Salinenstrasse and you'll be reminded of the saltworks that flourished here for centuries. The *Hall* in the town's name also derives from them. Brine was taken from a deep well, then simmered in large pans in the Hallplatz, now a riverside parking lot, until only the crystalline salt was left. The industry began to decline in the past century after the discovery of salt deposits in nearby Wilhelmsglück. Tradition still decrees, however, that descen-

dants of the salt-simmering families are given an annual pension.

Many of the old houses from the Neue Strasse down to the Milchmarkt have been gentrified to the point of blandness. The Middle Ages come alive, however, in an uneven triangle bounded by the Marktplatz, Hafenmarkt, Keckenhof, and Obere Herrngasse. Note the chain links still attached to the half-timbered building on the corner of Obere Herrngasse and the main square: They were part of chains that cordoned off the Marktplatz whenever Medieval knights settled their differences there. The last recorded duel in the Marktplatz took place between two brothers in 1523. Along the narrow, cobblestone Obere Herrngasse are several houses of special interest; the poet Eduard Mörike lived with his sister at number 7. Obere and Untere Herrngasse meet at Italian cook Cesare's **Gasthof zum Waldhorn**, which is locally renowned for its spaghetti alla puttanesca. From the tavern's terrace you can watch the Altstadt's ramparts slowly emerge as men and machines dig away where construction workers stumbled on a stretch of fortifications several years ago.

The Marktplatz's most prominent feature are 54 broad, curving steps at **St. Michaelskirche**. Every year, from June to August, this stairway is used as a slanting stage for the town's open-air theater festival. Past productions have starred some of the country's top actors in plays by Shakespeare, Brecht, and Schiller. Guests of honor invariably include members of the house of Hohenlohe-Oehringen, relatives of England's Windsor family. Part of the former's palatial edifice, just up the road in **Neuenstein**, is open to the public. Those of lesser lineage staying at the **Goldener Adler** in a room overlooking the Marktplatz can enjoy a royal view of the floodlit performance below.

# Schwäbisch Gmünd

On the B 19 and B 298, Schwäbisch Gmünd is less than an hour's drive south from Schwäbisch Hall and 52 km (33 miles) due east of Stuttgart on the B 29. A longer, scenic route, the Idyllische Strasse between Mainhardt and Fichtenberg, skirts the **Murrhardter Wald**, one of the unsung corners of the Schwäbische Wald. Great waves of forest seem to roll toward the horizon, particularly after a thunderstorm has shrouded them in mist. At dusk, deer lope over patches of farmland; at dawn, tattered feathers drifting through clearings are the only remainders of some fox's midnight feast. The local farming folk are tough and independent. Their dialect is down-to-earth Swabian, which incongruously attaches the diminutive *le* to nearly every noun, and thus sounds strangely sweet to German ears. Strangers who linger long enough in one of the remote villages like **Steinberg** are often invited to a *Hockele,* an impromptu gossip 'n' grub session at the end of the day. Bottles of the local *Apfelmost,* cider with a kick, are thumped down on long tables along with *Schärrkuchen,* savory pastries sprinkled with flakes of butter and cheese, straight out of the oven. For a wider range of rural fare, stop in at the **Gasthof Engel** in the little town of **Murrhardt**.

Schwäbisch Gmünd's main square, the **Marktplatz**, is 600 feet long, and a stroll across it is something of an expedition. The Baroque town-house façades around it appear standoffish and ornamental. As far as the original owners—wealthy merchants and craftsmen—were concerned, this was probably the desired effect.

As early as the 14th century municipal power passed from the local nobility to the guilds. The Swabians' entrepreneurial skill was admirably demonstrated in Gmünd by blacksmiths and cartwrights. As business slackened they turned their hand to forging scythes, and by 1580 were producing more than 270,000 a year and exporting them as far away as France and Spain. That trade dwindled during the devastating Thirty Years War. Splendid isolation was never an option in those turbulent days, however substantial the town fortifications, and Gmünd suffered considerable damage during the Peasants' War in 1525 and the religious feuds that followed. The town was also drawn into the War of Spanish Succession and the skirmishes triggered by the French Revolution in 1796.

A sizable **Altstadt**, which survived World War II unscathed, still surrounds the Marktplatz. As you walk around you will rub shoulders with off-duty GIs from the local military base. Several houses deserve special scrutiny. The **Kornhaus** (at the end of the Kornhausstrasse), a lofty, half-timbered tithe barn, dates from the 16th century. The **Fuggerei**, in the Münsterplatz, was a residence for visiting Medieval VIPs. Its Romanesque façade was elaborated with half-timbered frills in the 15th century. Of the town's three main churches, the **Johanniskirche** is outstanding. If you sample an ice cream at the Italian-run **Café Margrit**, you will have a wonderful view of the evening sun gilding the finely sculpted hunting scenes on the façade opposite.

Several bits of stonework are left from the Hohenstaufen era. Some can be found down narrow Bühlsgässle. One whole wall of the **Grät**, an early Medieval building, consists of *Buckelquader,* large stones each with a distinctive shape. Just a few miles south, between Schwäbisch Gmünd and Göppingen, following the brown Staufer Route signs with their lion-and-crown logo, this shape is repeated. The village of Hohenstaufen nestles below the ruins of one of the Holy Imperial family's hilltop castles. A steep path leads up to some fragments of wall, made of very similar stones. Here, the various Hohenstaufen emperors had a superb view of a fraction of their territory. They spent very little time in their Swabian homeland, however; leading Crusades and vying with successive popes for European supremacy kept them down south. The Hohenstaufen Friedrich II was even crowned king of Sicily in 1198. The last Hohenstaufen, Konradin, was beheaded in Naples in 1268, and these ruins are the last memento of an overambitious family that faded into oblivion. Stuttgart is only half an hour west of Schwäbish Gmünd.

# STUTTGART

Capitals are often populated with people who have a supercilious attitude toward their country cousins. However, Stuttgart's 600,000 citizens are an exception. When Baden and Württemberg were unified into a single political region in 1952, Stuttgart became the new federal state's capital. But those busy postwar decades did not lend themselves to the development of cosmopolitan airs and graces. Stuttgarters instead buckled down to rebuilding their city. During World War II, more than 50 air raids had destroyed an estimated 75 percent of the Altstadt. Up on the **Birkenkopf**, a hillock near the city center, a mount of rubble 40 feet high was dubbed Monte Scherbelino (Mount Smithereens) by the locals. It has since been landscaped into a memorial park. And there has been considerable industrial success—today Bosch, Bauknecht, Daimler-Benz, IBM, Kodak, Leitz, and Porsche are based in Stuttgart. Tour guides point out the Mercedes trademark rotating on top of the main railway station's tower as one of the city's major sights.

Today's Stuttgarters are a fascinating hybrid: children of an industrialized society, proud of their rural heritage. If you arrive at the Hauptbahnhof (main train station), you will sense this. Look uphill from the station's main entrance toward a vineyard that slopes down the **Kriegsberg** into the heart of town. These dusty vines, one of the world's surprising metropolitan sights, produce quite a reasonable red Trollinger wine. Property developers would love to grab them up, but because of their symbolic value they seem destined for survival. The steep valley that hems the city in on all sides used to be densely covered with vineyards. Like any ancient Neckar village downriver, Stuttgart still holds its *Weindorf* (wine festival) late every summer in the Kirch strasse and the Marktplatz.

Stuttgart's picturesque setting has drawbacks. In summer, early morning mist from the river mingles with exhaust fumes, and the resulting smog may not lift until well after noon. For the predominantly working-class community on the lower-altitude outskirts of the city, the days can be unbearably sultry. Those who are better off live up on the metropolitan basin's edge, in affluent districts such as Feuerbacher Heide, Degerloch, or Sillenbuch. Stuttgart's yellow municipal trams run on seven main lines and link up with the underground Stadtbahn's network. VVS, the public transport authority, offers a very reasonably priced *Tages-sparkarte*, or rover ticket, which entitles the bearer to a full day's use of all its services. Short of hiring a plane there is hardly a quicker way to get your bearings than by tram-hopping. You have several options. Tram line number 5 climbs up to Degerloch to give you a splendid view of the city. For a different view, you can also board the network's one and only cable car from Heslach up to the Waldfriedhof, one of the city's main cemeteries. It runs every quarter of an hour until 8:45 P.M. in summer and 7:41 P.M. in winter. Equally exciting is the cogwheel tram ride (number 10) from the Marienplatz up to Degerloch. Late at night a cog-wheel taxi takes over, at no extra charge. These rides, with their choice of vistas, also serve a useful purpose: It quickly becomes clear that historic Stuttgart is compact enough to explore on foot.

## The Altstadt

Visitors with a sense of chronology start their walk in the Schillerplatz. This was the city's nucleus, the site of the *Stuatgarten* (stud farm) owned by Luitolf, one of the dukes of Swabia, in the tenth century.

One side of the square is the moated **Altes Schloss**, built in about 1320. The castle's delicately sculpted Renaissance arcades, added in the 16th century, frame weekend concerts held in the courtyard during the summer. Inside, the **Württembergisches Landesmuseum** has the former monar-

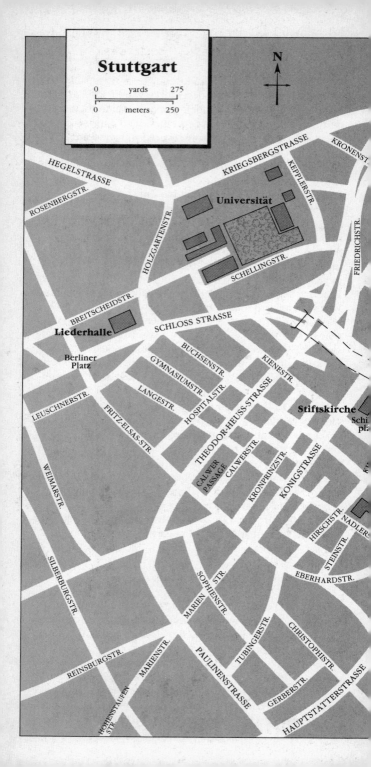

chy's crown jewels on display. Admission is free, as in most of the other town museums, except for special exhibitions.

The **Alte Kanzlei** restaurant on the square specializes in some of the region's staple dishes. *Gaisburger Marsch,* a beef stew served with radishes, onions, and *Spätzle,* Swabia's version of pasta, are worth sampling. The open-air section of the restaurant juts toward the middle of the square with its statue of a pensive Friedrich Schiller.

Just behind the cozy Schillerplatz is the Schlossplatz, laid out to overwhelm. Its prim and proper **Neues Schloss,** completed in 1807, embraces a symmetrical composition of segmented lawns, splashing fountains, and chestnut trees that could probably accommodate Trafalgar Square twice over.

This square amply reflects the past century's golden era. Pomp and circumstance became the order of the day when Napoleon elevated Duke Friedrich to first king of Württemberg, in 1806. Friedrich I commanded Württemberg's dukes to spend at least three months a year at court in Stuttgart and to address him as "Your Most Serene and Almighty Majesty." King and courtiers divided their time between Stuttgart and nearby Ludwigsburg, with its regal residence, **Monrepos,** and its Baroque palace. The special Franco-Swabian relationship cooled appreciably in 1812: Of 15,000 Württemberg soldiers forced to join Bonaparte on his disastrous Russian campaign, only 300 returned.

Save a whole afternoon for a walk through the **Schlossgarten,** a broad ribbon of a park that extends more than two miles from the Hauptbahnhof to where the Neckar river snakes its way out of the city. Some very senior citizens can remember spotting Württemberg's King Wilhelm II out walking his own Pomeranians in the park and at first mistaking him for a royal servant in shabby livery. Wilhelm II was never keen to have his photo taken in military uniform, and his pacifist views incurred Prussian Kaiser Wilhelm's displeasure. After World War I, he was deposed by a "tearful revolution," his former subjects affectionately but firmly retiring him to palatial lodgings next to a 12th-century Cistercian cloister in **Bebenhausen,** north of Tübingen. There he soon became a regular in the **Hirsch** tavern, partial to a *Viertel* (quarter-liter) of wine. His wife, Charlotte, lived in Bebenhausen until 1946.

The park's sunbathers adhere to the Swabian level of decorum: The nudist frolics seen in Munich's Englischer Garten have never caught on here. Stuttgarters often round off their Schlossgarten walk by dropping into the **Min-**

**eralbad Leuze**. Pungent mineral water said to be good for the digestion and all sorts of ailments gushes out of three taps, and you can help yourself to some with one of the ladles hanging on a chain. There is so much water to go around that it circulates copiously through the Leuze's pools and even rains out of a row of decorative fountains.

In the past, children from outlying villages fetched the "health water" in large cans. They came into town the old-fashioned way: down *Stäffele,* long flights of steps cut into the valley's flanks. The 306 Hasenberg steps and most of the other Stäffele are still used by joggers.

From the Leuze baths it is only a short walk to the **Wilhelma piers**, where the **Neckar-Personen-Schiffahrt**'s riverboats dock. There are eight river cruises daily during the summer, which go as far downstream as Lauffen. A favorite stopover is **Marbach**, Schiller's birthplace. The house the playwright was born in is on the Nikolastorstrasse. The **Schiller National-museum** (on the Schillerhöhe) has memorabilia associated with him.

## Museums in Stuttgart

A dozen major museums in Stuttgart chronicle several millennia of history. In the Schillerplatz you can go from one era to the next in minutes. The **Römisches Lapidarium**, in the Fruchtkasten, the city's Medieval wine depot, shows artifacts of the Roman occupation. A few doors away, the **Landesmuseum** takes up the story in the third century when the Alemanni, the Swabians' West Germanic forebears, over-ran the Roman Limes and settled between the Neckar and the Danube.

Many Stuttgarters, more interested in revs per minute than revolutions and the other events of history, prefer an era that has pride of place in the city's consciousness: the hundred-odd years of automobile manufacture. On weekends pilgrimage-size crowds flock to the **Gottlieb-Daimler-Gedächtnisstätte** (in Bad Cannstatt, a neighborhood on the north banks of the Neckar) to the converted shed in which Daimler, assisted by his friend Wilhelm Maybach, assembled the first high-speed gasoline engine, in 1883. The exhibits include his workbench and tools. The little museum is open from May to October. There is also a much larger **Daimler-Benz Museum** on the car plant's grounds in the Stuttgart-Untertürkheim district on the Mercedesstrasse. A full range of automobiles, from vintage to very latest, are on display. From Gate 1 of the plant, a shuttle bus carries visitors to the museum, which is open every day but Monday and public holidays year round. One of Daimler's best customers was Consul Jellinek, who had a daughter named Mercedes. As a token of gratitude, the Swabian engineer named his first models after her.

The **Staatsgalerie**'s new wing, designed by the British architect James Stirling, opened in 1984, and is the city's most entertaining piece of modern architecture. A flamingo-pink balustrade arches up to a slanted façade of local sandstone punctuated by broad, green-mullioned glass. Ivy has already spread up the walls of the inner courtyard, where art students sketch away in the shade of statues. Lovers of contemporary art can find regular exhibitions of the new masters, including Braque, Chagall, Dix, Kokoschka, Mondrian, and Dalí. The gallery owns one of the country's most respected collections of works by Picasso.

Unfortunately, in parts of Stuttgart slabs of concrete have replaced anything resembling a façade. One of the city's most blatant eyesores is the top-security prison in the Stammheim district, whose inmates include members of the terrorist organization Rote Armee Fraktion. The **Fernsehturm**, Stuttgart's concrete TV tower, much criticized on aesthetic grounds when it opened in 1956, has since been copied in Paris. Its restaurant, with magnificent views of the Alb and the Black Forest, is much frequented on weekends.

## The Arts in Stuttgart

Bordering the Oberer Schlossgarten, the **Landtag**, Baden-Württemberg's glass-plated House of Parliament, faces the pillared **Staatstheater**. After their debates, the state deputies often nip over to catch a performance. The State Theater is composed of the **Grosses Haus** (1,400 seats), the **Kleines Haus** (851 seats), and the **Kammertheater**. The latter, also designed by Stirling and known for its experimental repertoire, is actually in the Staatsgalerie and is connected to the main building by a pedestrian subway under the Konrad-Adenauer-Strasse. Guest performances by world-famous companies from abroad have often brought the theater good reviews; its own Staatsoper and Stuttgarter Ballet ensembles are popular in their own right. The Staatsoper was formed in the mid-18th century with the support of Duke Karl Eugen, an ardent patron. The ballet owes its present reputation to director John Cranko and to Marcia Haydée, who took over in 1976 after "miracle-worker" Cranko's death.

The **Variété-Theater**, in Hohenpark Killesberg, is the closest Stuttgart gets to old-time music-hall entertainment. It features afternoon and early evening performances by jugglers, clowns, acrobats, and assorted other entertainers. Artists from as far afield as Las Vegas have starred here. True to this theater's style, usherettes serve refreshments during, rather than between, acts. The theater is set in a beautiful park. **Theaterle der Käsreiter**, in the Rembrandtstrasse, offers a repertoire of sketches and fairy tales performed in the unmistakable Swabian dialect, which can stump even Northern Germans. Some of the dialogues in the **Theater am Faden**, in Hasenenstrasse, may be just as incomprehensible to Swabians, but the stars, intricately crafted marionettes, are worth seeing. The Liederhalls, on the Berliner Platz, is the venue for big rock, jazz, and classical concerts.

## Staying in Stuttgart

The postwar years here have ushered in a new generation of hotels geared to the needs of business guests. Modern business conveniences—central location, 6:00 A.M. breakfast—generally rank higher on the list of priorities than, say, atmosphere. The leaders in the efficiency stakes include the **Steigenberger-Hotel Graf Zeppelin**, in the Arnulf-Klett-Platz, and the **Inter-Continental**, at Neckarstrasse 60. Both are ideally situated if you fancy joining the executives who go for long prebusiness jogs in the Schlossgarten. Jet laggards opt for the **Airport Mövenpick-Hotel** on the Randstrasse. However, farther to the west and north along the rim of Stuttgart's valley, hotel life gets more interesting. From the **Relaxa Waldhotel Schatten**, Gewandschatten 2, you can conveniently sidetrack to Duke Karl Eugen's 17th-century Rococo residence. The **Messehotel Europe**, at Siemensstrasse 33, is handy to the big trade fairs held up on the Killesberg and to **Perkins Park**, the city's longtime top disco.

## Dining and Nightlife in Stuttgart

Spells of sultry weather assail the city from early spring to late autumn. But a redeeming feature of a hot, sticky day is that it often turns into a balmy night. When that is the case, early nightlife follows a simple traditional routine: several hours of starlit chat, regional wine served in squat *Viertel* glasses, and hearty Swabian food in a favorite *Gartenwirtschaft*. There are some 160 of these restaurants, which spill over onto pavements, courtyards, gardens, and parks. The huge **Amadeus**, in the Charlotteplatz, has 400 seats; the elegant **Cafe Künsterbund**, in the yard of an orphanage, attracts an artsy-craftsy clientele to its site under the Schlossplatz's arcades; the **Kachelofen**, on the Eberhardstrasse, tolerates casually dressed guests out on the pavement but not necessarily inside the restaurant proper; and the vine-draped **Rebgarten**, on the Hohenheimer Strasse, has an admirable choice of wines.

Very little pub crawling takes place in Stuttgart, where patrons' allegiance to a regular *Wirtschaft* is likely to waver only after a change in ownership. These establishments all have an egalitarian feel, but telltale signs distinguish them. You are in pricey territory if the wine list differentiates between fruity Badener vintages and their drier Württemberg counterparts. Prices are most reasonable where you are offered five variations on the theme of *Maultaschen,* the Swabian answer to ravioli. Members of the moderately bohemian "in" crowd congregate in the candlelit **Litfass** (halfway down to the Rathaus underground station), but would never set foot in the **Weinstube Schellenturm**, on the Weberstrasse, a favorite haunt of government officials. The Schellenturm got its name from the little bells stitched to the garments of the convicts who were formerly incarcerated here.

There are also Italian, Greek, Chinese, and vegetarian restaurants in Stuttgart. One of the few surviving fragments of the real Altstadt stretches from Fritz-Elsas-Strasse down the first hundred yards or so of the Calwerstrasse. This is where business people bring visiting associates for meals and deals. There is a row of popular restaurants: **Mira Garten**, **Da Vinci** (first and foremost a fast-serving pizzeria), **Das U-Boot**, and **St. Germain**. Their tables crowd the sidewalks, leaving just enough room for a thin trickle of pedestrians.

A sprinkling of discos, bistros, bars, peep shows, and nightclubs stay open into the wee hours. Observers attribute the state capital's straitlaced late-night style to Calvinist principles of the Reformation, and indeed, compared to other cities, Stuttgart manages only a blush-pink red-light district, in the **Bohnenviertel**. Bounded by the Charlottenstrasse, Esslinger Strasse, and Wagnerstrasse, this former low-rent area has seen seedier days. The professional classes have begun to move into the revamped terraced housing, and in streets full of dutifully fed parking meters, chic boutiques and wine parlors are fast replacing the *Stundenhotels,* where rooms are leased by the hour. Perhaps a slight air of mystery still surrounds bars like the **Nachtwächter** on the Brennerstrasse, which serves its clients behind an opaque glass front. **Basta,** on the Wagnerstrasse, is a middle-brow debating bistro where the day's newspapers, attached to long sticks, are scoured for financial tidbits and the like until well past midnight.

## Shopping in Stuttgart

The Swabians' alleged miserliness is nowhere in evidence on Saturday morning's spending spree in the **Königstrasse,** Stuttgart's shopping haven. Converted from city moat to elegant boulevard during King Friedrich I's reign in the early part of the 19th century, the street is now a mile-long pedestrian zone flanked by department stores. On weekdays it dies a sudden death at 6:30 P.M., when the shops close. Evening shopping (until 10:00 P.M.) continues in the subterranean **Klettpassage,** opposite the main railway station. The city's glitterati pop into the **Calwerpassage** between the Calwerstrasse and the Theodor-Heuss-Strasse for their more pricey upmarket needs. In the neon-flecked fashion boutiques you pay that little bit extra for the prestigious labels. The **Markthalle,** on the Dorotheenstrasse, celebrated its 75th anniversary in 1989; it's a cornucopia of fruit, vegetables, fish, meat, and spices. Outdoor markets are held on Tuesday, Thursday, and Saturday in the Schillerplatz and Marktplatz. Every Saturday, a flea market spreads over the Karlsplatz.

# *TÜBINGEN*

In its less modest moments Tübingen, or rather the town's promoters, refers to itself as a supplier of "seminal thinkers." An occasional lapse into hubris is excusable. The University of Tübingen is one of the country's oldest and best respected, and its 25,000 students make up a third of the city's population. The Hohe Schule was founded in 1477 when Pope Sixtus IV granted permission to a minor aristocrat, Count Eberhard, to do so. In 1536 Duke Ulrich added **the Stift,** originally a college to train the Protestant vicars needed to replace the Roman Catholic priests ousted by the Reformation, situated in a dissolved Augustinian monastery. Over the centuries the two merged into the present university. Graduates have included some outstanding figures: Philipp Melanchthon (1497–1560), who succeeded his mentor, Martin Luther, as leader of the German Reformation movement; the astronomer Johannes Kepler (1571–1630), who was one of the first to support Copernicus's theory of the universe and also advanced his own formulae, confirmed by the Sputnik space probe three centuries later; and the philosopher Georg Wilhelm Friedrich Hegel (1770–1831). Hegel shared a room in Tübingen with a student poet, Friedrich Hölderlin, and the philosopher Wilhelm Schelling. The poet Eduard Mörike and novelist Wilhelm Hauff were also students here.

Although many faculties have long since moved to modern buildings in the suburbs, the university's old core is still a photogenic jumble of half-timbered houses stretching down from Schloss Hohentübingen to the Neckar. Flotillas of swans and students in narrow flat-bottomed punts drift languidly past a skyline that is almost identical to the one shown in a 347-year-old copperplate etching by Mathäus Merian. Mörike waxed lyrical over the irresistible view from the **Eberhardsbrücke**: "My hands folded, as if of their own free will, and I felt my soul rejoice."

There are still a lot of romantics around, more than a million of whom visit Tübingen annually. (Tübingen is only 44 km/26 miles south up the Neckar from Stuttgart.) The **Altstadt** is at its time-warp best early in the morning or very late in the evening, when the crooked lanes are empty. At the northern end of the Eberhardsbrücke, turn down the path between the river and the **Zwingel**, the 13th-century remains of the town wall. Near the punt moorings, where willow branches trail in the Neckar, is the **Hölderlinturm**, a part of the old fortifications. Following a tragic love affair, theology graduate and tutor Hölderlin tumbled into the shadowy world of schizophrenia. In an act of charity, Ernst Friedrich Zimmer, a well-read carpenter who had been impressed by Hölderlin's novel *Hyperion,* took in the ailing man of letters as a lodger in the little tower above his workshop. There Hölderlin lived for nearly 40 tormented years. His lyrical genius was not fully appreciated until this century (Heidegger was one booster), when donations helped convert his refuge into a museum. Exhibits include first editions and some of the essays Hölderlin wrote as a university student.

Only 5,000 or so people actually live in the old part of town, no more than during Duke Karl Eugen's reign. The stately university buildings stand out from their half-timbered neighbors huddled above the Hölderlinturm. In 1477, the first 250 scholars studied, ate, and slept in the **Bursa**, on the Bursagasse. In those days only Latin was spoken within the college walls, a rule enforced by a *lupus,* or supervisor. Now the Alte Bursa houses art, history, and philosophy seminars.

The university has always been known for its pugnacious brand of theologian. On July 14, 1793, Hegel, Schelling, and Hölderlin danced a boisterous *carmagnole* together to celebrate the fourth anniversary of the storming of the Bastille. Young Hölderlin's enthusiasm in particular seems to have waned as the French Revolution's atrocities became apparent.

The first women students were admitted to the university in 1970. Today's students have proclaimed the university a "nuclear-free zone." Defiant graffiti line the Neckarhalde, a rambling lane in which several of the more militant ecology groups have their offices. Earnest political debate, a favorite student pastime in the evenings, is a public spectacle, witnessed in any of the *Gögenbeizen*. There are dozens of these wine taverns, from the **Gasthof Ritter** in the Am Stadtgraben, run by the same family for 70 years, to the **Wirtschaft am Hölderlinturm**, down by the river.

Some 600 students, often resplendent in colorful caps and sashes, belong to centuries-old fraternities. Some members still indulge in illegal initiation duels. The fraternities' traditional *Maisingen,* the singing of patriotic songs in the Marktplatz in May, sometimes leads to clashes with the less-conservative student faction. Under the town hall's Baroque-style gables, an astronomical clock has accurately recorded astral maneuvers, including solar eclipses, since 1511. Happily, its brilliant inventor, the mathematics professor Johannes Stöffler, was mistaken when he predicted the end of the world for February 25, 1524.

The town employs some 30 guides, many of them former academics who take visitors on individual tours. With a jangling bunch of keys they can get you into some of Tübingen's lesser-known nooks and crannies. They'll show you the **Karzer**, the tiny cell in which students had to spend hours or even days for minor offenses such as wearing the wrong attire, and the dank cellars beneath the Renaissance splendor of **Schloss Hohentübingen**. You'll hear bats squeaking and water dripping as the guide points out the gargantuan wine barrel that used to contain some 80,000 liters of Burgundy. Two nice, moderately priced hotels offer pleasant lodging in the old city: the **Am Schloss**, on the Burgsteige, and the **Hospiz**, on the Neckarholde.

# THE SCHWÄBISCHE ALB

East of Tübingen and more or less south of Stuttgart is the Schwäbische Alb, a high limestone plateau stretching from the Black Forest to the mountains of Bohemia. More than 175 million years ago it was part of a desert swept by scorching winds. As the millennia elapsed, the shifting surface compacted into a deep layer of red sandstone, which in turn disappeared under a gradually encroaching saltwater sea whose graveyard of shellfish and other crustaceans decomposed into limestone. Toward the end of the Mesozoic era, roughly 135 million years ago, the multitiered rock sandwich was topped off by three more strata of Jurassic limestone after yet another inland sea receded. In the course of seismic upheavals that ended some 15 million years ago, the formation reared up into a rough version of the upland we know today. Modern geologists liken the Alb to an enormous leaky barrel. Over the ages water has seeped through the porous limestone and accumulated carbonic acid, which is steadily eroding a subterranean tracery of largely uncharted streams, rivers, lakes, and caves.

Slate from the Alb's Jurassic layer has been quarried for centuries. At the end of the 19th century, a young man named Bernhard Hauff was the first to probe the area for fossilized remains of the denizens of those primeval seas. Many of these are in the Stattliches Museum für Naturkunde in Stuttgart. The fossil hunt is still on. Collectors crack open slate shards with little hammers, usually discovering dozens of fossils, mainly of mollusks.

# Dettingen/Kirchheim unter Teck

A particularly good view of the Alb, a shoal of dark humps beckoning southward, can be had from the cherry orchards overlooking Dettingen (south of Stuttgart to Metzingen, then east toward Bad Urich on route 28) and the neighboring town of Kirchheim unter Teck. Farmers in Dettingen pick fruit by hand from more than 10,000 trees. Part of the crop is traditionally distilled into *Kirschgeist,* a clear, fiery cherry brandy. Recently there has been a slump in production because of ever-higher duty and overhead, but many villagers nonetheless keep their cellars well stocked with their own moonshine. You can sample Kirschgeist at its best and punchiest in the **Gasthaus Grüner Baum**, the village's liveliest tavern, populated by a bunch of regulars versed in the coarser forms of Swabian humor. Genuine Kirschgeist generally comes in a bottle without a label, and is served in thimble-sized glasses. Connoisseurs dab a drop on the backs of their hands and sniff it for quality.

# Blaubeuren

Southeast of Dettingen, B 28 climbs toward Blaubeuren and Ulm into a less fertile region atop the Alb. The villages, clusters of red-roofed cottages in the upland's folds, look deceptively prosperous. The topsoil here is sometimes less than four inches deep. Rye and wheat grow only about half as tall as down in the Neckar valley. Rain falls frequently but is sucked rapidly into the Alb's porous limestone innards. Despite a great deal of research, the exact location of many huge underground reservoirs is still anyone's guess. One subterranean river route was traced simply enough, however, when dye allowed to trickle into the ground in Laichingen and Suppingen during a heavy rainfall resurfaced three days later just west of Ulm in Blaubeuren's **Blautopf**, a small crater filled with water that turns a brilliant shade of blue during dry periods.

The Blautopf's spring bubbles away, and its water is channeled up at high pressure through a series of limestone caves. Attempts to swim down the latter have claimed the lives of several divers. Jochen Hasenmayer, the most successful to date, was equipped with six aqualungs and a turbine-driven propeller when, in 1983, he fought and wriggled his way through 3,000 feet of tiny caves and lofty caverns. Groups of five and more can watch a 45-minute video film of his exploit in the tiny poolside cinema.

The poet Eduard Mörike found the intriguing blue pool "too wonderful to be adequately described." Its setting in a quiet valley has attracted generations of people who come to meditate and marvel. The first church here was built in the seventh century; a monastery was erected in 1085. The monks' cells are now used by a boarding school, and the magnificently sculpted **cloisters**, which frame an herbal garden, are open to the public. Some of the 500-year-old frescoes, especially those in the **Margarethenkapelle**, serve as a backdrop for the graffiti of generations of young boarders.

# Wimsener Höhle

Not all of the Alb's caves are restricted to intrepid explorers. A wooded ravine just off the scenic country road between Hayingen and, south of there, lying on B 312, Zwiefalten, camouflages the country's sole navigable cavern, the **Wimsener Höhle**. At the **Gasthaus Friedrichsmühle**, known for its trout dishes, you can rent essentials for the expedition: a guide and a flat-bottomed boat. At the cavern's lip a Latin inscription commemorates a ducal visit by Friedrich von Württemberg in 1803. Nothing much has changed in the dimly lit cave since then. The boatman claws the clammy walls with his fingertips to propel the vessel. The interior is just big enough, if passengers duck their heads, for a 200-foot foray. Beyond that are darkness and silence, except for the eerie drip of water. What people remember most about their short cruise is a rock about halfway along shaped spookily like an old man's head.

## Bad Buchau

The Alb's dry patches generate thermal currents that local gliders thrive on. Villages like **Hayingen**, on the southeast side of the Alb, have long, stubbly runways, called "airports," for their sailplane enthusiasts. Storks, flying in from Africa to breed, also benefit from the thermals. Generations of storks have homed in on the **Federsee**, a marshy lake at Bad Buchau (southeast of the Alb near Biberach) that the ornithological group Deutscher Bund für Vogelschutz has kept as a bird sanctuary since 1911. A mile-long boardwalk stretching out through the reeds provides a binoculars-aided view of some of the more than 200 bird species that congregate here. In Bad Buchau itself, the spa on the lake, a padded wicker nest made in the Bund's workshop tops the **Schloss**. Year after year the same pair of storks uses it. By autumn most of the birds, both parents and offspring, head for Africa. A few remain, to be fed through the winter by farmers in nearby Oggelshausen. In the 1960s Baden-Württemberg's population of itinerant storks dropped from 154 to 45, but recently there has been an upswing in their numbers.

## Hohenzollern Country

The facts of Prussian history are far removed from a fairy tale, although the royal family's last outpost, **Burg Hohenzollern**, suggests otherwise. Perched south of Tübingen at 2,700 feet on one of the Alb's westernmost pinnacles, the castle stabs the clouds with turrets that bring to mind damsels in distress awaiting rescue by knights errant. A narrow road winds up to the castle from **Hechingen**, its attendant town. Great echoing halls like the Grafensaal are a bit too monumental for domestic comfort. No one ever actually lived in Burg Hohenzollern until 1951, when Prussia's prince-in-waiting, Louis Ferdinand, and his wife, Kira, a great-niece of the last tsar, Nicholas II, brought a whiff of domesticity with them. Every summer the sound of children's laughter echoes through the castle. Princess Kira, who has since died, founded a charity for deprived Berlin youngsters, and the proceeds from an annual concert held in the Grafensaal go toward funding long therapeutic stays for them at the castle.

If a flag with the Prussian eagle is fluttering in the breeze, Louis Ferdinand is at home. During his sporadic stays the crown prince uses five of the castle's 250 salons, chambers, and banqueting halls. A retainer serves him breakfast, but Louis Ferdinand takes his other meals in the nearby **Burgschenke**, a restaurant that caters to nearly half a million visitors yearly.

His handful of employees address the prince as "Your Imperial Majesty," and their devotion borders on the effusive. One typical comment: "You could chop the prince into a hundred pieces and each bit would still be imperial." Prince Louis Ferdinand is a grandson of the last German kaiser, Wilhelm II. Although Prussia's royals were stripped of their political power at the end of World War I along with the rest of Germany's aristocracy, within their own circles the hierarchies of old, as set down in the Almanac de Gotha, the Continent's peerage register, still hold good.

The first castle on the present site was probably built in the 11th century. Although records are inconclusive, the original owners were probably forebears of the Hohenzollerns named Burchardinger. The seemingly impregnable castle has been wrested from the Hohenzollern grip twice: by Countess Henriette von Württemberg's army in 1423 and by French troops in 1744. It was rebuilt from ruins in 1846, when the Prussian and Swabian branches of the Hohenzollern family chose it as their joint ancestral residence.

At the foot of the castle rock you can take a shuttle bus up or opt for a steep walk through the woods. Crenellated walls lead up to the keep and the castle's neo-Gothic melodrama of flying buttresses, rib and shaft ceilings, pointed arches, and stained-glass windows.

The treasures on display in the **Schatzkammer** include a bejeweled Prussian crown that Kaiser Wilhelm II had made in 1889. The **Christuskapelle** holds the coffins of kings Frederick William I and Frederick the Great.

Hohenzollern territory extends south across the Alb to the town of **Sigmaringen**, an hour's drive away. **Schloss Sigmaringen**, seen from the Danube below, looks intimidating and aloof atop its sheer rock face. But its front section juts into the heart of town. In Medieval times the castle's occupants must have felt particularly vulnerable during periods of unrest. This is hinted at by the array of helmets, maces, and heavy muskets you'll pass on the way into the keep. Fortunately for Sigmaringen, the ruling family's diplomatic skills usually averted major showdowns. Even Napoleon was successfully appeased. Portraits of his relatives still abound in the stuccoed interior, which was largely refurnished after a devastating fire in 1893. Prince Franz, who lives here with his family, turns up as a guest of honor at local soccer club functions and joins in the fun at meetings of the Elferrat (carnival committee) wearing old Hohenzollern uniforms. The locals have nicknamed him Eierprinz (Egg Prince) because of the farm he owns and runs.

# Rottweil

Rottweil, 35 km (20 miles) southwest of Hechingen via the B 27, is Baden-Württemberg's oldest town, and exploring its past requires only some sensible walking shoes. Start down in the **Altstadt** on the banks of the Neckar. The river wends its way between the Alb's wooded flanks and the foothills of the Black Forest. Ancient Rome's empire builders risked a tentative settlement here that they called Arae Flaviae. From A.D. 73 on, the military encampment developed into a community. The **Römerbad**, remains of thermal baths in the Holderstrasse, is one of several archaeological sites. At the priest's house on the Pelagiusgasse the housekeeper will unlock a vault door in the church opposite and guide you down to the stone pipes of a Roman central heating system. Rottweil's most prized antique was excavated in 1834: a brilliant Roman mosaic of 570,000 pieces depicting Orpheus playing a lute. It is now in the **Stadtmuseum**.

The **Hochturm** and the **Schwarzes Tor** were key towers in the fortifications built during the Hohenstaufen era. For centuries Rottweil was a Free Imperial City with its own judicial and penal system, answerable only to the distant Holy Roman Emperor. From 1418 on, trials were held at the **Hofgerichtsstätte**, where you can see a replica of the judge's chair almost opposite the present Landgericht, on the Königstrasse. The finely sculpted baldachin, under which often Draconian sentencing took place, is an interesting misfit in the modern office setting of the **Einwohnermeldeamt** on the Königstrasse. The clerks in charge of the residents' register will show you which light switch illuminates the priceless stone relic in the corner.

Its long spells of imperial grandeur help to explain

Rottweil's strong sense of tradition. Local society is still very close knit. Its members keep tabs on one another and their assessment travels down the municipal grapevine, in taverns like **Zum Goldenen Becher** or cozy meeting places such as the **Café Armleder**, where slabs of Schwarzwälder Kirschtorte (Black Forest cherry cake) are served with great dollops of whipped cream.

The order of everyday life disappears during Rottweil's annual **Fasnet**, the Alemannic version of Carnival that takes place toward the end of winter. For several high-spirited days more than 2,000 townsfolk cavort behind exquisitely carved wooden masks and hand-painted linen robes, which are usually handed down from one generation to the next. As officially sanctioned *Narren* (jesters), plied with endless rounds of Champagne during tavern breathers, they roam the town recounting the year's events with a satirical bite that convention would normally forbid. Depending on their period of origin, from pagan to Baroque, the expressions on the masks range from bland to ferocious. Disguise is maintained for the duration of revelries; even during meals their wearers raise the masks just enough for the intake of food. The two main parades are held on Fasnet Monday and Shrove Tuesday. At 8:00 A.M. sharp all the *Narren* prance through the Schwarzes Tor and then tour the town for nearly three hours, cracking long whips, vaulting along on poles, and showering spectators with pretzels and sweets. This is all meant to banish winter's evil spirits. The high-pitched whoops the *Narren* excel in have a pagan ring, reverberating from the distant days when the first Alemannic tribes arrived to spoil the Roman idyll.

# Donaueschingen

First-time visitors to Donaueschingen, at the southwest end of A 16, 31 km (19 miles) south of Rottweil on route 27, are intrigued by the Art Nouveau façades they encounter on a crosstown stroll from, say, the Augustenstrasse to the Sennhofstrasse. A fire raged through the town in 1908, and the **Stadtkirche St. Johann** was one of the few major Baroque buildings to survive. There are other reminders of the past here: In the **Karlsbau Museum** is the best preserved of the three known handwritten Niebelungenlied scripts, and a fine collection of panel paintings, with works by Hans Holbein the Elder, on loan from the House of Fürstenberg, which has resided in the local **Schloss** since the 18th century.

The real crowd puller is the **Donauquelle**, the source of

the Danube, in the Schlosspark. The "glorious river" starts
out on its journey to the Black Sea as a tiny spring bubbling
into a shallow pool of water encircled by an ornamental
railing. Hundreds of coins, thrown in by tourists, glitter on
the pebble bed.

By the time it reaches Immendingen along B 311, the
Danube has grown into a full-fledged river, its banks dotted
with anglers. Here near its westernmost tip, however, the
river seems almost to disappear altogether—one more surprise that the Alb has in store. Just east of Immendingen
signs marked "Donauversinkung" lead to a secluded parking
lot near the river. Head toward Möhringen on a narrow path,
and you will watch the Danube slowly but surely peter out.
After a couple of hundred yards there is just about enough
Danube left to cover your feet. Then the last few puddles
disappear and the river seeps away into the pebble bed,
another case of the Alb at its most porous. The Danube
resurfaces in Aach (on B 31), where Germany's biggest
spring, the **Aachtopf**, bubbles. The dry riverbed, for its part,
meanders on from Immendingen toward Tuttlingen, to be
replenished by streams with, as yet, no waltzes named after
them.

# THE LAKE CONSTANCE AREA

Vineyards sloping down to crowded marinas on the north
shore and snow-capped Alps towering to the south face each
other across the waters of Central Europe's third-biggest
lake. Its 160 miles of hilly shoreline, more than 200 feet
above sea level, are shared by Switzerland, Austria, Bavaria,
and Baden-Württemberg, the latter claiming the lion's share.
In summer the water temperature rarely drops below 70° F
in the **Bodensee** (the lake's German name), which accounts
for the subtropical vegetation that in places fringes this
medium-altitude sun trap. Fierce winds from the mountains
occasionally whip up formidable seas, but on the whole this
is a lake popular with those who like their boating and
bathing on the tame side. Wide-scale pollution threatened
the waters more than a decade ago, but improved sewage
treatment has saved the day for tourism. All sorts of publicity
stunts were created to reassure doubters, including a photo
of Count Bernadotte, who runs the island of Mainau, sipping
a glass of lake water.

# Konstanz

Getting your bearings in Konstanz is a challenge. The oldest part of this former Free Imperial City is a German enclave in Swiss territory linked by the **Rheinbrücke** to its new suburbs in Baden-Württemberg. Scores of one-night emigrés from Zürich and St. Gallen cross the frontier and head for its roulette tables, which are forbidden in their own country.

Judging by the very thorough and very costly face-lift the Altstadt recently received, its venerable buildings will survive well into the next millennium. A case in point is the **Ober-markt** (formerly the place of public execution). Thanks to several coats of blue and gray paint, the **Malhaus** looks only half as old as its Renaissance bays. In fact, the pharmacy on its ground floor has been in business since the 14th century. That period will keep you in its grip all the way down Hussen-strasse to the **Schnetztor,** a former gate tower that looms over the half-timbered house in which Jan Hus is said to have spent three weeks in 1414 preparing to face the Council of Constance. The Bohemian teacher, preacher, and religious reformer had vehemently criticized church leaders, mainly on moral grounds. He was lured to Konstanz to defend his views with a promise of safe conduct. But the council interrogators threw him into jail, found him guilty of heresy, and burned him at the stake, in what is now Tägermoosstrasse. The martyr's former rooms were turned into a museum in 1922.

Hus was held prisoner in the Dominican monastery, which one of the country's big hotel chains has since transformed into the deluxe **Steinberger Insel-hotel** on the edge of the Stadtgarten. From here you can walk along the waterfront to the **Konzilgebäude,** built for the wealthy merchant class as its guild hall-cum-warehouse in 1388. Only 29 years later it was the venue for the council conclave that elected Cardinal Otto Colonna as Pope Martin V. A variety of conferences of a less momentous nature are still held in the main hall with its oak beams, pillars, and frescoed panels.

# Reichenau

From the little harbor at Konstanz, umpteen pleasure-boat cruises leave for destinations as distant as the Austrian town of Bregenz. In little more than an hour you can also travel by a roundabout but scenic water route to the island of Reichenau (only a few minutes' drive away via a causeway). As you pass beneath the **Rheinbrücke,** you will momentarily be on a continuation of the upper Rhine. A few hundred yards on, the channel widens into the branch of the lake, split into the **Gnadensee** and the **Untersee**, in which Reichenau basks.

Reichenau makes a first and lasting impression of sunlight glinting on greenhouse glass. The islanders export millions of cucumbers, tomatoes, and heads of lettuce annually. In this workaday setting, the three buttressed churches, all Romanesque in style, come as a surprise. **St. Georg** in Oberzell is the oldest such example north of the Alps. Its foundations date to the ninth century. Recent restoration, carried out according to the methods of that era, used a mixture of plaster and ox blood.

## Mainau

Within walking distance of modern Konstanz lies the more exotic of its two main islands, **Mainau**. Lennart Bernadotte moved into the Baroque island residence more than half a century ago. A trained agriculturist, the Swedish count spent years creating a botanical wonderland. Some 20 tons of bulbs are still planted annually. The season usually opens with an orchid show in the **Palmenhaus** toward the end of March, followed by the blossoming of rhododendrons, hyacinths, and more than 800 varieties of roses. Now and then King Carl Gustaf XVI, Bernadotte's great-nephew, drops in for a chat in the shade of Mainau's palm and citrus trees. A pedestrian causeway leads out to the island; a small entrance fee is charged.

## Meersburg

Ferries for Meersburg leave from the Konstanz-Staad dock every 15 minutes, and at hourly intervals during the night. As you steam northeast across the lake toward the old harbor, steep green cliffs covered with neatly planted vines rise to meet you. Some vineyards date from the Dark Ages, like the castle from which the town gets its name. The **Meersburg** presides over a two-tier cluster of half-timbered houses, the **Oberstadt** and the **Unterstadt**. Called Germany's oldest inhabited castle, the Meersburg was built in the seventh century at the command of King Dagobert I. Its fortifications withstood attack by the first-ever gunpowder cannons. In 1841 the author Annette von Droste-Hülshoff came here to stay with her brother-in-law, the owner, and wrote *Die Judenbuche* (*The Jew's Beech Tree*) and other works. Seven years later, after a lingering illness, she died in the castle. A small museum displays memorabilia associated with her, including the armchair in which she died.

With centuries of wine-growing experience, the local *Winzer* have perfected several Müller-Thurgau and Ruländer wines. Special praise must go to the fruity lakeside Spätburgunder Weissherbst, equally delicious in its rosé hue or its alternative amber color. The lake's premier delicacy, freshly netted whitefish (called *Felchen* on local menus), goes well with every variety of Weissherbst. Meersburg is on the northern shore's well-travelled gourmet trail, where vacations are often planned as culinary expeditions. Good, reasonably priced cooking can be found in any of the older establishments. One such is the **Wilder Mann**, down at the harbor, where latecomers, confronted by the locked town gates, used to stay more than 250 years ago.

# Überlingen

While Meersburg bursts at its Medieval seams during the summer, the rubbled lanes and squares of Überlingen (10 km/6 miles up the shore), only a couple of hundred years younger and endowed with such fine examples of Gothic and Baroque architecture as the **St. Nikolaus Münster** and the **Rathaus**, are comparatively serene. Even on the busiest weekends, the wine taverns between the Wiestorstrasse and Münsterplatz have enough elbow room for some serious sampling. A prowl through the Altstadt usually ends in the **Spitalkeller**, which has a selection of 65 wines in its cellars.

In the winter of 1904, ducal district doctor and medical counsellor Eduard Würth, to give him *almost* his full title, had a pavement of expensive Ticino gneiss laid from his favorite inn, the **Christophkeller**, to his house on the Mühlenstrasse. Ever since, local connoisseurs have prided themselves on making stylish exits, whatever their degree of inebriation, after a hard night's wine tasting.

**Unteruhldingen** 3 km (2 miles) east on B 31, warrants a stop. Archaeologists found remarkably well preserved remains of Stone Age and Bronze Age pile dwellings at the muddy bottom of the bay here. There was enough material to reconstruct a village on stilts, including such artifacts as a Stone Age oven and Bronze Age bellows. Long lines tend to form at the entrance to the open-air museum.

# Friedrichshafen

The 14 km (9 miles) between Friedrichshafen (east of Meersburg) and Romanshorn, on the Swiss shore opposite, is the widest part of Lake Constance. On hazy days, as the ferries, with their escort of squawking gulls, glide out of the harbor and fade into the distance, it is easy to see why lake transit burgeoned during the steamboat era. A regular ferry service between Friedrichshafen and the Swiss town of Rorschach began in 1824, when the steamer *Wilhelm* made a trial run on November 26. Buffeted by a storm, it still beat the sailboat carrying the day's mail by more than three hours. For decades Swabia had what amounted to a "Royal Württemberg" navy with captains decked out in full sword-toting regalia. Nowadays some three dozen diesel-engined ferries ply to and fro. They belong to the lake's white fleet, run as a joint venture by the Swiss, Austrian, and German railways.

A longish tramp steamer tour of the lake, with sorties into the hinterlands, is not expensive. The Deutsche Bundesbahn offers a reasonably priced *Bodenseepass,* valid for 15 days, that entitles you to ride ferries as well as trains, buses, and cable cars on and around the lake.

Both passenger vessels and car ferries call at Friedrichshafen. The broad sweep of its palm-studded esplanade is a reminder that this town, the lake's only real industrial sprawl, was a sleepy little royal spa at the turn of the century. Its career as a center of aeronautical engineering was triggered by Ferdinand von Zeppelin. On July 2, 1900, the count's first dirigible, filled with hydrogen and powered by twin Daimler gasoline engines, took off from a floating hangar moored off the village of **Manzell**.

One whole floor of the **Bodensee Museum**, in the north wing of the Rathaus, is devoted to the Zeppelin saga. At the touch of a button, a caterpillar of light crawls along a map of the airships' global routes.

# *THE BAROQUE ROAD*

Bounded by Lake Constance and the river Danube, and, to the east, the Iller, Upper (southern) Swabia's gently sloping hill country, dotted with isolated farms, hamlets, and villages, lulls one into a pastoral, straw-chewing mood. So, as you step out of the predictable prettiness of its dairy pastures into its abbeys, churches, mansions, and town halls, the lavish Baroque spectacles within are all the more over-whelming. The vivid blues, pinks, and yellows of the celestial scenes on the vaulting are offset by dazzling white walls and pillars dripping with stucco ornamentation. Gilded cherubs and angels, lips parted joyously, float over superbly carved altars, choir stalls, and pulpits.

If you are more an admirer of, say, Norman architectural austerity, this is rich fare indeed. The region's Baroque architecture was born of the Counter Reformation, instigated by the top echelons of the Roman Catholic Church in the 16th and 17th centuries. After the Reformation, roughly two thirds of Austria, to which most of Upper Swabia belonged at the time, had turned to Protestantism. To add insult to injury, Protestant troops from Sweden and Württemberg wrecked a considerable part of the region's finest architecture during the Thirty Years War. Large-scale rebuilding started toward the middle of the 17th century, when counts and abbots brought in painters, sculptors, and plasterers from as far afield as the Ticino. It was their goal to create imaginative and uplifting interiors that would help win back hearts and minds to the Roman Catholic faith. Their Baroque extravaganza here apparently did the trick, for most of today's Upper Swabians are Roman Catholic.

Plotting a route full of interesting examples of the Baroque style is easy enough. Endless permutations are possible, including an official **Schwäbische Barockstrasse** designated in 1966 (contact the German National Tourist Office for details). We suggest a looping run, less than 200 km (125 miles) in overall length, that will take you as far north as Ochsenhausen, near Biberach, and as far east as Eglofs.

A visit to the **Wallfahrtskirche St. Maria** in **Birnau** near Überlingen will whet your appetite. The angels portrayed on the nave's frescoes are traditional enough. The *Honig-schlecker,* in the transept, makes people smile; a stucco cherub holds a hive buzzing with golden bees and licks an apparently sticky index finger. This is Baroque at its most playful.

Drive south to Meersburg, then follow B 33 toward Ravensburg to Weingarten, less than an hour's drive away. Its **Pfarr- und Klosterkirche St. Martin und St. Oswald** is an unusually monumental example of German Baroque. The original Romanesque basilica was demolished at the beginning of the 18th century, and 200 craftsmen and artists, including the renowned fresco painter Cosmas Damian Asam, created what is often called "Swabia's answer to St. Peter's." The church is approximately half as big as the

Vatican structure. Priests, choirboys, and Benedictine monks from the adjacent monastery have perfected a decelerated delivery for sermons, hymns, and psalms to accommodate the echoes from the back of the church.

A pleasant country road, which bypasses heavy traffic on B 32 and B 30, meanders from Ravensburg to **Aulendorf**. Opposite the tiny spa's elegant Hofgarten, the **Pfarrkirche St. Martin** exemplifies Baroque's early and later phases. The life-size Madonna dates from 1656, the stucco ceiling in the nave from 1711. One of the altar shrines contains the bejeweled bones of Saint Felix, who was martyred in Rome. During the Middle Ages the local counts of Königsegg had the holy man's skeleton removed from Rome's catacombs and brought to Aulendorf.

**Bad Schussenried**, another of the region's spas, lies a few miles to the north. It, too, has several Baroque masterpieces. Connoisseurs regard the **Bibliotheksaal**, tucked away in a former monastery, as outstanding. Dominikus Zimmermann, one of Germany's most prolific Baroque artists, had a substantial hand in designing the library. Stucco heavens soar above balustrades, pillars, alabaster statues, and trompe l'oeil bookcases, in a wing of the ex-monastery that now houses a psychiatric clinic. To get to the Bibliotheksaal, pay the nominal fee at the entrance gates and then follow the signs to Stationen 14–17. Psychiatric wards and the library are at opposite ends of a long corridor. Patients attend church services in the Bibliotheksaal. Bad Buchau and the Federsee are only about 5 km (3 miles) to the north; see the Alb section above.

If you keep to minor roads, Degernau and Ummendorf are the only two sizable villages on the way east to **Ochsenhausen**, an unassuming town heralded by the **Pfarrkirche St. Georg** and its slender bell tower on a hill. Until the end of the 15th century, the basilica was a prime example of the Gothic style. It is now as ornate as a wedding cake, as a result of rebuilding from 1725 onward. The adjoining palatial structure was a Benedictine monastery until 1803, the year Napoleonic edicts put an end to most of the monastic life in this region. The buildings have proven to be a godsend to local clubs. The former monks' quarters are occupied by a school for Baden-Württemberg's promising young musicians.

From Ochsenhausen south to Wangen, follow the official Oberschwäbische Barockstrasse signs, showing a tilted cherub's head on a bluish background. The *Schloss* in **Bad Wurzach** is now a boarding school run by two dozen monks of the Salvator order. School holidays are an ideal time to visit it. From 8:00 A.M. until about 7:00 P.M. the monks leave the gates and the main door open, and anyone can stroll in. The building's staircase, its best-known feature, is another grand gesture of the Baroque, with Herculean torsos shouldering masonry and cherubs perched decoratively on the balustrades. The ceiling's fresco scenes are joyously pagan: Venus, Jupiter, Chronos, and other Greek deities seem to have just landed in a blaze of color.

**Schloss Wolfegg**, on a promontory between the Ach and Höll valleys, has belonged to the counts of Waldburg-Wolfegg since the 13th century. During the Thirty Years War it was burned down by Swedish troops while the head of the family was away defending Konstanz and Lindau. Restoration was supervised by the 17th-century master plasterer Balthasar Crinner. His magnificent Baroque ceiling spans the **Rittersaal**, a gallery flanked by 24 carved wooden knights representing prominent family ancestors. The Schloss is open to the public most mornings and afternoons. At noon the automatic main gate closes, like a portcullis of old.

Many smaller pieces of Baroque art are easily detachable, and thieves have frequently preyed on Upper Swabia's churches. The tiny market town of **Kisslegg**, just south of Bad Wurzach, had its **Pfarrkirche St. Gallus und Ulrich** wired with an alarm, but someone still made off with most of the cherubs on the choir stalls. Special alarms protect the church's "silver treasure": 21 shining statues of Christ, the apostles, and other biblical figures by the local artisan Christoph Mäderl. The silver can be viewed at close quarters only when a guide escorts visitors to their gallery. But by squeezing up against the opposite wall, you can catch a glimpse of the Christ figure from below.

Just south of Kisslegg is **Wangen**, with its surrounding sprawl of small factories. This is the biggest town on this Baroque itinerary, but the cobbled **Oberstadt** offers sanctuary. Stroll in through the **Frauentor**, one of three remaining gate towers, and the traffic will suddenly abate. Much of the Altstadt is now a pedestrian zone. For the past 20 years a history-conscious town council has allocated part of its budget to restoration. Many of the painted façades speak volumes: From a seat at one of the open-air cafés in the Herrengasse, you can peruse whole chapters of Wangen's history. Up on the Frauentor's outside wall, for example, Emperor Ferdinand is depicted holding an orb. As a Free Imperial City, Wangen owed allegiance to a succession of Holy Roman emperors. Ferdinand dropped in on the town with a retinue of 1,500, and municipal funds were greatly depleted by the ensuing days of merrymaking. The **Rathaus** and **Spitalkirche** are two more of Wangen's Baroque frills; the **Marktplatz** front of the Rathaus is decorated with cartouches, pillars, balconies, and gilded statuettes. In the back of the building is a conspicuous bulge under the ornate stonework: a segment of wall left over from distant imperial days.

**Eglofs** is little more than a sprinkling of farms some 8 km (5 miles) east of Wangen. Its elaborately stuccoed **Pfarr-kirche St. Martin**, however, will match most of what you have seen so far. You can enjoy a hearty meal in the **Gasthof zum Löwen von Josef Ellgass**, looking onto the village square with its patrician fountain and elegant half-timbered houses. Local families like Ellgass, Gollinger, and Egger are descended from forebears who were wealthy enough to qualify as *reichsfreie* farmers. In the 13th century that meant the little community was as autonomous as any of the Free Imperial towns. Later their privileges were rescinded, and a street called Freie Bauernstrasse is the only reminder of those decades of independence.

From Wangen it is only a 15-km (9-mile) drive south to Lindau, at the eastern end of Lake Constance.

## GETTING AROUND

Whether you plan a short trip into Swabia or an intense exploration of its heartland, Stuttgart is a good base from which to start. The state capital is linked by regular InterCity rail service with other major cities, and it is also at the intersection of Autobahns from Munich, Singen, Karlsruhe, Frankfurt, and Würzburg. The Stuttgart-Echterdingen airport had a distinctly provincial reputation for many years, but it has been upgraded, and domestic and international flights to and from Stuttgart-Echterdingen have increased in number. All the major car-rental agencies have desks at the airport and branch offices in even the smallest towns.

In general, motorists are pampered by a meticulously kept road network, with surfaces fit for an Autobahn. Be warned that the smooth ride encourages high-speed driving. Trunk road travel across the Swabian Alb's broad back is a pleasure, however. Traffic tends to build up only in the industrial sprawls around Stuttgart, Esslingen, Göppingen, Reutlingen, and Friedrichshafen. Lake Constance's northern shore road is also notorious for traffic jams during the summer months.

Roads are very well marked. Even the sites of minor tourist interest are well signposted. An exception is greater

Stuttgart, which makes no attempt at any semblance of a ring road and gives no warning that through traffic has no option but to struggle right down into the city basin and out the other side again.

A folk song that many Swabians know by heart immortalizes the regional railways and their plodding climbs up the Alb. Several of the trans-Alpine stretches, including Engstingen–Schelklingen (near Blaubeuren), have had their passenger services terminated. But enough lines remain in service for some extensive rail travel by *Bummelbahn,* or "dawdle trains," which stop at small country stations. One of the most scenic stretches meanders along the Danube from Tuttlingen to Ehingen. Fast, relatively direct rail links include Stuttgart–Rottweil and the Biberach-Ravensburg-Friedrichshafen run, which will bring you to the Lake Constance ferry services described above.

## ACCOMMODATIONS REFERENCE

▶ **Airport Mövenpick-Hotel.** Randstrasse, D-7000 **Stuttgart** 23. Tel: (711) 790-70; Fax: 793585.

▶ **Goldener Adler.** Am Markt 11, D-7170 **Schwäbisch Hall.** Tel: (791) 61-68.

▶ **Hospiz.** Neckarhalde 2, D-7400 **Tübingen.** Tel: (7071) 260-02; Telex: 7262841.

▶ **Inter-Continental.** Neckarstrasse 60, D-7000 **Stuttgart** 1. Tel: (711) 202-00; Fax: 202012.

▶ **Messehotel Europe.** Siemensstrasse 33, D-7000 **Stuttgart** 30. Tel: (711) 81-48-30.

▶ **Relaxa Waldhotel Schatten.** Gewandschatten 2, D-7000 **Stuttgart** 80. Tel: (711) 686-70; Fax: 6867999.

▶ **Am Schloss.** Burgsteige 18, D-7400 **Tübingen.** Tel: (7071) 210-77.

▶ **Steigenberger-Hotel Graf Zeppelin.** Arnulf-Klett-Platz 7, D-7000 **Stuttgart** 1. Tel: (711) 29-98-81; Fax: 722418.

▶ **Steigenberger Insel-Hotel.** Auf der Insel 1, 7750 **Konstanz.** Tel: (7531) 250-11.

# THE BLACK FOREST

## BADEN-BADEN AND FREIBURG

### By Ted Heck

*Ted Heck, a freelance travel and sports writer who lived in Germany for five years, contributes regularly to magazines and newspapers. He returns to Germany every year.*

Travellers come to Baden-Baden to bathe in thermal waters discovered by Roman soldiers or to gamble in the elegant casino. They also are drawn to the Medieval attractions of the university city of Freiburg. But both these cities are on the western edge of the forest, and the rest of the Schwarzwald (Black Forest) is frequently shortchanged by tourists with checklists of castles, museums, beer halls, and shops.

For Germans, however, the mountainous, legend-filled Schwarzwald is a favorite place to spend holidays. They come to this stretch of pine and fir trees and mountain meadows for lengthy vacations in hotels or for weekends in private retreats, where they can hike, wander in the woods—and take *die Kur* (the cure). The forest dominates the southwestern corner of Germany, running parallel to the Rhine river, which serves here as boundary with Switzerland on the south (Basel is right across the river) and France (Strasbourg, Alsace) to the west.

Health bubbles up from mineral springs in the Black Forest. Germans suffocating in highly industrialized cities look to the region's spas and Kur houses to heal assorted ailments. Resorts such as Wildbad, in the northern part of the forest, promise relief from rheumatic, respiratory, and circulatory disorders, even impotence. They offer motion therapy for accident victims and injured athletes, with more mechanical contraptions than a chain of physical fitness salons. Patrons don't just bathe in thermal springs; they drink water whose main ingredients are chlorine, salt, and sulphur. "Meet you for a drink" may be not an invitation for cocktails but a daily imbibing of hot mineral water. Unrefreshing as it sounds, many claim that it settles their stomachs.

A German need not be seriously ill to take the cure. Healing activities are supplemented with vigorous sports, varied cultural events, and culinary adventures. A week in a spa can be a healthy vacation, paid for by Germany's compulsory health-insurance system. Other vacationers prefer week-long walks from one Kur village to another. They lunch in mountain huts and sleep in first-class hotels, to which their bags have been moved by van. Hikers are encountered everywhere, and the hills are also alive with cyclists and horseback riders. Hang gliders make graceful swoops through the valleys; sailboats share mountain lakes with windsurfers.

In winter the Black Forest is popular with German skiers, but few North Americans are seen; with an average elevation of less than 3,000 feet, the tree-lined slopes do not appeal to transatlantic downhill skiers when high-altitude snowfields are only a few hours away in the Alps. The most impressive Black Forest resort, the **Feldberg**, in the southern region, is only 4,900 feet high. Cross-country skiers, however, find the forest a delight. Many of the 14,260 miles of hiking and walking paths become Nordic trails in winter.

Non-German travellers with limited time usually give the area's cure and sports aspects a low priority. They focus instead on the scenic pleasures of the forest the Roman soldiers called Silva Nigra. From a distance the dark green trees do indeed look black—and from inside the forest, too. Although logging is a major segment of the region's economy, lumberjacks have hardly made a dent. Tall trees are so close together here that the treetops merge to block out the sky. Sadly, about half the trees in the Black Forest suffer from *Waldsterben* (forest decline) caused by a mixture of acid rain, automobile emissions, and longer-distance industrial pollution, especially from France. The blight is a hot environmental issue in Germany, but the destruction is not yet apparent to the casual traveller.

Where trees open into meadows, quaint towns and vil-

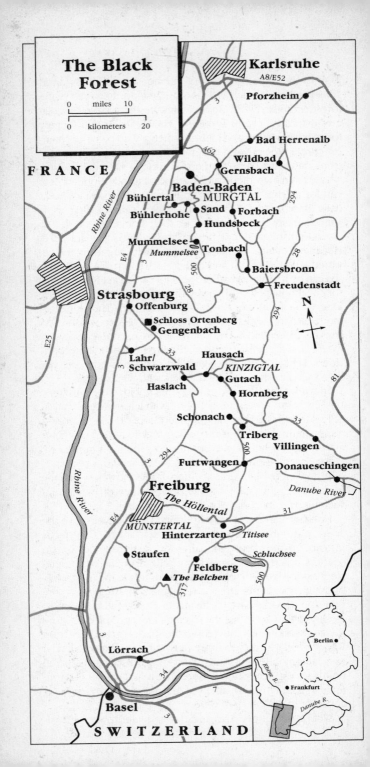

# The Black Forest

miles
0          10

kilometers
0                    20

FRANCE

Karlsruhe

A8/E52

Pforzheim

Bad Herrenalb

Wildbad
Gernsbach

462

Baden-Baden
MURGTAL

294

Bühlertal
Bühlerhöhe          Sand          Forbach
Hundsbeck

Mummelsee
*Mummelsee*          Tonbach          28

500          Baiersbronn

Freudenstadt

28          294

Strasbourg
Offenburg          N

Schloss Ortenberg
Gengenbach

81

Lahr/
Schwarzwald          Hausach
33          *KINZIGTAL*

Haslach          Gutach
Hornberg

Schonach
Triberg          33

500          Villingen

Furtwangen          Donaueschingen

Freiburg          *Danube River*

The Höllental

31

*MÜNSTERTAL*
Hinterzarten          *Titisee*

Staufen          *Schluchsee*

Feldberg
▲ *The Belchen*          500

317

Rhine River

E4

3

Lörrach

34

7

Basel          3

SWITZERLAND

Rhine R.          Berlin

Frankfurt          Danube R.

lages dot the landscape. Some have historical significance and may have figured in internecine conflicts in the days when princes ruled various segments of the land. Others are worth a look because of a folk museum or glass-blowing or even a cuckoo-clock factory.

### MAJOR INTEREST

Scenery, panoramas of forests and meadows
Mountain lakes and streams
Folk museums

**Baden-Baden**
Casino
Parks
Thermal baths

**Freiburg**
Old town
Cathedral
Museums

## The Food of the Black Forest

The Black Forest is a regional culinary paradise, in part because of its proximity to France and Switzerland, in part because of 20 centuries of cross-cultural influences. Some of the finest restaurants in Germany are scattered throughout the forest's towns and villages, most of them in charming inns where cooking odors complement the Old World atmosphere.

Regional specialties range from such farmhouse fare as *Schwarzwald Schinken* (smoked ham), bread, cheese, and wurst to various pork and veal plates to delicately prepared *Forelle* (trout). A typical Gasthof menu will have a sturdy soup, perhaps with floating pancake strips, and a variety of hot and cold wurst. The sausages are often surprising, because no two restaurants seem to make their *Hauswurst* the same way—and they guard their recipes.

*Spätzle* and other pastas are homemade, too. Typical main courses include various meat and fowl dishes with creamy sauces. Beef is usually on the menu, but rarely in the form of a large steak: Germans regard the cow primarily as a machine for making milk and cheese. Wild game is often offered, sometimes in a ragout of venison, hare, and boar, with wild mushrooms from the forest. Side dishes are mixed salads, potatoes, and red and green cabbage prepared in a variety of ways. Other members of the cabbage family are plentiful—and *Spargel* (asparagus), available in May, is a national passion.

Black Forest diners take wine with their meals, generally from a local vineyard on the Badische Weinstrasse (Baden Wine Road), which runs through the Rhine valley between the river and the mountains. Beer, of course, is also a staple on Black Forest tables, served chilled but not ice cold. Some beers require attention; ask for a *Pils vom Fass* (on tap) and you'll wait seven minutes while the bartender pauses several times in filling the stemmed glass to build a foamy head inch by inch.

Pastries and ice cream are popular desserts. The ice cream is served by the scoop, but often as part of an *Eisbecher,* a sundae smothered with fruit and whipped cream. A local specialty is *Schwarzwälder Kirschtorte* (Black Forest cake), a dense, chocolatey confection flavored with kirsch.

The challenge facing many visitors to the Black Forest is where to begin. Sightseeing strategy depends on available time, special interests, and points of access. Many travellers arrive in this southwestern corner of Germany from points north (Frankfurt and Heidelberg) or from Stuttgart to the east, and pass through the Karlsruhe area on the northern edge of the forest. From there, the international spa town of Baden-Baden, less than an hour south of Karlsruhe, is a good starting point—and it's there that we begin our coverage.

We follow Baden-Baden with two recommended motor trips into the forest. One is a scenic loop that begins on the Schwarzwald Hochstrasse (highway) and goes south to Freudenstadt and back. The other is a bit more ambitious, from Offenburg (west of Freudenstadt) through a series of small villages to Medieval Freiburg, the other city we cover in detail, farther south.

Other suggested itineraries then follow for visitors who enter the Black Forest from the south—from Basel, Switzerland, say—or from Swabia in the east.

# Baden-Baden

Marlene Dietrich once said, "The most beautiful casino in the whole world is in Baden-Baden—and I have seen them all."

Ms. Dietrich gets little argument from anyone who has gambled amidst the glitz of Las Vegas and Atlantic City. In

Baden-Baden's **casino** you picture James Bond tossing chips onto the roulette table or coolly studying fashionable women playing baccarat. There may be inner turmoil among the gamblers betting up to ten thousand marks at a time, but it doesn't show. Tones are hushed. Patrons (who pay a small entrance fee after providing passport identification) wear dresses or jackets and ties. The several salons of the casino look as if they were lifted from French palaces of the 17th and 18th centuries. Even if the wheel is going against you it is possible to feel like Louis XIV.

There are no slot machines at the casino; *Automaten* are found only at the old railroad station, which now houses a restaurant and art gallery. But another American game of chance, poker, is now available.

The casino is housed in the **Kurhaus**, a Neoclassical colonnade built in 1824 on the west bank of the river Oos. It is the centerpiece of the large riverside park and gardens where kings and queens and lesser nobles promenaded during Baden-Baden's heyday as the summer capital of Europe.

From the Kurhaus restaurant's patio, modern-day visitors can hear thrice-daily concerts from a bandshell nestled among chestnut trees. To the right of the shell are two rows of exclusive boutiques, where treasures in the windows can be contemplated to the strains of Brahms and other composers who lived for a time in Baden-Baden.

Near the Kurhaus is the **Trinkhalle** (Pump Room), a Romanesque colonnade where people meet for a drink of hot mineral water, a ritual that finds the faithful reading newspapers while sipping their way to health. Some travellers may be more interested in the frescoes of Black Forest legends outside.

Other major attractions in the park area are the **Kunsthalle**, an internationally recognized art gallery that shows travelling exhibits, and the Baroque **theater**. Concerts can often be heard in the Bénazet hall, upstairs in the Kurhaus.

A city of 50,000, including incorporated villages around it, Baden-Baden attracts 275,000 visitors a year, who stay on average three days. The head of the Kurverwaltung (tourist office) has the same status as the mayor. The office has its own impressive building, Haus des Kurgastes, on the Augustaplatz, a short distance across the river from the casino. It is a good place to book a room, get helpful information, or begin a walking tour.

The Baden-Baden *Guide in Color,* available in the tourist office, highlights strolls through the park and the Altstadt (Old Town). Note that the river Oos flows north through the city and separates the park area on the west bank from the commercial and residential areas on the east, right-bank side.

Before continuing, pay a quick visit to the Protestant **Stadtkirche**, probably the only church ever built in part by proceeds from a gambling casino. Depicted in its stained-glass windows are prominent figures of the Reformation.

Edouard Bénazet, a Frenchman whose family took over management of the casino in 1838, was responsible for much of the architecture of modern Baden-Baden. He not only helped finance churches but planned construction of other public buildings. The racecourse at nearby Iffezheim, where the twice-a-year horse races are still major social events, was another brainchild of his. The French feel that what Bénazet gave to the city may account for its being left unscarred in World War II. When Germany was divided into occupation zones, the French selected Baden-Baden for their headquarters.

The right-bank pedestrian zone of the **Lange Strasse** and the **Gernsbacher Strasse** is right across the Oos from the Trinkhalle. Shops of every description may slow you down here and on the neighboring, chestnut-tree–lined **Sophienstrasse**, where you'll find Ferragamo and other smart shops. On the western end of the Gernsbacher Strasse is the **Rathaus** (Town Hall), which dates back to 1632, when it was a Jesuit college. It was rebuilt in the 19th century.

The 13th-century **Stiftskirche** (Collegiate Church) is next door to the Rathaus. Its treasures include an exquisite Gothic crucifix and the tombstones of the margraves of Baden-Baden.

But the hot spot in this part of town is the baths. Half a million visitors a year use the bathing and sauna facilities of **Friedrichsbad** and **Caracalla Therme**. The former has been a therapeutic center for more than a century, offering various treatments, baths of different chemical composition, and stimulating massages. Underneath the Friedrichsbad are the **Römische Badruinen**, ruins of second-century baths built for Roman soldiers.

The ornate Caracalla baths feature indoor and outdoor pools and romantic grottoes, with warm water or cool. Built only in the mid-1980s, this spacious facility sits over mile-deep thermal springs whose water comes to the surface at more than 150 degrees Fahrenheit. Visitors may use the Caracalla's pools, saunas, solariums, and inhalatorium, paying at ticket-vending machines in the main lobby. An information desk helps first-time guests with details on lockers and fees for extra services, such as massages and mud wraps. A gymnastic area is set aside on the top floor for frequent visitors on a fitness regimen. Those who cannot wait to get home to replace lost energy can eat in a reasonably priced cafeteria with an outside terrace. Caracalla is open daily from 8:00 A.M. to 10:00 P.M. Take a towel and bathing suit; there are none for rent.

If you leave the baths with any energy, walk a short distance up the Florentine hill to the 15th-century **Neues Schloss** (New Castle) for its gardens and the view down into the town. Its residential rooms are furnished in an opulent Empire style.

There are many other sights in Baden-Baden; a brief list of some of them follows. The **Michaelsberg Stourdza Kapelle**, a Neoclassical crypt, is an uphill walk from the Trinkhalle on the west side of the Oos. A final resting place for Romanian noblemen, it sits among a waterfall, lake, and gardens. The **Russische Kirche** (Russian Church), with its onion-shaped dome, is on Lichtenthalerstrasse south of Bertoldplatz and the Stadtkirche. Farther south on Lichtenthalerstrasse, which roughly parallels the Oos river, is **Kloster Lichtenthal**, an abbey of Cistercian nuns dating to the 15th century and still active. Its museum displays handicraft work of the sisters. Music lovers should walk across the street to the **Brahmshaus**, where the famous German composer produced some of his best-known works. The **Kloster vom Heiligen Grab** (Holy Tomb) is another abbey, in the Altstadt, beside Friedrichsbad.

Wondering where to rest weary bones after a day of sightseeing? For just an ice-cream cone or tea and pastry, try a café at the **Palais Hamilton**, at the lower end of the Sophienstrasse. For something more substantial there are plenty of good restaurants in Baden-Baden. Consider the **Steigenberger Europäischer Hof** for a fashionable fling. Ask for a window table where you can see the casino and the Trinkhalle, a short distance away on the park side of the Oos. The service may be intimidating, but the food is superb. A humble farmer's plate of sausages is not on the menu, nor is onion cake. But the ubiquitous Black Forest *Forelle* (trout) is prepared exactly to your specifications. Be sure to have dessert; its presentation will convince you that the chef is really a moonlighting artist.

As to hotels, the **Europäischer Hof** has views of the park from many of its 200 rooms. It is a deluxe hotel, rich in tradition. Another hotel where you forget the budget and get superior meals and accommodations is **Brenner's Park-Hotel**, also near the Kurhaus. It is a favorite of celebrities and other well-to-do visitors seeking luxury. Style and grace are evident in the public halls, bedrooms, and spa facilities, for which Brenner's extracts the highest price in town.

For about half the Brenner's rates, you can stay in the small **Deutscher Kaiser**, on the Merkurstrasse near Augustaplatz. This family-run hotel has a *gemütliche* Bier-und-Weinstube, and its rooms are well equipped.

Some travellers to Baden-Baden find it worthwhile to stay in villages a bit farther into the forest. A hotel that anyone will be happy with is the reasonable **Rebstock** in Bühlertal. It's only 15 minutes south of the center of Baden. Ask for a room overlooking the patio.

# The Schwarzwald Hochstrasse

One of the most popular auto trips through the Black Forest is from Baden-Baden to Freudenstadt on the Schwarzwald Hochstrasse (route B 500). Follow the signs from Baden-Baden east up to Bühlerhohe. If you can talk your way past the gatehouse without a reservation, the **Schlosshotel Bühlerhohe** is worth seeing. This recently renovated castle with marble floors and tapestries has first-magnitude elegance (and its royal prices are at the upper end of the lodging spectrum in the Black Forest). It has been a favorite of world political leaders, and its well-to-do patrons use the beauty farm and health clinic that are part of its mountaintop complex.

From Bühlerhohe the Hochstrasse south passes through Hundseck, past two small ski areas, then by Sand to the **Mummelsee**. For all the attention Germans pay to the Mummelsee, foreign visitors are certain to be disappointed with this tiny lake. Mermaids in earlier days may have come out of the lake at night to cook and clean for sleeping farm wives, but nowadays the legend has been supplanted by the lakeside souvenir shop. One saving grace of the shop is the food section, featuring Schwarzwald specialties. You can make a spur-of-the-moment decision here to have a picnic of air-dried beef, smoked ham, cheese, hearty bread, and honey. Take along a Riesling wine from the Bühlertal or one of the neighboring villages of Baden-Baden and have your picnic at an *Aussichtpunkt* (lookout point). On a clear day at the Mummelsee, you can see across the broad expanse of the Rhine valley and pick out the famed Strasbourg cathedral in France.

**Freudenstadt**, about half an hour from the Mummelsee on the eastern side of the Schwarzwald mountains due east of Strasbourg, is a 400-year-old city that survived two sieges of the Black Death and the pillage of many wars. Shortly before VE day, the city center was literally destroyed by French soldiers who set the town on fire.

The ravages of war have long disappeared. The city has restored its buildings and preserved much of its colorful history. It was founded when Duke Friedrich of Württemberg commissioned an architect to create a new town in the center of his realm as a haven for Protestant refugees from religious persecution of the Catholic Hapsburg rulers in Austria, the duke being allied with French Huguenots. The architect explains his plan to the duke in a painting in the Schickhardt room of the **Gasthof zur Dreikönig**, on the Martin-Luther-Strasse, which is a comfortable place for lunch. (Another good choice is the **Ratskeller**, on the Marktplatz.)

Architect Schickhardt was a borrower—his **Stadtkirche**, on a corner of the market square, has Romanesque towers, Renaissance doors, and Gothic windows. It is an unusual church, having two naves: The congregation sits on two sides at right angles, men and women separated, with the pulpit in the juncture.

A museum in the **Stadthaus** depicts other aspects of Freudenstadt's past. An exhibit of raft making shows how trees were lashed together and floated down Black Forest rivers to the Rhine and on to Holland. (Many a vessel in the days of sailing ships had masts cut from the Black Forest.)

Take time in Freudenstadt to wander through the impressive shopping area. Two adjoining sections of arcades make a square more than 650 feet on a side. If the Schwarzwald is having one of its frequent showers, browse under cover in these delicatessens and boutiques.

A recommended route of return to Baden-Baden is through the Murgtal (*tal* means "valley") on highway 462. The small town of Baiersbronn-Mitteltal has a noted restaurant in the **Hotel Mitteltal**.

The ride along the Murg river passes a hydroelectrical plant in Forbach, but of more interest is **Schloss Eberstein**, near Gernsbach. The restaurant in this 13th-century castle mixes the menu with history; Medieval surroundings make food seem less important.

Look for the rock from which Count Wolf von Eberstein supposedly leapt into the Murg on horseback to escape his enemies. The Grafensprung (Count's Leap) is one of the legends depicted on the front wall of the Trinkhalle in Baden-Baden.

# The Kinzigtal

If you have time for an overnight stay in the Black Forest, it should be on this circle from Offenburg southeast up the Kinzigtal, on route B 33, to Hausach, through Gutach south to Triberg, continuing south to Furtwangen and Titisee on routes 500 and 31, and returning west on route 31 to the Rhine valley at Freiburg. (As with other recommended journeys into the Schwarzwald, this one works just as well in reverse, originating in Freiburg.)

**Offenburg**, 43 km (27 miles) south of Baden-Baden and due west of Freudenstadt across the Schwarzwald mountains, is a picturesque place, with fountains and buildings of stepped gables and a Baroque Rathaus. On the way up the valley you pass the imposing **castle of Ortenberg**, sitting on a promontory of vineyards, with fruit trees in the foreground.

**Gengenbach** will charm you. Half-timbered houses are rarely so colorful. Among the sights are the stunning market square with outdoor restaurants, narrow side streets, a cloister, and walls and gates from Medieval times.

The parking lot of the **Freilichtmuseum** at Gutach will be jammed with cars of visitors to this open-air museum that recreates Black Forest life of centuries ago. Original farmhouses with large sloping roofs that come almost to the ground were dismantled elsewhere in the Schwarzwald and reassembled here. The Vogtbauernhof, built in 1570 and the showpiece of the museum, gives a good picture of how an entire family, including grandparents, lived under the same thatched roof with their animals.

Along this route you may want to experience farmhouse living first hand. Local tourist bureaus often list private homes that take paying guests. But serendipity works, too. A *Zimmer Frei* (room free) sign pointing up a narrow lane can lead to an inexpensive night in a bona fide farmhouse, such as the **Kaltenbach Bauernhof** near Hornberg. Cows are in the stable underneath, a hayloft on the other side of the bedroom wall, and a bathroom down the hall. Breakfast is on a balcony with geranium-filled window boxes overlooking a meadow.

**Triberg** sits on the side of a mountain, its main street a long incline of shops, restaurants, and hotels, including the **Parkhotel Wehrle**, a charming hotel that serves gourmet meals, including more than 20 different trout dishes. Despite the old-fashioned look of the main building on the grassless thoroughfare, the Wehrle has an adjunct of modern villas with a park and swimming pool.

The **Heimatmuseum** here is one of the most comprehensive in the Schwarzwald, with elaborate exhibits of costumes, clocks, musical instruments, wood carvings, and farm tools. A model of the surrounding countryside and the Schwarzwaldbahn shows how the railroad pierces the mountains with tunnels between Freiburg and Triberg. Murals on one floor record Black Forest industry, including its extensive mining operations. Showcases in the basement are filled with exotic minerals from the region.

Triberg's most popular attraction is its **Wasserfälle**. Although they are only 531 feet high, the waterfalls are Germany's highest. The Gutach river cascades down the granite mountain in seven steps, its white water roaring through the forest. A walkway with guardrails allows visitors to follow the falls down through the gorge and into the town.

Once you leave Triberg (with its dozens of cuckoo-clock shops) do *not* be tempted to detour to Schonach to see the world's largest cuckoo clock. The façade of a one-room house is a clock face, from which an insipid cuckoo emerges. Anyone who pauses to see it moves on, embarrassed for having taken the time.

A worthwhile detour is to the **Uhrenmuseum** in **Furtwangen**, south on route B 500. Collectors are in heaven among the thousands of timepieces here, ranging from small gold pocket watches to pipe organs and player pianos that double as musical alarm clocks. There are cuckoo clocks here, too, but not as many as down the road at Titisee, a touristy town with a carnival flavor.

The Titisee (*see* means "lake") is claimed to be the most beautiful of the region's natural lakes, but that category leaves out the larger and more rustic **Schluchsee**, a lake to the south that was greatly enlarged by man. Moreover, the Titisee teems with sightseeing cruise boats, rowboats, motorboats, and children's paddle-wheelers.

The **Titisee Hotel** on the lake offers a temporary haven for visitors who want to lunch in relative quiet. The hotel becomes a lodge in winter for skiers on the Feldberg, which is less than half an hour away.

At **Hinterzarten**, near Titisee to the west on highway B 31, which after Hinterzarten goes down the Höllental toward Freiburg, you get a completely different feeling: Vacationers stroll through the nature preserve, and day hikers in heavy shoes and knapsacks roam the hills. One trail goes by the ski jump, a long incline in a clearing in the woods that is used for competitions in both winter and summer (in warm weather jumpers land on plastic grass).

Hinterzarten's **Parkhotel Adler** is a coat-and-tie establishment of Continental graciousness situated in the village near the ski jump. The Adler's annex, the Schwarzwaldhaus, has seven rooms for dining, with varying international menus. A dance band plays in one of the rooms. The hotel's 500-year history includes an overnight visit in 1770 by 15-year-old Marie Antoinette on her way to Paris to marry the future Louis XVI. Her mother, Empress Maria Theresa, ordered the road leading through Hinterzarten leveled and widened for the entourage.

Anyone who wants to tarry in Hinterzarten does not have to invest in deluxe accommodations. There are many more humble but perfectly satisfactory places to stay. The **Waldheim** pension, a few hundred yards from the Adler, is plain but comfortable at half the price. The birds singing in the fresh morning air will be just as melodious.

The drive west to Freiburg on route 31 is best done in daylight. It goes through the deep gorge of the **Höllental** (Hell Valley), with overhanging cliffs that almost touch over the highway to form tunnels. On one rocky precipice is a statue of a stag, the *Hirschsprung,* which in legend jumped across the gorge to avoid hunters.

# Freiburg

Freiburg, with 178,000 residents, is the largest city in the Black Forest and a thriving center of commerce. It is also a college town of 23,000 students; the philosopher Husserl worked here, as did the sociologist Max Weber, and Martin Heidegger taught at the university from 1927 to 1944. Despite extensive damage in World War II (including a bombing in error by the Luftwaffe), its Medieval charm has been preserved.

Because Freiburg has assimilated surrounding villages, it has 1,600 acres of vineyards, the most of any city in the nation. On the last weekend each June, during a four-day festival in the Münsterplatz, wines from these vineyards are sampled by the public.

Freiburgers know how to revel, as the number and variety of their festivals will attest. They boast of their *Fasnet* as one of Germany's better pre-Lenten carnivals, with bonfires on Shrove Tuesday and parades of jesters the day before. The May *Frühlingsfest* and October *Herbstfest* both last ten days, and the mid-August *Weinfest* nine. June visitors can also take in the fortnight-long International Tent Music Festival.

Freiburg is a fairly easy city to get your bearings in: The Hauptbahnhof (railroad station) is on the west side of the inner city; trains run north and south between Karlsruhe and Basel. On the south side is the Dreisam river, running east–west. Most of what you want to see is in the area bounded by the railroad and the river and, on the east side, by the Schlossberg. This is the **Altstadt**, where you walk back into the Middle Ages.

A good starting point is the Freiburg tourist information office on Rotteckring, several blocks east of the station and across the street from Colombipark. A palace in the park houses the **Ur-und-Frühgeschichte Museum** (Early and Pre-history Museum), with archaeological finds from the Paleolithic period to the Middle Ages. Next door to the tourist office is the modern-looking **Colombi Hotel**, costly and popular with business travellers.

**Münsterplatz** is where all travellers eventually congregate—with or without festivals. It is easy to spot; just look for the Gothic spire of the rosy-stone **Münster** (cathedral), the dominant feature of the Altstadt. Even if you don't include churches on your itinerary in other parts of the region, take time here to marvel at the artistry of the master builders, who began this church around 1200. A magnificent Gothic openwork spire soars above a front doorway of religious friezes and life-size statues. Inside the church are stained-glass windows of incomparable beauty; pray for the sun to be shining through. The triptych on the high altar, by Hans Baldung Grien, is widely acclaimed. The cathedral's imposing pipe organs are played in special Tuesday-evening concerts.

The area around the cathedral is often a marketplace of bright colors—flowers, vegetables, handicraft works, Kugelhopf ceramic cake molds. When you tire of browsing, draw up a chair outside the **Hotel Oberkirch**'s Weinstube and people-watch over a piece of *Zwiebelkuchen* (onion tart). Note the coat of arms on the dashing red Kaufhaus (merchants' hall) adjacent and its exotically tiled roof. Look up at the cathedral roof to the projecting gargoyles (one with his backside turned toward the bishop's house, said to convey the architect's contempt for the city fathers). Enjoy the street musicians if there are any about. Most are university students; the campus is six blocks away in the middle of town.

Inside the dark-wood-paneled Weinstube and out, locals fork up their Spätzle. In May they make a ceremony of eating long white spears of asparagus. For dessert they might choose a piece of *Zwetchgentorte* (plum pastry), another specialty of the region. If you like the food and the location, the Oberkirch also has 50 beds at moderate prices.

Other points of interest in Freiburg: the Kaiser-Joseph-Strasse is a north–south street that separates the Münsterplatz on the east side from several worthwhile buildings on the west. At the Renaissance **Rathaus** (Town Hall) a carillon peals at noon, and a wedding party is not an unusual sight—you might even see a farmer's daughter emerge from under an arch of shovels. The **Martinskirche**, also on the Rathausplatz, is a former Franciscan monastery that dates back to 1300. The **Haus zum Walfisch** (House of the Whale), nearby, has impressive Gothic doors. It was briefly the home of the Dutch humanist Desiderius Erasmus, who took refuge here at the height of the Reformation.

On the Kaiser-Joseph-Strasse you are back in the 20th century, amid arcades of modern shops. Streetcar tracks run down the middle of the street. The *Bächle,* shallow runnels lining both sides of the street, were formerly used to water livestock and as a fire precaution. More than four miles of these two-foot-wide minicanals lace the town, clean enough to wade in (and traps to the unwary pedestrian).

On this same street is the **Martinstor**, one of two surviving gates from the Middle Ages, when Freiburg was a walled city. On the southeast edge of the Altstadt is the **Schwabentor**, the other old city gate, built around 1200. Paintings on the tower include one of Saint George, the city's patron saint. In this cobblestoned area are restored buildings, narrow streets, and a canal whose water moved the wheels of tanneries and gem-cutting workshops. One of Germany's oldest inns, **Zum Roten Bären**, is a short distance from Schwabentor on Ober-lindenstrasse. In business since 1387, the moderately priced Roten Bären (Red Bear) is proud of its atmosphere, bed-rooms, and excellent kitchen.

The chief attraction in this vicinity is the **Augustiner-museum**, noted for its collection of art from Medieval times to the present. The museum is located in a former monastery with a yellow Baroque exterior. Gargoyles and stained glass from the Münster are on display, as are gold and silver relics and a memorable collection of wood carvings by such Upper Rhine masters as Hans Wydyz. The museum's treasures also include paintings by Grien, Grünewald, Cranach, and others.

A city proud of its history and culture, Freiburg has many museums. Some of the more prominent are: **Völkerkunde** (Ethnographic Museum), on Gerberaustrasse, near the Au-gustiner; **Naturkunde** (Natural History Museum), with Black

Forest minerals, gems, flora, and fauna, in the same location as the Völkerkunde; **Neue Kunst** (Modern Art Museum), featuring Expressionist and abstract paintings, on the Marienstrasse; and **Zinnfigurenklause** (Tin Figure Collection), in the Schwabentor.

# The Wiesental

For vacationers in Switzerland who want to add a day trip to Germany, the Black Forest is perfect, just a short distance across the Rhine from Basel.

Route 317, running northeast from Basel, leads through Lörrach along the river Wiese, where textile plants and lumber mills interrupt the landscape. As the road winds up the Wiesental, look for farmers cutting hay with scythes. Purple lupines and yellow buttercups make the hills look like a Pointillist painting. Deciduous trees that are a riot of color in the fall ultimately yield at higher altitudes to dark evergreens. Some travellers consider this the sunniest and prettiest part of the Schwarzwald.

The goal here is the **Belchen**, a rounded mountain nearly a mile high, with wandering trails haloing its grassy peak. A ski lift on one side takes visitors up the steep hill. The view from the top is spectacular: The Feldberg and other mountains are identifiable in the distance; pastures of different shades of green roll down from the Belchen; tile roofs in small villages in the valleys reflect the sunlight. Sightseers can relax or have lunch after their walk on the balcony of the **Hotel Belchen**, the only large structure on the mountain, with a pleasant restaurant and welcome *Bier vom Fass* (beer on tap).

Continue the journey down the Münstertal west from the Belchen to **Staufen**, a village on the Neumagen river. Ruins of a castle destroyed in the Thirty Years War tower over vineyards on the edge of town. Narrow gutters of running water flow before the gabled Rathaus, whose flower-crammed window boxes complement its mustard color.

Lunch or dinner in the nearby **Gasthof zum Löwen** is worth lingering over, if only for dessert. The chef has a heavy hand with the Kirschwasser in the Schwarzwälder Kirschtorte (Black Forest cake). (By now you may have noticed the many guesthouses called *zum Löwen*—lion—and other animal names, and may wonder at the apparent lack of originality. But most people could not read in the Middle Ages when these houses opened, and symbols of lions, bears, and eagles were instantly recognizable.) In this particular Gasthof zum Löwen, you may be less interested in lunch than legend. Doctor Faustus, the Medieval alchemist, whose deal with the Devil became the plot for Marlowe's *Doctor Faustus* and subsequent works of Goethe and Gounod, lived here in the early 16th century. Baron von Staufen had invited the alchemist to town to use his skills in making gold. Faustus conducted his experiments in the Löwen. One day the house was rocked by an explosion and a terrible smell of sulphur filled the air. Everyone rushed to Faustus's room; he lay dead on the floor, his face blackened, his neck broken.

You can ponder the legend while driving back toward Freiburg on the Autobahn, past the vineyards of the **Badische Weinstrasse** (Baden Wine Road). Vintners here produce a variety of wines well known in Germany and now on the lips of English-speaking connoisseurs everywhere: Riesling, Weissburgunder, Spätburgunder, Müller-Thurgau. Said to lift the spirits is a Silvaner from the Kaiserstuhl, an extinct volcano west of Freiburg. It is the wine to order at the **Schwarzer Adler** restaurant in Vogtsburg-Oberbergen on the west side of the Kaiserstuhl. The dining room is considered one of the finest in Germany.

## Other Parts of the Forest

Routes described above are oriented toward visiting the Schwarzwald from the *west* side—the Rhine valley and major cities of Karlsruhe, Baden-Baden, and Freiburg in Germany, and Basel in Switzerland. But access points along the *eastern,* Württemberg, side of the Baden-Württemberg state offer additional adventures, perhaps as side trips from the Stuttgart-Swabia area (for which see the preceding chapter).

It is a comfortable drive from Pforzheim on the Karlsruhe-Stuttgart Autobahn south to the spa town of **Wildbad**, where kings have come to seek a cure for rheumatism. Present-day business people like the conference facilities (and the mountaintop view) of the **Sommerberg Hotel**, which can be reached by car or funicular. For commercial travellers this hotel in the forest has all the amenities of a large metropolitan hotel. Its bonuses are a large indoor pool, a sauna, and massage rooms. Popular three seasons a year for nature walks, Sommerberg draws skiers in winter to its cross-country trails and lighted downhill slope.

If you want to have your main meal at noon, as most Germans do, try the *Vesperteller* at the **Hotel Bären**, on the main street of Wildbad beside the rushing Enz river. The wooden plate of cold sausages and cheese and dark bread you will eat is the hearty fare a logger takes into the forest. (Your beer, of course, will be colder.)

From the Stuttgart-Bodensee (Lake Constance) Autobahn, it is a short jaunt from the Horb, Rottweil, and Villingen exits to destinations like Freudenstadt, covered above in the Schwarzwald Hochstrasse section.

## GETTING AROUND

The vastness of the Black Forest makes transportation an important consideration. You can ride trains through the region on major service from Karlsruhe to Freudenstadt and on to Lake Constance. Scenic rail excursions run through the forest from several cities. Connections can be made from the main north–south rail route from Frankfurt to Basel, which runs through the Rhine valley, past Baden-Baden and Freiburg.

It is even possible to get a taste of the Black Forest by streetcar. Residents of Karlsruhe, northwest of the forest, ride trolleys on day trips up into the hills to **Bad Herrenalb**, a spa with ruins of a 14th-century monastery.

Trolley and train rides offer vistas with comfort. So do buses, which operate from many cities near the forest, but you may find yourself at the mercy of a driver who gets commissions from souvenir shops. Not everyone relishes waiting an hour to watch hundreds of cuckoo clocks chirp on cue.

The ideal way to see the Black Forest is by automobile. Most visitors to the area who do not arrive by bus will rent cars at major airports in Frankfurt and Stuttgart in Germany and Zurich and Basel in Switzerland.

Lufthansa is the major carrier to German cities, Swissair to Swiss cities. Many foreign carriers also offer service. Airlines from the United States include Pan Am and TWA. Balair, a public charter subsidiary of Swissair, offers direct flights to Basel at reduced rates.

When you pick up your rental car, get the largest-scale road map you can find, as well as a panorama map of the Schwarzwald, a yard-long foldout relief map from which to choose one or more trips into the mountains. The map clearly shows points of access, whether you start in Baden-Baden, Freiburg, or from the Stuttgart Autobahn. It also indicates how easy it is to hook the Black Forest onto a visit to Switzerland. It's also good for route-number guidance. Some tourist offices may have free English versions, but unfortunately, the map cannot usually be found outside of Germany.

## ACCOMMODATIONS REFERENCE

► **Brenner's Park-Hotel.** Schillerstrasse 4-6, D-7570 **Baden-Baden.** Tel: (7221) 35-30.

► **Colombi Hotel.** Rotteckring 16, D-7800 **Freiburg-im-Breisgau.** Tel: (761) 314-15.

► **Deutscher Kaiser.** Merkurstrasse 9, D-7570 **Baden-Baden.** Tel: (7221) 330-36.

► **Kaltenbach Bauernhof.** Obergiesshof 34, D-7746 Hornberg/Niederwasser. Tel: (7833) 69-78.

► **Hotel Oberkirch.** Münsterplatz, D-7800 **Freiburg-im-Breisgau.** Tel: (761) 310-11.

► **Park-Hotel Adler.** Adlerplatz 3, D-7824 **Hinterzarten.** Tel: (7652) 711.

► **Parkhotel Wehrle.** Markplatz, D-7740 **Triberg.** Tel: (7722) 860-20; Fax: 860290.

► **Rebstock.** D-7582 **Bühlertal.** Tel: (7323) 731-18.

► **Zum Roten Bären.** Zum Roten, Oberlinden 12, D-7800 Freiburg-im-Breisgau. Tel: (761) 369-13.

► **Schlosshotel Bühlerhohe.** Schwarzwaldhochstrasse 1, D-7580 **Bühl.** Tel: (7223) 550.

► **Sommerberg Hotel.** D-7547 **Wildbad.** Tel: (7081) 17-40.

► **Steigenberger Europäischer Hof.** Kaiserallee 2, D-7570 Baden-Baden. Tel: (7221) 235-61.

► **Titisee Hotel.** Seestrasse, D-7820 **Titisee-Neustadt.** Tel: (7651) 80-80.

► **Waldheim.** Windeckweg 9, D-7824 **Hinterzarten.** Tel: (7652) 286.

# CHRONOLOGY OF THE HISTORY OF GERMANY

For pre-Christian and pre-Roman days, German history consists of a chronicle of migrating Slavic and Germanic tribes, who managed to displace many of the Celts and make their mark on lands as far north as southern Scandinavia and as far south as the Lower Rhine and the Vistula. Modern Germany began in the tenth century, when the Bavarians, Franks, Frisians, Lombards, Saxons, and Thuringians joined the Holy Roman Empire.

## The Roman Period

- **First Century A.D.:** The Roman sphere of influence (read "control") extends well into the borders of present-day Germany (including Regensburg and Augsburg, for example, and Cologne but never very far or firmly beyond the Rhine and the Main). As early as 53 B.C. Julius Caesar leads his troops all the way to the banks of the Mosel, the Neckar, and the Rhine. The vineyards and villages that brighten those valleys today trace their legacy to the peripatetic Romans.
- **313:** With the Edict of Milan, Constantine I puts an end to Christian persecution. Trier becomes the "Second Rome," and site of the first bishopric in Germany. The city's Porta Nigra (which will be restored by Napoleon in the early 19th century) stands as perhaps the prime relic of Germany's Roman period. An inscription on one of the old town's 19th-century mansions informs passersby, "Trier lived for 1,300 years before Rome came into being."
- **400:** The Romans withdraw from Germany.

# The Franks

- **486**: Clovis crowned king of the Franks, most powerful of the various Germanic tribes that ultimately bring about the fall of the Roman Empire.
- **744**: Benedictine abbey founded at Fulda (near present-day Frankfurt-am-Main) by a follower of Saint Boniface. From this great center, Christianity and learning spreads throughout central Germany, to Cologne, St. Gallen, Aachen, and elsewhere. Einhard, for example, the famous biographer of Charlemagne and himself a figure in the so-called Carolingian renaissance centered around Charlemagne's court at Aachen, was educated at Fulda at the end of the eighth century.
- **788**: Charlemagne (a.k.a. Charles the Great, Charles I, Karl-der-Grosse, and Carolus Magnus) overcomes Tasso of Bavaria and annexes his lands.
- **800**: On Christmas Day in Rome, Pope Leo III crowns Charlemagne emperor of all the Romans, giving him jurisdiction over the new empire of the West (formerly Gaul and Germania). Four years later, Charlemagne defeats the Saxons, extending his empire to the Elbe. Charlemagne's court at Aachen is the scene of one of the first cultural renaissances after the collapse of the Roman Empire.
- **843**: At the Treaty of Verdun, the erstwhile Roman Empire is divided into a western portion (later France), a central portion (including the Low Countries, Lorraine, Alsace, Burgundy, Provence, and most of Italy), and an eastern portion, which ultimately becomes the German Empire.

# Church and Empire

- **962**: Otto I crowned "King of the Franks and the Lombards" in Rome, becoming ruler of both Germany and the Holy Roman Empire of the German Nation. At the end of the tenth century, weakened Carolingian rule over their domains is threatened by Slavs, Norsemen, Magyars, and others. The ensuing breakdown leads to the rise of the manorial system and the growth of feudalism.
- **1152–1190**: During the reign of the Hohenstaufen Frederick I (known as Frederick Barbarossa), the term "Holy Roman Empire" first comes into use.

Throughout nearly 40 years the empire is enlarged, and internal peace is maintained. During his reign, Barbarossa breaks the hold of Duke Henry the Lion over Saxony and Bavaria—the last great independent German domain of the time. Until the end of the Holy Roman Empire in 1806, Germany remains a collection of small principalities and free cities.

## The Merchant Princedom

- **1358**: The Hanseatic League, a merchants' guild that links the majority of the towns throughout northern Germany, is formed. Lübeck ("Queen of the Hanse") is named its capital. The city's Gothic Altstadt, still a gem, was recently added to UNESCO's World Heritage list.
- **1386**: Heidelberg university, Germany's oldest, is founded. (Sigmund Romberg put the town, its school, and its Neckar river on the operetta map of the world in *The Student Prince,* in 1924.)
- **1398**: Johannes Gutenberg is born in Mainz. Inventor of printing from movable type, he publishes the first printed Bible c. 1455.

## Artists and Humanists

- **1465**: Hans Holbein the Elder is born in Augsburg. His masterpiece, the Saint Sebastian altarpiece, is considered one of the prize possessions of Munich's Alte Pinakothek.
- **1471**: Albrecht Dürer, who would become the leader of the German Renaissance school of painting, is born in Nürnberg. His *Four Apostles* is also in the Alte Pinakothek in Munich.
- **1472**: Lucas Cranach, known as the Elder, is born in Kronach, near Bamberg. His great work, *Portrait of Martin Luther,* merits a special trip to the Germanisches National-Museum in Nürnberg.

## The Reformation

- **1483**: Martin Luther, destined to become the father of the Reformation, is born in Eisleben. In 1517 he posts his 95 "theses" on the door of the castle church at Wittenberg. In 1520 he burns the Papal Bull (the fundamental laws of the empire). These actions cause Pope Leo X to excommunicate him, triggering the Protestant Reformation. Clearly, Luther lived up to his description: "the last Medieval man and the first modern one, a political conservative and a spiritual revolutionary."

- **1545–1563**: The Council of Trent, which established the basic doctrines of the Counter-Reformation, moves to reform church abuses.
- **1618**: The Thirty Years War (basically, northern Protestants against the Catholic south) breaks out in Bohemia, and continues until the Peace of Westphalia in 1648. Results: the realignment of much of Europe, the laying waste and carving up of Germany, and an equal-rights guarantee to German Catholics and Protestants.
- **1685**: Johann Sebastian Bach is born into a musically gifted family in Eisenach. Georg Friedrich Handel is born in Halle.

## Prussia Ascendant

- **1724**: Immanuel Kant, founder of critical philosophy, in which he sought to determine the limits of man's knowledge, is born in Königsberg, in Prussia. His *Critique of Pure Reason* is published in 1781.
- **1733**: Munich's Asamkirche is built by the Asam brothers (Cosmas Damian and Egid Quirin), creators of some of southern Germany's most enduring examples of Baroque architecture and decoration.
- **1740**: Frederick II (aka Frederick the Great) ascends the Prussian throne.
- **1747**: Johann Sebastian Bach composes *The Musical Offering* and presents it to Frederick the Great as a token of gratitude for the warm reception the king accorded him during his visit to the court in Potsdam.
- **1749**: Johann Wolfgang von Goethe, whose tragedy *Götz von Berlichingen* was the first major drama of the German literary movement known as "Sturm und Drang," is born in Frankfurt-am-Main.
- **1759**: Johann Christoph Friedrich von Schiller, first among German dramatists (*Don Carlos, Maria Stuart, Die Jungfrau von Orléans, Wilhelm Tell*), is born in Marbach.
- **1770**: Georg Wilhelm Friedrich Hegel, whose philosophy of the Absolute (known as Hegelianism) becomes the leading system of metaphysics during the second quarter of the 19th century, is born in

Stuttgart. His *Phenomenology of the Spirit* is published in 1807. Ludwig van Beethoven is born in Bonn. A true musical revolutionary, he not only achieves unprecedented heights as a composer in the prevailing classical mode, but is responsible for launching the Romantic era in music.

- **1785–1786:** Jakob Ludwig and Wilhelm Karl Grimm (destined to gain renown as the Brothers Grimm) are born. In 1812 and 1815 they publish *Kinder- und Hausmärchen,* known to every child in the English-speaking world as *Grimm's Fairy Tales*.
- **1806:** Nürnberg withdraws from the Holy Roman Empire and becomes part of the kingdom of Bavaria. Hapsburg Kaiser Franz II abdicates; the Holy Roman Empire comes to an end, in good part under military pressure from Napoleon, who marches into Berlin.
- **1810:** Wilhelm von Humboldt founds the university of Berlin. Munich's first Oktoberfest is staged to celebrate the engagement of Crown Prince Ludwig and Princess Theresa.
- **1813:** Napoleon's armies forced to retreat across the Rhine back into France. Richard Wagner is born in Leipzig.
- **1815:** The Holy Alliance between Austria, Prussia, and Russia is signed on September 26.
- **1818:** Karl Marx, founder of Marxism, is born in Trier.
- **1833:** Johannes Brahms is born in Hamburg. The electromagnetic telegraph is invented by Carl Friedrich Gauss and Wilhelm Eduard Weber.
- **1835:** The first German railway, between Nürnberg and Fürth, goes into service.

# A United Germany

- **1848:** The law concerning the basic rights of the German people is passed by the Frankfurt national assembly, as the revolutions of 1848 threaten the German states. Germany's first parliament meets in Frankfurt.
- **1862:** Otto von Bismarck is appointed Prussian prime minister.
- **1867:** Käthe Kollwitz, graphic artist and sculptor, and ardent socialist and pacifist, is born. She becomes widely known for her powerful woodcuts and litho-

graphs depicting the misery and hunger of society's dispossessed.

- **1870–1871**: The Franco-Prussian War results in the collapse of the French and ultimately Bismarck's success in having Wilhelm I proclaimed German emperor (in the Hall of Mirrors at Versailles)—laying the groundwork for the unification of Germany.
- **1875**: That patchwork of imperial cities, principalities, and territories now known as Germany is finally unified by Bismarck, who is named first chancellor of the German Empire (with Berlin as its capital) and created prince. Thomas Mann is born in Lübeck.
- **1876**: The Bayreuth Festival Theater celebrates its premiere on August 13 with Wagner's *Das Rheingold*. Marx publishes *Das Kapital*.
- **1883**: Friedrich Wilhelm Nietzsche proclaims the gospel of the Superman. (*Thus Spake Zarathustra* begins publication in this year.)
- **1889**: Adolf Hitler is born in Braunau, Austria.
- **1890**: Bismarck is dismissed as Reich chancellor and Prussian prime minister.

## Twentieth-Century Germany

- **1901**: Wilhelm Conrad Roentgen, discoverer of the X-ray, wins the first Nobel Prize for Physics.
- **1911**: Wassily Kandinsky, together with Paul Klee, Franz Marc, and others, founds the *Blaue Reiter* movement of German Expressionist art, in Munich.
- **1914**: On June 28, Archduke Franz Ferdinand is assassinated in Sarajevo. On August 1, Germany declares war on Russia; on August 3, Germany declares war on France; on August 4, Great Britain declares war on Germany. World War I is off and running.
- **1917**: The United States declares war on Germany.
- **1918**: At war's end, Wilhelm II (the last kaiser) is forced to abdicate as part of the price of Allied peace terms. Max Karl Ernst Ludwig Planck, who originated and developed the quantum theory, is awarded the Nobel Prize for Physics.
- **1919**: The Treaty of Versailles is signed, Germany is demilitarized, and the so-called Weimar Republic is established. Walter Gropius founds the Bauhaus school of architecture (celebrated for achievement in abstract art and functionalism in architecture) in Weimar. In 1925 the Bauhaus moves to Dessau and

later to Berlin, before being shut down by the Nazis in 1933.

- **1921**: Albert Einstein is awarded the Nobel Prize for Physics.
- **1926**: Germany is admitted to the League of Nations.
- **1928**: The Brecht/Weill *Threepenny Opera* premieres in Berlin.
- **1929**: Thomas Mann receives the Nobel Prize for Literature.
- **1933**: On January 31 Hitler is named Reich chancellor. On February 27 the Reichstag is burned. On October 14, Germany withdraws from the League of Nations. The National Socialist Party comes to power. Hitler receives dictatorial powers, and embarks upon the "Third (or 1000-year) Reich," a concept patterned after the Holy Roman Empire of the German Nation. Thomas Mann goes to Switzerland in self-imposed exile, as a protest against the Nazi regime.
- **1934**: In June, Hitler's opponents within the party, including Ernst Roehm, are eliminated in the "Blood Purge." On the death of President Hindenburg (August 2), Hitler is appointed Führer.
- **1935**: The Nürnberg Laws deprive German Jews of citizenship, prohibit marriage between Jewish and non-Jewish Germans, and bar Jews from the liberal professions.
- **1936**: Nazis strip Thomas Mann of his German citizenship. On August 1, the Olympic Games open in Berlin.
- **1937**: Walter Gropius emigrates to the United States.
- **1938**: The Munich Pact marks the culmination of British and French attempts to appease Germany, on the assumption that Hitler's aims are limited.
- **1939**: Germany invades Czechoslovakia and Poland, precipitating the outbreak of World War II. On September 3 Great Britain and France declare war on Germany.
- **1945**: At the Yalta Conference, in February, the "Big Three" (Churchill, Roosevelt, and Stalin) determine the course of occupation policy. Berlin is to be partitioned into East (Soviet) and West (American, British, and French) zones. Germany is invaded from east and west, its cities in ruins. In April, Hitler commits suicide. Just over a week later, on May 8, World War II ends and the Allies occupy Germany. After twelve years of destruction and horror, the "Thousand Year Reich" is at an end. In August, Truman, Attlee, and

Stalin meet at Potsdam to determine the future of postwar Germany. The Nuremberg War Tribunal begins in November.

- **1946**: The Iron Curtain (Churchill coins the term) rings down.
- **1947**: West German reindustrialization and recovery, the fabulous Wirtschaftswunder (Economic Miracle), gets under way, with U.S. assistance in the form of the Marshall Plan, or European Recovery Program.
- **1948**: Beginning of Marshall Plan aid in Europe. The June 26 Soviet blockade of West Berlin results in the Anglo/American airlift, which continues until May 12, 1949. Bertolt Brecht returns to East Berlin, where, with his wife, Helene Weigel, he founds the Berliner Ensemble.
- **1949**: On May 23, the German Federal Republic is proclaimed in the zones occupied by the Allies. On October 7, the German Democratic Republic is established in the Soviet-occupied zone. NATO is founded.
- **1950**: Nuremberg celebrates its 900th anniversary. The first German Toy Fair (now the International Toy Fair) is held there.
- **1953**: Stalin dies in March. A people's uprising in East Berlin on June 17 is quashed with the help of Soviet tanks.
- **1955**: On May 5, President Konrad Adenauer declares, "The occcupation is over. The Federal Republic of Germany is sovereign."
- **1957**: On March 25, the Federal Republic joins Belgium, France, Luxembourg, and the Netherlands in establishing the European Economic Community (now the E.C., the European Community).
- **1961**: The Berlin Wall begins to go up on August 13.
- **1971**: On March 9, the Four Powers Pact on Berlin is signed. Chancellor Willy Brandt wins the Nobel Peace Prize.
- **1972**: Munich hosts the Summer Olympics, a politically tragic event at which nine Israeli athletes are kidnapped by Arab terrorists (and subsequently killed).
- **1973**: Both Germanys join the United Nations.
- **1989**: The Berlin Wall opens on November 9.
- **1990**: In June, the deutsche mark becomes the currency of East Germany, a sign of that nation's economic union with the West.

—*Robert Sammons*

# INDEX